The Twentieth Century
A Brief Global History

ARCTIC OCEAN

RUSSIAN EMPIRE

ALASKA

CHINA
Port Arthur *(RUS.)*
Weihaiwei *(BR.)*
Tsingtao *(GER.)*
KOREA
JAPAN

AFGHANISTAN
NEPAL
BHUTAN
INDIA
Hong Kong *(BR.)*
FORMOSA *(JAP.)*
HAWAII

Diu *(PORT.)*
Kwangchow *(FR.)*
TONKIN
Macao *(PORT.)*
BURMA
SIAM
FRENCH
INDOCHINA
GUAM
MARIANA IS.

Goa *(PORT.)*
Pondicherry *(FR.)*
Karikal *(FR.)*
PHILLIPINES
MARSHALL IS.

PACIFIC OCEA

CEYLON
BRITISH BORNEO
MALAYA
CAROLINE IS.
GILBERT IS.

MALDIVES
SINGAPORE
DUTCH EAST INDIES
ELLICE IS.

CHAGOS ARCHIPELAGO
NEW GUINEA
SOLOMON IS.

TIMOR *(PORT.)*
SAMOA
(GER.) *(U.S.)*

COCOS IS.
NEW HEBRIDES
FIJI
(BR.)
TAHITI *(FR.)*

NEW CALEDONIA
TONGA *(BR.)*

AUSTRALIA
NORFOLK IS. *(AUST.)*

INDIAN OCEAN

NEW ZEALAND

TASMANIA

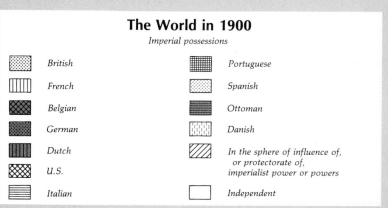

The World in 1900
Imperial possessions

British		Portuguese
French		Spanish
Belgian		Ottoman
German		Danish
Dutch		In the sphere of influence of, or protectorate of, imperialist power or powers
U.S.		
Italian		Independent

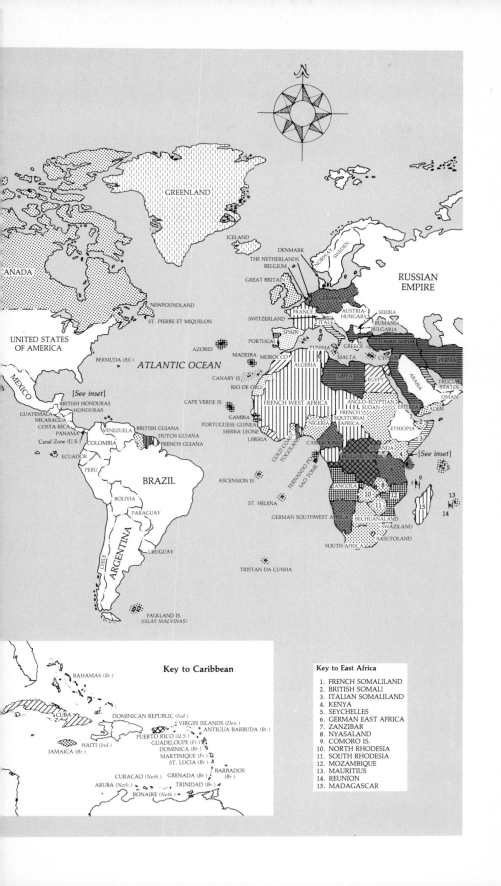

GREENLAND

ICELAND

DENMARK
THE NETHERLANDS
BELGIUM

GREAT BRITAIN

NORWAY SWEDEN

GERMANY

RUSSIAN
EMPIRE

ANADA

NEWFOUNDLAND

ST. PIERRE ET MIQUELON

FRANCE
SWITZERLAND
SPAIN
ITALY

AUSTRIA-
HUNGARY

SERBIA
RUMANIA
BULGARIA

UNITED STATES
OF AMERICA

PORTUGAL

ATLANTIC OCEAN

AZORES

MADEIRA MOROCCO

TUNISIA
GREECE
MALTA
CYPRUS

OTTOMAN EMPIRE

PERSIA

MEXICO

BERMUDA (BR.)

CANARY IS.

ALGERIA

LIBYA

EGYPT

ARABIA

TRUCIAL
STATES
OMAN

[See inset]

RIO DE ORO

BRITISH HONDURAS
HONDURAS

CAPE VERDE IS.

FRENCH WEST AFRICA

ANGLO-EGYPTIAN
SUDAN

ERITREA ADEN

GUATEMALA
NICARAGUA
COSTA RICA
PANAMA
Canal Zone (U.S.)

GAMBIA

PORTUGUESE GUINEA
SIERRA LEONE

NIGERIA

FRENCH
EQUATORIAL
AFRICA

VENEZUELA BRITISH GUIANA
DUTCH GUIANA

ETHIOPIA

1
2
3

COLOMBIA

FRENCH GUIANA

LIBERIA

GOLD COAST

ECUADOR

PERU

BRAZIL

CAPE

BELGIAN CONGO

4 [See inset]

5

BOLIVIA

ASCENSION IS.

FERNANDO PO
SAO TOME

ANGOLA

8

PARAGUAY

ST. HELENA

10
11

9

12

13

ARGENTINA

CHILE

URUGUAY

GERMAN SOUTHWEST AFRICA

BECHUANALAND

15

14

SWAZILAND

BASUTOLAND

SOUTH AFRICA

TRISTAN DA CUNHA

FALKLAND IS.
(ISLAS MALVINAS)

[See inset]

Key to Caribbean

BAHAMAS (Br.)

CUBA

DOMINICAN REPUBLIC (Ind.)
VIRGIN ISLANDS (Den.)
ANTIGUA BARBUDA (Br.)
PUERTO RICO (U.S.)
GUADELOUPE (Fr.)
DOMINICA (Br.)
MARTINIQUE (Fr.)
ST. LUCIA (Br.)
BARBADOS
(Br.)

HAITI (Ind.)

JAMAICA (Br.)

CURACAO (Neth.) GRENADA (Br.)
ARUBA (Neth.) TRINIDAD (Br.)
BONAIRE (Neth.)

Key to East Africa

1. FRENCH SOMALILAND
2. BRITISH SOMALI
3. ITALIAN SOMALILAND
4. KENYA
5. SEYCHELLES
6. GERMAN EAST AFRICA
7. ZANZIBAR
8. NYASALAND
9. COMORO IS.
10. NORTH RHODESIA
11. SOUTH RHODESIA
12. MOZAMBIQUE
13. MAURITIUS
14. REUNION
15. MADAGASCAR

The Twentieth Century

A Brief Global History

Richard Goff
Walter Moss
Janice Terry
Jiu-Hwa Upshur

Eastern Michigan University

THIRD EDITION

McGraw-Hill Publishing Company
New York   St. Louis   San Francisco   Auckland   Bogotá
Caracas   Hamburg   Lisbon   London   Madrid   Mexico   Milan
Montreal   New Delhi   Oklahoma City   Paris   San Juan   São Paulo
Singapore   Sydney   Tokyo   Toronto

This book was set in Times Roman by the College Composition Unit
in cooperation with General Graphic Services, Inc.
The editors were Christopher J. Rogers and Jean Akers;
the production supervisor was Friederich W. Schulte.
The cover was designed by Karen Quigley.
R. R. Donnelley & Sons Company was printer and binder.

Part opening photo credits:
Part 1: The Mansell Collection.
Part 2: (Mussolini) UPI/Bettmann Newsphotos; (Hitler) AP/Wide World Photos; (Hirohito)
UPI/Bettmann Newsphotos; (Nuremberg) The Bettmann Archive.
Part 3: (Astronaut) NASA; (atomic explosion) Defense Nuclear Agency.

The Twentieth Century
A Brief Global History

1 2 3 4 5 6 7 8 9 0   DOC   DOC   9 5 4 3 2 1 0

ISBN 0-07-023536-8

Library of Congress Cataloging-in Publication Data

The Twentieth century: a brief global history / Richard Goff ... [et al.]—3rd ed.
    p.   cm.
    Includes bibliographical references.
    ISBN 0–07–023536–8
    1. History, Modern—20th Century.   I. Goff, Richard D.
  II. Title: 20th century.
  D421.T9   1990
  909.82—dc20   89-13263

Contents

PART THREE
The Contemporary Era   271

Maps and Charts

Preface

This book is designed to facilitate the teaching of twentieth-century world history. As experienced instructors, we have seen the need for a compact text that would provide a balanced perspective and would be pedagogically helpful to students in introductory college history courses.

The Twentieth Century: A Brief Global History combines thematic and chronological approaches. The third edition contains thirty-three chapters, divided into three chronological parts, which lead the student from about 1900 to the present with a firm sense of historical order. The first chapter, new to the third edition, sets up five areas to be covered throughout the text: science and technology, economics, political and social developments, international trends, and culture. Each of the three chronological parts opens with a "general trends" chapter that explains how the five areas of discussion set out in the first chapter pertain to that particular portion of the twentieth century. In each part, the chapters following the "general trends" chapter provide basic historical information on specific regions of the world and key developments in major nations. While attempting to present both sufficient historical information and principal trends, we have kept the book brief, thus allowing instructors flexibility to use supplemental material.

In the third edition we have replaced the young persons fictional biographical sketches with excerpts from autobiographies and diaries of significant twentieth-century figures. The excerpts show, by and large, the actions and attitudes of these persons when they were young adults.

Since the first edition, the text has been strengthened by the inclusion of more social history. We have also added a number of new maps and a new appendix depicting the interrelationships and contrast in economic standing among nations of the world. We have, of course, kept the text up to date; in the process, Part Three has been substantially reorganized and extended. Finally, in the third edition we have extensively streamlined our presentation of the twentieth century by giving greater emphasis to the main themes and concentrating on a smaller number of nations.

In all editions, the text has had the student in mind. It is short enough not to be intimidating and includes many learning aids. Short annotated lists of additional sources appear at the end of each chapter. These lists stress readability and include historical sources, relevant fiction, and films and television programs that the student might be able to see outside the classroom. We have also prepared a set of uncluttered time charts. Maps that illustrate key historical concepts are presented throughout. Since most college students lack knowledge of geography, there is an appendix that briefly discusses world demographic and economic patterns. Instructors may find it useful to assign this geographical survey as an introduction to the text.

In the absence of a uniform practice on transliteration of proper names, we have used our own. For Chinese names, we have employed the pingying convention in reference to the People's Republic since 1949; otherwise we have employed Wade-Giles and other traditional usages. For Arabic, we have generally employed the commonly accepted Western usage.

ACKNOWLEDGMENTS

For the third edition we are pleased to be associated with McGraw-Hill Publishing Company and particularly appreciate the support provided by our editor, Christopher Rogers, and our project editor, Jean Akers. We would also like to thank the reviewers of the various editions for their extremely helpful insights: Erick Dorn Brose, Drexel University; William B. Cohen, Indiana University; C. Stewart Doty, University of Maine-Orono; Louis Menashe, Polytechnic Institute of New York; William Morris, Shelby State Community College; Gersham Nelson, Frostburg State University; Robina Quale, Albion College; Barbara Reinfeld, New York Institute of Technology; Paul Scherer, Indiana University at South Bend; and John G. Snetsinger, California Polytechnic State University. We are particularly indebted to Sally Marks of Rhode Island College for her encouragement and her effective critiques.

Many of our colleagues, unfortunately too many to name here, graciously assisted in our quest for accuracy throughout three editions. We are especially indebted to those colleagues at Eastern Michigan University who were kind enough to read and comment on major portions of the original manuscript: Richard Abbott, Donald Briggs, Donald Disbrow, Della Flusche, James McDonald, and Lester Scherer. Michael Homel was particularly helpful in revising material pertaining to the United States. George Cassar, Joseph Engwenyu, Louis Gimelli, Theodore Hefley, Neil McLarty, and Reinhard Wittke provided professional advice; James Waltz and Ira Wheatley gave administrative support. Deborah Mayfield, Geneva Trochet, Brian Dunn, Darren Herflicker, Martin Neil, Janice Swiger, and most especially Nancy Snyder have graciously assisted us with clerical and other help in the preparation of the various editions.

Richard Goff

Walter Moss

Janice Terry

Jiu-Hwa Upshur

1

1900: A Preview of the Twentieth Century

In 1900, on the sandy and breezy shores of Kitty Hawk, North Carolina, two bicycle mechanics from Dayton, Ohio, tested their first flying machine, a glider weighing fifty pounds. Within a few years, these brothers, Orville and Wilbur Wright, managed to keep a powered airplane aloft for more than half an hour. Other aviation pioneers were right on their heels.

The Wrights' airplane symbolizes the kind of technological innovation, based on new scientific knowledge, that occurred at an increasingly rapid pace in subsequent decades and became one of the central forces determining twentieth-century life. In the following decades, scientists rapidly expanded their insights into the basic properties of chemistry, biology, and agronomy. Medical and sanitation practices based on these insights dramatically improved health and longevity. New concepts of mathematics, physics, space, and time revolutionized the thinking of many on the meaning of history and the nature of the universe.

This notable twentieth-century advance in scientific knowledge led to a spectacular technological explosion. Automobiles and airliners, motion pictures and television, atomic energy and computers, plastics and synthetics, vaccines and antibiotics, satellites and space probes, missiles and lasers are only a few examples of the technological outpouring of the decades after 1900.

The results of twentieth-century science and technology came with increasing rapidity and ensured that each new generation lived in a world markedly different from that of preceding generations. Few living in 1900 could have imagined, for example, that by 1930 some people would be spending evenings listening to something called a radio or going to motion pictures where people talked on the screen. Even fewer dreamt that in 1969 hundreds of millions of people around the world would sit in their homes and see men walking on the moon.

Scientific and technological breakthroughs often had negative as well as positive consequences, and often strained humanity's capacity to adapt to them.

1

By 1989, life expectancy for many people had doubled since 1900; at the same time, all human life could perish in a few hours in a nuclear war.

At the same time that the Wright brothers were pursuing their dream, famine was destroying hundreds of thousands of lives in India. Observers wrote of the sunken eyes, hollow stomachs, and emaciated arms and legs of multitudes of suffering Indians; by the end of 1900, over a million had died. According to one estimate, fifteen million Indians died from famine in the years 1875–1900, ten times the number who had died from hunger in the first fifty years of the nineteenth century.

The 1899–1900 famine in India dramatically illustrated the role that another force, economics, would play in the twentieth century. Although the famine was precipitated by drought, its more fundamental cause lay with India's changing economy. The ruling British government tried to provide relief and blamed the tragedy primarily on rapid population growth, but British land taxes and agricultural policies had gradually driven more and more Indian peasants into poverty. Furthermore, a key factor that contributed to the impoverishment of the Indian masses was Great Britain's encouragement of the production of export crops for its global trading empire. The opening of the Suez Canal in 1869 and the rapid expansion of the Indian railroad network had dramatically cut the time and costs of importing Indian products to Great Britain and around the Empire. Landowners were encouraged to put their lands and peasant labor into producing jute, cotton, tea, and wheat for sale abroad rather than to cultivate food crops for the growing population. In 1901, when some were still perishing from hunger, landowners in India exported two and one-half times more food grains than they had in 1858.

As illustrated by the situation in India in 1900, a major economic theme of the twentieth century was the continuing disparity between impoverished and affluent areas of the world. Particularly in Asia, Africa, and Latin America, malnourished people remained tied to meager local economic resources, while at the same time the great international business cartels that controlled the world's resources brought prosperity to a few favored nations, particularly in Europe, North America, and parts of the Middle East and East Asia. Despite scientific and technological improvements that increased the production of food, global companies controlling the supply of essential grains often created an unequal distribution of such foodstuffs.

Climatic conditions, overpopulation, political rivalries, civil war, and domestic and international economic policies all contributed to the frequently reappearing tragedy of famine, a tragedy which occurred in nations of varying economic systems. In the 1930s, for example, millions starved in the Soviet Ukraine due to the policies of Joseph Stalin, even though the Ukrainians produced enough food to feed themselves. In the quarter century following 1960, millions died of hunger in the People's Republic of China, Nigeria, Bangladesh, India, Cambodia, Ethiopia, and Mozambique. In the same period, on the other hand, the international marketing of an array of industrial and consumer products brought a comfortable standard of living not only to many in the United

States, Canada, and Western Europe but also to increasing numbers in Japan, South Korea, Taiwan, Hong Kong, and Singapore.

Economic inequality helped to stimulate another significant phenomenon of the twentieth century: social and political conflict. No one personifies these tendencies better then Emma Goldman, a dynamic Russian Jewish emigré to the United States who was a major figure in the rise of anarchism. In the belief that the rich exploited the poor and that the state was merely a tool of wealthy interests, anarchists advocated doing away with all government. Leo Tolstoy, the famous Russian nobleman writer who was also an anarchist, urged the use of nonviolent means to bring about this goal, but most anarchists advocated violence.

In 1900, Goldman was a delegate to the Anarchist Conference in Paris. Sitting in a café one day, Goldman read of the assassination of the Italian King Humbert by a fellow anarchist who had come from the United States to perform the deed. Her reaction was that such acts were inevitable as long as centralized governments continued to exist. King Humbert had been the fourth royal figure or chief of state to be assassinated within six years. In 1901, a young man named Leon Czolgosz made U.S. President William McKinley a fifth victim. Earlier in the year, Czolgosz had attended a Goldman lecture, and he allegedly stated later that her fiery rhetoric had influenced his decision to commit his bloody act.

Goldman viewed herself as a spokesperson not only for the economically downtrodden but also for all oppressed people, including women. Although she criticized U.S. suffragettes for seeking what seemed to her meaningless voting power and ignoring the problems of working women, her thoughts on the liberation of women echoed down through the decades. Goldman argued that a woman had the "right to support herself; to live for herself; to love whomever she pleases, or as many as she pleases."[1]

Anarchism and women's rights became just two of the many ideas and ideologies stirring political waters after 1900. Marxism, liberalism, conservatism, syndicalism, populism, and progressivism were some of the others. Later in the century, communism, fascism, and Nazism became particularly powerful examples of the quest of men and women for political solutions to their various problems. Much blood would flow in many parts of the world as a result of the conflicts among these ideologies and the men and women who espoused them.

The Boxer Rebellion in China was one of the most dramatic events of 1900. An anti-foreign group known as the "Boxers" (the Society of Harmonious Fists) besieged the compound which housed the diplomatic community in Peking. Persistent Chinese hostility to predatory outsiders, coupled with a drought and other natural disasters in north China, culminated in the Boxer fury. Almost two months after the beginning of the siege of the foreign legations, an eight-nation force rescued the survivors. Before his soldiers departed

---

1. Quoted in Alice Wexler, *Emma Goldman: An Intimate Life* (1984), p. 94.

from Germany on this mission, the bombastic Kaiser Wilhelm II encouraged them to be as merciless as the barbarian followers of Attilla the Hun had been. Upon occupying Peking, many soldiers from the invading armies did their best to live up to the kaiser's exhortations.

The Boxer Rebellion and its quick suppression illustrated another dynamic force of the twentieth century: international relations. It was a major example of the key roles that nationalism, imperialism, and militarism would play in the twentieth century. For decades, foreign powers had used imperialist policies and their superior military might to impose unfair treaties on the Chinese and to carve China into spheres of influence. Even the United States's so-called Open Door policy was little more than a U.S. plan to gain its share of the wealth of helpless China.

The imperialism that crushed China continued throughout the twentieth century, as great powers imposed their rule over many weak nations. Early in the century, for example, France forced Morocco to accept its "protection," the United States took de facto control of a number of Caribbean nations, and Japan annexed Korea. In the 1930s and 1940s, Japanese militarists sought to impose their will on China; Hitler saw it as a German right to conquer and dominate the nations of Europe; Stalin annexed the Baltic republics (Estonia, Latvia, and Lithuania).

As China's twentieth-century resurgence from the Boxer defeat of 1900 would show, however, the force wielded by powerful nations to impose their will on weaker states often failed to snuff out the nationalistic aspirations of conquered peoples to be free from outside controls. Thus France failed to "assimilate" the Moroccans, and Latin Americans resisted "Yankee imperialism." Harsh Japanese colonial policy failed to make Koreans into docile subjects, and the Soviet Union failed to make the Baltic peoples into happy Soviet citizens. After World War II, one after another of the colonial powers collapsed, and hundreds of millions of the peoples of Asia and Africa became citizens of independent nations.

In 1900, the philosopher Friedrich Nietzsche died in Weimar, Germany, at the age of fifty-five. For the last eleven years of his life, this son of a Lutheran minister had been insane. His ideas posed a major challenge to the traditional Western religious beliefs and morality of his day. At a time when Western imperialists thought of themselves (in the words of the poet Rudyard Kipling) as taking up "the white man's burden" to bring their civilization to inferior peoples in Africa and Asia, Nietzsche's writings undermined confidence in Western civilization itself. He preached that "God is dead" and that Christianity— "the one great curse"—was a strategy of the weak, intended to enslave the strong. He advised individuals who dared to go "beyond good and evil" to become new "supermen." He had contempt not only for the spirit of Christianity and much of the Western culture that had evolved from it but also for democracy and the ideal of equality. He predicted a future of uncertainty, revolution, war, and turmoil.

Even after Nietzsche's death, his ideas lived on, testifying to the importance of culture—that is, philosophical ideas and cultural values—as another force that shaped the twentieth century. Many European poets, artists, playwrights, and composers fell under the sway of Nietzsche's ideas. During the twentieth century, a world increasingly interconnected by ever more effective systems of communication presented individuals with an unprecedented array of often conflicting ideas and values. Both new ideas from thinkers in technologically advanced nations and older ideas from traditional cultures were propagated around the world. Although Nietzsche's ideas represented, for many, a very powerful challenge to traditional Western values, even more of the world's people in the twentieth century felt liberated—or threatened—by the theories of Charles Darwin, Karl Marx, and Sigmund Freud. Some observers repudiated what they considered to be the cultural and religious anarchy of the modern era; others celebrated the multiplication of cultural and religious choices.

The discontent with traditional Western values that Nietzsche stimulated led some to seek enlightenment from other cultures. The French artist Paul Gauguin, disenchanted with Western materialism, sought what he considered a nobler existence in Tahiti, while Nietzsche's faithful friend Paul Deussen became one of Europe's leading experts on the religious philosophies of ancient India. Later, some in Europe and the United States adopted Zen Buddhism, or, like the boxer Muhammad Ali, converted to Islam.

To conclude, these five sketches from 1900—the Wright brothers at Kitty Hawk, the famine in India, Emma Goldman's activities in Paris, the Boxer Rebellion, and the death of Nietzsche—offer a preview of the years ahead. They illustrate the five major forces that this text will focus on throughout its discussions of the history of the twentieth century—rapid scientific and technological innovation; an increasingly global economy coupled with persistent economic inequality; continuing social and political conflict; aggression in international relations; and the broad dissemination of conflicting philosophical ideas and cultural values. These forces did not work in isolation but combined in unique patterns to create important results throughout the twentieth century. A Boxer leaflet citing technological change and the clash of cultural values in explaining the Boxers' hostility to outsiders is an example of how these factors intertwine:

> The arrival of calamities is because of the foreign devils. They have come to China to propagate their teachings, to build telegraph lines and to construct railways. They do not believe in spirits and they desecrate the gods. It is the desire of the gods to cut up the telegraph lines, to rip up the railroads, and to cut off the heads of the foreign devils.[2]

This book will show how the forces underlying the events set forth in this chapter combined in different ways to shape the history of the twentieth century.

2. Quoted in William J. Duiker, *Cultures in Collision: The Boxer Rebellion* (1978), p. 37.

PART ONE

The Era of Imperialism

TIME CHART I
1900–1918

Year	South & East Asia	Middle East & Africa	Europe	Western Hemisphere	Trends in Culture, Science, Technology
	AGE OF IMPERIAL DOMINATION			UNITED STATES PREDOMINANT IN LATIN AMERICA	Industrial West
1900	Boxer Rebellion	Boer War, 1899–1902	Triple Alliance in effect (1882)		
1901	Philippine insurrection, 1898–1913				
1902					Growing influence of Darwinism, Marxism
1903					
1904	Russo–Japanese War, 1904–05				
1905	All–India Muslim League formed	First Moroccan crisis	Continuing British– German naval race	Roosevelt Corollary	Einstein's theory of relativity
1906					Decade of arms build–up

Birth of modern art and music |

8

Year				
1907		Triple Entente completed		
1908	South Africa self-governing	Austria annexes Bosnia and Herzegovina		
1909				Advent of motion pictures, airplanes, automobiles
1910	Japan annexes Korea			
1911	Manchus overthrown in China		Beginning of Mexican Revolution	
1912	French protectorate in Morocco	Balkan Wars, 1912–13		
1913				Tagore first non-European to win Nobel Prize for Literature
1914	Ottoman Empire joins Central Powers / German colonies taken by allies, 1914–18	**WORLD WAR I**		Panama Canal completed / Submarines, trench warfare
1915	Japan serves 21 demands on China			
1916				
1917		Russian Revolution, 1917	United States enters war	Dadaism founded
1918	United States–Japanese intervention in Siberia, 1918–25	Allied intervention and civil war in Russia, 1918–20		

2

General Trends before World War I

The twentieth century opened on a world dominated by the West. Major European nations and the United States led the world in scientific discoveries and technological advances and controlled it with overwhelming economic and military power. Among non-Western nations, only the partially Westernized nation of Japan had joined a Western-dominated world.

Westerners believed that their preeminent position reflected their superior culture. By the beginning of the twentieth century, most Western peoples enjoyed an unmatched standard of living as well as the opportunity for better education, health care, and social services. For the West, at least, the future offered the prospect of continued progress.

Western power was not as overwhelming as it seemed, however, because it was weakened by internal strains in many Western nations and by hostilities among them. Many nations were beset by ethnic and religious strife as well as by political conflicts among liberal, conservative, and socialist forces. In addition, most European nations nursed hostilities against their neighbors. These tensions stemmed from long histories of national rivalries and competition for control of territory around the world. When European nations embarked on military build-ups and alliances for additional security, these policies added to the stresses of the era and eventually led to a general war. This war, World War I, weakened European power around the world.

SCIENCE AND TECHNOLOGY

The people of Europe and the United States took great pride in Western scientific discoveries and technological improvements in the nineteenth and early twentieth centuries. In biology, Charles Darwin's *On the Origin of Species by Means of Natural Selection* (1859) and *The Descent of Man* (1871) had revolutionized perceptions of humanity's history. Darwin had theorized that different animal species, including humans, might have originated through a process

10

of natural selection whereby the "fittest" survived and flourished. His concept became widely accepted, although many could not reconcile it with the Biblical account of creation. Darwin's ideas, along with advances in the study of geology and paleontology (fossils), led to further discoveries that brought many to a greater understanding of early humans and their society.

Psychologists brought forth a new field of investigation which opened human mental functions to study and interpretation. At the beginning of the twentieth century, Sigmund Freud was in the vanguard of psychological practitioners. His theories revolved around his belief that humans were driven by

An age of science: Marie Curie, twice a recipient of the Nobel Prize, in her laboratory. (American Institute of Physics/Niels Bohr Library)

unconscious pleasure-seeking forces such as sexuality. The conflict of these unconscious desires with other psychological forces more attuned to social "reality" often led to inner psychological conflict. To deal with serious cases, Freud developed psychoanalysis, a method of probing the unconscious mind, frequently by analyzing dreams. Freud's theories and methods were both supported and attacked by later experts in the field.

In 1895, Wilhelm Roentgen discovered a form of radiation that could penetrate opaque materials. These "x-rays," as he called them, were gradually applied in many areas of physics and medicine. Meanwhile, Antoine Becquerel discovered the radioactivity of uranium. Starting from this discovery, Marie and Pierre Curie investigated other radioactive elements, discovering radium and polonium in 1898. Their work helped to provide a foundation for twentieth-century research in the composition of atoms.

As Darwin changed thinking about the nature of humans, Albert Einstein in the first two decades of the twentieth century changed thinking about the nature of the universe. Einstein demonstrated that energy is mass multiplied by the square of the velocity of light. Joined with the conclusion of Ernest Rutherford and others that the atom is a combination of particles moving at enormous velocity, Einstein's theorem suggested that useful thermal energy would be released if the nuclei of atoms could be altered.

In addition to his studies of the atom, Einstein's theory of relativity and other discoveries changed scientific understanding of the forces that make up the universe. During the two centuries before 1900, scientists believed that the universe was a three-dimensional spatial arrangement and that its properties could be measured from an absolute point of reference. Einstein demonstrated that time was the "fourth dimension" interrelated with the other three. According to Einstein, the velocity of light is the same whether or not the observer is in motion, and thus there is no absolute point of reference. Measurement is in that sense "relative."

Westerners were particularly proud of the advances in health and longevity that had taken place. The work of Joseph Lister in the nineteenth century improved hygienic conditions in hospitals; puerperal fever, the main cause of death for women in childbirth, was eradicated. The introduction of anesthesia techniques enabled doctors to perform more complicated operations, which saved countless lives. Louis Pasteur and Robert Koch proved that bacteria were the cause of many previously incurable diseases and could be controlled through inoculations, medication, and hygienic measures. As a result, anthrax and rabies, which had destroyed many animals around the world, were coming under control, and four major causes of child mortality—smallpox, diphtheria, typhoid fever, and scarlet fever—were beginning to be eliminated in the Western world. Soon after 1900, chemists discovered vitamins and developed sulfa drugs, which helped humanity combat disease-causing bacteria.

Improvement in health care and in the control of disease contributed to a marked population increase late in the nineteenth century, not only in Europe and the United States but also throughout much of the world. The population of Europe more than doubled between 1800 and 1900, primarily through a low-ered death rate. On the other hand, increased population often created over-crowding in many Western cities, and as better health care spread through the rest of the world to areas such as India and China, it contributed to population increases that outstripped the available food supply.

Scientific insights spawned a multitude of technological breakthroughs. Engineers who developed turbines and dynamos dramatically accelerated the production of electro-power. New petroleum-refining techniques produced gas-oline and diesel fuels to power the new internal combustion engines. The chem-ists and technicians who produced rayon and artificial dyes in the laboratory brought in a new era of synthetic material, while their discovery of new metal alloys promised greater diversity in manufactured products. Industrial innova-tors used interchangeable parts and created the assembly line to make produc-tion more efficient, thus making manufactured goods cheaper. The develop-ment of structural steel, reinforced concrete, and the electric elevator allowed cities to grow upward as well as outward.

By 1900 physicists studying electricity and its relationship to magnetic waves had already revolutionized concepts of communication. The telegraph had been well established in the nineteenth century, and underseas cables al-ready linked the world's continents. The telephone also began to make its im-pact in urban centers at the beginning of the twentieth century. Perhaps the most exciting development in communication came in 1895, when Guglielmo Marconi sent messages through space with the "wireless" transmitter. The age of the radio soon followed. Advances in photography created a new wonder, the motion picture.

For those living early in the twentieth century, perhaps no single inven-tion marked the breakthrough into a new era more than the electric light. Thomas Edison had rolled back the darkness and promised a revolution in the pattern of daily life. For many in the West, in particular, home illumination was now safer, cleaner, and more effective, allowing a greater variety of family occu-pations over a longer period of the day. Activities of every kind could now be carried on around the clock.

In transportation, the advent in the nineteenth century of the steam-driven locomotive and the steamship had already greatly accelerated travel on land and water. After 1903, through the efforts of Orville and Wilbur Wright and many others, the age-old dream of air travel was realized. The achievement in aviation soon meant that people could traverse the world in a matter of days or hours instead of months or weeks. More important to the average Westerner was the development of the internal combustion engine, which led to the au-tomobile. While only in its infancy in 1900, the automobile already promised to transform work and leisure patterns throughout the West and eventually around the world.

Ironically, the same spirit of scientific and technological advance that was enhancing the life of human beings was also busily devising new means to de-stroy them. Scientists and metallurgists produced explosives and propellants such as cordite, TNT, and nitroglycerin. Their improvements in the techniques of rifling and metal casting brought forth a new class of artillery—howitzers, mortars, and long-range naval guns—and new or improved fragmentation weapons, such as shrapnel shells, antipersonnel mines, and hand grenades. These projectiles could now be delivered with great accuracy through new guidance systems, thus increasing the number of casualties per projectile expended. Technicians working on new fuel and hydraulic technology produced the submarine; additional propellants and guidance technology armed the submarine with a reliable torpedo. Applications of chemistry and physics created poison gas, the flame thrower, and the machine gun.

The military establishment also adapted a number of techniques originally intended for civilian use. Mass production of textiles and clothing, plus the invention of canning and refrigeration, meant that nations could raise, equip, and feed larger armies and navies. Utilizing new modes of transportation and communication, military leaders could move about, supply, and coordinate their forces over long distances.

Whether for good or ill, there is no doubt that there was an explosion of scientific and technological advances in this period. Indeed, it was difficult for many to see how this pace could be sustained. In 1899, the head of the U.S. Patent Office asked President William McKinley to abolish the office: "Everything that can be invented has been invented."

ECONOMIC TRENDS

The dawn of the twentieth century saw the West in economic control of the world. Before the eighteenth century, economic systems had been primarily local and regional, but by 1900 the rapid expansion of the Industrial Revolution, coupled with advances in transportation and communication, had created a worldwide economy. The heart of this new global economy lay in Western Europe, particularly Great Britain and Germany, and in the United States. These nations had created a complex of heavy industry in which iron ore, petroleum, and electricity provided the power for the production of iron and steel, machinery, chemicals, and textiles. Great Britain had been the world's greatest industrial nation early in the nineteenth century, but by 1900 Britain was losing its lead to Germany and the United States.

The rise of industry in Western nations had a major impact on other areas of the world. As their industries outgrew local resources and markets, industrialized Western nations began to pursue a policy of imperialism (see below), seizing economic control over parts of Latin America, Africa, and Asia in order to ensure a ready supply of raw materials for their factories and to gain secure markets for their surplus goods. The growing power and aggressiveness of the established industrial powers spurred less developed nations such as Russia and Japan to protect themselves by commencing intensive industrialization programs of their own.

Although European investors had built a few textile factories around the globe, overall there was little in the way of heavy industry outside Europe, the United States, and Japan. The most widespread form of manufacturing in non-industrialized areas was the processing of minerals, fibers, and hides in the British dominions of Canada, Australia, New Zealand, and South Africa and in the Latin American nations of Mexico, Brazil, Argentina, Uruguay, and Chile. These nations depended on Western Europe and the United States for the bulk of their manufactured goods.

Paralleling their industrial expansion, Westerners over the centuries had been developing a global network for producing and distributing agricultural products. By 1900 they had organized many areas of the world into large plantations, "agricultural factories" that poured out enormous quantities of foodstuffs. As a result, citizens in Western Europe and the United States could sit at their dinner tables and enjoy Hcnduran bananas, Brazilian coffee, East Indian spices, Cuban sugar, Hawaiian pineapple, Ceylonese tea, and many other products from all over the world.

As the industrial and agricultural factory system spread around the world, people moved—or were forced to move—from continent to continent to provide the labor necessary for economic development. For centuries, Westerners had imported African blacks into the Western Hemisphere to work as slaves on the plantations. By 1900 the slave trade was over, but new movements were underway. Millions of Europeans were encouraged to settle in North and South America, Australia, and New Zealand. Chinese and Japanese—many of them contract laborers—went to work on the plantations of Hawaii and the railroads of North America. Asian Indians labored in the mines of eastern and southern Africa and on the Caribbean plantations. Many of them later rose in economic and social status in their new homes.

An effective worldwide economy would have been impossible without a concurrent revolution in the technology of commercial transportation. Ships of ever greater capacity and speed, paced by the British merchant marine, hauled raw materials and finished products into every nook and cranny of the globe. Where water traffic was impeded by land formations, engineers constructed the Suez and Panama canals, created canal networks in Western Europe and the United States, and built or enlarged harbors all over the world.

On land, the tremendous cargo-hauling capacity of the steam-driven engine operating on rails gave an enormous boost to economic development. Railroads crisscrossed northwestern Europe, Japan, and much of North America. Elsewhere in the world, however, railroads were much rarer. The cargo-hauling potential of the internal combustion engine used in automobiles remained problematic because no cheap permanent road surface had been developed.

The massive economic development underway around the world was fueled by investment money; Great Britain was overwhelmingly dominant at the turn of the century. London was the center of world finance, setting the standards in investment, banking, and insurance. "Insured by Lloyds of London" was the ultimate guarantee of protection and security.

SOCIAL AND POLITICAL TRENDS

The rapid transformation in the world economy had brought many social changes by the opening decades of the twentieth century, particularly in the nations of Western Europe. These changes were also apparent in the United States and, to a lesser degree, in Latin America and Japan. As the century progressed, some of these social changes spread to other parts of the world.

Population Mobility and Social Classes

One social consequence of the industrialization process was that many people left the countryside to work in urban areas. As a result, old cities grew rapidly and new ones appeared. The population of the new urban areas grew so rapidly that the authorities were technologically and psychologically unprepared to deal with the situation. Industrialized nations soon faced a host of problems—poor sanitation and housing, crime, a shortage of schools and hospitals, and many others—in their urban centers.

The impact of industrialization and worldwide commercial activity created changes in the three social classes in the Western nations. The upper class was now comprised of an uneasy combination of the traditional titled, landed aristocracy (except in the United States) and a new group of wealthy industrial and commercial entrepreneurs. Whatever their background, the members of the upper class dominated their nations. In Great Britain, 5 percent of the population controlled 75 percent of the earnings from private property. The European hereditary aristocracy still occupied most of the high civil and military posts in their governments, but an increasing percentage of the important posts were beginning to be filled by men with a "common," though often affluent, background. The new rich, although usually products of the "work ethic," matched the traditional aristocrats in life styles of "conspicuous consumption." They built mansions; consumed huge quantities of expensive food and clothing; bought technological marvels such as automobiles, phonographs, telephones, and radios; patronized the arts; and indulged in expensive travel and recreation.

The middle class, while sharply separated from the upper class in income and status, was growing in size, prosperity, and complexity. Traditionally, the middle class had consisted of shopkeepers, skilled artisans, and such "white-collar" professionals as academics, physicians, and clergymen. By the twentieth century it also included new professionals such as engineers, business managers, and architects. These newcomers were joined by a large mass of less affluent teachers, business clerks, and civil servants who came in with the major expansion in public education, business, and government bureaucracy. Living in modest comfort, they saved money for a better home, for their children's education, and, if not protected by one of the new business or government pension plans, for retirement.

Perhaps the greatest social change brought about by the changing economy was the improvement in the condition of the urban working classes. Mass production and improved agricultural techniques were providing cheaper clothing, shoes, and food at the same time that wage increases were outstripping inflation. In Western Europe just before World War I, two-thirds of the urban work force, now rapidly outnumbering the rural labor force, made wages above the subsistence level. A small minority of skilled workers and foremen possessed an income greater than some people in the lower middle class. Many workers could afford to add meat, dairy products, and vegetables to a diet that had previously consisted almost entirely of bread and potatoes. Better nutrition and improved health care increased average life expectancy in Western Europe from around forty years old in the mid-nineteenth century to about fifty years old just before World War I. Increased wages and new laws forbidding child labor (although not in the United States) increased the opportunities for children to go to school.

Despite improvements for the upper reaches of the working class, however, many problems remained. Housing was cramped and uncomfortable; workplaces usually remained noisy, unhealthy, and dangerous. One-third of the urban workers, especially those employed in textiles, mining, hauling, and other relatively unskilled occupations, still eked out a living at a bare subsistence level. In 1900 in the United States, the average work week was fifty-nine hours at $13 a week. Some were no better off, and some were worse off, than farmers or peasants working on agricultural estates. It was estimated that in 1900, one-third of the inhabitants of New York and London lived in poverty.

There were some modest but noticeable shifts in the status of women. The advent of the typewriter and other office machines opened new opportunities for "respectable" women, especially single women, to work in business offices instead of remaining at home. Others became teachers. On the other hand, the rise in income for many working-class families allowed some wives to leave factory work and stay home to look after their children and households. The statement "My wife doesn't have to work" became a status symbol for many working-class husbands. Some upper- and middle-class women, particularly in the United States, obtained higher education and entered the professions. Many women wanted political power commensurate with their heightened economic and social status, and increasing numbers of women agitated for the right to vote.

In Western and Central Europe, two trends were underway in the countryside. Peasants who already owned substantial land expanded their holdings and mechanized their operations. Along with the nobles on the great estates, many of them converted from producing grain to raising beef, dairy herds, and vegetables in order to meet the changing consumption patterns of the city dwellers. These peasants were able to maintain a comfortable life style, but their incomes often barely kept pace with inflation. At the same time, small farmers often lost their lands and joined the mass of farmhands who were struggling to subsist in the countryside. Millions went to work in the factories, where they had to make the difficult transition from the sporadic work habits of the country to the continuous discipline demanded by the factory work routine. Millions more emigrated to the Western Hemisphere, where some secured farms of their own. Most immigrants, however, competed for factory jobs in the New World with other immigrants and with local workers.

Outside the industrialized West, social changes came much more slowly. In Japan, and to a much lesser extent in China and India, partial industrialization had enlarged the traditional middle class and created a small class of factory workers. Most of the non-West (as well as Eastern and southern Europe, the southern United States, and most of Latin America) remained a rural world, with a few affluent landowners and many impoverished laborers and tenant farmers. Because of imperial domination, local landowners in parts of Africa and Asia had been displaced by European settlers and corporations. In any case, whether dominated by a local feudal elite or by Westerners, the rural masses lived below or close to subsistence levels.

Competing Political Forces

The struggle between liberals and conservatives was a major source of dissension in the Western world. Conservatives usually came from the more privileged groups in society and supported existing class distinctions, autocratic government, and special economic privileges for the upper classes. They also generally defended institutions that embodied traditional practices and values— the established church, divine right monarchy, and a powerful military. Conservatism was still a powerful force in such Central and Eastern European nations as Germany and Austria-Hungary, and particularly in Russia.

Liberals tended to come from the rising business and professional classes and wanted to change society so that they would have a secure and powerful place in it. They wanted freedom of speech, press, religion, and assembly; the right, for men with modest amounts of property, to vote and hold office; elected governments responsible to the voters; and commerce free from restrictions. Some who were very liberal wished to allow all adult males, even those without property, the right to vote and hold office. Americans had achieved this for white males by the middle of the nineteenth century. Generally speaking, liberalism had been gaining power in Europe since the French Revolution in 1789, and by 1900 was a strong force in Great Britain and France, among some groups in Italy, and in some of the small Western European nations. By the turn of the century, some liberals, hoping to avoid socialist revolution, advocated welfare state programs such as unemployment compensation and pensions.

Liberal-conservative differences were often contests between persons of property, and such battles did not seem particularly relevant to many factory workers. One response of Western workers to their exploitation was to organize into trade unions to force improvements from their employers through collective bargaining, picketing, strikes, and boycotts. Trade unionists were not necessarily interested in bringing an end to the capitalist system, but instead concentrated on improving their wages and working conditions and on acquiring pensions and other forms of security. Trade unions met with great resistance from employers and their political allies, but they slowly gained strength, especially in Great Britain, after the turn of the century. Other people concerned with the plight of the workers turned to a more radical approach than trade unionism: the destruction of capitalism through socialism.

Karl Marx, who died in 1883, was one of the world's most important political theorists. The core of Marx's "scientific socialism," which he developed along with his fellow German Friedrich Engels, was the theory of historical or dialectical materialism. This theory proclaimed that such productive forces as technology, material resources, and labor determined economic relationships. According to Marx, the productive forces and economic relationships together made up the foundation of society and in turn determined the "superstructure" of government, laws, religions, and culture that the dominant class in any historical period used to strengthen its position.

Productive forces, Marx declared, had changed in the course of history. Therefore, economic relationships had changed, and as a result new classes had emerged to replace the old dominant classes and create new superstructures. However, no ruling class ever surrendered its power peacefully. It had to be overthrown by the rising class associated with the new productive forces. Thus class conflict was inevitable and would continue until the golden era of

Karl Marx, founder of one of the most influential modern ideologies. (The Mansell Collection)

communism was established. In his own time, Marx believed that he was witnessing in Western Europe the overthrow of the feudal landowning class by the capitalist merchants and industrialists. Just as inevitably, said Marx, the industrial working class, or "proletariat," would associate itself with still newer productive forces even then evolving out of capitalist society. This working class would clash with the capitalist class and would eventually overthrow it. It would then establish a "dictatorship of the proletariat" in order to set up a new socialist system and deal with any remaining class enemies. That dictatorship and all the machinery of government would then wither away, to be followed by an age of equitable social relations, humanized labor, and increased leisure.

By the turn of the century, both trade unionism and Marxism in its various interpretations had numerous followers in the industrial nations. It was clear that both liberals and conservatives faced formidable political opposition. Despite their differences, Marxists and trade unionists influenced one another. Marx had stated that the conditions of the workers under capitalism would grow worse and that the workers would become increasingly radical. On the contrary, salaries and working and living conditions in capitalist countries such as Great Britain and Germany began to improve, as capitalist politicians instituted reforms in order to ward off socialism. Many workers became more interested in continuing such improvements, and perhaps gaining a share of political power, than in overthrowing capitalism through revolution.

Before World War I, responding to the moderate outlook of most workers, many socialists in Europe and in the United States decided to work through the political party system rather than advocate revolution to replace capitalism. In those nations that allowed a popular vote, Marxist parties such as the German Social Democratic party increased rapidly in size. In the United States, the presidential candidate of the Socialist party, Eugene Debs, twice received approximately one million votes.

As some Socialist parties became less revolutionary, two other movements, anarchism and syndicalism, became more prominent. Anarchists believed that governments exploited people on behalf of the wealthier classes, and so they wished to destroy all governments and to reconstruct the social order without them. From 1894 to 1912, anarchists assassinated a president of France and one of the United States, two Spanish premiers, the king of Italy, and the empress of Austria. Syndicalists believed that a trade union–led general strike would paralyze society and destroy its government, after which the unions would be the basic organizing structures of society. The movement developed in France but influenced workers and radicals elsewhere. In the United States, the Industrial Workers of the World (the "Wobblies") was the largest group that reflected syndicalist ideas.

Liberalism, conservatism, socialism, and other political movements also had some impact outside the West. At the start of the twentieth century, liberalism was already strong among Indians educated in Great Britain, some of whom founded the Indian National Congress in 1885. At about the same time, some Japanese, influenced by Western ideas, advocated adopting a constitution, which was finally granted in 1889. Although Marxism eventually proved to be a potent influence among non-Westerners, it was a negligible one before World War I. However, the Westernized Sun Yat-sen overthrew the old regime in China in 1911 and attempted to replace it with one founded on democratic, liberal, and moderate socialist principles.

Although Western political ideas gained some ground in non-Western areas, most traditional leaders sought to perpetuate the old customs and cultures of their societies and often used religion as a powerful force to prevent or limit Westernization. Because these traditional leaders sought to maintain the status quo, they bore some resemblance to European conservatives.

Nationalism

At the turn of the century, nationalism was another political force at work in the West; later it spread around the world. Nationalism is a learned emotional loyalty that individuals direct toward a large group, organized as a state, with which they perceive certain common bonds. It gives to individuals a sense of membership and belonging. Nationalism is nurtured by a common heritage of ethnic similarity, language, religion, and traditions; a distinct territory; and a common history. It is not necessary, however, for a group to share all these characteristics. For example, the Swiss have a long national history, but they comprise several major languages.

National systems of education helped to foster nationalist sentiments. Leaders in Western Europe and the United States, where literacy was the highest, used the printed word and the educational system to indoctrinate individuals to find kinship with the national group and to identify with the government as one symbol of the nation.

A common history is an important ingredient in nationalism. National groups and states glorify their past and sometimes create or rediscover one if it is lacking. For example, Germans sought to overcome regional, political, and religious differences by emphasizing triumphs in their distant tribal past. Nationalistic Indians, chafing under British rule, rediscovered Asoka, an emperor of the third century *b.c.* under whom the subcontinent was unified and made powerful. His insignia, the wheel and the lion, became the symbols of the newly independent state of India in 1947.

In nationalism, the nation itself is often glorified. Nationalists evoked old, even primitive, feelings based on myths that nations are eternal. As the Italian writer Joseph Mazzini expressed it, "Our country is our Home, the house that God has given us. In laboring for our own country, on the right principle, we labor for humanity."

By the turn of the century, nationalism as a unifying force was well established in Western Europe and the United States. The dramatic unification of Germany and of Italy in the 1860s and 1870s exemplified the power of nationalism in Europe. Many Germans, however, considered their unification incomplete because millions of Germans still lived outside the boundaries of the new Germany. Nationalistic German demands for *Anschluss* (union) of all Germans into a single state disrupted the history of Europe well into the twentieth century.

In many areas, nationalism was a divisive rather than a unifying force, because it sometimes inspired a dominant group to persecute minorities within a nation. These actions were often based on ethnic antagonism, economic jealousy, and religious hatred. Pogroms (government-instigated mob attacks) in Russia against the Jews and Turkish suppression of the Armenians were examples of such persecutions at the beginning of the twentieth century.

Nationalistic sentiments were also divisive because in some nations, certain populations that were under the dominance of other groups aspired to break away from that control. Depending on the circumstances, they wanted either to form their own independent nations or to join their kindred who were already in control of a neighboring nation. Austria-Hungary and the Ottoman Empire, in particular, were torn by nationalistic dissension, because these states governed a host ethnic minority groups that were becoming increasingly nationalistic. The Austro-Hungarian Empire was largely held together by loyalty to the monarchy and the Catholic Church. When the dominant Germans and Magyars (Hungarians) began to stress that the empire was primarily a German one or a Magyar one, the Slavs and other minority ethnic groups within the empire responded by pushing for their own national states. The tensions and hatreds of nationalism made the Balkans the "Tinderbox of Europe." In the Ottoman Empire, which had been held together by a common belief in Islam, religious bonds were no longer sufficient, as both the Arabs and the Kurds sought their own national independence. In both cases, the development of local nationalisms and ethnic prejudices contributed to the collapse of these formerly great empires.

In the early part of the twentieth century, Western doctrines flourished that asserted the inherent superiority of the so-called Aryan group and of Aryan nations and stressed the inferiority of other groups—Jews, Slavs, Gypsies. This was the clearest example of the use of racial myths to foster nationalism.

By 1900 nationalism in its different forms was also taking hold in Asia. The Japanese justified their aggressiveness in Asia by asserting that they were a superior race. A small Indian elite, influenced by the West, worked to throw off British rule by attempting to instill the concept of a united India into a population divided by ethnicity, language, and religion. In China, another Western-influenced elite worked to rally the Chinese on two nationalistic crusades simultaneously. They channeled Chinese resentment of the ruling Manchu minority into plots to overthrow the Manchu dynasty, while at the same time they tried to rally all peoples of China to resist Western and Japanese imperialism.

INTERNATIONAL RELATIONS

At the beginning of the twentieth century, international relations around the world were poisoned by tensions emanating from a number of sources. New levels of nationalistic pride spilled over into international affairs, heightening fears and hostilities already inherited from the past. Often, nationalism manifested itself in general feelings of national or racial superiority; the British referred to non-Westerners as "wogs," to the French as "Frogs," and to the Germans as "Huns." More concretely, nations fought one another over territory and power while accusing their opponents of having a vicious character and a history of wrongdoing. "The policy of the German Empire...has always been one of undisguised blackmail," asserted a British official in 1899. Imperialist competition for control of territory around the world added more fuel to the flames, driving nations to search for security in arms races, alliances, and plans for war.

Imperialism

Imperialism, the process by which a small number of industrial nations extended their economic and political control over much of the rest of the world, was the main driving force in international relations at the turn of the century. As one of Great Britain's leading imperialists put it, "The day of small nations has passed away; the day of empires has come." Actually, the process was not new; Europeans had been engaged in imperialist practices for centuries. From the fifteenth through the eighteenth centuries, Europeans searching for foods, fibers, and precious metals had taken control of the entire Western Hemisphere, Australasia, large sections of Asia, and a few spots in Africa. Thereafter, although imperialist conquests never entirely ceased, they proceeded at a somewhat slower pace before imperialism intensified dramatically in the last third of the nineteenth century. The cast of imperialist nations had now changed. Spain, Portugal, and the Netherlands, three stalwarts of an earlier era, were no longer very active. However, three other traditional imperial powers, Great Britain, France, and Russia, were fully involved in the new era. They were now joined by Belgium, Germany, Italy, the United States, and Japan.

There were many reasons for the resurgence of imperialism, economic considerations being one of the most important. With new economic forces at work, Western and Japanese industrialists continually searched for new markets, cheap labor, resources, and places for investment. Often, complex patterns of economic interdependence developed. For example, British textile manufacturers encouraged the planting of cotton in India and Egypt, both crucial parts of the vast British Empire. Cheap local labor grew and harvested the cotton, which was shipped to Great Britain to be manufactured into cloth. Cotton cloth was then made into shirts and other articles of clothing, which were, in turn, sold back to the laborers in India and Egypt. In such a fashion, industrialists not only enjoyed cheap labor and raw materials, but also profited from new markets for their manufactured goods.

Imperialism was also fueled by nationalism, which engendered in many nations a relentless urge to compete with other nations to become the most powerful in the world. Frequently, interest groups or lobbyists such as explorers and adventurers encouraged national governments to extend their influence.

Strategic imperialism, a concern for control of key waterways, ports, and military outposts, was another important factor leading nations to take over distant territories. The British government, for example, always had as its first priority keeping the seas of the world safe for its commerce, protected by a powerful navy operating out of strategically located bases. The Suez Canal and the surrounding Middle Eastern territory, in particular, were viewed as crucial for controlling the lifeline to India and the Far East. The British took over Singapore, Aden, and other territories as bases to protect this vital trade route.

One complex aspect of imperialism, part motive, part rationalization, part result, has been termed "cultural imperialism." On the basis of the alleged natural superiority of the white race, Westerners argued that it was the "white man's burden" to bring the benefits of superior Western civilization—its technology, its religion, its institutions—to the inferior nonwhites of the world living in darkness and ignorance. The virulently imperialistic Kaiser Wilhelm II of Germany proclaimed, "God has called us to civilize the world. We are missionaries of human progress." A U.S. senator put it in a more folksy way: "We will lift Shanghai up and up, ever up, until it is just like Kansas City." Some Westerners went even further, arguing that nonwhites had few cultural or historical achievements to their credit and could never reach the cultural, political, or technical heights the predominantly white societies of the West had attained.

Social Darwinists such as Herbert Spencer argued that biological evolution, which involved competition, elimination of the weak, and "survival of the fittest," should be applied to competition among cultures, nations, and peoples. They argued that it was right or "natural" for the strong, "superior" cultures to control or even to eliminate weaker, "inferior" cultures. Thus, after France conquered Algeria, it attempted to eradicate all local traditions, language, and religion. When the Algerians fought against the destruction of their society, the French responded that there was no such thing as an Algerian nation, and that they were bringing the benefits of the superior French civilization to wandering, ignorant tribes.

Christian missionary zeal was another manifestation of cultural imperialism. It was often said that the flag followed the cross. Missionaries from Europe and the United States sought to spread Christianity in Africa and Asia, as they had earlier in Latin America. Missionary groups frequently competed with one another in their enthusiasm for propagating their particular denominational beliefs.

For cultural, religious, and racial reasons, many imperialists believed that the West's domination over the globe would never end. Western nations at-

The Outlook of a Young Imperialist

It did seem a pity that . . . the age of civilized wars had come to an end forever. If it had only been 100 years earlier what splendid times we should have had! Fancy being nineteen in 1793 with more than twenty years of war against Napoleon in front of one! However, all that was finished. The British army had never fired on white troops since the Crimea, and now that the world was growing so sensible and pacific—and so democratic too—the great days were over. Luckily, however, there were . . . Zulus and Afghans, also the . . . [Mahdi's followers] in the Sudan. Some of these might, if they were well-disposed "put up a show" someday. There might even be a revolt in India. . . . These thoughts were only partially consoling, for fighting the poor Indians, compared to taking part in a real European war, was only like riding in a paper-chase instead of in the Grand National.*

Here Winston Churchill, a member of one of the great political ruling families of Great Britain, reflects on his outlook when he was a cavalry cadet in the 1890s. The confidence in Western superiority to non-Western peoples that young Winston depicted here, as well as his assumption that warfare ought to be reserved for gentlemen, typifies the era before World War I. Churchill retained his imperialist attitudes throughout his career and resisted the dissolution of the British Empire after World War II.

*From *My Early Life: A Roving Commission* by Winston Churchill. Copyright 1930 Charles Scribner's Sons; copyright renewed © 1958 Winston Churchill. Reprinted by permission of Charles Scribner's Sons, an imprint of Macmillan Publishing Company.

tempted to recreate their empires in their own images. In the process, they attacked and modified local values, institutions, and achievements. Entire societies in Africa, Asia, and Latin America were uprooted and, in some cases, totally destroyed. In virtually all instances of imperial domination, the conquered people were changed. In many instances, the conquered people fought back and sought to overthrow outside control and to recapture control over their own destinies, but failed.

Sometimes, imperialist competition led rivals to the brink of war. One dangerous situation in Africa was a prime example. The British were interested in building a colonial dominion, and perhaps a transcontinental railroad, that would extend from Capetown in South Africa to Cairo in Egypt. Equally enthusiastic French imperialists dreamed of a transcontinental empire extending from western Africa to the east coast. This rivalry brought about a confrontation in 1898 at the Sudanese village of Fashoda. The Fashoda crisis was an outstanding example of extreme nationalism, or jingoism ("We don't want to fight,/ But by Jingo! if we do/ We've got the ships,/ We've got the men/ And got the money, too!"—a British beer hall song). Goaded by articles in the new mass media of journals and newspapers, people in France and Great Britain rushed thoughtlessly to support their nations—"my country right or wrong." Neither the French nor the British gave a thought to the Sudanese in the conflict. Only the intercession of more moderate diplomats, and second thoughts by the French, averted open warfare between Great Britain and France in 1898.

On a few occasions, imperialists went to war with one another to further their interests, but in most cases nations settled their rivalries peacefully. For example, Japan and Russia went to war over Korea and Manchuria, and the British fought the Dutch settlers in South Africa. For the most part, however, the imperialists preferred to hammer out diplomatic agreements, in which territories were parceled out as in some gigantic Monopoly game. For example, fourteen nations met at the Berlin Colonial Conference of 1885 to decide the fate of the Congo in Africa. No Congolese were included, and the European nations decided the fate of one of Africa's largest areas without ever asking the people of that region what they wanted.

Although major powers generally had not gone to war over imperialist claims, a number of them continued to nurse grievances. Japan, Germany, Russia, and Italy, in particular, believed they did not have their fair share of possessions and looked for ways to increase their global holdings. Some nations, such as Great Britain, France, and the United States, were essentially satisfied with the territories and the indirect economic controls they had accumulated.

Arms Races, Militarism, and Alliances

In a period filled with nationalistic and imperialistic tensions, the major nations moved to strengthen their security. They stockpiled the new weapons of the era, built up the size of their military establishments, and made alliances. In the nineteenth century, Prussia had led the way in military build-up, creating a mass army of short-term conscripts. Men were drafted, trained, and then sent home to their civilian occupations. This procedure created a large reserve of trained men that could be called up to form a formidable army at the outbreak of war. Prussia also set up a general staff organization that was charged with planning and conducting future wars. Prussia's large army of conscripts and reservists, well trained, equipped, and led, defeated France's smaller army of long-term professional soldiers in 1870. Learning from its defeat, France switched to the Prussian system and built up its own mass army. Such a system required huge amounts of money and disrupted the civilian occupations of a large percentage of a nation's population.

To protect itself from Western imperialism, Japan built up a Western-style military machine and demonstrated its strength by winning wars against China in 1895 and Russia in 1905. It won more praise from the West for these victories than for any other aspect of its modernization, and gained equality in international affairs. Japan saw that a strong military paid, and thereafter steered an increasingly militaristic and imperialistic course. On the other hand, Great Britain and the United States, which were protected by the sea and which regarded large standing armies as possible threats to popular government, maintained relatively small armies. By 1914, however, both nations were building up reserves and both had created general staffs.

The build-up in armies was matched by a naval arms race. Until the 1880s, the naval situation had been relatively stable. The British navy led in both size and quality. The French navy was a distant second, and France was not disposed to challenge Great Britain. Germany, however, began a naval building program in the 1890s, and the United States and Japan followed with more modest efforts. Both Germany and the United States were rapidly developing interests around the world and needed substantial navies to protect their supply lines. Japan's interests were regional, but it also sought to protect them with a strong navy. Great Britain feared that the German naval building program was intended not only to protect German interests outside Europe but also to threaten Great Britain itself. As a consequence, the British launched a determined effort to keep their navy well ahead of Germany's. The naval race was enormously expensive and created a further strain on the economic resources of both nations.

The arms race, begun as a defensive measure, only created more tension and fear, leading planners to the conclusion that if war broke out, the best pro-

A symbol of the arms race: In 1906, the New British battleship *Dreadnought* made other battleships obsolete and spurred expensive naval building programs in several major nations. (U.S. Navy Department)

tection would be to take the military offensive. Basing their calculations on the Austro-Prussian and Franco-Prussian wars of 1866 and 1870, European military planners believed that the next war would be a short one of open maneuver, although the Civil War in the United States and wars in the Balkans forewarned that the next war might be a long one of trenches and attrition.

The build-up of armies and navies was accompanied by the rise of militarism, the concept that military aspects of a society are the most important. The German general Friedrich von Bernhardi, reflecting the influence of Charles Darwin, wrote that war was a biological necessity, a law of nature. Darwin's ideas led the Russian writer Leo Tolstoy to lament in 1906 that science "has decided that the struggle and enmity of all against all is a necessary, unavoidable, and beneficent condition of human life." Friedrich Nietzsche wrote, "You say it is the good cause that hallows even war? I say unto you; it is the war that hallows any cause. War and courage have accomplished more great things than love of the neighbor."

Advocates of militarism stressed that war was good because it developed in individuals the qualities of loyalty, cooperation, courage, and sacrifice that were important for the development of humanity. President Theodore Roosevelt and Kaiser Wilhelm II agreed on the bracing effect of war on a nation's population. Roosevelt said, "No triumph of peace is quite as great as the sublime triumphs of war." Japanese patriotic writings glorified both war and the warrior. This Japanese attitude owed much to the sense of solidarity and sacrifice among the *samurai* (the former hereditary warrior class). A code of conduct, called *Bushido* (Way of the Warrior), governed *samurai* behavior. It taught service, loyalty, and willingness to die for nation and cause. The traditional respect that the Japanese accorded to their *samurai* superiors made it easy for Japan's leaders to inculcate the same values in the ordinary citizen.

In addition to building up their military forces, European countries sought to obtain security in a balance of power between blocs of nations. Long before 1900, European nations had made it a leading principle of diplomacy to balance their economic, military, and strategic power against competing nations so that a rival nation would not have a clear-cut advantage and seize that advantage to attack. Often, a major power, unsure of having parity with a competitor, sought to create a balance by forming a partnership with a third nation. Great Britain, for example, traditionally maintained a balance of power by formulating understandings with other nations based on loans and other economic arrangements. Other nations, such as France and Germany, believed their security lay in constructing formal military alliances.

Occasionally, smaller nations used the concept of balance of power to protect themselves from more powerful nations. For many decades the Ottoman Empire, the so-called Sick Man of Europe, prevented Russia and others from taking its territory by playing off the competitors against each other. Thus, while Russia envisioned carting the sick man off to the undertaker, the British, fearing an upset in the balance of power in the Eastern Mediterranean in that event, kept the patient alive. The Ottomans were thereby able to keep vast amounts of territory that otherwise would have been lost to more powerful nations. Likewise, China resorted to "using barbarians to control barbarians" in an attempt to play off the Western nations against Japan. Thailand remained independent because it served as a buffer state between British Burma and French Indochina. Similarly, Ethiopia's emperors preserved their sovereignty by propagating the idea that if one European nation controlled Ethiopia, the balance of power in Africa would be destroyed.

The balance of power idea was also used in a global context. Great Britain, fearing growing German strength in East Asia, concluded a rare formal peacetime alliance with Japan in 1902. Leaving Japan to watch the Germans in Asia, Great Britain concentrated its forces to meet opponents elsewhere in the world, for example, confronting Russia in Persia.

At times, the attempt to achieve a balance of power, especially through alliance systems, fomented war rather than sustaining peace. Nations were not content to maintain the balance of power in all its various aspects—military, economic, and diplomatic; they also struggled to shift that balance in their own favor. Consequently, the balance of power concept became a source of everspiraling economic and military competition and, eventually, war.

The atmosphere of increasing nationalistic tensions heightened interest in international cooperation to preserve the peace. Delegates met at international peace conferences at The Hague in the Netherlands in 1899 and 1907, where they worked on disarmament propositions and international arbitration techniques and established the Hague Tribunal for the arbitration of disputes. The presence of the tribunal induced a number of nations to settle their disputes through arbitration. The peace movement also benefited from the participation of prominent individuals. Alfred Nobel, the inventor of dynamite, instituted the Nobel Peace Prize. The iron and steel magnate Andrew Carnegie set up the Carnegie Endowment for International Peace and also built the Peace Palace at The Hague. Compared to the onrush of nationalistic hostilities, however, the international peace movement proved to be feeble; the Hague Tribunal was given only insignificant cases such as technical boundary questions. Meanwhile, the major nations continued to put their energy into building up their war machines.

CULTURAL TRENDS

In the West, many significant new forms of expression developed in religion, literature, and the arts. Non-Western cultures were modified to varying extents by contacts with the West. Non-Western cultures also had some impact in the West, but not nearly to the same degree.

The West before World War I witnessed continuing conflict between secularism and traditional religions. In Europe and the United States, secularists (persons who would greatly limit the role of the churches and their teachings in society) strongly challenged the privileged position of the established churches. Scientific and technological changes, urbanization, and the increased production of consumer goods disrupted traditional living patterns, which in turn affected religious customs and beliefs. Despite their differences, the ideas of Darwin, Marx, Nietzsche, and Freud all challenged, in whole or in part, longstanding religious beliefs.

Within Judaism and Christianity, some individuals tried to reconcile their religious beliefs with some of the new influences and ideas. Reform Judaism and liberal Protestantism were two such responses, but Orthodox Jews and Protestant fundamentalists were much less ready for compromise. The Catholic and Orthodox Churches also were not generally enthusiastic about modern ideas.

Another conflict in Western culture concerned differences among Western thinkers and artists about how to view and depict the world around them and inside themselves. In the decades immediately before 1914, many began to question the dominance of an objective, scientific, and strictly rational approach to reality. Einstein's theory of relativity seemed to deny certainty in science; the French philosopher Henri Bergson emphasized intuition rather than reason; and Freud, preceded by Nietzsche, stressed the role of unconscious, nonrational motivation. Writers and artists increasingly questioned the realistic modes of artistic expression that had been dominant since the mid-nineteenth century and that tended to be dependent on an objective, scientific approach.

Out of this questioning, and out of new ways of seeing and portraying not only the external world but also the reality within oneself, came modern art, music, and literature. Modern art embraced a range of expression, from the post-impressionist paintings of Paul Cézanne, Vincent van Gogh, Paul Gauguin, and Georges Seurat to the fauvism of Henri Matisse, the cubism of Pablo Picasso, and the abstractionism of Wassily Kandinsky. In music, Arnold Schoenberg was the most significant innovator. Between 1906 and 1909, he developed what came to be called atonal music, a step that led the artist Kandinsky to write that Schoenberg was "almost alone in abandoning conventional beauty and [in] sanctioning every means of expression," and that he had "discovered mines of new beauty in his search for spiritual structure." In literature, the symbolist poets of France and Russia, such as Stephane Mallarmé and Alexander Blok, were among the most notable challengers of literary realism and naturalism and the world they continued to depict. By using words as symbols, they attempted to suggest a more meaningful, mysterious, and hidden reality.

In addition to changes inside Western culture, another noteworthy trend was that non-Westerners sometimes altered their values after contacts with the West. In particular, non-Western religions found themselves challenged by Western value systems. The adherents of the major religions of Africa and Asia, such as Islam, Confucianism, Buddhism, and Hinduism, faced Christianity, secularism, and other aspects of Western culture. While some local religions were destroyed or transformed, in general the major world faiths were little affected before 1914. In India, Hindu reformers attempted to reconcile traditional teachings with modern science and the concept of the equality of all human beings. Some Chinese scholars attempted a reinterpretation of Confucianism to accord with democratic ideals. In both instances, however, such attempts were rejected by the orthodox majority.

While the influence of Western culture on the non-Western world was certainly greater than the reverse, there were also some notable non-Western influences on Western artists, writers, and thinkers. As a result of imperialistic expansion, Westerners became increasingly familiar with foreign cultures. The publication of the first two volumes of Sir James Frazer's *The Golden Bough* in 1890 opened the world of "primitive" societies to many, including Freud and others, who eventually made use of Frazer's material in formulating some of their psychological theories. Some modern Western artists who rejected traditional Western perspectives were influenced by Japanese, South Pacific, and African art. Paul Gauguin, for example, went to Tahiti in 1891 and was influenced by its art. Picasso was studying African art when, along with Georges

Picasso's *Young Ladies of Avignon* (1907) reflects the movement away from realistic representational art and also the influence on Picasso of primitive art. (Pablo Picasso, *Les Desmoiselles d'Avignon* [1907]. Oil on canvas, 8'×7'8". Collection, The Museum of Modern Art, New York. Acquired through the Lillie P. Bliss Bequest.)

Braque, he founded Cubism in 1907–1908. By the mid-nineteenth century, religious ideas of India had already begun to influence such Western thinkers as the German philosopher Arthur Schopenhauer and the American writer Ralph Waldo Emerson. In 1912, the famous Irish poet William Butler Yeats called attention to the poetic writings of the Indian religious thinker and writer Rabindranath Tagore, who the following year would become the first non-European writer to win the Nobel Prize for Literature. Commenting on Tagore's writings, Yeats noted, "They stirred my blood as nothing has for years."

SUGGESTED SOURCES

Barraclough, Geoffrey, *An Introduction to Contemporary History* (1968). A brief review of twentieth-century trends.*

Churchill, Winston S., *My Early Life: A Roving Commission* (1930). A recounting of Churchill's youthful experiences as a soldier and correspondent at home and abroad; gives insights into the British aristocracy and imperialism.* (Also a film, "Young Winston.")

Gollwitzer, Heinz, *Europe in the Age of Imperialism, 1880–1914* (1979). A well-illustrated book that focuses on the connection of imperialism to internal developments in Europe.*

Knapp, Vincent J., *Europe in the Era of Social Transformation: 1700–Present* (1976). A penetrating study of the changes in the lives of Europeans, with emphasis on the nineteenth and twentieth centuries.

Mosse, George L., *The Culture of Western Europe,* 3rd ed. (1988). Standard cultural history, with analysis of links between romanticism and nationalism.

Palmer, Alan, *Dictionary of Twentieth Century History, 1900–1982,* 2nd ed. (1983). Useful and readable resource.

Ruis (Eduardo del Rio), *Marx for Beginners* (1979). A humorous but sophisticated explanation of Marx by means of cartoons.*

Shafer, Boyd C., *Nationalism: Myth and Reality* (1955). A general treatment of the subject that deals with myths regarding both nationalism and its historic development.*

Tuchman, Barbara W., *The Proud Tower* (1972). A detailed and well-written look at politicians, anarchists, socialists, imperialists, nationalists, militarists, and leading figures in the arts in Europe and the United States from 1890 to 1914.*

Ward, Barbara, *Five Ideas That Change the World* (1984). A survey of five important ideologies that have had and continue to have a significant impact.*

Ware, Caroline F., K. M. Panikkar, and J. M. Romein, eds., *History of Mankind: Cultural and Scientific Development,* Vol. VI, *The Twentieth Century* (1966). A comprehensive overview of twentieth-century trends.

*Paperback available.

3

The Great Powers of Europe

The history of the period before World War I can be best understood by examining the characteristics of the powerful European nations that dominated much of the globe. Although each of these nations had its unique historical experiences, strengths, and weaknesses, each was also heavily influenced by the major trends discussed in the previous chapter. These nations will be taken up beginning with the more democratic nations in Western Europe, then moving eastward to consider the more autocratic nations.

GREAT BRITAIN

In 1900, Great Britain was generally considered to be the most liberal and prosperous nation in Europe. The British people enjoyed the benefits of a highly industrialized economy fueled by raw materials shipped in from a huge colonial empire. The empire also supplied many vital foodstuffs, for Great Britain's large urban population needed far more food than the farmers of the small island nation could provide. With the general economic prosperity, old landed aristocrats and new industrialists both were inclined to agree that it was "the best of all possible worlds."

Political life in Great Britain, a constitutional monarchy, was characterized by growing tendencies toward social reform and liberalism. The Reform Bill of 1867 and the Franchise Bill of 1884 had created virtually universal adult male suffrage. The Parliament Bill of 1911 in effect gave the House of Commons, the elected chamber of the British Parliament, control over the government budget. It also somewhat diminished the "gentlemen's club" atmosphere that had previously pervaded the Parliament. British politics developed along the lines of a system dominated by two parties, in contrast to the multi-party system common in France and many other European nations. The two-party system eliminated the necessity of forming party coalitions in order to gain a governing majority, and thereby contributed to a more stable political system. As a result, the British were able to modify many of their economic and political institutions without bloody and divisive revolutions. However, ethnic sep-

Europe in 1914

Triple Entente
Triple Alliance
Area of Russian–Austrian competition for influence
Area sought by France
Area sought by Italy
3 largest European armies
3 largest European navies
(Bosnia) region of larger nation

NORWAY
Oslo
SWEDEN
Stockholm
DENMARK
Copenhagen
Moscow
RUSSIA
Warsaw
(Poland)
GERMANY
Berlin
NETHER-
LANDS
Amsterdam
BELGIUM
Brussels
LUX.
Alsace-
Lorraine
SWITZ.
Bern
Vienna
AUSTRIA – HUNGARY
(S. Tyrol)
(Istria)
(Bosnia)
Sarajevo
MONTENEGRO
ITALY
Rome
Sardinia
Corsica
GREAT
BRITAIN
(Ireland)
London
FRANCE
Paris
PORTUGAL
Lisbon
SPAIN
Madrid
RUMANIA
Bucharest
BULGARIA
Sofia
SERBIA
Belgrade
ALBANIA
GREECE
Athens
Istanbul
OTTOMAN EMPIRE
Cyprus
Crete

NORTH SEA
BALTIC SEA
BLACK SEA
MEDITERRANEAN SEA
ATLANTIC OCEAN
AFRICA

Scale of miles
0   200   400

aratist movements in Wales and Scotland and the struggle for "Home Rule" in Ireland placed continued demands on the centralized political structures.

The industrialization of Great Britain during the eighteenth and nineteenth centuries had brought with it oppressive working conditions, and many remained so poor that the poet Alfred Lord Tennyson could write: "White chalk and alum and plaster are sold to the poor for bread." As a consequence, workers demanded better pay, improved working conditions, and fringe benefits. In contrast, industrialists believed in the laissez-faire system, in which the government kept a "hands-off" policy toward business, which permitted them to do precisely as they wished. Relatively unhampered by government controls, the industrialists tenaciously fought labor union demands for better working conditions. In spite of the owners' opposition, however, labor unions steadily gained power and influence. Workers rallied around the new Labour party, whose rapid growth demonstrated the rising political power of workers and their supporters and threatened to displace the Liberals, one of the traditional gentry-dominated political parties. Labour politicians and their political friends in Parliament created legislation limiting monopolies, assisting the unemployed, and bettering working conditions. They also made similar reforms in the fields of education and social welfare.

Beyond the British Isles, the British Empire was the largest in the world. A popular saying declared that "The sun never sets on the British Empire." In northern Africa, Great Britain dominated Egypt and the vital Suez Canal; it held Nigeria and other territory in western Africa. In eastern and southern Africa, Great Britain had taken control of Kenya, Uganda, the Rhodesias, and South Africa. In Asia, it held Hong Kong, other concessions on the China coast, the Malay peninsula, Burma, Ceylon, key areas along the Persian Gulf, and

Suffragettes, attempting to extend voting rights to women, are escorted away from Buckingham Palace by police in 1914. (BBC Hulton/The Bettmann Archive)

above all India, "the Jewel in the Crown." Halfway around the world, Great Britain had created two new "Britains" in Australia and New Zealand, almost completely displacing the original populations and populating the areas with settlers from the British Isles. Through its control of Canada, many Caribbean possessions, and islands off South America, Great Britain still maintained a formidable presence in the Western Hemisphere. Self-governing dominions such as Canada, Australia, and New Zealand had their own armed services, but relied on the British navy for overall protection and followed Great Britain's lead in foreign policy.

This vast imperial domain, so vital to the survival of Great Britain, required a large navy to protect the colonies and the supply lines from them, in addition to securing the British Isles from invasion. "Rule Britannia! Britannia rules the waves," the British sang as they spent millions of pounds to support their navy, the largest in the world. Conservatives seeking to increase the number of dreadnaughts, battleships with heavy caliber guns, adopted the slogan, "We want eight and we won't wait." Units of that huge navy were stationed around the world at strategic outposts such as Gibraltar, Alexandria, the Cape of Good Hope, Aden, and Singapore. The British also used numerous islands in the oceans of the world as coaling, watering, and supply stations for the navy.

In contrast to their enormous navy, the British maintained a small but efficient volunteer army. Britain did not aspire to make conquests on the Continent and was primarily protected by the navy, and therefore had no need for a huge standing army of conscripts. Nor did the empire require large land forces. A surprisingly small number of British officers and men, supported by a substantial number of local troops commanded by British officers, kept the peace throughout the colonies. For example, only 4,000 Britons were stationed in the entire Indian subcontinent.

FRANCE

France was also an industrialized nation with a large empire; compared with Great Britain, France had a much more substantial agricultural base, but a less developed industrial system. As in Great Britain, the French had been moving toward liberalization; French liberals advocating more democratic political forms clashed with conservatives who tended to support more authoritarian policies. The multi-party system of French politics before World War I reflected many gradations of conservatism, liberalism, and radicalism, and often made French governments unstable. After France's disastrous defeat in the Franco-Prussian war in 1870–71, an essentially moderate, middle-class group of politicians founded the Third Republic. They were opposed by forces on the Right that wanted a return to conservative monarchy, or what was jokingly called "the man on horseback," and by forces on the Left that wanted a more revolutionary, socialist government.

The Dreyfus case, which dragged on from 1894 to 1906, reflected the deep divisions within French society. Alfred Dreyfus, a French Jew and a junior army officer, was wrongly convicted of selling military secrets to a foreign power. Many Frenchmen, including noted intellectuals such as Emile Zola, were convinced that Dreyfus was innocent and that he had been used as a scapegoat to protect important judicial and military officials. The case became a cause célèbre and brought into serious question the extent to which French society had eradicated age-old privileges and prejudices. Dreyfus was finally found innocent in 1906. His exoneration resulted in the downfall of the conservative forces and the victory of the republicans and the socialists.

Successive coalition governments moved to reform the military, to subordinate it to the civilian government, and to limit the political power of the Catholic Church. One politician stated unequivocally, "Clericalism, there is the enemy." Organized labor sought to institute sweeping economic reforms and gained widespread political support. With increased power within the Chamber of Deputies, French radicals from 1905 to 1910 pushed through measures formally separating church and state and creating old-age pensions and other legislation to improve the lot of working people. However, prior to World War I, British workers still had more basic rights than did unionists in France.

France also faced particular problems in international affairs. Compared with other major continental powers, its population was small and growing more slowly. In addition, French industry lagged behind that of Great Britain, Germany, and, later, the United States. These problems in turn led to military weakness. The French army was smaller and less efficient than that of its neighboring enemy Germany, and its navy had fallen to fourth place behind those of Great Britain, Germany, and the United States.

To compensate for these weaknesses, the French government sought to create an alliance system that would bolster French power. Concerned about further German expansion, France sought to limit German power on the Continent by finding allies to counterbalance Germany and its Triple Alliance. In 1894, France signed a secret convention with Russia whereby if France were attacked by Germany or Italy, Russia would attack Germany, and conversely, if Russia were attacked by Germany or Austria, France would move against Germany. France later enlarged this agreement by including Great Britain. Traditionally suspicious of European alliances, Great Britain hesitated before finally joining in an informal understanding, or entente, with France in 1904 and Russia in 1907. With the resulting Triple Entente, which was in part no more than a "gentlemen's agreement," the French believed they had formed a powerful balance to Germany's growing strength in Central Europe.

France controlled the second-largest colonial empire. In North Africa, France held Algeria and Tunisia and, by 1912, Morocco. In sub-Saharan Africa, France dominated vast stretches of West and Equatorial Africa. In Asia, the French held Indochina, which was subdivided into Vietnam, Laos, and Cambodia. In the Western Hemisphere, France possessed a number of Caribbean islands and French

Guiana in South America. France also controlled numerous small islands in the South Pacific and in the Indian Ocean.

GERMANY

The opening of the twentieth century also witnessed the emergence of Germany, perhaps the most powerful European nation. Although not unified until 1871, Germany moved forward rapidly. Germany had a sound agricultural base and had become one of the world's leading industrial nations by the opening of the twentieth century, because of its large resources of coal and iron ore. By and large, Germany's industrial plant was newer and more efficient than that of its major economic rival, Great Britain.

Politically, the German government reflected autocratic tendencies that had been a predominant characteristic of the preceding Prussian monarchy. Prussia remained the dominant state within the federal system, while the constitution provided the chancellor with wide executive powers. The German Reichstag, elected by males over the age of twenty-five, was never as powerful a voice for citizen representation as was the British House of Commons or the French Chamber of Deputies.

As in other industrialized nations, Germany's growing industrial strength caused a rapid movement toward unionization. Ironically, it was Otto von Bismarck, the conservative "Blood and Iron Chancellor" who had masterminded the unification of Germany, who brought about many of the changes the workers desired. Hoping to cripple the socialist movement in Germany, the conservative and paternalistic Bismarck inaugurated social welfare programs in the 1880s, several decades before the more liberal governments of France and Great Britain and half a century before the United States. Through his social welfare program, Bismarck instituted social insurance compensating workers for illness or accidents and providing the aged with pensions.

German successes in the Franco-Prussian war of 1870–1871 not only completed the unification of Germany, but also shifted the center of European politics. Under the Treaty of Frankfurt, France was forced to surrender the provinces of Alsace-Lorraine to Germany, to pay an indemnity of about $1 billion, and to allow Germany to occupy key French fortresses until the amount owed was paid. Bismarck knew France would be set on revenge. Indeed, the unification of Germany was viewed with hostility and fear not only by the French but also by other European nations, particularly Russia and Great Britain.

Fearing French retaliation, Bismarck set out to form new political and military alliances; he compared this diplomatic maneuvering to a giant chess game. In order to isolate France and to avoid fighting a two-front war against France and Russia, Bismarck sought alliances with Austria-Hungary and Russia. He failed to conclude a lasting agreement with Russia, but he did forge an alliance with the declining Austro-Hungarian Empire, which wanted support to protect itself from possible conflict with Russia. In 1879, Germany and Austria-Hungary signed a secret Dual Alliance whereby both would make war together if either were attacked by Russia, and if either were attacked by another power, the other would remain neutral.

Three years later, in 1882, the Dual Alliance was enlarged to include Italy. Under the secret terms of the Triple Alliance, all three nations would fight together if Italy or Germany were attacked by France; if any one of these nations were attacked by any two great powers, all three would give mutual assistance. The Italians, fearing British naval power, stipulated that the treaty did not apply if Great Britain were involved in any of the attacks. Italy was willing to align itself with Germany because it was angry over the 1881 French takeover of Tunisia and because Germany offered to assist in securing Libya for the Italian empire.

Bismarck also tried to prevent Austrian-Russian conflict in the Balkans, but such efforts were often threatened by Austria-Hungary's ambitions for territorial gains there. Indeed, Austria's aggressive foreign policy against both Italy and the Balkan nations directly conflicted with the surging nationalism in these areas and contributed to the destruction of Bismarck's carefully constructed alliance system. Initially, Great Britain, secure with its naval superiority, remained aloof from these maneuverings. However, after Germany announced that it intended to build a first-class navy and in general to become a major industrial and military power, Great Britain's policy of isolation rapidly changed.

In 1890, Bismarck resigned under pressure from Kaiser Wilhelm II, who wanted to be his own chief minister. Wilhelm II sought to reestablish a more autocratic government, a move that was opposed by the German socialists. Wilhelm also supported the growth of the German military and the stockpiling of armaments. With continued economic prosperity and successes in expanding the German empire, Wilhelm II had little difficulty in repelling socialist attempts to take control of the government.

Like Italy, Germany came late to the imperial scramble and had to pick up the leftover pieces. Germany acquired a block of islands in the western Pacific and a sphere of influence in China. The Germans also obtained several scattered territories in Africa: Togoland and Cameroon in western Africa, German East Africa (Tanzania), and German Southwest Africa (Namibia). Other imperial powers, hardly pacifists themselves, considered the Germans particularly aggressive in their prowling around the world looking for opportunities to expand their colonial power. The United States feared that the Germans were even trying to establish a base of power in the Western Hemisphere.

RUSSIA

To Western European eyes, tsarist Russia was a gigantic but backward nation. Territorially three times as large as the continental United States, it was overwhelmingly populated by peasants. Despite significant industrial growth in the preceding quarter century, in 1914 there were only about three million industrial workers out of a population of approximately 170 million. Nor was it a homogeneous population. The Russians (or Great Russians) were not quite half of the population of the empire. Ukrainians, Byelorussians, Poles, Lithuanians, Latvians, Estonians, Finns, Jews, Armenians, Georgians, and various Muslim Turkish groups made up the bulk of the remaining population, and numerous smaller ethnic groups also existed within the vast borders. Most of the non-Russians had their own cultural and religious traditions, and were held in the empire only by the greater strength of the Russians. The Russian school system had recently been expanded, but on the eve of World War I, less than half of the Russian population was literate.

Like his predecessors, Nicholas II, "Tsar of all the Russias" from 1894 to 1917, believed that he alone was chosen by God to rule the Russian Empire. Only a revolt in 1905 persuaded him of the necessity of allowing the creation of a Duma, or Parliament, which had very limited legislative powers. Once the turmoil quieted, Nicholas promptly began to retreat from reforms. When he found the composition of the first two Dumas not to his liking, he changed the electoral law in 1907 so as to obtain more conservative representatives. Disparaging the determination of the tsar to remain an autocratic ruler, his opponents grumbled, "The Duma is dead, long live the Duma." As a result of the tsar's interference, the next Duma was so cooperative that it was allowed to serve the maximum five-year term. The Fourth Duma had almost completed a full term when the first 1917 revolution occurred.

A symbol of the old order: Russian Tsar Nicholas II and his family around the turn of the century. (UPI/Bettmann Newsphotos)

Finding it difficult because of geographic constraints to move overseas to acquire colonies, Russians participated in the imperialism of the era by moving overland. By the nineteenth century, the Russian Empire had expanded overland eastward to the shores of the Pacific and southeastward to central Asia, or Turkestan. This growth was in some ways comparable to the westward expansion in the United States. Both American and Russian settlers pushed aside scattered tribes. Like the United States with Mexico, Russia also made extensive gains at the expense of established nations, including the Ottoman Empire, Persia, Afghanistan, and China. In 1891, the Russian government began building a transcontinental railroad, the Trans-Siberian Railway, to knit together the vast stretches of its domain. In 1903, Russian railroad workers completed their task, having built a 5,500-mile single track from Moscow to Vladivostok on the Pacific Ocean. Since Vladivostok was icebound for part of the year, Russia in 1896 forced China to allow a branch line of the railroad to pass through Chinese Manchuria to ice-free Port Arthur on the Yellow Sea. In Manchuria and Korea, Russian imperialism openly confronted Japanese imperialism, which sought to expand into the same territories.

SUMMARY

Before World War I, Europe was rich and powerful, but it was also plagued with internal problems. Domestically, all European governments struggled with the conflict among the forces of conservatism, liberalism, and socialism. In Great Britain, France, and even Germany, these internal political divisions resulted in reforms that improved the lives of middle-class and working-class people. In Russia, however, the conservative aristocrats continued to be the dominant political force. While both Britain and France were characterized by a trend toward liberalization, the more autocratic governments of Germany and Russia continued to maintain their ascendancy.

The continued and mounting trend of nationalism also escalated old rivalries among the various European nations. These nationalist rivalries poisoned the atmosphere and led European nations to increase their armaments and to forge alliances in order to achieve security. Despite the known problems in creating and maintaining alliances, both Germany and France designed alliance systems that were as likely to cause war as to keep the peace. Increased arms stockpiles and the alliances added to tensions instead of providing a sense of calm or security.

Finally, Europeans felt superior to the Asians and Africans whom they were eagerly incorporating into vast empires. Great Britain and France had the largest empires. Having unified late in the nineteenth century, both Germany and Italy were relative newcomers, and struggled to secure whatever territories remained independent in Africa and Asia. Russia was another major European imperialist power, whose interests clashed with Austria-Hungary in the Balkans. These imperialist rivalries added to the international tensions and further exacerbated hostilities among European nations.

SUGGESTED SOURCES

Gilbert, Felix, *Europe Since 1890,* 2nd. ed. (1979). A brief, general survey for students, with illustrations.*

Hale, Oron J., *The Great Illusion, 1900–1914* (1971). A survey of technological, economic, cultural, and political developments in Europe before World War I.*

Massie, Robert K., *Nicholas and Alexandra* (1967). A popular, sympathetic biography of the last Russian tsar and tsarina. Gives a feeling for the world of royalty before World War I.* (Also a film.)

Stone, Norman, *Europe Transformed, 1878–1919* (1984). A scholarly, readable, and comprehensive work that emphasizes the decline of liberalism.*

Tannenbaum, Edward R., *1900* (1977). A depiction of Europe in 1900 with special emphasis on the European response to modernization.*

"Upstairs-Downstairs," BBC series. A look at life among the British upper class and their servants during the early part of the twentieth century.

*Paperback available.

4

The European Conquest
of Africa

In the late nineteenth and early twentieth centuries, the major European nations were in full tide of imperialistic conquest all over the world. The most spectacular example of this process occurred in Africa. Until the last quarter of the nineteenth century, European nations controlled only a scattering of outposts on the African coast and some settlements in Algeria and the southern tip of Africa. Within thirty years, they had partitioned nearly all of the continent and incorporated vast areas into their colonial empires.

By 1914 only two states in Africa, Liberia and Ethiopia, remained independent. Liberia, partly settled by former slaves from the United States, remained heavily dependent economically on U.S. companies such as Firestone. The other independent nation, Ethiopia, had the unique distinction of defeating a European nation, Italy, when that country attempted to conquer it in 1896.

AFRICAN SOCIETIES

Africa contained a vast mosaic of tribal peoples who lived in the varied landscape of desert, rain forest, savannah, mountain, and coastal lands. All these peoples had adapted their social and economic organizations to their environments; hence some were hunters, others agriculturalists, nomads, food gatherers, or herders. Their political systems varied from tribal groupings under chieftains to large empires. From the eleventh century onward, Africa south of the Sahara had also experienced an influx of newcomers from Islamic-Arabized North Africa and from western Asia, and, beginning in the seventeenth century, also from Europe. As a result of the confrontations among these different groups, many traditional tribal patterns had been disrupted and some destroyed.

THE PARTITION OF AFRICA

European nations looked on Africa as a target for imperialism from a broad spectrum of motives—economic, strategic, cultural, and nationalistic. Leaders of several of these nations watched with particular interest the activities of a private trade association organized by King Leopold II of Belgium in 1876 with the purpose of exploiting the resources of the Congo basin. As Leopold had commented, "I want my share of this wonderful African cake." The Congo Free State, as it was called, was headed by Leopold in his private capacity, although his prestige as king of the Belgians was crucial to the success of the association. His oppressive policies there justified accusations that modern tropical colonization by Europeans was motivated only by economic greed. As Joseph Conrad put it in his novel *Heart of Darkness,* "To tear treasure out of the bowels of the land was their desire, with no more moral purpose at the back of it than there is in burglars breaking into a safe." The charge of shameless exploitation of the natives so embarrassed the Belgian people that in 1908 the government forced the king to hand over his territory, and replaced the purely exploitative regime of the Congo Free State with a paternalistic and more benevolent one.

Leopold's early success played a key role in sharpening the mutual suspicions of European nations about each other's intentions in Africa, and they began to elbow one another in earnest after 1880 to get what they wanted on that continent. At an international conference held in Berlin in 1884–85, European colonial powers agreed on "first come, first served" as the basic rule of dividing Africa. Any power that effectively occupied an African territory and notified others would be recognized as having established sole possession. After 1884, the scramble intensified as the older colonial powers—Portugal, Spain, and particularly Great Britain and France—expanded inland from their original outposts on the coast. The new nations of Italy and Germany got footholds on the African coast, often in neglected areas, and pushed inland as well. By 1912 almost all Africa was under European control. Between 1871 and 1900, Britain added about 4.3 million square miles of territory and sixty-six million people to its African empire, and France about 3.5 million square miles and twenty-six million people. The possessions of the other imperial powers were smaller and less populous. Since Great Britain and France dominated the conquest of Africa, their actions will be the focus of this chapter.

As Europeans sought to consolidate their holdings, Africans saw in the coming of the Europeans the destruction of their traditional ways of life. They resisted bitterly, although, with the exception of the Ethiopians, all of them lost. There were at least twenty-five conflicts with Europeans before World War I. Examples of resisters were the Ashanti in Dahomey and Benin, the Herreros in German Southwest Africa, and numerous peoples in Islamic northern Africa. Two of the most determined groups that fought for years before succumbing were the followers of the Mahdi in the Sudan and the Zulus of southern Africa, both treated in the following discussion.

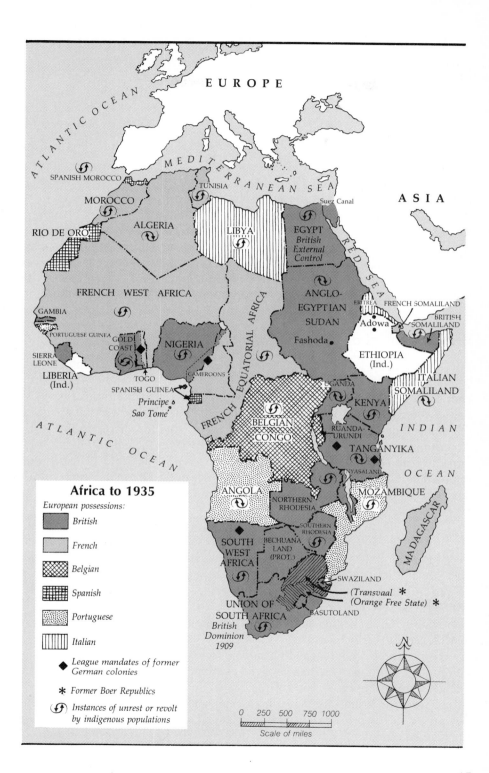

EUROPE

ATLANTIC OCEAN

MEDITERRANEAN SEA

ASIA

SPANISH MOROCCO

MOROCCO

TUNISIA

Suez Canal

ALGERIA

LIBYA

EGYPT
*British
External
Control*

RED SEA

RIO DE ORO

FRENCH WEST AFRICA

ANGLO-
EGYPTIAN
SUDAN

ERITREA

FRENCH SOMALILAND

BRITISH
SOMALILAND

GAMBIA

PORTUGUESE GUINEA

GOLD
COAST

NIGERIA

FRENCH EQUATORIAL AFRICA

Adowa

Fashoda

ETHIOPIA
(Ind.)

ITALIAN
SOMALILAND

SIERRA
LEONE

LIBERIA
(Ind.)

TOGO

CAMEROONS

SPANISH GUINEA

Principe
Sao Tome

UGANDA

KENYA

INDIAN

BELGIAN
CONGO

RUANDA-
URUNDI

TANGANYIKA

ATLANTIC OCEAN

OCEAN

NYASALAND

ANGOLA

NORTHERN
RHODESIA

MOZAMBIQUE

MADAGASCAR

Africa to 1935

European possessions:

British

French

Belgian

Spanish

Portuguese

Italian

♦ League mandates of former
German colonies

✳ Former Boer Republics

Ⓕ Instances of unrest or revolt
by indigenous populations

SOUTHERN
RHODESIA

SOUTH
WEST
AFRICA

BECHUANA-
LAND
(PROT.)

SWAZILAND

(Transvaal ✳
(Orange Free State) ✳

UNION OF
SOUTH AFRICA
*British
Dominion
1909*

BASUTOLAND

N

0   250   500   750 1000

Scale of miles

45

The scramble to divide Africa created a number of intense hostilities, particularly among Great Britain, France, Germany, and Italy. Nevertheless, these problems were settled peacefully in European capitals. After partitioning Africa, Europeans found through surveying and exploration that few areas could produce immediate wealth without large capital investments. Therefore it is not surprising that once Africa had been divided up and there was no longer a reason to fear rivals, most European governments lost some of their interest in their newly acquired possessions.

NORTH AFRICA

North Africa between the Mediterranean Sea and the Sahara Desert was a land of ancient civilizations. Since the eighth century *a.d.*, most peoples of this region had been Muslim. This land was called the *Mahgrib,* which means "the west" in Arabic, since it was the westernmost extension of Arab culture.

British Control of Egypt and the Sudan

The Suez Canal, designed by a French engineer and built by an international company, was opened in 1869. The canal provided a shortcut between Europe and Asia. Because of their far-flung empire and global trading network, the British were the most interested in the canal. In 1875, Great Britain acquired the controlling interest when the ruler of Egypt sold his shares to the British government to avert bankruptcy. In order to protect the canal, Great Britain moved to dominate Egypt. In 1882, Egypt became a de facto British protectorate, although it nominally remained a province of the Ottoman Empire. British advisors filled all important Egyptian government offices and were the real rulers of that land.

Egypt claimed possession of the Sudan, which controlled the water supply of the Nile River. The Sudanese, who resented Egyptian control, rose in revolt in 1883 under the Mahdi (Rightly Guided One), the leader of a nationalist Muslim movement. Since Great Britain controlled Egypt, it became involved in putting down the Sudanese uprising. Between 1896 and 1898, General Sir Herbert Kitchener undertook the reconquest of the Sudan. On its pacification, Great Britain and Egypt established joint rule over the land, which in effect meant British control.

When the British reached Fashoda in southern Sudan in 1898, they found a French expedition, which had arrived overland from the west, occupying that village. France hoped to control the Sudan so that its African empire might extend from the Atlantic to the Indian Ocean, and in order to pressure the British downriver in Egypt by controlling the Nile. The ensuing standoff was called the Fashoda Incident. France backed down in 1899 and renounced all claims to the Nile valley in return for British recognition of its claims in the Sahara. This

In 1898, an Anglo-Egyptian force commanded by General Kitchener conquered the Sudan. Here the Twenty-first Lancers charge at the battle of Omdurman. (Walker Art Gallery, Liverpool)

crisis illustrates the intensity of colonial rivalries in Africa, although these rivalries never led directly to war.

The French Conquest and Settlement of Northwest Africa

France was the dominant colonial power north of the Sahara. Between 1830 and 1869, France had conquered Algeria, which it then used as a base for further advances. By the end of the century, in spite of rival Italian interest, the French had made Tunisia to the east a protectorate, although, as in Egypt, a facade of native government continued to exist. The French also moved southward across the Sahara, and finally westward into Morocco.

Unlike the British, who made no attempt to send settlers to Egypt, the French from the start encouraged the immigration of Europeans into Algeria. Algerians found themselves pushed off their best agricultural lands to make room for European colonists. By 1911, out of a total population of 5.6 million people in Algeria, 752,000 were Europeans. Tunisia had a European population of 130,000.

In both Algeria and Tunisia, there was friction between the privileged European minority and the Arab majority. The Muslims were treated in every respect as a conquered people. Under the circumstances, it is hardly surprising that a "racial problem" developed between the Europeans and Muslims. In no other part of the Islamic world were Muslims confronted with so large a number of aliens settled in their midst.

In addition to economic advantages, the privileged European settlers enjoyed the right of political representation in the legislature of metropolitan France. Under the French constitution, the *colons* (French settlers) in Algeria sent six deputies and three senators to the French parliament in 1900. The Muslims had no representation. Established in a position of superiority, many *colons* regarded the Algerians with open contempt. "The Arab must accept the fate of the conquered," wrote one *colon*. "He must either become assimilated to our civilization or disappear. European civilization can have no sympathy for the life of the savage."

Gradually, the abuses of the colonial system became widely known in France and a spirited debate on colonial policy ensued in the Chamber of Deputies (French legislature), which enacted reforms early in the twentieth century. Given the tenor of French thought, the ideal of most reformers was progressive assimilation. Upper-class Algerian Muslims were encouraged to attend French schools and adopt French ways, for which they would be rewarded with a share in the power structure of the French Empire.

The policy of assimilation failed, however, for three basic reasons. One was the resistance of most Algerians, who were not prepared to renounce their culture and their religious law for those of their masters. Secondly, not all French opinion supported the assimilation plan, and it was limited in the scope of its execution. The *colons* were another factor. Unwilling to give up their privileges, they opposed most measures designed to lessen or dilute their power.

Morocco was the last French acquisition in North Africa. At the beginning of the twentieth century, Morocco was an independent kingdom beset by internal problems. For a time, the government of Morocco was able to delay the French imperialistic advances by exploiting the Franco-German rivalry in international affairs and appealing to the German government for help. Germany was at first happy to play this game, but in the face of European opposition it eventually backed down and recognized Morocco as a French sphere of influence. In 1912, the Sultan of Morocco was forced to sign a treaty that handed his country over to French protection.

WEST AFRICA

This huge territory contained some of the harshest deserts and some of the lushest rain forests in Africa. Before European colonization, the peoples in this area lived in societies ranging in scope from large empires like that of the Muslim Hausa-Fulani peoples in today's northern Nigeria, through well-organized kingdoms like that of the Ashanti in today's Ghana, to small groups who still lived by hunting and gathering in the equatorial rain forests. Except for those areas south of the Sahara that had become largely Islamic, traditional religions prevailed in West Africa.

Indirect Rule in Great Britain's Scattered Colonies

In West Africa, Great Britain ruled four colonies strung out on the coast and mostly surrounded by French possessions. There the British opened mines and encouraged cash crops worked by African peasants. They made this development profitable by building railroads to connect the coast with the interior. The Gold Coast (Ghana) was the best example of a successful and prosperous colony. Here, the railroad system made it possible to exploit timber, open up cocoa plantations, and develop gold mines in the hinterland. British-owned trading companies and their shareholders became rich from these operations. This economic process also provided jobs for some Africans, but it disrupted the previous subsistence economy.

In administering Africa, the British applied no preconceived notions of colonial government but devised practical, day-by-day solutions to the problems of governing. The policy Great Britain eventually applied in West Africa was called "indirect rule," a system developed by Lord Lugard, governor-general of Nigeria, Great Britain's largest West African colony. First developed as a pragmatic device to administer a district easily and cheaply, the concept soon spread throughout British African holdings. Because the British administrative staff was small, the African chief and his tribal council were delegated the task of running the day-to-day matters of government. They were supervised by a British official who also saw to it that British interests in the area were upheld.

Climatic conditions and an already large native population made West Africa unsuitable and unattractive for British immigration. The absence of a British immigrant group eager to compete for local jobs meant more opportunities for Africans. Many were very anxious to acquire a Western education to qualify them for the new skilled positions that the rapidly developing economy opened up. British official opinion was responsive and sometimes even enthusiastic about West African demands for more schools and job opportunities. Sir Frederick Guggisberg, governor of the Gold Coast during World War I, appointed a committee that drew up a new educational plan for that colony. This plan provided a foundation for the modernization of the Gold Coast, which paved the way for the independent nation of Ghana.

France's Vast West African Empire

By the twentieth century, France had acquired a huge block of colonial territory south of the Sahara that stretched 3,000 miles from the extreme west coast of Africa to the Congo River deep in central Africa. In Senegal, the oldest French colony in West Africa, the colonial administration encouraged the population to grow groundnuts on their farms as a cash crop. The peasants sold the nuts for cash, part of which they used to pay the head tax that was for many years the chief source of revenue for the government of Senegal. The French worked hard to implant French culture in Senegal, with some success. The capital at Dakar, with its boulevards and shops filled with French-speaking Africans and Europeans, was often referred to as the "Paris of Africa." Senegalese units fought in the French army around the world.

The colonies in the interior were sparsely populated, lacking in resources, and difficult to reach. The three major river systems in this area—the Congo, the Senegal, and the Niger—were difficult to navigate because of rapids that limited traffic. New cash crops, such as cotton in Niger, were introduced, but until railroads could be built to penetrate the interior, few products could be brought out. These colonies were therefore a financial drain on France. Cash crops such as palm oil and cocoa were introduced to the coastal colonies of Guinea, the Ivory Coast, and Dahomey, and proved profitable.

Pending the completion of new railroads to move the products to market, economic efficiency led the French government in 1904 to gather the West African territories into a single unit, called the Federation of French West Africa, under a governor-general who ruled from Dakar. The economic benefits that resulted from the federation of French West Africa led the French government to follow the same policy in its territories in the Congo basin, joining them into the Federation of French Equatorial Africa in 1910 under a governor-general who ruled from Brazzaville. In both cases, the greater resources of a federated colonial government resulted in faster economic development.

BRITISH EAST AFRICA: THE ADVENT OF A MULTIRACIAL SOCIETY

Geographically, this area is dominated by a chain of mountains and high plateaus that extends southward from Kenya to the Cape of Good Hope. The temperate uplands soon attracted British settlers. To the British Colonial Office in search of revenue, the prospect of settlement by British farmers seemed a good bet for economic development. Up to World War I, the number of British settlers in East Africa and central Africa remained small—around 3,000 in what is now Kenya, and a few hundred in Uganda. English settlers congregated in what were previously sparsely populated lands and did not intrude into areas of the dense and prosperous African population of Ugandans around Lake Victoria. However, from a long-term perspective, the British colonists became a disruptive factor in the region, competing with the Africans for land and exploiting labor. Many Africans became migrant laborers on European farms. This development caused political and social problems in the next generation.

The interracial tensions of East Africa were further inflamed when the British government allowed large numbers of Indians to be imported to build railroads and to work as clerks in government offices and commercial companies. Indians settled in towns and villages, and many also became traders. In the early decades, it was the Europeans who resented the numerous and articulate Indians in their midst. In a later era, as a result of growing African nationalism, Indian British subjects became the victims of African majorities who did not think Indians belonged in Africa. Thus, in British East Africa, a pluralist society was formed in the early twentieth century that had disturbing consequences in later years.

SOUTHERN AFRICA

In this temperate part of the continent, European colonies dated back to the beginning of the age of exploration and European settlement made by far its largest penetration. The early inhabitants of southern Africa were a scattered population of Bushmen and Hottentots, who lived by hunting and gathering and who were easily subdued by white settlers. Starting in the late eighteenth century, Bantus, who engaged in both herding and agriculture, began to immigrate from the north in large numbers. Clashes among the Bantu tribes and between the Bantus and Europeans resulted in the emergence of the warlike Zulus. Zulu leaders forged their people into a fighting nation that subjugated other tribes and fought the white man in several Zulu wars. While the whites eventually defeated the Zulus, they were not able to prevent the influx of these peoples into southern Africa. South Africa became a land with a black majority and white minority, the basis for race problems in the twentieth century.

The Birth and Death of the Boer Republics

South Africa attracted large numbers of white colonists over the years because of benign climate, good soil, and, in the late nineteenth century, the discovery of large gold and diamond deposits. When Great Britain acquired the Dutch colony located at the Cape of Good Hope in 1815, it also inherited the Dutch colonists of the land, who called themselves Boers (farmers). The Boers resented British rule, particularly a law which forbade slavery and forced the Boers to emancipate their slaves. To escape British control, the Boers in the 1830s and 1840s made a mass migration called the Great Trek (journey) into the interior of Africa. There they founded two independent republics, the Orange Free State and the Transvaal. Meanwhile, British settlers poured into the Cape Province and into Natal, the new colony to the east. The relationship between the Boer republics and Great Britain was tense, especially after gold was discovered in the Transvaal, and the Boer-controlled government discriminated against the non-Boer whites who had immigrated to the republics.

In 1899, war broke out between Great Britain and the two Boer republics. The Boers were ably led by Paul Kruger, the president of the Transvaal, and for three years Boer commandos (guerrillas), who perfected hit-and-run tactics of combat, successfully resisted the might of the British Empire. British forces resorted to the same harsh but effective anti-guerrilla measures used by the Spanish in Cuba and Americans in the Philippines in that period. They burned farms and herded women and children into concentration camps to deprive the commandos of refuge and resources. The Boers finally surrendered in 1902.

Out of their dogged resistance emerged modern Boer, or Afrikaner, nationalism. In an attempt to conciliate the defeated Boers, Great Britain let them decide whether blacks and other nonwhites should be given the vote; true to their white supremacist tradition, the Boers denied them suffrage. When the two former Boer states federated with the two British colonies of Natal and the Cape in 1909 to form the Union of South Africa, a self-governing dominion in the British Empire, blacks were denied political rights.

The Rhodesias: One-Man Imperialism

While trouble was brewing with the Boer republics, north of them was an area of high plains and good soil that in previous centuries had been the location of an African state centered at Great Zimbabwe. This area became the scene of one of the classic examples of European imperialism, built upon the exploits of the "Empire Builder" Cecil Rhodes, a British adventurer who had made a fortune from diamond mining in South Africa. An unabashed imperialist, he once exclaimed, "I would annex the planets if I could!"

At Rhodes's request, the British government annexed two territories which it named Northern Rhodesia and Southern Rhodesia, and delegated the government of those lands to his South Africa Company. During the 1890s, the company's army was responsible for winning Portuguese acquiescence in the British takeover of that area and for the defeat of the Matabele and Mashona tribes, who bitterly resented the company's demands on their land and labor. Fighting did not stop until 1897, after which company-sponsored European immigrants began to arrive, eventually constituting 5 percent of the total population.

THE IMPACT OF COLONIAL RULE ON AFRICA

The positive and negative effects of colonial rule of Africans varied greatly and differed from society to society. As always happens under conditions of change, some groups benefited. They were either lucky or farsighted enough to cooperate with the new masters and to take advantage of new circumstances, thereby winning favors, prestige, and sometimes additional land. Such beneficiaries were the Baganda people of Uganda and the Ibos in Nigeria, who welcomed chances for a British education and cooperated with the British authorities. They were rewarded with positions in the colonial bureaucracy.

Conversely, large numbers suffered from colonial rule, especially in areas where Europeans sought to settle or to extract minerals. In some instances, tribes were split under different European jurisdictions, while in others several traditionally hostile tribes were grouped under a single administration. In parts of Kenya and the Rhodesias, for example, hundreds of thousands of Africans lost their land. Many were forced to inferior lands designated as "native reserves" or became tenants of and laborers for the new white landowners.

It would be an exaggeration, however, to imagine that all Africans were directly affected when whites took over their areas. Large areas, in fact, remained untouched by white rule. Up until World War I, colonial officials frequently had little control over the local scene and had to work within the restraints of local kinship groups, village communities, and tribal ties. In Morocco and Tunisia, European diplomatic entanglements compelled the French to retain native rulers in power.

The indirect effects were much more widespread. Europeans investing in Africa demanded laborers to work in mines and on plantations and to build roads and railroads. Whether laborers were paid or not, their service was compulsory. On the issue of forced labor, European reaction was contradictory and tinged with hypocrisy. Although Europeans abhorred slavery, they permitted the forced labor of Africans. Yet when facts about King Leopold's methods to exact labor services in the Congo Free State were made public, adverse European public opinion forced the Belgian government to take over responsibility for its administration in 1908.

Despite the violence generated by the imposition of colonial rule, some forms of violence in Africa decreased after colonization. Colonial authorities suppressed the tribal wars, cattle rustling, and slave raids that had caused much bloodshed before the European takeover. Peace, better public health programs, development of cash crops, and agricultural improvements led to large increases in population. In some areas, rural peoples moved into the newly established cities for work, causing problems of social adjustment.

European control was invariably accompanied by Christian missionary activity, which had an important impact. In many inaccessible villages, the missionary teacher and preacher was much more likely than the colonial administrator to be the white person that the African encountered. In the early days, the teachers in the missionary "bush schools" were Europeans, but soon the first African pupils themselves became teachers and missionaries. By the early twentieth century, in many parts of Africa, Western education and Christian religion were expanding hand in hand. Christian missionaries and teachers brought with them not only new religion and education but also medical care and a general acquaintance with the scientific, technological, and intellectual bases of Western civilization.

In North Africa and areas immediately south of the Sahara, Islam remained the rallying point of the people and Christianity had little impact. Thus, in Algeria, the majority of Algerians resisted assimilation into an alien religion and culture, as did the peoples of Morocco, Tunisia, and Libya. At the same time, Muslim missionaries were equally active and spread their religion and culture south of the Sahara.

Western cultural impact on Africa: A drawing of missionary Robert Moffat preaching to the Tswanas. (African Museum, Johannesburg)

Early in the twentieth century, a new kind of leadership began to emerge in Africa. It consisted of Western-educated black Africans who rejected the authority of the traditional chiefs and willingly seized the new opportunities created by colonialism. Some of the new elite received further education in the ruling nations, where they gained new standards for judging the colonial administrations of their lands. They found that compared with the ideals professed by Western democracies, the actual policies of the colonial administrations invariably fell short. As a result, these Africans developed anticolonial movements. Even before World War I, these new leaders were demanding that African Christian churches be placed under black African leadership and that African independent states be established based on modern democratic concepts.

SUMMARY

In the late nineteenth and early twentieth centuries, European imperialism, based on a mixture of economic, strategic, cultural, and nationalistic motives, expressed itself in the partition of the African continent. The preeminence of European nations in industrial, technical, and military development made it relatively easy for them to defeat tribal societies and seize their territories. Although nationalism created intense rivalries between the imperialist states, diplomacy triumphed and they were able to avoid war against each other as they carved up Africa.

During this period, Great Britain and France seized the largest amount of African territory, but Germany, Italy, and Belgium also made extensive acquisitions. Spanish holdings in North Africa dated to an earlier century, as did those of Portugal, which were enlarged by expanding into the interior. Africans often resisted European imperialism, but with the exception of the Ethiopians and Liberians, all Africans were eventually subjugated. Many African groups were dislocated or destroyed in the process.

Europeans in Africa extensively exploited the mineral and agricultural products there, often by means of forced labor, sometimes with labor imported from other parts of their empires. On the other hand, colonial authorities sometimes introduced programs for health, education, and social welfare, and suppressed intertribal violence. While Europeans ruled some areas of Africa indirectly and allowed the local traditional cultural patterns to continue, in many cases their colonial administrations eliminated the traditional political leadership and imposed Western systems of government, taxation, and justice. Both Christian and Muslim missionaries worked to win converts from adherents of traditional African religions.

SUGGESTED SOURCES

Achebe, Chinua, *Things Fall Apart* (1978). A study of the disastrous effects of European contact on the African tribal society in Nigeria.*

The Horizon History of Africa (1971). A thoughtful text, with lavish illustrations and maps.

Kenyatta, Jomo, *Facing Mount Kenya* (1962). A collection of studies that depict in a favorable light the life and customs of Kenya's Kikuyu tribe before they were altered by the impact of imperialism.*

Morsy, Magali, *North Africa 1800–1900: A Survey from the Nile Valley to the Atlantic* (1984). An account and analysis of the peoples and societies of North Africa before and during the period of European imperial expansion.

Oliver, Roland, and Anthony Atomore, *Africa Since 1800,* 3rd ed. (1981). A standard survey of Africa and European imperialism.*

Robinson, Roland and John Gallagher, with Alice Denny, *Africa and the Victorians* (1961). A study of European expansion and the strategic reasons for imperialism.*

"Search for the Nile," BBC series. A six-part account of British explorers in Africa. A good visual account with numerous personal vignettes of nineteenth-century imperialists.

*Paperback available.

5

The United States
and Latin America

By 1900 the United States had emerged as the first world power from the Western Hemisphere. It was already one of the world's major industrialized states,
and as its economy, military, and national pride grew, it began to expand and
defend its interests throughout the region. In the process, it became one of the
leading imperialist powers.

THE UNITED STATES AT THE TURN
OF THE CENTURY

General Characteristics

By tradition, most citizens of the United States of America looked upon themselves as heaven-blessed. Far from the tumults of Europe, Americans had been
left alone for almost a century to develop one of the richest areas of the globe.
The United States was the second-largest nation in the Western Hemisphere in
total area and the largest in arable land. It contained five times the population
of the next-largest nation in the hemisphere and ranked fourth in population
worldwide. Whether measured in terms of property ownership or of per capita
income, the standard of living for most Americans far exceeded that of the other
nations in the hemisphere and rivaled that of the powerful European nations.
The overall affluence and high educational level of Americans made possible a
stable political system. The nation's farmers and ranchers produced an enormous quantity of food and fibers, enough to feed and clothe its citizens cheaply
and to lead the world in the value of its agricultural exports. The United States
dwarfed the rest of the hemisphere in general manufacturing and led all nations
in railroad mileage, iron ore and coal output, and iron and steel production.
Business leaders were aggressively entering the world of international trade and
finance and were gaining rapidly on European nations in the value of capital
invested abroad and the value of all exports to other areas of the world. To

protect its rapidly growing international trade, especially with Europe, the United States had built up the third-largest navy in the world.

Populist and Progressive Struggles

Despite its general affluence, economic power, and self-confidence, the United States at the turn of the century was beset by divisions. Most Americans were raised on farms and in small towns and had to learn how to adapt to a rapidly industrializing and urbanizing society. Major businesses, such as Standard Oil, U.S. Steel, and the Morgan Bank, amassed great power as monopolies. Like their European counterparts, U.S. factory workers worked long hours under unsafe conditions, were paid low wages, and lived in city slums and rundown housing in company towns. Some workers organized for collective bargaining to improve their situation. The American Federation of Labor, an association of skilled craftsmen led by Samuel Gompers, was the most effective of the early labor organizations. Unskilled workers trying to improve working conditions in the steel industry participated in massive strikes, such as the one at Homestead, Pennsylvania, where they fought with police and armed strikebreakers. After 1900, labor unrest spread to the mining towns and lumber camps in the West, where some workers were led by the syndicalist Industrial Workers of the World, or Wobblies. On the whole, however, unionization lagged behind industrialized Europe; only about 4 percent of all industrial workers were organized at the turn of the century.

Farmers, especially in the South and in the Plains states, comprised another major group that felt threatened by business consolidation. They found themselves facing monopolies in railroad shipping, commodity storage, and meat packing. They received low prices for the products they sold and paid high prices for the goods they purchased. To remedy their plight, the farmers organized politically, capturing control of several states in the agricultural belt. These farmer-controlled state legislatures then passed legislation regulating the operation of railroads, grain elevators, cotton gins, and stockyards.

On the national level, farmers formed the Populist party and seized temporary control of the Democratic party. Populist politicians then allied with small business interests and other reformers to frame national legislation that curbed the growing trend toward monopoly. The Populists and their allies were basically responsible for creating the first independent regulatory commission, the Interstate Commerce Commission, which they empowered to regulate railroad freight rates. The reformist political coalition also secured the first antitrust legislation and a graduated income tax. Populists also tried but failed to manipulate the value of currency for the benefit of debtors.

However, farmers and workers weakened their causes by fighting one another. Supreme Court decisions also tended to favor big business interests. Thus, in 1900, big business essentially controlled politics at every level and was stronger than ever.

After 1900, the growing middle class of small businessmen, professionals, and white-collar employees in towns and cities, especially in the East and

Confronted by Poverty

[We were] taken to the East End [the London slums] to witness the Saturday night sale of decaying vegetables and fruit, . . . [W]e saw two huge masses of ill-clad people clamoring around two hucksters' carts. They were bidding their farthings and ha'pennies for a vegetable held up by the auctioneer, which he at last scornfully flung, with a gibe for its cheapness, to the successful bidder. . . . [T]he final impression was not of ragged, tawdry clothing, nor of pinched and sallow faces, but of myriads of hands, empty, pathetic, nerveless and workworn, showing white in the uncertain light of the street, and clutching forward for food that was already unfit to eat.

I have never since been able to see a number of hands held upward, . . . without a certain revival of this memory, a clutching at the heart reminiscent of the despair and resentment which seized me then.*

This 1880s scene in London, which might have been witnessed in urban centers all over the world at the turn of the century, was one of the experiences that propelled Jane Addams to take action to combat poverty. An upper-middle-class young woman from a small town in Illinois, Addams had come to believe that her college education and comfortable financial circumstances not only put her in an elite minority among women but also made her responsible to help the less fortunate. In 1889, she founded Hull House, the famous urban complex in Chicago that addressed itself through a broad spectrum of programs to the needs of the poor. She became a powerful advocate, through her work and writing, of improved working conditions, women's rights, and peace. She received the Nobel Peace Prize in 1931. The "settlement house" and the new profession of social work were major components of the reform spirit that marked the Progressive era.

*From *Twenty Years at Hull House* by Jane Addams. Copyright © 1910 by Macmillan Co. Reprinted by permission.

Midwest, took the lead in working for reform. While they had different goals, when united they constituted a formidable constituency in support of change. Small businessmen found it difficult to survive in a corporate world, and were afraid of political and social polarization between supporters of the big business interests and those of the farmers and workers. Some of them resented the corrupt subservience of politicians to big business and detested the political machines that manipulated the new immigrants. Still others demanded equality for women, the abolition of child labor, and the elimination of gambling, prostitution, and alcohol. This restless middle class, at times in uneasy alliance with certain business interests, led the nation into an era of reform called Progressivism. The movement spread through both the Democratic and Republican parties, although in one election it fielded its own slate of candidates. Presidents Theodore Roosevelt, William Howard Taft, and Woodrow Wilson gave varying measures of support to the Progressive movement.

The Progressive era was one of extensive reforms in political structure and process. The most important were the vote for women in national elections in 1920, the direct election of senators, and the institution of party primaries. Progressives also reformed the structure of city government. New procedures, especially the initiative, the referendum, and the recall, gave citizens more leverage in creating legislation and in reducing corruption in office.

In addition, the Progressives expanded the power of both the state and the national government to regulate the economy, to protect the public from big business, and to provide increased public services. Using this power, they secured legislation that improved sanitation and education and upgraded working conditions, especially for women, children, and those in dangerous occupations. At the national level, they made monetary reforms and introduced the graduated income tax, the eight-hour day for railroad workers, pure food and drug regulations, laws mandating conservation of natural resources, and lower tariffs. They increased the network of laws and agencies for regulating big business, and through the Federal Reserve System improved the nation's financial structure. The wave of reform was in full tide by 1917, but the entry of the United States into World War I turned energies toward the war effort, and the reform spirit ebbed.

Racial and Ethnic Problems

Ethnic and racial prejudice and repression constituted another major problem in the United States. Blacks, Hispanics, and Asians were subjected to legal segregation in housing and education, and Asians were prohibited from owning land. In the South and elsewhere, the white majority was in the process of depriving blacks of the political and legal gains made during Reconstruction by such tactics as literacy tests, poll taxes, threats of job loss, and lynchings. While some blacks fought back through the press, the courts, and the NAACP (National Association for the Advancement of Colored People), most submitted to the dominance of the white majority.

Moreover, many of the white Americans of northern European descent, who controlled the economy and politics and set the social norms of the nation, looked down upon whites of Eastern and southern European descent. These "nativist" Americans attacked the traditional policy of open immigration because it allowed millions of new immigrants, mostly Slavs, Jews, Italians, and Greeks, to enter the United States annually. They sought to restrict immigration, and they were successful after World War I.

The Turn toward Imperialism

When Americans looked overseas at the turn of the century, they saw that imperialism was the dominant phenomenon in world affairs. The ambivalence Americans

Mulberry Street, New York: A neighborhood of new immigrants, a sight that often aroused fears in many Americans at the turn of the century. (Library of Congress)

felt toward imperialism accounted for some of the contradictions in U.S. foreign policy since independence. On one hand, the Americans were the prime example of a people who had won freedom from European colonial control. They had supported, at least in words, freedom for suppressed peoples elsewhere. On the other hand, most Americans believed that they were a chosen people and that it was their "Manifest Destiny" to expand throughout North America, and perhaps the whole hemisphere. They had at times aggressively expanded across the continent, at the expense of the Indians, Spain, and Mexico, in particular. U.S. capitalists were beginning to exploit the economies and to influence the public affairs of some Latin American nations.

By the 1890s, most Americans considered their nation a great global power. Although many still opposed imperialism, an increasing number had concluded that as a great nation the United States should have its share of colonies, protectorates, and spheres of influence, as did the other great powers. They agreed with Europeans that, as a part of the superior Western civilization, they were justified in joining the European march to rule the more "backward" parts of the world. Rather than seize colonies in non-Western areas across the oceans, however, Americans pursued their primary imperialist interests quite differently. The United States, chiefly through indirect means, took economic and political control of neighbors that were also a part of Western culture—the nations of Latin America.

SOCIAL, ECONOMIC, AND POLITICAL PATTERNS IN LATIN AMERICA

Latin America was the only major area of the world where substantial numbers of persons from three races lived together. However, the region was dominated by whites, who had conquered the region and controlled it for four centuries. The white population of Latin America had been in the distinct minority for most of this period until a wave of immigration from Europe in the late nineteenth century substantially increased the proportion of whites in southern South America. While whites had virtually destroyed the Indian population in some parts of Latin America, Indians were still in the majority in parts of Central America, the Amazon jungles, and the Andes mountains. Cohabitation between Indians and whites had resulted in large numbers of *mestizos* (persons of mixed white and Indian parentage), a group that would play a major role in twentieth-century developments. Whites had also brought millions of black slaves from Africa to the Caribbean and to sections of Brazil, where they had become the majority of the population. Cohabitation between whites and blacks had also created a significant number of mixed-blood mulattoes.

European conquerors also dominated Latin America culturally. Indian customs and languages survived to some extent in areas where they remained a majority, but in most places Indian culture had been supplanted by the values and customs of Europe, particularly those of Spain and Portugal. The vast majority of people, whatever their race or origin, spoke Spanish (Portuguese in Brazil; various European languages in the Caribbean) and were members of the Roman Catholic Church. Literature, art, and music, while distinctively Latin American, were based on the cultural forms of Latin Europe.

In the early twentieth century, most Latin American nations were characterized by two classes separated by a great gulf. At the top were a small group of European-descended whites, the *patrones* (landlords or patrons), who, along with foreign investors, owned the ranches, mines, and plantations of each nation. Like the established families of most societies elsewhere in the world, the *patrones* monopolized the wealth, social prestige, education, and cultural attainments of their nations. Many of them aspired to the ideal of nobility, with high standards of personal morality and a parental concern for those who worked for them. Some *patrones* lived up to these ideals, but most, consciously or unconsciously, exploited their workers. Allied with the *patrones* was another small group, the socially inferior middle-class professionals who wanted to join the propertied class.

In general, Latin American landowners, many of them content to preserve an aristocratic life-style, had not efficiently exploited the extensive array of natural resources in their region. For the most part, they neglected their abundant industrial raw materials while they clung to producing traditional colonial agricultural products—sugar, tobacco, coffee, and meat—that faced stiff competition on the world market. Agricultural production was low because of poor land-use methods. The owners preferred to employ cheap hoe-wielding hand labor rather than use expensive plows and tractors. They did not fertilize the soil, and much of the land was left fallow after having been depleted of its nutrients. As a result, a number of Latin American nations had to import food. Late in the nineteenth century, investors from Great Britain, France, and the United States began to move in. They reorganized plantations for efficient sugar and fruit production, mined ores for industry elsewhere, created factories to process agricultural and ranching products, and built up transportation and communications networks. In the process, Latin America became an economic colony of the advanced Western nations.

Far below the "establishment," the huge mass of rural and urban workers— Indians, *mestizos,* blacks, mulattoes, and some of the newly arrived white immigrants—comprised the great majority of the population. In the rural areas, the *campesinos* (country people) worked generation after generation on the estates of the elite, bound to the land by tradition, ignorance, and debt. A few *campesinos* owned tiny parcels of land that were often too small to support their families. They lived in shacks with dirt floors, lacked water and sanitation facilities, and had little medical attention or education. Malnutrition was common, and starvation also occurred. The high birth rate was paralleled by a high death rate, especially for infants. Life expectancy in some areas was in the thirties. Some of the rural people were Indians, most of whom spoke no Spanish or Portuguese and followed their traditional culture. Most *campesinos* were docile, respectful, and orderly; on the whole they complained little and rarely rioted or rebelled.

By 1900 several Latin American nations, such as Mexico, Argentina, Brazil, and Chile, were beginning to expand mining operations and to industrialize, and as a consequence an urban working class was swiftly developing. In the city neighborhoods and at the mines, factories, and workshops, the workers experienced the same miserable conditions commonly found all over the world at the onset of industrialization: overcrowded housing, poor sanitation, inadequate health care, unsafe working conditions, low wages, and no provision for accident, sickness, or layoff.

When the Latin American nations became independent early in the nineteenth century, their leaders placed republican forms and procedures in their national constitutions. However, widespread poverty and illiteracy and the lack of a democratic tradition quickly produced a system in which political power was often seized and held by a dictator, the *caudillo*. The *caudillo* ruled with the support of the dominant elements—the Church, the armed forces, the landlords, and foreign investors—and by force of personality. The *caudillo* system, however, was unstable and was often marked by violent changes in leadership.

THE UNITED STATES TAKES OVER THE CARIBBEAN

U.S. interests in Latin America were centered in the Caribbean and the nations adjacent to it. Economically, the United States wanted to control investment and trade in the area in order to import needed fruit, coffee, minerals, and petroleum and to monopolize the sale of foodstuffs and manufactured items. Strategically, U.S. leaders were worried that the political instability and military weakness of the republics of Central America, coupled with the economic attractions of the region, would tempt European powers to interfere. As early as 1823, through the Monroe Doctrine, the United States had opposed the expansion of European colonies in the Western Hemisphere. Although it was initially too weak to enforce its position without the concurrence of Great Britain, by the end of the nineteenth century the United States was powerful enough to enforce this policy. Thus, in 1895, it intervened in a boundary dispute between Venezuela and Great Britain with the ringing declaration that "the United States is practically sovereign on this continent."

The Spanish-American War and Its Results

In 1898, an opportunity arose for U.S. expansion into the Caribbean. For many years Americans had been particularly interested in the Spanish colony of Cuba; some had wanted to annex it, some to free it, and some to exploit it economically whether it remained a colony or became independent. Since 1869, some

Central America and the Caribbean to 1935

Scenes of U.S. intervention

Canal Zone   U.S. acquisitions

0   200   400   600

Scales of miles

Cubans had been fighting a predominantly guerrilla war for independence. The Spanish government had retaliated with an internment program that confined civilians to detention camps. On February 15, 1898, the battleship *Maine,* sent to Havana to demonstrate U.S. concern, was blown up and 260 men were killed. An influential segment of the U.S. public and press blamed Spain and clamored for revenge, and Congress declared war on Spain. The U.S. navy easily destroyed Spanish squadrons in Cuba and the Philippines, while a small U.S. volunteer army forced the Spanish garrisons in Cuba and Puerto Rico to sue for peace. Admiral George Dewey and Theodore Roosevelt's Rough Riders became the heroes of the day as the public hailed them for winning a "splendid little war" in four months.

In the peace treaty, Spain ceded Puerto Rico to the United States and gave Cuba its independence. U.S. imperialists and anti-imperialists clashed vehemently over what to do with the Spanish possessions now under the military control of the United States. The imperialists favored annexation of Cuba, but the anti-imperialists in Congress were able to push through the Teller Amendment, in which the United States disavowed any intention of exercising "sovereignty, jurisdiction, or control" over that island. However, situated only ninety miles from the Florida coast, Cuba was too important strategically for the United States to ignore, and in the long run imperialism won out. Cuba became a virtual U.S. protectorate, as its constitution permitted the United States to intervene in time of political or economic crisis. During the first decade of its so-called independence, Cuba was twice under U.S. military rule. Cuba also agreed to lease military sites to the United States. The navy developed a base at Guantanamo Bay that, along with facilities in Puerto Rico, enabled the United States to dominate the Caribbean and the routes to the future Panama Canal. Puerto Rico became a possession and not an integral part of the United States. The Supreme Court ruled that "the Constitution does not follow the flag"; that is, Puerto Ricans did not have the full range of constitutional rights that citizens of the continental United States enjoyed. In 1917, the United States purchased the Danish section of the Virgin Islands, which completed its strategic grasp of the Caribbean region. Great Britain gave tacit recognition to that fact by withdrawing its naval forces from the region.

Acquiring the Panama Canal

President Theodore Roosevelt, a dedicated imperialist, next pressed for the completion of an old project of both U.S. and international interest—the construction of a canal through Central America that would link the Atlantic and the Pacific oceans. The government of Colombia had earlier granted to a French company the right to build a canal through its Panamanian province to link up the Pacific and Atlantic oceans. When this company failed, the United States pressed Colombia for treaty rights to build the canal. The Colombian Senate, which was irritated by the pressure and also interested in holding out for more money, rejected a treaty that had been negotiated by Colombian representatives and ratified by the U.S. Senate. President Roosevelt was enraged by the action of those he termed "contemptible little creatures . . . the Bogotá lot of jackrabbits," and was determined to get a canal that could be controlled by the United States. In 1903, a motley group of Panamanians, Europeans, and Colombian soldiers revolted and declared Panama an independent country. The U.S. navy blocked Colombian attempts to recapture the province, and the U.S. government immediately recognized Panama as a sovereign state. In return, the new nation, in fact a new U.S. protectorate, granted to the United States a permanent lease to a zone across the isthmus enclosing the partially built canal. The United States fortified the zone and completed the Panama Canal in 1914, conquering both yellow fever and rugged terrain in the process.

U.S. imperialism in Latin America: President "Teddy" Roosevelt helps dig the canal he "took." (Harvard College Library)

Increased U.S. Intervention in Latin America

As it was building the canal, the United States also took action to defend its expanded interests against European intervention in the region. Several European nations had sent naval expeditions to the Caribbean either to force Latin American states to honor their debts or to protect European residents and their property in times of turmoil. In 1902, several European powers jointly blockaded and bombarded Venezuela in a typical example of imperialist "gunboat diplomacy" against a weak nation. Roosevelt feared that if European nations were allowed to continue this practice, they might take over in the Caribbean and threaten U.S. interests there. The United States therefore made a statement to express its concern over continued European armed interference in the region. To preempt future European intervention, President Roosevelt then declared that in the future the United States would assume the "international police power" against those Latin American nations that were guilty of "chronic wrongdoing." This was called the Roosevelt Corollary to the Monroe Doctrine. No European nation directly challenged this doctrine by attempting new interventions.

On the other hand, in applying its new doctrine, the United States repeatedly intervened in the Caribbean. Between 1900 and 1934, the United States sent armed forces at least once into Cuba, Mexico, Honduras, Haiti, the Dominican Republic, and Nicaragua. In the last three nations, the marines stayed for many years.

Whereas the United States restricted direct military intervention to the Caribbean, its economic penetration, called "dollar diplomacy" by critics, was applied throughout Latin America. Two-thirds of all U.S. foreign investment dollars were spent in Canada and Latin America. U.S. capitalists were attracted to Mexican petroleum, Chilean copper, Colombian coffee, Brazilian rubber, Central American bananas, and numerous other products. In addition to importing these raw materials and foodstuffs, U.S. businessmen competed aggressively in selling their products, and by 1913 the value of U.S. exports to Latin America outstripped those sent by any other nation. With extensive economic and strategic interests at stake, the U.S. government was interested in stability in Latin America and backed dictators if democratic governments failed to maintain order.

The Impact of U.S. Imperialism

By 1914 the United States had emerged as a major world power. It was the dominant power in the Western Hemisphere, and one with a stake in the Pacific and Far East (see Chapter 7). It was a heady time for Americans and their leaders, for events of the preceding twenty years had confirmed their self-perception as a special people, with a glorious future.

Problems attended the exercise of imperialist power. While some Latin Americans benefited from and supported U.S. economic, political, and military activities in their nations, many reacted with hostility. They resented the seemingly incessant interference by the "Colossus of the North" and called it "Yankee imperialism." The fact that the United States often supported dictatorships was interpreted as indifference or hostility to the masses of peasants exploited in such nations. Later in the twentieth century, many Latin American reform leaders came to regard the United States as their chief enemy.

THE UNITED STATES AND CANADA

From the days of the War for Independence, Americans had been interested in absorbing the British possessions to the north, and as late as the middle of the nineteenth century many Americans still expected to incorporate that area. Between 1867 and 1871, however, Canadians frustrated U.S. hopes by uniting several different colonies and the possessions of the Hudson's Bay Company into a federation called the Dominion of Canada. Initially, the new dominion was firmly attached to Great Britain through an arrangement in which the Canadians governed their internal affairs while Great Britain controlled trade, foreign policy, and military matters. By the twentieth century, Great Britain had granted Canada substantial control over its external affairs as well. This development was the first example of an imperial nation's peacefully granting political freedom to a former colony, a process called devolution.

By 1900 few Americans still expected to annex Canada; instead, they sought to dominate it economically. By 1914 almost one-quarter of U.S. foreign investments were concentrated in Canada, although this was less than one-third of British investment there. Initially, U.S. investments centered in Canadian mines and transportation; later they expanded into manufacturing as that sector developed during and after World War I.

SUMMARY

By the end of the nineteenth century, the United States had emerged as the greatest power in the Western Hemisphere and was ready to press its interests around the world. Despite several internal social and economic tensions, Americans lived in a relatively affluent and stable nation. By 1914, the United States was an economic power on a par with the most powerful European nations. It was also ready to exercise that economic power, often in conjunction with its naval might, in other regions of the world, especially in Latin America, but also in Asia and the Pacific.

Between 1898 and 1917, the United States turned the Caribbean into a U.S. lake through war and intimidation. It acquired Puerto Rico, Guantanamo, the Canal Zone, and the Danish Virgin Islands, and established economic and political control over Cuba, Panama, and other Caribbean nations. By assuming the responsibility of policing the Western Hemisphere, the United States made sure that European powers had no grounds for intervention in the region. Conversely, U.S. military and economic domination aroused hostility among other peoples of the Western Hemisphere and led to the charge of Yankee imperialism.

SUGGESTED SOURCES

Burns, E. Bradford, *Latin America: A Concise Interpretative History,* 3rd ed. (1982). A well-written text; opening chapters provide historical background for twentieth-century Latin America.

Freidel, Frank, *The Splendid Little War* (1962). A lively account of the Spanish-American War.

Goldman, Eric F., *Rendezvous with Destiny* (1972). An impressionistic survey of the Progressive era.*

Link, Arthur S., and Richard L. McCormick, *Progressivism* (1983). A short, lively overview of the period.*

Morgan, H. Wayne, *America's Road to Empire* (1968). A description of the beginnings of U.S. imperialism.

Sinclair, Upton, *The Jungle* (1906). A searing novel depicting the plight of exploited immigrants in Chicago at the turn of the century. The book ends with a socialist appeal.*

Woodward, C. Vann, *The Strange Career of Jim Crow* (1974). An account of the segregation of blacks in the United States, challenged in part by later scholarship.*

*Paperback available.

6

European Imperialism in Asia and the Pacific

Western domination of Asia was almost complete by the year 1900. In that year, a last futile attempt at resistance in China was crushed by a joint imperialist force. With a few exceptions, Europeans (and the United States and Japan, whose interests on the Asian continent will be taken up in Chapter 7) were primarily interested in raw materials and markets in Asia and not in settlement. Industrialized European nations prized Asia's mineral wealth and also needed agricultural raw materials, such as rubber, hemp, sugar, and other tropical products. On plantations developed to grow these items, local or imported labor under European supervision produced goods for a world market. In addition, Europeans coveted the markets that the peoples of Asia would supply for their manufactured goods. The large population of China especially excited the imagination of European merchants. As one wishful thinker said, if every Chinese would buy a British-made shirt each year, Manchester shirt manufacturers would never suffer economic recession! Only Japan, China, Thailand, Nepal, Afghanistan, Persia, and the Ottoman Empire still retained a form of independence. However, with the exception of Japan, these nations were really no more than "semicolonies," which Europeans influenced or controlled indirectly.

Western states gained and maintained dominion over Asia for a number of reasons. They possessed overwhelming military power, backed by advanced technology and a modern industrial base. Nationalism was another important factor, as highly competitive Western nation-states vied constantly with one another for real and imagined advantages. Conversely, citizens of Asian states, except for the Japanese, lacked a sense of modern nationalism. Because of these factors, as well as local circumstances and ineffective governments, Asian states unsuccessfully resisted foreign intervention and domination—and sometimes even invited it. Eventually, European rule exposed Asians to the ideas of modern nationalism, which in the end provided the impetus for the dominated peoples to revolt against European imperialism. It also made available to Asians European science, technology, and cultural norms. Thus, while Western im-

69

South and East Asia to 1935

Possessions of:

Great Britain

France

The Netherlands

U.S.A.

League mandates of
former German colonies

Japanese Empire

Instances of unrest
by indigenous population

"Modernization" under
Western influence

Chiang's Northern Expedition,
1926-28

Communist Chinese, 1933

Communist Long March,
1934-35

UNION OF SOVIET SOCIALIST REPUBLICS

TANNU TUVA

MONGOLIA
(U.S.S.R. protectorate)

MANCHUKUO
(1931-33)

Sakhalin I.
(1905)

Kurile Is.

JAPAN
Tokyo

Bonin Is.

PACIFIC OCEAN

Korea
(1910)

Ryukyu Is.

Formosa (1895)

Mariana Is.

Guam (U.S.)

Japanese

Caroline Is.

NEW
GUINEA
Australian

AUSTRALIA
British dominion, 1901

Peking

Nanking

Yenan

REPUBLIC OF CHINA

Hong Kong
(Br.)

Canton

Macao
(Port.)

Hanoi

FRENCH
INDO-
CHINA

CHINA

PHILIPPINES

Manila

N.
BORNEO

SARAWAK

DUTCH EAST IN

Batavia

Timor
(Port.)

Scale of miles

0   500

BHUTAN

NEPAL

(BURMA)

Rangoon

SIAM

Bangkok

MALAYA

Singapore

INDIA

New Delhi

Pondichery
(Fr.)

CEYLON

Maldives (Br.)

Goa
(Port.)

Diu
(Port.)

AFGHANI-
STAN
British sphere
of influence

INDIAN OCEAN

perialism was at its height, European empires had already sown the seeds of their own destruction. In the twentieth century, Asians would use what they had learned from the West to compete with it.

INDIA

India: A Fragmented Society

India boasted one of the world's oldest continuous civilizations, dating from approximately 3000 b.c. It was the home of many religions and philosophies. One was Hinduism, which was the religion of the vast majority of Indians; another was Buddhism, which was almost extinct in its homeland but was a major world religion.

Hinduism taught its believers that each person's life was predetermined by his or her behavior in previous lives. Only spiritual perfection, or nirvana, attainable through a combination of devotion, good works, and spiritual learning, released one from the wheel of births and rebirths. Hinduism divided people into hereditary castes, from the exalted Brahman, or priest-scholar, caste on top of society to the outcastes, or untouchables, at the bottom.

Throughout its history, India had been the victim of many invasions. After the seventh century a.d., most invaders were Muslims of Arab, Turkish, and Persian ethnic groups, some of whom had settled in India. In time, many Indians, especially those from lower castes, attracted by Islam's promise of equality among believers, had converted to the conquerors' religion. The northwestern and northeastern parts of the subcontinent had Muslim majorities, while they constituted the minority community in the rest of the land. Many languages further divided the Indian people.

Europeans came to India by sea and eventually became a new threat to the land. When they first came in the sixteenth century, the Moghul Empire was in control. Moghuls were Muslim in religion, Turkish in race, and Persian in culture. The first Moghul rulers were great builders who left behind many impressive monuments (one of the seven wonders of the world, the Taj Mahal, was the mausoleum of a famous Moghul empress). However, by the eighteenth century, the Moghul dynasty was in decline, challenged by both its Hindu and its Muslim subjects.

British Rule in India

The disintegration of Moghul political power was accompanied by civil wars and foreign intervention. By the middle of the eighteenth century, Great Britain and France were fighting for colonial supremacy throughout the world, and India became one prey of the imperialist rivals. Great Britain won out over France, and wars in the nineteenth century against Indian princes consolidated British rule over the subcontinent. The British put parts of India directly under their rule, while other parts were ruled by Indian princes under British supervision.

In order to protect India, the British, by one means or another, took control over territories adjacent to it. To the east, they defeated the Burmese in three wars and incorporated Burma into the Indian Empire. To the south, they secured the island of Ceylon from the Dutch by treaty, creating a new colony. To the west and northwest, Great Britain sought to protect India from raiding Afghans and expansionist Russia by creating a protectorate over Afghanistan and a sphere of influence in eastern Persia (see below). The Himalaya mountains protected India from attack out of the north. The British also purchased Singapore, situated on the tip of the Malay peninsula, from a Malay ruler. They developed Singapore into a free port and a major naval base that protected British trade routes to China.

Since the main motive for their control of India was commercial, the British paid close attention to developing the economy in order to expand trade. They undertook large irrigation projects to bring new land into cultivation and introduced new crops such as tea and coffee. Old crops such as cotton and jute were revitalized to supply raw material to British mills. To bring the crops to the seaports and to transport their manufactured goods to the Indian consumer, the British built railroads that linked the coast to the interior. They opened coal and other mines to extract minerals from the land and to fuel new industries that were introduced to India.

The British administration also introduced measures to correct Indian practices that were considered wrong by Western standards. They abolished *suttee* (burning upper-caste widows alive on their husbands' funeral pyres) and suppressed the *thuggees,* who robbed and murdered in the name of religion. Many Indians accepted the reforms as beneficial and responded to the Western challenge to their traditional values by reexamining and reevaluating their religion and society. As a result, many Indians actively supported such reform measures as the Age of Consent Act of 1891, which raised the marriageable age of girls. Hindu traditionalists, however, bitterly resented this act as an example of British interference in Indian society, and organized riots in several cities to protest it.

Gradually, the lines of contact between British and Indians broadened and new ideas about social reform, popular sovereignty, and modern nationalism took root among the Western-educated Indian elite. In 1885, a group of British-educated Indians, mostly lawyers, and some of their British friends formed an organization called the Indian National Congress, whose goal was to gain for Indians the same political rights enjoyed by Britons in their homeland. The Congress met in annual sessions to formulate goals and programs. Between sessions, its members lobbied for reforms. All Indians were welcome to join the Congress, which professed no religious biases. However, few Muslims joined, for they feared that majority rule would result in Hindu suppression of the Muslim minority. As a result, Muslims regarded the Congress as a Hindu group that represented only the Hindu majority of India.

Without question, nationalism was the most powerful force in India from 1900 onward. Western liberal ideas and modern nationalistic feelings, either introduced by the British or generated in reaction to British rule, profoundly changed the nature of Indian upper-class society. Most Indian nationalists of the twentieth century wanted not only independence, but independence based on Western concepts of nationhood. They sought democracy and representative government, not a return to the authoritarian monarchies of ancient India. Confident of the superiority of its educational system, Great Britain had since the early nineteenth century used public revenues in India to support British-style schools. Christian missionary schools, Catholic and Protestant, had also been established in many cities. Christian missionaries had not converted many Indians to Christianity, but had succeeded in teaching Western values and knowledge to many Indians. British-educated Indians now turned the tables on Great Britain, insisting that democracy and self-government were universally applicable ideals; therefore, Indians should govern themselves and the British should leave India. Great Britain, on the other hand, had no clear vision of where it wanted to move, but it slowly and reluctantly made concessions to Indian demands for self-government.

Early in the twentieth century, in response to political agitation by the Congress and other nationalist groups, Great Britain began to formulate plans for granting a measure of self-government to India. Indian Muslims were ambivalent about self-government, since they feared that in a representative government, the Hindu majority would override the interests of their community. To safeguard their interests against possible Hindu oppression, the All-India Muslim League was founded in 1906. The League demanded "separate electorates" for Muslims (Muslims electing their own representatives) in any elected Indian legislature. The Congress from the beginning vehemently opposed the idea of separate electorates, but its opposition merely made the Muslims more adamant.

In the face of determined Indian pressure, Great Britain began to retreat. The British Parliament passed the Indian Councils Act in 1909, popularly known as the Morley-Minto reforms after its authors, which gave Indians limited franchise and representation in elective councils and assemblies at both the provincial and central government levels. This was not self-government, however; British-appointed governors and officials still held the reins of power and made most of the important decisions. The reforms did, however, provide a constitutional platform where Indian representatives could voice their opinions, and they introduced Indians to the concept and practice of elections and representative government. They also set the pattern for future constitutional development. Muslims won their right to separate electorates and insisted on being guaranteed separate electorates in the future. Finally, they demanded separate nationhood as the only way for them to protect their religion, rights, and interests. Conversely, Hindus and the Congress interpreted separate electorates and other British concessions to Muslims as a means for Britain to prolong its dominance of the subcontinent by a deliberate policy of divide and rule.

Neither the Congress nor the League was satisfied with the concessions of the Morley-Minto reforms. Both saw self-government as the logical goal of

English ladies and gentlemen served afternoon tea by Indian servants. Even minor British officers and officials lived well in India. ("Afternoon Tea," © 1976, Aperture, Inc., as published in *The Last Empire, Photography in British India, 1855–1911*, Aperture, 1976.)

Indian nationalism. They coined a new word, *Swaraj,* or self-rule, to represent their goal. By 1914, the cry *"Swaraj"* was on the lips of every Indian political activist.

A faraway event added to Indian restlessness—news of Japanese victory on land and sea over Russia in the Russo-Japanese war of 1904–05, the first victory by an Asian nation in modern times over a great power of the West. As a foreign traveler observed at the time: "Even the remote villages talked over the victories of Japan as they sat in their circles and passed around the pipe at night."

AUSTRALASIA

In addition to carving out a vast empire in Asia, the British also took control of Australasia (Australia and New Zealand). The climate of part of Australasia resembled that of Europe, and imperialism in this area stressed the settlement of Europeans, a pattern similar to colonizing North America in previous centuries. British immigrants easily defeated and in some cases exterminated the numerically small and technologically unsophisticated local populations they found there. Australia and New Zealand became British in population, culture, and institutions.

Australia, although first discovered and explored by the Dutch, was colonized by Great Britain, beginning in 1788, as a dumping ground for convicts, who could no longer be sent to the former North American colonies. Some parts of Australia, however, were not set up as penal colonies, and soon all of the continent became a land of free British immigration. A total of six colonies were established "Down Under." In 1901, the six self-governing colonies federated to form the Commonwealth of Australia, a self-governing dominion in the British Empire. Until World War II, Australia remained overwhelmingly British in race and sentiment and enjoyed the protection of the British navy. With the exception of a small number of native aborigines, Australians maintained racial and cultural homogeneity by keeping out Asian immigrants through the White Australia Policy.

New Zealand was also discovered by Dutch explorers in the seventeenth century. British settlers came in the early nineteenth century and subjugated the Maoris, natives of Polynesian descent. New Zealand was never a penal colony, and Great Britain had no hesitation about granting the settlers self-government. In 1907, the North and South Islands joined to form a dominion within the British Empire. Like Australia, New Zealand passed laws to restrict Asian immigration, which ensured the British heritage of the white New Zealanders.

The small populations of Australia and New Zealand enjoyed a high standard of living in an economy that emphasized export-oriented farming and animal husbandry, and mining where applicable. Both Australia and New Zealand exported wheat, wool, meat, and dairy products, mainly to Britain, and depended on Britain for manufactured products. By the early twentieth century, the few industries that existed mainly processed the primary products or locally mined metals.

The labor movement, expressed in unions and in labor parties, was strong in both Australia and New Zealand, with the result that both nations were in the vanguard of social legislation in such areas as old-age pensions, financed by heavy taxes on large properties. New Zealand granted women suffrage in 1893 and the Australian states did so beginning in 1894. In 1910, as evidence of growing national maturity, Australia instituted compulsory military training for its young men and began to organize a regular military force. New Zealand followed suit in 1911.

FRENCH INDOCHINA

Although French Catholic missionaries had been active in Indochina since the seventeenth century, French imperial ambitions in the region did not become a factor until the middle of the nineteenth century. France was interested in the area for several reasons: for natural resources, as a domain for Catholic missionary work, as a back door to southern China, and as a foil to British imperialism. The advance of French power in Vietnam during the nineteenth century was often occasioned by native attacks on French missionaries and native converts. In 1885, France defeated China in war; China was forced to give up its position as overlord of Vietnam, which was annexed by France. In 1887, France joined together Cochin-China, Tonkin, Annam (the three components of Vietnam), Laos, and Cambodia to form the Indochina Union. Within the Union, France ruled Cochin-China directly and the others as protectorates. The governor-general, headquartered in Hanoi, controlled overall policy, while the native rulers in the protectorates were allowed to supervise routine administration. The French aimed at the gradual extension of their control by employing the policy of association, whereby French resident officials closely supervised the administration of the native states.

As it had in Africa, France pursued a policy of cultural "assimilation," a concept aimed at creating a "New France" in Indochina by establishing French schools and promoting French language, culture, and customs. France hoped that eventually a new elite class sympathetic to French rule would emerge among the Indochinese. Instead, the small minority of Indochinese who acquired French culture, like the British-educated Indians, used their new knowledge to oppose colonial rule and to advocate independence for their nations.

Economically, French policy aimed at exploiting Indochinese, especially Vietnamese, resources. The French greatly expanded rice and rubber production and developed the mining of coal and metals. To facilitate economic development, they built roads and railroads, expanded the irrigation system, and introduced modern public health and educational facilities. The average Vietnamese paid dearly for these improvements and benefited little from them. As late as 1939, only 15 percent of school-age children in Indochina were receiving any education.

The Vietnamese elite who did receive a French education became the standard-bearers of modern Vietnamese nationalism. Japan's victory over Russia in 1904–05 spurred Vietnamese nationalists to organize and publicize their aims and goals. Vietnamese students in Japan organized and openly agitated for throwing out the French. Chinese reform movements that culminated in the successful revolution of 1911 gave additional stimulus to the Vietnamese anti-French activities. They were so widespread that the years after 1905 were known as the "era of plots," all of which failed. An example of the contradiction inherent in France's colonial policy was the closing down of the University of Hanoi because it was a center of revolutionary activities. The University was a creation of the French colonial government, opened to promote its policy of assimilation and to impart French culture and values to the Vietnamese. Yet it was precisely these French-trained Vietnamese who led the nationalist movement to oust the French from Vietnam. Temporarily, the French repression succeeded. Some activists fled to China to continue their work; others, most notably Ho Chi Minh, went to Europe, where they kept up their anti-French activities.

THE DUTCH EAST INDIES (INDONESIA)

The Dutch had been involved in the East Indies since early in the seventeenth century. However, the Netherlands did not extend effective control outside Java to the rest of Indonesia until early in the nineteenth century. From the beginning, the Dutch showed little interest in exporting their culture or religion to their colonies; rather, they regarded them as valuable sources of raw materials, and later as a market for the sale of manufactured goods. Their plantation system, financed by the Netherlands and other Western nations and worked by Javanese and Chinese laborers, produced goods for export, including tea, coffee, indigo, tobacco, spices, sugar, palm oil, petroleum, and tin.

At the turn of the century, the Dutch introduced the "ethical policy," a program aimed at protecting the ordinary Indonesian from the more flagrant forms of economic exploitation. This paternalistic policy established state-supported elementary schools and stressed the moral obligation of the Netherlands to improve the welfare of the local people. Despite this policy, economic prosperity benefited the Dutch rather than the Indonesians.

Dutch rule in Indonesia until World War I was authoritarian. A governor-general ruled from Batavia (renamed Jakarta after independence) in Java; he was assisted by an advisory council and a cabinet, the members of which were all Dutch. No popular assemblies of any kind existed beyond the village level. Even though the Dutch rulers did not attempt to bring Western ideas and methods to the natives, nevertheless by the early twentieth century young Indonesians were beginning to embrace them. Indonesians were also impressed by the rising stature of Japan and the respect the European powers accorded to it; for example, in 1899 the Japanese were granted equal status with Europeans in Indonesia.

An Indonesian nationalist movement emerged in reaction to Dutch colonial rule. Most notable among the nationalist groups was the Sarekat Islam, formed in 1910. As the title indicates, the movement stood for the Muslim faith; in this way, it appealed to the religious feelings of the majority of the people. In 1911, the Sarekat Islam organized anti-Chinese riots, a reflection of native resentment of the strong economic role of the Chinese community in Indonesian life. By World War I the Sarekat Islam had become a mass movement, aimed at religious revival, independence, and eliminating the economic power of the Chinese community.

CHINA

A Tradition-Bound Society

For millennia, China, geographically isolated from other major cultures, dominated East Asia. Like India, China boasted a continuous civilization spanning some 4,000 years. In the third century *b.c.*, to protect itself from the nomadic peoples on its northern borders, China built the Great Wall, the biggest man-made structure on earth (and the only one that can be seen from the moon), over 1,500 miles long. In its isolation, China developed a unique writing system (ideograms and pictograms), local religions (ancestor worship and Taoism), and a political and moral philosophy (Confucianism). Although caravans and sailing boats had carried goods between China and the eastern Mediterranean since ancient times, the only outside culture that had an influence on it before the coming of modern Westerners was that of India. Indian Buddhism was accepted enthusiastically by the Chinese in the early centuries of the Christian era, at a time of social and political disruption, but was transformed to suit Chinese needs and ideals.

Since China was the largest, most advanced, and strongest state in East Asia, its civilization, even more than its political power, dominated the area. Korea and Vietnam were under direct or indirect Chinese political control for two thousand years and absorbed major aspects of Chinese culture. Even though Japan was never under China's political sway, it voluntarily adopted much of China's culture. China's traditional role as the giver but not the receiver of cultures contributed to its reluctance to learn from other peoples, which proved to be disastrous during the era of imperialism.

From its traditional cultural and political perspective, China thought of itself as the "Central Kingdom" and all foreign nations as tributary vassal states. When the monarchs of the Manchu (or Ch'ing) dynasty received modern seaborne Westerners in the late seventeenth century, they, like their predecessors of the Ming dynasty, regarded the foreigners as barbarian vassals bearing tribute.

In fact, the Westerners had come to China to trade. Tea, silks, and porcelains from China were in great demand in Europe. Until the late eighteenth century, however, Europeans had little to trade in return. This balance of trade in China's favor further reinforced China's self-perception of superiority and indispensability. Westerners, however, rejected China's claim of superiority; they not only believed in legal equality between nations, but in fact often looked down on the Chinese as inferiors.

The Twilight of the Manchu Dynasty

In the nineteenth century, Chinese traditional culture and Western imperialism met in headlong confrontation as China became the main target for imperialism in Asia. Differences on such issues as diplomatic equality, international relations, laws, and trade all made conflict inevitable, but opium precipitated the clash. The Chinese government had banned opium, but opium was a lucrative trade item for Western merchants. Great Britain's insistence that its merchants had the right to sell opium to the Chinese triggered war between the two nations in 1840 and again in 1858–60. In each case, China was defeated and forced not only to open the opium trade but also to cede territory and pay an indemnity. The Chinese had to grant extraterritorial rights to Westerners residing in China; that is, Westerners were exempted from Chinese laws which were too harsh and punishments which were barbarous by Western standards. By 1900

Extraterritorial rights and wealth gave Westerners special privileges in China. Two well-dressed gentlemen carried in litters as they sightsee. (Museum of American China Trade, Milton, Mass.)

China had been carved up into spheres of influence by Russia, Germany, Britain, France, and Japan (Germany alone could exploit the resources, and placed many restrictions on the Chinese government in the German sphere of influence, for example), and seemed destined for full colonization by the Western powers and Japan.

These humiliations weakened and discredited the ruling Manchu dynasty. During the last decades of the nineteenth century, China was plagued internally with rebellions, brigandage, and natural disasters, while externally it struggled unsuccessfully to maintain itself against increasing foreign encroachments. It was China's misfortune that in the most critical years of its contact with the West, its destiny was in the hands of an ignorant, corrupt, and unscrupulous woman, Yehonala, better known to the world as the Dowager Empress Tz'u Hsi. From 1862, when she became co-regent for her infant son, to her death in 1908 (with the exception of a few short years), she ruled China as an autocrat. Hating all foreigners, she threw her support behind a militant group who shared her xenophobia (fear of outsiders), popularly called the Boxers.

In the summer of 1900, the Boxers inflicted a reign of terror on Peking, the capital city, and its environs, and besieged the foreign legation quarters

A Foe of the Manchus

From 1885, i.e., from the time of our defeat in the war with France, I set before myself the object of the overthrow of the Ch'ing [Manchu] dynasty and the establishment of a Chinese Republic on its ruins. At the very beginning I selected for my propaganda the college at which I was studying, regarding medical science as the kindly aunt who would bring me out onto the high road of politics.

Ten years passed like one day. In Canton Medical School, I made friends with Chen-Shih-Liang, who had a very large circle of acquaintances amongst widely traveled people who knew China well. When I began talking of revolution, advocating its ideas, he gladly agreed with me, and declared that he would immediately enter a revolutionary party if I would agree to lead it. After staying a year in the school at Canton, I learned that an English Medical School with a wider program than that of the Canton School had been opened in Hong Kong. Thereupon, attracted also by the thought that there I should have a wider field for my revolutionary propaganda, I went to Hong Kong to continue my education. For four years I gave up all my free time from studies to the cause of revolutionary propaganda, traveling backward and forward between Hong Kong and Amoy.*

Dr. Sun Yat-sen, 1866–1925, father of the Chinese Republic, wrote here about how he became a revolutionary and his early career as a student revolutionary.

*From *Memoirs of a Chinese Revolutionary* (1918), quoted in *The China Reader*, Vol. 2, *Republican China, 1911–1919*, edited by Franz Schurmann and Orville Schell. Copyright © 1967 by Random House, Inc. Reprinted by permission of Random House, Inc.

there. Meanwhile, their ally Tz'u Hsi went so far as to declare war on all the Western nations and to order all foreigners in China killed. Fortunately for China, its diplomats abroad refused to obey her order, and many local authorities at home also ignored her and succeeded in restricting Boxer activity to Peking and parts of north China. Eight nations with nationals in China organized an international force to relieve the besieged foreigners, and succeeded in doing so in August 1900. Just before the relief forces entered Peking, Tz'u Hsi fled the capital disguised as a peasant woman.

The Boxer fiasco ended in 1901 with China's acceptance of a Protocol dictated to it by the victorious powers. It provided for punishment of Boxer leaders, an indemnity, and an armed and walled legation quarters for the foreign diplomatic community in Peking.

After the Boxer Rebellion, China was prostrate. In the words of U.S.-educated Dr. Sun Yat-sen, who later led the overthrow of the Manchu dynasty, China in the early twentieth century was a semicolony, the prey to all and the responsibility of none. The impotent Manchu dynasty remained in power until 1911, at least partly because the imperialist nations were for the moment satisfied with their gains and did not wish to risk war among one another by demanding additional concessions from China.

THE MIDDLE EAST

Middle Eastern Society: The Bond of Islam

Like China, the Middle East was held together by a common history. Residents of that area could look back on the glorious Golden Age of Islam from about 800 to 1100, which occurred at the time Europe was in the depths of economic and cultural depression, the so-called Dark Ages. During this period, Islamic culture, economy, and political power reached its zenith.

The Islamic religion was another important cohesive factor in the Middle East. Islam came out of the same traditions as Judaism and Christianity. Muslims (submitters to Islam) believe in one God (Allah) and in his prophets of the Old and New Testaments, including Jesus, who is considered a great prophet but not God. All people who accept the belief in one God and in Muhammad as his prophet are seen as equal before that God and as equals within the Muslim community. It was largely on the basis of this egalitarian teaching that Islam spread rapidly within many diverse cultures.

The Koran, the Muslim holy book, contains instructions for every aspect of a Muslim's life. The leaders in Islam were viewed as both political and religious figures; in its early formation Islamic society did not separate the role of the government from that of religion. For millions of Muslims, Islam was perceived as a dynamic force for social change, particularly in the treatment of women, who could inherit property, initiate divorces, and remarry in the event of widowhood or divorce. Largely as a result of its stable and complete nature, Islamic society remained resistant to outside forces. Thus, while the political apparatus of the Arab world fell to Western colonialism, the culture and religion remained relatively unchanged. As in Africa, Asian Muslims rarely, if ever, converted to Christianity, nor did they lose their traditional values of respect for the family and loyalty to one another. Hence Islam was to be an important factor for many Muslims in their struggle against Western domination.

European Imperialist Inroads

By 1900 the states of the Middle East, which had long been in decline, were at a low ebb. The Persian and Ottoman dynasties, which had formerly produced able and vigorous leaders, were headed by incompetent and sometimes unstable men. These governments had lost much territory and in some cases had to submit to European control in areas that remained in their nominal jurisdiction. They had, however, managed to play off competing foreign forces and maintain control in parts of their empires. Great Britain and Russia were rivals who had interests and ambitions in both the Persian and Ottoman empires, while Germany had extended its influence over the Ottoman Empire. The German government sent officers to train the Ottoman army, and planned to build a Berlin to Baghdad railway; German banks loaned money to the Ottoman government and invested in financial enterprises in the Ottoman Empire.

Competition between the British and the Russians came to a head in Persia. Sharing a long border with Persia, Russia was in an advantageous position to infiltrate and penetrate that nation. Russian officers had been sent to Persia to organize the Persian army; Russian banks loaned money to the Persian government; and Russian firms built Persian railroads. In return, Russia controlled the Persian customs office and other departments of the Persian government.

Great Britain was afraid that Russia coveted India and believed that the easiest way for Russia to attack India was via the eastern frontier of Persia and Afghanistan. Based on this assumption, the key to British policy toward Persia was to thwart Russia's southward advance. For this reason, Great Britain was satisfied with the results of the Russo-Japanese War, which forced Russia to turn its attentions elsewhere and to retrench in Persia. It was in this context that Russia and Great Britain began to negotiate their outstanding differences in 1907, which resulted in the Anglo-Russian Convention and Entente. In the Convention, Russia agreed not to encroach on Afghanistan and conceded it as an exclusive British sphere of influence. Both powers agreed to "respect" Persian "independence," but they then proceeded to divide the nation into their respective spheres of influence. Russia got the lion's share, or the entire northern half of the nation, including the capital city, Tehran. Great Britain's sphere in the southeast was smaller, but was strategically located on the border of Afghanistan and India. The remainder of the nation was designated a neutral zone. As a result of this settlement, tension between Russia and Great Britain eased.

Meanwhile, Persians who had traveled and studied in Europe were convinced that Persia needed to reform its antiquated political system if it was to survive. They launched a dual program that involved agitation for Westernization and constitutional reforms, on the one hand, and on the other for the creation of a national consciousness based on deep-rooted traditions and Persia's long history. In a bloodless revolution in 1906, the shah (ruler of Persia) was forced to give up his absolute powers and convene an elected parliament to draw up a constitution, which was promulgated in December of that year. Persia was neutral during World War I, when Western pressures on it were much reduced.

In Europe during the nineteenth century, the Ottoman Empire was often called the "Sick Man of Europe" and was viewed as a dangerous power vacuum that tempted major European powers to intervene. The Austro-Hungarians, Russians, and Germans had conflicting imperial ambitions in the Balkan part of the Ottoman Empire. They encouraged such subject nationalities of the Turks as the Serbians, Bulgarians, Rumanians, Albanians, and Greeks to undertake a series of successful rebellions that created new independent states. By 1914 the Ottoman Empire retained only a foothold in Europe. However, the British and French encouraged the Ottomans to keep this foothold and to retain their hold on the vital Dardanelles Straits, thereby preventing Russian access to the Mediterranean.

In Asia, restlessness among the unassimilated Christian Armenian minority caused the Turkish-Ottoman government great alarm and resulted in harsh repression. A sizeable Arab subject population in the Middle East (which, indeed, outnumbered the ruling Turkish population) had also awakened to the pulls of nationalism and was threatening secession from the empire. North Africa and Egypt, still technically Ottoman provinces, had long since come under French and British control respectively. Italy annexed the Ottoman Empire's last African possession, Libya, in 1912.

In attempting to hold on to what remained of the crumbling empire, the Ottoman government had enlisted German aid. Kaiser Wilhelm II was only too happy to comply, for he saw in such aid an opportunity to expand German influence into the Middle East. German instructors helped to modernize the Ottoman army and, in so doing, helped to awaken a spirit of nationalism among its Turkish officers. They formed an organization dedicated to the modernization of the Ottoman Empire and called themselves the Young Turks. In 1908, the Young Turks staged a successful revolution, and their leader, Enver Bey, became the de facto ruler of the empire. Between 1909 and 1914, the Young Turks attempted a program of "Turkification" of Armenians, Arabs, and other subject nationalities of the empire; this, however, only served to deepen local nationalistic feelings among these minority groups. The Ottoman Empire fought alongside Germany in World War I.

From the experience of the Arabs, Armenians, and others, it can be seen that Western nations were not alone guilty of imperialism. The Ottoman Empire provided an ironic example of a state that was the victim of European imperialism, but which in turn imposed a harsh rule on its subject nationalities.

SUMMARY

Western imperialism was at its height in Asia in the beginning of the twentieth century. With the exception of Japan, all of Asia was under either the direct or the indirect control of Western imperial nations. Large areas and ancient civilizations —the Indian subcontinent, Indochina, the East Indies, and other smaller territories—had fallen to colonial status. Other once-powerful empires were in decay and only nominally independent. This category included Persia and the Ottoman Empire, both of which had been reduced in size by successful revolts of subject nationalities and the encroachments of Russian and other imperialisms. Another example was China, which had been stripped of vassal states and was but a semicolony itself.

Even as Western imperialism stood at its height, however, movements had been set in motion that would eventually topple it. Victims of imperialism, Asian peoples were among the first non-Westerners to experience a new sense of nationalism. This desire to control their own destinies inspired a new generation of

Asian nationalists not only to be free of Western imperialism, but to be rid of their traditional governments and, in some cases, moribund cultures. Asian nationalist movements were clearly influenced by Western ideas of society and democracy. Traditional life in Asia was also changing, as a result of the technological and scientific innovations introduced by Western imperial powers. Traditionalists in China, India, and other lands had resisted changes and reforms in accordance with modern Western ideas. In China, the ignominious defeat of the Boxer movement, which sought to counter Western science and technology by superstition and magic, opened the way for forward-looking leaders. These leaders set as their goal learning from advanced Western nations so that their peoples could throw off the yoke of subjugation.

Australasia was different. This area had been colonized by people of predominantly British stock who enjoyed a prosperous economy. Great Britain did not repeat the mistake it had made with the Thirteen Colonies; by the early twentieth century, all its remaining colonies of white settlement had gained self-government within the British Empire.

SUGGESTED SOURCES

Clavell, James, *Tai-Pan* (1966). An epic novel about British traders on the China coast in the mid-nineteenth century.* (Also a film.)

Dean, Vera M., *The Nature of the Non-Western World* (1966). An easy-to-read introduction to general problems of modernization and culture clash.*

Elegant, Robert, *Mandarin* (1984). A novel set in late-nineteenth century China showing interplay between the old and new, Chinese and Western ways.*

Forster, E. M., *A Passage to India* (1924). A novel about English men and women in India and their interactions with Indians.* (Also a film.)

Goldschmidt, Arthur, *A Concise History of the Middle East,* 2nd ed. (1983). A readable summary.*

Lowe, Cedric J., *The Reluctant Imperialist* (1967). An introduction to the Arab world by a journalist.*

MacMillan, Margaret, *Women of the Raj* (1988). Concentrates on the role of English women in India c. 1650–1947; richly illustrated.

Mansfield, Peter, *The Arab World* (1976). An introduction to the Arab world by a journalist.*

Robinson, Donald H., *The Raj* (1981). An interesting view of British rule in India.* (Also a BBC television production.)

Tan, Chester C., *The Boxer Catastrophe* (1967). The best book on the uprising of the Boxers and their effort to drive Westerners out of China.*

*Paperback available.

7

The United States and Japan in Asia and the Pacific

As European nations consolidated their hold over most of Asia, two rising powers—the United States and Japan—also began to push their claims in that region. Many in the United States believed in its "Manifest Destiny," and the Japanese felt great pride because Japan alone among non-Western nations had successfully modernized and escaped the fate of other Asians. Nationalistic pride became imperialism as both the upstart Americans and Japanese elbowed their way into Asia against European nations already established there. Each defeated relatively weak European rivals in the process. Eventually the United States and Japan would each see the other, not European nations, as the main threat to its interests in Asia.

THE UNITED STATES CROSSES THE PACIFIC

Taking over Hawaii and the Philippines

While the United States was primarily absorbed in Latin America, it also showed strong interest in Asia. Throughout the nineteenth century, U.S. merchants had engaged in the famous "clipper ship" trade for silk, tea, and porcelain from China and spices from the Dutch East Indies. To ensure its share of widening trade possibilities, the United States had sent naval squadrons to force the opening of commercial contacts with Japan and Korea. In 1867, the United States purchased Alaska from Russia and occupied Midway Island in the central Pacific for use as a coaling station for its commercial and naval vessels.

In the 1890s, a rush of events propelled the United States into a dominant position in the northern Pacific. One of the main centers of activity was the Hawaiian Islands, the key to controlling the area. This Polynesian kingdom had already been conquered economically by U.S. sugar and pineapple planters, who imported Chinese and Japanese labor to work the plantations. By 1887 the United States had concluded commercial treaties with Hawaii and acquired Pearl Harbor

85

for a future naval base, in effect making the islands a U.S. protectorate. In 1893, U.S. settlers toppled the Hawaiian monarchy, and in 1898, by mutual agreement, the United States annexed Hawaii. Unlike Puerto Rico, Hawaii was given territorial status, a stepping-stone to statehood. The United States rapidly developed Pearl Harbor into a major naval base, which made it supreme in the northern Pacific. One year later, the United States annexed Wake Island, thereby filling a gap in its mid-Pacific supply line.

Also in 1898, as a result of the Spanish-American War, and after payment of $20 million to Spain, the United States acquired the Philippines and the strategically important Pacific island of Guam. As with Cuba and Puerto Rico, the question of what to do with the populous Philippine Islands became the chief focus of debate between pro- and anti-imperialist politicians. Anti-imperialists argued that the Philippines possessed a hodgepodge of unassimilable peoples and cultures and that the islands were not necessary for the security of the United States; therefore, annexation of these islands would be a deplorable act of imperialism and a repudiation of U.S. ideals.

Those who supported annexation argued that the Philippines were valuable economically as a producer of such items as sugar, coconut oil, and hemp, and as a consumer of U.S. products. They were also concerned that some powerful European nation or Japan might seize the islands if the United States did not. In Subic Bay, they saw an excellent base for a U.S. naval squadron that would protect U.S. trade and other interests in Asia. Imperialists further argued that the backward Filipinos needed a period of tutelage under the United States before they could operate successfully as an independent nation. In annexing the islands, therefore, the United States was only assuming its responsibility, as the British imperialist writer Rudyard Kipling had advocated when he urged Americans to "take up the white man's burden." Protestant ministers also favored annexation as an opportunity to save souls for Christ, even though the majority of Filipinos were already Catholics.

At a crucial point in the debate, President William McKinley told the public that prayerful contemplation had convinced him that the United States should keep possession of the Philippines. The annexationist point of view prevailed both in Congress and in the election of 1900, when anti-expansionist William Jennings Bryan was defeated by McKinley for the second time. Thus, like Puerto Rico, the Philippines became a U.S. possession.

Politically active Filipinos, who had already been fighting the Spanish for independence, opposed annexation by the United States. In 1899, they proclaimed a Philippine republic. Emilio Aguinaldo, a hero of the fight against Spain, was named its first president. However, the United States refused to recognize this government and waged war to suppress it. In 1901, General Arthur MacArthur (father of General Douglas MacArthur) captured Aguinaldo. The independence movement eventually collapsed, but the Muslim Moros, who were a minority community that lived on several islands of the archipelago, continued their rebellion until 1913.

The United States had sent many more troops to conquer the Philippines than it had sent to Cuba. On occasion, U.S. soldiers committed the same atrocities and pursued the same policies of internment that Americans had condemned when they were used by the Spanish in Cuba and the British in South Africa. Some 200,000 Filipinos died from various causes during the fighting. U.S. dead numbered over 4,000.

From this first unhappy experience, U.S. attitudes toward the Philippines were tinged with guilt. While it suppressed movements for immediate independence, the U.S. government also played an active role in the preparation for its eventual realization. In 1913, and again in 1919, President Wilson formally pledged that it was U.S. policy to grant independence to the Philippines at an early date. To prepare Filipinos for the responsibility of independence, Governor-General William Howard Taft and his successors launched an ambitious program of public education that doubled the literacy rate in just over a generation and introduced English as the second language for a significant minority.

Qualified Filipinos found the doors to the civil service open to them. By 1912 half of all ranking judges were Filipinos. In 1907, local elections were held for an Assembly, in which two major political parties competed for power. This Assembly was the first popularly elected legislative body in Southeast Asia. An upper house in which Filipinos had a majority was added in 1913. However, political reforms were not matched by economic ones. Wealth in the

Imperialism in Asia: U.S. troops suppress insurrection in the Philippines. (Culver Pictures)

Philippines remained in the hands of U.S. business firms and a few rich Filipinos and Chinese.

Expanding U.S. Stakes in China

By the turn of the century the United States controlled a string of possessions and bases across the Pacific to the threshold of the Asian mainland. Now that their trade routes were protected, U.S. businesses wished to expand their share of Asian commerce. Missionaries were equally anxious to spread the Gospel among the "heathen." Unfortunately for U.S. capitalists, most of the Asian trade had already been preempted by European nations through their colonial possessions and their spheres of influence in China. In 1899, and again in 1900, Secretary of State John Hay announced that he had secured an agreement from the European powers and Japan for an "Open Door" policy that would allow all nations equal opportunity to trade throughout China while respecting its territorial integrity. In fact, there had been no uniform agreement, but the Open Door principle became the cornerstone of United States policy toward China up to World War II. In contradiction to its own policy, however, the United States also attempted to carve out a sphere of influence on the Fukien coast of China; it was thwarted by Japanese opposition.

The pace of U.S. contacts with China accelerated in the twentieth century. In 1900, U.S. marines joined the international relief force that rescued the besieged Westerners in Peking and suppressed the Boxer rebellion. Although some U.S. merchants and missionaries moved into the interior, the majority remained clustered in the autonomous foreign settlements in coastal cities. Like other privileged foreigners protected by unequal treaty rights, Americans enjoyed immunity from Chinese justice wherever they were. To safeguard U.S. lives and property, its gunboats patrolled the Chinese coast and along the Yangtze River.

Although the United States had become a significant imperialist presence in East Asia and the Pacific, and had developed economic, strategic, and cultural stakes in the entire area, its position there was much weaker than in Latin America. Whereas U.S. interests in the Western Hemisphere were backed by overwhelming and unchallenged military might, in Asia the United States faced strongly entrenched European interests and the rapidly rising economic and military might of Japan. The U.S. presence in the Far East was also weakened by divisions inside the United States concerning the legitimacy of its presence in Asia. As a result, U.S. policy in Asia tended to be reactive.

THE RISE OF JAPAN AS A GREAT POWER

The transformation of Japan from an isolated, traditional nation to a respected modern industrial power in record time has fascinated the world. How Japan accomplished this remarkable feat has been the subject of study by those anxious to unlock the secrets of its phenomenal success. In 1900, Japan was the only Asian nation that had made the transformation to modern nationhood, had broken the shackles that the West had placed upon it half a century earlier, and was ready to challenge Western dominance of Asia.

The Opening of Japan and the Meiji Restoration

Whereas Great Britain had taken the lead in the opening of China, the United States was responsible for forcing Japan to open its doors to the world. In 1853, it sent a naval squadron commanded by Commodore Matthew Perry to Japan with an ultimatum that Japan sign a treaty with the United States. Perry invited leaders of Japan aboard his ships and showed them their formidable cannons, as well as displays of U.S. science and technology, including model trains and tracks that had been brought and set up for this purpose. The Japanese were suitably impressed. They knew what had happened to the Chinese who tried to resist British might, and they bowed to the inevitable. Japan signed the treaty as demanded, as well as similar treaties with Great Britain, Russia, France, and the Netherlands, who followed in the wake of the United States. These treaties opened up Japanese ports for trade with the West, fixed the tariff that the government of Japan could charge on imported goods, and granted extraterritorial rights to the Western signatory states.

In 1868, a revolution overthrew the ineffective feudal government that had bowed to the humiliating Western demands, and returned authority to the emperor and his advisors. The event was called the Meiji Restoration, named after the young emperor who gained power as a result of the revolution. During the early years of the Meiji Restoration, Japan reconciled itself to the limitations that the unequal treaties had placed on its sovereignty. With the same zeal that they had manifested in learning from a more advanced China over a thousand years earlier, the emperor and his youthful advisors began a program of reforms, which were based on what they perceived to be the best Western models. As the emperor officially proclaimed at the Restoration: "Knowledge shall be sought throughout the world so as to strengthen the foundation of imperial rule." For example, the Japanese decided to build an army on the French model because everyone then thought that the French army was the best in the world. When France was resoundingly defeated by Germany in the war of 1870–1871, the Japanese quickly switched and patterned their army on that of Germany. Following the same logic, they began a navy based on the British model.

The crowning political achievement of the Meiji Restoration was the promulgation of the constitution in 1889, which made Japan the first Asian nation to commit itself to the daring innovation of constitutional government. In the early 1880s, a constitutional commission had spent several years studying the forms of government of Western nations. They found the political system of Germany most congenial to Japan's needs, and drafted a constitution that approximated it closely. The Meiji Constitution, promulgated as a gift of the emperor to the people, pro-

The Meiji emperor proclaiming the constitution in 1889.

nounced the imperial line as divinely descended, protected many imperial prerogatives, and made the emperor commander-in-chief of the military forces. However, in a dramatic departure from Japanese traditions, it created a bicameral legislature, known in English as the Diet, which consisted of a largely hereditary House of Peers and a popularly elected lower house. The Diet's consent was needed in all money matters and in the making of permanent laws. About 5 percent of adult males, those who paid a certain level of taxes, were eligible to vote in the 1890 election (the male franchise was progressively extended, but women were denied the vote until after World War II). Political parties were permitted to contest the elections. The constitution also provided for government by a prime minister and a cabinet under him, and in time it was accepted that the prime minister and cabinet must receive majority endorsement by the Diet. The constitution also guaranteed a host of freedoms.

The goals of these reforms were, first, to strengthen Japan so that it would not have to suffer further losses to its sovereignty, and thereafter to recover lost sovereign rights by convincing Western powers that the Japanese were as good as Westerners. In the following pages we will look at some specific areas of change and modernization.

A Modern Economy

Japan's successful transition from an agricultural to an industrial nation was the result of government planning and cooperation between the government and private enterprise. The government took the lead in developing a modern economy, by providing a modern transportation and communication network and by denoting as national enterprises certain key industries and mines. Japan was leery of contracting foreign loans because of the onerous conditions that borrowing money entailed, and so it financed modernization by squeezing tax revenues out of the farming sector. After it defeated China in war in 1895, Japan received a monetary indemnity from China and used that money to finance further industrial expansion. A ministry of industry was created to coordinate the strategic nationalized industries with nonstrategic private enterprises such as the textile industry.

After the key industries were firmly established, the government sold them at low prices to private capitalists. A strong private sector developed, dominated by a few large firms called *zaibatsu,* conglomerates that worked hand in glove with the government. The two largest *zaibatsu* were Mitsui and Mitsubishi, each of which had many affiliates that straddled all segments of the economy. Up to World War I, Japan's heavy industries were mainly designed to meet its strategic and military needs. Since Japan lacked key raw materials such as iron ore and coal, its military strategists were concerned about the security of the sea lanes and the reliability of the foreign sources of raw materials. In light industry, the early emphasis was on building silk and cotton mills, which required little capital, had a traditional base, and employed mostly low-paid, docile women from the farms.

Japan's transition from an agrarian to an industrial society was not without dislocations and problems, but as its industrialization came relatively late, these problems were not as acute as those experienced by earlier industrialized nations such as Great Britain. As "latecomers," Japanese planners, like those in Germany, benefited from knowing and avoiding many of the economic problems that had beset Great Britain and other nations. The Japanese government desired not only a rapid industrialization but also a peaceful one. Thus it outlawed strikes in the Peace Preservation Law of 1900, while at the same time it also passed laws that ensured factory safety and provided workers with some welfare programs to forestall industrial unrest.

The pattern of Japanese industrialization differed from those of European nations and the United States. This was partly due to the uniquely Japanese employment system, which had three distinctive and interrelated characteristics that have persisted throughout the twentieth century. First was the low turnover rate in the labor force. Second was a strong mutual loyalty between employer and employee; both prefer a lifelong commitment to each other, and workers identify with their employer, who tries not to lay them off. Third was the prevalence of company-provided welfare and benefits programs for employees. These factors contributed to Japan's successful and rapid industrialization.

Farmers, through paying high taxes, financed Japan's industrialization and supplied its labor force. They also produced agricultural goods for export in exchange for foreign machinery and raw materials, and grew the food for the growing urban population. Adoption of modern farming techniques and the introduction of chemical fertilizers increased the yield on the limited farmlands. Thus, up to about 1900, the Japanese farmers were able to feed an increasing population and maintain a tolerable standard of living despite the high burden of taxes they endured.

Whereas the population had been relatively stable in the premodern era, the introduction of modern science and medicine resulted in a rapid increase. Between 1903 and 1919, the population grew from forty-six to fifty-six million people, about 20 percent. Since all arable land was already under intense cultivation, the land could not support additional people. The growth was then siphoned off to the new commercial and industrial cities such as Tokyo, Yokohama, Nagoya, Osaka, and Kobe. In 1900, only about half of the population remained on the land, and even in a period of rapid industrial growth, the supply of labor increased faster than demand. Wages, therefore, remained low, and the standard of living for the average person did not improve significantly during the early twentieth century.

After 1900, food made up a significant part of Japanese imports. This growing dependence on imported food, a situation similar to that faced by Great Britain, worried planners who feared what this might mean in wartime. Since Great Britain's situation was eased by the dominance of its navy and by food produced in its colonies and dominions, Japanese leaders also sought colonies for a secure food source and consequently created a strong military force to conquer colonies.

Modernizing Education, the Bureaucracy, and the Military

A fundamental reason behind Japan's successful modernization was the system of universal education instituted in the early years of the Meiji Restoration. By 1907, universal compulsory education lasted for six years, and about five million boys and girls were attending 27,000 elementary schools. Schools taught a large dose of patriotism in addition to the basic curriculum of reading, writing, and arithmetic. Secondary schools emphasized vocational and technical training and thus provided a firm base for Japan's industrial advance. The imperial universities trained the sons of the elite for the bureaucracy and the professions. A highly organized educational bureaucracy monitored the school system and, after 1903, compiled all textbooks. Illiteracy virtually disappeared.

Several themes were stressed in textbooks for the Japanese student: loyalty to the emperor and the state, selfless patriotism, and duty to family. An Imperial Rescript on Education which stated these values was issued in 1890. A copy of the Rescript was hung beside the emperor's portrait in every classroom. It became the basis of the moral and ethical instruction of all Japanese children.

Military education, however, was rigidly specialized, and produced an officer corps with a distinctive outlook and experience. Japanese officers viewed themselves as heirs of the nation's ancient military tradition, and since their education was narrowly limited, they tended to propose simple solutions to complex modern problems. The ordinary citizen, accustomed to respecting rulers from the hereditary military class, or *samurai,* looked up to the military as tradition dictated. Successful in war, the military provided the people with national heroes. Its image was also helped by government propaganda that placed great emphasis on loyalty and devotion to the imperial cause and to its champions, the army and navy. To strengthen the state's claim of unquestioning obedience and loyalty from its citizens, the Meiji Constitution made Shintoism Japan's official religion. Shinto means "The Way of the Gods," and is unique to Japan. Shinto myths tell of the divine origin of the imperial house. Until 1945, Shintoism was used to instill patriotism among the Japanese and in part to justify Japanese aggression.

Japan's modern education was the foundation of its efficient bureaucracy. At the heart of the civil service were several thousand graduates of the elite Imperial (later Tokyo) University. Civil servants enjoyed high respect, both because of their rigorous academic training and as "officials of the emperor." They drafted legislation for the Diet, had access to cabinet ministers, and generally controlled the administration. As members of a career bureaucracy, they were immune from outside political influences, popular favor, or special interests. Therefore they acted as a stabilizing factor in society.

The bureaucracy and the military were the twin pillars of Meiji Japan. For centuries the *samurai* had ruled Japan. After the Meiji Restoration, all males were liable for military service. The end of the monopoly of the *samurai* class on the military by no means diminished the importance of the armed forces, which continued to dominate society and command respect. In an imperialistic age, the army and navy had no difficulty demonstrating their importance. The emperor was commander-in-chief of the armed forces under the Meiji Constitution of 1889. He was advised in military matters by ministers who were active senior officers of the army and the navy, nominated by their respective services. In time, the military establishment came to control the civilian cabinets and cabinet policy. They did so by refusing to nominate men to serve in the army and navy posts in a cabinet not to their liking, or by ordering their respective ministers to resign from cabinets that did not do the military's bidding. Since no cabinet could survive without the army and navy ministers, the armed services in effect exercised veto power over the formation and survival of governments. In both absolute and proportional terms, military expenditures increased year by year, from about one-third of the national budget in 1894 to nearly one-half by 1913.

The Transformation of Japanese Society

Industrialization and modernization depended on new skills, attitudes, and knowledge. Japan's success in these endeavors was due to farsighted leadership as well as to the responsiveness of tens of thousands of its citizens, who felt that Westernization was the wave of the future and were willing to make sacrifices to bring it about. Some of the copying was indiscriminate, such as the adoption of Western dress and hair styles, hand-shaking, and ballroom dancing. Many mansions of the rich began to sport "Western rooms" furnished in the Victorian manner.

On the other hand, some of the changes were fundamental. Legal reform was one; to win acceptance by the West, it was necessary to change Japanese legal institutions, which was done in the 1890s on the German model. This paved the way for the end of unequal treaties and extraterritorial rights for Westerners. However, Western legal forms brought with them the Western concepts and value judgments on which they were based. Although it was easier to understand and accept Western fashion and scientific techniques than morals and ideas, the latter also began to make inroads. Westernization was speeded along by the hundreds of Westerners hired to work in Japan as experts and teachers, by Christian missionaries, and by the thousands of young Japanese men and women who went to the West to study.

The many rapid changes of the Meiji era were nothing short of revolutionary. Old legal class distinctions were abolished, old laws were replaced, and many old norms were regarded as obsolete. The old static but stable society was replaced by shifting populations and unstable social relationships in the new industrial cities. While there was no turning back, some social critics nevertheless lamented the passing of the old ways.

JAPAN BECOMES AN IMPERIALIST POWER

Leaders of Meiji Japan turned to imperialism when they saw that their modernization programs were successful, and continued on that course until 1945. There were several reasons for this quest for conquest and empire. One was historical precedent. In the late sixteenth century, powerful Japanese warlords had dreamt of conquering China, and invaded Korea as a first step. Another reason was the prevailing mood of the late nineteenth century, which glorified imperialism as a symbol of international success and racial superiority. Having suffered humiliation by Western powers, Meiji leaders sought international recognition and equality with the great powers by demonstrating military prowess and by conquering colonies. Finally, economic motivation was also important; resource-poor Japan sought security in colonies that would provide raw materials and secure markets.

Japanese diplomatic efforts in the late nineteenth century focused on treaty revision, or the negotiation of new, equal treaties to replace the old unequal ones. It was argued that the constitution of 1889 had placed Japan among the modern civilized nations, and further that the adoption of modern legal codes no longer justified the enjoyment of extraterritorial rights by citizens of Western nations in Japan. Japanese arguments were apparently persuasive, for Great

Britain signed a new treaty in 1894 that ended extraterritorial rights for British subjects in Japan within five years and also restored tariff autonomy to Japan. Other nations, impressed by Great Britain's leadership and by Japan's resounding victory over China in 1895, followed suit. By 1911 all treaties between Japan and Western nations were based on equality.

Despite its formal treaty status, however, Japanese pride was continually rankled by Western racist attitudes about Asians, especially about Japanese living in Western nations. It was most hurt by the treatment of Japanese nationals as inferior people in the United States. When the governments of the United States and Japan began negotiations over Japanese immigration to the United States and the treatment of Japanese by white Americans, Japan's foremost concern was that its people should not in any way be treated as inferiors to peoples of European background. The U.S. government pressured local governments to modify their anti-Japanese ordinances, but the Japanese government ultimately decided that the only way to avoid international humiliation was to forbid some of its own nationals to emigrate to the United States, to which the United States agreed. The arrangement was called the Gentlemen's Agreement of 1908. Despite this, the U.S. Congress passed an Exclusion Act in 1924 which specifically designated Japanese immigrants as ineligible for citizenship.

Japan's First Victims: China and Korea

From the 1890s on, Japanese foreign policy had the twin goals of self-aggrandizement and the reduction of Western influence in East Asia. It defeated China resoundingly in the Sino-Japanese War of 1894–1895, and forced China to cede Taiwan (Formosa), which became Japan's first overseas colony. Victory against China also brought Japan an indemnity, and Japanese citizens in China obtained the extraterritorial rights enjoyed by Westerners.

Japan was now gaining confidence to seek equality with Western nations. The main issue that had led to the Sino-Japanese War had been control of Korea, a Chinese vassal state that Japan coveted. The 1894–1895 war eliminated Chinese influence from Korea, and the impotent Korean government could ward off neither Japanese nor Russian imperialistic advances. Russia was interested in Korea for its ice-free ports, resources, and for the prestige that control of that state would give. Similar reasons motivated Japan, except that Japanese industries were more in need of Korean raw materials, such as iron ore and coal. Thus Japan regarded the possibility of Russian control over Korea as "a dagger pointed at her heart," which it must prevent at all costs.

Beyond Korea, both powers also coveted Manchuria, a sparsely populated part of northeast China that was rich in both agricultural and mineral resources. During 1900, using suppression of the Boxer disturbances as an excuse, Russia poured 175,000 troops into Manchuria, and refused to evacuate them after the Boxer Rebellion had been put down. In 1903, in a blatant gesture of imperialism, the Russian government created a new position of Viceroy of the Far East, and gave its appointee authority to advance Russian interests in Manchuria and Korea. The pro-expansion faction was definitely in the ascendant in the Russian court, and Russia seemed determined to have its way in the Far East.

Since Japan was equally determined not to concede, it began to prepare for war. Between 1893 and 1903, the Japanese military budget increased by more than 300 percent. Japanese leaders also realized the need for allies who could give it support in times of international crisis, and found one in Great Britain. In the Anglo-Japanese Alliance of 1902, the two powers agreed to aid each other in their respective imperialist goals in East and South Asia. The treaty was the first modern military pact between a Western and a non-Western nation concluded on the basis of equality. It also provided for British neutrality if Japan went to war against one enemy, and British assistance should it become embroiled in war against two or more nations. This last provision, more than any other, strengthened Japan's hand in its rivalry with Russia.

The Russo-Japanese War: Japan Electrifies the World

While completing its military preparations, Japan negotiated with Russia. Since each side stubbornly held to its stand, however, the talks bogged down. The Japanese navy then made a surprise attack and sank the Russian Far Eastern Fleet in its harbor at Port Arthur in southern Manchuria (a Russian sphere of influence in northeastern China). Two days later, Japan declared war.

Most of the battles of the Russo-Japanese War were fought in Manchuria, although China was technically neutral. It was a measure of China's impotence that it could do nothing to prevent the two antagonists from conducting their campaigns on its territory. In Japan, the war was popular and morale was high. Conversely, the Russians were divided by social unrest and felt no unity of purpose in waging the war; the morale of Russian troops was low.

Japan's modern military machine won spectacular victories on both land and sea. Russian troops were first expelled from Korea, and then surrendered in Port Arthur after suffering a five-month siege. In March 1905, Japan captured Mukden, the chief city of Manchuria, after a battle in which about 400,000 troops were engaged on each side. In May, the Russian Baltic Fleet, which had sailed from Europe via South Africa, was destroyed in the Korean Straits by the Japanese navy under Admiral Togo Heihachiro. This last feat roused admiration for the Japanese all over the world, evident in President Roosevelt's excitement as he wrote: "This is the greatest phenomenon the world has ever seen. Even the battle of Trafalgar could not match this."

Defeated on both land and sea, Russia sought peace. Japan, too, was exhausted. When President Roosevelt offered to mediate, both sides accepted eagerly, and the peace conference opened in August 1905 in Portsmouth, New Hampshire. Many of the negotiating sessions were held on a yacht loaned by banking magnate J. P. Morgan. Roosevelt was motivated partly by a desire to achieve a settlement before either side gained a complete victory, which would jeopardize the Open Door policy the United States was trying to uphold in Manchuria. Ability to host a major peace conference and mediate a peace treaty would also enhance U.S. international prestige. Although both China and Korea were to be vitally affected by the peace terms, neither was invited to the conference.

In the Treaty of Portsmouth, Russia acknowledged Japan's "paramount interests" in Korea and agreed to cede to Japan its railroad rights and sphere of influence in southern Manchuria. Russia also ceded to Japan the southern half of the island of Sakhalin, but paid no indemnity. The Japanese people had expected more for their sacrifices, and riots broke out in many Japanese cities when terms of the treaty were published. The Japanese negotiators literally had to sneak home to avoid physical harm from popular anger. Roosevelt received the Nobel Peace Prize.

Japan interpreted its "paramount" position in Korea to mean control of key Korean government agencies, which it proceeded to force on the weak Korean government. Those Koreans who did not wish to be ruled by Japan rioted and in other ways tried to register their protest. In 1907, the king of Korea secretly sent a delegation with an appeal against Japanese imperialism to the Hague International Peace Conference, then in session, but the conference refused to receive it. Next, Japan forced the Korean king to abdicate and placed his feebleminded son on the throne instead. In late 1909, a Korean patriot assassinated the Japanese resident-general in Korea. This event gave Japan the pretext it needed, and it annexed Korea on August 22, 1910. Thus began a harsh colonial rule that lasted until 1945.

The Russo-Japanese War was a landmark conflict for both Japan and the world. There was now little doubt about Japan's great-power status. Its victory gave inspiration to peoples under or threatened by Western imperialism. As Jawaharlal Nehru, later prime minister of independent India, said in his autobiography, it was a "great pick-me-up for Asia." Territorial gains from both wars and the potential for more definitely set Japan on the path of imperialism that would end only with its defeat in World War II.

SUMMARY

Drawn westward by prospects for a lucrative Asian trade, the United States acquired a string of island bases across the Pacific and conquered the Philippines, where it created a relatively enlightened colonial administration. U.S. merchants who had acquired a share of the Chinese market were anxious that their government act on their behalf to preserve and expand that share. The United States did not establish an exclusive sphere of influence in China, but instead formulated an Open Door policy aimed at equal opportunity for all foreigners in that nation.

Japan was opened to the modern world by the threat of force by the United States. Failure of the government to defend the nation brought about a political revolution in Japan, called the Meiji Restoration. The new rulers of Japan, supported by the people, set about to learn everything they could from the Western world, which they did with astonishing success and record speed. In one generation, Japan was transformed from an isolated, traditional land to a modern nation with industries, an infrastructure, competent schools, Western-influenced law codes, and a constitutional government which gave a voice to the people. Its accomplishments inspired admiration, won for it formal international equality, and made it the inspiration of other peoples who also aspired to success.

Japanese leaders were first and foremost motivated by national security considerations when they embarked on their modernization program. Once they were secure, the nature of Japanese national goals changed; Japanese nationalism became imperialism. The Japanese believed that they had to control the raw materials and markets of Asia if their progress in industrialization and modernization was to continue. Japan went to war against China and Russia to achieve those goals and succeeded, acquiring Formosa and Korea as colonies, and extensive economic rights in resource-rich northeastern China.

The rapidity and success of Japanese expansion in Asia in general and its defeat of Russia in particular surprised and impressed the Western powers and was a matter of great pride for the Japanese. Asians admired Japan for defeating Europeans but feared its mounting aggressiveness. The United States and Japan were initially interested in competing with the established European imperialist powers, but tensions between the two new imperialist nations augured greater conflicts to come.

SUGGESTED SOURCES

Conroy, Hillary, *The Japanese Seizure of Korea, 1868–1910* (1974). An account of Japanese imperialism at work in its early phase.*

Creighton Miller, Stuart, *"Benevolent Assimilation": The American Conquest of the Philippines, 1899–1903* (1982). A colorful account of the Philippine-American War, drawing heavily from contemporary American newspaper materials.

Griswold, A. Whitney, *The Far Eastern Policy of the United States* (1966). A well-written and comprehensive overview of U.S. action in the Philippines and China.

Jansen, Marius B., *Japan and China: From War to Peace, 1894–1972* (1975). A survey of Sino-Japanese relations in modern times.

Michener, James, *Hawaii* (1978). A saga about Hawaiians, missionaries, white traders, Chinese and Japanese settlers.* (Also a film.)

Neumann, William L., *America Encounters Japan* (1969). A study of the ideas and attitudes that shaped U.S. foreign policy toward Japan.*

Reischauer, Edwin O., *The United States and Japan*, 4th ed. (1978). A brief, interesting survey of the relationship between the two nations by a former U.S. ambassador to Japan.*

*Paperback available.

8

The Origins of World War I

On June 28, 1914, a Serbian nationalist assassinated the Austrian archduke and heir to the throne, Franz Ferdinand, in Sarajevo, Bosnia. While Ferdinand was sitting in the open back seat of a car—it was a beautiful sunny day—a nineteen-year-old youth stepped out into the street and fired several shots. Before the archduke himself expired—after several times dismissing his wound as "nothing"—his wife Sophie had already died from a bullet in the stomach. The assassin was Gavrilo Princip, a Bosnian of Serbian nationality. Himself stricken with tuberculosis, he was fond of quoting Nietzsche's lines from *Ecce Homo:* "Insatiable as the flame, I glow and consume myself." Princip wished to see Bosnia break away from the Austro-Hungarian Empire and become part of a Greater Serbia. Austria-Hungary soon declared war on Serbia, and by August 4 most of the major European powers were involved in World War I. To understand how a major war could follow from the shooting of an Austrian archduke, it is necessary to investigate the combustible atmosphere that transformed the spark of an assassination into an all-consuming fire that would bring about the deaths of millions.

NATIONALISM

Nationalism was the first element at work. This passion was especially strong in the Balkans. Serbia had gained complete independence from the Ottoman Empire in 1878. In that year, major European powers at the Congress of Berlin allowed Austria-Hungary to occupy Bosnia and Herzegovina despite the fact that they were still legally part of the Ottoman Empire and that most of the population in both provinces consisted of Serbians. After King Peter I came to the throne in 1903, Serbia stepped up its efforts to incorporate ethnic Serbian areas still outside of its national borders; it was outraged when Austria completely annexed Bosnia and Herzegovina in 1908. Serbia made threats and appealed to Russia for help. Germany promised Austria its backing and sent the Russians a note demanding that the tsarist government recognize the annex-

99

Sarajevo, 1914: Austrian Archduke Franz Ferdinand and his wife in the rear of the automobile in which they would soon be assassinated. (UPI/Bettmann Newsphotos)

ation and not support Serbia in the matter. Russia yielded, and without Russian support Serbia had to acknowledge the annexation. As a result of strong Austrian pressure, Serbia also promised to cease activities that were hostile to its northern neighbor.

Despite its promise, however, Serbia failed to curtail such actions. In fact, within a short period, several new nationalistic societies appeared. One of these was the conspiratorial group Unity or Death, commonly referred to as the Black Hand, which specialized in encouraging ethnic Serbs in areas such as Bosnia to work for unification with Serbia. It helped to smuggle men, guns, and propaganda to sympathetic individuals still outside Serbian borders. Led by the chief of intelligence of the Serbian army, the Black Hand organized Princip's bloody deed.

Although this act of Serbian nationalism had precipitated the crisis, the nationalism displayed by other powers widened it. Kaiser Wilhelm II and segments of the German public, including many intellectuals and politicians, believed in the superiority of the German nation and culture. Some Germans dreamed of uniting all members of the German race in a Pan-German state that would include large areas of Austria-Hungary.

Pan-Germanists were countered by Russian Pan-Slavists, who dreamed of politically uniting with Russia the many Orthodox Slavs who populated the Balkans. As the control of the Ottoman Empire in the Balkans weakened during the century preceding World War I, the Russians planned to exercise increasing influence in the area, but instead suffered a number of disappointments there. Russia lost the influence it once had in Bulgaria, and, along with Serbia, suffered a diplomatic defeat when Austria-Hungary annexed Bosnia and Herzegovina in 1908.

A quickening of French nationalism was also apparent. An anti-German disturbance in late 1913 in a French town in the German provinces of Alsace-Lorraine dramatized to the French the pain of the loss of those provinces to Germany in the Franco-Prussian War. Ten-year-old Raymond Poincaré had watched the Germans march through his hometown in Lorraine in 1870. Elected premier of France in 1912 and president in 1913, he played an active role in leading France into war with Germany in 1914.

Nor were the Serbians, Germans, Russians, and French alone in their nationalism. As Winston Churchill later wrote about this period, "National passions, unduly exalted in the decline of religion, burned beneath the surface of every land with fierce, if shrouded fires." Not even the rival faith of socialism could compete with nationalism. For twenty-five years, the Second International Workingman's Association had preached the international brotherhood of the working class. It had also often criticized war, attributing it to capitalist forces. Yet the vast majority of its members supported their nations in the crucial days of early August 1914.

IMPERIALISM

Imperialism was the second combustible element in the prewar atmosphere. As the major European powers competed in various areas of the world, conflicts naturally arose among them. The first Moroccan crisis of 1905 serves as an excellent illustration. In 1904, Great Britain and France had concluded the Entente Cordiale, an understanding concerning their overseas spheres of influence. As part of the agreement, Great Britain recognized France's desire to control Morocco. Germany disliked the Entente and thought that a stiff challenge to the French position in Morocco might split it apart. In 1905, Kaiser Wilhelm II landed at Tangier and recognized the sultan of Morocco as a ruler independent of French control. Wilhelm also demanded an international conference, which assembled in 1906, to discuss the situation. Meanwhile, the British had become so alarmed at German belligerence over Morocco, as well as at the continuing German naval build-up, that they moved much closer to France. While not going as far as the French would have liked—a promise of British support in case of war with Germany—Great Britain's foreign minister, Sir Edward Grey, did authorize informal military conversations with the French. These conversations continued from time to time over the years and strengthened the impression among some French statesmen that Great Britain would back it in case of a war with Germany.

In addition to bringing Great Britain closer to France, the Moroccan crisis also helped to bring about the Anglo-Russian Entente in 1907. It was not an alliance, but primarily a settlement over spheres of influence in Persia, Afghanistan, and Tibet. Nevertheless, it brought Great Britain closer to France's ally. The entente increased the Germans' fear of encirclement, and to some extent induced them to vigorously back the dual monarchy in the annexation crisis of 1908. Again in 1914, Germany's uncompromising support of Austria-Hungary reflected its fear of losing its only real ally.

MILITARISM

Militarism also contributed to the outbreak of World War I, as European nations feverishly expanded their military forces and armaments in the years immediately before 1914. German and Austrian military spending doubled between 1910 and 1914, and other European nations increased their expenditures markedly. By 1914 both Germany and France had each assembled standing armies of 800,000 men, with a million more in the reserves. About 1.2 million Russians were under arms, although the Russian army was inferior in equipment, training, and leadership. By 1905 the British had begun construction on a new battleship, the *Dreadnought,* designed to be the most powerful ship ever built. Germany responded with increased naval expenditures of its own. From 1900 to 1911, German naval spending nearly tripled. Such contests did little to increase the security of either side; instead they heightened the hostility and mistrust already existing among nations.

Another manifestation of the militarism of the era was the failure of the peace conferences of 1899 and 1907. Most government and military leaders were more concerned with keeping up in the arms race and maintaining absolute national sovereignty than with achieving disarmament and arbitrating disputes. At the 1907 conference, the delegates quickly postponed the issue of disarmament and passed a resolution calling for further study of the question. The delegates then spent weeks thrashing out the guidelines for the proper conduct of warfare. It was as if they were saying to the world, "Disarmament is a fool's dream, but war will surely come. So let us agree on the rules."

In this militaristic era, the plans and advice of military leaders played an increasingly influential role in government decisions. For example, Germany's Schlieffen Plan, which the French and Russian generals knew in broad outline, was a key factor in the peace options and war plans of several nations. In the plan, the German general staff had assumed that in a two-front war with France and Russia, Germany could not defeat both opponents simultaneously. Germany had therefore decided to knock out France first by an invasion through Belgium, while holding off the slow-mobilizing Russians. After defeating France, Germany would then concentrate its forces in the east and crush the Russians. For this plan to work, the German military could not give the Russians a significant head start in mobilizing their forces. Russia, on the other hand, reacting in part to strong French pressure, had to do just what the Germans hoped they could not do—divert German troops to the Russian front before France could be defeated. Other nations had their own military plans that demanded lead time for mobilization and deployment of troops. Thus, in those final hectic days, military considerations afforded diplomacy little time to reach a peaceful settlement. Because it included the military necessity of invading neutral Belgium, the Schlieffen Plan was also likely to bring Great Britain, which wanted nearby Belgium free from either French or German control, into the war.

THE ALLIANCE SYSTEM AND WAR PREPARATION

As the events of July and August 1914 clearly indicate, the two European alliance systems were the mechanisms that transformed a local conflict into World War I. After the shooting of Ferdinand, Austria was convinced that the Serbian government was implicated. The government in Vienna believed that, one way or another, it must crush the threat to its empire posed by advocates of Greater Serbia. Before acting, however, Austria sought assurance that Germany would back it in case the Russians intervened on behalf of Serbia. Having received Germany's almost unconditional backing, or "blank check," in early July, Austria sent an ultimatum to Serbia on July 23. Austria demanded an end to anti-Austrian organizations and propaganda, the removal of officers and officials accused by Austria of being hostile, Austrian participation in the investigation of the assassination plot, and the suppression of subversive movements directed against Austria-Hungary. The Serbian government was given forty-eight hours to reply.

Serbia was aware that Russia, its chief supporter, advised caution but would nevertheless ultimately back Serbia in case of hostilities. Russia supported Serbia because after the diplomatic defeat of 1908 it did not wish to lose further influence and power in the Balkans to Austria-Hungary. Serbia was Russia's last bastion of influence in the area. If Austria were allowed to crush Serbia, either diplomatically or militarily, Russia's hopes in the Balkans would be finally smashed. After hearing of Austria's ultimatum, the Russian foreign minister, Sergei Sazanov, declared: "It means a European war!" He accused Austria of "setting fire to Europe," and on July 25 his government approved preliminary military preparations. This was done in the hope that it would frighten Austria into arriving at some sort of compromise. Russia also wished to be prepared in case it was necessary to come to the aid of Serbia.

In addition to its concern about Austria, the tsarist government had also become increasingly troubled about growing German influence in the Ottoman Empire. It is not difficult, therefore, to understand why some Russian officials perceived the demands placed on Serbia as part of a united effort by Austria and Germany to strengthen the "Germanic" influence in areas long considered of special interest to the Russians.

Partly because of Russian support, Serbia did not accept all the Austrian demands. Nevertheless, Serbia's carefully worded reply reflected a conciliatory spirit. Austria, however, despite some belated German qualms, would recognize nothing less than unconditional acceptance. On July 28, Austria declared war on Serbia and bombarded Belgrade, the Serbian capital.

Meanwhile, Russia's ally, France, had been giving strong support to the tsarist government. The French remembered the 1870 war with Prussia (Germany, 1871) and did not wish to be isolated again in a struggle with Germany. Accordingly, they were prepared to give full backing to their major ally, Russia. In addition, a war against Germany, if won, held out the hope of recovering the lost provinces of Alsace and Lorraine. From July 20 to 23, French President Poincaré and Premier Viviani were in St. Petersburg encouraging the Russians to stand firm.

After some indecisiveness about how to mobilize, on July 30 Russia finally decided on a general mobilization of its troops. The French encouraged such an action because France knew of the general thrust of the Schlieffen Plan. If Russia mobilized substantially ahead of Germany, there was less likelihood that Germany could swiftly defeat France.

Because of Germany's war plan, it was no surprise that after several warnings on previous days, on July 31 Germany sent an ultimatum with a twelve-hour limit demanding that Russia end its war preparations along the German frontier. On that same day, Germany asked the French government what its position would be in case of a Russian-German war. On August 1, the French replied that France would consult its own interests. On the same day, the government in Paris ordered mobilization. Germany also mobilized on that day and, having received no reply to its ultimatum, declared war on Russia. Two days later, certain that France was preparing to aid Russia, and unwilling to lose any more time, Germany declared war on France and directed its attack through neutral Belgium.

As a result of British-French friendship and military conversations that followed from their entente and the Moroccan crisis of 1905, Great Britain had

Serbia, Austria, Russia, Germany, France, and Great Britain in a cartoon suggesting how the alliance systems would work. (Brooklyn Eagle)

Enflamed with Patriotism

To me those hours seemed like a release from the painful feelings of my youth. . . . Overpowered by stormy enthusiasm, I fell down on my knees and thanked Heaven from an overflowing heart for granting me the good fortune of being permitted to live at this time.

A fight for freedom had begun, mightier than the earth had ever seen; for once Destiny had begun its course, the conviction dawned on even the broad masses that this time not the fate of Serbia or Austria was involved, but whether the German nation was to be or not to be. . . .

As a boy and young man I had so often felt the desire to prove at least once by deeds that for me national enthusiasm was no empty whim. . . . Thus my heart, like that of a million others, overflowed with proud joy that at last I would be able to redeem myself from this paralyzing feeling. I had so often sung "Deutschland uber Alles" and shouted "Heil" at the top of my lungs, that it seemed to me almost a belated act of grace to be allowed to stand as a witness in the divine court of the eternal judge and proclaim the sincerity of this convic-tion. . . . [I] was ready at any time to die for my people and for the Reich which embodied it. . . . [D]ays later I was wearing the tunic which I was not to doff until nearly six years later.*

Adolf Hitler, describing his feelings at the start of World War I, when he was twenty-five and living an impoverished life in Munich. On August 3, 1914, he volunteered to enlist in the German army. See Chapter 13 for more on Hitler's youth.

*From *Mein Kampf* by Adolf Hitler, translated by Ralph Manheim. Copyright © 1943 by Houghton Mifflin Company. Reprinted by permission.

already been moving toward support of France. A few days before, for exam-ple, the British cabinet had voted to give assurance to the French that the British navy would protect the French coast and shipping against any German attack. The invasion of Belgium made it much easier, however, to decide on a decla-ration of war. The neutrality of Belgium, just across the English Channel from Great Britain, was considered essential to the British interest. Great Britain, along with France, Germany, Austria, and Russia, had been one of the guar-antors of that neutrality since the Treaty of London in 1839. Thus, on August 4, Great Britain declared war on Germany. "All for just a word—'neutrality'—just for a scrap of paper," lamented Germany's Chancellor Bethmann-Hollweg, who nevertheless had earlier in the day stated: "Whatever our lot may be, Au-gust 4, 1914, will remain for all eternity one of Germany's greatest days."

With the British declaration, almost all the major European powers that would enter the war were committed. Great Britain, France, and Russia opposed Germany and Austria-Hungary. The fear of being left without an ally helped ensure such a widespread war. Italy, the ally of Germany and Austria-Hungary in the Triple Alliance, did not enter the war at this time on the grounds that the alliance was a defensive one, and that Germany had taken the offensive.

SUMMARY

The assassination of Archduke Franz Ferdinand was the immediate cause of World War I, but four prominent background factors helped to explain how such an event could lead to a war as vast as World War I. As with the Boxer Rebellion of 1900, nationalism, imperialism, and militarism again all played a part. So too did a fourth factor: the alliance system.

Historians have debated and will continue to debate which nation was most at fault, but none of the nations that went to war in the summer of 1914 had done all they might have to prevent the conflict from occurring. Despite some late and relatively weak diplomatic efforts to slow the rapid escalation of events, in the end each nation valued security, prestige, influence, and allies more than peace. Only after years of death and destruction did many realize that in 1914 they had undervalued the fruits of peace and underestimated the human and material costs of modern warfare.

SUGGESTED SOURCES

Dedijer, Vladimir, *The Road to Sarajevo* (1966). A detailed but fascinating account of the events leading up to the assassination of Archduke Franz Ferdinand; sympathetic with the idealism of the conspirators.

Fischer, Fritz, *World Power or Decline* (1975). A summation of the author's controversial case for blaming primarily Germany's imperialist aims for causing World War I.*

Joll, James, *The Origins of the First World War* (1984). A concise overview of the causes of the war and a reexamination of differing historical interpretations of them.*

Kennedy, Paul M., ed., *The War Plans of the Great Powers, 1880–1914* (1985). An excellent and comprehensive collection of essays on the war.*

Koch, H. W., ed., *The Origins of the First World War*, 2d ed. (1984). A collection of essays with different interpretations of the causes of World War I and the responsibility of the belligerents.*

Lafore, Laurence, *The Long Fuse* (1981). A readable work on the origins of the war that while emphasizing Serbian-Austrian tensions also examines the concerns of the other major powers.*

Lieven, D. C. B., *Russia and the Origins of the First World War* (1983). A clear, well-balanced analysis of why Russia became involved in World War I.*

Remak, Joachim, *The Origin of World War I: 1871–1914* (1980). A good, brief, balanced introduction to the subject.*

Remak, Joachim, *Sarajevo* (1959). An interesting brief look at the events surrounding the assassination.

Turner, L. C. F., *Origins of the First World War* (1970). A brief, balanced account of the origin and causes of the war, especially good on the significance of military considerations.*

*Paperback available.

9

World War I

Those who lived during the conflict that broke out in July and August 1914 called it the Great War, but later it became known as World War I. Both names are appropriate, for sixty-five million people from thirty-five nations served in the armed forces, hundreds of millions of civilians were directly involved, and fighting occurred on three continents and throughout the oceans. The main struggle, however, was on the continent of Europe and the adjacent North Atlantic waters. In the beginning, it was a popular war. The citizens of the participating powers, conditioned by years of nationalistic propaganda, greeted the declarations of war with enthusiasm. Cheering crowds showered flowers and gifts on the proud troops departing for the front. Most thought it would be a short war; they expected an early rout of the enemy and a glorious and profitable peace settlement for their nation. "You will be home before the leaves have fallen from the trees," Kaiser Wilhelm told his departing troops.

THE OPENING PHASE OF THE WAR

After declaring war, Germany, carrying out its Schlieffen Plan, concentrated the bulk of its powerful army against France while assigning limited forces to hold off the slowly mobilizing Russians. German planners had modified the Schlieffen Plan, however, placing proportionately fewer troops on the right wing that was to attack through Belgium than had originally been specified. Still, the German high command was confident that there were enough men to move the bulk of the German army in a great arc through northern France, swinging around west of Paris and crushing the enemy in a vise in eastern France. All through August, the German armies moved through Belgium and across northern France, persistently pushing back the French, British, and Belgian troops. By early September when the Germans approached Paris, they had modified their course to swing southward to the east of Paris. They were also behind schedule, fatigued, and plagued with supply problems.

Under the leadership of General Joseph Joffre, the French and British reorganized the front. Beginning on September 5, at the Marne River, they threw

108

their last reserves, some of them rushed by taxicabs through Paris, into a series of counterattacks. Although the counterattacks made only a limited penetration, the Germans decided to pull back to the Aisne river. The Schlieffen Plan had failed; subsequently, both sides tried to outflank each other, and in the process extended their line to the seacoast, digging in along the way. By the middle of October 1914, a heavily fortified trench system, the Western Front, meandered 450 miles across Belgium and France from the North Sea to the Swiss border.

As the Germans were advancing across France in August, the Russians attacked more quickly than the Germans had expected. Two Russian armies swept into East Prussia and defeated German forces on the Prussian frontier. The German command diverted troops from the Western Front, but they arrived in East Prussia too late. Meanwhile, German forces already in East Prussia recovered quickly. Maneuvering their outnumbered forces brilliantly, General Paul von Hindenburg and his chief of staff, Erich von Ludendorff, annihilated one Russian army at Tannenberg and routed the other at the Masurian Lakes. Hindenburg became a popular hero, and Ludendorff eventually went on to direct all German army operations. However, the Germans were not yet strong enough to follow up their victories and invade Russia. Meanwhile, the Ottoman Empire and Bulgaria, each for its own reasons, joined Germany and Austria-Hungary. These four nations are traditionally called the Central Powers, and their opponents, the Allies.

THE PERIOD OF STALEMATE

As the war bogged down in Western Europe and East Prussia in the autumn of 1914, an extended period of stalemate began that spread to other battlefronts in Europe over the next two years. Lured by British and French promises of Austrian and Turkish territory, Italy attacked Austria in 1915. The new front, located in mountainous terrain, soon became deadlocked. In a major strategic move, an Allied expeditionary force attempted to seize the Dardanelles with the object of defeating the Ottoman Empire and opening a water route to supply the faltering Russian war effort. Ottoman forces pinned down the attackers at Gallipoli near the mouth of the Dardanelles and forced them to withdraw. In the Balkans, where the war had begun, German, Austrian, and Bulgarian troops overran Serbia. The British and French, always sensitive to any potential threat to their Mediterranean supply lines, rushed forces to northern Greece, but no active front developed there.

For almost two years, there was considerable movement on the Eastern Front. In 1915 and 1916, both sides launched major offensives that gained ground and lost it again, but the Germans steadily gained the upper hand and eventually conquered the Russian provinces of Poland and Lithuania. In 1916, German, Austrian, and Bulgarian forces overran Rumania, forcing the Russians to enter eastern Rumania in order to prevent an invasion of southern Russia. The East-

Europe in World War I

Central powers
Allied powers
Neutral
Main battlefronts throughout much of the war
Conquered by Central powers
Major battles

St. Petersburg

RUSSIA

BLACK SEA

OTTOMAN EMPIRE

Cyprus

RUMANIA
Bucharest
Istanbul

Warsaw

AUSTRIA – HUNGARY

BULGARIA
Sofia

SERBIA
Belgrade

GREECE
Athens

Crete

NORWAY

SWEDEN

Oslo

Stockholm

BALTIC SEA

Copenhagen

Tannenberg

Vienna

Berlin

GERMANY

DENMARK

Sarajevo

MONTEN.

ALBANIA

NETHER-
LANDS

BELG.

LUX.

Bern
SWITZ.

ITALY

Rome

Sardinia

MEDITERRANEAN SEA

NORTH SEA

Amsterdam

Brussels

Verdun

Marne

FRANCE

Somme

Paris

London

GREAT BRITAIN

Corsica

AFRICA

ATLANTIC OCEAN

Madrid

SPAIN

PORTUGAL

Lisbon

0   200   400

Scale of miles

110

ern Front now extended 1,200 miles from the Baltic to the Black Sea. Most of the front consisted of lightly defended sectors interspersed with heavily defended strong points. Some areas of heavy forests and extensive swamps were not defended at all. Germany did not have sufficient forces to launch a decisive invasion of Russia; in that sense, the Eastern Front also became a stalemate.

THE WAR OUTSIDE EUROPE

Between 1914 and 1918, fighting spread around the world, although nowhere did it remotely attain the magnitude of the struggle in Europe. In Africa, Allied colonial troops captured German colonies isolated by the blockade. Togo, Cameroons, and German Southwest Africa were quickly overrun, but a small German force held out in part of German East Africa until the armistice.

In Asia, World War I gave Japan an opportunity to improve its position in the Far East and in the western Pacific, and it lost little time in making the most of it. Following the terms of the Anglo-Japanese Alliance, Japan declared war on Germany. Japanese and British military units cleared German forces from China before the end of 1914. While ANZAC (Australian and New Zealand) forces were occupying German colonies south of the equator, units of the Japanese navy seized German-held islands north of it. After these conquests, Japan became essentially a noncombatant.

Japan also took advantage of the war to advance its imperialist designs on China. On January 18, 1915, the Japanese presented to the Chinese government the Twenty-One Demands, which would have turned China into an economic protectorate. In effect, Japan insisted on virtually direct controls over Manchuria, eastern Inner Mongolia, and the Shantung peninsula, and demanded a monopoly of iron ore and coal mining in the Yangtze valley. Japan also "requested" the right to build railroads in southern China and to share control over Chinese police units and arsenals. China looked for outside support, especially from the United States, in vain; alone and feeble, China capitulated on nearly all points on May 15, 1915. Japan subsequently secured pledges from Great Britain, France, Italy, and Russia that they would back Japan's claims in postwar negotiations. The United States, however, in a joint agreement with Japan, would only assent to the vague statement that "Japan has special interests in China, particularly in that part to which her possessions are contiguous."

In the Middle East, the Allies faced a more formidable problem. Unlike Germany, which could not adequately defend its African and Asian colonies, the Ottoman Empire could devote a significant portion of its military forces to defending its Middle Eastern territories. The Ottoman army was on the whole not well trained or led, but it was initially able to keep the Russians from advancing deep into Armenia, to repulse a British invasion of Iraq, to watch the British in Egypt, and to contain an Arab revolt in the Arabian peninsula. By 1917, however, Great Britain had assembled British, ANZAC, and colonial forces and began driving into Palestine and Iraq. In addition, the romantic hero Colonel T. E. Lawrence, among others, helped the Arabs to mount a more effective revolt. By 1918 Ottoman control of the Middle East had collapsed and the region was fully in control of Allied and Arab forces.

Not only was the war fought outside Europe, but in a reversal of recent European encroachment on the rest of the world, World War I saw military forces from the outside world appear in Europe. Contingents of troops from the British Empire, French colonial troops from Africa and Vietnam, and token units from Latin American nations saw service on the Allied side on the Western Front. A Japanese destroyer force patrolled the Mediterranean. In addition, the United States intervened massively. The presence of personnel from the other continents in Europe was a harbinger of the decline of European power later in the twentieth century.

THE WAR OF ATTRITION BECOMES "TOTAL WAR"

Bogged down in a stalemate, the leaders of the warring powers nevertheless refused to end the struggle and settle for "peace without victory," as President Wilson later advised. Some began to doubt that a decisive battlefront breakthrough would win the war, however, and considered another approach to winning wars—attrition. In a war of attrition, instead of a decisive battlefield victory, a nation wins if it outlasts the other side. There are two general ways, singly or in combination, to win a war of attrition. One is to bleed the enemy by causing so many casualties they can no longer sustain effective military operations and are finally forced to sue for peace. Another is to cut off supplies coming to the enemy from abroad, hampering the output of vital war materials. Such a cutoff also deprives the enemy's civilians of food, clothing, and fuel. Faced with mounting losses of loved ones on the battlefront and/or increasing deprivation at home, the civilians of the enemy power will force their government to make peace.

As the war settled more into one of attrition, each government attempted to mobilize all the resources of its nation to win the war. In the process, the difference between the civilian population and the military forces became less distinct than it had been in earlier wars. Governments became more authoritarian, increasing their control over the economic, social, political, and cultural lives of their peoples. This process has been referred to by many historians as "total war."

The War on Land

Although there were extensive military activities elsewhere, both sides invested their main effort in the Western Front, where six million troops were massed. The troops had fortified themselves in an intricate network of multiple trenches, underground bunkers, barbed wire, and mine fields integrated with extensive deployment of artillery, mortars, and machine guns. Elaborate support facilities, including railroad systems that reached back into the civilian support areas, supplied the front-line troops.

This combination of fortifications and weapons made it impossible for attacking infantry to break through to victory; frontal attacks produced enormous losses and insignificant gains. Throughout 1915, 1916, and 1917, the same grim scenario was played and replayed. The attackers would commence with a massive artillery bombardment along a front sometimes fifty miles wide. The bombardment might last for several days and was intended to clear out the mines and barbed wire, smash in the front-line trench system, and kill and wound many of the defenders, while others suffered shellshock and hysteria. The defenders would take refuge in their underground bunkers while reinforcements and artillery would be rushed up and held ready in the rear. When the attackers' artillery barrage lifted and the attacking infantry surged forward, the defenders' artillery would rain shells on the attackers, and the defending infantry, reinforced, would come out of the bunkers, set up machine guns, and mow down the attacking infantry. The attackers would in their turn be reinforced, and occasionally penetrate a few miles or so, but eventually both the attackers and the defenders would become exhausted.

As the war progressed, commanders would send their men into battle hoping for a breakthrough but willing to settle for killing and incapacitating more of the enemy's men than they lost of their own. "I am nibbling them," Joffre explained. Two of the most gruesome encounters came in 1916, when two million men were killed and wounded in battles at the Somme River and at Verdun.

Death on the Western Front: A German patrol fires on a French patrol between the lines. (Acme/UPI/Bettmann Newsphotos)

"Humanity . . . must be mad. . . . What scenes of horror and carnage! . . . Hell cannot be so terrible," wrote a French soldier at Verdun. Since the casualty rates were approximately equal, neither side "won." Other major offensives had the same results.

Between battles, men died from sniper fire, front-line patrols, random mortar fire, disease, exposure, and spoiled and adulterated rations. In Erich Remarque's novel *All Quiet on the Western Front,* the hero commented:

> Although we need reinforcement, the recruits give us almost more
> trouble than they are worth. They are helpless in these grim fighting
> areas, they fall like flies . . . a man must have a feeling for the contours
> of the ground, an ear for the sound and character of shells, must be able
> to decide beforehand where they will drop, how they will burst, and how
> to shelter from them.
>
> The young recruits of course know none of these things. They get
> killed simply because they hardly can tell shrapnel from high-
> explosives, they are mown down. . . . They flock together like sheep
> instead of scattering. . . . Some of them in a shell hole took off their
> gas masks too soon; they did not know that the gas lies longest in the
> hollows. . . . Their condition is hopeless, they choke to death with
> haemorrhages and suffocation.

Survivors had to endure crowded quarters, trench foot, rats, lice, mud, loss of comrades, and the probability of death during the next offensive. Under such conditions, men became living automatons. "We are not leading the lives of men at all," one British soldier wrote, "but that of animals, living in holes in the ground, and only showing outside to fight and to feed." Some deserted, and on occasions there were mutinies. Most of the troops, however, kept on fighting loyally.

In an attempt to find a way out of the stalemate, each side invented new weapons. They used poison gas and flame-throwers, but in particular, special hopes were pinned on breaking through entrenchments by developing effective airplanes and tanks. Both sides used airplanes and dirigibles (propelled lighter-than-air craft) for observation and for attacks on the front lines and the rear support areas. Airplanes fought each other in spectacular "dogfights," and skill-ful pilots ("aces") became romantic heroes in an otherwise grim war of impersonal death. Airplanes and dirigibles also attacked cities behind the battlefronts, often for the specific purpose of demoralizing the civilian population. The phenomenon of civilians suffering the same grisly deaths as soldiers and sailors foretold the nature of wars to come. Tanks became a major supporting weapon for infantry attacks late in the war. When used in conjunction with airplanes, they gave the promise of breaking through entrenched positions and thus re-turning combat to a war of maneuver. However, neither the airplane nor the tank was fully developed during the war, and they were not decisive in bring-ing victory to either side.

The War at Sea

While attempting to wear down the enemy on the battlefield, military leaders also pursued another goal of the war of attrition—cutting off supplies coming to the enemy by sea. Germany and particularly Great Britain depended on overseas sources of raw materials and food, and both nations were thus vulnerable to enemy navies. To protect its own trade and to cut off the commerce of any wartime enemy, Great Britain had built up the world's largest navy. Early in the war, the British mined the North Sea approaches to Germany and cleared German surface raiders from the sea. In addition, the British seized all merchant ships carrying contraband, which Great Britain in effect defined as any product that might help the enemy war effort. The British even seized neutral ships heading for neutral nations if the British suspected their cargoes would be reshipped to Germany. Neutral nations, including the United States, protested; but despite the seizures U.S. shipping to Europe continued. Since little could get through to Germany, U.S. trade benefited the Allies almost exclusively. Although some supplies continued to get through, as time passed German imports declined precipitously, and it was clear that in the long run the British blockade would strangle Germany.

Germany could also play the blockading game. Great Britain depended on large numbers of ships docking at its ports daily to feed its people and to keep its factories running. If its supplies were cut off, Great Britain would crumble much faster than Germany, and if Great Britain dropped out of the war, France would not last long. To starve out the British, the Germans had developed the submarine, an effective new weapon labeled by a British admiral as "under-handed, unfair, and un-English."

Beginning in earnest in 1915, German U-boats fanned out over the western approaches to Great Britain, destroying shipping at a rapid rate. At first, even though their submarines were vulnerable to attacks by airplanes and destroyers when they surfaced, German commanders tried to follow the rules of war by warning British merchant vessels so that their crews could take to the lifeboats. The British began to arm merchant ships, have merchant ships ram submarines, send war supplies and soldiers on passenger ships, fly the flags of neutral nations, and register British ships under foreign governments. The Germans began sinking merchant ships without warning, killing many more seamen and passengers. These German actions, exaggerated by Allied propaganda ministries, provoked international outcries. The climax came on May 7, 1915, when a U-boat sank the British passenger liner *Lusitania,* with the loss of 1,198 lives, including 128 Americans. The Germans claimed, possibly correctly, that the ship was carrying munitions and soldiers, and there is some evidence that the vessel was armed as well. By 1916 after repeated incidents, the reaction of the U.S. government became so threatening that the German government restricted the aggressive tactics of its submarines. With the submarine campaign hampered, the German surface fleet steamed out in an attempt to break the blockade, but at the Battle of Jutland on May 31–June 1, 1916, the British fleet forced the German navy back into port, from which it did not emerge for the remainder of the war. British admiral John Jellicoe, "the man who could have lost the war in a single hour," had held on.

The War at Home

If a nation expected to outlast its enemy in a war of attrition, it had to mobilize its civilian population effectively and create a new war front—the "home front." Since the warring governments had believed the conflict would be short, none of them had stockpiled resources or made plans to allocate them in the event of a lengthy struggle. As a war of attrition emerged, belligerent governments, whether authoritarian or democratic, took increasing control of broad facets of the economy and social life at home. The men who planned the centralization of the home front now became the pivotal figures of the war. Some were technicians, such as Walter Rathenau in Germany and Bernard Baruch in the United States; others were political leaders, such as David Lloyd George in Great Britain and Georges Clemenceau in France.

The managers of the home front had numerous responsibilities, none more crucial than the allocation of manpower. General Kitchener contributed substantially to the Allied war effort when he transformed the small professional army of Great Britain into a mass conscript army without a notable loss of ef-

World War I war production needs eased restrictions on what activities were possible for "respectable" women. (National Archives)

ficiency. In time, all the major belligerents conscripted able-bodied men and in some cases took teenagers, the elderly, and the marginally disabled. To replace these men in their civilian occupations, cultural tradition was swept aside as women were recruited for labor in the factories and offices and on the farms. Governments seized complete control of the production of industrial raw materials, and when key commodities such as natural nitrates and food were in short supply, governments financed research, development, and production of substitutes. Germany created many *ersatz* (substitute) commodities, such as artificial nitrates, cellulose clothing, bark coffee, and turnip bread. Civilians contributed to the war effort by working overtime, sending packages to the servicemen, planting gardens, investing in government bonds, supplementing rationing with fast days and meatless days, and watching for spies and saboteurs.

Because of the tremendous strains on the civilian populations, government propaganda ministries became a crucial aspect of the war effort, inciting citizens to work harder, love their government, and hate the enemy. Vivid propaganda posters portrayed opponents as slavering inhuman beasts fit only to be exterminated. At the same time, governments suppressed dissent through censorship and arrests for sedition.

THE BREAK IN THE STALEMATE

The decisive point in the war came in the winter of 1916–17. Germany was staggering under the pressure of the British blockade and other factors, and its population was suffering severe deprivation. German leaders feared that unless something was done to break the impasse, Germany would lose the war. The German naval command pressed for permission to resume unrestricted submarine warfare, sinking all ships heading for the British Isles. The German leaders understood that such a campaign would probably bring the United States into the war, but it was already a virtual ally of Great Britain, providing millions of dollars of war materials to Germany's enemies. They derided the United States as a "disorganized and undisciplined" nation that would not be effective in the war, and some German officers pledged that "not one American will land on the Continent." Even the more cautious officers estimated that it would take a year for the United States to place substantial troops on the Western Front. Long before the Americans could effectively intervene, they reasoned, Great Britain would be starved out and would surrender, and the other Allies would have collapsed. Over the protest of the civilian leaders, the kaiser reluctantly gave his approval.

On February 1, 1917, the reopening of unrestricted submarine warfare marked the beginning of the final phase of the war. For two months, the submarine campaign was spectacularly effective, and by April the British found themselves without reserves of industrial raw materials and with only six weeks' supply of food. Meanwhile, on April 6, the United States declared war on Germany. President Wilson, while personally a supporter of the Allied cause, had been a sincere advocate of neutrality. However, the new submarine campaign not only cost U.S. lives, but also, in Wilson's eyes, demonstrated a malignant militarism that threatened liberal institutions all over the world. This last point had been brought home to Americans when they discovered that Germany had promised to return the U.S. Southwest to Mexico if Mexico would attack the United States. Congress supported the president, and Americans entered the war believing they were fighting to "make the world safe for democracy."

Soon after the United States entered the war, it was apparent that the Germans had miscalculated. While the U.S. army did take many months to train and transport, the powerful U.S. navy was immediately ready to deal with the submarines. The U.S. and British navies created a convoy system and began to use new antisubmarine weapons such as depth charges and hydrophone detectors. During the summer and autumn of 1917, the combined navies sank an increasing number of submarines, while more and more merchant ships got through to Great Britain and France. By the end of 1917, as U.S. supplies poured in, it was clear the U-boat offensive had failed. If the Germans could not win a quick victory on the battlefield, the Allies, reinforced by the Americans, would win the war.

In fact, the Germans in late 1917 believed that victory on the Western Front was still possible because Russia was about to collapse. Russia had held on grimly throughout 1915 and 1916, absorbing millions of casualties, yet saved by the fact that the Germans and Austrians were too committed elsewhere to undertake a decisive offensive across the vast spaces of western Russia. Finally, however, the government of the tsar became the first casualty of the war of attrition. War-weariness and privation spurred civilians and soldiers alike to take to the streets and drive Tsar Nicholas from power in March 1917. The new provisional government attempted to carry on the war but was crippled by desertion at the front and political dissension at home (see Chapter 12). In November 1917, the Bolsheviks toppled the government, seized power, and immediately began negotiations for peace. On March 3, 1918, at Brest-Litovsk, Russia signed a humiliating peace treaty with Germany and dropped out of the war.

Russia's collapse allowed Germany to send its best troops in the east to the Western Front during the winter of 1917–18. Fearing these soldiers might have been infected with Bolshevik propaganda, the German government set up "mental delousing stations" to reindoctrinate them with the correct loyal attitudes. Bolstered by this additional manpower arriving on the Western Front, the Germans prepared to launch a decisive offensive. As Ludendorff put it, "Our general situation requires that we should strike at the earliest possible moment . . . before the Americans throw strong forces into the scale." Meanwhile, U.S. industry was pouring out an enormous quantity of war materiel to bolster the French and British armies, and U.S. troops began landing in France in numbers that eventually reached 250,000 a month. U.S. commander John "Black Jack" Pershing ringingly announced on his arrival in France, "Lafayette, we are here," in memory of France's contribution to victory in the U.S. War for Independence.

In March 1918, the Germans commenced their do-or-die offensive. They successfully used a new technique of sudden, overwhelming onslaughts on a narrow front to achieve a breakthrough, followed by rolling up the flanks of the break. They drove the French and British back for miles in a series of offensives lasting into July. The Allies, increasingly reinforced by the Americans, did not allow a major breakthrough: "There is no course open to us but to fight it out....each one of us must fight on to the end," read a typical headquarters command. As the Germans paused in exhaustion, Marshal Ferdinand Foch, the newly created commander-in-chief of the Allied forces, coordinated a series of counterattacks that steadily drove the Germans back through their main positions and out into open country. The increasing presence of U.S. troops at the front, plus a spectacular breakthrough on August 8 by British troops supported by large numbers of tanks, signaled the approaching end of the war. By September the German army, though not broken, had been pushed out of most of the territory it had conquered in France. On September 29, Ludendorff informed the kaiser that Germany could not win the war and recommended that the German government should explore avenues for peace while its military forces were still formidable.

THE ENDING OF THE WAR

Feverish diplomatic maneuverings punctuated the last weeks of the war. Wilson, convinced that demands of unconditional surrender would prolong the war, had outlined in January 1918 his Fourteen Points. The proposal contained three broad goals. The first goal was to prevent future wars by eliminating practices that had helped to precipitate the current war: trade barriers, interference with freedom of the seas, secret diplomacy, colonial tensions, and arms races. The second goal, aimed at settling particular problems in Europe, was a series of specific proposals concerning territorial integrity, national boundaries, and ethnic nationalism. To Wilson, his third goal was the most important: a League of Nations to preserve peace in the future. In addition to the Fourteen Points, Wilson had another condition for peace—the end of authoritarian government in Germany. He did not call for harsh terms to punish the Central Powers. The other Allies, which had suffered much more than the United States, were not particularly happy with Wilson's idea of leniency toward Germany, but they eventually agreed, with some reservations.

During September and October, while the Germans made overtures for peace on the basis of the Fourteen Points and tinkered with coalition governments that might satisfy Wilson that Germany was no longer an autocracy, the war wound down. Bulgaria surrendered on September 30 and Turkey on October 30. Ethnic minorities in Austria-Hungary began declaring their independence, and on November 3, Austria surrendered, with Kaiser Karl going into exile shortly afterward. On the same day, the German sailors at Kiel mutinied, running up the Socialist red flag. Councils of workers and soldiers began springing up in the major German cities in imitation of the Russian Soviets. During the days that followed, Socialist leaders encouraged wildcat strikes in many German cities, and the military leaders forced Kaiser Wilhelm II to abdicate. He then went into exile in the Netherlands.

When representatives of the new German republic went to France prepared to sign an armistice on the basis of the Fourteen Points, they found to their dismay that the Allies had additional terms that would make it impossible for Germany to renew the fighting. The Allied officials demanded that the German army withdraw to the east bank of the Rhine so that the Allied armies could occupy the west bank and several bridgeheads. Germany was to surrender the bulk of its surface fleet, its submarines, its air force, much of its machine guns and artillery, and its motorized transport. Finally, Germany was to renounce the Treaty of Brest-Litovsk and make reparations for damages sustained by civilians in the occupied territories. The German representatives reluctantly and bitterly agreed: "I saw [the German delegation leader] brandish his pen and grind his teeth, . . . the business was settled," Foch recalled. On November 11, 1918, at 11:00 *a.m.*, the guns fell silent on the Western Front. World War I was over.

SUMMARY

World War I was primarily fought in Europe and the North Atlantic, although some fighting occurred in Asia and Africa and elsewhere on the world's oceans. The French and British halted the Germans at the Battle of the Marne and both sides dug in, creating a stalemate on the Western Front. In the east, German forces routed invading Russian armies, but the Eastern Front also ended in a stalemate, as did secondary fronts in Italy and northern Greece. Elsewhere, Allied forces conquered German colonies in Asia and Africa and cleared German vessels out of the Indian and Pacific oceans.

As the stalemate persisted, each side attempted to wear down the opponent's armed forces and break the morale of the opponents' civilian populations. The war of attrition on the Western Front entailed rituals of mass slaughter, as assaulting infantry was almost invariably turned back by entrenched defenders. Great Britain conducted a surface and mine blockade that slowly strangled the German economy and caused great deprivation among German civilians. Germany responded with a submarine blockade of Great Britain, but temporarily ceased sinking neutral ships when threatened by the United States. Governments of the warring nations urged their "home front" populations to make greater and greater sacrifices and to hate the enemy.

In 1917, two major occurrences broke the stalemate. One was the German decision to resume unrestricted warfare, which brought the United States into the war on the side of the Allies. Anglo-American naval cooperation broke the submarine blockade, and U.S. war materiel and U.S. soldiers began to pour into Europe. The second major event was the revolution that knocked Russia out of the war and freed German troops to fight on the Western Front. In March 1918, the Germans launched their last offensive but were thrown back by Allied troops, who launched a counteroffensive that slowly drove German troops out of France. Unable to stop the Allied offensive, faced with social revolution, and deserted by its allies, Germany agreed to a harsh armistice, which went into effect on November 11, 1918.

SUGGESTED SOURCES

Cobb, Humphrey, *Paths of Glory* (1935). A fictional account of the French army that attacks the high command. (Also a film.)

Falls, Cyril B., *The First World War* (1960). An extremely well-written account by a noted British expert in military history.

Ferro, Marc, *The Great War 1914–18* (1973). A concise interpretive account stressing the overall economic, political, and psychological context of the struggle.*

Lincoln, W. Bruce, *Passage Through Armageddon: The Russians in War and Revolution, 1914–1918* (1986). A lively presentation of the Russian war effort.*

Remarque, Erich Maria, *All Quiet on the Western Front* (1928). A classic novel about the nature of modern war, emphasizing the lives of the soldiers.* (Also a film and a television program.)

Stokesbury, James L., *A Short History of World War I* (1981). A well-written general survey of the conflict.*

Tansill, Charles C., *America Goes to War* (1963). A survey of U.S. involvement.

Tuchman, Barbara, *The Guns of August* (1982). A lively account of individuals and events at the opening of World War I.* (Also a film.)

*Paperback available.

PART TWO

The Era of Revolution and War

TIME CHART II
1918–1945

Year	South & East Asia	Middle East & Africa	Europe	Western Hemisphere	Trends in Culture, Science, Technology
1918	Chinese Republican Revolution, 1911–26		Russian Revolution and civil war, 1917–20	UNITED STATES PREDOMINANT IN LATIN AMERICA Revolution and civil war in Mexico, 1910–24	Popularization of Freudian analysis
1919	PARIS PEACE CONFERENCE AND FORMATION OF THE LEAGUE OF NATIONS				
	GROWING NATIONALISM Wafd party in Egypt, 1919–52		Rebellion and civil war in Ireland, 1916–23		
		Ataturk in Turkey			
1920					
1921					The Roaring Twenties
1922	Gandhi leads non-violent independence movement in India, 1920s–40s		Mussolini assumes power in Italy		
1923					Decade of the popularization of motion pictures and radio
1924			Lenin dies		Advent of surrealism
1925		Reza shah in Iran	Locarno treaties	U.S. military withdrawal from Latin America, 1920s–1930s	Scopes trial
1926	Chiang leads northern expedition in China, 1926–28	Ibn Saud in Saudi Arabia			

1927	
1928	
1929	Stalin begins collectivization and first Five–Year plan
1930	THE GREAT DEPRESSION BEGINS — Stock market collapses — Decade of popularization of air travel
1931	Japan occupies Manchuria
1932	
1933	Hitler assumes power in Germany — Roosevelt launches New Deal — Mexican muralist Rivera
1934	Communist Long March in China, 1934–35 — Purges in U.S.S.R., 1934–35 — U.S. Good Neighbor Policy, 1930s
1935	Italy conquers Ethiopia, 1935–36 — Period of appeasement, 1935–39
1936	Spanish Civil War, 1936–39
1937	Japan invades China
1938	Munich Agreement
1939	Nazi-Soviet Pact
1940	**WORLD WAR II** — North African campaigns
1941	Japanese conquest of Southeast Asia — German invasion of U.S.S.R. — Japan attacks Pearl Harbor — Tank and air warfare
1942	Battle of Stalingrad
1943	U.S. war industries build-up — Amphibious warfare
1944	Normandy invasion
1945	Atomic bombs dropped on Hiroshima and Nagasaki — Mistral – first Latin American writer to win Nobel Prize for literature

10

General Trends in the Interwar Years

The global trends that characterized the opening of the twentieth century—nationalism, imperialism, political diversity, economic disparity, and social and cultural upheaval—continued to dominate events during the interwar years of 1919 through 1939. After World War I, nationalists intensified their struggles for self-determination, while many Western and Japanese leaders sought to maintain and increase their national empires. Nations escalated their races for military supremacy, while at the same time individuals and organizations worked toward disarmament and the formation of meaningful international organizations. Many had fought in World War I believing that victory would lead to more liberal, progressive governments. However, after the war, authoritarian regimes steadily increased in both numbers and power. During the interwar years, it was by no means clear which forces would emerge victorious.

PROGRESS IN SCIENCE AND TECHNOLOGY

During the interwar years, scientists and technicians refined and expanded theories in physics, biology, and engineering. Chemists and biologists took major steps toward understanding and explaining the structure and the genetic composition of the cell. Medical researchers improved techniques for inoculating against disease, thereby further prolonging the span of human life. Ironically, such improvements in health care also contributed to the population explosion in the colonized world, at the very time that increased use of birth control methods slowed or stabilized population growth in the industrialized world.

In engineering, structural designers were able to create larger and taller buildings, and propulsion experts brought forth an infant rocket industry. The armament industries in many nations continued to prosper as their technicians developed bigger and more deadly weapons, particularly airplanes, tanks, and submarines. Both airplanes and tanks, introduced during World War I, played a major role during the world conflict that was to follow.

Beyond these advances, the interwar years produced two developments that profoundly changed how humanity lived. In the first of these, building upon conceptual breakthroughs of the pre-World War I era, Henry Ford's mass production techniques and Frederick Taylor's labor efficiency studies contributed to increased production of consumer goods. The automobile and many other items came within the purchasing power of the average Western worker. By 1930 there were more than five million automobile owners in Europe. In Great Britain, there were seven times as many in 1930 as in 1913; in France, almost twelve times as many. In the United States, Henry Ford's Model T, which was always painted black, ushered in a new era of mobility. In Africa, Asia, and Latin America, however, such consumer goods remained luxury items only the very rich could afford.

The automobile also fostered a number of new industries, such as manufacturing tires and constructing extensive asphalt and concrete road networks. A mass-market tourist industry came into being. The aircraft industry developed more slowly, but by the 1930s, commercial air travel, catering to wealthy vacationers and enterprising business executives, was well established.

Widespread use of automotive and air travel created escalating demands for gasoline. To meet this demand, the petroleum industry increased its operations on a global scale. In the process, entrepreneurs created huge international corporations that monopolized petroleum resources. After World War II, these international corporations directly clashed with petroleum-producing nations in the Middle East, Africa, and Latin America, as these nations sought a more advantageous distribution of the profits from this vital industry.

The radio was a major development in the field of mass communication. Because of mass production, most Western families could afford a radio, which became the leading form of home entertainment. There were about three million radios in Great Britain and Germany by 1930. Such figures were small, however, compared to those of the United States, which far surpassed the rest of the world in producing and owning consumer goods.

Motion pictures also became popular: millions flocked to see "movies" featuring Rudolph Valentino, Jean Harlow, Douglas Fairbanks, Edward G. Robinson, and others. These "stars" were featured everywhere, and the public avidly followed not only the professional careers of the stars but also their private lives. Radio, newspapers, films, and magazines fueled public interest in sports, society, and crime. Media coverage popularized personalities from the gangster Al Capone to Charles "Lucky Lindy" Lindbergh, the first person to fly solo, nonstop across the Atlantic.

Radio, news broadcasts, and film newsreels had both positive and negative effects. The Western public became more informed about public affairs and about the politicians who made decisions. Regional suspicions inside nations were often reduced, as their inhabitants identified with the practices and ideals displayed in the national media. On the negative side, politicians sought to manipulate the media to present themselves in the most favorable light. As a result, the superficial media image of political leaders often became more important than substantive issues and programs. Thus, at the very time masses of people throughout the world were becoming better informed, they were also often being misled by charismatic figures.

Scientists conducting theoretical research on the nature and potential of the atom brought about the second profound development of this period. After decades of prior research, scientists during World War II succeeded in creating a reliable "chain reaction" in uranium-235 and plutonium. By "splitting the atom," scientists were able to release and ultimately to harness the energy that had been "locked up" inside the atom. In this process, an atom that had been split (atomic fission) shot out neutrons that struck and split other atoms, releasing immense power. When encased in a bomb, the chain reaction produced the blast effect of hundreds of conventional bombs, plus radioactive effects that killed and maimed over an extended period.

ECONOMIC CRISES

After World War I, economic conditions varied widely from nation to nation. The United States emerged from the war with a huge industrial capacity, no wartime damage at home, and enormous amounts of capital owed to it from wartime loans to other Allied nations. U.S. business prospered; despite the unflattering portraits of businessmen created by Sinclair Lewis in his novels *Main Street* and *Babbitt,* the businessman became the ideal of Americans, compared by one enthusiast to Jesus. "The business of this country is business," summed up President Calvin Coolidge.

In contrast, many businesses and industries in Europe never recovered the dynamism they had displayed before the war. Europe's share of world trade diminished; nations remained deeply in debt, particularly to the United States. In Great Britain and other European nations, unemployment remained almost constantly above 10 percent.

Galloping inflation, except in the United States, was another global legacy of the war. By 1919, prices in Great Britain were three times as high as in 1913. By 1926 prices in France were at least seven times as high as in 1913. In Germany, the government tried to cope with the inflationary spiral by printing more and more money. Confidence in the German mark fell on the international exchange; however, because of attractive interest rates, U.S. creditors continued to advance money to German borrowers. At home, Germans attempted to invest in durable goods that would maintain their value. This only furthered price increases. By 1923, the German mark was worth only one-trillionth of its prewar value. People demanded that they be paid every day so they could rush to the stores to buy anything in sight before their money became even more worthless. Although the German statesman Gustav Stresemann took energetic steps to end the crisis, social and psychological scars remained, for the German people had witnessed the destruction of the value of their savings.

Many parts of the British and French empires also suffered economic difficulties. Western nations had fought the war not only with their own resources

The ravages of postwar inflation: German bank officials in 1923 carrying money that declined in value as the walked. (The Granger Collection).

but also with those of their vast empires, enlarging the agricultural and industrial sectors of their colonial holdings to support the war effort. Once the war was over, there were surpluses of some goods, but those surpluses were often accompanied by scarcities in vital commodities such as bread and kerosene for cooking and heating. Mounting unemployment forced peasants into the cities in search of employment and the "easy life," but there were few jobs in the cities, which were ill-equipped to provide even minimal services for this rapid influx of humanity. Asian, Latin, and African cities were soon plagued with the same kind of social and economic problems that Western cities had endured during the industrialization of the nineteenth century.

Through the expansion of mass media, even poor peasants became more aware of the high standard of living in the West and in urban areas around the world. In poor agricultural areas, where the economy was still at a subsistence level, people began to demand an improvement in their daily lives. A widening gap existed between those societies that enjoyed high living standards and those that remained relatively poor. Such a gap had existed in the beginning of the twentieth century; the difference in the interwar years was that many had now become aware of those differences and therefore had become impatient for change.

Many nationalist leaders in the colonized world believed that their particular economic woes—unemployment, inflation, poverty, scarcities of consumer goods—were caused by imperial domination. As a result, the middle-class elites in nations such as India and Egypt concluded that their goal should be economic as well as political independence. Indeed, demands for more local participation in economic spheres often went hand-in-hand with demands for political autonomy. For example, Egyptian nationalists established an Egyptian bank (Bank Misr) and a locally owned cigarette factory, and urged all patriotic Egyptians to boycott British goods and to "buy Egyptian." In India, nationalist leaders urged Indians to adopt *Swadeshi;* that is, to buy only Indian-made goods.

However, total economic self-sufficiency, whether in poor or in rich nations, was an impossible goal in the twentieth century. The economies of nations had become too interrelated through trade, credit systems, markets, and resource needs to be separated into individual independent entities. International corporations were only one evidence of the economic interdependency that surpassed narrow national interests. Most African and Asian nations ultimately secured political independence but remained economically tied to the industrialized nations who controlled the majority of the world's industrial might.

By 1929 the economic imbalances and problems of the global economic systems resulted in a worldwide economic depression. The Great Depression was a global economic crisis which lasted in many areas until World War II and which vividly demonstrated the interdependency of twentieth-century economies. There were several specific causes. Production far exceeded consumption. Staggering amounts of credit had been extended during the war. Individuals, businesses, and nations had become obligated to one another in a vast web of indebtedness. In addition, many individuals and nations had estimated their wealth, not by tangible goods or resources, but by paper assets such as money or stocks. Paper assets printed (as they were in postwar Germany) without real productivity or tangible assets such as gold to support them were, in fact, worthless. Finally, many gambled recklessly in the stock market.

The Great Depression began on October 24, 1929, when the U.S. stock market started to plummet; soon the U.S. economy began to crumble. By early 1933 the United States was deeply mired in business cutbacks, unemployment, and bankruptcies. Europe soon felt the impact of the economic disaster. In 1930, as the collapse hit Germany, five bankrupt Berlin businessmen committed suicide in one week. Chancellor Heinrich Bruning became known as "The Chancellor of Hunger." As a result of the economic crisis in Germany, the Allies were forced first to postpone German payment of the reparations. Payment of the reparations had become one of the major sources of economic dispute among the major powers after World War I. Under the Dawes Plan, in 1924, an initial foreign loan was promised and Germany's annual reparation payments were reduced. Again in 1929, under the U.S.-devised Young Plan, the reparations were further reduced. Finally, in 1932, the Allies admitted—albeit with great reluctance—that Germany would no longer pay reparations.

The economic crisis created by the Great Depression was felt in other European nations as well; by 1932, one man in four in Great Britain was on "the dole" (welfare) and production fell 28 percent in France and 33 percent in

Italy. In early 1930, the Depression hit Japan. The Japanese public blamed the politicians, and many argued that the solution to the economic disaster lay in military expansion and the creation of a self-sufficient empire. Many Japanese viewed Germany's turning from democracy to authoritarian policies as a positive object lesson. Although Japan was the first major industrialized nation to recover from the Depression, Japanese democracy and parliamentary government never really recovered from the effects of the Depression.

The Depression also had devastating economic consequences on the largely agricultural economies of Asia, Africa, and Latin America, since most of the nations on those continents were linked through imperial ties and trade with the industrialized world. As most of the people in these nations already lived at the poverty level, the loss of even a few pennies of income per capita could mean economic ruin. Leaders of the poor nations emphasized that when a man's belt was already pulled to the last notch, it was impossible to ask him to tighten it further.

SOCIAL AND POLITICAL TURMOIL

The interwar years also ushered in sweeping social changes. With their new-found economic strength, many Western women demanded, and eventually obtained, the right to vote; they also gained more influence in political circles. In Africa, Asia, and the Middle East, aristocratic and middle-class women were

Unemployment was a problem in Japan through the 1920s and became worse with the world Depression. Here, priests march through Tokyo soliciting money for victims of an earthquake and for the unemployed. (The Bettmann Archive)

often in the vanguard of nationalist movements. They, too, struggled for political and social rights and joined in the larger international women's movement.

As more and more women entered the labor force, old social patterns—already altered by the war and technological developments—changed. In most of the industrialized world, the birth rate continued to drop, and throughout most of the world, the average adult lived longer and the trend toward urbanization accelerated. To some extent, in Great Britain and elsewhere, upper-class privilege and its monopoly over the political and economic systems began to decline. Superficially, the war ended in a victory for liberal, democratic forces. In reality, the conservatives on the Right and socialists on the Left were far from destroyed. Struggles between socialist and conservative forces became particularly intense in the defeated nations; in Italy and Germany, leftists and conservatives battled openly and violently in the streets of major cities.

Protracted political clashes and economic crises throughout Europe forced more and more people toward the extremes of the political spectrum, leaving fewer and fewer to support the center. Europeans became increasingly unwilling to compromise and grew more fearful of social and political anarchy. By promising easy, quick solutions, authoritarian forces, generally from the Right, gained support. One by one, moderate or progressive governments in Italy, Portugal, Spain, Germany, and Eastern Europe fell to dictatorial regimes.

Faced with defeats in the heartland of Europe, Marxists redefined their immediate goals during the interwar years. In the first fervor of the 1917 revolution, Vladimir Lenin and Leon Trotsky had both argued that the Russian Revolution was merely the first link in a chain of revolutions that would soon sweep the world. The goal of the Third International, or Comintern, dominated by the Soviet Union, was to hasten that process by supporting local Communist parties in their fight against capitalism and imperialism. By the mid-1920s, with continued domestic problems and a new leadership under Stalin, the Soviets began to place less emphasis on international revolution and more stress on increasing the strength of the Soviet Union.

Before World War II, Marxist ideology had little impact on the masses of people within Africa or Asia. The few Marxist leaders who did emerge generally came from the educated middle class, and they met severe opposition not only from the ruling classes in their own nations but also from the imperial powers. However, as demands for national autonomy were continually rejected by the colonial powers, some nationalist leaders began to turn to the Soviet Union for support. Some, like Sun Yat-sen in China, did not intend to institute Marxist revolutions but only to secure Soviet assistance in ousting the imperial powers and internal enemies. Two Asian leaders, Mao Tse-tung in China and Ho Chi Minh in French Indochina, did expect to make their nations Marxist states. However, both were faced with the task of converting Marx's ideas, which presumed an industrialized environment, to the needs of peasant societies.

The prewar politics of ethnic nationalism continued to be a divisive issue after the war. The delegates at Paris had carved out new nations in Eastern

Europe in an attempt to grant self-determination to peoples living within them. However, many of these new nations still contained minority groups inside their boundaries. The conflicts between these new governments and minority groups who wanted autonomy contributed to the next global confrontation.

INTERNATIONAL AFFAIRS: CONFLICTS AND THE SEARCH FOR PEACE

The Rise of Anticolonialism

One international trend during the interwar years was the increasing pressure applied by colonial nationalists for an end to imperialism. World War I had badly weakened the great European nations, and the relative importance of Europe to the rest of the world declined after the war. The war also hastened the day when European colonial empires would disappear. Wartime statements in support of self-determination had stimulated anticolonialism at the same time that the war had weakened the colonial powers' ability to hold on to their possessions in the face of such rising nationalism. In fact, the seeds were germinating for the post-World War II breakup of colonial empires.

None of this was foreseen at the Paris Peace Conference, where old-fashioned imperialism was "business as usual." Western representatives, who controlled the conference, made it clear that self-determination applied to national groups in Central and Eastern Europe, but not to demands from Arabs, Zionists, Indians, and others under imperial control. In their last major effort to enlarge their empires, Great Britain, France, and Japan used the mandate system created after World War I to govern the colonies of the defeated powers. It was, however, at best a stopgap measure in halting the overwhelming push toward national independence throughout the world.

By the early 1930s, imperial powers, with varying degrees of reluctance, were beginning to make concessions to the rising pressures of anti-imperial nationalism. The British responded to the moves toward independence in their possessions first by making accommodations with their colonies that had been settled and controlled by white Europeans, usually of British descent. These dominions— Canada, Newfoundland, Australia, New Zealand, and South Africa—had provided substantial financial and military assistance in the war effort. After the war, Great Britain acknowledged this support by agreeing to individual membership in the League of Nations for all of these dominions and for India as well. Later, Great Britain went further down the path of devolution. The Statute of Westminister in 1931 recognized these white-controlled dominions as "autonomous communities." Economic and military links to Great Britain were preserved through the Commonwealth, which was a loosely knit association of the dominions, a few former colonies, and Great Britain.

However, in the interwar period, Great Britain was willing to grant autonomy only to those parts of the empire with which it retained close racial and cultural ties. The more heterogeneous and less Westernized parts of the empire were kept under controls that were as tight as the British—given their weakened world status—could sustain. Similarly, the French fought tenaciously to maintain their far-flung empire. British and French determination to safeguard their empires provoked peoples living under their domination to increase their demands for freedom.

In another major example of the decline of imperialism, the United States began to back off from its interventionist approach in Latin America. The United States had intervened repeatedly in the affairs of nations in the Caribbean area, and by 1924, U.S. military and Treasury personnel directed fiscal affairs in ten nations. Many Latin Americans bitterly resented this intervention by the "Colossus of the North." Mexican leaders sometimes bitterly complained that being a neighbor of the U.S. was like being a mouse sleeping next to an elephant: If the elephant rolled over, the mouse was crushed. Realizing that the policy of direct interference was often counterproductive, the United States began to withdraw its forces, and after the marines left Haiti in 1934, no U.S. troops remained on Latin American soil.

The more relaxed policy of the United States was sharply tested in Mexico. President Laźaro Cárdenas had moved to nationalize foreign petroleum companies, including U.S. corporation holdings valued by the companies at $500 million. The U.S. business community clamored for action against Mexico, but the Roosevelt administration was determined to pursue a "Good Neighbor" policy and chose to negotiate. As a result, the U.S. government agreed to loan the Mexican government $24 million, to be used to pay off the petroleum companies. In a further retreat from imperialism, the United States recognized the independence of Cuba in 1932; however, Cuba remained a diplomatic and economic protectorate.

The Revival of Militarism

During the interwar years, extreme forms of nationalism developed that fed and encouraged the rise of militarism, particularly in Italy, Germany, and Japan. The rise of fascism in Italy and Nazism in Germany stimulated an upsurge of aggressive nationalism that in Nazi Germany was also based on beliefs of racial and cultural superiority. In Japan, nationalism coupled with long-held beliefs of cultural superiority resulted in an aggressive, expansionist foreign policy aimed at acquiring an Asian empire.

Extreme nationalism led to military build-ups. In Japan, the military exercised substantial power within political circles, stockpiling arms and building up Japan's land and sea forces. As a defeated power, Germany's armaments were strictly limited under the terms of the Versailles treaty. However, as it became evident that the Allies would not enforce their own treaty, the Germans moved to rebuild their armed forces. By the mid-1930s it was apparent that the Versailles treaty had failed to prevent Germany from becoming, for a second time in the twentieth century, a major military power. Russia also expanded its military capabilities, preparing for the looming conflict that would again pit the major powers of the globe against one another.

The Search for Collective Security

Recognizing the problems inherent in a world of conflicting nationalisms, Wilson and others urged the formation of effective international organizations that would prevent future great wars. Wilson also spoke extensively about the need for disarmament. There was general agreement that stockpiles of arms had contributed to the martial spirit prevalent before 1914 and had prolonged the war.

The League of Nations represented the major postwar attempt to seek peaceful means of settling disputes and sharing responsibility for the protection of its members from aggression. The League contained an Assembly (where all members participated), a Council composed of the great powers (Great Britain, France, Italy, and Japan) and four lesser nations, and a Secretariat. The International Court was also established to settle disputes referred to it.

The League was fairly successful in settling border disputes between Latin American nations and between minor European nations such as Sweden, Finland, Greece, Albania, and Poland. It also administered the free city of Danzig and the Saar district, both taken from Germany after the war. In addition, many noted humanists and philanthropists from around the world participated in and lent their energies to League activities.

In matters concerning the interests of major nations, however, the League was a failure. Over and over again, nations refused to work collectively either to settle disputes or to stop aggression. The most powerful nations also refused to commit themselves to mutual armed action against aggressors, nor would they act against their own self-interest for the larger good. The League was also hampered by the refusal of the United States to join and, in its early years, by the absence of the Soviet Union and the powers defeated in World War I. In the final analysis, the League's greatest achievements were its efforts in the fields of social welfare, its support of agencies for refugees and the poor, and its sponsorship of medical research.

Internationalism on a regional basis, in the form of a Pan-American association, was well established in the Western Hemisphere. Initiated in 1889 by the United States as a thinly disguised arrangement to facilitate its own goals in the region, the Pan-American association displayed elements of genuine cooperation in the interwar years. At five-year intervals, Pan-American conferences forged a number of agreements on, and created special organizations concerning, copyrights, labor codes, agriculture, child protection, and arbitration procedures. However, these agreements were often ignored in practice.

In the interwar years, several international agreements addressing specific problems appeared to offer the greatest hope for a lasting peace. The Locarno treaties (1925) addressed a number of European issues, and the Washington Naval Conference (1922) and the Kellogg-Briand Peace Pact (1928) were concerned with knotty problems of arms limitation and war.

With the failure of the powers to settle their economic, political, and national rivalries, it was almost inevitable that moves toward disarmament should also fail and that, in the interwar years, nations should take steps to protect their interests by military means. European and U.S. leaders spoke eloquently of peace and disarmament during the 1920s, but they remained suspicious that their enemies were continuing the race toward armed superiority.

Despite the Washington Naval Conference and the Kellogg-Briand Peace Pact, by the 1930s most nations still emphasized stockpiling weapons in order to be prepared for the next war. After World War I, the total arms expenditures of Great Britain, France, and Italy actually increased. France refused to limit its armaments and subsidized arms for Central European nations as a safeguard against Germany. France also built, at great expense and effort, the famous Maginot Line, purported to be an impregnable defense. Only the United States, far removed from the trouble areas of the world, greatly reduced its army. By 1932 fifteen nations, including Turkey and Rumania, had larger armies than that of the United States. In the final analysis, the major trend of nationalism far outweighed the opposing movement toward international peace, dooming the League of Nations and other international agreements to failure.

IDEAS AND CULTURE

In the period between the wars, as people continued to search for deeper meanings to life and the world around them, the works of thinkers such as Marx, Darwin, Freud, and Nietzsche continued to exercise considerable influence. To some, the experiences of World War I made the ideas of these important intellectuals seem more relevant than ever.

The combined impact of these thinkers was particularly evident in the continuing battle between secularism and traditional religious beliefs. The most dramatic struggle took place in the Soviet Union. The new Marxist-Leninist government not only removed the Russian Orthodox Church from its exalted position as the state religion, but also encouraged atheistic beliefs and in general persecuted and discriminated against religious believers.

In the United States and Western Europe, secularists and proponents of traditional religious teachings generally waged their battles in more democratic arenas, such as in law courts and on the pages of journals. One example was the spectacular Scopes "Monkey Trial" of 1925, where a high school biology teacher was found guilty of teaching Darwinian evolution instead of the Biblical account of creation. One of the leading and most influential opponents of organized religion in the United States was H.L. Mencken, a writer and editor, who as a young man had been greatly influenced by the ideas of Nietzsche. In colorful, exaggerated language, Mencken railed against theologians, censorship, middle-class values, and Prohibition—to name just a few of his favorite targets.

Secularists were also active in Latin America and in non-Western areas of the world. In 1917, Mexican revolutionaries pushed through a secular constitution which limited the power of the Catholic Church. In Asia, secularists, often strongly influenced by the West, challenged advocates of traditional re-

Defense attorney Clarence Darrow (left) and former Secretary of State William Jennings Bryan, who differed on the interpretation of the Bible at the Scopes "Monkey Trial." (Historical Picture Services)

ligions such as Islam, Hinduism, or Buddhism. For example, Mustafa Kemal (Ataturk), head of the Turkish government through most of the 1920s and 1930s, set out to break the centuries-old dominance of Islamic tradition over Turkish life, and in many ways succeeded.

Technological changes such as the motion picture and the automobile fostered challenges to traditional values in the United States and Europe, especially regarding sex and marriage. People became more familiar with the psychology of Freud, whose analysis of human psychological behavior was often misinterpreted by popularizers to mean that frustrating the sex drive was harmful. Advocates of the new life style spoke in the name of increased freedom. An affluent "smart set" stressed self-indulgent individualism through fast cars, bathtub gin, sex, and "hot" dance music. Many women began to discard the traditional demure female image and to wear short skirts, bob their hair, dance, drink, smoke, and "neck." A U.S. college president expressed feelings shared by many conservative Americans when he said, "The low cut gowns, the rolled hose, and the short skirts were born of the Devil." Despite all of these new challenges, however, most people continued to be heavily influenced by traditional religious beliefs. For example, Protestant fundamentalists were largely responsible for prohibiting the manufacture and sale of intoxicating beverages in the United States from 1919 until 1933.

Many of the new enthusiasms, often fed by newspapers, radio, and motion pictures, increased appetites for the novel and bizarre, while reflecting a nervous rootlessness and an attempt to escape from the harsh realities of the war years. Thus people turned increasingly to expending their energies on the enjoyments offered by the abundance of consumer goods and services: automobiles, radios, jazz records, movies, night clubs, and cabarets. In London, Paris, and Berlin, as in Chicago and New York, the 1920s often "roared." A penchant for new pleasures swept over many European cities. The Austrian writer Stefan Zweig noted that "all values were changed, and . . . Berlin was transformed into the Babylon of the world." He also wrote that "anything that gave hope of newer and greater thrills . . . anything in the way of narcotics, morphine, cocaine, heroin, found a tremendous market." For a girl "to be sixteen and still under suspicion of virginity," he added, perhaps exaggerating, "would have been considered a disgrace in any school of Berlin."

The rapid change in values and practices frightened traditionalists. A growing number of people throughout the world echoed U.S. President Warren Harding's cry for a return to "normalcy." The cry was echoed in Great Britain, where politicians called for a return to "tranquility" and "honesty." However, in a transformed world in which so much had been destroyed, a return to a pre-1914 existence was impossible.

In the interwar years, people not only challenged traditional religious values and escaped into new pleasures and fads, but also questioned a whole range of more traditional beliefs, such as loyalty to one's nation and faith in progress, science, reason, and civilization itself. For some disillusioned intellectuals, the experiences of the war underscored the validity of many of Nietzsche's earlier criticisms. One of the most popular books of 1919 was *The Decline of the West,* by Oswald Spengler, who thought of Nietzsche as Europe's greatest modern prophet. Spengler was an unknown former schoolteacher when his book was first published in the summer of 1918; in it he attempted to build upon Nietzsche's pessimistic view of the West and to construct a total survey (past, present, and future) of the rise and fall of Western civilization, comparing the destiny of the West with the fate of previous societies. Even in the more down-to-earth, less rarefied intellectual atmosphere of the 1930s, the ideas of Nietzsche continued to appeal to some, especially in Germany, where his ideas of a superman were often selectively used to justify the new Nazi order. Hitler himself, although he lacked any sound knowledge of Nietzsche's ideas, was fond of quoting several of his lines, and on Mussolini's sixtieth birthday, the Führer sent the philosopher's complete works to him as a present.

Developments in art and literature paralleled those in philosophy. While fighting men were still in the trenches, a group known as the Dadaists founded an artistic and literary movement in Zurich, Switzerland, which, for a short time, symbolized the disenchantment with all the old values; one of the founders wrote, "I loathe fat objectivity and harmony" and "Logic was always false." After the war, the Dadaists returned to Paris and Berlin and resorted to displays such as reading poetry while ringing bells. When their actions created disbelief, they replied that their audiences were not the only ones who did not understand their actions—they themselves did not.

Dadaism soon gave way to surrealism, another artistic and literary move-ment begun in France. Influenced by Freud, surrealists expressed the belief that the unconscious world of dreams and fantasies represented a higher, more real and significant world than the practical one of everyday life. In their writ-ings, paintings, and films, they attempted to portray this unconscious dream world. James Joyce's *Ulysses* (1922), one of the most significant novels of the interwar period, strongly reflected the author's interest in the subconscious life of his characters. Although surrealism as a distinct movement ended at the be-ginning of World War II, surrealist ideas continued to have an effect on writ-ers, artists, and film directors wishing to go beyond traditional realism.

From the beginning to the end of the 1920s, literature mirrored the disil-lusionment of the decade, as indicated by the title alone of T. S. Eliot's widely acclaimed poem "The Waste Land" (1922). Frederick Henry, a character in Ernest Hemingway's 1929 novel of World War I, *A Farewell to Arms,* came to the conclusion that "abstract words such as glory, honor, courage or hallow were obscene."

Following the Great Depression and the rise of Hitler, writers and artists in the West became more concerned with concrete social and political issues. The realistic style, more easily understood than that of Joyce or Eliot, regained some of the popularity it had lost in the 1920s. Writers like John Steinbeck, author of the novel *The Grapes of Wrath* (1939), expressed sympathy for the poor and stressed the brotherhood of man. The Depression also led some West-ern writers to embrace Marxist ideas. For example, the Mexican artist Diego Rivera and the Chilean poet Pablo Neruda were influenced not only by European artistic ideas but also by those of Marx and Lenin, who helped to fuel their already critical view of a West that they perceived to be both capitalistic and imperialistic.

Cultural developments and conflicts in the West had only a limited im-pact on the non-West. The mass media helped to transmit Western cultural ideas to cities such as Cairo and Shanghai, where the upper and middle classes at-tempted to copy the example of those who "roared" in New York, Paris, and Berlin. On the other hand, despite some Western-oriented secularist leaders such as Jawaharlal Nehru, most Indian Hindus and Muslims regarded religion and religious customs as all-important. The traditional values advocated by Mohandas Gandhi dominated Indian culture. Although Gandhi worked together with Nehru to obtain Indian independence and was tolerant of Islam and of some Western ideas, Gandhi's solutions for India's future were largely based on his own understanding of Hinduism, and he remained deeply suspicious of modern secularized Western states.

In China, as in India, people differed over the relative merits of synthe-sizing Western ideas with Chinese tradition. The older faiths of Buddhism, Confucianism, and Taoism did not generally exclude one another, and many Chinese practiced teachings from several faiths. Some tried to assimilate be-liefs and ideas from the West. For example, Sun Yat-sen, the most outstanding leader of China until his death in 1925, was a Protestant who greatly admired

Darwin's teachings and yet respected the Confucian tradition. His successor, Chiang Kai-shek, became a Protestant but retained respect for traditional Confucian ideas. The Chinese constitution of 1923 stated that a "citizen of the Republic of China shall be free to honor Confucius and to prefer any religion." By the late 1930s, the Chinese Communists were Chiang Kai-shek's chief rivals for power, and their leaders had little respect for either Eastern or Western religious teachings. They agreed with another Western concept: Marx's statement that religion was "the opium of the people."

Some writers educated in Europe were torn, appreciating aspects of both the new Western culture and the traditions of their homelands. A good example was Leopold Senghor of Senegal, who spent much of the 1930s in France. A poet as well as a future politician, Senghor helped to develop and to popularize the idea of Negritude during the 1930s. The concept of Negritude was partly based on ideas adopted from Caribbean writers, including Claude McKay, who in the 1920s had become a prominent figure in the black or Harlem Renaissance in the United States. Senghor defined Negritude as "the sum total of the values of the African world." Although a Catholic married to a Frenchwoman, and admittedly influenced by European writers and thinkers, Senghor in his poetry praised the "Africanness" of his native land and people.

SUGGESTED SOURCES

Barraclough, Geoffrey, *An Introduction to Contemporary History* (1968). A brief treatise on twentieth-century trends.*

The Blue Angel (1930). One of the great German films made in Berlin prior to Hitler's rule.

Galbraith, J. Kenneth, *The Great Crash, 1929,* 50th anniv. ed. (1979). A readable work by one of the leading U.S. liberal economists.*

Inherit the Wind (1960). A remarkable film starring Spencer Tracy about the famous Scopes "Monkey Trial."

Isherwood, Christopher, *The Berlin Stories* (1979). A fictionalized reflection of the author's experiences during the Depression in Berlin.* The film *Cabaret* was based on Isherwood's Berlin experiences.

Koestler, Arthur, et al., *The God That Failed* (1950). A collection of six autobiographical sketches by U.S. and European writers who relate why they were attracted to communism in the interwar years.

Landes, David S., *The Unbound Prometheus* (1976). A work containing insights on technological, industrial, and economic developments between the wars.*

Solomon, Barbara H., *Ain't We Got Fun* (1980). A collection of essays, lyrics, and stories that capture the cultural changes occurring in the United States during the 1920s.*

Taylor, A. J. P., *From Sarajevo to Potsdam* (1974). A lively, liberally illustrated survey of European affairs.*

*Paperback available.

11

Postwar Settlements

World War I was a shattering experience, particularly for European nations. At the international conferences that followed the war, the victors decided the terms and imposed them on the defeated nations. Both the process and the results bred nationalistic resentments among the defeated powers, especially Germany. Even some of the victorious nations, particularly Italy and Japan, were frustrated by the postwar settlements. These resentments and frustrations, coupled with extensive economic dislocations stemming from the war, caused considerable international tension in the postwar period. Many historians have claimed that the roots of World War II lay in the soil of the 1919 treaties.

THE DEVASTATION OF THE GREAT WAR

It has been estimated that some ten million fighting men lost their lives in World War I, victims not only of their enemies but also of the technology of a more modern military warfare. Three-quarters of the dead were from Russia, Germany, France, Austria-Hungary, Great Britain, and Italy. Those wounded in combat numbered about twice the military deaths. One of every ten men in France was killed, and three of every ten between the ages of eighteen and twenty-eight. Since the United States entered the war late, U.S. losses were numerically and proportionally less than those of any of the major European countries. For example, despite a population almost two and one-half times larger than that of France, U.S. combat losses were less than one-tenth of those suffered by the French. An extremely high percentage of well-educated young Europeans, many of them junior officers, lost their lives. The lack of vitality and leadership Great Britain and France displayed in the 1930s was due in part to the war deaths of so many potential leaders.

Besides the military deaths, countless civilians died between 1914 and 1918 as a result of the war. Some estimates place the figure higher than that of military deaths. The Turks massacred nearly one million Armenians in 1915. While some civilians died as a result of shells or bullets, many others, especially in Eastern Europe, were attacked by the maladies that accompanied war: influenza, typhus, cholera, and malnutrition. Even after the war ended, many more millions of men and women continued to die in the chaos of the Russian civil war and the postwar worldwide influenza epidemic. The ravages of World War I contributed to both disasters.

Accompanying the loss of lives was a great loss of property, especially in Belgium, France, and Eastern Europe. German property suffered little in comparison to that of France, where it was estimated that 300,000 homes, 8,000 factories and mines (including steel plants and coal mines, the basis of French heavy industry), 52,000 kilometers of roads, and 6,000 kilometers of railroads had been destroyed. About seven million acres of arable land in France were also devastated.

The estimated overall direct cost of the war was $180 billion; the indirect cost was approximately $150 billion. The Carnegie Endowment for International Peace estimated that with the money spent on the war every family in England, Wales, Ireland, Scotland, Belgium, Russia, Germany, the United States, Canada, and Australia could have been provided with a home of its own. In addition, all the property and wealth of Great Britain and France could have been purchased, and a considerable sum would still have remained. From 1870 to 1914, Europe had been the world's banker, with financial investments spread across the world's continents. By 1918, however, many of these investments had been lost or withdrawn to help pay for the war. In addition, Europe was now in debt, principally to the United States, which had now become the great creditor of the world.

THE PARIS PEACE CONFERENCE AND GERMANY

The Paris Peace Conference opened on January 18, 1919, with twenty-seven of the victorious nations represented. This was to be a gathering only of the victors; Germany and other defeated powers were not allowed representation at the conference. Nor was Russia; the victors resented the new Bolshevik government, which had made a separate peace with Germany, and a civil war then being waged in Russia provided a pretext for not inviting a Russian delegation to Paris. Originally, the victors made plans for a peace congress to follow the conference, and it would have included the defeated powers, but this idea was later dropped.

The important decisions at the conference were made by a Supreme Council made up of the heads of state and foreign ministers of the United States, Great Britain, France, Italy, and Japan. The dominant figures at the conference proved to be the scholarly U.S. President Wilson, the colorful British Prime Minister David Lloyd George, and the French Prime Minister Georges Clemenceau, "The Tiger of France," who was in his late seventies and still a formidable figure. Wilson was primarily concerned with ensuring that agreement would be reached on a covenant for a League of Nations and that, to the extent possible, the peace would be based on his Fourteen Points. Clemenceau's

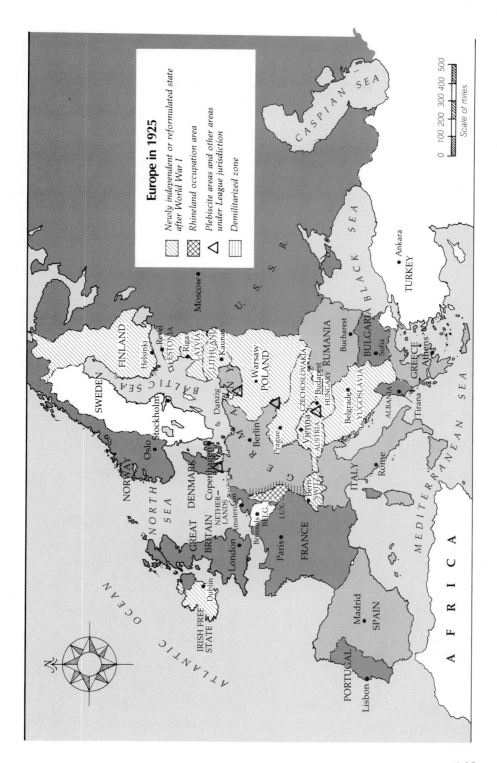

Europe in 1925

Newly independent or reformulated state after World War I

Rhineland occupation area

Plebiscite areas and other areas under League jurisdiction

Demilitarized zone

main preoccupation was to ensure that Germany would never again threaten French security. Lloyd George was not as inclined as Clemenceau to be harsh toward the Germans, but he had just been returned to office after his party had promised to hang the kaiser and to "squeeze the German lemon until the pips squeaked."

Through the spring and into the summer of 1919, the conference moved at a rapid but often disorderly pace. "A riot in a parrot house," one member of the British delegation described it. On June 28, exactly five years after the assassination of Archduke Franz Ferdinand, the attending nations signed the Treaty of Versailles with Germany. Germany had protested that the terms were too harsh and not in keeping with Wilson's Fourteen Points, on which basis Germany had agreed to lay down its arms. Undoubtedly, the German perception of the treaty was influenced by the fact that almost all the war had been fought on non-German soil, and to many Germans it seemed more a stalemate than a decisive Allied victory. However, Germany had little choice but to sign.

According to the terms of the treaty, Germany lost Alsace-Lorraine to France, several small districts to Belgium, one to Czechoslovakia, and a large portion of eastern Germany to Poland. In addition, plebiscites were to be held in several areas, such as northern Schleswig on the Danish border; Germany eventually lost some of these territories as well. Several German areas were to be put under control of the newly formed League of Nations. The Saar district and the city of Danzig fell into this category. The city of Memel was also taken away and eventually ceded to Lithuania. Many of the lost German territories contained only a minority of Germans. In the Saar, Danzig, and Memel, however, Germans predominated. Germany also lost all her overseas colonies, which

At the Paris Peace Conference: Lloyd George, Orlando (of Italy), Clemenceau, and Wilson. (Brown Brothers)

came under the control of the victors.

According to the treaty, Germany and its allies were guilty of aggression in imposing a war on the Allies. The kaiser was to be tried for offenses against "international morality and the sanctity of treaties," and hundreds of German military officers were charged with war crimes. Although no significant individuals came to trial, Germany was assessed reparations to pay for the war damages. The exact figure was not settled at the time of the conference, but the Allies stipulated that Germany would make payments totaling the equivalent of $5 billion by 1921. At that time the final sum, understood to be much higher, would be announced.

Germany also had to observe various strict limitations on its armed forces and weapons. As an additional safeguard for France, Allied forces were to occupy the Rhineland area west of the Rhine and control three of the river's bridgeheads, in both cases for periods ranging from five to fifteen years. In addition, the Rhineland and a thirty-mile zone east of the river were to be permanently demilitarized.

While Germany regarded the Treaty of Versailles as severe, the treaty would have been even harsher if French desires had been fully realized. Concerned for its future security, France had suggested, among other propositions, that the territory west of the Rhine be made into a separate buffer state under French influence. Wilson, however, was successful in reducing France's demands on Germany by agreeing, along with Great Britain, to guarantee France against any future German invasion, a guarantee that never became operative because of the U.S. Senate's later refusal to support Wilson's pledge. However, Wilson also found it necessary to make concessions so that the Covenant of the League of Nations would be accepted.

ARRANGEMENTS FOR THE REST OF EUROPE

The Allies at the conference dictated terms to the other defeated powers as well as to Germany. All had to pay reparations, limit their armies, and acknowledge the loss of some territory. To some extent, drafting treaties for the other defeated nations involved sanctioning what had already occurred in Central and Eastern Europe, particularly in the case of Austria-Hungary. By 1919 little was left of the old Austro-Hungarian Empire. Led by the able and respected Thomas Masaryk, Czechoslovakians had appealed for recognition to Allied leaders on the basis of Wilson's principle of self-determination. Even before the November armistice had been signed, the Allies had recognized Czechoslovakia's right to an independent existence, and a separate government was already functioning there. A month before the convening of the Paris Peace Conference, the Kingdom of the Serbs, Croats, and Slovenes (or Yugoslavia, as it would later be officially known) was proclaimed. It included, or soon would include, formerly independent Serbia and Montenegro, combined with the former Austro-Hungarian areas of Croatia, Slovenia, Bosnia, and Herzegovina. In addition,

Rumania had seized the Transylvania region from Hungary.

The Poles also gained their independence. Poland had not existed as a nation since it had been divided in the eighteenth century among Prussia (now part of Germany), Russia, and Austria. Woodrow Wilson's thirteenth point, proclaimed a full year before the convening of the conference, called for an "independent Poland, to include the territories indisputably Polish, with free and secure access to the sea." By the time the Allied diplomats assembled in 1919, a Polish republic had been proclaimed, and the Poles had already taken control of Polish segments of Austria-Hungary, as well as Polish-claimed portions of Germany and Russia. The key territory Poland annexed from Germany was the "Polish Corridor," primarily peopled by Poles. The corridor, along with Danzig (under the League of Nations' control), provided Poland with an outlet to the sea and severed East Prussia from the rest of Germany. The final Polish gains at the expense of Austria-Hungary and Russia were not determined until after Polish success in the Russian-Polish War of 1920.

The Allies ended the union of Austria and Hungary in the Treaty of St. Germain (1919) with Austria and the Treaty of Trianon (1920) with Hungary. Austria and Hungary recognized the losses to Czechoslovakia, Yugoslavia, Poland, and Rumania; in addition, Austria recognized the loss of territory to Italy. Fearing the possibility of German dominance over Central Europe, the Allies also forbade Austria, now composed of only a German-speaking population, any future union (*Anschluss*) with Germany. Both Austria and Hungary agreed to reparations payments and to limitations on their armies.

In general, the conference delegates divided Austria-Hungary according to principles of ethnic nationalist self-determination. There were exceptions, however, partly because some nationalities were tightly intermingled and partly because of a number of other important considerations. Bargains had been made, for example, with Italy and Rumania in order to bring them into the war. When the boundaries of Italy were drawn through the Alps, Italy was given control over several hundred thousand Germans in the South Tyrol and tens of thousands of Slavs in Istria. When Italy further demanded the Adriatic port of Fiume, also claimed by the Yugoslavs, Wilson refused. At that point, Italy stormed out of the Paris Peace Conference. Rumania, too, was granted control over other ethnic groups. In the Transylvanian territory annexed by Rumania there were two Magyars for every three Rumanians.

Economic or strategic considerations also came into conflict with the principle of self-determination. Both factors, for example, played a role in persuading Allied statesmen to recognize as part of Czechoslovakia a German-speaking area of the former Austro-Hungarian territory that the Nazis later claimed as the Germanic Sudetenland.

As for the treaties with Bulgaria and Turkey, the latter was especially severe. Bulgaria lost a few border areas to its neighbors, but the former Ottoman Empire was torn to pieces. The Turks lost their Arab-populated territories in the Middle East, which came under either British or French control or, as in the case of the Arabian peninsula, became independent. In addition, much of the Anatolian (Turkish) peninsula was put under the temporary occupation of European nations.

As already noted, Russia was not invited to the peace conference, and neither the "Red" Bolsheviks nor the "White" anti-Bolsheviks were officially recognized by any of the Allied powers as the legitimate government of Russia. The fate of Finland, Estonia, Latvia, and Lithuania, all parts of the former Russian Empire, was not officially dealt with at the conference. Nevertheless, the conference diplomats were concerned by 1919 with the possible spread of communism. Their favorable treatment of Poland and Rumania partly reflected a desire to set up strong bulwarks against communism and to create a *cordon sanitaire,* or quarantine zone, to keep communism out of Central and Western Europe. Hence, between 1918 and 1921, European powers supported independence for the four Baltic nations as part of the *cordon sanitaire.*

EUROPEAN REFUGEES, EMIGRANTS, AND MINORITIES

Faced with new governments and changing boundaries, several million people left their homes and settled elsewhere. Some left their nation behind, as, for example, the Russians who left the new Soviet state to live in such cities as Berlin, Paris, and Shanghai. Some took up a new life in a nation for which they felt kinship, such as the Germans who moved inside the new borders of Germany from areas that had been part of prewar Germany but were now French or Polish.

Not all minorities, however, were able to move. Between the wars, minority problems, especially in Central and Eastern Europe, would remain a serious cause of tension. Of particular significance were the German minorities in Poland and especially Czechoslovakia, where more than one out of every five individuals was German. Other notable minorities were the Slavic and German minorities in Italy; the Hungarian (Magyar) minorities in Rumania, Czechoslovakia, and Yugoslavia; the sizeable Ukrainian and White Russian minorities in Poland; the Ukrainians in Rumania; and the Great Russians in Estonia, Latvia, and Rumania. In Yugoslavia, made up of a variety of ethnic groups, dissatisfied Croats and Slovenes in particular threatened to upset a state dominated by Serbs.

Between the wars, minorities and the dominant national groups continued to view each other with hostility. In addition, when some members of an ethnic group were separated from their home nation, as the Germans of Memel and Danzig were from Germany, this provided a convenient grievance and excuse for one nation to interfere in the affairs of another.

EUROPEAN AND JAPANESE IMPERIALISM AT THE PEACE CONFERENCE

Although President Wilson had called for a peace without "annexations," the prewar imperialist drive to acquire new possessions showed up strongly again at the conference. Great Britain, France, South Africa, and Belgium divided up Germany's holdings in Africa. The conference also parceled out former German-held islands in the Pacific to Australia, New Zealand, and Japan. These former German territories and a portion of the defeated Ottoman Turkish Empire (See Chapter 17) were to be ruled by the victorious powers as "mandates" of the League of Nations. The new mandates were divided into A, B, and C categories. Type A mandates were nations that were almost ready for independence; these included most of the Middle East, formerly part of the Ottoman Empire. In Type B mandates, it would be several generations before independence would be granted; this applied to most of the African territory. Finally, in Type C mandates, the peoples would not be ready for independence any time in the foreseeable future; this applied to the Pacific islands. The League of Nations was to safeguard the interests of the peoples in the mandates, but in practice the powers that received the mandates exercised unrestricted authority.

Although the participation of Japan in the war had been marginal, it also benefited at the Paris Peace Conference, especially when compared to China, which had no real voice in the proceedings. Japan and its delegates were accorded a special position on the Supreme Council and voiced three specific demands: (1) the transfer of the former German islands in the North Pacific (the Marianas, the Carolines, and the Marshalls) to Japanese control, (2) the confirmation of Japan's claim to former German rights in China's Shantung province, and (3) a declaration of racial equality in the Covenant of the League of Nations. Japan's first demand was essentially met when it received the German islands in the North Pacific to administer as mandates under the League of Nations. Due to Wilson's reservations, Japan was persuaded to drop its third demand for a declaration of racial equality. Japan considered this a particularly galling defeat, since the race issue was a symbol of discrimination. Because of its defeat on the racial equality issue, Japan threatened to walk out of the conference unless its second demand was met.

Sovereignty over the Shantung province was the one specific demand of the Chinese, who, like the Japanese, had participated marginally in the war. China also sought an international forum to air its grievances concerning the unequal treaties and to seek their abolition. In particular, the Chinese hoped Woodrow Wilson would champion their cause. The Japanese got their way, however, and as a result, Japan signed the peace treaty with Germany and China did not.

Although China lost on Shantung, and although its demand for a discussion on ending the unequal treaty system was ruled out of order, the balance sheet was not entirely negative. World War I had broken the solidarity of Western imperialism against China. The Soviet government had denounced tsarist Russia's unequal treaties with China and soon began to negotiate with China on the basis of equality. The Chinese also established new relations based on equality in separate treaties signed with Germany, Austria, and Hungary.

THE UNITED STATES REJECTS THE TREATY OF VERSAILLES

When the U.S. Senate began its consideration of the Treaty of Versailles, one of the most dramatic struggles in U.S. political history occurred. The Republican Senate majority, led by Senator Henry Cabot Lodge and joined by some Democrats, raised a number of objections to the treaty. Some senators criticized the peace as too harsh, a falling-off from the ideals of the Fourteen Points; others opposed the treaty from motives of partisanship and personal dislike of the president; still others denounced Wilson for the surrender of Shantung to Japan. Most senators, however, were apparently troubled by Article 10, which obligated members of the League of Nations to repel aggression against League members by means "the Council shall advise." They feared, incorrectly, that if the United States ratified the treaty and became a member of the League of Nations, the League could order the United States into wars around the world, even if Americans were opposed. Some shared the disdain of a former Senate colleague, Albert Beveridge of Indiana, who declared the League to be the work of "amiable old male grannies who, over their afternoon tea, are planning to denationalize America and denationalize the Nation's manhood." In order to preserve U.S. freedom of action in world affairs, many senators insisted that a number of reservations be added to the treaty. The reservation receiving the most support asserted that Congress must approve any U.S. involvement in League-sponsored actions to curb aggression.

President Wilson adamantly opposed any compromise that might curtail his fervent vision of a League of Nations to preserve the peace. He would not agree to any of the proposed reservations and was self-righteously shrill and partisan in dealing with doubters and opponents. While attempting to mobilize "grass roots" opinion, he suffered a stroke and was removed from an active role in the ratification struggle. When the treaty finally came up for a vote in November 1919, treaty supporters failed to muster the constitutional two-thirds majority, and it was not ratified.

In 1921, the United States signed a separate treaty with Germany that ratified most of the provisions of the Treaty of Versailles, but forbade the participation of the United States in any international agencies created by the Versailles treaty without the consent of both houses of Congress. Americans were not yet ready for peace through collective security if that concept limited the U.S. tradition of unilateral action. The refusal of the United States to join the League was a blow to the League's prestige and to its effectiveness.

SUMMARY

World War I brought with it an unprecedented loss of life and property and the decline of European wealth and prestige. The postwar settlements pleased some nations, angered others, and left others with decidedly mixed feelings. The new nations of Eastern Europe—Finland, Estonia, Latvia, Lithuania, Poland, Czechoslovakia, and Yugoslavia—gained the most from the conflict: their independence. Although Austria and Hungary were now also separate nations, they were not happy with their fate; nor were Bulgaria and Turkey. Germany was the most aggrieved, having incurred various territorial losses, the payment of reparations, and other stipulations such as the occupation of the Rhineland. Each of the Allied powers, including Japan, achieved only part of its goals in the postwar settlements. While gaining Alsace-Lorraine, for example, France did not weaken Germany as much as it would have liked. President Wilson achieved his primary goal of establishing a League of Nations, only to have the U.S. Senate block his nation's membership in that body. The postwar settlements, along with subsequent diplomacy, thus failed to foster security and stability. Whether as a result primarily of the attitudes and actions of the victors or of the vanquished, postwar resentment continued to exist, especially in Germany, and eventually helped lead to another war. The French writer Romain Rolland was more prophetic than he knew when on June 23, 1919, he wrote: "Sad peace! Laughable interlude between the massacres of peoples!"

SUGGESTED SOURCES

Birdsall, Paul, *Versailles Twenty Years After* (1962). An interesting summary of the conference and of its long-term effects by one sympathetic with Wilson's goals.

House, E. M., and C. Seymour, *What Really Happened at Paris* (1921). Includes accounts of the conference by various members of the U.S. delegation.

Klingaman, William K., *1919: The Year Our World Began* (1987). A vivid political, social, cultural narrative of the world's main events and personalities in 1919.

Lederer, Ivo J., ed., *The Versailles Settlement: Was It Foredoomed to Failure?* (1960). A collection of essays in the Heath series representing various viewpoints.*

Mayer, Arno J., *The Politics and Diplomacy of Peacemaking* (1968). A look at the political climate and especially the effects of the Bolshevik Revolution that influenced decisions at the Paris Peace Conference.

Mee, Charles L., Jr., *The End of Order: Versailles, 1919* (1980). A well-written, if not penetrating, account, critical of Wilson.

Nicolson, Harold, *Peacemaking, 1919* (1933). The highly personal memoirs of a British participant.*

Walworth, Arthur, *Wilson and His Peacemakers* (1986). A first-rate, comprehensive narrative history of Wilson at the Paris Peace Conference.

*Paperback available.

12

The Transformation of Russia, 1917–1932

One of the offspring of World War I was the 1917 Bolshevik Revolution in Russia. The war contributed to the instability that helped to bring about the upheaval, and had it not been for the war it is possible that Russia could have avoided revolution.

Even before that calamitous world conflict, however, the Russians and the empire's numerous other nationalities were becoming increasingly discontented, both in the countryside and in the cities. In the year prior to the beginning of the war, 50 percent of the empire's industrial workers engaged in labor protests. Facing worse working and living conditions than their counterparts in Western Europe, they became more and more receptive to the ideas and ideologies preached by Russian radicals. From his distant throne, an aloof and ineffective Tsar Nicholas II, despite the scare of the 1905 revolt, remained virtually oblivious to the rampant dissatisfaction.

When war broke out in 1914, Russia was unprepared to meet the challenge. Once again, as in the Russo-Japanese War of 1904–1905, a combination of industrial-technological backwardness, governmental and military inefficiency, and corruption led to a series of military defeats. Nicholas II listened too much to the wrong advisors, including his wife, Tsarina Alexandra. At a crucial point in late 1915, he left the capital in her hands in order to assume personal command of the armies at the front. The tsarina was under the strong influence of the notorious Gregory Rasputin, a self-proclaimed holy man who specialized in seducing women. Thus, as one expert on Russia puts it, the fate of Russia was in the hands of "a narrow-minded, reactionary, hysterical woman and an ignorant, weird peasant—who apparently made decisions simply in terms of his personal interest, and whose exalted position depended on the empress's belief that he could protect her son from hemophilia and that he had been sent by God to guide her, her husband, and Russia."[1] Rasputin's death, on December

---

1. Nicholas V. Riasanovsky, *A History of Russia,* 4th ed. (New York: Oxford University Press, 1984), p. 421.

30, 1916—he was heavily poisoned, shot several times, kicked and beaten, and finally tied up and pushed through a hole in the icy Neva River—was not enough to restore popular confidence in the government. The tsar remained at the front, as ineffective as ever. In January 1917, the French ambassador wrote to his government: "I am obliged to report that, at the present moment, the Russian Empire is run by lunatics."

THE REVOLUTIONS OF MARCH AND NOVEMBER 1917

Early in March,[2] food shortages in the capital of Petrograd triggered bread riots, demonstrations, and strikes. With the best soldiers at the front, the government tried to end the disturbances by using inexperienced recruits, who soon fraternized with the demonstrators. Chaos followed, and on March 15, Nicholas II abdicated the throne.

With the collapse of the monarchy, leaders from Russia's legislative Duma formed the Provisional Government. It was composed primarily of moderates with only one Socialist in its cabinet, the Minister of Justice, Alexander Kerensky. The power of the new government was soon challenged by a rival organization, the Petrograd Soviet (Council) of Workers' and Soldiers' Deputies. At first this body was led by the moderate Marxist Mensheviks and the peasant-oriented Socialist Revolutionaries, and it enjoyed the support of many Petrograd soldiers and workers. As a result of the encouragement and example of the Petrograd Soviet, radicals soon formed local Soviets throughout Russia, including some within military units. Both the Mensheviks and the Socialist Revolutionaries were reluctant to bring down the Provisional Government. They were influenced by the Marxist view of history, which held that a country could not begin a socialist stage until it had first undergone a capitalist one. In their eyes, Russia had just overthrown a feudal order, and a lengthy capitalist period would have to ensue before this capitalist state could be replaced by a socialist one.

The party of Lenin, the Bolsheviks, did not play a major role in the opening weeks of the revolution. Its leader, Vladimir Ulyanov (Lenin), was born in 1870, the son of a provincial school inspector. Young Lenin had been profoundly affected by the execution of his brother for revolutionary activities and had himself become an opponent of the tsar. By his twenties, Lenin had become a Marxist. He engaged in revolutionary activities that were punished by almost five years of prison and Siberian exile. These experiences were followed by Marxist activities in Western Europe, where in 1903 he played a leading role in splitting the Russian Marxists into two factions: the Mensheviks and his own Bolsheviks. The Mensheviks favored a large, broad-based workers' party, while the Bolsheviks demanded a small, well-disciplined party of dedicated revolutionaries.

2. Until 1918, Russia still used the old Julian calendar, which was thirteen days behind the Gregorian calendar in use in the West. All dates here, however, are from the Gregorian calendar.

On April 16, 1917, after seventeen years of exile in Western Europe, Lenin returned by train from Switzerland to Petrograd. Knowing of Lenin's opposition to Russia's involvement in an "imperialist war," the Germans allowed him to pass through German territory, but quarantined him from contact with any Germans, who might be infected by his ideas. While Winston Churchill later compared the arrival of this short, balding, goateed, forty-six-year-old radical to that of a "plague bacillus," Lenin was not an alien infection but a Russian who well understood the volatile mood of the masses. He immediately challenged the dominance of the Mensheviks and Socialist Revolutionaries within the Soviets. He called for "all power to the Soviets," hoping that his own Bolshevik party could soon assume a commanding position within them. He wanted a Marxist revolution to occur in Russia and quickly spread from there to some of the more industrialized nations. These nations could, in turn, help Russia build up the industrial base necessary to construct Marxist socialism.

Following his return, Lenin strongly criticized the war, which the Provisional Government, supported by the Soviets, continued to wage, in part because of strong Allied pressure. He also advocated the seizure of landed estates and worker control of the factories. Although at first encountering strong opposition to his radical demands, as 1917 proceeded his party gradually gained support. As early as May, representatives of the Mensheviks and Socialist Revolutionaries had become cabinet members in the Provisional Government; the Bolsheviks thus had the advantage of being the only major party of the Left not implicated in an unpopular government. Some peasant soldiers began to desert the front and go home, often hoping to benefit from the seizure of property in the countryside. As Lenin later said, they "voted for peace with their feet."

By October 1917, Bolshevik strength had substantially increased. By October, the Bolsheviks had gained a majority in both the Petrograd and the Moscow Soviets; Leon Trotsky, who had returned to Russia in 1917 and decided to become a Bolshevik, was now the chairman of the Petrograd Soviet.

Late in October, Lenin returned to the capital after temporarily hiding in Finland, and immediately called for a takeover of power. Lenin's urgings and Trotsky's persuasive and dynamic speeches to Soviet deputies, soldiers, and workers moved preparations steadily forward. On the evening of November 6 and the morning of November 7, troops under the control of the Bolshevik-dominated Petrograd Soviet took control of the bridges, railroad and electric stations, state bank, post office, and central telephone station. Finally, after a siege marked more by noise and confusion than by loss of blood, the revolutionaries broke into the Winter Palace during the early morning of November 8. Members of the Provisional Government (except for Prime Minister Alexander Kerensky, who had left the capital in order to seek out loyal troops) surrendered to representatives of the Petrograd Soviet.

Meanwhile, at a meeting of the Second All Russian Congress of Soviets, deputies of the Mensheviks and many of the moderate Socialist Revolutionaries strongly objected to the armed takeover that was in progress, but they were

Vladimir Lenin speaking to Soviet citizens during a May Day celebration. (Brown Brothers)

outnumbered. Finally, in frustration, they stormed out in protest. Trotsky mocked those who left: "You are bankrupt. Your role is played out. Go where you belong: into the dustbin of history." On November 9, the delegates who remained approved a new government with Lenin as chairman of the Council of People's Commissars and Trotsky as commissar of foreign affairs.

CIVIL WAR AND ALLIED INTERVENTION

Although the Bolsheviks had an extensive following among workers and soldiers, the peasant-oriented Socialist Revolutionaries remained more popular in the country as a whole. When the previously scheduled elections for a Constituent Assembly took place in late November 1917, the Socialist Revolutionaries won more than twice as many seats as the Bolsheviks. When the Assembly met in January 1918, however, Lenin disbanded the Assembly after a day, and no major force was able to effectively challenge his action. As the year progressed, the Bolsheviks used their newly founded secret police, the Cheka, not only against conservative and liberal parties and groups, but also against other radical parties such as the Mensheviks and Socialist Revolutionaries. Nevertheless, Bolshevik control was primarily restricted to the ethnic Russian heartland. In other areas of the empire, many of the non-Russian nationalities refused to accept Bolshevik rule.

In March 1918, after months of trying by diplomatic means to prevent it, the militarily weakened Russians signed with Germany the Treaty of Brest-Litovsk, which recognized the surrender of huge areas to the west and southwest. According to the treaty, former areas of the tsar's empire—Finland, Lithuania, Estonia, Latvia, the Ukraine, and Poland—gained independence from

Russia. All were ethnically non-Russian and already, or soon to be, controlled by Germany.

If the Bolsheviks were willing, however reluctantly, to come to terms with Germany, Russia's former allies in the war were not. One of the Allies' concerns was to see that the military supplies they had sent to such ports as Archangel and Murmansk did not fall into German hands. The Allies also desired to prevent even greater numbers of German troops from being transferred to the Western Front. They decided to send military forces into Russia, and eventually fourteen nations became involved, particularly Great Britain, France, the United States, and Japan. Allied intervention was also motivated by the Bolsheviks' call for "international socialist revolution" and their cancellation of several billion dollars of tsarist debt to Western creditors. Following the end of the war in November 1918, the Allies remained in Russia, supporting the anti-Bolshevik (White) forces that had organized during that year to challenge the Soviet government in a full-scale civil war.

The Whites were made up of various groups, including many former officers, Cossacks, and followers of political parties ranging from the far Right to the leftist Socialist Revolutionaries. For two years, they fought against the Bolsheviks, or Reds, on many fronts. In Siberia, they were supported for a time by a Czechoslovakian Legion of some 40,000 former Czech prisoners of war who had served in the Austro-Hungarian army. The point of greatest danger for the Bolsheviks was probably in October 1919, when White forces threatened both Moscow and Petrograd.

In 1920, Poland attacked Russia. After seesaw campaigning, Poland gained ethnically non-Polish areas of the Ukraine and Byelorussia that Poland considered its own by historical right. Despite losing the war with Poland, the Bolsheviks pushed forward on all fronts against the Whites during 1920. In November, Red troops in the south forced the last major White army contingent to evacuate in Allied ships. Most Allied forces also withdrew, leaving only the Japanese in Siberia, who finally left the mainland in 1922 and the Russian part of the island of Sakhalin in 1925. All in all, the intervention was a failure, leaving behind only a legacy of mistrust.

Despite Allied intervention, a war with Poland, and the opposition of powerful forces inside Russia, the Bolsheviks had been able to win the civil war for a number of reasons. They were more unified than their many enemies, who found it almost impossible to work together. Despite differences among themselves—for example, between Trotsky and Stalin—party discipline and the leadership of Lenin kept the Bolsheviks working together. Trotsky, as head of the Red Army, displayed impressive organizational and leadership abilities, rushing in his special train from one front to another. The Bolsheviks also had the advantage of controlling the heartland of Russia, while their enemies were scattered around the periphery. Finally, a Red victory held out more hope to the peasants and the many minority nationalities than did a White victory. While both sides forcibly requisitioned food from them, peasants feared that the Whites might try to restore the rights of landowners. In addition, minorities feared that the Whites would reestablish the Russian Empire and that they would be dominated once again by the Great Russian ethnic group. The Communists at least promised something better.

THE YEARS OF THE NEW ECONOMIC POLICY, 1921–28

Although the Bolsheviks had won the civil war, they had inherited an exhausted and shrunken nation. After heavy losses in World War I, millions of additional lives had been lost in the strife that followed. Drought, epidemics, famine, and starvation had accompanied and followed the years of war. Numerous cities and villages had been destroyed. Many factories sat idle, and the transportation system had almost ceased to function. Crop production had fallen off drastically. Not only had territory been lost to Poland, but in a series of 1920 treaties the Soviets had also found it necessary to recognize the independence of Finland, Estonia, Latvia, and Lithuania. Parts of the Asiatic portion of the nation were still not firmly under Bolshevik control.

In March 1921, the sailors of the Kronstadt naval base, early supporters of the Bolsheviks who had grown tired of Communist authoritarianism, revolted, but the government crushed the uprising. The anarchist Emma Goldman, then in Petrograd, stated that the brutal slaughter of the sailors severed the last strand which had once united her with the Bolshevik cause. Such expressions were commonplace by 1921 among many non-Bolsheviks who had enthusiastically backed the November 1917 revolution.

Faced with widespread economic and political unrest, Lenin decided to make concessions, and in 1921 instituted the New Economic Policy (NEP). Following the revolution, the Communists had instituted War Communism, which had nationalized industry and land, all but abolished private trade, and forced the peasants to turn over most of their crops to the state. Under the NEP, the state continued to maintain control over major industry, transportation, banking, and foreign and wholesale trade, but now the new policy allowed a measure of private enterprise in small industries and retail trade. In addition, the state no longer forcibly requisitioned peasant produce. After paying a tax, first in kind and later in money, peasants were free to sell what remained on the open market.

Economically, the NEP was a notable success. By 1928 the program had reached and in some cases surpassed prewar levels of agriculture and industrial production. Given the devastation of the economy from 1914 through 1920, this was no small accomplishment.

From the beginning, the Communist party had dominated the state, and during the NEP years, while easing economic controls, the party tightened its control over all levels of government. Inside the party, the hierarchy strengthened its hold on the rank-and-file membership. According to the Constitution of 1924, the nation was a federation of republics, the Union of Soviet Socialist Republics (U.S.S.R.). Supreme power resided in an All-Union Congress of So-

A Young Man in Lenin's Russia

I became a Bolshevik and a member of the Communist Party after the Revolution and a short time later joined the Red Army as a political worker and propagandist. As soon as I returned from the Front after the Civil War, the Yuzovka Party organization made me a deputy manager of the Ruchenkov mines. . . .

There was famine in the mines of the Donbass in 1922, and even isolated incidents of cannibalism. The villages were even more ravaged than the mines. My first wife, Galina, died during the famine in 1921. Her death was a great sadness to me. I was left with two children to look after, my son Leonid and my daughter Julia. In 1924 I married again to Nina Petrovna. Those first years of Soviet Power were years of struggle and hardship and self-sacrifice. But the people still believed in the Party; even the most illiterate of our citizens understood the Party's slogans and rallying cries. The people knew that these hardships were being thrust upon us by the bourgeoisie—both by our own bourgeoisie and by the bourgeoisie of the world at large, which was instigating counterrevolution and intervention against us. We told ourselves that no matter how bad things were, they had been worse in the old days, before the Revolution.*

From the memoirs of Nikita Khrushchev, who headed the Soviet Union's Communist Party from 1953 until 1964. He was in his mid- and late twenties in the period described above.

*From _Khrushchev Remembers_, Vol. I, by Nikita Khrushchev, translated and edited by Strobe Talbott. Copyright © 1971 by Little, Brown & Co. Reprinted by permission.

viets (after 1936 the Supreme Soviet). This body was to elect the Council of People's Commissars (after 1946 the Council of Ministers) and also an Executive Committee and a smaller Presidium that acted for the Congress between sessions. The Communist party, especially its Central Committee (sixty-three members in 1926), Politburo, and Secretariat, filled the government posts. Important central government figures were members of the party and followed the instructions of the central party leadership; this was also true throughout all the republics. Claims of any real autonomous powers for the republics were mere propaganda.

During the NEP years, Joseph Stalin replaced Lenin as the most important Communist political figure. In 1922, Lenin suffered a stroke, and in January 1924 he died. Although after his death Russian Communists revered him, even before his death other leaders began to maneuver to fill the power vacuum that resulted from his stroke. The man who seemed to be the frontrunner for Lenin's mantle was Leon Trotsky. Unfortunately for Trotsky, others united against him. Trotsky's main opponent was Joseph Stalin, who was forty-four years old when Lenin died. Born in Georgia in the Caucasus, Stalin was a long-time Marxist who had been made general secretary of the Communist party when the office was created in 1922. In 1923, Lenin concluded that Stalin "was too rude" and should be replaced in his position by someone "more patient, more loyal, more courteous, and more considerate of his comrades." But Lenin was too sick to engineer Stalin's removal. After Lenin's death, Stalin used his position as general secretary to strengthen his control over the party, cleverly playing on the ambitions of others and making useful political allies when he needed them. By 1927, Stalin had Trotsky and a few of his other political opponents expelled from the party. In 1929, Trotsky was forced to leave the Soviet Union; he eventually settled in Mexico. He watched from afar as "Stalinism," which he referred to as "the syphilis of socialism," was gradually imposed. In 1940, he was axed in the head by a Stalinist agent.

The NEP years were also ones of social and cultural experimentation. The power of husbands and fathers was curtailed. Divorces increased by 1927 to a ratio of one for every four marriages. The government legalized abortions, confiscated Church land and possessions, and inculcated antireligious and pro-Communist propaganda through the educational system and media. The state stressed technical, vocational, and adult education and also briefly experimented with progressive educational techniques. By 1939 about 81 percent of Soviet citizens were literate, compared with 51 percent in 1926.

Benefiting from the presence of some gifted writers and thinkers who decided not to follow many of their fellow intellectuals into exile, the NEP period was culturally richer than were subsequent Stalinist years. Some "true believers" in the revolution—such as the film director Sergei Eisenstein and, for a time, the poet Vladimir Mayakovsky—shared with their audience a sense of excitement. Many others, such as the poet Boris Pasternak, who later wrote *Doctor Zhivago,* were not so enthusiastic, yet created works of merit. Censorship was not yet complete, and there was still room for experimentation, but the increasing power of Stalin and the party slowly dissipated vital intellectual forces.

Soviet foreign policy was still another area of change during the NEP period. In 1919, the Communist International, or Comintern, was established amid hopes of establishing Communist governments elsewhere; it succeeded briefly in parts of Germany and Hungary (see Chapter 13). The Comintern eventually came to consist of Communist parties of various nations, parties which in many cases had split from larger Socialist parties. The Comintern was run from Moscow and was correctly perceived by other nations as a force that encouraged Communist agitation and revolution outside of the Soviet Union. In 1923, for example, its agents attempted to take advantage of the unsettled conditions in Germany to encourage Communist takeovers.

While leaving such foreign activities to the nominally independent Comintern, the Soviet government sought to gain diplomatic recognition, trade, and credits from other nations. In 1921, it signed a trade agreement with the British; "One can trade even with cannibals," British Prime Minister Lloyd George once stated in defense of such trade. The Treaty of Rapallo with Germany in 1922 marked a further breakthrough, as the two nations agreed to restore normal diplomatic and commercial relations. In 1924, Great Britain, France, Italy, China, and a number of other nations also officially recognized the Soviet Union.

By the middle of the 1920s, the Soviet government appeared to be becoming less revolutionary. In fact, Trotsky and a few others accused Stalin of a lack of enthusiasm for encouraging revolutions abroad. They accurately charged that Stalin's slogan of "socialism in one nation" deemphasized fomenting revolution abroad and stressed instead the construction of a socialist society within the Soviet Union, even if it had to be done without much aid from the more industrialized West.

In spite of a decline of revolutionary action on the part of the Comintern in the second half of the 1920s, however, Soviet foreign policy still continued to reflect its origins. In 1927, Great Britain broke relations with the U.S.S.R. on discovering extensive Soviet espionage and propaganda activities in London.

COLLECTIVIZATION AND THE FIRST FIVE-YEAR PLAN

Despite the many changes Russia had undergone in the decade following 1917, the lives of Soviet peasants were still similar in many ways to those of the prerevolutionary era. They still made up about 80 percent of the total Soviet population; more than half of them were illiterate, and their communal work and leisure habits, social organization, and suspicious attitude toward authority had changed little. Many, especially the older peasants, also retained their prerevolutionary religious beliefs and, to the extent possible, their religious ceremonies and customs.

In 1928, Stalin began to change the lives of the peasants profoundly. That year the party inaugurated the collectivization of agriculture and the first Five-Year Plan, which emphasized the building up of heavy industry. The reasons Stalin introduced his new policies at this time are subject to debate, but five have been frequently mentioned. (1) Peasants were not selling enough grain to the state at the low prices the government was willing to pay, and more grain was needed to help feed the urban population, which was expected to increase. (2) More rapid industrialization, especially by heavy industry, was necessary if the Soviet Union was to become a stronger military power. ("If in ten years we do not cover the distance that other countries took fifty or a hundred years to traverse, we will be crushed," Stalin warned.) (3) Marxist ideology based socialism on a developed industrial order, and therefore the continued development of a Soviet socialist state was thought by many to depend on the expansion of Soviet industry. (4) Both the Five-Year Plan and collectivization would increase the control of the party over the economy and over the lives of Soviet citizens. (5) If he now rejected the NEP approach, Stalin would at the same time discredit his remaining major political opponents, who had consistently supported it.

With the inauguration in 1928 of the first Five-Year Plan, the Soviet economy took on the characteristics that would mark it for the next six decades. Government officials decided what should be produced in the Soviet Union, and in what quantity; consumers' desires had relatively little effect. The government, following party orders as always, established target figures for the next five years that significantly increased metals and chemicals production, electricity and petroleum output, new factory construction, and other industrial growth. The government obtained capital for expansion in these areas by squeezing high indirect taxes from its population. The purchasing power of Soviet citizens declined, and few consumer goods were available.

At the end of 1932, the government claimed that it had already met the goals of the first Five-Year Plan in a little over four years. While it is impossible to be sure of the exact figures, and while haste in meeting production quotas often caused shoddy workmanship, it does appear certain that in some areas production increased significantly. Most Western estimates agree that iron and steel output was up by about 50 percent during the Five-Year Plan. The output of chemicals, machinery, equipment, fertilizers, petroleum, and electricity increased even more dramatically. New factories, industrial complexes, and cities sprang up in a few years, often located far in the interior, away from vulnerable borders.

The record in agriculture was not as impressive. Russian peasants in 1933 produced less food than before collectivization, and the amount of livestock markedly declined. In addition, famine occurred in 1932–33. The poor record was largely due to the peasants' resistance to collectivization and the government's use of force. Stalin was determined to push most peasants into either collective farms or state farms. In the collectives, peasants worked the land collectively, and after meeting all other obligations, they divided what was left of their produce according to what percentage they had earned by their work. On a state farm, on the other hand, workers worked directly for the state and were paid wages.

Both collective and state farms were unpopular with the peasants, and few were willing to give up their old ways. Peasants slaughtered their animals rather than turn them over to the collective farms. In response to such resistance, the government killed millions of peasants and sent additional millions to premature deaths in forced labor camps. Stalin waged war especially on those designated as ''kulaks,'' who were supposedly prosperous peasants guilty of hoarding. Actually, almost any peasant who was in trouble with the authorities was liable to be included in this category. Children learned:

> A bad kulak, *he's* our foe,
> A good kulak?—the *same*, don'cha know!

Stalin also deliberately kept food from Ukrainians, always too independent-minded for his taste, and, according to some estimates, caused five million

Some of the millions of Soviet peasants who were deported from villages during the collectivization process. (© Illustrated London News)

deaths in the Ukraine alone during the famine of 1932–33. The overall toll of deaths resulting from Stalin's collectivization policies and the famine has been estimated by the historian Robert Conquest at 14.5 million people.

Despite the resistance, however, Stalin succeeded in forcing many peasants onto collective or state farms. He granted only one noteworthy concession when he allowed collectivized peasants to maintain small private garden plots and a few animals. By the end of the first Five-Year Plan, more than 60 percent of the cultivated land in Russia was under the control of collective farms and about 10 percent under state farms.

In subsequent years, the collectivization thrust continued, placing most of the remaining peasants and their produce effectively under the control of the party and state. At a time when Soviet peasants were starving to death, the government forced them to turn over grain to government agencies in order to feed the expanding cities, to add to grain reserves, and even to export.

SUMMARY

The years 1917–32 witnessed cataclysmic changes in Russian life. The overthrow of the tsar, the establishment of the Provisional Government, the Bolshevik Revolution, the civil war, the NEP, and finally the first five-Year Plan and collectivization all had helped to greatly transform Russia. By 1932, it had changed from an overwhelmingly agrarian, religious, and traditional empire with an autocratic government to a Marxist society moving rapidly toward industrialization. Its official values were atheistic and revolutionary, and the Communist party and Soviet government interfered more actively in the lives of the people than had the old tsarist government. Collectivization, in particular, transformed patterns of work. The increased use of education and the media and the use of terror also made it increasingly difficult to ignore or oppose the desires of the authorities. In the immediate postwar years, the revolutionary nature of the government and its aggressive Marxist-Leninist ideas made it a threat to international stability. By 1932, however, it was more concerned with continuing the internal transformation of the Soviet Union than with causing Communist revolutions in other nations.

SUGGESTED SOURCES

Chamberlain, William Henry, *The Russian Revolution, 1917–1921,* 2 vols. (1935). A readable and still valuable overview of the revolution and civil war.*

Conquest, Robert, *The Harvest of Sorrow: Soviet Collectivization and the Terror-Famine* (1986). The appalling story of Stalin's policies which cost millions of Soviet lives.* (A fifty-five-minute documentary on the same subject, called *Harvest of Despair,* is available on video.)

———, *V. I. Lenin* (1972). A brief introduction and analysis of the life, ideas, and policies of Lenin.*

Fitzpatrick, Sheila, *The Russian Revolution, 1917–32* (1984). A clear, brief, and objective account.*

Goldman, Emma, *My Disillusionment in Russia* (1970). Recounts her experiences in Russia in 1920–21 after she was deported from the United States.*

Mawdsley, Evan, *The Russian Civil War* (1987). An excellent treatment which emphasizes the military aspects of the conflict.*

Pasternak, Boris, *Doctor Zhivago* (1958). A great novel conveying the chaotic conditions of Russia during World War I, the revolution, and the civil war, and the reactions of a sensitive man to it all.* (Also a film.)

Potemkin (1926). One of Sergei Eisenstein's most famous films, it deals with a mutiny on a battleship during the revolt of 1905.

Reed, John, *Ten Days That Shook the World* (1919). A first-hand account of the Bolshevik revolt by the famous American Marxist.* (Several films have also appeared with this title: the first, an Eisenstein film, was originally called *October* and is now available on video tape under its original title; a more recent film narrated by Orsen Welles is also available on videotape.)

Thompson, John M., *Revolutionary Russia, 1917,* 2d ed. (1989). A brief and accurate book; a good introduction to the subject.*

Trotsky, Leon, *My Life* (1930). The autobiography (up to 1929) of one of the leading activists of revolutionary Russia and one who also knew how to write well.*

*Paperback available.

13

Europe in the 1920s

The period from the end of World War I up to the Great Depression of 1929 was one in which Europe tried to adjust to the results of the war and to the Russian Revolution. From 1919 until 1923–24, instability pervaded Europe. By the middle of the decade, there were signs that a more stable atmosphere was returning, but to some extent these signs were illusory.

1919–1923: A PERIOD OF FLUX

Economic and Social Adjustments

One of the greatest problems European governments faced after the war was how to reintegrate millions of returning servicemen into their peacetime economies. Some men were unable to find jobs and became part of a severe unemployment problem in Europe during the postwar decade. After years of combat, many servicemen also found it difficult to settle down into a normal routine. They believed that those who had not been through combat were not in a position to hold themselves up as guides and teachers. Some veterans blamed their elders for the folly of the war, and some, especially in Germany and Italy, objected to the peace settlements. While many servicemen stayed out of politics or supported traditional political leaders, some of the early followers of Benito Mussolini and Adolf Hitler, both veterans themselves, were fellow veterans.

Europeans also found it difficult to adjust to inflation. It affected mostly clerks, civil servants, teachers, and others on fixed incomes, and old people on pensions. Many of these pople had prided themselves on their "white-collar" middle-class status and now often saw their wages fall behind those of unionized "blue-collar" workers, who were in a better position to bargain for salary increases. Many feared that inflation would eat up their savings and that they would be destitute in their old age. Economic insecurities in Italy and Germany, later heightened in Germany by the Great Depression, led white-collar workers increasingly to despair of moderate government solutions. But fearful that the blue-collar parties of the Left would bring social disorder and loss of their status, many white-collar workers turned to the policies of Mussolini and Hitler.

The postwar period saw the gap between the aristocracy and the rest of society lessen. Ever since citizens had been encouraged to make sacrifices during the war, flagrant displays of wealth had gone out of style. The 1917 revolution had destroyed the aristocracy in Russia, and its status was in decline in Germany and Austria-Hungary with the collapse of the monarchies there. The aristocracy elsewhere in Europe often found their real wealth eroded by taxes and inflation.

At the other end of the social scale, the working class and its unions became more respectable. Most wartime governments had realized the need for cooperating with the unions, and this had conferred on the unions a new prestige. Immediately after the war, there was extensive labor unrest, but by the middle of the 1920s, the situation was more stable. In 1924, Great Britain acquired its first Labour government.

During the war, women had been permitted for the first time to engage in a number of occupations previously reserved for men. With the presence of so many men at the front, it had become more acceptable for respectable women to be seen in public without male escorts. Women also secured the right to vote in a number of nations; Great Britain enfranchised those over thirty in 1918, and German women got the vote in 1919. During the 1920s, it became more common to see women smoking and drinking in public. All these changes contributed to breaking down some of the traditional cultural distinctions between men and women.

Ethnic Nationalism and the Conflict in Ireland

During the immediate postwar period, the Irish, like many ethnic nationalities in Eastern Europe, struggled for their independence. The Catholic Irish majority on the island had long regarded the Protestant British rulers and Scots-Irish minority as exploiters and religious enemies. The Irish had already been agitating for the right to run their own internal affairs (Home Rule) for some fifty years. A Home Rule bill was enacted in 1914, but because of the outbreak of the war and resistance among Protestants in northern Ireland, the British government decided not to put it into effect until the hostilities ended. After the British government in 1916 executed fourteen ringleaders for attempting an uprising, the radical Sinn Fein party, with Eamon De Valera at its head, became more popular among the Irish.

In December 1918, the Sinn Fein party won a smashing victory in the election of Irish members to the British Parliament. The next month, they organized an Irish parliament of their own and declared their independence from Great Britain. The British, supported by the Protestants, sent in forces to crush the rebels. A vicious cycle of terror and counterterror followed, marked by bombs, arson, and torture. In December 1921, the British government and rebel leaders signed a treaty that recognized the Irish Free State, a self-governing dominion comprising most of Ireland. Much of Ulster in the north, where the Protestants were dominant, remained a part of Great Britain.

The trouble was still not over. Some of the Irish nationalists, led by De Valera, were not willing to write off Northern Ireland or accept anything other than complete independence, and continued to wage an unsuccessful civil war until De Valera's arrest in 1923. De Valera later returned and became the outstanding figure in Irish politics for decades. After World War II, the Republic of Ireland would declare its complete independence. Northern Ireland, with its Protestant majority, continued to be united with Great Britain. The Catholic minority in Northern Ireland, however, opposed the union with Great Britain and wanted to be incorporated into the Republic of Ireland. The "Irish question" continued to be an unsettled problem.

Challenges from the Left and Right in Europe

With the collapse of the monarchies in Russia, Germany, and Austria-Hungary, champions of democracy hoped that the postwar period might be a golden age for democracy. They had been further encouraged by Woodrow Wilson, who had proclaimed in 1917 that the Unites States would fight "for the right of those who submit to authority to have a voice in their own government." The hope proved to be utopian. Instead, undemocratic movements of the Left and the Right, by challenging and at times overcoming fragile democratic institutions, contributed to the instability of the period.

The Marxist revolution in Russia not only helped to set off a chain of events that kept Russia in a chaotic condition until 1921, but also contributed to "Red Scares" in other European nations. In January 1919, disturbances involving leftists broke out in Berlin, after which two leading German Communists, Rosa Luxemburg and Karl Liebknecht, were murdered. Later in 1919, Communists established governments in Hungary and in Bavaria for a short time, until Rumanian troops helped to oust the first and German regular troops and *Freikorps* (free corps) volunteers the second. In 1920, German leftist forces were put down in the Ruhr mining districts.

There were also threats from the far Right during these early postwar years. In March 1920, Berlin was taken over for several days by rightist military forces during the Kapp Putsch. The putsch failed when the Socialist party and trade unions began a general strike. In 1923 in Munich, former army corporal Adolf Hitler unsuccessfully attempted to topple both the local Bavarian government and that of the German republic. In that same year in Spain, General Miguel Primo de Rivera took over the government in a military coup and established a dictatorship.

Fascist Italy

The most important and successful right-wing movement of the immediate postwar years was that of the Italian Fascist Benito Mussolini. Before the war,

Mussolini had been one of Italy's most prominent Socialists and the editor of the official Socialist newspaper. In addition to the ideas of Karl Marx, those of Nietzsche also strongly influenced him. "To comprehend Nietzsche," he wrote in 1908, "we must imagine a new race of 'free spirits,' strengthened in war . . . spirits endowed with a sort of sublime perversity, spirits that will free us from the love of our neighbor." Such macho statements were typical of Mussolini, who also thought of himself as a virile man—he reportedly had 169 mistresses during his lifetime. He also said that "war is to man as maternity to women," and that "the Italians must learn to grow less likeable and to become hard, implacable, and full of hatred."

Shortly after the outbreak of World War I, his call for Italian participation on the side of France and Great Britain led the Italian Socialist party to expel him. He then became the editor of his own newspaper and continued a campaign for Italian intervention. Soon after Italy entered the war in 1915, Mussolini was sent to the front but did not see combat. After the war, Mussolini emerged as the leader of a group that soon came to be known as Fascists after they had labeled themselves *Fasci di Combattimento*, meaning "combat groups."

A number of factors explain how Mussolini was able to rise from the leader of a small group of malcontents to the legitimate head of the Italian government by late 1922. Although Italy possessed a parliamentary system, it did not possess a strong democratic tradition. After the war, its prime ministers and the Chamber of Deputies had to deal with a number of serious problems, including an inflation rate that by 1920 had reduced the lira to one-fifth of its prewar value. Italy also faced, as did other nations, the difficulty of reintegrating veterans into its society and economy and of once again putting society on a peacetime basis. In addition, the government had to contend with the anger of those disappointed over the failure of Italy to gain more territory from the postwar settlements. Mussolini and his black-shirted Fascists helped to magnify these problems and added others of their own. Aided by the alarm created by strikes and land seizures in 1919 and 1920, Mussolini played on the fears of communism and socialism that were shared by those afraid to lose their property and by those opposed to Marxist atheism. The Fascists attacked and at times killed their leftist opponents. Semilawlessness soon existed as violence countered violence. Many of the rich and powerful were willing to countenance Fascist brutality in the hope it would destroy leftist forces. In the face of these difficulties, the various parties in the Chamber of Deputies found it increasingly difficult to work together. Finally, confronted with the threat of Fascist bands marching on Rome, the constitutional monarch, Victor Emmanuel III, asked Mussolini to form a new government in 1922.

Since his party still possessed only a small number of representatives in the Chamber of Deputies, Mussolini's first government included only four Fascists among the fourteen ministers. Undoubtedly, some Italians hoped that, once saddled with the responsibilities of government, Mussolini and his followers would become more moderate. Mussolini did consolidate his power cautiously,

A defiant-looking Mussolini with some of his followers before assuming power in 1922. (The Granger Collection)

but his goal was still authoritarian government. For a short period, other parties continued to exist and to criticize the Fascists. In May 1924, for example, the Socialist deputy Giacomo Matteotti stood up in the Chamber of Deputies, amidst flying inkwells and insults, and accused the Fascists of rigging the recent elections and of resorting to murdering their political opponents. When he finished, he said to a colleague: "Now you may write the eulogy for my funeral." Eleven days later, he was stabbed to death by a Fascist gang. The public outrage that followed created the most serious crisis Mussolini had yet faced. Once again, however, the other political parties were unable to effectively move against Mussolini, and by 1925 all political parties except the Fascists were outlawed.

The Weimar Republic in Germany

In February 1919, a Constituent Assembly was convened at Weimar, Germany. By July it had adopted a democratic constitution, which was to remain in effect until Hitler began circumventing it in 1933. Both before and after the adoption of the constitution, political conditions remained in a state of flux. Even more than the Italians, the Germans had no tradition of democracy. Parties on the extreme Right and Left opposed both the leadership of various moderate coalitions and the Weimar constitution itself. Political instability was partly a result of the Weimar system of representation: parties in the Reichstag (lower house of parliament) received seats in proportion to the votes each had gained in general elections. This virtually ensured a multiplicity of parties, and made coalition governments almost inevitable. As was often the case in other European nations with similar systems, Weimar coalition governments disintegrated quickly. While the moderate Socialist Friedrich Ebert was president from 1919 until 1925, cabinets under a variety of chancellors changed on the average of about once a year.

Stability was also difficult to achieve in Germany because of the resentment Germans felt toward the Treaty of Versailles. The Right, as well as many politically moderate Germans, believed their nation had not really been defeated but in fact had been tricked by the Allies or betrayed by their own leaders. Extreme right-wing enemies of the republic insisted that the military had been betrayed in World War I by some of the same politicians who now supported the new form of government, and insisted that the Versailles treaty could have been resisted by again taking up arms. Partly in an effort to discredit further attacks from the Right, but also because most Germans were indignant regarding the treaty, most German politicians did their best to prevent it from being fully enforced. This helped lead to continual tensions with the Versailles "winners," which in turn further contributed to the unsettled conditions in Germany, especially before 1924.

The French Search for Security

In international affairs, France's search for security created tension and instability in Europe. France had fought two wars with Germany in fifty years and had twice seen German soldiers occupy its lands. The cost in lives and economic damage had been great. Yet Germany, despite its defeat in World War I, remained a potentially stronger nation, with a population considerably larger than that of France. Growing British and French differences over treatment of Germany, as well as other international issues, left the French in an especially difficult position. Great Britain's pledge to support France if Germany should attack in the future had lapsed when the United States had failed to ratify a similar commitment. Great Britain feared German resurgence less and seemed more concerned with restoring prewar trade with Germany. This often led, in turn, to differences of opinion concerning the level of German reparations payments. Neither the League of Nations, dominated by the Europeans but with no real power, nor treaties signed with Eastern European nations offered much reassurance to the French.

Meanwhile, France became increasingly frustrated by the German attempts to evade the Versailles treaty. Because of opposition to the treaty at home, and because German statesmen also sensed a lack of Allied unity, Germany had no reservations about trying to subvert it. Germany attempted to evade full compliance with disarmament provisions, failed to comply with some boundary commission decisions, and failed to meet many of its reparations payments on schedule. In 1922, Germany's Rapallo Agreement with Russia caused further French fears.

Against the background of these events, and because of the insistence of the United States that Allied nations repay large wartime loans, France, Belgium, and Italy occupied the Ruhr industrial region in early 1923 when Germany failed to meet a reparations obligation. The Germans in the Ruhr responded with passive resistance, a resistance that inadvertently dealt a final blow to the already unstable German currency. As the economy faltered and inflation skyrocketed—paying a billion marks for a restaurant meal was not unusual—the Allies held firm, and the German government of Wilhelm Cuno collapsed. The French encouraged separatist movements in the occupied territories, and the Soviet-dominated Comintern helped stir up unrest in central Germany. Thus, in mid-1923, both German society and European international relations were still unsettled.

1924–1929: THE RETURN OF STABILITY?

By the middle of the 1920s, it appeared that settled conditions had returned to Europe. By early 1924 the conflicts in Ireland and Russia had ended, and in that year a number of major powers recognized the Soviet government. In Germany, Chancellor Gustav Stresemann dealt in late 1923 with the threats by Hitler and the Communists, reformed the ridiculously inflated currency, and began a foreign policy that appeared to be more accommodating than that of his predecessors. After being replaced as chancellor in November 1923—after only 100 days—he remained in various cabinets as foreign minister until his death in 1929. Stresemann helped Germany to improve relations with the former Allies and to scale down reparations payments. The latter accomplishment was aided by the Dawes Plan of 1924, which also provided for U.S. loans, and the Young Plan of 1929.

International Agreements: The Search for a Lasting Peace

One aspect of the apparent equilibrium of the middle and late 1920s was a series of agreements and adjustments in which some of the major European powers participated. The momentum for international accords that characterized the period began with a series of treaties at Washington in 1921–22.

After World War I, the major naval powers feared that a new naval shipbuilding race would escalate tensions and increase expenses. In particular, many nations were concerned about the aggressive actions of Japan. The United States invited delegates from eight other nations to attend a conference in Washington, and during 1921 and 1922 several agreements were worked out there. One agreement was the Five-Power Naval Treaty, which provided for scrapping seventy ships, a ten-year moratorium on new construction of capital ships, and a global tonnage ratio for capital ships (United States 5: Great Britain 5: Japan 3: France 1.75: Italy 1.75). The treaty also provided for a halt in naval fortifications in most of the Pacific area. Another agreement, the Four-Power Treaty, ended the Anglo-Japanese alliance and replaced it with an agreement between the United States, Great Britain, Japan, and France for mutual consultation in case of threats to the security of any territories belonging to any of them. The Nine-Power Treaty provided for the continuation of the Open Door policy and the preservation of China's sovereignty but continued the unequal treaties of the imperialist era. In addition, Japan agreed to make a compensated, gradual withdrawal from the Shantung peninsula in China and also to remove its troops from Siberia.

The agreements made at Washington in effect recognized that World War I had weakened the global power of Europe and augmented the military strength of the United States and Japan. In particular, in return for curbing aggressive tendencies on the Asian mainland, Japan gained de facto recognition as the dominant naval power in Asian waters.

For many, the Locarno treaties of 1925 represented the greatest sign of hope for a more tranquil era. The most important of these treaties confirmed the existing Franco-German and Belgian-German frontiers, and the treaty was guaranteed by Great Britain and Italy. Germany, France, Belgium, Poland, and Czechoslovakia also signed a series of agreements promising to submit any conflict to arbitration. Finally, France signed treaties with Poland and Czechoslovakia providing for mutual assistance in case of a German attack.

While it might appear that the treaties signified no great gain for Germany, the rewards were significant. As the price for apparent German willingness to accept the western frontier imposed on it by the Versailles treaty, France agreed to give way on a number of points that considerably weakened its powers of coercion over Germany. The right of the Allies to inspect Germany's compliance with the disarmament provisions of Versailles now became almost meaningless. The evacuation of part of the Rhineland, which was scheduled to occur that year, went forward. Germany was also to join the League of Nations and to be given a permanent seat on its Council. Finally, it was significant that Germany refused at Locarno to confirm its eastern borders, a situation that increased the fears of Czechoslovakia and Poland and helped drive them into the arms of the French.

In 1926, Stresemann and the French and British foreign ministers, Aristide Briand and Austen Chamberlain, were all awarded the Nobel Peace Prize for their Locarno efforts. Europeans talked of the new spirit of conciliation that was in the air. This "Spirit of Locarno" was further in evidence in 1928 when the U.S. Secretary of State, Frank Kellogg, joined Briand in creating the Kellogg-Briand Pact in which sixty-four nations renounced war as an "instrument of national policy." Paradoxically, the same nations reiterated their right to take up arms in self-defense.

Despite all these agreements, however, international stability proved illusory. Europe's economic recovery had in general been sluggish. Germany's economy and reparations payments were partly dependent on U.S. loans. Thus, a serious curtailment of the U.S. loans could have a ripple effect on Germany and the European Allies. Between a Germany bent on revision of the Treaty of Versailles and a France attempting to maintain its security, the potential for

Three foreign ministers, Gustav Stresemann (center, Germany), Sir Austen Chamberlain (left, Great Britain), and Aristide Briand (far right, France), discuss the future of Europe in 1928. (Bilderdienst Süddeutscher Verlag)

serious conflict remained. Germany's unwillingness at Locarno to recognize its eastern frontiers as permanent was also an ill omen.

In the case of the Washington Naval Conference agreements, there was no guarantee the signatories would continue to honor them once they no longer felt it was in their interest to do so. The Kellogg-Briand Pact contained no provisions for dealing with aggression. In fact, it was little more than a pious wish, an "international kiss," in the words of one U.S. senator. Attempts in the late 1920s and early 1930s to deal with concrete issues of aggression and disarmament also proved fruitless.

European Governments: The Veneer of Stability

The ambiguous nature of international developments in the 1920s was also reflected in European governments, particularly in Germany. Despite the continuation of a multiplicity of political parties and coalition governments, the German governments following Stresemann from 1924 to 1929 appeared to be stable, as threats from the Left and the Right subsided. Nevertheless, important segments of German public opinion still criticized the new republican form of government or only grudgingly tolerated it. Despite the accomplishments of Stresemann as foreign minister, many nationalists believed that the government was moving too slowly in removing the shackles of the Versailles treaty. By 1929 such discontent took the form of organized opposition to the Young Plan and to continuing reparations payments.

Part of the opposition to paying reparations came from Adolf Hitler and his small Nazi party. Although few guessed in 1929 how important Hitler would soon become, he had already come a long way from rather humble beginnings.

Born in 1889, the son of a minor Austrian customs official, he failed to graduate from high school and had gone to Vienna hoping to enter art school. He was unsuccessful, but he remained in the Austro-Hungarian capital, living an impoverished life as a creator of advertising cards and small paintings. In 1913, he left Vienna for Munich in southern Germany. When World War I broke out, he enlisted in the German army. During the war he was wounded several times and was also cited and decorated for bravery on a number of occasions.

After the war, Hitler became involved in Munich with a small, rather insignificant nationalistic political group that called itself the German Workers' party. Within a couple of years he became its Führer, or leader. After leading the unsuccessful "Beer-Hall Putsch" in Munich in 1923, he spent nine months in prison. He used the time to write *Mein Kampf* (*My Struggle*), a work he originally wished to call "Four and a Half Years of Struggle against Lies, Stupidity, and Cowardice." In it he spelled out his nationalism, anti-Semitism, racism, and totalitarianism. After his release from prison he continued to build up his party, by then called the National Socialist German Workers'(Nazi) party. In the 1928 Reichstag elections, despite its 108,000 paid members, the Nazis won only about 3 percent of the total vote.

In 1930, the beginnings of the Great Depression and continued national resentment over the Versailles provisions led to impressive Nazi gains in the Reichstag elections. As a result, the Nazis gained 18 percent of the total vote and became the second-largest party in that body, and the illusory nature of the German stability of the late 1920s soon became more evident.

In Great Britain, the Conservative party under Stanley Baldwin replaced a shaky Labour government in 1924 and remained in power for the next five years. Baldwin prided himself on being a plain and ordinary man, full of common sense. Under the Conservatives, the British appeared to be returning to happier times; the general standard of living went up, and the state provided even more benefits for the old, widowed, orphaned, and unemployed. But Britain's economic foundation was weak. Basic industries such as iron and steel, coal, cotton, and shipbuilding were in decline as a result of a combination of foreign competition, outdated business practices and technology, and legislation that prohibited general strikes and hampered the unionization of civil servants.

In France, it took longer for matters to stabilize. After Edouard Herriot, the leader of the Radical Socialist party, had governed for ten months, six successive governments followed each other in the period from April 1925 to July 1926, most of them brought down when they failed to deal with inflation. Only in July 1926, when Raymond Poincaré became prime minister of a broad-based National Union Coalition, was inflation brought under control. Poincaré's government lasted three years, a long time in French politics, and it was instrumental in bringing to France a measure of the calm that characterized the last part of the decade. Unfortunately for France, however, fundamental problems remained. The temporary equilibrium was largely a result of Poincaré's leadership rather than of change in the basically rickety French political system. In addition, French industry could not successfully compete with that of Germany, and both its industry and its agriculture remained inefficient compared to those of the United States.

While the larger nations of Europe struggled with their particular social and economic problems, two basic economic difficulties continued to lurk in the background of most of the smaller nations of Eastern and southern Europe: rural overpopulation and small markets for their goods, a problem exacerbated by increasing foreign tariffs. Concurrently, there were disturbing signs of a movement toward the authoritarian Right in these nations. Right-wing seizures of power took place in Portugal and Poland in 1926, bringing about more ordered conditions than had previously existed, but at the cost of civil liberties and political freedom. In addition, a host of social, minority, and nationalistic rivalries in Eastern Europe, although less apparent than in the early 1920s, continued to simmer.

SUMMARY

The immediate postwar years presented the West with a number of problems: the reintegration of soldiers into a peacetime economy, reparations, the repayment of loans, unemployment and inflation, social and cultural adjustments, political conflicts in Russia and Ireland, and challenges from the Left and the Right to fragile democratic governments. For the time being, some governments were able to withstand the pressure, but others were not; the most notable case was that of Italy, where Mussolini came to power in 1922.

By the middle and latter part of the decade, most of the major powers appeared to be less troubled, as their economies apparently recovered. Agreements such as the Washington Naval Conference treaties, the Locarno treaties, and the Kellogg-Briand Pact all promised greater international equilibrium. Governments also seemed more stable. Stresemann remained Germany's foreign minister from 1923 to 1929, Baldwin was prime minister in Great Britain from 1924 to 1929, and Poincaré was prime minister in France from 1926 to 1929.

Underneath the apparent stabilizing developments of the late 1920s, however, there were problems. The economic underpinnings of many nations remained weak, and in Europe allegiance to democratic political forms was tentative. German resentment toward the Allies also was never far below the surface. All the international agreements, in turn, depended largely on the domestic stability and prosperity of the signatories, as well as continuing successful diplomacy. Beginning in 1929 and continuing into the 1930s, these problems became manifested in depression, aggression, and, finally, total war.

SUGGESTED SOURCES

Friedrich, Otto, *Before the Deluge* (1972). A portrait for the general reader of various aspects of Berlin life during the Weimar Republic.*

Graves, Robert, and Alan Hodge, *The Long Week-End* (1936). An interesting portrayal of British life and customs from 1918 to 1939.*

Kolb, Eberhard, *The Weimar Republic* (1988). A good overview by a German scholar.*

Mack Smith, Denis, *Mussolini* (1982). A well-written analysis by a leading scholar.*

Marks, Sally, *The Illusion of Peace* (1976). A brief and clear examination of international relations in the 1918–33 period.*

Mussolini (The Twentieth Century series). A twenty-seven-minute film dealing with the Italian dictator from the end of World War I until his death in 1945.

Shirer, William L., *20th Century Journey* (1985). More than 300 pages are devoted to the 1920s in this U.S. journalist's account of experiences in the United States and in Paris, London, and other European cities.*

Silone, Ignazio, *Fontamara* (1934). A leading Italian novelist's depiction of conflict in the 1920s between the village of Fontamara and Mussolini's Fascists.*

Waite, Robert G., *The Psychopathic God: Adolf Hitler* (1983). A fascinating look at the personality of Hitler and the historical context in which he flourished; an example of psycho-history.*

*Paperback available.

14

Economic and Social Upheaval in the United States and Latin America

During the 1920s and 1930s, the Western Hemisphere was largely spared the horrors of war, but nonetheless the period was one of social discord and economic turmoil. The United States experienced social dislocations in the 1920s and plunged into the economic nightmare of the Great Depression during the 1930s. In Latin America, the entrenched privileged classes were subject to challenges ranging from violence and social revolution in Mexico to more orderly reform movements in Chile. In international relations, the United States abandoned its policy of direct intervention in the Caribbean area, but its remaining economic and political controls continued to cause hostility to "the Colossus of the North." By the late 1930s, however, there were hopeful signs of a recovering economy and more equitable social systems in both the United States and Latin America.

THE UNITED STATES: BOOM TO BUST

Postwar Discord in the United States

The United States, like Europe, found the postwar years unsettling. The Senate rejected the Versailles treaty and the United States refused to join the League of Nations. Wilson spent his last months in office as a reclusive invalid. Warren Harding called for a return to "normalcy" upon taking office in 1921, but his administration was troubled by corruption, and soon after his death in 1923 a number of political scandals surfaced. In 1919, workers conducted widespread strikes and Attorney General A. Mitchell Palmer orchestrated a "Red Scare," jailing and deporting Marxists and anarchists. In Massachusetts in 1921, two anarchists, Nicola Sacco and Bartolomeo Vanzetti, were convicted of robbery and murder and eventually executed. In view of the actions of the judge and others connected with the trial, many claimed that the men were convicted in part because of their beliefs. Anticapitalists around the world proclaimed that the trial was a symbol of capitalist repression.

The ethnic and racial tensions already on the rise before World War I came to a climax after the war. Anti-Semitism continued, and lynchings of blacks and race riots punctuated the scene. Nativist Americans of northern European descent had enough political clout to persuade Congress in 1921 and 1924 to limit annual immigration to a low figure, to establish quotas that discriminated against those who did not come from northern Europe, and to exclude the Japanese. The revived Ku Klux Klan gained political control of several states across the nation. At its peak in the early 1920s, the Klan contested control of the Democratic party and staged a massive march in Washington before it collapsed from internal bickering. In addition to political and racial tensions, there was often a cultural hostility between advocates of the new values of the "Roaring Twenties," usually city dwellers, and those from smaller towns and rural areas who defended Prohibition and conservative religious values.

"Prosperity"

During President Calvin Coolidge's years in office, from late 1923 until early 1929, the United States apparently entered a period of quiet and stability; many in the United States believed that "normalcy" had finally arrived. Coolidge himself claimed in 1928 that "in the domestic field there is tranquility and contentment . . . . In the foreign field there is peace." One measure of "tranquility" appeared to be a booming economy; industrial production doubled between 1921 and 1929. Republican administrations fostered the growth of business through high tariffs and low corporate and income taxes. Many business corporations merged into larger and more efficient conglomerates, and new technology spawned an increasing array of consumer goods for Americans and for world markets. The growing middle class bought up an enormous number of automobiles, telephones, radios, and electric appliances, taking advantage of an exciting new credit concept—the installment plan. Many Americans also found extra money to invest in the stock market, which moved ever higher.

Despite the apparent prosperity, however, there were grave problems in the U.S. economy. Railroads, textiles, and coal were depressed industries; many workers faced layoffs and wage cuts. Only those workers in the skilled trades benefited from union organization. In the South, children and women labored in the textile mills for up to sixty hours a week for a few cents per hour.

Problems among the nation's farmers constituted another sign of impending economic trouble. Having overexpanded production in World War I to produce the bumper crops demanded by the Allies, U.S. farmers throughout the 1920s faced both a drop in demand and increased worldwide competition. As a result, crop prices plummeted and many farmers could not make enough money to pay their mortgages. Some of the larger landholders saved themselves by mechanizing their operations, but many sharecroppers and tenant farmers lost their jobs, and a growing number of marginal farmers had to abandon their farms. Farm belt politicians created a political furor, but Republican administrations failed to find any effective policies for relief.

By 1929 when Herbert Hoover became president, additional economic problems beset the nation, although they were largely unseen at the time. Production far exceeded consumption; stockpiles accumulated as consumers lacked the money and even the credit to purchase the vast array of goods available. In addition, many individuals and banking institutions were speculating on the stock market. There were no laws controlling the amount of stock that could be purchased on credit; speculators could and did buy a maximum amount of stocks with a minimum amount of cash. When prices went high enough, speculators sold their stocks, paid their debt, and kept the remainder as a profit. However, if prices dropped or even remained steady, speculators could easily owe enormous sums of money they did not have. Few seemed worried. "Stocks have reached a permanently high plateau," commented a distinguished professor of economics on October 17, 1929.

On "Black Thursday," October 24, 1929, the stock market on Wall Street began to collapse, and the United States headed toward a full-fledged crisis. Within a matter of hours, most speculators were ruined. Despite assurances from authority figures from Hoover on down that the worst was over, stock prices moved steadily lower until December 1932. During this three-year period, a devastating downward spiral of business cutbacks, unemployment, and bankruptcies ensued. Many unemployed families lost their homes when they could no longer meet their mortgage payments. Other families lost their savings when their banks failed. By early 1933 the U.S. economy was in a disastrous condition, with industrial production cut back, 25 percent of the work force unemployed, and more and more banks going under. Hoover, a devout capitalist and a Constitutional conservative, believed that the best way to pull out of the Depression was to let the economy alone to work its way through the crisis. In his view, the U.S. federal Constitutional system placed responsibility for providing relief on the private sector and the states; the national government's role was limited to expanding public works, providing loans to big business (the benefits would "trickle down" to the average American), and raising the tariff to keep out competing foreign goods. Hoover's policies did not work; the economy continued to deteriorate, and he was defeated in his bid for a second term in 1932 by Democrat Franklin Roosevelt.

The New Deal

When Roosevelt took the oath of office on March 4, 1933, the United States faced its greatest threat since the Civil War. With the Republican party and its policies discredited by economic collapse and three years of failure to bring about recovery, the American people had turned to the Democratic party. Roosevelt was a rather traditional politician from a wealthy family; he wished to preserve U.S. capitalism, but was willing to experiment with new programs

President Franklin D. Roosevelt projects a cheerful image during the New Deal.
(AP/Wide World Photos)

to ensure that capitalism survived. Because state governments and the private
sector had failed to cope with the economic disaster, Roosevelt was willing to
extend the national government's regulatory power deep into the economic and
social fabric of the nation. "The only thing we have to fear is fear itself," he
assured his fellow Americans. Roosevelt and the Democrats called their collection of programs the New Deal.

Roosevelt was concerned for the suffering of the poor and unemployed,
and was willing to run up large budget deficits to provide relief and stimulate
recovery. "Our greatest primary task is to put people to work," he declared,
and most of his relief programs focused on providing employment to put purchasing power back into the hands of U.S. families and to rekindle a sense of
pride and worth. Various federal programs gave people jobs in reforestation
and in constructing government buildings, schools, airports, hospitals, parks,
and dams. Where possible, the government employed writers, musicians, ac-
tors, artists, and archivists in their own professions. The national government
also provided grants-in-aid to the states to supplement their relief programs.
The government assisted tenant farmers, resettled farm families, and provided
home loans to pay off mortgages.

Although the New Dealers were willing to spend money on relief projects
for the short run, they were more interested in creating programs that would solve
basic problems in the U.S. economy. Under Roosevelt's sponsorship, the U.S.
government regulated the financial community, monitored the stock market, pro-

vided loans for banks to regain solvency, and insured savings deposits. When Roosevelt took the nation off the gold standard, Roosevelt's conservative Director of the Budget moaned, "This is the end of Western civilization."

In order to assist business, improve wages and working conditions, and protect consumer interests, the Roosevelt administration set up the National Recovery Administration (NRA), charged with creating codes regulating production standards in business. In practice, the NRA codes often turned out to benefit big business; they were plagued with noncompliance, and they were eventually struck down by the Supreme Court. The government succeeded in regulating certain industries, such as coal, petroleum, and trucking. In the interests of developing depressed regions, the government went beyond regulation. For example, in the Tennessee Valley Authority and in similar projects in the West, the government constructed dams that not only controlled floods but also produced cheap electrical power, thus putting the government in competition with privately owned utilities.

To stimulate wage increases and thereby increase purchasing power, the federal government supported collective bargaining. The craft unions, long organized under the American Federation of Labor, grew stronger. After a period of strikes and violence, industrial workers, under the umbrella of the Congress of Industrial Organizations, established unions in the automobile, steel, mining, and other industries. Once unionized, workers made substantial headway in improving wages, working conditions, and grievance procedures. Labor leaders, such as the dynamic John L. Lewis of the United Mine Workers, became powerful national figures.

The Roosevelt administration also took strong measures to end the farm depression. Farmers limited production in certain basic commodities by voting to submit to government production and marketing quotas. In return, the government set a fair price level (parity) and guaranteed to subsidize the difference or most of the difference if market prices fell below the parity level. Under this approach and through related programs, farm income, especially for those with large holdings, began to rise steadily.

The New Deal also rapidly expanded the welfare state. The welfare state in the United States came later than did similar modifications of capitalism in other industrialized nations, and it was less complete. It was not a reflection of a coherent overall policy, but a collection of specific programs, some administered by the national government and some by the states, which provided sketchy cradle-to-the-grave protection against personal catastrophes. It included aid to women with dependent children, aid to the blind and handicapped, unemployment compensation, workmen's compensation for injuries and illnesses sustained on the job, minimum wage and maximum hour limits, public housing, old-age pensions, and limitations on child labor. Some Americans regarded the welfare state as socialism, but it proved to be popular with most of the U.S. public, even though benefits were low and many people were excluded.

By 1939 the New Deal had brought about a partial economic recovery. On the positive side, the percentage of families above the poverty level had increased and the percentage of the national income owned by the upper classes had declined, indicating a more equitable distribution of the national wealth. Middle-class Americans had been bolstered financially and psychologically, and lower-class Americans, especially minorities, had been saved from destitution. On the other hand, unemployment ran at 15 percent, and real wages were still below those of 1929. Meanwhile, the budget deficit of the national government had risen from $7 million to $20 billion. It took the outbreak of the war in Europe, with the subsequent rise in military spending, to bring an end to the Depression.

While only partially successful in bringing back economic prosperity, the New Deal created substantial changes in U.S. living patterns. Through their national government, Americans increasingly regulated capitalism and expanded the welfare state. Agriculture continued to be subsidized, and the trade union movement remained powerful in the basic industries. Roosevelt's aggressive leadership expanded the groundwork laid by Theodore Roosevelt and Wilson in strengthening the power of the presidency. In politics, the Roosevelt coalition of southern whites, blacks, union labor, ethnics, and urban voters made the Democratic party the majority party in Congress for most of the next fifty-seven years. In the larger context, the people of the United States had strongly affirmed the historic democratic experience of their nation. In the face of heavy economic pressures, they had demonstrated that they could work out their problems inside the traditional democratic political system and reject totalitarian solutions of the Right and of the Left.

REVOLUTION IN MEXICO

By the early twentieth century many dictatorships, especially among the smaller and poorer nations, were essentially the same as in the nineteenth century. They were usually run by military "strongmen," or *jefes,* and the tone of these regimes varied with the personalities of the leaders.

Gradually, however, certain groups began to challenge the ruling order. Some members of the small middle class of businessmen and professionals, traditionally subservient to the landlord families, wished to replace *caudillo* (strongman) rule with representative governments, hoping they would thereby be able to secure political power. They also wanted to reduce foreign investment and thus gain a greater share in the financial and industrial development of their nations. Some members of the elite and the middle class were idealistic and wished to improve the living conditions of the lower classes and bring them into the political system.

The rapidly growing masses of impoverished urban workers also challenged *caudillo* rule. Many workers were white immigrants from Europe who were often escaping from repression at home and had no tradition of obedience to the ruling elites. They were joined by peasants fleeing the poverty in the countryside, many of whom had abandoned their traditional passive subservience. The urban workers were interested in obtaining minimum wage and maximum hour laws, sickness and accident protection, health and safety regulations, and pensions; but they showed little interest in education or democratic political systems. They represented an explosive new force in Latin American politics, and tradionalists were uncertain whether they should suppress the urban masses if they became unruly or appease them with welfare legislation in order to obtain their political support.

The Díaz Dictatorship

Although the middle class and the urban workers appeared the most likely to bring social change to Latin America, the most radical social and economic revolution came in Mexico. The middle class furnished the catalyst for revolution, and the urban workers pitched in, but the Indian and *mestizo* peasants who had recently lost their land provided the driving force. In 1910, Mexico had been in the grip of a classic strongman, Porfirio Díaz, for thirty-five years. Díaz, a *mestizo,* was supported by Mexico's ruling families and foreign corporations. The Church also backed Díaz, as did the military. The mass of Indians and *mestizos* were considered fit only to be laborers. One element of Díaz's supporters claimed that Indians were inferior and that progress would come by attracting white settlement, in the pattern set by the United States, Canada, Argentina, Uruguay, Brazil, and Chile.

Díaz once said, "Poor Mexico, so far from God and so close to the United States." These may well have been problems, but most Mexicans found that their main torment was the dictator himself. Díaz used classic strongman tactics to perpetuate his regime. The *rurales,* his rural police, kept order in the countryside by shooting opponents and suppressing the riots sparked by angry Indians who had lost their land. The growing urban working class, especially in the new textile industry, was closely watched by the authorities; strikes were forbidden and wildcat walkouts were crushed. Díaz conciliated some in the rapidly growing middle class by expanding the bureaucracy and giving them employment. Political opponents were watched; the press was partially censored and the judiciary controlled. Díaz manipulated the political process by nominating his allies to congress and himself to the presidency and declaring everyone elected after votes were cast at the end of each term.

During the rule of Díaz, the great landlords of Mexico—a few thousand *hacienderos*—expanded their holdings, often at the expense of the Indian communities, in order to increase the production of staples for sale in the international market. Food production dropped and food had to be imported; the standard of living for the majority of the population declined. In some states, over 95 percent of the population were landless. Díaz encouraged foreign investors to build up the railroad system, to create electric power, and especially to develop the petroleum industry, which rose to become the third largest in the world. He also invited them to become *hacienderos* by purchasing large tracts of mining, timber, and farmland. In 1910, Americans owned 22 percent of the land of Mexico. To outsiders, the Díaz regime appeared a stable and economically progressive administration. The United States and European nations extended their support. The U.S. millionaire Andrew Carnegie, for example, stated after a visit that "in every corner of the Republic reigned prosperity and peace."

Revolt, Civil War, and Revolution

Despite his dictatorial controls, Díaz's regime was overthrown. In 1910, Francisco Madero, a moderate liberal who was working for political freedom for the middle class, raised the standard of revolt. Madero was quickly joined by two charismatic leaders who became folk heroes of Mexico. In northern Mexico, Francisco "Pancho" Villa led a group of cowboys and small farmers who wanted to oust foreign property owners. In the south, Madero received support from Emiliano Zapata, who led a group of dispossessed peasants who wanted legal reforms and land. Díaz fled, reputedly remarking, "Madero has unleashed a tiger; let us see if he can control it." Madero and Zapata were both assassinated, and a bloody struggle between revolutionary factions raged across Mexico for ten years. Relations with the United States deteriorated in the wake of Mexican border raids and two major punitive expeditions by the United States into Mexico. As many as two million Mexicans perished.

As the fighting raged on, it became apparent that what had begun as a relatively limited reform movement was changing into a broad-scale social, economic, and political revolution. Some of the Indian and *mestizo* leaders wished

A brief moment of unity in the Mexican Revolution: Francisco Villa (left) sits in the presidential chair with Emiliano Zapata beside him. (Special Collections, University of Texas at El Paso)

Declaring against the Caudillo

[My college landlady boasted] that she had gone to the ball given for Porfirio Díaz, . . .

"He bears the stamp of the hero," she said.

"Of the assassin," I interrupted. . . .

Why my violent reaction against the Mexican caudillo? I had not thought it out. Perhaps I merely absorbed my hatred from my surroundings. He was never publicly attacked, but you breathed in the very air a violent dislike of him. . . .

The latent social distress of the country had at last taken form in the mind of . . . Francisco Madero. . . . He was looking for independent men, men of decision; he invited me to a meeting. . . .

Anything rather than Mexico under Díaz—corrupt, militaristic, murderous. Going home, I looked adoringly at my son, a few months old, smiling and vigorous, and I thought, "I wish he might die if this does not change."*

Thus the young Mexican philosopher José Vasconcelos discusses how his anti-Díaz sentiments were crystallized into action by the influence of Francisco Madero, the man who toppled Porfirio Díaz and launched the Mexican Revolution. Vasconcelos later became a major, but controversial, politician and educator in revolutionary Mexico. As Minister of Education and head of the National University, he supported secularism and championed Mexico's Indian/mestizo heritage. Later, however, he repudiated this outlook and embraced the Catholic Church and the Spanish traditon of Mexico.

*From A Mexican Ulysses: An Autobiography, by José Vasconcelos, translated and abridged by W. Rex Crawford. Copyright © 1963 by the University of Indiana Press. Reprinted by permission.

to destroy white rule in Mexico; secularists and religious reformers wished to curb the power of the Catholic Church; Indian villagers wanted their communal lands returned; farm workers wanted land of their own; urban laborers wanted higher wages and improved working conditions; the middle class wanted a liberal republic, both for idealistic reasons and because of a desire to assume control of the political process. Nearly all agreed that foreign controls over the Mexican economy had to be rolled back. As the struggle continued, a new Mexico evolved as Mexican revolutionaries incorporated the reforms sought by the major contending groups.

The Constitution of 1917, the most radical constitution in the world at that time, laid out the goals of the Mexican Revolution. The aspirations of the Indian and *mestizo* middle and lower classes of Mexico dominated the document, which ended the rule of the predominantly white upper class. The constitution was traditional in its political provisions, setting up a typical Latin American government coupling democratic processes with a strong presidency. On the other hand, the social and economic provisions of the constitution were revolutionary. It reduced the power of the Catholic Church in Mexico, stripping it of its remaining lands, removing the Church from primary education, and forbidding clerics to engage in politics. It empowered the government to take and redistribute private land, while at the same time it recognized Indian communal landholding. Petroleum, minerals, and water were declared common national resources, and foreign companies were made subject to government control. The constitution outlined a complete labor code, recognized the right to unionize and strike, called for minimum wage and maximum hour standards, and promised insurance and pension plans.

By 1921 order had been generally restored; as one general grumbled, "This revolution has now degenerated into a government." The men who controlled Mexico during the 1920s and 1930s were interested in restoring political stability. They wished to provide reforms at a moderate pace rather than stirring up new convulsions by immediately implementing the social and economic clauses of the Constitution of 1917. They brought the army and the Church under civilian control and created what became essentially a one-party state. The new party, The Party of the Revolution, institutionalized the revolution and turned it away from violence. The party was pledged to carry forward the revolution; its support was so broad that it prevented effective opposition parties from developing. In time, the party organization became more important than individuals; party leaders agreed in advance on who would succeed to the presidency, thus providing for an orderly transfer of power at each election. Meanwhile, the government inaugurated a modest program of rural schools and slowly proceeded with land redistribution. This expanded the small farmer class, which concentrated on producing badly needed foodstuffs.

The revolution bore its greatest fruit under President Lázaro Cárdenas, who held office from 1934 to 1940. Remembering his roots in a grindingly poor village, Cárdenas was determined to improve the lot of his downtrodden countrymen. In a term in office paralleling the New Deal years in the United States, Cárdenas built up enormous popularity as he toured villages to learn of local problems and to make arrangements for relief. He accelerated the process of taking land from the *haciendros* and giving it to landless peasants, giving particular emphasis to restoring land lost by the Indian communities. By 1940 the accumulated land reforms of twenty years had put almost half of the cropland of Mexico in the hands of small farmers. Cárdenas also ordered more schools built and supported improved working conditions and wage raises for urban workers.

To the widespread acclaim of Mexicans of all classes, Cárdenas also clamped down on foreign-owned companies. He nationalized the railroads, and after the petroleum companies had ignored a Mexican supreme court ruling on paying minimum wages, he nationalized the petroleum industry. The national petroleum corporation was soon operating more efficiently than the foreign owners had, and the government earmarked the petroleum for domestic development instead of foreign consumption. The United States and European nations were angry, but eventually acquiesced.

In another major consequence of the Mexican Revolution, governments after Díaz began to recast the national image away from the Latin history of Mexico toward its Indian heritage. The *mestizos,* who now dominated Mexican affairs, encouraged books and murals about Indian history and culture. The new motion picture medium made a marked impression on the masses, as they saw films about contemporary life in the Indian villages and about the Aztec and Mayan past. The population began to celebrate their Indian background and to identify with the nation and the new revolutionary party.

By the 1940s, however, revolutionary fervor began to fade, and Mexican society fell well short of fulfilling its revolutionary goals. *Haciendaros* still controlled half the productive acreage, and one-third of the population still worked as serfs. Graft and mismanagement dissipated the effects of many of Cárdenas's programs. Still, Mexico had come a long way from the days of Díaz.

The Mexican Revolution occurred at the same time as the Bolshevik Revolution, but its ideology, pace, and results were quite different. The Bolsheviks had two successive long-term leaders, supported by a highly disciplined minority party determined to fulfill a blueprint for a new order. They gained control of their nation relatively quickly, and with clearly defined goals made profound changes in Russian society. The Mexican Revolution was rooted in Mexican problems and worked its way toward a uniquely Mexican resolution. It had many leaders, none of whom had any significant connection with the revolutionary ideologies sweeping Europe. The civil war lasted for a decade and revolutionary goals varied widely among different groups, and a disciplined party and a consensus on goals were therefore slow to develop. Although substantial progress was made toward fundamental change, the revolution in Mexico was not pushed through to completion.

OTHER CHALLENGES TO THE TRADITIONAL *CAUDILLO* IN LATIN AMERICA

Mexico, with its partly realized social revolution and its one-party state, was unique in its overthrow of *caudillo* government in the interwar period. However, pressure from events outside Latin America, the influence of the Mexican Revolution, and developments inside particular nations brought about either threats to or modifications of the rule of the strongman.

In response to the great movements sweeping Europe, the authoritarian regimes were staunchly anti-Marxist, but some urban workers did join Marxist organizations. Some regimes flirted with fascism, but they did not become self-conscious ideological regimes like Hitler's Germany, nor did

**South America
Before World War II**

△ Major boundary or
territorial dispute

⚔ Major War

FALKLAND ISLANDS (Br.) Claimed by
Argentina as Islas Malvinas

0 200 400 600 800 1000

Scale of miles

they actively indoctrinate the public through an extensive propaganda apparatus.

In some of the larger Latin American nations that had a more complicated economic and social order, there was a movement toward a new pattern of authoritarian rule. These governments featured dynamic personalities, some of whom were attracted to the Latin tone of Mussolini's fascism, who ruled by manipulating the vote and making concessions to the volatile masses of the urban centers. Brazil was a good example of this trend. The largest Latin American nation and one with abundant natural resources, Brazil had been a traditional feudal nation in the nineteenth century, but began to industrialize rapidly in the twentieth. Urban workers had been slow to unionize before 1930, but the Depression produced such disastrous effects on the workers that they quickly organized into unions and in some cases became involved in Marxist revolutionary activities. Getulio Vargas, who ruled from 1930 to 1945, moved quickly to win the support of the urban workers by creating a welfare state, with benefits such as minimum wages, pension plans, and guaranteed jobs. Vargas organized the workers into government-controlled unions that were forbidden to strike but had the benevolent support of the government when involved in negotiations with employers. With the support of the workers, Vargas kept the coffee planters, who had previously run the nation, at bay. Vargas accommodated the planters to some extent by refusing to extend labor protection to rural workers. In effect, the urban workers, in return for security, supported the rule of a strongman.

In a region marked by authoritarian rule of one type or another, a few nations, particularly Chile, had managed to make democracy work during significant stretches of their history. In many ways, Chile displayed the same economic and social characteristics as other Latin American states. The nation was short on arable land, which was held by a few families who were inefficient agriculturalists; food supplies were often inadequate for the urban poor, which constituted an ever-growing—and hungry—segment of the population. Foreign companies controlled Chile's main exports—copper ore and nitrates—as well as its public utilities.

Still, Chile was different. Its population was more racially homogeneous than most Latin American nations, overwhelmingly *mestizo* at all social levels, making social mobility easier. The Church was relatively liberal, supporting programs to help the underprivileged. What made Chile unique, however, was that the nation was developing a democratic political tradition, later to be accompanied by a commitment to social welfare. During the late nineteenth and early twentieth centuries, a multi-party parliamentary process similar to those in France and Italy had developed. This process was based on free elections and a tradition that the military ought not intervene in civilian affairs. By and large, this was a liberal era. Political leaders removed many Church controls over the state, enlarged the electorate, and inaugurated a few modest improvements in health services and education. Up through World War I, Chile earned substantial income from taxes on large exports of nitrates and copper ore.

The interwar years, however, demonstrated that both democracy and liberalism in Chile were still shallow-rooted compared to its older traditions of authoritarian social patterns, class exploitation, and antagonisms between the various regions of the nation. The great mass of peasants and the growing numbers of miners and factory workers were still miserably exploited, living in rural slums and urban tenements, with inadequate food and medical care; over half were illiterate. In the grip of strong tradition, the rural peasants were relatively quiet; but the miners, factory workers, and urban unemployed struck back through unionization, strikes, riots, and support for the Socialist and Communist parties. The government was paralyzed by infighting among a host of political parties representing narrow regional and group interests. Meanwhile, with World War I over, the bottom fell out of the nitrate market.

The result was twenty years of an economic and political rollercoaster. The economy gained ground in the 1920s, collapsed in the global Depression of the early 1930s, and revived again in the late 1930s. Meanwhile, Chile began to squeeze out European holdings in transportation and nitrates, but only mildly regulated U.S. business interests in nitrate and copper mining. Politically, a new constitution was established that promised more stability. It separated church and state and raised the office of president from that of a figurehead to that of coordinate power with the congress. On the other hand, this was a period of military revolts and coups, juntas, rigged elections, dictatorships, and the rise of fascist and Nazi paramilitary forces.

The dominant figure of this period was Arturo Allesandri Palma, who led the nation three times between 1920 and 1938. A political chameleon who in many ways resembled Vargas in Brazil, Allesandri began as a liberal reformer and ended as a crypto-fascist dictator. Allesandri and many other Chilean political leaders of this period, whether authoritarian or democratic, saw the need to make concessions to the miners and the urban masses. They instituted a number of social reforms, particularly a labor code (similar to Mexico's) that guaranteed the right to unionize and engage in collective bargaining, restricted child labor, and provided health insurance. The public school system was extended and wages and government salaries increased. By World War II, Chile appeared to have come out well from its tumultuous interwar period. The economy had been revived, diversified, and modernized; there had been an advance in social justice; there was greater constitutional stability; and, as it turned out, the democratic tradition of free elections was in the process of being restored.

SUMMARY

The interwar period was one of social and economic upheaval in the United States and Latin America. The United States experienced an era of ethnic and racial discord. The upper classes profited from a major expansion of the industrial economy, but some areas of the economy remained depressed and the purchasing power of the general public remained low. The stock market collapsed in 1929, triggering a massive depression which prostrated the nation by 1932. Roosevelt's New Deal brought some reforms and relief, but recovery was still incomplete in 1939.

In Mexico, the initial political revolt of 1910 was followed by a decade of civil war before the revolution became institutionalized in an umbrella political party. The new revolutionary party was committed to implementing a broad spectrum of social, economic, and political reforms and made a significant start in this direction during the 1920s and 1930s before revolutionary fervor faded.

Traditional elites still ruled most of the nations elsewhere in Latin America, but new political patterns and steps toward social reform were making an appearance in some places. In Chile, democratic institutions and social reforms were trying to survive a chaotic period. In Brazil, the Vargas dictatorship rested in large part on the support of the urban masses, rather than on the aristocracy.

SUGGESTED SOURCES

Allen, Frederick Lewis, *Only Yesterday* (1931). A colorful history of U.S. fads and much more during the 1920s.*

Azuela, Mariano, *The Underdogs* (1962). A moving novel about the Mexican Revolution.*

Knight, Alan, *The Mexican Revolution* (1986). Insightful and well written.

Leuchtenberg, William E., *Franklin Roosevelt and the New Deal, 1932–1940* (1963). Still the best general account.*

Loveman, Brian, *Chile: The Legacy of Hispanic Capitalism* (1979). A sound general study.

Steinbeck, John, *The Grapes of Wrath* (1939). A powerful novel depicting the plight of an American farm family dispossessed by poverty and drought during the Depression.* (Also a film.)

Womack, John, Jr., *Zapata and the Mexican Revolution* (1972). An outstanding biography of an outstanding revolutionary.*

*Paperback available.

15

East Asia between the World Wars

In the early twentieth century, China and Japan followed two very different paths. China was absorbed in a process of revolution and tentative beginnings that affected every part of society and every aspect of its civilization. The revolution of 1911 ended the world's longest continuous imperial system of government and institutions and an ideology that had sustained that government system. As the Chinese groped for a new order, they had to endure decades of civil war. As the twentieth century advanced, the Chinese continued their quest to find institutions and ideology to replace what was discredited and outdated.

Japan, on the other hand, was a success story; it had not only shaken off the shackles of inequality, but had emerged from World War I and the peace conferences as an undisputed great power. It continued to move forward in all fields with amazing speed, and to close the technological gap between itself and the West. Politically, Japan moved toward greater democratization, following a trend that was also characteristic of the Western world in the post-World War I era. Japan's very success in modernization, however, brought in its wake little-understood problems which led it along the path of disaster in the 1930s.

WAR AND REVOLUTION IN CHINA

From Dynasty to Republic

After the humiliation of the 1900 Boxer fiasco, the moral authority of the Manchu empire was shattered, its hold on the people weakened. The imperial government, in a desperate attempt to win popular support, approved all sorts of proposals for change. A constitutional mission sent to Europe and the United States to study their government forms recommended the gradual introduction of parliamentary government. A new educational policy called for Western-style schools and a modern curriculum.

In spite of its eleventh-hour reform attempts, however, the dynasty was doomed, as new forces emerged to challenge a government that had outlived its usefulness. The merchants and industrialists in the port cities opposed the dying Manchu dynasty because the unequal treaties gave foreign products an unfair competitive edge over Chinese goods. Another group was the Western-educated students, who wanted rapid modernization and resented the reactionary court. Opponents of the dynasty organized for revolution abroad or in the foreign concession areas in Chinese cities, which were outside the jurisdiction of the Chinese government. China was ready for revolution. All it needed was a catalyst.

The anti-dynastic forces found a leader in Sun Yat-sen. Sun was born in 1866 of poor peasant parents near Canton in southern China. Thanks to an elder brother who had established a successful business in Hawaii, he was sent to school there and later studied medicine in Hong Kong, the British colony on China's southern coast. In his studies and travels, Sun became very impressed with the progress of the West and correspondingly disgusted with China's backwardness. He gradually turned to revolution, and after 1890 devoted himself to traveling, recruiting, and fund-raising to prepare for it.

Sun's ideology and the particular ways he proposed to put it into effect clearly displayed Western cultural influence. He formulated a program known as the Three People's Principles. These principles were, first, nationalism, which stressed the overthrow of the Manchus (who were a minority ethnic-cultural group in China) as well as the recovery of China's rights from the imperialists; second, democracy, under a liberal republic where the people would be sovereign; and, third, livelihood, a combination of industrial socialism and land reform to give land to the peasants.

In 1905, Sun organized a group of students, literati, and military officers into a political party that later adopted the name Kuomintang (the National People's party or Nationalist party, hereafter cited as KMT). Between 1906 and 1911, Sun and his KMT followers attempted ten unsuccessful uprisings to overthrow the Manchus. The eleventh occurred on October 10, 1911 (hence called the Double Tenth in China), at Wuhan, an important industrial center. The revolt spread quickly across central and southern China. Sun was on a fund-raising tour in the United States and quickly made his way back to China, arriving in Shanghai on December 25. Four days later, he was elected provisional president of the Chinese republic by provincial delegates meeting in Nanking.

Frightened and leaderless, the Manchus were not prepared to fight the revolutionaries. On February 12, 1912, the boy emperor abdicated the throne, and the ancient dynastic principle came to an end. China became the first republic in Asia, but Sun did not remain the president of the Chinese Republic. The post went to Yuan Shih-k'ai, an ambitious general who commanded the largest and most modern units of the Manchu army.

The Era of Warlordism

Ineffectiveness and frustration marked the first years of the republic. Most of Sun's followers were satisfied once the Manchus had been overthrown, and did little to fight for his other, little-understood, ideals. Yuan Shih-k'ai, not content with the title of president, proclaimed himself emperor in 1915; but the monarchical concept was now in disrepute and, faced with revolt, Yuan was forced to resign in humiliation.

The death of Yuan in 1916, shortly after his resignation, was the end of an effective central government in China, and chaos set in. The KMT remained an organization of politicians without political power. Force, now the main criterion for power in China, rested in the hands of local military leaders, or "warlords," who ruled parts of China alone or in coalition and who fought frequent wars with each other. Warlords came in all descriptions. Manchuria, an area as big as France and Germany combined, was ruled by a former bandit; Szechwan, another huge province, was for years the battleground of two men surnamed Liu, uncle and nephew; parts of northwestern China were ruled for years by Feng Yu-hsiang, a poorly educated son of a bricklayer who was in succession a Christian, a Communist, and a member of the KMT. During his Christian phase, warlord Feng reputedly baptized his soldiers with a firehose. Associating cleanliness with godliness, he also personally inspected their fingernails. The capital remained in Peking, but obtaining the presidency after Yuan's departure became a game of musical chairs, won by whatever group happened to control Peking and its environs at the time. The government at Peking controlled little of the countryside and relied mainly on foreign loans for revenue.

Between 1914 and 1918, Western nations were too preoccupied with the war in Europe to meddle further in China. As Great Britain's ally, Japan declared war against Germany in 1914, but the Japanese, for their own reasons, kept China out of the war until 1917. At the end of 1914, a Japanese force landed in Shantung and expelled the German garrison from this province in north China, which it proceeded to control. China did not participate in any fighting in World War I, but 700,000 Chinese laborers were sent to work in factories and mines in Europe and the Middle East.

World War I dealt drastic blows to European industries and trade in China and allowed native industries and trade to develop, relatively unhindered by competition. All aspects of the Chinese industrial sector grew—textiles, iron and steel, coal, flour mills, and modern banking. New industries and enterprises created new merchant and laboring classes in growing urban centers, where the new schools were also located and where a new intelligentsia was also emerging, all of whom were receptive to the calls of nationalism.

The Russian Revolution of 1917 and the U.S. role in the world war also profoundly influenced the Chinese nationalist movement. President Wilson's calls for national self-determination and abolition of secret diplomacy appealed to some Chinese intellectuals. The Communist revolution in Russia, with its promise of world revolution and its anti-imperialist ideology, made converts of others. Both stirred intellectual ferment in China, with far-reaching results.

Viewed as a period, the years between 1900 and 1918 brought both chaos and hope. Unrestrained by authority, all sorts of new theories were aired and experiments tried. Increasing numbers of young men, and even women, were attending modern schools or going to the West and Japan to study. They formed a new social class of intellectuals who both represented and demanded change. They were nationalistic and were determined to create a strong China that could break the shackles the imperialist nations had placed on it.

Intellectual Revolution: The May Fourth Movement

On May 4, 1919, students demonstrated in Peking to protest the awarding of Shantung to Japan at the Paris Peace Conference. This became known as the May Fourth Movement, a wide-ranging outburst of social and intellectual protest that had been fermenting for some time. This movement paved the way for the revival of the KMT and the rise of the Chinese Communist party (hereafter, CCP), founded in 1921. The center of the intellectual revolution was National Peking University, where a group of progressive faculty and bright students had set as their task the reexamination of old values and systems. Hu Shih, a professor of philosophy at Peking University, began a movement to replace the classical language, used only by scholars, with the vernacular form in order to facilitate mass literacy. Hu's language reform was so popular that by the 1920s the vernacular was used in school textbooks, newspapers, and popular journals. A new literature, influenced by Western trends, followed.

Immediately, the May Fourth demonstrations in Peking became a nationwide protest movement, as merchants and workers struck in sympathy with the student cause. They forced the government to refrain from signing the Paris Peace Treaty and to dismiss blatantly pro-Japanese officials; more significantly, they showed widespread nationalist and anti-imperialist feelings. The movement also inaugurated a new era of political and intellectual activism in China. Many of the young patriots of the May Fourth Movement joined and helped to revitalize the KMT, while others turned to the Soviet Union and Marxism.

Nationalist Triumph

Deeply disappointed with the warlords, the Western powers, and the incompetence of his loosely organized KMT, Sun Yat-sen turned for help where he could get it—to Soviet Russia. In return for aid in the form of Soviet advisors and arms, Sun agreed to admit the 300 members of the Chinese Communist party, as individuals, into the KMT.

After 1923, Soviet advisors assisted Sun to reorganize the KMT and win for it mass support. Sun sent his young ally Chiang Kai-shek to Russia for three months during 1923, where he learned training methods from the Red Army. From his trip, Chiang also learned to distrust Communist aims in China. On his

return from Moscow, Chiang established a military academy to train and indoctrinate officers for the KMT army.

Sun died of cancer in 1925 and was afterwards revered as Father of the
Republic. Chiang Kai-shek emerged the leader. Born of a gentry family and
trained in military academies in China and Japan as an army officer, he had
taken part in the 1911 revolution. As commandant of the Nationalist military
academy in Canton, he was responsible for creating the Nationalist army that
he commanded. In 1926, Chiang was elected commander-in-chief of the KMT
armies and began his Northern Expedition to unify China. By harnessing and
riding the wave of a popular nationalist movement, Chiang's army was able
within a few months to conquer all warlords as it marched north to the Yangtze
valley in central China. The KMT and CCP cooperated with each other so long
as both were still weak. Communist strategy was to help the KMT during the
Northern Expedition, and, in Stalin's phrase, to drop it like so many ''squeezed-
out lemons'' when victory was at hand. In 1927, however, after conquering
only half of China, Chiang squeezed first. Supported by the anti-Communist
faction of the KMT, Chiang expelled the CCP from the Kuomintang and killed

Sun Yat-sen (seated), father of the Chinese republic, with his lieutenant,
Chiang Kai-shek in 1924. (Camera Press)

as many of them as he could. He also expelled Soviet advisors from China. In Canton, the Communists started a last-ditch uprising in December 1927. After it failed, Communists were identified by the red dye marks on their necks left by their discarded red scarves and were summarily shot. The purified KMT resumed its march in 1928. In June, Peking surrendered, and in December the warlord of Manchuria declared his allegiance to the KMT government. With this act, all of China was nominally unified under the KMT.

For ten years between 1928 and 1937, Chiang Kai-shek's Nationalist government ruled China. Between 1928 and 1931, Chiang's enemies within the KMT rose either singly or in coalition to challenge his power. One by one he defeated them, and in the process slowly expanded the power of the central government, the most modern government China had known. The Nationalists made significant advances in broadening and enlarging the modern sector during this period. They built factories, created new universities for men and women, and improved the road and railroad networks. New legal codes based on European models gave women equality for the first time.

A high priority of the KMT during and after the Northern Expedition was the "rights recovery" movement, an effort to end the unequal treaties and restore sovereignty. In 1928, under pressure from the Nationalist government, all powers except Japan recognized China's tariff autonomy (Japan was compelled to follow later). For the first time since 1842, China was able to set its own tariff rates. After promulgating new civil and criminal codes based on Western models, China demanded an end to extraterritorial rights that nationals of some Western nations and Japan still enjoyed in China. While several small Western nations agreed to do so, Great Britain, the United States, France, Italy, and Japan refused. China then began to negotiate with these powers to provide for a gradual ending of extraterritoriality, which did not finally come until 1943. Most foreign concessions in Chinese cities were also restored to China during this period.

With its very existence threatened by Japanese aggression after 1931, China deferred pressing Western powers on two additional remaining items that compromised its sovereignty: the right of Western powers to station troops and naval vessels in certain designated areas of China, and the right of Western naval vessels to patrol Chinese rivers. The Chinese also reasoned that Western presence might deter Japan from becoming too aggressive, and hoped that Great Britain and the United States might come to China's aid against Japan. It is clear from this that the Chinese after the 1920s were much less fearful of Western European and U.S. imperialism, which was indeed in retreat, than of Japanese and Russian imperialism. To non-Marxist Chinese, tsarist Russian imperialism had been replaced by Soviet Marxist imperialism. It is clear from the foregoing that in general terms the KMT government had performed well in representing Chinese nationalistic aspirations and in recovering lost sovereign rights.

The Nationalist government failed decisively, however, to carry out Sun's principles of democracy and livelihood. Chiang's narrow military training limited his vision of China's needs and his choice of tactics to achieve reforms. The Nationalists made no real effort to train the people for the practice of democracy, which was an alien concept to the Chinese, and ruled in an authoritarian manner. No comprehensive plan was devised to redistribute the land and revitalize the farm economy. Even where the KMT enacted rent control laws, it made little effort to enforce them, so that most farmers remained poverty-stricken. On social issues, the KMT lost its revolutionary mission after attaining power. Chiang and his confederates feared the force of social and political change that any real economic reform would unleash. While they enacted reforms such as the new marriage laws and a law prohibiting foot-binding, enforcement was sporadic. Mass movements of the early 1920s, which had significantly helped to win popular support for the KMT, were now suppressed. Unwilling to tinker with the social fabric, the KMT let rising demands for reform pass it by.

The Resurgence of the CCP

Intra-KMT civil wars between 1928 and 1931 and major Japanese assaults against China after 1931 gave the CCP remnants a chance to rebuild. Those who had survived the 1927 purges had either gone into hiding in the cities or taken to the hills in southern China, where Mao Tse-tung collected about 10,000 escapees in the winter of 1927–28. Mao, the son of a rich peasant and later a library assistant at Peking University during the May Fourth Movement, was a founding member of the CCP in 1921 and organized peasants during the Northern Expedition. Now, with the assistance of Chu Teh, father of the Chinese Red Army, Mao and others developed a guerrilla army and a Soviet-style government.

Since the Communists were hiding out in an economically backward area that contained no industries and therefore had no proletariat, Mao abandoned traditional Marxist concepts of reliance on the urban proletariat as the core of the revolution and turned to the poor peasantry as his "revolutionary vanguard" in China. During the late 1920s and 1930s, Mao wrote extensively to reinterpret Marxism and to apply it to the underdeveloped agricultural parts of the world. Since most of the world was populated by peasants, Mao's modification of Marxian doctrine would eventually give Marxism an enormous impact around the globe.

In CCP-controlled areas, land was redistributed by force in the name of class warfare. In November 1931, a Chinese Soviet Republic was proclaimed at Juichin, a small town in the mountains of Kiangsi province, under Mao as president. It claimed control over 2.5 million people.

Between 1930 and 1933, KMT armies launched four successive "Extermination Campaigns" against the Communists. In each case, Mao's guerrilla tactics, peasant support, and other factors contributed to the defeat of the better-equipped and numerically superior KMT forces. The tide turned in Chiang's favor in 1934 during the fifth Extermination Campaign, mostly as a result of the strategy of economic blockade, carried out in conjunction with economic

Organizing Peasants for Revolution

During my recent visit to Hunan I conducted an investigation on the spot into the conditions. . . . I called together for fact finding conferences experienced peasants and comrades working for the peasant movement, listened attentively to their reports, and collected a lot of material. . . .

All kinds of arguments against the peasant movement must be speedily set right. The erroneous measures taken by the revolutionary authorities concerning the peasant movement must be speedily changed. Only thus can any good be done for the future of the revolution. For the rise of the present peasant movement is a colossal event. In a very short time, in China's central, southern, and northern provinces, several hundred million peasants will rise like a tornado or tempest, a force so extraordinarily swift and violent that no power, however great, will be able to suppress it. They will break all trammels that now bind them and rush forward along the road to liberation. They will send all imperialists, warlords, corrupt officials, local bullies, and bad gentry to their graves.*

Mao Tse-tung contributed to the development of Marxism-Leninism by recognizing the importance of peasants as a potentially important revolution, ry force in China, and, by implication, in non-Western, nonindustrial parts of the world. He was sent to his native province, Hunan, in 1925, to investigate the conditions of the peasants there, and this report, partly reproduced above, was the result.

*From "Report on an Investigation of the Hunan Peasant Movement" by Mao Tse-tung (Zedong), quoted in William T. DeBary, ed, *Sources of Chinese Tradition*. Copyright © 1960 by Columbia University Press. Reprinted by permission.

reforms for the peasants in the disputed areas. Defeat forced the CCP to flee. About 100,000 men and women of the CCP army and government broke through the blockading army and began a 6,000-mile march from southern China to the northwest, while it constantly fought off pursuing KMT forces.

The legendary Long March took 370 days to complete. Of the 100,000 who started, about 20,000 made it to the finish, with Mao Tse-tung in control and his power consolidated. Most of the leaders survived. In 1936, the Communists established their headquarters in Yenan in the remote and poor hinterland area in northern China, and there they remained until after the end of World War II. The main advantage of Yenan was its location, far from Chiang's army and bases. Chiang had now to rely on the unreliable troops of his Manchurian warlord ally to continue the fight against the Communists.

JAPAN IN THE 1920s

While China was preoccupied with domestic struggles, Japan consolidated its position as a great power at the Paris Peace Conference as one of the Big Five. It won former German rights in Shantung province and received German islands in the North Pacific as mandates. In the newly formed League of Nations, Japan was the equal of Great Britain, France, and Italy, and at the Washington Naval Conference it had achieved naval supremacy in Asia.

Liberal Democracy Gains Ground

Developments in Japan after World War I reflected the intellectual, social, and economic changes within the nation and worldwide. Within Japan a new generation had come to maturity since the Meiji Restoration that was better acquainted with the outside world and more confident than its predecessors. The tremendous industrial and commercial expansion that took place in Japan during the war had made the business classes more important in Japanese life. As Japanese businesses expanded in Asia after the war, they offered the prospect of commercial growth unaccompanied by force of arms. The overwhelming victory of democratic Western powers in World War I and the defeat of the least democratic ones also convinced many Japanese of the merits of democratic government.

The ascendancy of liberal and democratic tendencies was evident in many ways. In 1926, the Diet enfranchised all males over twenty-five, increasing the size of the electorate from three to over twelve million. Another bill reduced the hereditary component of the House of Peers. The Japanese began to accept government by the political party that controlled a majority of votes in the lower house. Two important political parties emerged, providing considerable stability. In addition, many small political parties and groups were allowed to operate as long as they did not advocate changing the "national polity" or abolishing private property.

The Diet also enacted social legislation favorable to labor. It abolished an earlier law that restricted labor unions, and legalized union support of nonrevolutionary socialist movements. A revised Factory Law, a National Health Insurance Law, and a Labor Disputes Mediation Law improved the life of the worker. As a result, a variety of political and social organizations mushroomed that campaigned for further reforms, including women's rights.

In foreign policy, internationalism and international cooperation gained at the expense of militarism. At the Washington Conference in 1921, Japan joined the signing of a Naval Limitation Treaty and agreed to return many of its privileges in Shantung to China. The government reduced the military share of the budget from 42 percent in 1922 to 28 percent in 1928; four divisions were cut out of the army.

Underlying Weaknesses in Japanese Democracy

The progress toward democracy and liberalism in the postwar years was not, however, built upon firm foundations. Thus, when the world Depression hit Japan in 1930, the conditions it created easily undermined many of the progressive trends of the previous decade, and finally led to the fall of the democratic experiment in the 1930s. Because of its newness, Japanese democratic constitutional government was not deeply rooted. Despite its democratic trappings in the 1920s, the Japanese political system was closer to that of pre-Weimar Germany than to those of Great Britain and the United States. With its deeply rooted autocratic traditions, its traditional respect for the military, and its veneration of the imperial institution, Japanese society was more akin to that of the German Empire. The Meiji Constitution was closely modeled on that of imperial Germany.

Despite several very able men at the helm, most Japanese citizens, like many in Germany and Italy at this time, had little faith in or respect for elected party governments. The mud-slinging and often corrupt election campaigns did nothing to dispel the image of politicians as venal. The *zaibatsu,* or large conglomerates, contributed heavily to the political parties that they favored, and after an election, the winning party returned the favor by awarding contracts to the *zaibatsu* that had supported it. Thus governments came to be called the "Mitsui cabinet" or the "Mitsubishi cabinet." Amidst charges of unethical conduct, antidemocratic forces that demanded a form of government that was above parties and other interest groups grew in appeal to disenchanted citizens. Corruption under party governments came under slashing attack from both the Left and the Right after the onset of the Depression, when popular suffering made such behavior seem more blatantly immoral.

Even before the Great Depression changed the political and economic climate, and even while party governments were in control, antidemocratic forces were at work which would later bring down the shallowly rooted liberal experiment. Some legislation reflected the strength of traditional authoritarian tendencies, even in an era of liberalism. An example of this was the Peace Preservation Law of 1925, amended in 1928, which stipulated stiff penalties for membership in the Communist party, and for activities considered subversive.

A more important sign of danger for Japanese democracy was the renewed tilt towards militarism and a military solution to problems. Within and outside of the armed forces, ultranationalists willing to use private force to gain their ends became glamorous. For example, in 1921, Prime Minister Hara, a noted believer in constitutional government, was assassinated by an ultranationalist. In 1927, ultranationalist junior officers of the Japanese army in Manchuria blew up a train to assassinate the Chinese warlord of that region for fear that he would not be subservient enough to Japanese interests in the future. In the Manchurian case, the military blocked an inquiry that might have resulted in punishment of the guilty, and caused the fall of the government that demanded it. Even when fanatical assassins were brought to justice, ordinary citizens increasingly sympathized with them as pure-hearted patriots opposed to venal politicians.

The Depression

The Depression of 1930 marked the watershed between the liberal decade of the 1920s and the militarism of the 1930s. Since a domestic depression in 1926, the Japanese economy had been on shaky ground. When the global Depression hit Japan in early 1930, it touched off a major catastrophe. The value of exports dropped 50 percent from 1929 to 1931; workers' real income dropped by about a third in the same period, and unemployment rose to three million. The hardest hit, however, were the farmers, who could not recover production costs despite a bumper crop in 1931. This was followed by widespread crop failures in 1932, which brought conditions of near-starvation in several areas. Some tenants and poor farmers, who had few reserves in the best of times, were reduced to selling their daughters.

The politicians, the party government, and the *zaibatsu,* who composed the "parliamentary coalition," were blamed for the Depression, despite the fact that the party government acted effectively to counter it. Japan went off the gold standard in December 1931, which led to a boom in exports. Japan was thus the first major industrial nation to recover from the Depression, but the recovery did not benefit the parties and democratic government. The Depression also called into question the validity of the postwar international economic order, which now lay in ruins. As nations erected protectionist tariff walls, Japanese worried about their raw material and market needs in the future. The failure of the postwar international economy caused Japanese also to doubt the international political order led by Western democratic nations. The rise of Nazism in Germany further discredited democratic forces in Japan and cast doubts on its parliamentary government, for Germany had been Japan's constitutional model and was one of the Western nations the Japanese admired most.

Amidst the rough and tumble of political life and economic ups and downs, the armed forces alone retained an untarnished image. Those who opposed democracy and advocated a greater role for the army and navy in government argued that the military best expressed the will of the emperor and the interest of the people. They further argued that military expansion would assure steady supplies of raw materials and markets for Japanese manufactured products. This was the background that permitted the Japanese army to act independently of civilian authorities in the 1930s and finally to topple them.

SUMMARY

China and Japan during this period were a study in contrasts. The Chinese revolution of 1911 overturned a discredited dynasty, but the Republic that replaced the Manchus was even less capable of preserving Chinese independence than its predecessor. Warlords struggled against each other and signed away Chinese rights to Japanese governments, who replaced Europeans as the primary imperialist nation against China. Sun Yat-sen, father of the Chinese Republic, eventually turned to the Soviet Union to revitalize his political party, the Kuomintang. Shortly after his death, Sun's political heir, Chiang Kai-shek, led a military expedition that defeated the warlords and gave China its first effective and modernizing government in the twentieth century. Chiang's Nationalist government strove with success to realize Chinese nationalism and to recover rights lost to Western imperialists, but it neglected Sun's other principles, livelihood and democracy. Thus the Chinese Communists, who promised a drastic social and economic revolution, gained support which the superior military force of the KMT could not eradicate.

World War I enhanced Japan's international stature and boosted its industries and economy. Japan emerged from the war as the preeminent imperial power in East Asia. World trends that favored democratic and egalitarian political and social forces in the 1920s were also strong in Japan in the same period, evidenced by reforms that gave universal manhood suffrage, greater political freedoms, and social betterment. However, the shallowly rooted democratic forces were fatally undermined by the Depression, which aided the triumph of militarism.

SUGGESTED SOURCES

Bosse, Malcolm, *Warlord* (1983). A historical novel set in China in the 1920s, where Nationalists, Communists, Soviets, White Russians, and others intrigued to secure their goals.*

Duus, Peter, *Party Rivalry and Political Change in Taisho Japan* (1968). A study of Japan's experiment with democracy.

McKenna, Richard, *The Sand Pebbles* (1964). A novel set in the mid-1920s that pits American sailors who patrol the Yangtze River against each other and against Chinese. (Also a film.)

Pa Chin, *Family* (1972). A translation of a novel first published in China in 1931 that deals with the conflict between forces of tradition and those of change.*

Snow, Edgar, *Red Star Over China*, rev. ed. (1978). Snow was the first Western journalist to travel to Communist-held territory in China in the 1930s. This book is his lively account of that experience.*

Wilson, Dick, *The Long March, 1935* (1982). An account of the Chinese Communist Long March that is both scholarly and good reading.*

*Paperback available.

16

Nationalist Struggles in India and Southeast Asia

Although the movement for self-government in India and Southeast Asia had its roots in an earlier era, World War I and the years that followed accelerated its development. Before 1914, most nationalist movements of the area merely sought participation in the colonial government, but by the late 1920s many would be satisfied only with independence.

INDIA

India during World War I

India remained definitely loyal to Great Britain throughout World War I. Articulate and thoughtful Indians realized that Great Britain and its allies were more liberal and democratic than the Central Powers. The Indian press was nearly unanimous in supporting the British war effort and in expressing shock at Germany's invasion of neutral Belgium. In any case, India and even self-governing dominions such as Canada had no choice in the matter of declaration of war, because George V, as king and emperor, declared war on behalf of the entire British Empire. India contributed substantially to the Allied war cause: 800,000 soldiers went to Europe and the Middle East, 500,000 noncombatant laborers worked in factories and mines in Europe, and many Indians made monetary contributions and war loans. In return, Great Britain appointed more Indians to high government positions, and an Indian delegation was allowed to participate in postwar peace negotiations.

In August 1917, the British government for the first time proclaimed its goal to be self-government for India, to be granted in stages. Toward its eventual realization, the British Parliament passed the Government of India Act in 1919. By this act, an electorate of middle-class voters was permitted to elect representatives to provincial assemblies, where the party with a majority formed a government that controlled a number of departments of the provincial administration. However, public security and the provincial budget remained under the control of the British-appointed governor. This system of sharing power in the provinces between the British and the Indians was called dyarchy. In the central government, a British-appointed viceroy retained supreme power and appointed a cabinet of Britons and Indians to assist him in the administration. The national assembly of elected Indian representatives could only advise the viceroy. At the insistence of Muslims, separate electorates, whereby Muslims and Hindus elected their separate representatives, were continued. The act of 1919 was intended to remain in effect for ten years, after which there would be evaluation for changes. Indian moderates welcomed these reforms, but radicals denounced them as inadequate.

In 1918, a government commission recommended legislation to empower provincial governments to jail suspected political subversives without trial and to try political cases without jury. When the recommendations were enacted into law, known as the Rowlatt Act, Indian nationalists were outraged. The Congress party launched public meetings to protest this law. The protests turned violent in Punjab province, where a mob murdered four Europeans in Amritsar. Shortly after that, about 10,000 people, without official permission, gathered in a large enclosed square in that city for a meeting. Without warning, the British commanding general in the city ordered troops to fire upon the assembled crowd. The official estimate of casualties was 379 killed and over 1,200 wounded. The Amritsar Massacre crystalized anti-British feelings and became a rallying point for the Indian independence movement.

The Rise of Gandhi

Mohandas K. Gandhi was commonly called Mahatma ("Great Soul" or "Holy One") by his followers. He was born in 1869 of prosperous and devout Hindu parents, and was educated in law in London, where he also studied the New Testament and the works of Tolstoy and Thoreau. After a brief and unsuccessful attempt to practice law in India, he took his family to South Africa to represent some Indian clients. He quickly gained a reputation there as the champion of Indian immigrant workers against white South African bigotry and discrimination. He perfected techniques of nonviolent protest demonstrations, and called his nonviolent movement *Satyagraha* (truth force). He taught his followers the tactics of noncooperation to protest unjust laws. Gandhi returned to India in 1915 and organized an ambulance corps for noncombatant duty to assist the British war effort.

The immediate postwar years were disturbed ones in India. There were severe economic problems associated with demobilization. There was also widespread dissatisfaction with the slow pace of political reform, and outrage over the Rowlatt Act and the Amritsar Massacre. Muslims were, in addition, resentful about the fate of the Ottoman Empire and the humiliating treatment of Muslims in the Middle East by the Allies at the Paris Peace Conference.

A New Weapon in the Struggle for Freedom

News was received that the Rowlatt Bill had been published as an Act. That night I fell asleep while thinking over the question. Towards the small hours of the morning I woke up somewhat earlier than usual. I was still in that twilight condition between sleep and consciousness when suddenly the idea broke upon me—it was as if in a dream. Early in the morning I related the whole story to Rajagopalachari [a Congress leader].

> The idea came to me last night in a dream that we should call upon the country to observe a general hartal. Satyagraha is a process of self-purification, and ours is a sacred fight, and it seems to me to be the fitness of things that it should be commenced with an act of self-purification. Let all the people of India, therefore, suspend their business on that day and observe the day as one of fasting and prayer. The Musalmans [Muslims] may not fast for more than one day; so the duration of the fast should be 24 hours. . . .

Rajagopalachari was at once taken up with my suggestion. Other friends too welcomed it. . . . I drafted a brief appeal. The date of the hartal was first fixed on the 30th March 1919, but was subsequently changed to 6th April. . . . The whole of India from one end to the other, towns as well as villages, observed a complete hartal on that day. It was a most wonderful experience.*

Mohandas K. Gandhi (1869–1948) became a leader of the Indian National Congress during World War I. He was responsible for changing its direction into a mass movement by such actions as the hartal _described above. A_ hartal _is a strike with a moral purpose, accompanied by fasting. Gandhi first employed it as a protest against the British-imposed Rowlatt Act, which cracked down on Indian protests._

*From _The Story of My Experiments with Truth_ by Mohandas K. Gandhi. Copyright © 1927 by Viking Penguin Company.

It was at this critical juncture of the Indian nationalist movement that Gandhi entered the struggle for independence. His ideas were simple. He argued that since fewer than 200,000 Britons ruled 400 million Indians, the maintenance of British authority had to be based on Indian cooperation. Consequently, if Indians withdrew their cooperation, British rule could not continue. Gandhi also realized that the nationalist movement, previously mostly middle-class, must be broadened to include the masses. Toward this end, he visited villages throughout India, dressed in simple homespun garb, where he identified with the poor, preached his message in simple terms, and taught the goal of national unity and the tactics of nonviolence to the peasants. Gandhi's understanding of peasant mentality was his greatest strength, and he broadened the nationalist movement into one for the masses. He persuaded the Indian National Congress to lower its membership dues to a nominal sum to attract poor members, and to publish its messages in Indian languages as well as in English. Gandhi also attempted to narrow the gap that divided Hindus from Muslims by such acts as endorsing Indian Muslim demands for lenient treatment of the Ottoman dynasty, but he opposed separate electorates.

Gandhi was not only interested in driving out the British. He also crusaded in favor of social reform to rid Hindu society of customs and usages that oppressed and abused women and certain social classes. He spoke eloquently in opposition to child marriage for girls, the prohibition against widow remarriage, and, above all, the oppression of the untouchables. He spoke of independence as something one must deserve, and implied that Hindus did not deserve self-rule when they oppressed whole categories of their own people. He renamed the outcastes, or untouchables, *Harijans,* which means "children of god," to signify their common humanity with other Indians. He founded a journal named *The Harijan,* where his writings were published, and often insisted that he be quartered in the untouchable part of a town that he was visiting. In his *ashram,* or retreat, he made sure that all shared in doing unpleasant work that was otherwise the lot of the untouchable. The name *Harijan* is still widely used today.

Gandhi mobilized the masses in repeated *Satyagraha* movements against the British. He organized them in peaceful demonstrations and strikes and told them to meet police brutality by "offering the other cheek." Thus, when Indians rioted during demonstrations, a disappointed Gandhi would call off his *Satyagraha,* and go on a fast to atone for the violence. Some Indians who did not care about the means used so long as they achieved their desired end blamed Gandhi's moral scruples for delaying the attainment of Indian independence. He also fasted as a means to persuade his British adversaries and his Indian followers to see the error of their ways and to change as a result of their own moral awakening.

Gandhi's Salt March of 1930 was a good example of his method of protest. In India, the British government had a monopoly on the manufacture and sale of salt and taxed it for revenue. Gandhi chose to protest the salt tax as a burden to the poor and as a symbol of those British laws that violated Indian civil rights. In March 1930, Gandhi led seventy-eight followers on a "Great Salt March." In a well-publicized media event, they slowly walked 200 miles to the seacoast. Daily, thousands turned out to cheer them on, and some joined the march. When he reached the coast, Gandhi waded into the water and drew out a pitcherful, which he boiled to extract the salt. In so doing, he defied the salt monopoly and the salt tax law. Indians responded with a general strike and with *Swadeshi,* which entailed the boycott of British manufactured goods, especially British woven cotton textiles, and their replacement with Indian home-

A protest march organized by the Indian National Congress against the British in 1928. (BBC Hulton/The Bettmann Archive)

spun cotton cloths. The boycott put many British laborers out of work, thus placing additional pressure on the British government. Gandhi and 60,000 of his supporters were arrested, but the civil disobedience campaign persisted. Finally the government capitulated. Gandhi and his supporters were released from jail, the salt tax was reduced, and some restrictive laws were rescinded.

The campaign showed Gandhi at his most brilliant. As a humanitarian, he abhorred violence, and, as a political realist, he understood that his cause would most benefit by winning the sympathy of world public opinion. He further understood that democratic Great Britain was sensitive to public opinion and that the British government could be forced to make concessions in response to public pressure.

In many ways, Gandhi was a traditionalist. He loved Hindu customs and dreamed of an independent India true to its ancient heritage, one that turned its back on modern technology and industrial society. Gandhi advocated reviving cottage industries not only to support the *Swadeshi* movement, but also for their intrinsic economic and social value. For several hours nearly every day, he spun and wove his own cloth, which he wore exclusively after he gave up wearing Western-style clothing. Millions of Indians, of high station and low, also took up the weaving of homespun cloth, so that the spinning wheel came to symbolize the Indian nationalist movement. At his insistence, the Congress required its members to spend a portion of their day working at the handloom, to the annoyance of some.

Gandhi and Nehru in 1938: Both had discarded Western clothes in favor of Indian garb, Gandhi for homespuns. (Nehru Memorial Library)

The Hindu-Muslim Communal Problem

Gandhi advocated a policy of generosity toward Muslims. He welcomed all, especially the Muslims, to join the Indian National Congress, which he sought to make into a body that represented all Indian nationalists. Thus he disapproved of separate electorates for Muslims or any other minority. Instead, he suggested that Muslims should be given a guaranteed number of representatives on the Congress ticket. In this he failed, however, for several reasons. One was that militant Hindus in the Congress smelled victory in elections and refused to set aside a percentage of seats for Muslim representatives. The other was that the Muslims were now largely represented by the All India Muslim League. League leaders, most of whom were Western-trained lawyers, objected to Gandhi's nonconstitutional methods of protest and did not share his rejection of Western values. Moreover, the League relied on separate electorates to protect Muslim rights. Thus any Muslim who joined the Congress was not recognized as a representative of the Muslim community.

As a result, in the rancor that surfaced in the post-1919 election campaigns and competition for power, the relative communal peace of the war years quickly evaporated. Congress Hindus sought to capture and hold the power their numbers guaranteed to them. On the other hand, Muslims feared the potential tyranny of Hindu majority rule and sought safeguards for their rights in any negotiations for a settlement.

From the late 1920s on, Great Britain stepped up the timetable for Indian independence in response to Indian demands. However, no proposal the British made was acceptable to both the Congress and the League, and neither accepted the other's suggested solutions. Whatever the specific issue at hand, both Hindus and Muslims looked at it in terms of who would dominate an independent India and who would be dominated. Mutual hatred between Hindus and Muslims (Muslim fear of Hindu numbers and Hindu fear of possible new Muslim inroads by conversion) came to outweigh hatred for the foreign ruler. In the final analysis, the inability of Indians to solve their communal problem delayed the process of attaining self-government.

The India Act of 1935

After several years of intensive consultations with the representatives of different interests, the British government concluded that India should become a federation of princely states and self-governing provinces. The Government of India Act of 1935 enlarged the electorate to 18 percent of the population, which would elect representatives to both provincial and federal legislatures. In each province, the party with a majority of representatives would form the government, which was to be entirely self-governing. The British-appointed governor became largely a figurehead, except in emergencies, when he could veto actions by the elected government. At the federal level, the British-appointed viceroy was advised by an Executive Council chosen from the elected members of the federal legislature. He also had the power of veto and emergency powers. At the Muslim League's insistence, separate electorates were retained for Muslims. In addition, the India Act provided that other minorities and special interest groups such as Christians, untouchables, women, Europeans, laborers, and landlords could also have their own representatives in every assembly, in reserved seats through a quota system. The more than five hundred princely states were also given representation in the federal legislature, according to their size and population. This act attempted to ensure that all Indians received representation and had a voice in the government. The federal form of government, in which each province had broad rights, was an attempt to satisfy Muslim demands that they should rule themselves in areas where they had a majority.

While the Indian National Congress criticized portions of the act as either insufficient or reactionary, it nevertheless set about to capture as much power as possible in the elections the act mandated. Although the Muslim League won majorities in the few Muslim-dominated provinces in the provincial elections of 1936, the Congress captured a majority in all the remaining provinces. Greatly encouraged by its effective organization and vote-getting power, Congress leader Jawaharlal Nehru bragged: "There are only two parties in the country—the Congress and the British." Such statements only aggravated the fears of Muslims over their fate in a Hindu-dominated India. The India Act separated Burma from India. The Burmese, however, received self-government comparable to that of Indians, also in 1935.

NATIONALIST MOVEMENTS IN SOUTHEAST ASIA

In the Dutch East Indies, a Muslim-rooted nationalist movement had been active since the early twentieth century; the Dutch government had made only slow progress in accommodation to it. The Dutch-created People's Council, which began in 1918, was a mere debating society compared with the legislatures of the same period in British India. Such halfhearted measures were condemned as absolutely inadequate by the Indonesian Communist party, the first established in Southeast Asia, and by nationalists led by Sukarno; these forces, however, were in the political wilderness until the outbreak of World War II.

In Indochina, French tactics of combining direct and indirect rule, the cultivation of the native elite, and local ethnic diversity all retarded the nationalist movement. Among all Indochinese, the Vietnamese offered the greatest resistance to French rule. The failure of moderate Vietnamese nationalists to persuade the French to make concessions opened the way for the more extreme elements. Ho Chi Minh emerged during the interwar years as the most prominent nationalist leader. He went to France as a young man and helped to organize the French Communist party there after World War I. In 1925, he surfaced in Canton, where he worked for Soviet advisors who were then helping the KMT in China. It was not until 1930 that he drew together various dissident Vietnamese groups in Hong Kong and formed the Communist party of Indochina. In that same year, French authorities crushed all peasant and nationalist revolts in Vietnam. The repression that followed ruled out any further Communist activities until World War II.

In the Philippines, in contrast, a bicameral legislature of elected representatives had taken over lawmaking since 1916. Only the governor-general, the vice-governors, and the judges of the supreme court were still appointed from Washington. In 1919, President Wilson promised complete independence, but it took the Depression of 1930 to hasten its realization.

Since the Philippines was a U.S. possession, both Filipino products (notably sugar, tobacco, and coconut oil) and Filipino immigrants could freely enter the United States. During the Depression, U.S. industry, in particular the sugar industry, and U.S. labor unions agitated in favor of granting independence to the Philippines so that its cheap products and labor could be shut out of the United States. Others argued that the defense of the islands would be a military liability to the United States. The U.S. Congress passed the Tydings-McDuffie Act in 1934, whereby the Philippines immediately became fully self-governing, except for control of its foreign policy by Washington for ten years. Complete independence was promised for July 4, 1944.

SUMMARY

European imperialism was on the retreat and nationalism was on the rise throughout the colonial world in South and Southeast Asia between the two world wars. As before, India led the way. As a result of Indian contributions in World War I, Britain agreed to grant India self-government, which it proceeded to implement in the acts of 1919 and 1935. Sharp disagreements emerged, however, over the timing and over how Hindus and Muslims would share power in a self-governing India. Led by Mahatma Gandhi, who applied tactics of non-violent protest he had earlier developed in South Africa to the Indian independence struggle, the Congress developed grass-roots support, but increasingly represented Hindu aspirations. The prospect of a Hindu-dominated self-governing India led Muslims to cling to separate electorates and to follow the All India Muslim League and its president, M. A. Jinnah, as their champions. In elections held in accordance with the India Act of 1935, the Congress won majorities in Hindu-populated states and the League in Muslim ones.

By comparison, the Dutch East Indies was far behind in the progress of its nationalist struggles. In Indochina, likewise, French authoritarian rule continued supreme, after successfully suppressing peasant revolts in 1930. In the same year, however, Ho Chi Minh organized the Indochinese Communist party in exile. The U.S.-ruled Philippines was the only colony in Southeast Asia where there was significant progress toward independence, as U.S. policy progressively associated Filipinos in the process of self-government. In 1934, the U.S. Congress passed an act that immediately granted autonomy to the Philippines, with full independence to follow in ten years.

SUGGESTED SOURCES

Bolitho, Hector, *Jinnah: Creator of Pakistan* (1982). A good, readable biography of the founder of Pakistan and champion of Muslim rights.

Bondurant, Joan V., *Conquest of Violence: The Gandhian Philosophy of Conflict*, new rev. ed. (1988). Good book on Gandhi's political thought and philosophy.*

Embree, Ainslie T., *India's Search for National Identity* (1981). A brief, readable, and objective introduction.*

Fischer, Louis, *Gandhi* (1983). A concise biography, full of human interest.*

Gandhi (1982). A sympathetic film portraying the powerful impact of the great Indian leader.

Khanh, Huynh Kim, *Vietnamese Communism, 1925-1945* (1986). A description of the origins and development of Vietnamese communism and the role of the party in the anticolonial struggle.*

Lewis, Martin Deming, ed., *The British in India: Imperialism or Trusteeship?* (1962). A collection of essays in the Heath series that presents different points of view on the question.*

Nehru, Jawaharlal, *The Discovery of India* (1946). The first prime minister of independent India wrote this book while in a British jail for his part in his country's nationalist struggle. His love for India and its culture is very movingly demonstrated.

*Paperback available.

17

Anticolonialism in the Middle East and Africa

As the anticolonial struggle swept India in the period between the wars, nationalists were also intensifying their efforts in the Middle East and Africa. The strength and extent of these nationalist movements differed widely from area to area. The Middle East was often in a state of turmoil, as Arab nationalists shifted their activity from resisting the Ottomans to opposing British and French control, and Jews attempted to establish a homeland in Palestine. Even those states that were nominally independent, such as Iran and Turkey, witnessed the stirring of a new nationalism. In both nations, dynamic leaders emerged who sought modernization and Westernization precisely in order to repel Western domination and to make their homelands independent in fact as well as in name. African nationalist movements developed later in the century than did their Asian counterparts. Nevertheless, the interwar period witnessed the beginning of anti-Western independence movements throughout the continent.

NATIONALIST UNREST IN THE MIDDLE EAST

Allied political considerations during World War I aided nationalist movements throughout the Middle East. The British were generally willing to assist Arab nationalism, not because they necessarily believed in its aims, but because they hoped that an Arab revolt would weaken Ottoman forces and thus help to protect the Suez Canal. Kitchener, as British high commissioner in Egypt and later secretary of war, discussed the possibility of Arab independence with Abdullah, a son of Sherif Husayn (sherif is a title indicating both a religious and political leader). Sherif Husayn was the ruler of the Muslim holy city of Mecca. To implement their war and postwar plans, the British made three agreements involving the Middle East that sowed the seeds for a struggle—the Arab-Israeli conflict—that has yet to be resolved.

The Middle East in the Interwar Years

Conflicting Wartime Agreements

The first wartime agreement was the secret correspondence (1915–16) between Henry McMahon, the British high commissioner in Egypt, and Sherif Husayn, acting in the self-appointed role of champion of Arab independence. The British promised to support an independent Arab nation after the war in return for Arab support during the war. The negotiations were protracted because of the conflict over the boundaries for the proposed Arab nation. Husayn originally demanded all of the Arab Middle East south of Turkey, including most of the Arabian peninsula. The British countered that they had interests in Iraq and that the French had religious and economic interests in the territory that is to-day Lebanon. While pointing out that all the territory was clearly Arab, Husayn finally agreed to compromise on Iraq and Lebanon. As a result, the Arabs raised the standard of revolt against the Ottoman Empire and fought on the Allied side, believing that after the war they would receive independence.

However, the British had made a second commitment, which in parts con-tradicted their agreement with Husayn. In the Sykes-Picot Agreement (1916), the British and the French agreed to divide the Ottoman Empire among European nations. The Anatolian peninsula was to be partitioned, and the French were to secure Lebanon and Syria, while the British were to receive

Iraq and Palestine and a sphere of influence over the Arabian peninsula. The British probably did not demand direct control over what is today Saudi Arabia because in 1916 the vast petroleum reserves in that nation had not yet been discovered. Because both European terms and Ottoman administrative divisions for these areas were used in both agreements, after the war there was some confusion and argument over the exact terms and borders.

The Balfour Declaration of November 1917 was the third British statement regarding the Middle East. To understand this pronouncement it is necessary to discuss briefly the Zionist movement, which was fervently supported by some Jews in Europe and the United States. The Zionists sought to establish a Jewish state in Palestine. Theodor Herzl, a Hungarian journalist and Zionist leader, had advocated in his book *Der Judenstaat* (The Jewish State) that Jews have a nation of their own in order to avoid anti-Semitism (anti-Jewish attitudes and behavior), which he believed was an evil inherent in Western civilization. The Dreyfus case in France and the pogroms in Poland and Russia had convinced Herzl and other Jewish leaders that Jews needed a state of their own. Herzl favored accepting any territory; parts of Argentina and Uganda were even suggested. However, Chaim Weizmann, a chemist of Polish origin, argued that Palestine, the location of the ancient Jewish state, was the only place in which the Zionists could realize their aspirations. In 1897, at the First Zionist Congress, Zionists pledged to work for the creation of a Jewish state in Palestine.

In November 1917, British Foreign Secretary, Arthur Balfour, wrote to a prominent British Zionist, Lord Rothschild, publicly stating British support for "the establishment in Palestine of a national home for the Jewish people." Balfour also stated that "nothing shall be done which may prejudice" the rights of the "non-Jewish" communities (the Arab majority) in Palestine or the rights of Jews in other nations. In such a manner, the British hoped to assuage those Jews, particularly in Great Britain, who opposed the Zionist idea of creating a Jewish state because they feared the existence of such a state would only increase anti-Semitism. Prime Minister David Lloyd George favored the Balfour Declaration because he wanted more support for the war effort. Zionists hailed the Balfour Declaration as a major step toward the realization of their dream. Although Balfour had not promised that Great Britain would support an independent Jewish state in Palestine, many Jews and non-Jews believed that an independent Jewish state would eventually be established.

Arab leaders promptly condemned the Balfour Declaration and vowed to oppose the creation of a Jewish state in Palestine, where about 90 percent of the population was composed of Arabs living in rural villages. Many Westerners who knew little of the area concluded—on the basis of the Balfour Declaration, which had referred only to the "non-Jewish population"—that only a few nomads lived in what was otherwise a sparsely populated territory. Consequently, many Westerners failed to recognize that if Jewish settlements were supported, another group, the Palestinians, might well lose their homeland. This laid the foundation for the Arab-Israeli conflict.

A Vision of Zion

In the winter of 1918 the American Jewish Congress held its first convention in Philadelphia. The main purpose was the formulation of a program (to be presented at the Peace Conference in Versailles) for the safeguarding of the civil rights of the Jews in Europe. To my astonishment . . . I was chosen to be one of the delegates from Milwaukee. It was a marvelously stimulating experience; I can still remember how proud I was to have been chosen to represent my own community and what it was like sitting with the rest of the delegation in the overheated train on our way to Philadelphia. I was (as always in that period) the youngest in the group and, in a way, everyone pampered me—except when it came to giving me assignments. Today when journalists ask me when my political career actually began, my mind always flashes back to that convention, to the smoke-filled hall in a Philadelphia hotel where I sat for hours listening, completely absorbed, to the details of the program being thrashed out, to the excitement of the debates and of being able to cast my own vote.*

In her autobiography, Golda Meir remembered the exciting times in her early twenties when she had just entered her political career as an ardent supporter of the Zionist movement for an independent Jewish state. She went on to become Prime Minister of Israel.

*From *My Life* by Golda Meir. The Putnam Publishing Group. Copyright © 1975 by Golda Meir.

The contradictions inherent in the three agreements became clear at the Paris Peace Conference. Sherif Husayn's son Faysal, Weizmann, and a host of other nationalist leaders appeared in Paris with their documents. Their hopes for national self-determination had been fueled by Wilson's Fourteen Points and declarations favoring self-determination. Although a champion of self-determination, Wilson was willing to back European interests in the Middle East instead of Arab aspirations in order to secure Allied support for the League of Nations and other parts of his program. As a result, the British and the French were able to implement their territorial ambitions in the Middle East. Under the terms agreed on at the San Remo Conference in 1920, the British got mandated control over Iraq and Palestine, including what is today Jordan, and the French got mandates over Syria and Lebanon. When it became clear that the Arabs were not to receive independence, one Arab leader remarked, "Independence is never given, it is taken." In fact, several decades were to pass before Arab national aspirations were realized.

Postwar Developments

Following the Paris conference, France immediately moved troops into Syria and Lebanon. In the last days of the war, the populace in Syria had proclaimed Faysal the king of the newly independent Arab nation. However, in the face of superior French military force, Faysal was forced to flee from Syria, although the Syrian Arabs never accepted the French occupation and continued to fight against it. In Lebanon, the French created a more autonomous government by relying heavily on the Maronite Christian Lebanese, who were about half the total population. They also enlarged the nation by including within its boundaries several predominantly Muslim areas that had previously been under Syrian domination. By relying on one religious group, the French helped to intensify religious differences in Lebanon that persisted into the 1980s.

Meanwhile, Great Britain proceeded with its own arrangements. The British attempted to provide a facade of independence in Iraq by crowning Faysal king of a constitutional monarchy that was bound by treaty in a close alliance with Great Britain. British troops remained in Iraq, and British advisors were, in fact, the actual rulers.

Great Britain divided the Palestinian mandate into two sections, making Abdullah the amir (prince) of the new state, Transjordan, in the interior, which historically had never been part of Palestine and which had been ruled under the Ottoman Empire from Damascus. (This state was later known as Jordan.) In the coastal area of Palestine proper, the British attempted to balance the conflicting Zionist and Palestinian Arab demands for independence. The 1920s and 1930s were marked by continued political confrontation and sporadic armed conflict between the Zionists and the Palestinian Arabs.

Meanwhile, the Zionists worked to translate their goals into reality through Jewish immigration, colonization, and Western support. The Palestinians opposed both Zionist and British activities; by the 1930s, Palestinian opposition was directed largely against the British. The British, responding in the old imperial tradition, sent out a series of commissions to investigate the problems. By 1937 it appeared to the British commission that the conflict was irreconcilable and that Palestine should be partitioned into a Jewish and an Arab state. The Palestinian Arabs, who viewed the territory as theirs, rejected the partition scheme, which allotted about 50 percent of the land to the Jews, who numbered only 30 percent of the population. Many Zionists also opposed the plan because it failed to allot to them all of the territory that had been part of historic Israel.

As a result of the mounting Zionist presence that the British had permitted and sometimes encouraged and also of continued British imperial control, the Palestinians openly fought British troops from 1936 to 1939. With superior weapons and organization, the British inflicted heavy losses and destroyed the Palestinian armed opposition. However, as World War II drew closer, the British sought to placate Arab leaders. The White Paper of 1939 proposed limiting Jewish immigration for five years, after which time immigration quotas were to be subject to Palestinian acquiescence. Further, British control over Palestine was to be discussed after ten years. The Zionists immediately rejected the 1939 plan, which they dubbed the "Black Paper." Thus the British wavered between the Zionists and the Palestinians, while both remained opposed to continued British domination.

In Mecca, Sherif Husayn, who had proclaimed himself king during World War I, was having troubles of his own. Throughout the war, Husayn had fought not only the Central Powers but also local rivals. Ironically, Husayn's major rival, Ibn Saud (a follower of the *Wahhabi* movement, which advocated the establishment of a puritanical Islamic government), had also received British subsidies during the war. Saud had the advantages of religious zeal, better organization, and military strength; by 1925, he succeeded in ousting Husayn. He then established the Saudi Arabian monarchy based on strict adherence to Islamic precepts.

SECULARISM VERSUS SPIRITUALISM

In the Middle East and the Islamic world in general, so-called modernizing leaders wanted to create secular nation-states that were largely modeled on Western ones. They sought to industrialize the economies of their nations while simultaneously adopting largely Western models in dress, culture, education, and behavior. More traditional or conservative forces in these societies argued against the wholesale adoption of Western institutions. They sought to preserve and reinforce traditional spiritual and societal values based on Islam.

After World War I, new, Western-looking leaders seemed to predominate, instituting sweeping changes in Turkey and Iran. To a much lesser extent, Afghanistan was also affected by similar conflicts between modernizing leaders and a largely conservative traditional populace. In both Turkey and Iran, largely Muslim and traditional nations, modernizing but authoritarian rulers sought to diminish the importance of religion and religious institutions and to force secularization on the Western model. In both nations, changes were forced from above rather than from the grass-roots level. Perhaps nowhere else in the postwar world were the lines between the conflicting forces of religion and secularism more clearly drawn.

In Turkey, Mustafa Kemal, or Ataturk (Father of the Turks), emerged as the leader following the collapse of the old Ottoman government. A professional soldier by training, Ataturk embarked on an ambitious program of Westernization. He eliminated both the old Ottoman sultanate and the caliphate and created a parliamentary state with himself as the president. Using nationalism and his enormous personal popularity, Ataturk attempted to alter the entire structure of Turkish society. He banned the wearing of the veil by women, forced men to wear Western hats rather than the traditional fez, and even had a new alphabet created, based on Western models. Ataturk used to tour the countryside with a portable blackboard on which he personally taught the new alphabet, thereby turning Turkey into one vast classroom.

Turkey also managed to avoid imperial domination or foreign entanglements while steering a careful course of neutrality. Although Ataturk was certainly an authoritarian ruler, he bequeathed to Turkey a relatively effective legislative democracy which survived long after his death. In contrast, many of his reforms regarding religion and the status of women were not as permanent.

In neighboring Iran (formerly Persia), another military officer, Reza Khan, overthrew the Qajar dynasty and also moved to Westernize and secularize the nation. Unlike Ataturk, however, Reza Khan retained the monarchy, with himself at the helm. The Pahlavi dynasty that Reza Khan established lasted until 1979, when it was overthrown in a popular revolution. Reza Shah was able to avoid imperial domination by either the Soviet Union or Great Britain, but his personal ambition and his moves to undercut the power of the clergy and religion eventually brought down his dynasty.

NATIONALIST STIRRINGS IN AFRICA

As in Asia, people throughout Africa had been swayed by Wilson's persuasive statements regarding self-determination. However, African nationalist movements did not generally reach maturity until after World War II. In general, the first generation of African nationalist leaders represented the educated elites, who often came from old established tribes and who had enjoyed positions of power long before the arrival of the Europeans. These leaders, while well-meaning, often failed to reach the masses of the people who lived in isolated, remote villages. Ironically, during World War II, there was a brief rapprochement, as both Africans and European settlers fought against Fascist and Nazi aggression. This cooperation ended after the war when the settlers moved to maintain their superior political and economic status and the black African majority struggled for independence.

Contrasting Imperial Policies

As previously indicated, the imperial policies of the European nations differed widely within Africa. For their African empire, the British had developed a system of working through the traditional political institutions, known as indirect rule. However, the application of this policy varied tremendously from colony to colony. The policy tended to be most successful in areas where there were identifiable tribal authorities, as in Nigeria and the Gold Coast (Ghana), and was less successful in areas where there were conflicting local leaders or where there were white settlers, as in Rhodesia and Kenya.

The British also continuously reaffirmed their intention to grant self-government as soon as they deemed the African peoples ready to assume the responsibilities of national independence. In British eyes, this would not occur, for the most part, for several more generations. During that time, local African elites were to be exposed to and educated in the British system. Once these elites were educated, the local bureaucracies would be turned over to the African leaders. However, the British still planned to retain overall control for a period of time well into the future. In areas where there were white settlers, the British anticipated turning over the government to them after an unscheduled period had elapsed. Anticipation of eventual self-government intensified African nationalism, causing open breaks between African nationalist movements and the British government.

In contrast to the British, the French claimed to be dedicated to a policy of maintaining close economic ties with their African colonies and of assimilating Africans into French society. Although the process of assimilation was never realized, it did seem to avoid the implication of African racial inferiority that was sometimes charged to the British approach of maintaining local and British systems in isolation from each other. Both approaches were, in the final analysis, based on the notion of cultural superiority.

In short, the British policies seemed to be based upon the notion that Africans could never be like the British, so there was no point in trying to assimilate them. On the other hand, French policies were based on belief in the superiority of French culture and the absolute assurance of the French that, given the opportunity, all people would, in fact, wish to become French. As a result of these conflicting policies, there tended to be greater nationalist political activity in British-held African territories than in those held by the French, Portuguese, or Belgians.

Revolts in North Africa

The French kept firm control over their North African empire of Morocco, Algeria, and Tunisia. Political movements by local nationalists were swiftly curtailed. In the 1920s, the Rif rebellion in Morocco, led by the Krim brothers, was brutally crushed by Spanish and French forces. Likewise, the Senussi religious and nationalist movement in Libya was attacked and bombed by the Italians. Throughout North Africa, nationalist leaders were closely watched and frequently jailed or sent into exile. In the Western world, nationalist forces and their opponents, such as the French Foreign Legion, were often pictured through the distorted lens of Hollywood cameras. The area became a favorite subject for romanticized tales of adventure like *The Sheik* and *Beau Geste,* two popular films of the era. These fictionalized accounts created a false impression that the peoples of North Africa were all either desert sheiks, living in exotic desert cities and oases, or poverty-stricken nomads. These stereotyped images distorted Western perceptions not only of North Africa but also of Arab and Islamic society in general.

In Egypt, Britain faced a fully developed nationalist movement. Encouraged by the Fourteen Points and Allied declarations, a group of Egyptians led by Saad Zaghlul formed a delegation, or *Wafd,* to ask for Egyptian independence after the war. However, Egyptian demands were thwarted by British determination to control the vital Suez Canal. The British rejected the Egyptian

Toward liberation: Moroccan fighters against Spanish colonial rule during the rebellion of 1924–26. (BBC Hulton/The Bettmann Archive)

demands, which resulted in a full-scale revolution in 1919. Although Wafdist leaders were exiled, the Wafd party became the chief political and nationalist organization from 1919 to 1952, and nationalist revolts persisted. The interwar years saw a protracted tricornered conflict for political power among the British, King Fu'ad and his successor King Faruk, and the Wafd. As a means of maintaining their presence in Egypt while undercutting the nationalist movement, the British unilaterally proclaimed Egyptian independence under the constitutional monarchy of King Fu'ad in 1922. Some Egyptian nationalist demands were furthered under the Anglo-Egyptian treaty of 1936, but the British continued to hold the Suez Canal, to base soldiers on Egyptian territory, and to exercise widespread influence over Egyptian political life. As nationalist demands for complete independence failed, both the monarchy and the Wafd became increasingly corrupt and lost the support of the Egyptian population, which turned to more radical groups on the Left and Right and finally to the army for realization of their nationalist aspirations.

Rumblings in West Africa

Although West African colonies had given loyal support to the Allied efforts in World War I, nationalist discontent became apparent immediately following the peace settlement, particularly in the British colonies. Groups from the Gold Coast (Ghana) led the first demands for greater autonomy. Under the leadership of Casely Hayford, educated Africans from the four British colonies in West Africa met in Accra, the capital of the Gold Coast, in 1920 to discuss the implementation of reforms that would lead to independence. This group formed

Egyptian women demonstrate against the Bristish occupation and in support of Wafdist demands for independence. (From *A Woman Tenderfoot in Egypt* by Grace Thompson Sexton [New York: Dodd, Mead and Co., 1923])

the nucleus of the National Congress of British West Africa, which met periodically for the next decade; after Hayford's death in 1930, however, the Congress withered away, its demands still far from realization.

Nigeria, the largest and one of the most important British territories, was one of the focal points for nationalist outbreaks. In opposition to British domination, women merchants led demonstrations and riots in 1919 and again in 1928. Under the leadership of Herbert Macaulay, Lagos, the capital city, soon became the center of the well-organized and effective nationalist opposition. Macaulay organized the Nigerian National Democratic party, which pushed for more Nigerian participation within the British-dominated political system. Similarly, Blaise Diagne, a customs official who became the first African to be elected to the French Chamber of Deputies, pushed for African national causes in French-held Senegal. However, after the pattern of the rest of Africa, West African nationalists in both British and French territories faced an uphill battle, and their demands for independence were not met until after World War II.

Nationalists in the Belgian Congo faced even greater difficulties. Although the Belgians had established a local school system, few graduates went on to European universities, and, in general, the Belgians continued to pursue a highly paternalistic policy in the Congo. Not surprisingly, repressive tactics by the Belgians only increased the number of nationalist sympathizers, who, in the Congo, frequently used religious fervor to popularize their programs. The Belgian government responded by reinforcing its authoritarian system.

Multiracial Tensions in British East Africa

Nationalist fervor varied greatly in British-dominated East Africa. In Uganda, where British authorities worked through local leaders who exercised local government duties, nationalist demonstrations were rare. In contrast, Kenya was far from quiescent during the interwar years. The continued racial and class divisions among elements of the diverse population caused ongoing conflict. Indians from the subcontinent had settled in fairly large numbers in Kenya and in Uganda and had gradually become the dominant merchants. Owing to their superior social and economic status within the British imperial system, the Indians never assimilated with the indigenous African population. On the other hand, they were never fully accepted by the white European settlers or by the British officials. Consequently, the issue of Indian citizenship and national participation irrevocably separated the East African population from the Indian immigrants, who generally sought to attain British citizenship.

British policy in Kenya attempted to balance the rights of the Africans with the goal of furthering white settlement of the rich agricultural land in the Kenyan highlands. The Kikuyu, the largest tribe in the highlands, were particularly alienated by British policies. Not surprisingly, the Kikuyu resented the loss of their traditional landholdings and were also angered by British taxes. By the 1920s, Kenyan nationalists had established several groups, including the Kikuyu Central Association (KCA). The British responded by arresting Kikuyu leaders, which only increased local hostility. Membership in the KCA grew as younger Kenyans joined the ranks. In 1928, a key Kikuyu leader, Jomo Kenyatta, became secretary of the KCA and presented Kikuyu grievances to the British government in London. Kenyatta remained in Europe until the late 1940s, when he returned to take up the leadership of the Kenyan nationalist movement.

Southern Africa: Nationalism versus White Settler Rule

Nationalist movements in southern Africa faced many of the same problems as those in East Africa. In the Portuguese colonies of Angola and Mozambique, *prazos* (huge feudal estates) held by a very small white minority dominated agricultural and business activities. Like the *colons* in Algeria and the British settlers in Kenya, the *prazeros* clung tenaciously to these colonies and were the major force behind authoritarian Portuguese policies that were similar to those adopted in the Belgian Congo.

As in Mozambique and Angola, European settlers in British-held Rhodesia controlled economic and political power, placing the majority blacks in a subordinate position and depriving them of effective political participation. The relative poverty and economic dependence of the Africans prevented them from forming effective nationalist organizations in the Portuguese colonies and Rhodesia; the result would be protracted struggles for national independence after World War II.

The racial and political divisions in the Union of South Africa were complex. After winning a victory over the Boers in South Africa and enjoying considerable support by many European settlers in South Africa during World War I, the British government first incorporated Boer territory and then granted it Dominion status within the Commonwealth, a position which implied an equal partnership with the mother country rather than a role as a subordinate. The British also embarked on a program of economic rehabilitation and assimilation of the Boers. While the economic programs were fairly successful, attempts to assimilate the Boers failed, and a new brand of Afrikaner (Dutch) nationalism emerged.

The Afrikaners, as the Boers called themselves, formed political parties led by the military heroes of the Boer War. The Afrikaners moved to maintain their superior political and economic status through the United Party, which was established in 1934 by Generals Jan Christian Smuts and James Hertzog. By 1934 the segregationist policies which formed the foundation for apartheid ("separate development," a strict government policy of racial segregation) had already become apparent.

With vast natural resources, rich agricultural land, minerals, and water, the Union of South Africa, dominated by the white Afrikaners, prospered. However, the Bantu tribal peoples who constituted over 80 percent of the population were kept in subordinate positions as tenant farmers, manual laborers, or workers in the mines and factories. As they became increasingly disenfranchised from the political and economic centers of power, educated blacks responded in 1912 by forming the South African Native National Congress (ANC), the first political coalition of its type in Africa. The ANC developed into the major nationalist organization for black participation and self-determination in South Africa. As in East Africa, Indians formed a small but generally prosperous minority. Here too, whites, particularly the Boers, tended to discriminate against the Indians solely on the basis of race. Indeed, it was in South Africa that Gandhi first began his struggles for equality and began to formalize his commitment to nonviolent struggle.

A small group of settlers of British origin attempted to liberalize the society of South Africa, but failed, and the Afrikaners kept their dominant positions. To perpetuate their privileged status, the Afrikaners tried a policy of divide and rule, and encouraged intertribal differences. As a result of their tribal policies and their vastly superior economic position, the Afrikaners continued to subordinate the majority black African population, and to ignore or repress nationalist demands.

THE EMERGENCE OF PAN-AFRICANISM

By the turn of the century, African leaders, who were increasingly alienated by European economic, political, and cultural domination, called for the unity of all Africans, or Pan-Africanism. Called by Henry Sylvester-Williams, the first Pan-African Conference was held in Trinidad in 1900. Later conferences, supported by blacks in Latin America and the United States, were held in South Africa in 1910 and in West Africa in 1920. U.S.-born W. E. B. DuBois, who was also involved with the NAACP, helped to popularize the movement in the West; he was often called the father of Pan-Africanism.

Marcus Garvey, another U.S. black leader, was one of the most outspoken champions of black nationalism. In the United States, Garvey enjoyed enormous personal popularity among many blacks. With slogans like "Africa for the Africans!" "Renaissance of the Negro Race," and "Back to Africa," Garvey attracted widespread support from blacks in the Western Hemisphere; his Back to Africa movement had over two million followers. The Pan-African and Back to Africa movements tended to be dominated by educated Africans who advocated an appreciation of African cultures, better education, and racial equality. However, the movement secured few concrete results prior to World War II.

SUMMARY

During the postwar era, British and French refusals to grant full autonomy assured continued nationalist upheavals in the Middle East. Nationalist leaders, generally from the middle class, persisted in their demands for political and economic power. Their demands, whether presented through diplomatic channels or in revolutions, were consistently rebuffed. The British and French governments were determined to control the Middle Eastern oil fields and the strategic Suez Canal and Persian Gulf. When the middle-class political parties and nationalists failed to secure national independence, as in Egypt or Iraq, masses of people in the region turned to more radical groups and often concluded that only military actions would achieve national liberation.

As in India, nationalism in the Arab world was highly developed. Also as in India, nationalism was segmented, both as a result of Arab heritage and of circumstance and because of the division of Arab lands between the British and the French. The progress of Arab nationalism was further complicated by the extension of Jewish nationalism (Zionism) in Palestine.

Nationalist discontent in Africa also continued to mount during the interwar years. The first generation of African nationalists failed to achieve their goals, and in many parts of the continent, as in the areas under the repressive domination of Belgium and Portugal, mobilized only a small fraction of the local populations. Economically and politically, most Africans, in the East and West, remained subordinated to the imperial powers and to the European settlers. In South Africa, as the minority Afrikaner population sought to perpetuate its dominant position, the political and economic gaps between the minority white population and the majority black population deepened. However, the more repressive the settlers and Western imperial governments became, the more the opposition increased. After 1945, another generation of African leaders emerged to demand and ultimately to achieve national independence.

SUGGESTED SOURCES

Antonius, George, *The Arab Awakening* (1976). A straightforward description of the growth of Arab nationalism.*

Geiss, Imanuel, *The Pan African Movement* (1974). A study of the origins and development of the Pan-African movement.*

I Stand for Your Dreams (n.d., video, available from Turkish Embassy). Highly laudatory Turkish film on Ataturk's military and political career.

Lion of the Desert (1981). An action-packed film depicting the revolt of some Libyan Arabs against the Italian invasions during the 1920s and 1930s.

Mahfouz, Naguib, *Midhaq Alley* (1981). One of a trilogy by a Nobel Prize-winning Egyptian novelist detailing lives of people living in Cairo during World War II.*

Oliver, Roland and J.D. Fage, *A Short History of Africa*, 4th ed. (1975). A basic overview of African political and cultural developments.*

Paton, Alan, *Cry, the Beloved Country* (1961). A compelling novel about the black experience in South Africa.* (Also a film.)

Rose, Norman, *Chaim Weizmann: A Biography* (1986). An excellent introduction to Zionism and a sympathetic account of one of Israel's founding fathers.

*Paperback available.

18

Dictatorship and Democracy in Europe during the 1930s

During the 1930s, authoritarian government became increasingly prevalent in Europe. Democratic ideals, which Woodrow Wilson popularized at the end of World War I, had subsequently been buffeted during the 1920s by dictators such as Lenin, Stalin, and Mussolini, and by authoritarian movements in the Iberian peninsula and parts of Eastern Europe. After 1929, the devastating economic effects of the Great Depression posed another serious challenge to democracy throughout Europe. By 1932 unemployment was skyrocketing, and both in cities and on farms people were struggling. Such an atmosphere was conducive to would-be dictators who promised people an end to their misery. Adolf Hitler, who came to power in 1933, was not the only authoritarian politician in the 1930s to benefit from people's misery and longing for better times, but he was the most infamous. By 1939 democracy survived only in Western and northern Europe.

HITLER AND THE CONSOLIDATION OF NAZI POWER IN GERMANY

By 1930 Hitler was a rising political leader. While Hitler's primary appeal to the German people was his outspoken nationalism and criticism of the Allied treatment of Germany, the Depression also contributed significantly to his rise to political power. Many Germans blamed their economic ills on the Allies and the imposition of reparations payments. Others agreed with Hitler that the Jews were somehow to blame. Hitler's extreme criticism of the Versailles settlement grew in appeal as the economic situation worsened. In the autumn of 1930, as the 107 brown-uniformed Nazi delegates goose-stepped into the Reichstag building, the Depression was still in its early stages. In the summer elections of 1932, by which time economic conditions had worsened considerably—roughly two out of every five German workers were unemployed—the Nazis received 230 seats. This was almost a hundred more than their nearest rival, but still only 37 percent of the Reichstag seats. As the leader of the largest party in the Reichstag,

Hitler was now a major political power. Despite a loss of thirty-four seats in an autumn election, the Nazis remained by far the largest party.

After 1930, German governments, unable to command a parliamentary majority, increasingly resorted to ruling by emergency decrees signed by President Paul von Hindenburg. Such decrees were allowed by the Weimar constitution. Nevertheless, parliamentary government ceased to function as originally envisioned, and the situation became more chaotic. Finally, Hindenburg reluctantly bowed to pressure from conservative politicians and businessmen who were impressed by the size of the Nazi following. They convinced the aging president that they could use Hitler for their own purposes. Thus Hindenburg, who two years earlier had said contemptuously that the highest office Hitler could ever hope to obtain was head of the Postal Department, appointed him chancellor of Germany on January 30, 1933.

After assuming the office, Adolf Hitler moved quickly and skillfully to strengthen his control. First, he blamed a fire that had destroyed the Reichstag building on the German Communists. He then convinced Hindenburg to sign an emergency decree that indefinitely suspended basic liberties and the due process of law. Hitler also stepped up his accusations and bullying tactics against the Communists. In elections to the Reichstag in early March 1933, the Communist vote declined and the Nazi vote increased to 44 percent of the total. Many of the Communist deputies were imprisoned, and none was allowed to take his seat in the new Reichstag. Later that month, using threats and promises, Hitler obtained the agreement of the Reichstag to the Enabling Act, which transferred legislative power to Hitler and his cabinet and allowed him to suspend parts of the Weimar constitution. The other political parties had thus allowed Hitler to assume dictatorial powers. By the summer of 1933, all political parties except the Nazis were outlawed.

Hitler's next move was to deal with a potential threat within his own Nazi party. The Storm Troopers (SA), who had been the "street fighters" of the party, were under the leadership of Ernst Röhm. Röhm and others wanted the "Nazi revolution" to be a true revolution that would destroy the old aristocratic and conservative elements, including those within the army. Hitler, however, had perceived the desirability of using these groups for his own purposes. On June 30, 1934, the "Night of the Long Knives," he set his elite guard, the SS (*Schutzstaffel*, or black-shirts), on the SA. Röhm, other SA leaders, and some of Hitler's non-Nazi political opponents were killed.

As a result of Hitler's handling of the more radical elements within his party, the conservative army leaders became more cooperative. After President von Hindenburg died in August 1934, Hitler assumed the presidency. He then ordered the armed forces to swear an oath of personal loyalty to him as Führer (leader). Meanwhile, the Nazi party took control of state and local governments and the judiciary. The secret police (Gestapo) ferreted out the remnants of political dissent. Arrest, torture, imprisonment, and death were commonplace. Special concentration camps were set up to hold political opponents and other so-called undesirables.

Despite earlier Nazi attacks on capitalism, Hitler's economic program after he came to power was based on supporting big business while making labor happy and controlling both. Pleased with the Nazis' strident anti-Communism, many businessmen had supported Hitler. Once in power, Hitler allowed major industries and large businesses to dominate the economy, as long as they supported his regime. Hitler's military rebuilding program, in particular, allowed German industrialists to enjoy favorable contracts and to make large profits. Meanwhile, Hitler put German workers back to work constructing public buildings and superhighways (*Autobahns*) and producing armaments for the German war machine. Forbidding any threats to his authority, Hitler dissolved the old labor unions and prohibited strikes. Workers were enrolled in a powerless national labor organization and were pacified with better wages and working conditions, vacations, pensions, and children's camps.

Nazism was by now a potent stew of the half-cooked ideas of Darwin, Nietzsche, and the nineteenth-century German nationalist composer Richard Wagner, combined with anti-Semitism and anti-Communism. Hitler's most important idea, and one that would soon cause much misery in the world, was the theory of the superiority of the German race (Aryans). In 1927, he had said: "Man owes everything that is of any importance to the principle of struggle and to one race which has carried itself forward successfully. Take away the Nordic Germans and nothing remains but the dance of apes." In the mind of Hitler, who had been anti-Semitic since his youth, Jews had polluted the pure Aryan blood and were behind many of the evils confronting Germany: the Versailles treaty, democracy, communism, and the Depression. Although Hitler's ideas were bogus, he believed deeply in them, and their emotional appeal was great, especially when delivered by the master orator himself. At giant rallies, such as the one in Nuremberg in 1934 in which hundreds of thousands participated amidst 130 giant searchlights and 20,000 flags, Hitler stirred his crowds to a frenzy by appealing to German romantic nationalism, asking his listeners to pledge themselves to put the *Volk* (the German folk or nation) above all.

In order to entrench Nazism in Germany in both the present and the future, Hitler and his party created an elaborate program to indoctrinate the German people to be loyal to the Führer and to Nazi ideology. A ministry of culture supervised art, music, drama, literature, architecture, radio, films, and the press to ensure that all media instilled the Nazi program. The Nazis burned publications with opposing or "incorrect" views in public bonfire ceremonies and silenced dissenters.

The Nazis concentrated particularly on indoctrinating young Germans. They inculcated Nazism and an almost godlike reverence for Hitler in the schools, while Nazi-approved professors taught college youth racial pseudo-science and other "correct" subjects. The party also trained adolescent boys in the Hitler Youth to fight and die for the Führer, while adolescent girls were taught that the home was their rightful place and they should have many babies to propagate the superior German race. Hitler once said "a woman must be a cute, cuddly, naive little thing—tender, sweet, and stupid."

Meanwhile, Hitler began his special campaign to isolate and degrade the Jews of Germany. In the spring and summer of 1933, they were removed from the civil service and from leading positions in German cultural life. In September 1935, the Nuremberg Laws deprived German Jews of their citizenship and forbade marriages between Jews and those defined as Germans. The Nazis gradually increased the use of terroristic methods against them. On November 9 and 10, 1938, Nazi thugs and others destroyed or ransacked well over 10,000 Jewish shops, homes, and synagogues, killed scores of Jews, and arrested and sent tens of thousands of Jews to concentration camps. But despite Crystal Night (as the Nazis labeled the event), until World War II broke out, more Jews emigrated than were imprisoned, including such notables as Albert Einstein. Only after the beginning of the war did Hitler begin a massive slaughter of Jews who fell under Nazi control.

Despite Hitler's many successes in a short time, not all Germans approved of his policies. Some leaders of the German Catholic and Protestant churches, for example, resented Hitler's attempt to foster and propagate Nazi ideals contrary to the spirit of Christianity. A papal encyclical of 1937 criticized Nazi racism and paganism. Those German clergymen and lay leaders who spoke out openly often suffered persecution.

In general, however, the Nazi regime was popular in Germany. In a general sense, the Nazi indoctrination was effective. It stimulated pride in the German past and promoted the determination to overcome Germany's humiliation and to become a great power in the future. The violations of the rights of Jews and of those who opposed Hitler's policies were less important to many Germans than were Hitler's apparent successes. While Nazi terror helped keep Germans in line, many apparently would have supported Hitler in any case, in appreciation for his restoration of German economic and political power.

Two of Europe's leading dictators, Hitler and Mussolini, at a German military review in 1937. (Brown Brothers)

THE CORPORATE STATE IN ITALY

By the time Hitler became chancellor of Germany, Mussolini had already been in power in Italy for a decade, and his Fascist state continued to evolve toward greater authoritarian controls. Until 1929, the Catholic papacy continued, as it had for almost sixty years, to have serious differences with the Italian state. In that year, Pope Pius XI and Mussolini came to an agreement, the Lateran Treaty, that recognized papal control over Vatican City and its political independence. At the same time, Catholicism was recognized as the religion of the Italian state. Catholic religious education was allowed in the public schools, and Catholic marriage laws were to become the norm for state law. While this pragmatic agreement by the atheist Mussolini and the Catholic pope proved quite popular among Italy's overwhelmingly Catholic population and greatly increased Mussolini's support, strains between the Italian state and the papacy soon reappeared. In 1930, the pope denounced the government's attempts to train the young in "a pagan worship of the State." While not causing Mussolini serious problems, relations with the papacy were strained for the rest of the decade.

In the 1930s, Mussolini's "corporate state" became something of a reality. In theory, such a state would overcome class conflict by bringing representatives of employers, employees, and the government together in corporations to decide on such questions as wages and working hours. By 1934 twenty-two of these corporations had been brought together, representing such areas as the clothing trades and mining. Since only Fascist trade unions were allowed to exist and represent the workers in the corporations, the interest of the workers was sacrificed to that of the Fascist party and the employers. The party, appreciative of the financial and political backing of big business, allowed business to help run an economy more and more dominated by large firms and monopolies. When some businesses found themselves near bankruptcy during the Depression, the government invested in them to keep them afloat. As a result, by 1937 the government possessed the controlling interest in shipping, electricity, heavy machinery, steel, and telephones. In 1938, the Chamber of Deputies, a carry-over from a more democratic Italy long since dominated by the Fascists, was replaced by the Chamber of Fasces and Corporations. While no real power changed hands, this move symbolized Mussolini's dislike of liberal democracy and his fondness for his own type of "corporatism."

AUTHORITARIAN GOVERNMENTS ELSEWHERE IN EUROPE

At the beginning of the 1920s, parliamentary governments, democratic in form, existed almost everywhere in Europe west of the Soviet Union. By 1939, rightist authoritarian dictators had taken over most of the nations of Europe, and few republics remained outside Western Europe and Scandinavia. However, none of the other governments was as oppressive as Hitler's.

On the Iberian peninsula, Spain and Portugal had already witnessed the collapse of democracy in the 1920s. In Spain, General Primo de Rivera, who took power in 1923, held it until 1930. In 1931, democratic forces succeeded in restoring democracy until civil war broke out in Spain in 1936 and General Francisco Franco eventually established a dictatorship (see Chapter 19). In Portugal, the military uprising of 1926 led to the eventual dictatorial control of Antonio de Oliviera Salazar, who became prime minister in 1932. Both Franco and Salazar would continue in power for over three decades.

The authoritarianism of Primo de Rivera, Salazar, and Franco had just as much in common with Catholic traditionalist ideas as it did with those of Mussolini, perhaps more. Papal encyclicals such as Leo XIII's *Rerum Novarum* (1891) and Pius XI's *Quadragesimo Anno* (1931) and the writings of Catholic intellectuals such as Gilbert Chesterton and Charles Peguy criticized modern individualism as well as some of the inequities and abuses of both capitalism and Marxism. They emphasized subordinating individual and economic interests and rights to the good of the whole, as understood in the light of Catholic teaching. The Iberian dictators felt they were best qualified to interpret how this was to be done. From 1933 until 1938, Austria pursued a path similar to the Iberian states: Englebert Dollfuss, sometimes referred to as "Mickey Mouse" because of his small stature, and his successor, Kurt von Schuschnigg, attempted to rule in an authoritarian fashion, which Dollfuss claimed was to be based on the *Quadragesimo Anno*.

In the Eastern European nations, a variety of authoritarian governments appeared and disappeared during the 1920s and 1930s. In some nations, real power was exercised by kings, as for a time in Yugoslavia, Rumania, and Bulgaria. In other nations, it was held by men of military background, such as Marshal Joseph Pilsudski in Poland and Admiral Miklos Horthy in Hungary. The trend toward authoritarian right-wing regimes sped up following the onset of the Depression, as did economic and political nationalism and hostility toward minorities, especially the Jews. The involvement of some Jews in the region's banking, industry, and trade made them convenient scapegoats at a time of economic misery. By 1938 only Czechoslovakia maintained a viable democratic government in Eastern Europe, but its German minority became increasingly troublesome as a result of the Depression and Nazi-generated propaganda.

STALINISM IN THE SOVIET UNION: 1933–1939

Aware of the rising power of Germany and Japan, Stalin believed that it was more important than ever for the Soviet Union to strengthen its industrial base and its armed forces. As a result, the Second Soviet Five-Year Plan, begun in 1933, continued to emphasize the build-up of heavy industry. While increasing Communist party and personal control over the nation, Stalin began to downplay some of the ideological innovations introduced after the revolution, especially if they appeared to interfere with industrial productivity. The Communist ideal of egalitarianism, for example, was increasingly ignored. Thus, in order to get workers and managers to produce more, the party introduced various types of wage incentives and established a variety of incentives on the collective farms. The wages and privileges of technocrats, party and government bureaucrats, and military officers were also increased. A new privileged class of leaders came into existence, but the life of the average agricultural or industrial worker improved little. During the middle and late 1930s, the Soviet people had to cope with cramped housing, food shortages, and a dearth of consumer goods. The regime also retreated from earlier innovations regarding family life and education, making divorce and abortions more difficult to obtain and introducing new incentives for having children. In education, some of the earlier progressive experiments were scrapped, and hard work, discipline, and academic standards were reemphasized.

Stalin, it seemed, was motivated to make these retreats because he realized that communist ideology and its radical innovations had not won the hearts of the Soviet people. As the German and Japanese danger became greater, he increasingly appealed to the patriotic rather than Marxist feelings of the people. There was no relaxation of the party's attempt to control people's ideas, however; in fact, Stalin tightened party control over books, films, and other media. They now displayed a much more respectful attitude than previously toward such figures from the tsarist past as Ivan the Terrible and Peter the Great. Even the Orthodox Church, which was so intricately connected with the tsarist past, began to receive somewhat better treatment.

As another tool to motivate the Soviet people to work harder for their nation, Stalin also forced writers and artists to use the techniques of approved "Socialist realism" for artistic and literary expression. Basically, this meant that artists and writers were to portray reality as the party wished it portrayed, in a clear, simple form that the average worker could understand. To the party, "reality" during the 1930s often meant the image of pure, courageous workers overcoming all sorts of obstacles and enemies in order to help increase productivity and thereby make the Soviet Union stronger.

Although Stalin was very anxious to strengthen the Soviet Union, he became even more interested in increasing his personal power. Political opposition to him was by most standards minimal, being confined within the party and to fairly minor matters. Stalin could not tolerate any opposition, however, no matter how limited, and he instituted massive purges of his political opponents and their followers. The purges began with the assassination of one of the most popular Communist party leaders, Sergei Kirov, in 1934. Although Stalin himself apparently approved of the killing, he blamed it on his political opponents. Additional false accusations were soon produced, and arrest followed arrest. Imprisonment, exile to Siberian prison camps, and execution awaited many. Important former political figures were executed after staged show trials at which the defendants often confessed to crimes they could not possibly have committed. Despite the need for a strong military, a majority of the generals and colonels in the army were imprisoned, exiled, or executed. Of the members of the Central Committee of the party in 1934, the most powerful governing group in the Soviet Union, only about 20 percent were still free in 1939. Even the head of the secret police, Yezhov, who directed the purge for Stalin during its most intense phase, was removed in 1938 and eventually executed—only to be replaced by the infamous Beria, who once said: "[Give me someone] for one night, and I'll have him confessing he's the king of England." The flood of arrests did not abate until 1939.

While the purges of former leaders and party members were the most dramatic events, others also suffered in these years. Prominent among them were intellectuals and those minorities accused of "bourgeois nationalistic tendencies." At times the police arrested ordinary individuals for no apparent reason other than to fill "arrest quotas" and to terrorize Soviet citizens into becoming more docile. In all, it has been estimated that at least eight million people were arrested during the purges of the late 1930s and that a few million of them were shot or otherwise died in the prison camps to which most of them were sent.

TOTALITARIANISM

In practice, German Nazism and Stalin's Soviet communism had much in common. Both Hitler and Stalin were dictators, and the respective parties they dominated exercised almost complete control over all phases of life: government, the judiciary, the military, police forces, the economy, ideology, education, the press, and cultural institutions. Massive propaganda, as well as terror and fear, were regular instruments of their policy. Before their deaths, Hitler and Stalin would be responsible for the execution of millions. While figures are far from exact, Hitler was responsible for the murder of perhaps six million European Jews and seven million other Europeans; from 1928 to 1953, Stalin was responsible for the extermination of an even higher total number of Soviet citizens. "One death is a tragedy, a million just statistics," Stalin once said.

Systems such as those of Germany and the Soviet Union in the 1930s, where the government attempted to maintain total control over the hearts, minds, and actions of the populace, are commonly referred to as totalitarianism. The term was a favorite of Mussolini (although not of Hitler or Stalin), who thought of his Fascist Italy as a totalitarian state. In some ways it was, but in actuality his control was never as "total" as that exercised by the other two dictators. In general, other authoritarian regimes of this time could not be classified as totalitarian. Even though each was run by a dictator or small elite group, its control over various phases of life did not approximate that of Hitler or Stalin. Nevertheless, some type of censorship, restriction of civil liberties, and limitation on political opposition was practiced in all these regimes.

Despite the similarities between Stalin's U.S.S.R. and other nondemocratic societies, some distinctions existed that were also important. When Communists came to power in Russia, they effected a social and cultural revolution and dealt harshly with the prerevolutionary upper and middle classes and with traditional religious beliefs and values. While Hitler certainly weakened the power of the old German aristocracy, he and men such as Mussolini and Franco benefited from the fear and support of conservative classes and individuals who saw the Communists as a much more serious threat to their status, property, and beliefs. Another difference was that though Stalin increasingly appealed in the 1930s to Russian nationalism, he continued to reconcile it, at least in theory, with the internationalist emphasis that had long characterized communist ideology. The right-wing authoritarian governments, especially those of Hitler and Mussolini, were aggressively nationalistic.

SOCIAL AND POLITICAL CHANGES IN THE EUROPEAN DEMOCRACIES

The Depression and the rise of Nazism greatly affected the European democracies during the 1930s. Unemployment and other hardships experienced by many during the 1930s produced numerous significant social consequences, including a decline in the birth rate in most of the Western democracies and a corresponding proportional increase in the number of older people. Numerous couples were apparently unwilling to have children while they remained in precarious economic circumstances.

Another change was the increasing attraction of workers to more militant unionism and more radical political ideas than those that appealed to workers in the late 1920s. As the Depression threw more and more workers out of jobs, they demanded an end to the liberal laissez-faire policies of their governments. Some felt that the Depression had proved the failure of capitalism. In Scandinavia, where democratic Socialist parties had alternated in power with more conservative parties during the 1920s, Socialists became dominant in the 1930s. In France, support for the Socialist and Communist parties increased, and a leftist coalition Popular Front government was formed in 1936, under France's first Socialist premier, Léon Blum. Blum's government took a more active role in the economy by increasing public spending and helping workers gain salary increases. Like President Franklin Roosevelt in the United States, he hoped to help France out of the lingering Depression by stimulating purchasing power. Blum strengthened the rights of unions and helped workers gain a forty-hour work week and two-week paid vacations every year. Like most French governments in the interwar years, however, Blum's coalition government was unstable. Its reforms had the effect of decreasing production in the area of armaments, which was significant, considering the Nazi threat.

In Great Britain, the socialist-oriented Labour party was already in power when the Depression hit the nation, and it did not cope effectively with the downturn's early stages. In August 1931, the Labour government fell when half the cabinet refused to go along with cuts in government benefits, cuts that U.S.

and British bankers insisted were necessary before further U.S. loans could be issued to stabilize the British currency. For the remainder of the decade, the Conservative party ruled with mixed success by dominating successive National Coalition governments. Despite being more cautious than the Labour party, the Conservatives were moved by high unemployment and the public mood to enact some welfare-state provisions—for example, in regard to public housing and expanded social insurance coverage.

SUMMARY

Undermined by the Depression, democracy seemed an outdated concept to many in Europe during the 1930s. Right-wing dictatorial and authoritarian personalities such as Hitler, Franco, and many Eastern European leaders joined the earlier victorious Mussolini in opposing democracy, individualism, and equality with ideas of national or racial superiority, the superiority of the state over the individual, and various forms of elitism. In Russia, Stalin praised democracy and equality; but no less than Hitler, he aspired to totalitarian control of his country's actions and thoughts. While democratic governments survived in Scandinavia, Great Britain, and France, these governments had to increase their control over economic life in order to combat the effects of the Depression. By 1939 governments that advocated traditional laissez-faire economic policies seemed outmoded. To many, either the dictatorships or the democratic welfare states represented the future.

SUGGESTED SOURCES

Bullock, Alan, *Hitler, A Study in Tyranny,* rev. ed. (1971). The best overall work on Hitler and his domestic and foreign policies. Also available in an abridged edition.*

De Jonge, Alex, *Stalin and the Shaping of the Soviet Union* (1986). The most readable up-to-date biography of the Soviet dictator.*

Englemann, Bernt, *In Hitler's Germany: Everyday Life in the Third Reich* (1986). A fascinating book which uses interviews to weave a story of everyday life from the early 1930s to 1945.

Fischer, Louis, *Men and Politics* (1941). A lively account of politics and personalities in Europe between the wars by a leading U.S. correspondent.*

Koestler, Arthur, *Darkness at Noon* (1941). A novel that captures something of the atmosphere of the 1930s Soviet purges and show trials.*

Shirer, William L., *Twentieth Century Journey,* Vol. II, *The Nightmare Years, 1930–1940* (1984). A foreign correspondent's account of the important events of the 1930s, many of which he witnessed firsthand.*

Solzhenitsyn, Aleksandr I., *The Gulag Archipelago: 1918-1956,* 3 vols. (1973-78). A fascinating collection of materials about the treatment of those whom the Soviet government has considered "enemies" of the state.*

Spielvogel, Jackson J., *Hitler and Nazi Germany: A History* (1988). A blend of biography and history with special emphasis on social history and the Holocaust.*

Triumph of the Will. The infamous 110-minute propaganda film of the 1934 Nazi Nuremberg rallies. (Also available on video.)

Wiskemann, Elizabeth, *Fascism in Italy* (1970). A short, well-written, and scholarly treatment of fascism in Italy and of its ideological influence in other European nations.*

*Paperback available.

19

Aggression in the 1930s

During the 1930s, the fragile system of international order broke down as some of the major world powers resorted to force to achieve their national goals and to settle real or imagined grievances. The rise to power of Japanese militarists, Hitler, and other European dictators, coupled with the hardships of the Depression, brought on more aggressive policies. While Japan used military force in expanding its holdings at the expense of China, Hitler made advances by relying on a combination of diplomacy and implicit or explicit threats of force, up until the invasion of Poland on September 1, 1939. Both Japanese aggressions and the actions of Hitler and other European right-wing dictators met with little more than empty protests and appeasement.

JAPANESE AGGRESSION AND CHINESE RESPONSE

Japan Seizes Manchuria

Witnessing the trade barriers erected following the onset of the Depression, the Japanese became more convinced than ever of the need for a self-sufficient empire. Dependent upon importing industrial raw materials and food from the mainland of Asia, particularly from China, Japanese leaders were now determined to seize those parts of Asia that would give Japan a secure supply of these commodities. In addition, ultranationalists in Japan saw their nation as the rightful ruler of Asia. By either measure, China was Japan's next victim. During the same period, China was slowly inching toward modernization and national unity. Japanese militarists could not tolerate this, since a strong China would preclude Japanese dominance on the Asian mainland.

In the 1930s, the Chinese and the Japanese embarked on a collision course in Manchuria, as both intensified their moves to control the area. Japan had been satisfied to maintain a facade of Chinese sovereignty in Manchuria as long as a disunited China allowed Japan to control the warlord there. Japan called Manchuria its "lifeline" and relied on it for such vital resources as iron ore, coal, and grain. The Chinese called Manchuria the "granary of China," where poor peasants from north China migrated to pioneer the virgin land. The KMT had targeted Manchuria as a key area in its movement to recover sovereign rights lost to outside powers. After 1929, the pro-Chiang warlord of Manchuria began a program of economic development, which included the building of Chinese-controlled railroad lines and seaports in competition with those already established by Japan.

These KMT initiatives led militant Japanese to fear that unless they acted quickly, Chinese authority would be reestablished in Manchuria. On September 18, 1931, junior officers of the Japanese army in Manchuria, whose goal was to conquer Manchuria and then take over the rest of China, engineered the Manchurian, or Mukden, Incident. Late that evening, the Japanese army staged an explosion on the tracks of the Japanese-controlled South Manchurian Railway. Blaming the Chinese, the entire Japanese army in Manchuria swung into action. Within days, they had captured all the important cities in the region.

It was a critical moment for party government in Japan. A strong government might have restrained the army's action and postponed a reckoning with China, but the government in Tokyo was weak and dared not risk its existence by forcing a showdown with the army. The army ignored civilian calls for restraint and completed its conquest of Manchuria by the end of 1931. In March 1932, Manchuria, renamed Manchukuo (Land of the Manchus), was proclaimed an independent state headed by the last Manchu emperor, who had abdicated the Chinese throne in 1912 when he was a little boy. In reality, Japan controlled every department of the new government, which it ran as a de facto colony until 1945. These events led to the resignation of the Japanese prime minister and cabinet.

China appealed to the League of Nations and the international community for help. After futile debates, the League appointed an international commission headed by a British chairman, Lord Lytton, whose report condemned Japan for aggression and called on it to withdraw from its conquests. The League Assembly unanimously adopted the report, and Japan withdrew from the League. The League did nothing further. This was the first major crisis of war and peace to confront the League of Nations, and it had shown itself to be ineffective. U.S. protests were also not successful in deterring the Japanese.

Japan Attacks China

In the years following the Manchurian Incident, the Japanese pushed farther into China, brushing aside ineffective Chinese resistance. In 1933, Jehol, a province that linked Manchuria to northern China, was conquered by Japanese and puppet Manchukuo troops. Japan's next step south was to form the five provinces of north China into a neutral zone and oust the Chinese central government from the region. In response, Chiang Kai-shek clung to the strategy of "unification before resistance." Translated, this meant that Chiang wished to eliminate the Communists and warlords first, to build up the military next, and finally to resist Japan. Meanwhile, he would trade space for time, negotiate, temporize, but not commit his ill-prepared army to battle. In conventional military terms, Chiang's strategy made sense, but he discounted the potential power of nonmilitary and guerrilla forces when mobilized in support of a conventional war.

Above all, Chiang was insensitive to popular opinion, which demanded active resistance to Japan. Chinese students took to the streets calling for an end to civil wars and for all Chinese to form an anti-Japanese united front. The CCP was quick to take up the student cause. Hard-pressed as it was in Yenan, it wanted a united front, if only to relieve KMT pressure on the Communists. The Soviet Union also came out for a Chinese united front, because a Sino-Japanese war would take Japanese pressure off Soviet Siberia and allow the Soviet Union to concentrate on the German menace in Europe. In 1937, Chiang bowed to public pressure and began negotiations for a united front with the CCP.

Given their ambition to dominate China, the last thing the Japanese wanted was the creation of a united front in China to resist them, and they decided to strike before Chinese progress could foil their plans. On the night of July 7, 1937, at an important railroad junction near Peking called the Marco Polo Bridge, the Japanese army attacked. Popular feeling in China was so strongly in favor of resistance that no government could have survived unless it complied. In Tokyo, the Japanese cabinet vainly attempted to halt the spreading conflict. It failed because it could neither restrain its men at the front nor offer terms the Chinese government could accept. By August, serious fighting had spread to several fronts in north and central China. This was the beginning of World War II in Asia, which in China would last a full eight years.

Japanese troops overrunning part of the devastated Shanghai in the war against China. (Historical Pictures Service)

China during the War

From 1937 to 1941, China fought alone. Until mid-1941, the isolationist United States continued to sell the essentials of war, such as petroleum and iron, to Japan. Great Britain and France were too preoccupied with their own problems in Europe and elsewhere to come to China's aid. The Soviet Union assisted China in the first two years of war, supplying a volunteer air force and loans. Soviet aid ended in 1939, however, because of the threat of war in Europe between the Soviet Union and Germany.

With inadequate aid from abroad, China was no match for Japan. With its modern war machine, Japan had little trouble conquering major cities along China's coast and rivers. However, Japanese mechanized warfare was tied to an inadequate Chinese road and railroad system for logistical support, and eventually Japan's war effort bogged down. Its occupation of the countryside was ineffective, limited to forays and punitive expeditions. In spite of, or because of, the barbarous behavior of Japanese troops, China would not surrender. The Chinese government retreated westward to the mountainous interior to get out of reach of the Japanese tanks, although that area was still within range of Japanese planes. The retreating Chinese army used the "scorched earth" policy, destroying what it could not take with it. Stage by stage, the Chinese government retreated westward up the gorges of the Yangtze River, taking with it whole arsenals, factories, libraries, and groups of people, until it attained safety in Chungking. It was one of humanity's largest migrations.

After 1939, a war of attrition began, as Japan was both unable and disinclined to occupy all of China. The Chinese government continued to hold on, convinced that in its fanaticism Japan would eventually widen the war and thus bring other nations to China's aid. In the occupied areas, Japanese-sponsored puppet governments emerged in northern and southern China, but they were unable to attract to them many men or women of stature.

The full-scale war with Japan compelled the KMT and CCP to form the United Front in September 1937. Under its terms, the CCP agreed to abide by Dr. Sun's Three People's Principles, abandon its Marxist policies and Soviet-style government in areas it controlled, and abolish its Red Army. In return, the KMT agreed to reorganize the 40,000-strong Red Army into the national army, in separate units under CCP command, and to recognize CCP control of Yenan and some other areas.

From the beginning, the CCP regarded the Sino-Japanese War as an opportunity to build up its strength while the Japanese destroyed the KMT. While Nationalist armies were preoccupied with the Japanese, the Communists greatly expanded their area of control in the northwest. Shortly after the United Front was formally proclaimed, the Central Committee of the CCP issued the following directive to its cadres: "Our fixed policy should be 70 percent expansion, 20 percent dealing with the Kuomintang, and 10 percent resisting Japan." Besides territorial expansion, the CCP attempted to increase its army to one million men and the party to one million members. During the next eight years,

Communist units were very successful in slipping behind Japanese lines and organizing peasant guerrilla bands to harass the Japanese.

The United States Moves toward Confronting Japan

From the beginning, the United States strongly opposed Japanese aggression in China. Although Americans living in China enjoyed the benefits of extraterritoriality and other benefits of Western imperialism, the U.S. public fancied itself as a longtime friend of China. Most Americans regarded Japan not only as a brutal attacker of a nation friendly to the United States, but also as a threat to U.S. interests in Asia. When Japan seized Manchuria in 1931, the United States was opposed, but, unwilling to intervene militarily or to deepen the Depression by imposing economic sanctions, had to content itself with a strong diplomatic protest. Secretary of State Henry Stimson announced that the United States would not recognize Japan's seizure of Manchuria because it impaired U.S. rights, violated the Open Door policy, and flouted the Kellogg-Briand Peace Pact. This statement, plus a U.S. threat to build up military strength in the Pacific, failed to deter the Japanese; meanwhile, normal business relationships continued.

When Japan invaded China in 1937, the United States again protested. Roosevelt stated that aggression was becoming "epidemic" and that a "quarantine" was needed. This time the United States government went beyond rhetoric. It arranged limited economic and military aid to the Chinese, embargoed the sale of airplanes to Japan, and abrogated the Commercial Treaty of 1911. In order to increase military preparedness, Congress authorized the construction of aircraft carriers and battleships. None of these actions halted the Japanese in China or materially aided the Chinese, and extensive U.S. trade with Japan continued until 1941. Japanese actions and U.S. reactions rapidly soured relations between the two nations, and many officials on both sides of the Pacific believed that a direct confrontation might well occur in the near future.

THE NAZI THREAT TO PEACE AND THE ALLIED RESPONSE

During the 1930s, Great Britain and France failed to deal effectively with the increasing aggressiveness of Nazi Germany and Fascist Italy. In the first half of the decade, before Hitler made his most conspicuous international moves, the major European democratic powers had already been unable to halt aggression. Following Japan's 1931 occupation of Chinese Manchuria, Italy attacked Ethiopia in late 1935. In the second case, as in the first, the British and French delegates to the League of Nations were critical of this aggression but put forward little effective response. Despite a personal appeal by Ethiopian Emperor Haile Selassie, the League imposed only halfhearted, short-lived, and limited economic sanctions. Nor did Great Britain and France take any meaningful action when, in early 1935, Hitler announced that, in violation of the Treaty of Versailles, he intended to reintroduce military conscription and increase the size of the German armed forces.

The German Occupation of the Rhineland

In March 1936, Hitler took the most daring gamble of his early years in power when he decided to send troops into the Rhineland, the German territory that according to the Versailles and Locarno treaties was to remain demilitarized. The French had removed their last troops from the area in 1930, but as long as the area was not fortified, a German attack on France was difficult. Many German diplomats, statesmen, and officers considered Hitler's gamble too risky. They believed French soldiers would be sent to turn back the Germans and feared that the German army was not yet ready for war with France. Hitler himself later stated: "If the French had then marched into the Rhineland, we would have had to withdraw with our tails between our legs." But he did not think the French would act. He was right; they did nothing.

There were a variety of reasons for the failure of France and Great Britain to take more decisive action. Among the most prominent were: (1) a genuine hatred of war on the part of many who remembered the horrors of World War I, accompanied by a lack of enthusiasm for heavy military spending; (2) a feeling, more common in Great Britain than France, that perhaps Germany had been dealt with too harshly in the Versailles treaty and that its desire for revision was understandable; (3) Hitler's ability to make some Allied statesmen believe he was a reasonable and peace-loving man with limited goals; and (4) a fear that if Hitler were overthrown in Germany, a worse situation might arise: a Communist government. In 1938, British Prime Minister Neville Chamberlain, prompted by a discussion of Hitler's possible overthrow, asked: "Who will guarantee that Germany will not become Bolshevik afterwards?"

Soviet Response to Japanese and German Aggression

Shortly after Hitler had assumed power and had demonstrated his hostility toward communism and the Soviet Union, Stalin began looking for assistance against this potential new threat. Already alarmed by Japan's movements near Soviet borders in Manchuria, in 1933 the Soviet Union achieved diplomatic recognition from the United States. In 1934, it joined the League of Nations, an organization that Lenin had earlier described as "an alliance of world bandits against the proletariat."

After 1934, Soviet delegates frequently attempted to arouse other nations to a realization of the dangers presented by Japan and Germany. In May 1935, the Soviet Union signed the Mutual Assistance Treaty with France, in which each party agreed to come to the assistance of the other in case of an unprovoked attack. That same year, the Soviet government concluded a similar treaty with

Czechoslovakia, except in this case neither party was obligated to aid the other unless France first came to the aid of the attacked nation. Both treaties clearly reflected the Soviet Union's growing fear of Germany.

Another important step taken in 1934 and 1935 was that Moscow directed foreign Communist parties to cooperate with other political parties in nations that were willing to take steps to check German aggression. In both Great Britain and France, however, fear and suspicion of Communist aims hindered close cooperation against Germany. In France, conservative distrust delayed ratification of the pact with Moscow until February 1936.

The Soviet Union's apprehensions about Germany and Japan were increased when the two nations signed the Anti-Comintern Pact in 1936. The following year, Italy, which had been moving closer to Germany, also affixed its signature. Although the pact did little more than record the signatories' opposition to international communism, it did symbolize the growing affinity of the three powers.

Franco Triumphs in Spain

In the Spanish Civil War (1936–1939), dictatorship won a significant victory over democracy. In the summer of 1936, General Francisco Franco invaded Spain from Spanish Morocco, seeking to oust the shaky leftist coalition government of the Spanish Republic. Franco was supported by most of the army, conservative elements in the Spanish Catholic Church, and the middle and upper classes, especially in agrarian areas. The Republican government, on the other hand, relied on support from most urban areas, including the capital, Madrid, and from many of the lower class, especially from the industrial workers. Portions of the Spanish air force and navy also remained loyal to the government. It was a cruel war, with atrocities on both sides; an estimated one million people lost their lives.

From the very beginning, however, the Spanish Civil War was more than a domestic problem. Ideological forces in Europe seized on the conflict as a symbolic test whose outcome would predict the future direction of European affairs. By 1937 Mussolini was assisting Franco with some 70,000 troops and technicians, plus planes and mechanized equipment. Germany had at least 10,000 troops in Spain, including the dreaded Condor Legion, an air force unit that bombed Madrid and other Spanish cities, causing many civilian casualties. On April 26, 1937, the Germans bombed and destroyed the market town and Basque religious center of Guernica, killing and maiming much of the population. "We bombed it, and bombed it, and bombed it, and why not?" one aviator was reputed to have said. The bombings, a preview of World War II terror bombings, outraged world opinion and inspired Pablo Picasso to create *Guernica,* one of the major paintings of the twentieth century.

To counter Fascist and Nazi efforts in Spain, the Soviet Union sent aid and advisors to the Spanish Republic and worked through the Comintern to help drum up volunteers to fight Franco. Even without Soviet promptings, foreigners volunteered to fight on the side of the Spanish government. There were several "international brigades," including the Abraham Lincoln Brigade from the United States and the Canadian McKenzie-Papineau Battalion. The anarchist Emma Goldman also came to Spain to aid in the fight against the Franco forces. For many politically inclined intellectuals, it was a chance, in one way or another, to demonstrate their hatred of fascism and the Nazis. The French novelist and adventurer André Malraux, who flew fighter planes for the Republican side, and the U.S. novelist Ernest Hemingway, who served as correspondent and fundraiser, were just two of the intellectuals who aided the Popular Front government. Leftist support to the Spanish government, however, was not as effective as that given by Italy and Germany to Franco. The Soviet Union appeared more concerned with using the war as an opportunity to control and expand the Spanish Communist party's role than it did with helping to win the war. Divided internally on the left/right political spectrum, Great Britain and France did little to counter outside support to Franco. Fearing that the civil war in Spain might spread, Great Britain and France ineffectually called on outside powers not to intervene in Spain. Thus Hitler and Mussolini once again witnessed the inability of Great Britain and France to check their actions. In 1939, Franco finally defeated the Republic and set up a repressive right-wing dictatorship.

German Aggression: March 1938 to March 1939

Hitler had indicated on the first page of his *Mein Kampf* that union with "German Austria" (*Anschluss*), forbidden in the post-World War I peace treaties signed by Germany and Austria, should be a German goal. He also stated that all German-speaking people should be united in an enlarged German Reich (realm or empire). Territory or living space (*Lebensraum*) for such an empire could be obtained, conquered if need be, in Eastern Europe. His activities during 1938 and 1939 were in keeping with these long-held beliefs.

In March 1938, Germany moved again. By pressure and bullying tactics, Hitler succeeded in bringing a Nazi to power in Austria and obtaining an invitation for Germany to occupy the nation. German troops marched in without resistance, and the forbidden *Anschluss* took place as Austria became a province of Germany. Once again, the French and British did nothing but protest.

In late 1938, Hitler demanded that Czechoslovakia cede what Hitler called "the Sudetenland" to Germany. This territory, which bordered on Germany and the former Austrian Republic, consisted primarily of ethnic Germans. But the area had been a part of the former Austro-Hungarian Empire and not of Germany. On September 15 and again on September 22, the British prime minister, Neville Chamberlain, flew to Germany to see Hitler and try to avert an international crisis. After his first meeting, Chamberlain wrote to his sister: "In spite of the hardness and ruthlessness I thought I saw in his face, I got the impression that here was a man who could be relied upon when he had given his word." On September 29, Chamberlain returned to Germany, where at Munich he and Hitler were joined by Mussolini and the French premier, Edouard

Daladier. Czechoslovakia was not invited to participate in the conference; neither was the Soviet Union, which had pledged to come to the aid of Czechoslovakia in case of aggression, providing France did so first.

Despite Soviet support for Czechoslovakia, the other major powers, including France, which had a defensive alliance with Czechoslovakia, agreed that the Sudetenland was to be given to Germany. Neither France nor Great Britain had kept up with the German rearmament, and neither was yet ready to risk war. French military thinking was symbolized by the Maginot Line, a long series of defensive fortifications built on France's eastern front between 1929 and 1934; such defensive-mindedness ill prepared France to come to the aid of her Czechoslovakian ally.

Poland and Hungary also took advantage of the situation and within a few months seized portions of Czechoslovakia. Altogether, Czechoslovakia lost about a third of its population, much of its heavy industry, and important defensive fortifications. When news of the Munich Agreement was received in Prague, people cried openly in the streets. Despite Chamberlain's claim that "peace for our time" had been achieved, the Munich Conference soon became a symbol of the dangers of "appeasement," and Hitler hardly seemed grateful. "If ever that silly old man comes interfering here again with his umbrella," Hitler said about Chamberlain, "I'll kick him downstairs and jump on his stomach in front of photographers."

The signatories of the Munich Agreement had promised to guarantee what remained of Czechoslovakia against aggression. In March 1939, however, Hitler took over most of what was left of that unfortunate nation except for an eastern portion, Ruthenia, that he allowed Hungary to add to its previous gains. A

After returning from the Munich Conference, British Prime Minister Chamberlain displayed a British-German declaration and predicted "peace for out time." (Central Press Photos)

little later that month, Lithuania, faced with an ultimatum, allowed Germany to annex its Germanic city of Memel. Hitler then began putting pressure on Poland for the return of the city of Danzig, with its overwhelmingly German population, and he also demanded special extraterritorial rail and road rights across the Polish Corridor separating East Prussia from the rest of Germany.

By this time, however, the British and French had finally seen the light. Despite continuing reservations about military readiness, public opinion, especially in Great Britain, had been awakened by the events of March 1939. Appeasement was not working; Hitler always came back for more. On the last day of March, Chamberlain announced that he and the French leaders had agreed to back Poland fully if it were threatened. This awakening, however, came too late for the small nation of Albania, which, already under strong Italian influence, was formally occupied by Mussolini's forces in early April 1939.

The United States Remains Neutral

Like Great Britain and France, the United States had great difficulty creating an effective response to Hitler's and Mussolini's aggressive actions in Europe. The U.S. public viewed the upheavals in Europe with mixed emotions. On the one hand, there was some concern about the persecution of Jews in Germany and some fear of Hitler's threat to European democracy and to the United States. On the other hand, some Americans, like many Europeans, regarded a strong Germany as a bulwark against Soviet communism. Many New Deal liberals feared that involvement in European conflicts would distract energy and money from domestic reforms. An even larger number of Americans simply believed that intervention in World War I had been a mistake and opposed any actions that would involve the United States in another war. Americans were on balance, therefore, isolationists, and when Congress passed a series of Neutrality Acts, 1935–37, it reflected public opinion. In this legislation, Congress prohibited U.S. vessels from transporting war materiel to belligerents, prohibited loans to belligerents, declared the United States neutral in the Spanish Civil War, and forbade U.S. citizens to travel on belligerent ships. By such action, Congress hoped to prevent U.S. trade from dragging the United States into war, as had happened in World War I. Roosevelt and his administration went along with Congress reluctantly, although the effect of the Neutrality Acts was to strengthen Hitler, Mussolini, Franco, and Japan.

As aggression in Europe mounted, the United States, distracted by Japanese advances in China, pursued a policy of appeasement like that of Great Britain and France, in hopes of preserving peace. Roosevelt raised little or no objection to Hitler's moves in the Rhineland, Austria, and the Sudetenland. However, Hitler's seizure of the rest of Czechoslovakia and Mussolini's conquest of Albania shocked Americans and began to bring them around to the belief that aggression in Europe should be stopped. Roosevelt appealed to Hitler to refrain from attacking a list of European nations, but Hitler (like the kaiser's advisors in World War I) viewed the United States as degenerate and incompetent and ridiculed Roosevelt's appeal. Despite Roosevelt's change of posi-

Europe, August 1939

German advances:

Reoccupation of the Rhineland, March 1936

Annexation of Austria, March 1938

Annexation of the Sudetenland, Oct. 1938

Occupation of Bohemia and Moravia, March 1939

Annexation of Memel, March 1939

Italian annexation of Albania, April 1939

Polish and Hungarian annexations of Czech territory

Authoritarian Regimes, 1939

(Austria) former independent nation

0 100 200 300 400 500
Scale of miles

ATLANTIC OCEAN

NORTH SEA

BALTIC SEA

CASPIAN SEA

BLACK SEA

MEDITERRANEAN SEA

AFRICA

U. S. S. R.

Moscow

FINLAND
Helsinki

SWEDEN
Stockholm

NORWAY
Oslo

ESTONIA
LATVIA
LITHUANIA

Memel
Danzig

POLAND
Warsaw

GERMANY
Berlin

Prague (CZECH)
AUSTRIA
Vienna

HUNGARY
Budapest

RUMANIA
Bucharest

BULGARIA
Sofia

YUGOSLAVIA
Belgrade

(ALBANIA)

GREECE
Athens

TURKEY
Istanbul

ITALY
Rome

SWITZ.
Bern

FRANCE
Paris

LUX.

BELG.
Brussels

NETHER-
LANDS
Amsterdam

DENMARK
Copenhagen

GREAT
BRITAIN
London

EIRE
Dublin

SPAIN
Madrid

PORTUGAL
Lisbon

tion, Congress refused to repeal the neutrality legislation, and the United States continued to remain a spectator.

Europe on the Eve of the War

Although the British, and to a somewhat lesser extent the French, were now more determined to oppose any further German moves, Hitler had no way of being sure that his opponents would not again back down. If France and Great Britain did support Poland against German aggression, however, he had to prevent the Soviet Union from becoming involved. If he could obtain a promise of neutrality from Stalin, perhaps Great Britain and France would once again retreat rather than support Poland alone. In any case, he did not want a war on two major fronts.

In 1939, the French government and many influential figures in Great Britain believed that a strong alliance with the Soviet Union was needed if they hoped to avert a war or defeat Hitler if one should come. However, despite their 1935 Mutual Assistance Treaty, France and the Soviet Union were suspicious of each other. Firm military arrangements in case of war, for example, were never worked out. Nor did France's other potential ally, Great Britain, have much faith in the Soviet Union. Chamberlain, especially, still distrusted the Communist giant.

Stalin, of course, had his own interests in mind, and when Hitler's needs inclined him to make a deal with the Soviet Union, Stalin proved willing. Stalin never trusted Great Britain or France and was not opposed to the idea of their fighting Germany in a war that might exhaust and weaken all three.

On August 23, 1939, the Soviet government signed a Non-Aggression Pact with Germany. It stipulated that for ten years both sides would refrain from attacking each other and would remain neutral in case the other became "the object of a belligerent action by a third power." A secret attached protocol, as later modified, divided Eastern Europe into spheres of influence. Finland, Latvia, Estonia, Lithuania, eastern Poland, and Bessarabia (in Rumania) were to be in the Soviet sphere, while Germany's was to be western Poland.

With the Soviet Union now neutralized, Germany was ready to attack Poland, and as a result of the pact Hitler now had reason to hope that Poland might be deserted by Great Britain and France. He attacked Poland on September 1. Two days later, however, Poland's Western allies declared war on Germany. World War II had begun in Europe.

SUMMARY

During the 1930s, both Japan and Germany pursued aggressive policies designed to expand their territories. Interested in controlling its sources of supply in East Asia and worried about China's efforts to strengthen itself, Japan moved first in the decade, seizing Manchuria in 1931. Japan's pace of aggression thereafter accelerated; Japan attacked China in 1937 and subsequently conquered much of it.

In Europe, Nazi Germany and Fascist Italy committed similar aggressions. Between 1936 and 1939, Adolf Hitler tore up the Treaty of Versailles by remilitarizing the Rhineland and annexing Austria, and later partitioned Czechoslovakia, all without effective opposition. Mussolini conquered Ethiopia, helped Franco win the civil war in Spain, and annexed Albania. Germany and Italy were aided, as was Japan, by the reluctance of Great Britain, France, and the United States to take stern measures to check aggression. The Soviet Union was somewhat more willing to stand up to Germany and Japan, but did not wish to do so alone. However, different ideologies and mutual mistrust on the part of the Soviet Union and the Western democracies prevented them from forming an effective coalition against the aggressors. In August 1939, after years of denouncing Nazi behavior, Stalin signed a pact with Hitler, clearing the way for a division of Poland between the two. Allied appeasement of Germany ended when Hitler attacked Poland, bringing on World War II.

SUGGESTED SOURCES

Bell, P. M. H., *The Origins of the Second World War in Europe* (1987). A clear survey suitable for undergraduates.*

Butow, Robert J.C., *Tojo and the Coming of the War* (1969). An excellent study of Japanese policy before and during World War II.*

Divine, Robert H., *The Illusion of Neutrality* (1968). A general account of neutrality legislation in the United States.*

Hemingway, Ernest, *For Whom the Bell Tolls* (1940). A novel depicting the Spanish Civil War by a famous American writer who participated in it.* (Also a film.)

Iriye, Akira, *The Origins of the Second World War in Asia and the Pacific* (1987). A clear introduction by a leading U.S. historian.*

Lafore, Laurence, *The End of Glory* (1970). An excellent introduction to the individuals and events of the 1920s and 1930s that helped lead to World War II.*

Malraux, André, *Man's Hope* (1938). A novel dealing with the Spanish Civil War by a leading French writer who helped organize, and flew for, the Spanish Republican air force.*

Murray, Williamson, *The Change in the European Balance of Power, 1938–1939* (1984). A comprehensive, well-written, and scholarly examination.*

Smith, Gene, *The Dark Summer: An Intimate History of the Events That Led to World War II* (1987). A very interesting narrative, full of colorful quotes which help to reveal the main statesmen and politicians of the time.

Taylor, A.J.P., *The Origins of the Second World War* (1983). A controversial work that questions to what extent Hitler was "guilty" of beginning the war.*

Thorne, Christopher, *The Approach of War, 1938–1939* (1973). A sound, readable account.*

*Paperback available.

20

World War II

Compared to World War I, World War II was a true global phenomenon. The warring nations mounted major land campaigns in Europe, North Africa, and East and Southeast Asia, waged amphibious warfare in the western Pacific, and conducted extensive naval operations throughout the world's oceans.

HITLER'S CONQUESTS IN EUROPE, 1939–1941

In the first year of war, Germany dramatically demonstrated that it had moved tactically far ahead of its opponents. To avoid the stalemate that had defeated them in the last war, the Germans intended to wage *Blitzkrieg* (lightning warfare); this was an effective combination of new weapons, tanks and aircraft, with traditional arms, infantry and artillery, designed to keep the fighting mobile and prevent the opponent from digging in. In early September 1939, masses of German tanks, supported by airplanes, broke through the Polish infantry and pushed behind the Polish lines, disrupting supplies and reinforcements. German infantry mopped up the isolated Polish remnants. The German air force bombed the Polish capital, Warsaw, and other cities, demoralizing the civilian population. The Polish campaign was over in three weeks; the entrenched stalemate that characterized World War I would not be repeated. Operating under prior secret agreement with the Germans, Soviet forces moved in to occupy eastern Poland, whose ethnic makeup was predominantly Byelorussian and Ukrainian. The conquering powers divided Poland, which once again disappeared from the map of Europe.

Hitler offered peace to Great Britain and France if they would recognize his conquest of Poland; when they refused, he made plans to defeat them in the spring and summer of 1940. As German preparations went forward, Great Britain contented itself with driving German surface vessels off the oceans, imposing a blockade, and sending a small army to assist France. The French waited behind the Maginot Line for the German attack, a strategy observers scorned as "sitzkrieg." In April 1940, the Germans thrust northward rather than westward, surprising their opponents. They seized Denmark without resistance and

250

World War II in Europe and Africa

Axis, 1939
U.S.S.R. annexations, 1939-40
Axis satellites, 1941
Axis conquests, 1939-1942
Allied powers and areas under
Allied control
Neutral nations
Axis offensives, 1939-42
Furthest Axis advance, 1941-42
Allied offensives, 1942-45
Junction of Soviet and Western
troops May, 1945

ATLANTIC OCEAN

Reykjavik
ICELAND
From U.S.
From Britain
Allied supply routes
From U.S.

NORTH SEA

EIRE
GREAT BRITAIN
Liverpool
London
NETHER-LANDS
DENMARK
BELG.
Paris
1940
Vichy FRANCE
June 6, 1944
SWITZ.
Elbe
GERMANY
Berlin
1939
1945
1944-45
1945
1944-45
1945
East Prussia
Warsaw
1944
1944
1944
SLOVAKIA
HUNGARY
YUGOSLAVIA
ALBANIA
ITALY
Rome
1943
1944

SWEDEN
NORWAY
1940
FINLAND
1944
Leningrad
Murmansk
Moscow
UNION OF SOVIET SOCIALIST REPUBLICS
1941
1943
Stalingrad
1942-43
ESTONIA
LATVIA
LITHUANIA

CASPIAN SEA
IRAN
IRAQ
SAUDI ARABIA
TRANS-JORDAN
SYRIA
LEBANON
PALESTINE
Suez Canal
EGYPT
El Alamein
1942
1942-43

BLACK SEA
TURKEY
Yalta
RUMANIA
BULGARIA
GREECE
Crete
CYPRUS

MEDITERRANEAN SEA
1944
1943
1943
TUNISIA
Tunis
Algiers
1942
ALGERIA
LIBYA
1943

SPAIN
PORTUGAL
1942
SP. MOROCCO
Casablanca
MOROCCO

Persian Gulf

Scale of miles
100   500

251

conquered Norway in two weeks, expelling British forces that had attempted to hold northern Norway. Germany now controlled the export of neutral Sweden's iron ore and could now use the Norwegian coast as a base for air and submarine attacks on British shipping. In Great Britain, the Chamberlain government collapsed and the dynamic Winston Churchill became prime minister of Great Britain.

In May, the Germans struck in Western Europe. They quickly overran the Dutch, and the Belgians soon surrendered. Instead of wheeling in an arc as in the previous war, the Germans launched a massive armored attack through a gap at Sedan, France, in the center of the Allied front in Western Europe. The German forces broke through and dashed to the English Channel, cutting off the British army and some French troops from the main body of French forces. Using almost every craft in Great Britain that would float, the British staged a spectacular rescue operation at Dunkirk. They were able to evacuate most of the soldiers but had to leave behind their supplies and heavy equipment, leaving the British army gravely weakened. In the face of the disaster, Churchill rallied the British people: "We shall fight on the beaches, we shall fight on the landing grounds, we shall fight in the fields and in the streets, we shall fight in the hills; we shall never surrender." In June, the Germans drove southward and westward across France, bypassing the Maginot Line. The French army was unable to consolidate a front. With the French near defeat, Italy declared war.

On June 22, France surrendered. For the surrender ceremony, Hitler chose the same spot and same railroad car where the German representatives had signed the armistice in 1918. Under the terms of surrender, Germany annexed Alsace-Lorraine and the Germans occupied northern and western France, enabling Hitler to use the French coastline for submarine and air bases against Great Britain. Unoccupied France, with its capital at Vichy, became an ally of Germany. A small contingent of French troops in Africa and refugee French soldiers and officials in Great Britain, led by General Charles de Gaulle, formed a government in exile and fought on at the side of the British. French underground "resistance" fighters harassed the Germans in France.

While Hitler was overrunning Western Europe, the Soviet Union was improving its position in Eastern Europe. It occupied the Baltic nations of Lithuania, Latvia, and Estonia, and a border province of Rumania; after a difficult war with the Finns, it annexed some border sections of Finland and a site for a naval base on the Baltic Sea. These moves, combined with its earlier incorporation of eastern Poland, enabled the Soviet Union to widen the buffer zone between Germany and the heart of the Soviet Union. These actions alienated and frightened the Eastern European authoritarian regimes and drove most of them to seek alliances with Hitler.

Meanwhile, Hitler turned his attention to his surviving enemy, Great Britain. He had never really been interested in fighting the British, and he made peace overtures to them based on the status quo. Great Britain rejected the German offers, although it was too crippled to attack Germany in Europe. Hitler then moved to invade Great Britain. He planned first to use his air force to destroy the British air force. With British planes destroyed, the Germans would be able to bomb or drive off the British fleet; the German army could then invade England. All through the summer and early autumn of 1940, a great air battle, the Battle of Britain, raged, but the Germans failed to destroy the British air force. "Never have so many owed so much to so few," said Churchill of the British airmen. The Germans turned to terror bombing the British cities, hoping to demoralize the British population, who would then force the British government to sue for peace. Despite extensive damage to some British cities and heavy loss of life, the British civilians persevered. Churchill was an inspirational leader and effectively exhorted the British to fight on: "Hitler knows that he must break us in this island or lose the war. . . . Let us therefore brace ourselves to our duty and so bear ourselves that . . . men will . . . say, 'This was their finest hour.'" By the winter of 1940–41, it was clear that Great Britain would continue in the war, although essentially on the defensive. Hitler hoped that a more intensive version of the World War I submarine blockade would eventually strangle the British.

Although the British remained unconquered, Hitler could not resist turning to his longstanding dream of destroying the Communist government in the Soviet Union, enslaving its people, and colonizing the East with Germanic peoples. He planned to throw his army and air force against the Soviet Union in mid-May 1941 and to destroy Stalin's regime in five months, before winter set in. In preparation for the assault, Hitler forged alliances with Hungary, Rumania, and Bulgaria, reached an understanding with Finland, and moved German and allied troops up to the Soviet border.

Hitler's plans to invade the Soviet Union were disrupted, however, by the difficulties of his ally Mussolini. The British had conquered Italian East Africa, driven into Libya, sunk most of the Italian navy, and supported the Greeks in repelling an Italian invasion. In April 1941, with Yugoslavia on the verge of joining the British and Greeks, Hitler acted. German forces and their allies overwhelmed Yugoslavia, but guerrillas, especially Communist units led by Joseph Tito, fought the Germans there throughout the war. The British tried to hold Greece and Crete to protect their Mediterranean supply route, but were driven out. Meanwhile, Hitler dispatched the famed Afrika Corps under General Erwin Rommel to aid the Italians, and Rommel pushed into Egypt toward the Suez Canal. Desperate, the British called on Indian and ANZAC troops to hold Egypt and to protect the Middle East petroleum fields. The Soviets and British deposed the pro-German shah of Iran, Reza Pahlavi, and installed his young son Mohammed as ruler. Turkey, caught between German success in Europe and British and Soviet power in Asia, remained neutral.

In the meantime, Hitler prepared to invade the Soviet Union. The Balkan campaign had been highly successful, but it had delayed the invasion of the Soviet Union for five precious weeks. Fearing British invasion, Hitler left a large number of troops and planes in Western Europe, and launched the invasion of the Soviet Union with the bulk of his armed forces on June 22, 1941, exactly a year after the surrender of France. Throughout the summer, *blitzkrieg* tactics worked spectacularly for the Germans and their allies. They destroyed the Soviet air force and surrounded entire Soviet armies; four million Soviet soldiers surrendered. "The Russians are finished. They have nothing left to throw against us," Hitler chortled.

By November 1941, the Germans did indeed appear to be on their way to victory. They had Leningrad surrounded on three sides, and Nazi forces were less than twenty miles from Moscow. In the south, the Germans had reached Rostov-on-the-Don. Despite these massive gains, the German offensive was in fact beginning to sag because of accumulated casualties, a shortage of transport, the climate, distance, and inadequate forces assigned to too many objectives. After an initial period of irresolution, Stalin rallied, encouraging dogged Soviet resistance in front of Moscow and Leningrad. In December, Hitler called a halt to his campaign for the winter. He had lost three-quarters of a million men, his armies were short on supplies and warm clothing, and his equipment was breaking down under extensive wear and intensive cold—on December 2 the Moscow temperature reached 40 degrees below zero. By no means defeated, the Soviets counterattacked during the winter and drove the Germans back from Moscow. Hitler was confident, however, that he could finish off the Soviets in the summer of 1942.

HITLER'S "NEW ORDER" AND THE HOLOCAUST

By the autumn of 1941, Hitler was the master of the continent of Europe and used his control to carry out his demonic vision of a "New Order." At the center of Europe he created the Greater German Nation, consisting of an enlarged Germany, much of Poland and Czechoslovakia, and parts of Yugoslavia and France. This would be the homeland of the superior Aryan race. Germany stripped the nations under its military control for the benefit of the German war effort, often to the point of causing severe deprivation and hunger. Hitler ordered his allies to supply his nation with products on terms favorable to it and to follow its lead in foreign and military affairs. Germany directed commanders in the occupied areas and the governments of the client states to deport "undesirables" to Germany for slave labor; the number eventually reached nine million. Farther to the east, Hitler planned to use the Soviet Union for the future expansion of the Aryan race. Germans were to be settled there in increasing numbers as a master class that would control the vast raw materials in that region. The Slavs and Asiatics there, considered subhumans, would be reduced to serfs.

As a part of the New Order, Hitler's regime decided to implement "The Final Solution," a program to exterminate the Jews and Gypsies of Europe that is now referred to as the Holocaust. The Final Solution is an example of genocide, a systematic process to destroy a particular national, ethnic, or racial group. History has recorded many instances of mankind's episodes of genocide, the Turkish massacre of Armenians during World War I being one of the more recent examples. In the east, the Nazis and local police forces rounded up Jews along with resistance fighters and Communist party members; special execution teams shot them and dumped them into mass graves. This method was soon deemed to be too slow and expensive, however, and after 1941, nearly

The Holocaust: After their uprising in the Warsaw Ghetto was crushed, surviving Jews are marched to the trains that would take them to extermination camps (above). The fate of these Jews, and millions like them, was to be gassed in batches and to have remains burned in ovens (below). (Above, YIVO Institute for Jewish Research; below, UPI/Bettmann Newsphotos)

Hitler's New Order: Millions of slave laborers and political prisoners who were not Jews were beaten, tortured, starved, and worked to death in concentration camps throughout Europe. (UPI/Bettmann Newsphotos)

every area of Europe under Hitler's control was ordered to send its Jews to special extermination camps located primarily in Poland. Arriving packed in railroad boxcars, they were systematically gassed, then cremated, and their remains processed for soap and blanket fibers. At Auschwitz, the Nazis killed an average of 12,000 people, including some non-Jews, a day.

By one means or another, approximately six million Jews, about 75 percent of the European Jewish population, were put to death. Millions of other Europeans perished in the slave labor camps from overwork, malnutrition, disease, and abuse. The Allies did little of consequence to aid the victims. How much and how soon the Allies knew about the situation, and how much the Allies could be accused of sharing the guilt for the Holocaust, has been the subject of historical debate. The horror of the Holocaust convinced many Jews to support the Zionist idea of setting up an independent Jewish state in Palestine. There Jews could control the government instead of being, as elsewhere, a minority group subject to the power and attitudes of the majority.

THE UNITED STATES AND EUROPEAN AFFAIRS

As the power of Hitler spread across Europe, the U.S. government became increasingly concerned. President Roosevelt believed that, unless halted, Nazism

Defying the Holocaust

We have been pointedly reminded that we are in hiding, that we are Jews in chains, chained to one spot, without any rights, but with a thousand duties. We Jews mustn't show our feelings, must be brave and strong, must accept all inconveniences and not grumble, must do what is within our power and trust in God. Sometime this terrible war will be over. Surely the time will come when we are people again, and not just Jews.

Who has inflicted this upon us? Who has made us Jews different from all other people? Who has allowed us to suffer so terribly up till now? It is God that has made us as we are, but it will be God, too, who will raise us up again. If we bear all this suffering and if there are still Jews left, when it is over, then Jews, instead of being doomed, will be held up as an example. . . .

If God lets me live . . . I shall not remain insignificant, I shall work in the world and for mankind!

And now I know that first and foremost I shall require courage and cheerfulness!*

Anne Frank was a fourteen-year-old German Jew in hiding in Amsterdam when this diary entry was written on 11 April 1944. Four months later she was arrested and sent to Auschwitz and later to the Belsen concentration camp, where she died in 1945.

*Excerpted from *Anne Frank: The Diary of a Young Girl* by Anne Frank, copyright 1952 by Otto H. Frank. Used by permission of Doubleday, a division of Bantam, Doubleday, Dell Publishing Group, Inc.

and fascism would wipe out democracy in Europe and would become a direct threat to the safety of the United States. The public at large, however, opposed any actions that might lead the United States into war. U.S. neutrality legislation was technically evenhanded, but its effect was to aid Great Britain, since the British could buy and transport U.S. goods to Great Britain while the British naval blockade prevented Germany from getting supplies.

While the U.S. public continued to hope for peace, U.S. leaders began to prepare for a possible war. By 1940, Congress was providing funds for a rapid increase in the armed forces, and later in the year created the first peacetime conscription act in U.S. history. Meanwhile, the U.S. economy was booming with orders from the U.S. and British governments for war materiel.

Events in 1940 and 1941 drew the United States ever closer to the war in Europe. In September 1940, the United States agreed to supply Great Britain with fifty old destroyers in exchange for British bases in the Caribbean, Bermuda, and Canada. By 1941, with Hitler's power spreading south and east across Europe, the U.S. government became more assertive. Congress created a massive Lend-Lease program by making billions of dollars' worth of military equipment available to Great Britain and the Soviet Union. U.S. military forces began to take control of the western Atlantic, sending forces to occupy Greenland and Iceland and escorting convoys to midpoint in the Atlantic. By the autumn of 1941, with U.S. destroyers taking casualties in conflicts with German submarines, and with the orders given to arm merchantmen, the United States was only one step short of war with Germany.

CONFRONTATION BETWEEN JAPAN AND THE UNITED STATES

While Germany was conquering Europe, Japan was continuing to expand in Asia. By 1940 Japan had secured the coal and iron ore of Manchuria and north China and controlled the major industrial centers and seaports of China. Much of the Japanese army was bogged down in China, but the Japanese were determined to fight on until they had finally defeated the Chinese. The Japanese were equally determined to press on into Southeast Asia to wrest the petroleum, rubber, and tin located there from Western colonial control.

The United States continued to be the main opponent of Japanese plans for Asia. Committed to open economic access to an independent China, the United States, along with Great Britain, did what little it could to supply Chinese military forces. The United States also made it clear to the Japanese that it opposed Japanese expansion in Southeast Asia. Japan was prepared to attack the United States if that became necessary to control East and Southeast Asia.

Japan was aided in its expansionist plans by the war in Europe. In the summer of 1940, with France defeated and Great Britain beleaguered, Japan forced the British to close the Burma Road supply route to China and pressured the Vichy government to agree to Japanese occupation of northern Indochina, thus cutting off another source of supplies to China. The United States responded with an embargo on sales of aviation fuel and scrap metal to Japan, although general trade continued. Japan countered by signing the Tripartite Pact with Germany and Italy, in which the three powers pledged to aid each other if any one of them was attacked by a new enemy, which in this case would have been the United States.

In the summer of 1941, the tension between the United States and Japan heated up. The Japanese moved into southern Indochina and appeared to be about to launch a military conquest of Southeast Asia. The United States responded by expanding the embargo and freezing Japanese assets in the United States, while beginning discussions with the Dutch and the British concerning the mutual defense of Southeast Asia. Meanwhile, the Japanese government began a two-pronged program. On the one hand, Japanese diplomats were instructed to continue to try to reach agreements with the United States that would guarantee Japan access to the raw materials of Southeast Asia and a free hand to deal with the Chinese. On the other hand, since the diplomats were likely to fail, the military laid plans for the conquest of Southeast Asia and the elimination of U.S. power in Asia. Throughout the late summer and the autumn of 1941, Japanese diplomats pressed their position on the United States, while the United States countered with the demand for Japanese withdrawal from Indochina and China. By the end of November, faced with the failure of negotiations, the new military-controlled cabinet of General Hideki Tojo decided to proceed with the military plans. Beginning on December 7, 1941, the Japanese attacked the British, Dutch, and Americans throughout Southeast Asia, highlighted by a surprise attack on the U.S. Pacific fleet at Pearl Harbor. The United States declared war on Japan on December 8; Germany and Italy declared war on the United States on December 11, 1941. World War II was now to be a massive struggle in Asia as well as in Europe.

JAPANESE CONQUESTS IN ASIA AND THE PACIFIC, 1941–1942

Japan's program for waging war was a mixture of offensive and defensive strategies. Japan intended to seize Southeast Asia and the vital supplies there, defeat Chiang Kai-shek, and drive the U.S. forces from the Philippines and the western Pacific. Japanese leaders believed that once they were in control of East Asia and had dug in behind a wall of fortified islands in the western Pacific, the Western powers would be unable to fight their way back into Asia and would agree to Japan's having a free hand there.

In the five months following December 7, the Japanese secured most of their goals. The Japanese war machine either destroyed Western military forces or drove them out of East Asia. The U.S. Pacific fleet was bombed into temporary impotence, although it was by no means destroyed, since it had its vital aircraft carriers. Thailand was forced into an alliance with Japan, and the British were driven from Burma and Malaya, surrendering 60,000 men at Singapore. The Japanese quickly overran the Dutch East Indies and forced the U.S. army in the Philippines to surrender. They seized American and British islands in the Western Pacific and secured a foothold in the Aleutian Islands and on New Guinea. Australia appeared to be Japan's next target, and Australians prepared for resistance. By April 1942 the Japanese had accumulated a vast land and water domain that geographically dwarfed the conquests of Adolf Hitler.

Japan's next step was to consolidate its conquests. Japan intended to eradicate the vestiges of Western colonialism and to exploit the conquered areas for its economic benefit. Toward these ends, Japan organized the Greater East Asia Co-Prosperity Sphere. Its ultimate aim was to make Southeast Asia an economically self-sufficient community that would blend into the rest of the Japanese Empire. In pursuing their goal, however, the Japanese made such heavy demands for manpower and materials and caused such hardship that they

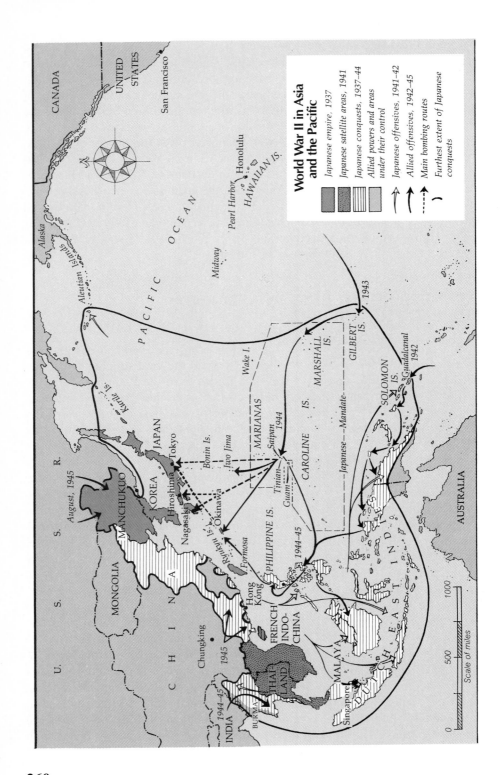

World War II in Asia and the Pacific

Japanese empire, 1937
Japanese satellite areas, 1941
Japanese conquests, 1937–44
Allied powers and areas under their control
Japanese offensives, 1941–42
Allied offensives, 1942–45
Main bombing routes
Furthest extent of Japanese conquests

eventually turned the local peoples against Japan. In the Philippines, where independence had been promised by the United States, resistance to the Japanese was strong and Japanese repression was especially brutal.

FORGING THE "GRAND ALLIANCE" AGAINST THE AXIS

By 1942 two different conflicts of unprecedented magnitude, waged simultaneously, raged across the globe. In the Pacific and East Asia, the United States and China, with limited aid from the British Empire, made war against Japan. In Europe and North Africa, the Soviet Union, Great Britain, the British Empire, and minor allies were locked in combat with Germany and its allies, with the United States about to bring its armed forces into action.

Germany, Italy, and Japan (the Axis powers) did not coordinate their side of the two struggles. Their opponents, however, realized it was necessary to come to an agreement on strategic priorities. Before U.S. entry into the war, Roosevelt and Churchill announced in the 1941 Atlantic Charter that opponents of the Axis would fight not to gain foreign territory but only to halt aggression. Stalin gave his qualified approval. From 1942 to 1945, Roosevelt, Churchill,

Yalta Summit Conference, 1945: Churchill, Roosevelt, and Stalin plan for the ending of World War II and for the postwar period. (AP/Wide World Photos)

and Stalin met at several conferences around the world to evolve a strategy for the defeat of the Axis powers. This was not easy; the Western Allies and the Soviet Union were suspicious of each other, and at times there were intense differences between the United States and Great Britain. Nevertheless, faced with a common peril, the leaders hammered out a series of broad agreements. The three men agreed that their nations would not make a separate peace but would fight the war through to the unconditional surrender of all the Axis powers. They concurred that Germany should be defeated first, both because it was a greater threat and because the Allies were in a better position to assist each other effectively in Europe. Stalin agreed that the Soviet Union would join in the war against Japan after Germany had been defeated. The leaders also decided to place all Allied forces in Western Europe under a single supreme commander, U.S. General Dwight Eisenhower.

By far the greatest point of friction between the Allies was the time and place to attack German forces from the west. The Soviet Union demanded that the United States and Great Britain land in Western Europe, presumably France, as soon as possible, creating a second front. This would take some of the pressure off the Soviet Union, whose people were desperately struggling against the main strength of the German armed forces. With an eye to postwar Europe as well as to the defeat of Germany, the British wanted to attack first what Churchill termed "the soft underbelly of Europe." This involved clearing North Africa, conquering Italy, and liberating the Balkans. This approach would fully open up supply routes to Great Britain and keep the Soviets out of the Mediterranean and Eastern Europe, but it involved fighting in difficult terrain in Italy and the Balkans. U.S. leaders vacillated. As the war progressed, the United States supported clearing the Mediterranean but opposed landing in the Balkans. It eventually supported opening a front in France at the earliest opportunity.

INDUSTRIAL MOBILIZATION FOR TOTAL WAR

The awesome industrial and agricultural output of the United States, which made that nation, in Roosevelt's words, "The Great Arsenal of Democracy," was a crucial factor in the Allied defeat of the Axis powers. As in World War I, the wartime enemies of the United States had fatally underestimated U.S. economic power, with Marshal Hermann Goering sneering that Americans "only knew how to make refrigerators and razor blades." U.S. factories not only equipped their own military establishment of twelve million men, but also underwrote part of the war effort of Great Britain, the Soviet Union, and other allies. During the war, U.S. factories and shipyards produced 300,000 airplanes, 88,000 tanks, 2.5 million trucks, 17.4 million rifles, 315,000 artillery pieces, and 3,000 ships. Some ships were built in as little as seventeen days. U.S. farmers increased production by one-third, enabling the United States to send food to other nations. U.S. military output doubled the combined production of the Axis powers; when Allied industrial output, particularly that of the Soviet Union later in the war, is added to that of the United States, one key reason for the eventual defeat of the Axis is clear.

The massive military production of the United States and other nations involved in World War II was one aspect of total war, made possible by an ever-increasing alliance between government, industry, and the military. Even more than in World War I, national governments closely regulated the production of raw materials, monitored labor, set production priorities, created manufacturing establishments where needed, and regulated the price and distribution of civilian and military products. Again, more than in World War I, home front populations were exhorted by government propaganda organizations through pamphlets, radio, and motion pictures to hate the enemy, make sacrifices, and work harder. When the war was over, the citizens of the Western democracies had become conditioned to function in a national environment in which the government was thoroughly integrated into economic and social life.

THE WAR AT SEA

Like World War I, World War II was largely one of attrition. In the new war, the airplane joined the submarine and the minefield as key weapons in the attempt to destroy the economy of opponents and to erode the morale of the enemy civilian populations. Early in the war, as in World War I, the British navy mined the approaches to Germany, cutting off all supplies to Germany from outside Europe. This time, however, the British were unable to close off a corridor within Norwegian territorial waters, a gap exploited by German submarines and naval surface raiders. In any case, during World War II Germany controlled the economy of most of Europe and was much less vulnerable to blockade than it had been in World War I.

Great Britain, on the other hand, was just as vulnerable to blockade as ever. Surprisingly, despite the proven effectiveness of its submarines during World War I, Germany had only a few of them ready for service in 1939. After the outbreak of war, Germany embarked on an intensive submarine building program, and by 1942 it had built a large number of U-boats that were capable of long-distance travel. U-boats prowled the entire North and South Atlantic, operating from well-defended bases on the coasts of occupied Norway and France. Clusters of submarines, "wolfpacks," tore into Allied convoys as far south as Brazil and South Africa, while other U-boats operated along the Atlantic and Gulf coasts of the United States. Land-based aircraft from Norway assisted German submarines in attacking convoys attempting to pass around Scandinavia with supplies for the Soviet Union.

The Allies fought the submarines with increasing success, using the convoy system, destroyers, and submarine-hunting escort carriers, and by late 1943 the worst of the submarine threat was over. Submarines failed to sink any of the hundreds of transports that carried over a million soldiers to Europe. Still, the Atlantic was a grim theater of war, in which thousands of merchantmen and sailors were blown up, burned in oil fires, or drowned.

In the Pacific, the war at sea featured numerous encounters between elements of the surface fleets of the United States and Japan. The largest encounters introduced a new mode of naval combat: carrier warfare. Earlier in the century, naval combat had been decided by large battleships raining heavy shells on the enemy fleet. In the Pacific in World War II, the heart of naval task forces consisted of aircraft carriers, surrounded like queen bees by supporting craft bristling with anti-aircraft batteries. Most battles were decided by the number of carriers sunk by the waves of dive bombers, high-altitude bombers, and torpedo planes launched by opposing naval squadrons hundreds of miles apart. The United States won the largest, most crucial naval battles, in part because it had cracked the Japanese naval code.

Submarine warfare was also extremely important to the Pacific, and here the roles were reversed. Like Great Britain, Japan was dependent on shipping to secure food and raw materials and to supply its armies on the Asian mainland and garrisons in the western Pacific. Realizing Japan's vulnerability, the United States mounted a campaign to sink its merchant shipping and thus strangle its war effort. By 1945, American submarines and aircraft had succeeded in destroying the bulk of the Japanese merchant marine and had virtually cut off Japan from Asia and the Pacific islands.

THE AIR WAR

While there was extensive tactical bombing in support of ground operations, the war in the air was dominated by the strategic bombardment of the enemy's economic and military installations, accompanied by the terror bombing of civilian population centers. These operations, in which helpless civilians were attacked with the same weapons used against military combatants, was another aspect of the total war concept that typified World War II. The Germans had used both strategic and terror bombing in their attacks on Poland, Western Europe, and Great Britain. After 1942, the air war began to turn against the Axis; Allied bombers probed deeper and deeper into Germany and Central Europe. Allied fighters furnished protection for the bombers and shot down German planes faster than they could be replaced. As German air resistance weakened, Allied bombers became increasingly effective in destroying factories, dams, roads, canals, and railroads, although the Germans rebuilt their factories underground. The Allies also used terror bombing. Certain raids on Hamburg and Berlin and the raid on Dresden killed hundreds of thousands of civilians.

To supplement the rapidly declining regular air force, German specialists in military technology came up with a series of new weapons. Jet-propelled aircraft appeared in the skies late in the war, but too late to become effective. Germany produced V-1 jet-powered flying bombs ("buzz bombs") and used them to strike at southeastern Britain. They also developed the V-2 liquid-fueled rockets. Because they traveled at a high speed and struck without warning, the V-2s had a particularly depressing psychological effect on British civilians. Nevertheless, Germany had too few of these rockets and used them too late in the war for them to be decisive. Like the airplane and the tank in World War I, the jet airplane and the guided missile pointed toward the nature of war in the future.

Strategic bombardment came late in the Pacific, but once underway it was devastating. Most of the war in the Pacific was centered around the U.S. forces working into positions from which they could bomb the Japanese homeland. The bombardment of Japan was not effective until late 1944, when bombers began to fly over Japan from bases in the Marianas. The Japanese air force was effectively wiped out by 1945, and by the spring and summer of 1945, U.S. bombers flew at will over the cities of Japan, using incendiary bombs to create raging "firestorms" that consumed the wooden buildings of the Japanese cities along with hundreds of thousands of Japanese civilians.

THE ALLIES DEFEAT THE AXIS, 1942–1945

Soviet Victories and Nazi Defeat

In 1942, the war in Europe centered on a titanic struggle in Russia. Here the bulk and the cream of the German armed forces was pitted against the capacity of the Soviet Union to fight on virtually alone and endure tremendous suffering while it built up its own massive war machine. Like the Japanese in China, the bulk of the German army and air force, including their best units, found themselves bogged down on a 1,000-mile front inside an enemy nation of vast geographical dimensions and huge population. Unlike the Japanese, however, Hitler had not taken his primary objectives; Leningrad and Moscow in the north and the Caucasus petroleum fields in the south remained in Soviet hands.

The Germans added to their problems in the Soviet Union by making a calamitous mistake in dealing with the civilians in the areas they had conquered. Although many non-Russian ethnic groups in the Soviet Union initially greeted the Germans as liberators, and some fought on the German side, the Nazis regarded all Slavs as subhuman. They inflicted so many atrocities that they unified most of the ethnic groups in the Soviet Union against them, stirring up a swarm of guerrillas who attacked German supply lines and installations. Another problem for the Germans was that their economy and their transportation system, increasingly disrupted by British and U.S. aerial bombardment, faltered in their efforts to keep the German armed forces effectively supplied over the vast sweep of the Russian front. In the autumn of 1942, Soviet forces began to drive the Germans back and surrounded a German army at Stalingrad. After a ferocious struggle, the Germans surrendered in January 1943, having incurred 300,000 casualties. Stalingrad effectively ended Germany's hope of defeating the Soviet Union.

By 1943 the Soviet Union, with some U.S. and British aid, had created an impressive armaments industry that now sustained a huge military machine— over six million men, more than double the German army. Soviet forces also outnumbered the Germans three to one in artillery, tanks, and airplanes. With this superiority, the Soviets could now attack along several sectors simulta-

This gigantic statue in Kiev is one of the memorials to the suffering and heroics of Soviet citizens in World War II.

neously. In July 1943, the Soviets destroyed the core of Germany's tank forces at Kursk and made advances all along the front. By the spring of 1944, Soviet troops had reconquered the Ukraine, and pushed into Rumania and Poland. They also lifted the 900-day siege of Leningrad, but not before a million of its citizens had perished—one graphic example of the massive suffering the German invasion inflicted on the Soviet Union, where over twenty million died. The defeat of German forces on the eastern front was now only a matter of time.

Attacking From the West and the Final Phases

With the Germans fully occupied in the Soviet Union, the Western Allies struck in the Mediterranean. In November 1942, the Americans and British used the new technology of amphibious warfare to land on the coasts of Vichy-held Morocco and Algeria, quickly overrunning these areas and pushing eastward. At the same time, British and Commonwealth forces pushed westward out of Egypt across Libya. Most of the German and Italian forces in North Africa were caught between the two drives and surrendered in Tunisia in May 1943. In July and August 1943, U.S. and British forces conquered Sicily. In September, Allied forces landed on the Italian peninsula, forcing the Italians to overthrow Mussolini and to surrender. The Germans pushed troops into Italy and dug in across the peninsula south of Rome, preventing further Allied advance. The armies bogged down in a winter warfare of fortification and mud resembling the trench warfare of World War I.

In the summer and autumn of 1944, the Allies opened the crucial campaigns that were to end the war in Europe. On June 6, 1944—''D-Day''—U.S., British, and Canadian forces launched a massive landing on the Normandy coast in France, opening a major second front. For a month, German forces held the Allies close to the beaches, but in July the Americans broke out and German resistance collapsed in France. By the autumn, German forces had withdrawn to the fortified western border of Germany. In Italy, the central part of the peninsula, including Rome, fell to the Allies, but the Germans retained control of the north.

During 1944, the Soviets continued their relentless drive westward. By December, the Soviet army had cleared most of the Balkans, and advanced to the outskirts of Budapest and Warsaw. Anti-Communist Poles in Warsaw rose in revolt against the Germans. Soviet troops did not cross the Vistula River to aid the Poles, and the Germans smashed the revolt. Finland, Rumania, and Bulgaria surrendered, and Tito's Communist partisans made headway against the Germans in Yugoslavia. British troops entered Greece to finish securing the Mediterranean and to prevent Soviet expansion in that area.

By the spring of 1945, Germany was caught in a massive vise. Allied forces crossed the Rhine and passed eastward, while Soviet forces moved in from the east and surrounded Berlin. Hitler committed suicide in his underground bunker in Berlin on April 30, as Western and Soviet forces met in the middle of Germany. By May 8, 1945, all German units in Europe had surrendered. The war in Europe was over.

Campaigns against Japan, 1942–1944

In mid-1942, the tide began to turn against Japan in the Pacific. The Japanese fleet was driven back from its advance on the Hawaiian Islands at the Battle of Midway, the first important reverse for the Japanese navy. In late 1942 and early 1943, in fighting centering at Guadalcanal, Allied forces gradually pushed the Japanese out of the islands northeast of Australia, relieving the Japanese threat.

By 1943 the enormous U.S. war effort was turning out enough war materiel and training enough men to press the war in the Pacific as well as in Europe. In 1943 and early 1944, U.S. forces in the Pacific attacked selected islands in the Central Pacific, in a strategy called ''island-hopping.'' Once secured, these islands served as bases for attacks on the main objective: islands in the Marianas close enough to Japan to serve as bases for long-range bombing. Meanwhile, General Douglas MacArthur worked his way along the coast of New Guinea, with the intention of eventually seizing the Philippines and Formosa and using them as a base for invading Japan. The Japanese garrisons on the remaining islands in the perimeter, cut off from supply or reinforcement, were left to starve in isolation.

In June and July 1944, Admiral Chester Nimitz's forces seized Saipan and Tinian in the Marianas. Here were set up major bases from which the new B-29 bomber could begin the regular bombardment of Japanese cities. MacArthur meanwhile began the reconquest of the Philippines. This, plus the destruction of the remainder of the Japanese fleet in a series of naval battles off the Philippines, effectively cut off Japanese forces in Southeast Asia from those in China and Japan.

The Atomic Bomb: The Climax of Total War

In the spring of 1945, the Japanese were in full retreat across Asia and the Pacific. The Chinese were pushing forward, while the British and Indians were reconquering Burma. The U.S. command needed air bases closer to Japan and captured the islands of Iwo Jima and Okinawa, sustaining heavy casualties.

The resolute Japanese defense of Iwo Jima and Okinawa, including the extensive use of *kamikaze* (suicide) air attacks, made it clear that invading the Japanese home islands would lead to a terrible loss of life for both sides. Mean-

The devastation of the atomic bomb dropped on Nagasaki on August 9, 1945. (UPI/Bettmann Newsphotos)

while, Allied scientists had created two atomic bombs; in July 1945, President Harry Truman, who had succeeded to office after Roosevelt's death in April 1945, authorized their use. On August 6, the U.S. air force dropped one bomb on Hiroshima; it delivered the other one on Nagasaki on August 9. The bombs, based on the power unleashed by splitting and fusing atoms, created tremendous explosive and radioactive effects that caused as much damage and death as hundreds of conventional bombs. They killed 200,000 Japanese, while the radioactive effects kept on killing long after the bombs were dropped.

Historians subsequently argued about whether or not Japan would have soon surrendered without having been hit with the atomic bombs. They have also debated whether the bomb was dropped primarily to end the war or to shape the postwar era (see Chapter 22). In any case, the fact that Truman did agree to drop the bombs, a decision which carried even further the trend of terror bombing masses of civilians, indicated how the "total war" concept now dominated the conflict. The huge, mushroom-shaped clouds towering over the doomed cities became the symbol of a new era: Humanity had pushed the concept of total war to the point where it had created the technology to destroy itself.

The detonation of the two atomic bombs quickly brought the war to its end. On August 8, the Soviet Union, as it had earlier agreed to do, declared war and attacked Japanese forces in Manchuria and Korea. The destruction caused by the bombs, coupled with the general military situation, convinced Emperor Hirohito that Japan had lost the war. On August 14, the Japanese announced their surrender, which was ratified at a ceremony on September 2, 1945, in Tokyo Bay. World War II was over.

SUMMARY

When World War II broke out in Europe in 1939 and in Asia in 1941, the Axis powers were far better prepared than their opponents. Using the new military technology of the improved tank and airplane effectively, German forces easily defeated and occupied Poland, Denmark, Norway, the Netherlands, Belgium, Luxemburg, and France. Great Britain held out despite submarine blockades and air bombardment, and the Germans and their Italian and East European allies turned their attention southward and eastward in 1941, conquering Yugoslavia and Greece, reinvading Egypt, and smashing into the Soviet Union. Although the Russians suffered immense losses, the Germans bogged down in front of Leningrad and Moscow in December 1941. Meanwhile, the Japanese decided that war was necessary to complete their designs on Southeast Asia. Accordingly, they invaded Southeast Asia and attacked U.S. naval forces in Hawaii in December 1941, quickly overrunning Southeast Asia and the western Pacific. German and Japanese administration of their conquered territories was brutal. In German-controlled Europe, mass enslavement and extermination campaigns led to millions of deaths and suffering for millions more.

In order to defeat the Axis powers, an effective alliance had to be forged by those nations allied against them, including—insofar as possible—common strategy and unified command. The United States became the economic and military backbone of the war against Germany from the west and of the war against Japan, while the Soviet Union engaged in a massive struggle with the main German forces. Extensive sea and air campaigns strangled the economies of Germany and Japan and inflicted heavy casualties on their civilian populations. The Allies finally defeated Germany by first clearing the Mediterranean and knocking Italy out of the war and then crushing Germany between massive advances from the east and west. The United States defeated Japan by isolating and ignoring the bulk of its armed forces in the Pacific and Asia and seizing selected islands in the Pacific. From these islands, U.S. fliers methodically bombed Japan. Japan surrendered after the United States dropped atomic bombs on Hiroshima and Nagasaki.

SUGGESTED SOURCES

Clark, Alan, *Barbarossa* (1965). A lively account of the Soviet-German struggle in Europe during World War II.*

Costello, John, *The Pacific War* (1981). A comprehensive account of the struggle between the Allies and Japan, based in part on recently released documents.

Kuznetsov, Anatoli V., *Babi Yar,* uncensored ed. (1970). A well-written, realistic novel of the German occupation of Kiev and the mass killing of Jews at Babi Yar.*

Monsarrat, Nicholas, *The Cruel Sea* (1965). A gripping novel about the destroyer-submarine struggle in the North Atlantic.*

Shaw, Irwin, *The Young Lions* (1958). A novel depicting the war in Europe and North Africa as experienced by American soldiers and a Nazi.* (Also a film.)

Shoah (1985). A long but gripping film about the Holocaust, based on the testimony of the surviving victims and their persecutors. (Also available on video).

Taylor, A.J.P., *The War Lords* (1977). A collection of descriptions of major leaders during World War II.*

Tregaskis, Richard W., *Guadalcanal Diary* (1943). A first-hand account of jungle warfare in the Pacific.*

"The World at War" (1973). A BBC television series that provides an account of the conflict compiled from newsreels and documentaries. Emphasizes the British role. available on video (Also available on video.)

Wright, Gordon, *The Ordeal of Total War, 1939–1945* (1969). A broad overview, with attention to the war's impact on the home front and on ideas.*

Young, Peter, *World War, 1939–1945: A Short History* (1966). A balanced survey of the war.

*Paperback available.

P A R T   T H R E E

The Contemporary Era

TIME CHART III
1945–1984

Year	South & East Asia	Middle East & Africa	Europe	Western Hemisphere	Trends in Culture, Science, Technology
1945		THE UNITED NATIONS ESTABLISHED	ORIGINS OF THE COLD WAR		The atomic age, 1945–present
1946	ERA OF ASIAN INDEPENDENCE, 1946–67			The Pérons in Argentina, 1946–55	
1947	First Indochina war, 1946–54; India and Pakistan independent		Truman Doctrine; Marshall Plan		Antibiotic drugs
1948		First Arab–Israeli war	Berlin airlift	Organization of American States established	
1949	Chinese Communist victory		NATO; First Soviet A–bomb tested		
1950	Korean War, 1950–53				
1951		ERA OF INDEPENDENCE IN NORTH, WEST, AND CENTRAL AFRICA, 1951–64			Decade of the popularization of television
1952		Independence struggles in Kenya, 1952–56			
1953			Stalin dies		
1954	SEATO; Geneva Agreement on Indochina	Algerian revolution, 1954–62		Arbenz government in Guatemala overthrown	Salk vaccine

Year				
1955		Warsaw Pact	Beginning of the civil rights struggle in United States	
1956	Second Arab–Israeli war	Hungarian revolt		
1957	Second Indochina War, 1957–75	Common Market founded		Sputnik launches the space age
1958		DeGaulle becomes President of fifth French Republic		
1959			Castro assumes power in Cuba	
1960	Sino-Soviet split			
1961		Berlin Wall	Bay of Pigs	
1962			Cuban Missile crisis	
1963	Organization of African Unity founded			Vatican II convened

ERA OF INTERMITTENT DÉTENTE, 1963–79

Year				
1964	Tonkin Gulf Resolution	Khrushchev ousted	Era of rightist coups in Latin America, 1964–76	Era of Green Revolution, 1960s–1970s
1965				
1966	Cultural revolution in China, 1966–76			
1967	Third Arab–Israeli war Civil war in Nigeria, 1967–70			

Year				
1968		Soviet intervention in Czechoslovakia	Decade of political and social turmoil in United States, 1965–75	
1969				Moon landing
1970				Growing environmental concerns, 1970s–1980s
1971				
1972	Nixon visits China	Strategic Arms Limitation Treaty (SALT)		
1973	Era of military coups in Africa		Allende government overthrown in Chile	Era of women's activism
	Fourth Arab–Israeli War			
1974	**INDEPENDENCE STRUGGLES IN SOUTHERN AFRICA, 1974–PRESENT**			
1975	Vietnam unified	Helsinki Accords		Era of the popularization of computers
1976	Mao dies			
1977				
1978	Iranian revolution, 1978–present		Social revolution and cold war struggles in Central America, 1970s–present	Resurgent Islam
1979	Egypt–Israel Accords	Thatcher becomes prime minister in Great Britain		Era of rising economic power of Asian rim
	Soviet invasion of Afghanistan, 1979–89			

Year			
1980	Deng Xiaoping in control of China	Iran–Iraq War, 1980–88	
1981		Reagan conservatism in United States	Martial law declared in Poland
1982		Israeli invasion of Lebanon	
1983		Civilian government restored in much of Latin America in 1980s	
1984	Continued resistance against apartheid in South Africa	Drought and famine in Africa	
1985		Gorbachev comes to power in U.S.S.R.	
1986	Marcos ousted in the Philippines		
1987	Intifada in Israeli-occupied territories, 1987–present		
1988	Benazir Bhutto first woman head of a Muslim state (elected in Pakistan)	INF ratified	
1989		New Soviet parliament convenes	

21

General Trends after World War II

In the decades following World War II, scientists and technicians brought the world nuclear energy, television, and computers; they put men in space and, by manipulating genes, produced new types of plants and animals. At the same time, however, scientific and technological advance was accompanied by environmental decline and the proliferation of thermonuclear weapons, both of which threatened to destroy the planet.

In the immediate postwar era, the United States emerged as the overwhelmingly dominant economic power, but by the late 1980s a more balanced world economy had developed, as Western Europe, Japan, and other Asian nations became increasingly competitive. Although the standard of living of much of the world's population improved dramatically in the first three decades following the war, by the end of the 1980s many in areas such as Africa and Latin America were worse off than they had been a decade earlier. Political leaders in these regions charged that the disparity between the rich and poor nations of the world was increasing.

Throughout the postwar era, the lower classes in many nations challenged the traditional political and economic controls that held them in their place. Many workers and peasants desired to improve their lives and pressed for a share of the power and property held by the privileged elites. In such a climate, Communist promises of land reform and economic justice had a considerable appeal, especially in poorer areas of the world where ruling groups ignored or suppressed cries for reforms and supported authoritarian right-wing anti-Communist governments. Such repression often spurred advocates of change to resort to guerrilla warfare and other forms of violence to obtain their ends. In the wealthier nations of the world, leaders became less ideological and more pragmatic. By the late 1980s, some Communist rulers were also stressing pragmatism more, and traditional Marxism less.

In the decades following World War II, more than 100 nations received their independence, and the major powers lost almost all of their former colonies. Competition and confrontation between the United States and the Soviet

Union, the two greatest military powers, also dominated most of the postwar period, creating a "Cold War" contest that affected every continent. By 1988, however, the world had become less bipolar and more multipolar, as a variety of nations became stronger and less dependent on one of the two superpowers. The United Nations and regional international organizations were created to preserve the peace, yet nationalism remained a major force as alliances and power blocs were formed and wars broke out frequently.

In the realm of ideas and culture, the battle between traditional religions and secularist forces continued. And as communications technology helped to spread Western cultural influences, non-Western thinkers, both religious and secular, increasingly reacted against any global dominance of Western ideas. Nevertheless, despite revolts against Western influence, such as in Iran under the Ayatollah Khomeini, the world continued to become more interdependent every year. Developments in telecommunications and transportation facilitated the spread of ideas and of global businesses and finance, as well as of fashions, fads, music, and television programming.

SCIENTIFIC–TECHNOLOGICAL ADVANCES AND ENVIRONMENTAL DECLINE

The postwar years witnessed a stunning display of scientific and technological achievements. One of the most important of these was the rapid development of atomic technology. By the 1950s scientists had learned how to fuse the atoms in hydrogen isotopes, thus creating the hydrogen bomb, which was a thousand times more destructive than the original atomic bomb. By the 1970s more than enough thermonuclear weapons existed to destroy all human life on the planet. The knowledge of such a possibility had effects on many aspects of civilization, from art to life styles. The overall effect was so profound that some labeled the postwar era "the Atomic Age."

Splitting the atom also provided a significant opportunity to create energy for peaceful purposes. Atomic energy was inexhaustible and could beneficially transform life on earth and displace reliance on shrinking and increasingly expensive supplies of petroleum and natural gas. By the 1980s a number of nuclear reactors were in service around the world. However, because of recurrent radioactive accidents, extensive opposition to the development of this energy source persisted.

In the decades after World War II, scientists and technicians brought forth an array of other mind-boggling developments, particularly in transportation and communication. In 1947, a piloted jet airplane first flew faster than the speed of sound; jet propulsion eventually became the prime mode of civilian and military air travel. Ballistics technology generated the power to push rockets bearing either space capsules or atomic warheads through the earth's gravitational field into outer space at a rate of thousands of miles in a few moments. In 1969, U.S. astronauts traveled to the moon—about 240,000 miles—in just four days.

Space technology also put satellites into orbit around the earth and created manned space stations.

In the field of communications, the invention of the transistor in 1947 eventually revolutionized radio communication, bringing broadcasts into the more remote areas of the world. Television also became a major phenomenon of the postwar era—contrary to the prediction of movie producer Darryl Zanuck, who said: "People will soon get tired of staring at a plywood box every night." In Mexico City in 1981, the government discovered that the average primary school child spent 1,460 hours a year watching television, as opposed to 920 hours in school. Polls in the United States reflected similar results. Television became an important instrument not only for entertainment and, less frequently, education, but also, depending on the society, for government propaganda and business advertising. In the United States in 1986, companies spent $22.6 billion on television advertising, which was more than the total spent by the federal government on education and environmental protection combined.

Information processing, as exemplified by the computer, was another dominant postwar development. Computers continually improved the storing, retrieving, and manipulating of enormous amounts of information, especially after the development of small silicon memory chips in the late 1950s. Combined with the most modern means of telecommunication, including communication satellites, computers could transfer data quickly from one part of the world to another. They brought about major changes in business and government practices, research and scholarship, military technology, and intelligence activities, and in general gradually transformed patterns of thought and behavior.

Despite their many advantages, computers also appeared to be a threat to privacy. Giant data bases available to creditors and advertisers included personal information on more than half of the people in the United States, and government data bases increasingly integrated the information they gathered concerning their citizens. The significance of the computer led some to refer to the present era as the "Computer Age" or "Information Age."

Some of the most dramatic scientific advances related to the study of genes. Scientists declared that DNA (deoxyribonucleic acid) was the key to heredity, leading scientists and doctors to become increasingly optimistic about the possibility of preventing certain inherited diseases and dealing with defective genes. In 1988, Harvard University was granted the first U.S. patent on an animal: a type of mouse genetically engineered for use in cancer experiments. Genetic engineering also opened up a whole new realm of possibilities in regard to the breeding of plant and animal food sources, but it simultaneously aroused fears of unforeseen results. Medical advances improved health care and decreased the world death rate while increasing life expectancy. As a result, the population of the world increased from 1.6 billion in 1900 to 2.4 billion in 1950 and to 5 billion by 1987. Even so, medicine still had far to go. Most chronic killers, such as heart disease and cancer, remained to be conquered, and a new incurable contagious disease, Acquired Immunity Deficiency Syndrome (AIDS), caused a rapidly increasing number of deaths, particularly in the United States and Africa.

During the 1960s and 1970s, many people, especially in advanced industrialized nations, became aware of environmental issues for the first time. One area of concern was the depletion of energy resources. The advanced technological and industrialized societies were rapidly consuming energy and other resources; many of these resources, like petroleum and natural gas, were nonrenewable. Between the end of World War II and the late 1970s, the Western nations and Japan used up more petroleum and minerals than had been consumed in all previous history; the United States was the biggest user, alone accounting for approximately 30 percent of world energy consumption during the 1970s. By the 1980s, however, the advanced industrialized democratic nations had begun to reduce their levels of energy consumption, and this trend continued, although unevenly, throughout the decade.

Just as population growth, industrialization, and urbanization all contributed to the need for more energy, so these factors also increased demand for a variety of other resources, such as food, forests, and water. To meet the growing need for food and fodder—also stimulated by an increased world demand for meat and dairy products—scientists and technicians developed new high-yield strains of wheat and rice. Other agricultural techniques, such as using more fertilizers, irrigating lands only marginally fit for agriculture, and reducing the periods in which land was allowed to rest, contributed to increasing food supplies. Between 1950 and 1985, as world population doubled, global food production almost tripled. In certain areas of the world, however, most dramatically in Africa, food production per capita decreased in the 1970s and 1980s. By the mid-1980s the African population was increasing twice as fast as food

Junked cars symbolize the heavy U.S. consumption of energy and world resources. (EPA Documeria)

resources. Deforestation on the southern fringes of the Sahara and overgrazing combined with a series of dry years to cause the desert to spread southward. This contributed to famine and countless deaths during the 1970s and early 1980s.

In economically advanced nations, scientific and technological developments and increasing industrialization polluted the air and water. In 1975 alone, more than 10,000 petroleum spills were reported in U.S. navigable waters. As industrial smokestacks continued spewing sulphur dioxide into the atmosphere, more and more nations became concerned about the destructive ecological effects of acid rain. During the 1980s, Canadians became increasingly upset with the administration of President Ronald Reagan for not doing more to curtail U.S. air pollutants which drifted into Canada and caused about half of their acid rain. A 1988 report documented for the first time the fact that nitrogen oxides in acid rain, caused mainly by automobiles and electric utilities, were also a major cause of the destruction of marine life along the U.S. Atlantic coast.

It was discovered, at times belatedly, that many new chemical compounds, such as DDT, PCB, and PBB, had adverse effects on the environment and on people's health. Pesticides such as DDT introduced a special dilemma into a world hungry for food. By killing crop-threatening insects, DDT and a number of other pesticides increased crop yields, yet caused illness and death in humans and animals. In the 1970s, an estimated 90 percent of Michigan residents ingested some traces of PBB, a suspected carcinogen, after it had been accidentally fed to cattle.

The development of nuclear power plants in the United States and other nations led to increased concern about radioactive accidents and waste disposal that could damage the environment. The worst accident occurred in 1986 at Chernobyl, near the Soviet city of Kiev, where a nuclear reactor exploded, spewing radioactive debris into the atmosphere. Thirty-one people were killed in the Soviet Union, and thousands of others were exposed to very high levels of radiation. Radioactive winds carried some contamination to various other nations; two years after the accident, most European nations continued to monitor radioactive levels of at least some food. Scientists estimated that the Chernobyl radiation could eventually cause thousands of cancer deaths.

Two major fears about the environment grew rapidly in the 1980s. Scientists worried that heavy emissions of chlorofluorocarbons were depleting atmospheric ozone and consequently increasing solar radiation. By 1988, they concluded that the problem was much worse than they had earlier thought, and that strong steps had to be taken to prevent a significant increase in skin cancer and uncalculated damage to food crops. Scientists also became increasingly concerned with the "greenhouse effect." They claimed that the increased burning of fossil fuels such as coal and petroleum was likely to cause an increase in global temperatures, possibly melting the polar ice caps, changing crop yields, and flooding low-lying parts of the world. Many of them also attributed the noticeable rise in global temperatures in the 1980s to the greenhouse effect.

As a result of increasing environmental concerns, a number of governments took steps to reverse deteriorating conditions. The first clean air act was passed in Great Britain in 1955, and as a result London was less polluted by the end of the 1970s than it had been a quarter century before. During the late 1960s and 1970s, the United States created a series of environmental protection laws, regulating in particular water and air pollution. At Montreal in 1987, forty-six nations agreed to a 50 percent reduction in the emissions of chlorofluorocarbons by 1999.

RICH NATIONS AND POOR NATIONS COMPETING IN A GLOBAL ECONOMY

By the end of World War II, the United States had emerged as by far the most powerful economic force in the world. Europe, the leading prewar producer of goods and services, and the Soviet Union were now devastated, and much of their capital had been depleted by the war. Japan lay in ruins, and China was on the verge of civil war. Toward the end of the war and shortly thereafter, the Allied powers agreed to encourage international economic growth and free trade by the formation of the International Monetary Fund (IMF), the International Bank for Reconstruction and Development (World Bank), and the General Agreement on Tariffs and Trade (GATT). The United States played a leading role in the formation of all three institutions, but the Soviet Union declined to participate or to permit its satellite states in Eastern Europe to do so. GATT, which became a permanent organization, was especially created to reduce tariffs and other trade barriers, reductions which were particularly important to the United States, the nation with the greatest productive capacity.

For several years, much of Europe faced unstable economic and political conditions, but in 1947 the U.S.-sponsored Marshall Plan stimulated industrial and agricultural production and trade, while also stabilizing postwar inflation and unemployment. By the early 1950s, Western Europe was well on the road to economic recovery. In Eastern Europe, which did not participate in the Marshall Plan, recovery was slower. The Soviet Union renewed its Five-Year Plans and once again squeezed economic sacrifices out of its people in order to rebuild heavy industry.

Between the early 1950s and the late 1980s, the unique postwar economic dominance of the United States slowly gave way to a more balanced world economy. By 1980 the United States produced only one quarter of the value of the world's goods and services (gross world product), down from its 40 percent share in the early 1950s, but roughly equivalent to its 1938 portion. Within the same postwar period, Japan's share went from 2 percent to 10 percent, and Western Europe's also increased, although not nearly as dramatically as Japan's. From 1973 to 1981, members of the Organization of Petroleum Exporting Countries (OPEC) increased the price per barrel of petroleum tenfold, almost doubling their per capita gross national product (GNP). From 1981 to late 1988, however, petroleum prices fell by more than 50 percent, and the OPEC share of global wealth declined.

Meanwhile, during the 1980s, a number of other nations sharply increased their share of the global production of goods and services. From 1973 to 1986, China, Taiwan, South Korea, Singapore, and Hong Kong all saw their economies expand at about triple the U.S. rate. China's economic growth was largely due to changes after the death of Mao Tse-tung in 1976; the new policies reduced state economic controls and made the economy more responsive to national and global market forces. In some other parts of the Communist world, especially in Hungary and Yugoslavia, economic reforms had also been attempted prior to the 1980s, and in the middle of the decade Mikhail Gorbachev began a major attempt to restructure the bureaucratic and inefficient Soviet economy.

By 1988 despite a U.S. economy more than twice the size of Japan's and about the same as that of the combined twelve nations of the European Economic Community (Common Market), Americans were becoming increasingly concerned about the economic competitiveness of other areas of the world. Foreign imports and investments in the United States, an unfavorable trade balance, and large government budget deficits (an accumulated $2.6 trillion by October 1988) were some of the major concerns. Some Americans seemed especially concerned about Japan's economic strength: It was estimated that at U.S. bond auctions, the Japanese were buying about 30 percent of U.S. thirty-year treasury notes and that in 1988, they invested about $16.5 billion in U.S. property. Despite free trade sentiments expressed by the major capitalist powers, all had previously taken some steps to protect domestic economies from too much foreign competition. Advocates of free trade now feared signs of increasing protectionism and rising economic nationalism.

After World War II, the economic status of most people in the world improved as their economies modernized; but the improvements were uneven, and economic modernization had its negative as well as its positive consequences. During the mid-1970s and again in the early 1980s, many of the nations of the world suffered through recessions; the latter one created record postwar unemployment in some nations, including the United States. Many nations in the poorer areas of the world saw some of their earlier economic gains erode during the 1970s and 1980s.

Throughout the postwar period, the poor nations saw their populations grow at a considerably higher rate than those of the more industrialized nations. They found especially burdensome the steep price hikes from 1973 to 1981 for petroleum, manufactured goods, and some foods. These increases caused them to borrow heavily and incur excessive debt. When petroleum prices fell, some of the less affluent petroleum-exporting nations were also hard hit: they had borrowed large amounts of money in the expectation that healthy petroleum revenues would pay off their debts, and now were more hard-pressed than ever to meet their obligations. Western banks continued to charge high interest rates, which raised the debts of the poorer nations still further. By 1988, estimates of Third World debt totaled $1.2 trillion, up from $98 billion in 1973 and $575 billion in 1982. The debt was owed to banks, governments, and international lending agencies such as the IMF and the World Bank.

The debt became so staggering for many nations that a few suspended repayments. Even more shared the sentiment of Peru's President Garcia: "We reject the usurious terms of the foreign debt." In an increasingly interdependent international economy, however, outright refusal to repay loans meant no new credits and unfavorable treatment by the major global economic powers. Therefore, most debtor nations worked with the IMF to extend and restructure their repayment schedules. But the IMF frequently demanded domestic financial reforms of debtor nations as the price for restructuring debts or for any new credits. These demands were often resented by indebted nations because they included calls for politically unpopular austerity programs, balanced budgets, and more private enterprise. Some charged that the IMF (composed of 151 nations in 1988) was a tool of its major capitalist contributors, particularly the United States. In their view, the IMF was part of an overall system whereby rich nations controlled world finance and trade in order to maintain high prices for their exports to poor nations while paying low prices for basic commodities imported from these states. For poor nations, the only real answer to the debt problem was for lending agencies to reduce the overall debt. Latin American nations, which owed about 30 percent of the total Third World debt, pointed out that while they attempted to repay their debt, their standard of living had declined.

The most essential need of poor nations after World War II was sufficient food. Although world per capita food production continued to increase, poverty and ineffective world distribution systems combined to deny enough of it to poorer peoples. During the early 1980s, for example, half the sugar, banana, and pineapple crops were exported from the Philippines, much of it by U.S. corporations, while most Philippine children were malnourished. Overall, experts contended that producer nations only earned about 15 percent of the final consumer costs of such tropical products.

Estimates varied widely on the extent of world hunger and undernourishment, but in the early 1980s, about one billion people a year suffered from serious caloric insufficiencies. During the 1970s and 1980s, millions of lives were lost as a result of famines in areas such as Bangladesh, India, Cambodia, the Sahel (the area immediately south of the Sahara), and eastern and southern Africa. During 1982, UNICEF estimated that some 40,000 children died each day in the poorer nations of the world as a result of hunger-related diseases, poor health, and deficient sanitation practices.

Not only did the gap between rich nations and many poor nations widen during the 1980s, but so did the difference between rich and poor inside many Third World nations. Peasants were often forced from land they once farmed, as big producers converted it to the production of export crops. In increasing numbers, these peasants migrated to urban centers to swell the size of city slums. In Latin America during the 1980s, 10 percent of rural landowners owned

Hope: An African woman plants crops as part of the growing effort to increase agricultural production across the continent. (Courtesy CARE)

90 percent of all farmland, while a majority of rural inhabitants owned none at all.

One of the most evident economic trends of the postwar period was that the interdependence of the economies of the world continued to increase. OPEC petroleum ministers during the 1970s, for example, greatly influenced the lives of Americans, and drought or bad harvest conditions in the United States affected the lives of millions of people dependent on U.S. food exports. The growing power of the multinational corporations also lessened the control of individual nations over their own economies. Businesses increasingly operated on a global scale. By the end of 1987, for example, there were over 400 Sheraton hotels in forty-two nations; the world's largest Kentucky Fried Chicken restaurant had opened in Beijing, and Coca-Cola earned more money from soft drinks sold in Japan than it did from U.S. sales. During 1988, McDonald's opened up its first outlets in Yugoslavia and Hungary and announced plans to open others in Moscow.

SOCIETY AND POLITICS: REBELLIONS AND CONFLICTING IDEOLOGIES

In the social sphere, the years after World War II witnessed a gradual but growing rebellion against the overwhelmingly dominant role that white adult males had held in the interwar years. Blacks in the United States and Africa increasingly demanded equality. In Africa, as well as in Asia, the challenge to the au-

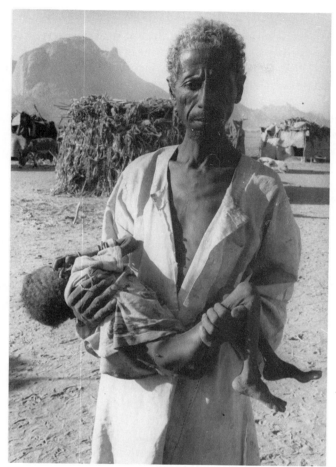

Despair: Over 1.2 million refugees in the southern Sudan
continue to suffer from the effects of drought, famine, civil
wars, and government mismanagement. (Sebastiao
Salgado/Magnum)

thority of the white man was part of a broad anticolonial movement. In addition, by the 1960s, youths in many nations were challenging the authority of societies dominated by older men and were becoming more aware of a "youth culture" of their own. This trend was especially noticeable in some affluent Western nations, where it was stimulated by media, music, and advertising that catered especially to youthful tastes. Women, particularly in the same affluent Western nations, increasingly demanded rights, pay, and career advancement opportunities equal to those of their male counterparts.

Some of these challenges to white male dominance were stimulated by demographic developments which helped to change family and social patterns. Family size gradually grew smaller, people lived longer, and the percentage of older people in societies increased. These trends were especially noticeable in the industrialized world, whereas in developing nations the size of families and percentage of younger people remained considerably higher than in richer nations. Yet even in most poorer nations the overall pattern was moving in the same direction; for example, from 1950 to 1979 average life expectancy increased in such nations by fourteen years. Increased urbanization and literacy were two other global trends, although here again significant gaps continued to exist among different states. By the early 1980s, more than 70 percent of the almost two billion people in China and India still lived in rural areas, as did about 60 percent of the world's total population; in the United States and Japan, almost 80 percent lived in urban areas, as did about two-thirds of Latin Americans. By the mid-1980s approximately one-fourth of Chinese adults and almost two-thirds of Indian adults were still illiterate, but most of the richer industrialized nations claimed 99 percent literacy rates.

Although also influenced at times by demographic changes, the rebellious attitudes of dissatisfied ethnic and cultural minorities in various countries were generally more influenced by long-standing rivalries. Some of these minorities, such as the French in Quebec Province in Canada, agitated for autonomy primarily through peaceful legal and constitutional means, interspersed with threats of complete separation. Other minorities, such as the Basques in Spain, who held less hope for obtaining autonomy or independence through peaceful means, resorted to sporadic terrorism. In Great Britain, the Irish Republican Army in Northern Ireland carried on intermittent guerrilla warfare against both British troops and armed Protestant paramilitary groups. In Africa, tribalism contributed to civil wars, and in Nigeria in 1967 it almost split the nation apart. In 1988, minority nationalities in the Soviet Union and some of the peoples of Yugoslavia expressed increasingly open demands for increased rights, and Hungarians demonstrated over Rumania's treatment of its Hungarian minority.

In postwar Europe right-wing governments declined. With Nazism, fascism, and East European conservative dictatorships destroyed, the only remaining European rightist governments were those of Salazar in Portugal and Franco in Spain. After these dictators died in the 1970s, both nations moved toward democracy. This development, along with the restoration of democracy in Greece in 1974–75 after seven years of military rule, meant that by the late 1970s, democracy prevailed in all the major non-Communist European nations.

By 1989 democracy was also advancing in other parts of the world, especially Latin America. Its success was partly due to an increase of educated middle classes and the growing interconnectedness of global communication and a global economy. As the economic and human-rights failures of dictators and oligarchs, of both the Right and the Left, became more apparent and their subjects increasingly contrasted their lives with the freer and generally more prosperous lives of those living in democracies, pressures from within joined demands from outside for reforms. Nevertheless, twentieth-century history was too full of examples of the collapse of democracies to safely predict that the trend toward them was permanent.

Liberalism and conservativism continued to evolve and exercise influence in Western Europe and the United States after 1945. The dominant note throughout most of the postwar era, however, was political pragmatism. Compared to the period before World War II, politics in Western Europe was more stable, dominated by moderate socialist or moderate conservative parties. In addition to differing with conservatives over economic policy, socialists tended to be less aggressive than conservatives concerning relations with the Soviet Union and more willing to grant independence to colonies. However, both moderate socialists and moderate conservatives in Europe were heirs of the liberal tradition of support for civil rights and individual liberties. In the United States, which continued to be associated with civil liberties and increasingly with the civil rights of minorities, liberalism was associated with an expanded government role, especially in behalf of the disadvantaged. U.S. liberals tended to be more sympathetic toward peaceful coexistence with the Soviet Union, while conservative administrations alternated between periods of confrontation and episodes of effective coexistence.

Communism also expanded throughout most of the postwar years, already spreading throughout Eastern Europe by 1948. Immediately following the war, the Communist parties of France and Italy were also strong and participated in coalition governments. Communism spread through much of Asia after World War II, and Marxist-influenced states appeared in Africa and Latin America in the 1960s and 1970s. On the other hand, after 1947, as Cold War tensions increased, Communists were excluded from cabinet participation in Western European governments until 1981, when they received minor and insignificant cabinet posts in the newly elected French socialist government.

World communism became less unified following Khrushchev's criticism of the dead Stalin in 1956. The Sino-Soviet split of the early 1960s split the Communist world and divided Asian and African Communist parties into pro-Peking and pro-Moscow factions. Western and Eastern European Communists began to display more independence. Yugoslavian Communism had already begun to develop along its own line following its split from the U.S.S.R. in 1948. But for most Eastern European nations there were limits on how far they could deviate from the Soviet interpretation of Marxism, as the Hungarians, Czechoslovakians, and Poles discovered between 1956 and 1981.

After 1985, however, the Soviet leadership itself, led by the pragmatic Mikhail Gorbachev, liberalized its own Marxism and called for more democratization, while at the same time encouraging similar steps in Eastern Europe. Although the Chinese Communists under Deng Xiaoping did not allow the types of political liberalization allowed by Gorbachev, they did, beginning in the late 1970s, push through various measures which liberalized the Chinese economy. By mid-1989, due to a whole series of developments (see Chapter 32), many Western observers were beginning to share British Prime Minister Margaret Thatcher's belief that "Marxism's had it."

This evaluation, however, was not as widely held by many in the non-Western nations of the world and in Latin America, where the chief competing postwar political forces often were Marxism and anti-Communism. Aided by the spread of the transistor radio, proponents of both forces broadened their indoctrination efforts to reach even peoples living in remote areas. Lenin had linked capitalism with imperialism and encouraged nationalist revolutions against the imperialist powers, thus building support for communism in areas in the grip of Western imperialism. In the Third World, leaders were also struck, especially prior to the Soviet economic stagnation of the 1980s, by the rapid industrialization that occurred in the Soviet Union and the planned economy that helped bring it about. As a revolutionary doctrine directed against the rich and powerful, communism also had an appeal in many nations where the disparity between the rich and poor was great.

Beginning in 1949, Marxist governments came to power in several nations outside Europe, such as China, Vietnam, Cuba, and Ethiopia. But these governments were not carbon copies of the Soviet Union. Non-Western Marxist governments were influenced by their own national traditions, and different interpretations of Marxism contributed to ideological conflicts in the Marxist world, especially between China and the Soviet Union in the 1960s and 1970s. By 1989, although certainly not dead, Marxism was being interpreted in hundreds of different ways and was definitely in a period of crisis and transition.

Many anti-Communist leaders of Asia, Africa, and Latin America had little in common except their opposition to communism, democracy, and civil liberties. They were generally supporters of the status quo and opposed to social reforms and the redistribution of property. Some, however, like the Shah of Iran, were sympathetic to technological modernization, a force that greatly changed many non-Western societies. Many of these Third World anti-Communist nations were dictatorships or one-party states. In contrast, several nations, such as India and Venezuela, maintained democratic institutions throughout most of the postwar period.

Certain Third World leaders were neither dogmatically Communist nor anti-Communist. Individuals like Jomo Kenyatta of Kenya and Nehru of India were interested in Western political ideas and attempted to blend them with "homegrown" ideas. Such leaders were primarily concerned with political order and economic development.

After 1945, religion continued to play an important role in politics. In the Islamic world, politicians at least paid lip service to Islam, and some nations such as Saudi Arabia and later Pakistan and Iran based their laws on interpretations of *Shari'a*, the traditional system of Islamic law. The Catholic Church also played a political role in much of Latin America and Europe, where its leadership had been traditionally allied with conservative forces. In the 1960s, however, Latin American Catholic clergy became increasingly critical of the social injustices perpetuated by right-wing governments. At times, they allied themselves with forces of rebellion. Liberal Protestants, Catholics, and Jews in the United States in the 1960s became more active in civil rights and anti-Vietnam War protests and followed the nonviolent resistance tactics of Baptist minister Martin Luther King, Jr. By the early 1980s, the momentum in U.S. Protestantism appeared to have swung back to conservative fundamentalists and evangelicals, who stressed the literal interpretation of the

Bible and religious rebirth in Christ; they also became more active in politics.

INTERNATIONAL RELATIONS: DECOLONIALIZATION AND THE COLD WAR

During the three decades following World War II, the great majority of former colonial territories in Asia and Africa, and some in the Caribbean and the Pacific, became independent. The United States, Belgium, France, Great Britain, Spain, Portugal, and Italy together relinquished control over more than one-quarter of the world's population. By 1980 the United Nations had welcomed over a hundred new nations since its founding in 1945, and during the 1980s additional colonial areas, especially in the Caribbean and Pacific, became independent.

The decolonization phenomenon came about for many reasons. World War II had weakened Western imperialistic control, especially in parts of Asia where Japan had temporarily taken over. Imperialistic controls were also weakened by growing disenchantment with imperialism by voters and parties within the Western nations, the economic cost of maintaining an empire on depleted resources, and increased resistance on the part of colonial peoples. In most cases, imperial powers granted independence peacefully, but some powers departed from certain colonies in Asia and Africa only after years of bloody struggle.

Decolonization did not mean, however, that the Western powers ceased to attempt to wield influence in former colonial territories. Many of France's African colonies retained close associations with France. Great Britain worked at maintaining a variety of ties with most of its former empire through the Commonwealth organization.

Developments in the colonies and former colonies were also affected by the Cold War between the United States and the Soviet Union, which developed immediately after World War II. Both superpowers often tried to support friendly, newly independent governments. At times, both the Soviet Union and the United States used economic and military aid, military advisors, and sometimes troops and covert operations. Many leaders of the new nations, which were particularly vulnerable to superpower imperialism because of their economic poverty, were opposed to joining either camp. These leaders feared being trapped by a form of "neo-imperialism" under which their nations would become the puppets of the superpowers. They also feared that their nations would become the battleground for superpower struggles. As an African saying goes, when elephants fight, it is the grass that gets trampled.

To resist this danger, Third World leaders of major nations not committed to the United States or the Soviet Union, such as Nehru of India, Sukarno of Indonesia, Tito of Yugoslavia, and Gamal Abdul Nasser of Egypt, sought to form a movement of nonaligned or neutral nations. In 1955, leaders of twenty Asian and African states met at Bandung, Indonesia, and resolved to adopt the

"We have always loved the black ones as our own! But if they demand freedom and independence—they are no longer blacks, they are reds!"

A Soviet cartoon indicates how independence and anticolonial movements could become involved in Cold War politics. (Courtesy of Rodger Swearingen)

principles of nonalignment, coexistence, and cooperation. In 1961, representatives of twenty-five nations met in Yugoslavia for the first Conference of Non-Aligned Heads of State. In 1986, 101 nations took part in this group's eighth summit. Throughout most of the 1970s and 1980s, the summits produced calls for a "new economic order" which would lessen the disparity between the rich and poorer nations of the world. Although its members, including such nations as Cuba and Vietnam, declared themselves to be "against great power and bloc politics," the group was more critical of the United States and its allies, especially Israel, than of the Soviet bloc.

Although the Soviet Union encouraged nationalistic movements against Western imperialism, it enjoyed imperialist successes of its own. In fact, by bringing Eastern Europe under its control in the late 1940s and by creating a new "Soviet Empire," the Soviet Union countered the postwar historical trend that witnessed the breakup of empires. Soviet imperialism, however, fostered nationalistic resentment, and unrest at various times in Yugoslavia, Hungary, Czechoslovakia, Poland, and Afghanistan indicated that nationalism remained alive within the Soviet sphere.

Partly in order to counter Soviet influence, some Western leaders encouraged regional and international economic and political cooperation. The Marshall

Plan, the North Atlantic Treaty Organization (NATO), the Organization of American States (OAS), and the formation of the European Economic Community (EEC) in 1957 and its subsequent broadening were examples of regional cooperation. Such continuing collaboration, however, often had to overcome nationalist obstacles such as the imposing General Charles de Gaulle, president of France from 1958 to 1969.

In Africa and the Middle East, as in the Soviet and Western blocs, some politicians promoted regional unity. Kwame Nkrumah, of Ghana, wrote a book entitled *Africa Must Unite,* and in 1963, the Organization of African Unity was founded. Islam was still another affiliation that transcended national boundaries. Many militant Muslims were critical of any nationalism that separated Muslims from one another. Militant Islam, always a force in Islamic nations, became stronger in the 1970s. Arab nationalism also transcended the boundaries of individual Arab states. However, despite some sincere efforts, Pan-Africanism and Islam were too weak to prevent conflict in Africa and the Middle East.

The major international organization of the postwar world, the United Nations (UN), was formed in 1945 by fifty-one nations to replace the League of Nations. It consisted of six bodies: the General Assembly (159 members as of 1988), the Security Council, the Secretariat, the Economic and Social Council, the Trusteeship Council, and the International Court of Justice. The Security Council had five permanent members: France, Great Britain, the United States, the Soviet Union, and the People's Republic of China (after taking the place of the Republic of China [Taiwan] in 1971). These permanent members could veto substantive Council action. In addition, the Council contained ten nonpermanent members (six up to 1965) elected for two-year terms by the Assembly. Under the secretary general, the Secretariat headed the administrative and civil service branch of the United Nations. The Economic and Social Council, elected by the General Assembly, coordinated various UN and autonomous commissions and agencies concerned with economics, social conditions, culture, education, and health. In 1945, the Trusteeship Council was given responsibility for eleven territories, most of which were earlier mandates of the League of Nations. By 1988, however, only the Pacific islands administered by the United States remained as a Trust Territory.

The record of the United Nations was mixed. As a forum for international opinion and as an organization that called attention to the economic and social needs of underdeveloped areas, it was often effective. It helped to channel aid to these areas, dependent of course on the willingness of the richer nations of the world to offer assistance.

As a peace-keeping force, the United Nations had a better record than that of the League of Nations. In 1946, it helped pressure the Soviet Union into leaving Iran. In 1950, largely as a result of a temporary Soviet boycott of the United Nations, it condemned North Korea for invading South Korea and sent an international force to aid South Korea. Since the late 1940s, UN peace-keeping forces have served, in some cases for decades, in various parts of the world—for example, Kashmir along the India-Pakistan border, the Congo,

Cyprus, and the Middle East. In 1988, the UN peace-keeping forces were awarded the Nobel Peace Prize for their continuing efforts.

Like the League of Nations, however, the United Nations was not very effective in preventing major powers from pursuing their vital interests. The United Nations was only as effective as its member states allowed it to be, and no major power was willing to give up sovereign decision-making powers. In 1956, despite the appeal of the Hungarian premier and a General Assembly demand that Soviet forces be withdrawn, the United Nations was unable to dislodge Soviet troops from Hungary.

Despite UN efforts and the absence of another world war, smaller wars and protracted guerrilla warfare became increasingly common. By one estimate, twenty-five million people lost their lives between the end of World War II and 1978 as a result of warfare. Civil war in China, Indo-Pakistani wars, the Korean War, Arab-Israeli wars, and the war in Indochina were just a few of the conflicts in that period. During the 1980s, the Iran-Iraq war and the war in Afghanistan were among the bloodiest conflicts. In addition, there were many crises and near wars. The Berlin crises in 1948–49 and 1961, the Cuban missile crisis of 1962, the Soviet-Chinese border skirmishes during the 1960s and 1970s, and a variety of Middle East crises throughout the postwar period all contributed to international tensions.

Beginning in the late 1940s, hostilities and suspicions also fueled a continuing escalation of global military spending and armaments. The United States and the Soviet Union, together with by their European allies, easily accounted for the largest percentage of world military spending. From 1975 to 1987, the United States and the Soviet Union alone accounted for about 60 percent of the world total. By 1987 the combined nations of the world were spending an estimated $1.8 million a minute for military purposes.

The destructive power and proliferation of nuclear weapons increased dramatically after the explosion of the A-bomb at Hiroshima. By the mid-1970s, the United States and the Soviet Union had developed combined nuclear arsenals with over a million times the destructive power of the bomb dropped on Hiroshima, enough to kill the population of the earth twelve times over. By that time, China, France, Great Britain, and India had also become nuclear powers, and a number of other nations, including India, Israel, Pakistan, and South Africa, were suspected of possessing nuclear weapons.

Amidst the spiraling military spending and developments, some super-power arms limitation treaties were signed, especially in 1972; and by 1988 the United States actually possessed fewer nuclear weapons, although more sophisticated ones, than it had two decades earlier. These developments, however, did not prevent a significant increase in military spending in almost all regions of the world. Most leaders apparently continued to share Theodore Roosevelt's belief that a navy was an "infinitely more potent factor for peace than all the peace societies."

In 1988, three years after Mikhail Gorbachev had become the leader of the Soviet Union, the United States and the Soviet Union ratified an INF (intermediate-range nuclear forces) treaty eliminating intermediate land-based missiles from Europe. They, along with other involved nations, also reached

This chart demonstrates the world's nuclear firepower in the early 1980s (represented by all the multi-dot squares) as compared to the firepower of all the bombs dropped in World War II (the single dot in the middle). (Courtesy Traprock Peace Center, Deerfield, MA)

an agreement on a Soviet withdrawal from Afghanistan. As Gorbachev and U.S. President Reagan exchanged visits to each other's nations in 1987 and 1988, and as both sides actually began destroying some of the newly banned missiles, leaders and citizens of both superpowers once again expressed hopes for further agreements that would deescalate the arms race and regional conflicts. Some even declared that the Cold War was over.

If superpower rivalry seemed on the decline by mid-1989, some other international threats to human life and health either increased or showed no signs of abating. One was the problem of international terrorism. Nations seemed at a loss as to how to prevent terrorist atrocities, which were sometimes supported by foreign governments. In 1986, the United States, angered by the killing of two U.S. servicemen in West Berlin, blamed Libya and bombed selected targets in that nation. International drug traffic also became a major problem in the 1980s, destroying the health of millions.

TRADITION AND THE GLOBALIZATION OF CULTURE

In the decades after World War II, the challenge to traditional religious beliefs and values that was best symbolized at the beginning of the century by Nietzsche continued throughout the world. As Communism spread to Eastern Europe, China, and Southeast Asia, traditional religions in those areas were usually persecuted or at most grudgingly tolerated. Although in a few cases, especially Poland, the Catholic Church remained strong, in most Catholic nations of Europe the influence of the Church continued to decline. Despite Church opposition, Italians legalized abortion in 1978; many Catholics in various parts of the world rejected papal teachings on birth control. In the United States, local "blue laws" regulating Sunday work, amusements, and drinking were gradually eased or revoked. In the early 1960s, the U.S. Supreme Court ruled against prayer and the devotional reading of the Bible in public schools. In the 1970s, it ruled that abortion was a woman's right under certain conditions. In the United States and Western Europe, censorship of pornography also eased, despite religious opposition. In the Third World, as urbanization, education, literacy, and mass media spread, more people became separated from traditional religious beliefs.

Secularism also strongly influenced many intellectuals. Some of them came to accept a view similar to that of the secular French existentialists, who were greatly influenced by Nietzsche. They believed that God did not exist, that the world was "absurd," and that the best one could do was try to live for the present in a responsible and honest manner. Writers such as Jean-Paul Sartre, Albert Camus, and Simone de Beauvoir helped make existentialism one of the most influential of Western postwar movements.

Despite an overall trend in the world toward secularization, many traditional religions remained vigorous. After his elevation in 1958, Pope John XXIII worked toward a revitalization of the Catholic Church and encouraged ecumenical initiatives. The election of the Polish John Paul II as pope in 1978 helped to strengthen the already strong Catholic forces in Poland and, to a lesser extent, those in some other Eastern European nations. Protestant fundamentalism and Islam also displayed signs of increased vigor during the late 1970s and the 1980s.

By the 1980s Communist values seemed increasingly unable to offer a meaningful alternative to traditional religious beliefs. Even the Soviet government under Gorbachev, concerned with Soviet alcoholism, corruption, and other signs of moral decline, spoke more favorably than in the past regarding religious values. The Soviet publication of Boris Pasternak's *Doctor Zhivago* and the showing of the film *Repentance,* both full of religious symbolism, were just two signs of this increased tolerance.

Some intellectuals supported traditional religions and their teachings. During the 1950s and early 1960s, the influence of the Anglo-Catholic poet T. S. Eliot was still strong. In France, Catholic writers and thinkers such as Gabriel Marcel and Pierre Teilhard de Chardin challenged the dominance of atheistic or agnostic existentialism. Beginning in the 1960s, the much-acclaimed Russian novelist Alexander Solzhenitsyn increasingly celebrated the values of traditional Russian Orthodoxy. Protestant theologians such as Karl Barth and Paul Tillich, and the Jewish thinker Martin Buber, continued to have significant followings, and the controversial Catholic theologian Hans Küng appealed to many liberal Christians. Popularizers of Christianity such as the U.S. evangelist Billy Graham reached millions through various media.

In nations where authoritarian or totalitarian measures were imposed, culture often suffered and was made to reflect propagandistic purposes. In nations as diverse as the U.S.S.R., China, Turkey, the Republic of South Africa, Chile, and Guatemala, writers were censored and persecuted. Some writers in these nations smuggled their work out, and others wrote freely only in exile after having been encouraged or forced to leave their homelands.

Cultural pluralism, the coexistence of many different subcultures and beliefs in a society, became increasingly common in nations that allowed freedom of expression. Pluralism was encouraged by the tremendous expansion of various forms of media. The media made possible the creation of instant fads and the popularizing of new trends, a phenomenon first witnessed in the 1920s but since accelerated. The average person in technologically advanced nations was able to select from an ever-increasing number of here-today-gone-tomorrow philosophies of life and role models. This was true not only in the West, but also in many other parts of the world where Western culture had an impact. On the other hand, movies, television, and transistor radios (especially valuable in areas of the world without electricity) also contributed to breaking down regional differences and to fostering standardization. Certain American television programs, such as "Dallas," which by 1988 was seen in more than 100 nations, became commonplace throughout the world.

Non-Western ideas also played an increasing role in world culture. For example, Zen Buddhism, Transcendental Meditation, the Hare Krishna sect, and various Muslim movements all had followings in the United States. In addition, many non-Western writers increasingly looked for inspiration within their own traditions. In Africa and the Caribbean, the *négritude* movement, founded between the wars, became increasingly popular after World War II. More non-Western writers and film makers achieved world recognition after 1945 than ever before, and their different perspectives exposed Westerners to non-Western viewpoints. Writers such as Chinua Achebe of Nigeria and Yasunari Kawabata of Japan, winner of the Nobel Prize for Literature in 1968, became international figures, as did the Japanese film director Akira Kurosawa, who directed such classics as *Rashomon* and *The Seven Samurai*.

After 1945, when the poet Gabriela Mistral of Chile became the first Latin American to win the Nobel Prize for Literature, Latin American writers pro-

duced some of the most celebrated literature in the Third World. Three other
Latin American writers in subsequent years were also awarded the prize: Miguel
Angel Asturias of Guatemala (1967), Pablo Neruda of Chile (1971), and Gabriel
García Márquez of Colombia (1982). Márquez and Jorge Luis Borges of Ar-
gentina were especially influential for American and European writers who con-
tinued the attempt of many twentieth-century writers and artists to go beyond
the techniques of literary or artistic realism. By 1981, Márquez's novel *One
Hundred Years of Solitude* (1969) had been translated into thirty-two languages.

Amid all these cultural currents, some individuals in various parts of the
world felt uncomfortable and wished to stress simpler "old-fashioned" ways
and values. Outside the West, as for example in Iran, where Islamic fundamentalism manifested itself strongly in the 1980s, such feelings were often connected with anti-Westernism. Modern Western, especially U.S., influences were
perceived, correctly or incorrectly, as the primary cause of the corruption of
more traditional, cohesive, and religious-based societies. In the words of Iran's
Ayatollah Khomeini, the United States was "the great Satan."

Most Third World intellectuals, however, rejected any simplistic attempts to
return to past traditions, especially if they involved intolerance of modern ideas.
After his wife had been killed in a bombing amidst the religious-political intolerance and chaos of Beirut in 1981, the Arabic poet Qabbani wrote: "Each day we
regress a thousand years." Writers like Qabbani and his fellow Arab poet Adonis
rejected conformity to traditional ideas no less than to foreign ones. Like many
Third World intellectuals, they advocated expanding upon their own tradition in a
creative way, in a manner open to the best ideas of other cultures.

The Islamic faithful, an important cultural and political force, at prayer in West
Africa. (Marc & Evelyne Bernheim/Woodfin Camp & Associates)

Thus, the battle continued between traditional and new beliefs and life styles, which were often fostered by global media influences. And despite signs in certain spheres of increasing standardization or globalization of culture, the world's peoples by the end of the 1980s seemed as divided as ever on fundamental values. In the 1930s, the poet T. S. Eliot wrote:

> Where is the wisdom we have lost in knowledge?
> Where is the knowledge we have lost in information?

A half century later, many still doubted whether the new "Information Age" had led to any significant moral progress, or made humankind any wiser.

SUGGESTED SOURCES

Blake, David H., and Robert S. Walters, *The Politics of Global Economic Relations,* 3rd ed. (1987). A clearly written overview of global economic relations since World War II; presents contrasting points of view concerning major developments.*

Brandt, Willy, *Arms and Hunger* (1987). The former West German chancellor combines useful data and analysis in his reflections on two of the major problems of the postwar era.*

Bundy, McGeorge, *Danger and Survival: Choices about the Bomb in the First Fifty Years* (1988). Interesting reflections by a former U.S. presidential advisor.

Egginton, Joyce, *The Poisoning of Michigan* (1980). Relates how PBB got into the food chain in Michigan in the early 1970s and deals with some of the effects of the accident.

Harrison, Paul, *Inside the Third World,* 2nd ed. (1987). A firsthand account and analysis of the poverty of many modern nations; 1987 printing contains an updated postscript.*

Jackson, Robert, ed., *Global Issues 89/90* (1989). A collection of fifty-five articles dealing with a wide variety of 1980s global problems.*

Miller, N., and Roderick Aya, eds., *National Liberation: Revolution in the Third World* (1971). A collection of incisive articles on Third World revolutions, primarily in the 1950s and 1960s.*

Morris, Charles R., *Iron Destinies, Lost Opportunities: The Arms Race between the U.S.A. and the U.S.S.R., 1945–87* (1988). An in-depth, balanced assessment of the arms race.

Rubin, Barry, *Modern Dictators* (1987). An interesting examination of Third World dictators of recent decades in Asia, Africa, Latin America, and the Middle East.*

Stromberg, Ronald N., *After Everything: Western Intellectual History since 1945* (1975). A clear overview of political, cultural, philosophical, artistic, and scientific trends in the first three postwar decades.*

Writings on the Sand (1965). An engaging film on birth control programs in India.

*Paperback available.

22

Postwar Settlements, Europe, and the Early Cold War

World War II was a catastrophe for the twentieth century. First, it brought about immense suffering, death, and destruction. Second, it was the catalyst for the onset of the Cold War, in which rivalry between the United States and the Soviet Union brought on a period of increasingly intense confrontation. When this rivalry was combined with the menace of atomic destruction at supersonic speeds, there began to be the distinct possibility of global holocaust, which in fact came fearsomely close in the Cuban missile crisis of 1962.

THE DESTRUCTIVE LEGACY OF WORLD WAR II

World War II caused even greater carnage than World War I. Casualty estimates vary, but even modest ones are astronomical: sixty million dead, thirty-five million injured, and three million missing. In this human disaster, the civilian losses were perhaps the most appalling: possibly thirty million noncombatants died from starvation and disease or perished in battles, air raids, labor and extermination camps, and deportations. Europe suffered thirty-five million dead, half of them Soviet citizens. Over one million Germans and more than one million ethnic Poles were killed. In Asia, twenty million Chinese and two million Japanese lost their lives. By comparison, British and U.S. wartime losses were of a much lower magnitude, in combination numbering 600,000 killed.

In addition to the casualties, war and postwar dislocation uprooted thirty million Europeans from their homes, and the initials "D.P." ("displaced person") became familiar. In many nations in postwar Europe, the ethnic majority in an area permanently expelled ethnic minorities. Some seventeen million Germans were driven out of Eastern Europe. In the Soviet Union, two million "unreliables," most of them ethnic minorities, were sent to Siberia. Greeks, Turks, Yugoslavs, and Hungarians fled from other nations to their homelands, and about a million of the surviving European Jews immigrated to Palestine (later Israel). Over a million people had no homeland, and the United

Nations struggled to resettle these refugees in Western Europe, the Western Hemisphere, and Australia. Five years after the war, most ethnic boundaries in Europe, with major exceptions in Czechoslovakia, Rumania, and Yugoslavia, coincided with national boundaries, at a terrible cost to millions of individuals. Asia and Africa also suffered population dislocations, but most occurred during the decolonization process well after the war.

Vast stretches of Europe and Asia were physically devastated. Most of the principal cities in Central and Eastern Europe had been bombed and shelled into rubble. The road, canal, and railroad systems of much of Europe had disappeared, and millions of acres of farmland had been damaged. In Asia, the cities of Japan had been obliterated under incendiary and atomic attacks, and many Chinese and other Asian cities had been substantially destroyed. Much of rural China had also been damaged in eight years of war. The cost of the war, both in damages and in war expenditures, has been estimated at one and one-half trillion dollars.

ANOTHER SEVERE POSTWAR SETTLEMENT

It is not surprising that the circumstances of the onset and conduct of World War II made the victors view the defeated aggressor nations with a mixture of hatred and vengefulness. The Allied powers were determined that neither Germany nor Japan would ever again threaten its neighbors. During the war, the Allies had forged a broad consensus on general terms for the defeated, but these wartime agreements broke down quickly after the war under the stress of antagonism among the victors. Instead of being settled at a formal peace conference, as was done after World War I, most issues were worked out in military conferences immediately after the war and at a series of conferences of foreign ministers lasting until 1963. Some of the agreements were ratified through bilateral treaties; some de facto arrangements, particularly those dealing with Germany, were not ratified until 1975.

Europe

The territorial arrangements in Europe were not as extensive as those made after World War I. The single largest change involved the agreement that the Soviet Union would retain the areas originally acquired in 1939–40 and again in their possession at the end of the war: Estonia, Latvia, Lithuania, portions of Rumania and Finland, and eastern Poland. In addition, the Soviet Union annexed a province of Czechoslovakia and the northern half of East Prussia. These acquisitions moved the Soviet border dramatically westward compared with 1939, but placed it at about the same place as the border of tsarist Russia in 1914. Although some nations refused to acknowledge the change, Poland received the eastern one-quarter of Germany in compensation for the loss of eastern Poland. Boundary changes in the rest of Europe were relatively minor. Hit-

Europe after World War II

ⓕ Ethnic and/or religious unrest

⚡ Unrest or revolt against Eastern European governments

▓ Member of the European Economic Community, 1984 (Common market)

░ Member of the Council for Mutual Economic Assistance (COMECON)

UNION OF SOVIET SOCIALIST REPUBLICS

CASPIAN SEA

GEORGIAN S. S. R.
AZERBAIJAN S. S. R.
ARMENIAN S. S. R.

BLACK SEA

TURKEY

ESTONIAN S. S. R.
LATVIAN S. S. R.
LITHUANIAN S. S. R.
BELORUSSIAN S. S. R.
UKRAINIAN S. S. R.
MOLDAVIAN S. S. R.

FINLAND

BALTIC SEA

(1956)
(1980–1982)
POLAND
(1968)
CZECHOSLOVAKIA
(1956)
HUNGARY

1953
GERMAN DEMOCRATIC REP.

RUMANIA

BULGARIA

GREECE

ALBANIA

YUGOSLAVIA ⓕ

SWEDEN

NORWAY

DENMARK

UNITED KINGDOM

NETHER-LANDS

FED. REP. OF GERMANY
BELG.
LUX.
AUSTRIA
SWITZ.

ITALY

NORTHERN IRELAND ⓕ

IRELAND

FRANCE

SPAIN ⓕ

PORTUGAL

ATLANTIC OCEAN

MEDITERRANEAN SEA

AFRICA

0 100 200 300 400 500
Scale of miles

ler's Axis allies—Finland, Hungary, Rumania, Bulgaria, and Italy—faced some territorial adjustments, reparations payments, and limitations on their military establishments; but the overall terms were not particularly harsh. The most notable change was Italy's surrender of the predominantly Slavic province of Istria to Yugoslavia. The western boundary of Germany was set as it had existed in 1937, which primarily involved returning Alsace-Lorraine to France. Austria was detached from Germany and occupied by the United States, Great Britain, France, and the Soviet Union. In 1955, the occupation forces were withdrawn and Austria regained its independence.

As at the Paris Peace Conference of 1919, the postwar status of Germany dominated the thinking of the victorious powers. During the war, Germany's enemies had considered permanently dismembering it or stripping it of industry and reducing it to a feeble agricultural region. By the war's end, the United States had changed to the belief that a healthy, united Germany would be essential to European recovery and to vigorous international trade. By 1945, the Allies had agreed to retain Germany as a single nation but hedged about with safeguards to prevent future aggression. To accomplish the latter, they agreed that Germany was to be disarmed and divided into four occupation zones: French, British, U.S., and Soviet. The occupying forces were to remain there until they could be sure that the German people had been de-Nazified and would no longer be aggressive. At some future time, a German government acceptable to the occupying forces would be set up, a treaty would then be concluded with this new government, and the occupying forces would withdraw. In 1945, most observers believed the occupation would be over in three to five years. Again, as after World War I, the victors were interested in reparations settlements and agreed that the heavily ravaged Soviet Union would receive the largest share. The Allies left the details concerning reparations for later resolution.

One feature of the arrangements for the occupation zones became extremely important in postwar years. During the war, the Western forces had agreed to halt west of Berlin while Soviet forces captured the city; this put Berlin in the Soviet occupation zone. After the war, the Western Allies insisted on sharing in the occupation of the city, and an awkward arrangement was worked out. Berlin became a separate occupation authority, divided into four occupation zones. The Soviet Union agreed that certain highways, railroads, and air corridors would be set aside in their German occupation zone for the Western powers to supply their three sectors in West Berlin. This arrangement left the Western forces in Berlin cut off behind Soviet lines, a precarious military situation.

Finally, there was the matter of war crimes. The Nazis had caused such horror before and during World War II that this time the victorious powers were determined to punish the leaders. An international judicial tribunal assembled at Nuremberg during 1945–46. The highest surviving Nazi leaders were put on trial for waging aggressive war and for committing crimes against humanity. Twelve were condemned to death, seven were imprisoned for terms up to life, and three were acquitted. While some attacked the process as "victor's justice,'' the precedent was set that brutal treatment of prisoners and non-combatants constituted a crime and that "following orders" was not a sufficient defense. Trials of lesser officials followed.

Asia

As in Europe, postwar arrangements in Asia devolved from basic agreements in the midwar conferences. The victors stripped Japan of its empire, divided its possessions among themselves, and occupied Japan. They set Japan's boundaries as those of 1854, which restricted Japan to the four home islands. The United States, which had carried the great burden of the war with Japan, was to be the sole occupying power in Japan and the Ryukyu Island chain with its important Okinawa air base. The United States also took over the western Pacific islands as a United Nations Trust Territory. The Soviet Union received the southern half of Sakhalin, the Kurile Islands, and railroad and seaport rights in Manchuria (all lost to Japan in 1905). China regained Taiwan (Formosa), which had been lost to Japan in 1895. Soviet and U.S. forces split Korea into two occupation zones until a mutually suitable government could be installed.

Defeated Japan received much the same treatment as Germany. Japan's armed forces were disbanded, and Japan, in a new constitution, was made to renounce war as an instrument of national policy. Japan was to be governed by a U.S. army of occupation under the direction of General MacArthur. U.S. forces would stay until the Japanese could demonstrate they were no longer an aggressive people, which they could do by creating a government acceptable to the United States. As at Nuremberg, Japanese leaders were put on trial in Tokyo and Manila for war crimes; seven were executed, and others were imprisoned. Unlike Germany, Japan retained its government, but it was purged of militarists. The emperor was also retained on the condition that he renounce his claim to divinity.

THE ONSET OF THE COLD WAR

As World War II came to a close, the alliance among the victorious powers began to dissolve. The United States, Great Britain, and the Soviet Union—nations very different in their political, social, and economic characteristics—had been united in a "shotgun marriage" against a fearsome enemy. Even as they were fighting the Axis, however, each of these allies looked ahead in one degree or another to arranging the postwar world along lines that would be best for its own nation. Great Britain wished to maintain its empire and retain its closed imperial economic system; the United States wished to retain its spheres of influence in the Western Hemisphere and Asia, but also wished to construct a worldwide system of free markets; the Soviet Union was determined to dominate Eastern Europe and to keep Germany militarily impotent in order to prevent another invasion out of the west. In addition, the Soviet Union was willing to exploit opportunities to advance Marxism and Soviet interests around the world if such opportunities did not embroil the Soviet Union in too much difficulty.

Reflecting such a diversity of interests, World War II, a "hot" war, was followed by the "Cold War," a confrontation between the United States and the Soviet Union that persisted to one degree or another throughout most of the postwar period. Historians strongly debated its causes and the responsibility of each power for its outbreak.

Phase One: Eastern Europe and Germany

At the last two wartime conferences, Yalta in February 1945 and Potsdam in July and August 1945, it became clear that strong disagreements about the future of Eastern Europe and the occupation of Germany were developing between the United States and Great Britain, on the one hand, and the Soviet Union, on the other. Soviet troops already occupied Eastern Europe and eastern Germany. The Soviet Union, with approximately seventeen million dead, was determined to weld Eastern Europe into a buffer zone of friendly nations, presumably with Communist governments, that would protect it from future invasion. Stalin believed the Soviet Union was entitled to a sphere of influence in Eastern Europe because the United States had spheres of influence in the Caribbean, Japan, and Western Europe. The United States wanted Eastern European governments to reflect the will of their people through democratic elections, partly from principle and partly from confidence that such elections would create governments that would be friendly to the United States. It pressed the Soviet Union to permit the creation of governments based on a broad political spectrum, particularly in Poland, but the Soviet Union made only token concessions.

The wartime allies also clashed over German reparations. All the victors believed they were entitled to wring reparations from Germany, and they had talked about setting the figure at $20 billion. On the other hand, the United States was undamaged by the war and its economy had prospered mightily. American leaders also remembered the German experience after World War I and were therefore more interested in rebuilding Germany as a trading partner than in burdening it with reparations. The Soviet Union, on the other hand, had been badly devastated during the war and wanted to rebuild its economy either through postwar loans from the United States or from reparations from defeated Germany, or both. To pressure the Soviets into opening Eastern Europe, the United States cut off Lend-Lease and refused to make loans to the Soviet Union. In addition, in 1946, the Western powers ended shipments of industrial materials out of their German zones to the Soviet Union, causing great bitterness in the Soviet Union. Meanwhile, the Soviets proceeded to strip their occupation zone in eastern Germany of materials useful to the Soviet economy.

The conflict between the United States and the Soviet Union stemmed from more than policy differences alone. In mid-1945, the two nations were led by Harry Truman and Joseph Stalin, men whose personalities contributed to the tensions. Truman's predecessor, President Roosevelt, was by temperament a pragmatist. Needing Soviet help during the war, he had tried to work in a cooperative spirit with Stalin. Truman was an intelligent, feisty politician who had come to the presidency by accident. He had little training in foreign affairs, but he had always been a critic of Stalinism; now that the war was over, he was temperamentally disposed to "get tough" with the Soviet Union. Premier Stalin was also a clever, determined political leader, but one with limited contacts with the outside world. Possessed of an iron will and not overly concerned about the morality of the means he used, he had displayed an almost paranoid obsession with acquiring and maintaining personal political power. He harbored strong suspicions of the nations of the West. He feared that the capitalist powers were determined to destroy the Soviet state, as they seemed bent on doing during the Allied intervention following the Bolshevik revolution.

The atomic bomb also harmed postwar relationships. The political fallout in U.S.-Soviet relations matched the atomic fallout over Japan. Most historians claimed that the bomb was used because intense Japanese resistance threatened to prolong the war at a cost of over a million additional casualties. On the other hand, some took the view that the bomb was dropped primarily to prevent the Soviet Union from making gains in Asia and to make that nation more amenable to U.S. desires concerning Germany and Eastern Europe. Whatever the case, U.S. possession of the atomic bomb made the Soviet Union fearful and suspicious, but it did not back down about Eastern Europe or Germany.

After Potsdam, relationships between the two superpowers deteriorated further. The United States blocked Soviet interests in Iran while strengthening its own interests in the area. The Soviet Union continued to suppress anti-Communist elements in Poland, Rumania, and Bulgaria, and to tighten the grip of Communist parties there. In addition, the Soviet Union began to work for control in Czechoslovakia and Hungary, where free elections had been held and where, in each case, the Communist party was in a minority. Meanwhile, the United States presented a plan for the control of atomic energy, the Baruch Plan, which specified that all nations give up control of fissionable materials to an independent international agency, submit to international inspection of existing facilities, and cease making atomic bombs. Because the United States and its Latin American and Western European allies controlled the United Nations, and through it would control the proposed international agency, the Soviet Union rejected the plan. At the same time, rhetoric escalated on both sides. In a speech at Fulton, Missouri, in 1946, Churchill charged that an "iron curtain" had fallen, dividing Moscow-controlled Eastern Europe from "free" Western Europe. Actually, the situation was still fluid in Eastern Europe. Stalin told the Soviet people that the Soviet Union was ringed by enemies bent upon destroying it, and that they would have to endure privations and return to Five-Year Plans to build up the economic and military strength needed to defend themselves.

Phase Two: The Truman Doctrine and European Developments

Late in 1946 and early in 1947, the focus of confrontation shifted to Turkey and Greece. The Soviet Union was interested in obtaining secure transit through Turkey's water passage from the Black Sea to the Mediterranean. The Soviet Union demanded joint Soviet-Turkish supervision of the waterway, but the Turkish government refused. Being much weaker than the Soviet Union, Turkey looked for help.

In Greece, the end of World War II had brought about a brutal, atrocity-filled civil war between the corrupt, authoritarian Greek government and Communist-dominated guerrillas. British army units backed the government, and Communist regimes in Bulgaria, Albania, and particularly Yugoslavia supported the guerrillas. Churchill had exacted from Stalin a promise not to support the guerrillas there, and Stalin, for reasons of his own, did not help them. In February 1947, unable to bear the costs, the British government announced it was pulling its troops out of Greece.

The Truman administration, faced with what it viewed as a Soviet threat to conquer smaller nations and break out onto the Mediterranean, formulated a policy that intensified the Cold War. Most U.S. diplomats and military leaders assumed that the Soviet Union was out to destroy the "free" (non-Communist) world, and they viewed the crisis in the Mediterranean as the crucial test. If aggression against Greece and Turkey could be halted, the Communists would be unlikely to attempt aggression elsewhere. Instead of using atomic bombs, the Truman administration put emphasis on "containing" communism, preventing its advance until the people in the Communist nations would tire of Marxism and overthrow their governments. The containment policy, as it came to be called, generally dominated U.S. strategic thought throughout the postwar period. As viewed in 1947, containment meant sending extensive economic and military aid to enable governments to defeat external or internal Communist threats through their own efforts. To carry out this policy, Truman and his advisors had to persuade the U.S. public and Congress to spend massive amounts of tax dollars for "peacetime" military aid.

In March 1947, President Truman called Congress into special session. He asked for money for military supplies and military advisors for Greece and Turkey, declaring, "I believe it must be the policy of the United States to support free peoples who are facing attempted subjugation by armed minorities or by outside pressures." Congress voted $400 million, and this policy became known as the Truman Doctrine. A naval squadron was already in the Mediterranean, and military aid and advisors were quickly rushed to Greece. Bolstered by the U.S. presence, the Turkish government continued to refuse to administer the waterway to the Mediterranean jointly with the Soviet Union. With U.S. aid, the reorganized and better-equipped Greek army became more effective against the guerrillas, and when Yugoslavia closed the border with Greece in 1949, cutting off supplies and a place of refuge, the guerrillas laid down their arms.

Western Europe was another source of Cold War tension. Despite several billion dollars in U.S. loans, by 1947 the economy of Western Europe had not

A step into the Cold War: President Truman addresses a joint session of Congress on March 12, 1947, calling for military aid to Greece and Turkey in order to block Communist expansion into the Mediterranean. (UPI/ Bettmann Newsphotos)

revived. France and Italy, in particular, were plagued with shortages, inflation, unemployment, and inadequate housing. This situation, plus the fact that leftists had played an important role in the wartime resistance movement against Nazism and fascism, induced many French and Italians to vote for Socialist and Communist candidates. The only other major political party in Italy and France that rivaled them in popularity was that of the Christian Democrats, called in France the Popular Republican Movement. Christian democracy developed out of Catholic wartime resistance movements and was at first inclined toward a moderate Catholic leftist position. It had significant support in many European nations and in Latin America as well. However, under both the Italian and French multi-party political systems, no one party was able to obtain a parliamentary majority, and coalition governments were usually necessary. The Socialists and Communists were able to obtain cabinet posts along with the Christian Democrats, but no Communist had yet become prime minister in Italy or France.

The Truman administration concluded that the economic and political situation in Western Europe demanded effective U.S. economic intervention. In June 1947, Secretary of State George Marshall proposed that the nations of Europe consult with one another and with the United States to determine the amount of economic assistance they would need to rebuild their economies. Marshall's offer was technically open to every European nation, including the Soviet Union, although U.S. leaders expected—and hoped—that the Soviet Union would refuse. Western European nations accepted quickly, but the Soviet Union, suspicious that U.S. aid meant U.S. economic penetration, refused and prevented Eastern European nations from participating.

The U.S. Congress at first balked at the novel idea of giving money away as peacetime foreign aid rather than lending it in wartime. Soviet actions in Eastern Europe during 1947 and 1948 finally convinced Congress that the United States should undertake foreign aid; in 1948, Congress created the European Recovery Program, usually referred to as the Marshall Plan, with an initial outlay of $4 billion. By 1951 Marshall Plan aid totaled over $13 billion, most of it going to Great Britain, Germany, France, and Italy. The Marshall Plan was a success; the economy of Western European nations recovered rapidly.

Even before the Marshall Plan went into effect, Communist political fortunes were already on the decline. In both Italy and France, Communists were excluded from cabinet positions after mid-1947. In the Italian general elections in April 1948, Alcide de Gasperi's Christian Democratic party attained a near majority and the Communist-Socialist vote dropped to 31 percent. While no single party would again come as close to an absolute majority in Italy, Christian Democrats would remain the most influential of Italy's numerous parties. Communist-led general strikes in 1947–48 in both Italy and France caused some disruption, but both were broken by government action. The popularity of the Italian Christian Democrats stemmed in part from the backing of more conservative elements, who saw the Christian Democrats as the only major alternative to the Socialists and Communists. During the late 1940s, this phenomenon also occurred in several other European nations, and it moved Christian Democratic parties toward more conservative policies than they had originally espoused.

In 1950, the United States extended the concept of foreign aid to the non-Western world in the hope that such aid would prevent new nations from turning to communism. The United States embodied this concept in the Point Four Program, which channeled millions and eventually billions of dollars into the economies of newly emerging nations.

The Soviet Union kept pace with the Truman Doctrine and Marshall Plan offensives by tightening its grip on Moscow-backed Eastern European governments. In 1947–48, Communist takeovers added Hungary and Czechoslovakia to the Soviet sphere, which already included Poland, Rumania, Bulgaria, and Albania. The takeover in Czechoslovakia, the only Eastern European nation with a solid interwar tradition of Western democracy, shocked the West and hastened Congress's approval of the Marshall Plan. In order to tighten its grip on Eastern Europe, the Soviet Union created bilateral economic treaties, later followed by COMECON, a Soviet-controlled economic organization that integrated the economies of Eastern European nations with one another and with the Soviet Union. COMECON assigned some nations (such as Czechoslovakia) industrial goals and other nations (such as Bulgaria) agricultural goals. To reinforce the unity of Communist regimes in Eastern Europe, the Soviet Union created Cominform, a new organization containing most of the European Communist parties.

There was a hole in the Soviet Eastern European buffer zone, however: Yugoslavia, although Communist, took an independent, nationalistic course under Marshal Tito and, after a bitter confrontation with the Soviet Union, was expelled from Cominform in 1948. Because of other problems, Stalin did not attack Yugoslavia. Tito cautiously maneuvered his nation into a position of neutrality, and eventually became important as one of the leaders of nonaligned nations around the world.

Although Stalin could do little more than expel Tito from Cominform, he was able to exert much more pressure on those he considered "Titoists" in other Eastern European nations. From 1949 to 1952, many of those so labeled were imprisoned, tried, and, on occasion, executed. Stalin also demanded that each government within the Eastern bloc follow the Soviet example more closely in such matters as centralized party control over the economy, acceleration of collectivized agriculture, persecution of religion, and establishment of a Soviet-style constitution. Nevertheless, these nations never became clones of the Soviet Union. For example, private agriculture and religion continued to be more significant forces in Eastern Europe than in the U.S.S.R., despite Stalin's efforts.

In a major application of the containment policy, the United States and its allies combined the three Western zones of occupation in Germany into a German national state. Although Germany had been a hated enemy and was still feared, by the French in particular, the West began to view a revived Germany as a buffer against the Soviet-controlled East. The Western powers united their zones in stages between 1946 and 1949, a process somewhat delayed because of French reluctance. By 1949 the Western powers were well advanced on a program to create a national economic unit and a new currency in western Germany and were building up the government from the local level. During 1948 and 1949, with Western supervision, the West Germans created a new constitution acceptable to the three occupying powers. The newly united nation, the Federal Republic of Germany, put its capital at the university town of Bonn. Its government was controlled by the Christian Democratic party, led by the anti-Communist Konrad Adenauer, who was already in his seventies when he came to power. His party held power for two decades. By September 1949 "West Germany" was operating as a sovereign state, although formal recognition would not come until later. Western troops remained, although less visible.

Of all the actions undertaken by the United States and its allies after World War II, the reestablishment of West Germany probably created the most hostility in the Soviet Union. After Russia's two twentieth-century experiences, the Soviet Union hated and feared a reborn Germany and believed that the West intended to rearm West Germany and use it against the Soviet Union. The Soviets countered by transforming their occupation zone into the Democratic Republic of Germany, but their main effort to derail the unification of West Germany centered on the spot where the West was most vulnerable: Berlin. In June 1948, the Soviets announced they had closed for repairs the railroads and highways in East Germany set aside to supply Western troops and the civilians in West Berlin. The Western governments immediately gathered all available cargo planes and used the air corridors to supply more than two million West Berliners and Western troops with food, clothing, coal, and other supplies. The Berlin Airlift, or "Operation Vittles," was a triumph of efficiency. At its peak, transport planes touched down at Berlin's Templehof airdrome every few minutes on an around-the-clock schedule. The blockade of Berlin lasted 300 days, until May 1949, when the Soviets conceded defeat and reopened the highways and railroads. The crisis was over, but Berlin remained a trouble spot for the future.

The Cold War tensions were not confined to international diplomacy; they also affected the people at home. For example, during the war, Americans had been friendly toward "Uncle Joe" Stalin and the Soviet Union. After the war, their attitude changed, and, taking their cues from the government, they began to view the Soviet Union as heading an international conspiracy to overthrow capitalism. It was a short step from hostility toward the Soviet Union to hostility toward those Americans who were perceived to be, or to have been, friendly to the Soviet Union. Americans were egged on by some leaders to worry about alleged "subversives," "Commie dupes," "parlor pinks," and "fellow travelers." Congress ran several investigations of alleged subversives in the United States and created legislation with such broad power to combat subversive organizations that it posed a threat to civil liberties. The executive branch created a government loyalty program designed to uncover subversives and unreliables in the federal government. Although there were indeed a few pro-Soviet Americans, most of the accused were innocent people, many of whom lost their jobs or saw their reputations tarnished. The climax of anti-Communist hysteria occurred from 1950 to 1954; it was intensified by the Communist takeover of China and the Korean War (see Chapter 24). Senator Joseph McCarthy made the term "McCarthyism" famous because of his unproven charges of subversion directed against a wide variety of Americans ranging from ordinary citizens to the army command.

As the economies of Western European nations recovered with the aid of the Marshall Plan, the influence of Communist parties continued to decline in France and Italy. West Germany under Adenauer recovered its full sovereignty. It also became increasingly prosperous, and in the 1950s there was talk of the German "economic miracle." Adenauer's relationship with a variety of French governments was better than that of any previous German leader of the century. Adenauer finally retired as chancellor in late 1963, but his Christian Democratic party continued in power for six more years. In 1951, aided at least in part by Cold War developments, the Conservative party in Great Britain returned to power after six postwar years of Labour party control marked by such social welfare policies as the institution of free medical care. The Conservatives, first under Churchill and then under Anthony Eden, Harold Macmillan, and Sir Alec Douglas-Home, remained in power until 1964. The Conservative dominance in Great Britain in the 1950s was symptomatic of a general European trend in that decade toward more conservative governments.

In the Soviet Union, Stalin tightened his hold over the nation. The enormous wartime loss of life and property necessitated massive economic reconstruction, and Stalin also distrusted the more friendly attitude toward the West that the war had generated in the Soviet Union. These factors, plus Stalin's continued concern with his own political power and Cold War tensions, all led to strict controls over the economic, social, and cultural life of Soviet citizens up to Stalin's death in 1953.

Phase Three: Global Nuclear Confrontation

The Cold War heated up further in 1949, as the United States abandoned its tradition of unilateral diplomacy and moved into a new era. After World War II, both the Soviet Union and the United States had demobilized the bulk of their armies. However, postwar events culminating in Czechoslovakia and Berlin convinced U.S. leaders that the Soviet Union represented a permanent aggressive menace in Europe that must be confronted with a permanent U.S. military presence, bolstered by an alliance system.

The era of alliances began in 1947 when the United States created the Rio Pact, a regional defensive alliance in which the United States and Latin American nations agreed to come to the aid of any member nation threatened with aggression. In 1949, the Truman administration set up the North Atlantic Treaty Organization (NATO), in which the United States, Canada, Iceland, Norway, Denmark, the Netherlands, Belgium, Luxemburg, Great Britain, France, Portugal, and Italy (and later Greece and Turkey) agreed to come to one another's aid if attacked. The alliance's goal was the eventual integration of the national armed forces of the member nations into a unified military command. In practical terms, NATO was dominated by the U.S. military establishment; a U.S. general (beginning with Eisenhower) was always the supreme commander. The United States Strategic Air Command (SAC) established air bases in Western Europe and the North Atlantic. The United States also began constructing air bases in non-NATO nations such as Spain and Libya, as well as developing bases in U.S.-occupied Japan and Okinawa. From all these bases, U.S. B-29s could drop atomic bombs on the Soviet Union.

Soviet reaction was twofold. First, the Soviet Union began to increase the size of its army in Europe until it heavily outnumbered the NATO forces opposing it, thus making it likely that the Soviet Union could overrun Western Europe if war broke out with the United States. This in effect turned Western

European nations into hostages in a superpower confrontation, and often stimulated these nations to urge restraint during U.S.-Soviet crises. The Soviets' second move was to create its own bristling array of atomic weapons. Only five months after NATO was organized, the Soviet Union surprised the world by detonating an atomic bomb.

In the early 1950s, the United States and the Soviet Union found themselves engaged in a fevered arms race, creating weapons of ever more destructive power. In 1952, the United States test-exploded a hydrogen bomb, followed in 1953 by the Soviet Union. The Eisenhower administration decided to base its military policy on "massive retaliation," the concept that in the event of any Soviet attack on the United States or its allies, SAC bombers would destroy the Soviet Union with atomic or thermonuclear bombs. Eisenhower's Secretary of State, John Foster Dulles, believed that U.S. military superiority would be an excellent backup for his "brinksmanship" policy of pressing selective issues with the Soviet Union to the limit. By 1955, both superpowers possessed bombers of intercontinental range that could hit the opponent's homeland. They carried four ten-megaton hydrogen bombs; each bomb was capable of substantially destroying a major urban center, such as Moscow or New York. Still, the U.S. air force maintained a four-to-one lead over the Soviet Union in aircraft capable of delivering bombs on the enemy's homeland.

Meanwhile, the United States continued to tighten its containment noose around the Soviet Union. By 1954, the Cold War had spread to Asia (see Chapter 24), and the United States organized the Southeast Asia Treaty Organization (SEATO). This alliance supported anti-Communist nations in Asia while enlarging the string of SAC air bases surrounding the Soviet Union. In the Middle East, the United States stood behind but was not a member of the Baghdad Pact, allying Great Britain with Iran, Turkey, Iraq, and Pakistan. This alliance system collapsed because of Middle Eastern politics and other factors, but in 1957, President Eisenhower pressured Congress into authorizing the president to commit U.S. troops to defend nations in the Middle East against "overt armed aggression from any nation controlled by international communism." Eisenhower used this policy to intervene briefly and unprofitably in Lebanon. The total result of these arrangements was that the United States could bomb the Soviet Union from virtually every direction, but the Soviet Union could bomb the United States only via the North Pole, and even that with difficulty because radar systems in Canada gave early warning of approaching Soviet aircraft.

Despite extensive U.S. military build-ups, the Soviet army, backed by medium-range missiles and bombers, still gave the Soviet Union a distinct advantage in Europe. In an effort to lessen the imbalance there, West Germany was admitted into NATO and permitted to rearm. To accomplish this, the United States had to pressure its reluctant NATO allies, who were caught between fear of the Soviet Union and suspicion of a rearmed Germany.

In 1955, the Soviet Union—with its own fears of a rearmed Germany— created its own military alliance system, the Warsaw Pact, integrating the armed forces of Eastern Europe into a unified force under Soviet command. In addition, the Soviets recognized East Germany as an independent state. Although the hope of unifying Germany still remained in some quarters, as of 1955 Germany had become two separate nations, each integrated into the sphere of influence of a superpower.

Eastern Europe remained a problem for the Soviet Union. Dissatisfaction with living conditions, plus the hopes raised by more liberal Soviet post-Stalinist policies, led to riots and other convulsions in East Germany in 1953. The East German disturbance was quickly suppressed, but disturbances occurred in Poland and Hungary in 1956. Wladyslaw Gomulka, considered an unreliable Polish "Titoist" by the Soviet Union, was made the head of the Polish Communist party. The Soviet Union threatened to intervene in Poland, but did not. In Hungary, some police officials were lynched, and some army units went over to the people. Premier Imre Nagy announced that Hungary would cease to be a one-party state or a member of the Warsaw Pact. This was unacceptable to the Soviet Union, and Soviet troops poured in to suppress the rebellion. The United States was caught in a dilemma. It had been the stated policy of the Eisenhower administration to "roll back the iron curtain" and to "liberate Eastern Europe." The Voice of America and Radio Free Europe had been beaming propaganda broadcasts into the region for years in an effort to stir up unrest there. Many Hungarian rebels expected that the United States would now intervene, but the Soviet Union made it plain that intervention meant war. The United States was not prepared to go to war over Eastern Europe; further, it was distracted at that time by a confrontation with its allies, Great Britain and France, over the Suez Canal (see Chapter 26). The United States did nothing, and the Soviet Union crushed the rebellion. About 25,000 Hungarians, including Nagy, lost their lives, and some 200,000 Hungarians fled to the West. Although the Soviet Union was, and would remain, supreme in Eastern Europe, there was to be no return to the policies of the 1949–52 period. Conditions gradually improved as living standards rose moderately and repressive policies were slowly relaxed.

A Thaw in the Cold War

Although the Cold War intensified at times during the 1950s, the superpowers also made sporadic attempts to negotiate their differences. The death of Stalin in 1953 opened the door to a possible relaxation of tensions. After Stalin died, a scramble for leadership ensued in the Soviet Union, resolved by the accession of Nikita Khrushchev to power. In 1956, Khrushchev made a daring "secret speech" to a closed session of the Twentieth Congress of the Communist party of the Soviet Union; he criticized Stalin's policies, including his elimination of many innocent people during the 1930s. From then until his removal in 1964, Khrushchev used criticism of Stalin and Stalinist policies to weaken the power of his political rivals within the party hierarchy. While motivated largely by political concerns, Khrushchev's de-Stalinization campaign did help lead to less censorship. In 1962, for example, Khrushchev personally approved the publi-

Stalin's Corpse

On March 5, 1953, an event took place which shattered Russia—Stalin died. I found it almost impossible to imagine him dead, so much had he been an indispensable part of life.

A sort of general paralysis came over the country. Trained to believe that they were all in Stalin's care, people were lost and bewildered without him. All Russia wept. And so did I. We wept sincerely, tears of grief—and perhaps also tears of fear for the future. . . .

I will never forget going to see Stalin's coffin. . . . The crowd closed tighter and tighter. I was saved by my height. Short people were smothered alive, falling and perishing. We were caught between the walls of houses on one side and a row of army trucks on the other.

"Get those trucks out of the way!" people howled. "Get them out of here!"

"I can't do it! I have no instructions," a very young, towheaded police officer shouted back from one of the trucks, almost crying with helplessness. And people were being hurtled against the trucks by the crowd, and their heads smashed. The sides of the trucks were splashed with blood. All at once I felt a savage hatred for everything that had given birth to that "I have no instructions," shouted at a moment when people were dying because of someone's stupidity. For the first time in my life I thought with hatred of the man we were burying. He could not be innocent of the disaster. It was the "No instructions" that had caused the chaos and bloodshed at his funeral.*

The Russian poet Yevgeny Yevtushenko, who was nineteen when Stalin died, describes the general sense of grief and shock at Stalin's death and the tragic deaths of an untold number lining up to view his corpse in Moscow on March 6, 1953.

*From *A Precocious Autobiography* by Yevgeny Yevtushenko, translated by Andrew R. McAndrew. Copyright © 1964 by E. P. Dutton. Reprinted by permission.

cation of Alexander Solzhenitsyn's *One Day in the Life of Ivan Denisovich,* the story of a man unjustly sent to a prison camp during Stalin's regime. By the late 1950s, the Communist party under Khrushchev's leadership had allowed millions of innocent people to be freed from the camps. Khrushchev also desired to improve living standards, including increasing agricultural output. In order to do this, he limited military spending more than some of his political rivals thought appropriate.

In 1953, there was also a change of leadership in the United States, as the moderate, easygoing Eisenhower ("Ike") succeeded Truman as president. Eisenhower and Khrushchev remained suspicious of each other, each determined to keep his country strong, but both were more willing than their pre-decessors to negotiate under appropriate circumstances. Concerned with the danger and cost of the escalating Cold War, and under pressure from world opinion, Khrushchev and Eisenhower met at a "summit conference" in Geneva during 1955. Although nothing of substance came from the meeting, enough momentum was established to lead to other meetings. In 1955, the occupying powers agreed to end the occupation of Austria, and the Soviet Union recognized the West German government. Selected groups of Americans and Soviet citizens began visiting each other's nations. At the same time, the U.S. media began to tone down its strident anti-Communist presentations. This thaw in the Cold War was limited in both accomplishments and duration, but neither superpower believed that it could bypass the opportunity for discussions. In the future, new discussions would accompany new alarms and distractions.

Phase Four: Missile Races

On October 4, 1957, the Cold War moved into a still more dangerous phase. On that day, the Soviet Union, using a powerful new rocket booster, launched a small satellite, Sputnik, into an orbit around the earth. The space age had

The Great Kitchen Debate: Premier Khrushchev and Vice-President Nixon argue the merits of Soviet and U.S. ways of life at a U.S. exhibition in Moscow in 1959. (UPI/Bettmann Newsphotos)

begun. Two months later, the Soviet Union launched an intercontinental ballistics missile (ICBM). The missile age had begun. The Soviets gloried in their achievements. "We will bury you," Khrushchev promised the West. His statement, probably a figurative assertion that Marxist concepts would triumph in the long run, was taken by some in the West to be a threat of imminent nuclear war. Shortly thereafter, in 1958, he pressed his advantage by putting pressure on Berlin. Terming Berlin "a bone in the throat," he warned Western powers that the multiforce occupation of Berlin must end in six months' time or the Soviet Union would turn over the responsibility for Berlin and the supply corridors to East Germany.

Sputnik, the ICBM, and the Berlin threat prompted several reactions in the United States. Americans took pride in leading the world in science and technology and were depressed by Soviet successes. One leading atomic scientist moaned, "[The United States] has lost a battle more important and greater than Pearl Harbor." Some feared attacks by Soviet ICBMs, and a political furor broke out. The Democrats charged the Republicans with having created a "missile gap," and made gains in the 1958 Congressional elections. The scientific and educational community was blamed as well, with charges that "Johnny" was not measuring up to "Ivan."

In the face of public outcry, the Eisenhower administration moved quickly. It poured money into scientific research in the universities, tying them more closely to the military-industrial-political complex. The government sent up a satellite in 1958 and created the National Aeronautics and Space Administration (NASA) to get Americans ahead in space. The administration also spent vast sums of money to launch a major ICBM program and to build submarine-launched missiles (SLBM) that offered the advantage of a portable missile-firing platform that could not easily be detected. To further strengthen U.S. missile response to the Soviet Union, the United States offered to base intermediate-range and medium-range ballistics missiles in NATO countries, but only Great Britain, Italy, and Turkey agreed to set up missile sites. By 1962–63 the United States had 450 missiles and 2,000 bombers capable of striking the Soviet Union, compared to 50 to 100 Soviet ICBMs and 200 bombers that could reach the United States. The "missile gap" had been reversed with a vengeance, and the U.S. margin widened monthly. Both sides could now inflict enormous damage on each other, and a new phrase, "balance of terror," came into use.

Despite the missile race, diplomatic exchanges continued. Khrushchev repeatedly postponed the Berlin "deadline" and pressed for more summit meetings. In 1959, he traveled to the United States and tried to make Americans see him as a jovial human being, interested in everything from pig farms to San Francisco. He was upset that security problems prevented his visit to Disneyland. "Is there an epidemic of cholera there or something?" he asked. "Do you have rocket-launching pads there? . . . Or have gangsters taken hold of the place?" He was, however, able to visit Hollywood, but was critical of the scantily clad chorus girls on the set of the movie musical *Can Can*. A meeting with Eisenhower at Camp David went well, and enthusiasts spoke of the "spirit of Camp David" while the Soviet premier explained away his threatening rheto-

The Global Cold War, 1989
As seen from space over the North Pole

HAWAIIAN IS.

U.S.A. and allies
U.S. nuclear missiles
U.S. B-52 bomber bases
U.S. fleets
Naval bases abroad or ports open to U.S. navy
U.S. combat troops
U.S. nuclear missile submarines
Chinese nuclear missiles

U.S.S.R. and allies
Soviet nuclear missiles
Soviet nuclear bomber bases
Soviet fleets
Naval bases abroad or ports open to U.S.S.R. navy
Soviet combat troops
Soviet nuclear missile submarines

North Pole

A EAST GERMANY
B POLAND
C CZECHOSLOVAKIA
D HUNGARY
E RUMANIA
F BULGARIA

1 DENMARK
2 NETHERLANDS
3 BELGIUM
4 WEST GERMANY

GREENLAND

ICELAND

NORWAY

UNITED KINGDOM

FRANCE

SPAIN

PORTUGAL

Azores

ATLANTIC OCEAN

ALASKA

CANADA

UNITED STATES

MEXICO

GUATEMALA
EL SALVADOR
HONDURAS
COSTA RICA
PANAMA
Canal Zone

CUBA

Puerto Rico

COLOMBIA
VENEZUELA
ECUADOR

PACIFIC OCEAN

UNION OF SOVIET SOCIALIST REPUBLICS

MONGOLIA

CHINA

JAPAN

NORTH KOREA
SOUTH KOREA

Okinawa

TAIWAN

PHILIPPINES

VIETNAM

THAILAND

SINGAPORE

INDIAN OCEAN

PAKISTAN

AFGHANISTAN

SAUDI ARABIA

OMAN

ISRAEL
SYRIA
TURKEY
GREECE
ITALY

EGYPT

LIBYA

S. YEMEN

SOCOTRA

SOMALIA

ETHIOPIA

Diego Garcia I.

ric. Nuclear disarmament talks were once again in the air, and the United States, the Soviet Union, and Great Britain (which now also had nuclear bombs) stopped testing nuclear weapons in the atmosphere.

Phase Five: To the Brink of Nuclear War

Beginning in 1960, the Cold War suddenly heated into a confrontation in which the two superpowers teetered on the edge of nuclear holocaust. In May 1960, two weeks before a scheduled summit conference at Paris, Soviet forces shot down a U-2, a U.S. high-altitude supersonic spy plane, that was violating Soviet airspace. Such planes were capable of flying from twelve to fourteen miles above the earth and taking photographs that when blown up could spot an object as small as a golf ball. The Soviet Union immediately turned that incident and the initial U.S. cover-up into a propaganda coup. At Paris, Khrushchev demanded an apology, plus punishment for those involved; when Eisenhower refused, he left the conference in a show of anger. The embarrassment of the Eisenhower administration and the missile gap controversy aided the election of John F. Kennedy, who promised new programs to restore U.S. prestige.

President Kennedy displayed many of the characteristics of President Truman. He was a tough political battler and a believer in the containment doctrine; he surrounded himself with advisors who were equally disposed to be "tough" with the Russians. His administration increased the defense budget and contributed notably to the U.S. surge in missile production. Kennedy was more aware than his predecessors of the necessity of dealing with struggles for independence and social reform in Asia, Africa, and Latin America, which Communists often supported as "wars of liberation." Kennedy therefore coupled to the old "massive retaliation" doctrine the new concept of "flexible response," which entailed building up the "conventional arms"—the army, navy, and marines—to fight in limited wars. As a part of this program, the United States stepped up commitments to train and supply the armed forces of allies in every quarter of the world. On the other hand, the Kennedy administration also created the Peace Corps, in which Americans volunteered to bring educational and technological skills to poorer nations.

Kennedy was soon tested by Khrushchev over the perennial trouble spot, Berlin. Berlin had become a double problem for the Soviet Union. In addition to housing a Western military garrison behind Soviet lines, it spotlighted the weaknesses of East Germany. The Communist regime in East Germany was so unpopular that masses of East Germans were fleeing annually, crossing from East Berlin into West Berlin and then to West Germany and beyond. In 1960, for example, 152,000 East Germans escaped via Berlin; on one day alone, August 6, 1961, 2,305 persons arrived in West Berlin from East Germany. Something had to be done to stop the outflow of population or East Germany would collapse and communism would be held up to worldwide disrepute. At the June 1961 summit conference in Vienna, Khrushchev once again threatened to turn Berlin over to the East Germans if the city were not demilitarized. Kennedy

U.S. and Soviet tanks confront each other in Berlin at a moment of heightened tension. (UPI/Bettmann Newsphotos)

rejected the solution, but not firmly enough to impress the Soviet premier, who apparently left Vienna with the idea that Kennedy could be pressured. Kennedy apparently also believed that he had left an impression of weakness. To dispel that notion, Kennedy announced that Berlin would be defended as a test of "Western courage and will." He called up reservists and asked Congress to institute a "civil defense" bomb shelter program. Kennedy's clear resolve to remain in Berlin prompted the Soviet Union to authorize East Germany to stop the exodus. The East German government put up the Berlin Wall in August 1961; in the eyes of the West, it became a major symbol of repression and of the failure of communism. Tensions remained high in the months that followed. Additional U.S. troops and equipment were sent to Europe, and Kennedy went to West Berlin to underscore U.S. determination to protect the city, telling an excited crowd, "Ich bin ein Berliner" ("I am a Berliner").

Berlin had been a serious confrontation, but it was in Cuba that the world stood at the brink of thermonuclear war. This crisis grew out of the nature of U.S. relationships in Latin America. Traditionally, the United States had not been overly scrupulous about the nature of political regimes in postwar Latin America, as long as they were "anti-Communist"—that is, anti-Soviet. The United States had previously toppled a government in Guatemala it had suspected of becoming Communist (see Chapter 23). Cuba in the 1950s was controlled by the dictator Fulgencio Batista, an ally of the U.S. government and a friend of U.S. businesses ranging from sugar refining to gambling. In return, the United States backed the Batista regime. Under Batista, Cuban urban areas maintained a relatively high standard of living, but the rural peasantry suffered from seasonal unemployment, inadequate medical facilities, and lack of education.

In 1953 and again in 1956, Fidel Castro, a young lawyer, attempted and failed to overthrow the Batista government. After his second defeat, he went into the hills to build up a guerrilla army. In 1959, Castro had created enough support to topple the regime, and Batista fled. Between 1959 and 1961, Castro, defying increasingly hostile U.S. reactions, rapidly moved Cuba toward a new society based on Marxist principles. During this period he consolidated his grip on power, becoming a leftist *caudillo* in tight control of a totalitarian apparatus. Accusing U.S. entrepreneurs and upper-class Cubans of exploiting the Cuban masses, Castro rapidly nationalized both domestic and foreign-owned corporations and instituted egalitarian social reform programs.

The Eisenhower administration, seeing Cuba heading out of the U.S. orbit, presumably toward the Soviet Union, reacted with increasing vigor. After its early protests were ignored, the United States organized an economic boycott and stopped buying Cuban sugar, measures designed to disrupt the Cuban economy and to bring Castro down. Faced with U.S. economic warfare, Castro accelerated his nationalization of U.S. business holdings in Cuba and began to build an economic relationship with the Soviet Union.

By 1960 the Eisenhower administration was convinced that the Castro regime was fast becoming a Soviet ally in the heart of the U.S. sphere of influence in the Caribbean; such a government was to be overthrown and replaced with a reliable ally. The United States broke diplomatic relations with Cuba. In addition, Eisenhower, following the program earlier used successfully to overthrow the government of Guatemala (see Chapter 23), authorized the CIA (Central Intelligence Agency) to recruit and train anti-Castro Cubans to invade Cuba and provide a rallying point for the Cuban population to overthrow Castro. This plan was based on the belief that few people wished to live under communism, and that now that the Cubans had had a taste of it, they would be ready to rebel.

On entering office in 1961, President Kennedy authorized the invasion plans to proceed, with the understanding that the United States was not to be involved in the landing itself. In April, the anti-Castro forces bombed Cuban air bases and landed at the Bay of Pigs, but the peasants did not revolt. Kennedy vetoed pleas for air support, Cuban militia moved in, and the invaders surrendered after two days.

The Bay of Pigs provoked a number of reactions that had a major effect on the Cold War. Castro, convinced that the United States would try to overthrow him again, quite possibly with a direct invasion, now sought the protection of the Soviet Union. In December 1961, he announced, "I am a Marxist-Leninist and will remain a Marxist-Leninist until the day I die." He also pledged that Cuba would work to spread Marxist revolution throughout Latin America.

More important to the future health of the world were the responses in Washington and Moscow. The fiasco was a sore blow to the prestige of the new young U.S. president. Kennedy was attacked for not supporting the invasion force, and he apparently decided to move with greater firmness in the future. Combined with Vienna, the incident apparently predisposed Khrushchev to consider Kennedy a weak leader; more ominously, it tempted Khrushchev to use Cuba to solve some of his own problems. The Chinese and some of his colleagues in Moscow had been criticizing Khrushchev for being insufficiently aggressive in Cold War confrontations with the United States. Some of his domestic policies, agricultural production in particular, were not working out, and he needed to distract attention. The Americans were clearly catching up and passing the Soviet Union in ICBM production, and Castro was calling for support.

These factors, plus the presence of fifteen U.S. Jupiter missiles in Turkey aimed at the Soviet Union, motivated the Soviet premier to make a daring, fundamental challenge to the United States by plunging into the heart of the U.S. sphere of influence. Khrushchev secretly began to send medium-range bombers and medium-range missiles to Cuba. These weapons could defend Cuba by hitting the southeastern United States, including Washington, D.C., but they could not hit most American ICBM installations or SAC bases. From Khrushchev's point of view, such a move would demonstrate that he could take a tough line, apply additional pressure to get the Western powers out of Berlin, moderate the imbalance in the arms race, and provide support for Castro.

In October 1962, U-2s discovered the missile sites in Cuba and found some almost operational. The Kennedy administration sprang into action. Cuba was for the United States the equivalent of Hungary for the Soviet Union. It was a direct challenge to a vital sphere of influence; U.S. leadership in Latin America and its credibility in Western Europe were on the line. In addition, President Kennedy seemed to consider it a personal test. Amid a flurry of pressures, including conflicting signals from Western Europe, the Kennedy administration worked out the U.S. position. The missiles and bombers must go. The Soviet Union would be given the opportunity to remove them voluntarily. If the Soviet Union refused, the United States would destroy the missiles by air strike or invasion. If such an action meant a collision with the Soviet Union, the United States would go to war. The military command sent some SAC bombers into the air and put others on fifteen-minute alert, while placing ICBMs in a preliminary state of readiness to fire. The command also moved army units into position in the Southeast and reinforced Guantanamo Bay. Pressuring the Soviet Union to withdraw the missiles and bombers, Kennedy imposed a "quarantine," a peacetime naval blockade of Cuba (by international law an act of war) that prevented additional missiles from reaching Cuba. Latin American nations, at a meeting of the Organization of American States, supported the blockade. On October 22, Kennedy appeared on television to demand that the Soviet Union "halt and eliminate this clandestine and provocative threat to world peace."

The decision now lay with Moscow, and for six days peace or war hung in the balance. President Kennedy privately estimated the chances of war to be "between one out of three and even." Faced with U.S. resolve backed by U.S. nuclear superiority, the Soviet premier retreated. He ordered the Soviet merchant ships carrying missiles to turn back and avoid confrontation with the U.S. navy. In an exchange of notes, Khrushchev and Kennedy agreed that the Soviet Union would remove the offending missiles and bombers and that the United States would make a public pledge not to invade Cuba. Unofficially, Attorney General Robert Kennedy also informed the Soviet ambassador that the United States would remove its missiles from Turkey at some time in the future. The armed forces of the two nations were ordered to stand down, and the shadow of nuclear war passed over—for the moment.

SUMMARY

World War II caused a ghastly human carnage of tens of millions and destroyed much of Europe and Asia. The victorious Allies prescribed severe peace terms for both Japan and Germany; both nations lost territory conquered in the course of the twentieth century, and Germany lost one-quarter of its former homeland to Poland. The victors demilitarized and occupied Japan and Germany and imprisoned or executed some of their surviving leaders as war criminals. The Soviet Union was the chief beneficiary of the territorial changes, annexing a large area along its western border and additional territory in Asia.

Near the end of World War II, strains appeared between the Soviet Union and its allies, in part based on differing programs concerning the control and reconstruction of postwar Europe. These differences sharply increased immediately after the war, complicated in particular by U.S. control of the atomic bomb. The Soviet Union was determined to protect itself against any future attack out of the West, and the United States perceived the Soviet Union to be bent on a program of worldwide conquest. By the late 1940s the Soviet Union had installed friendly Communist governments in Eastern Europe, and the United States dominated Western Europe through the NATO military alliance and the economic ties of the Marshall Plan.

During the 1950s, the Cold War further intensified. The United States pursued a policy of global containment of the Soviet Union and extended its network of agreements and alliances to Asia. As a consequence, by the late 1950s the United States had surrounded the Soviet Union with a circle of air bases and missile sites from which the United States could deliver nuclear warheads to the Soviet Union. The Soviet Union could respond by attacking Western Europe. Germany was in effect divided into two nations, with East and West Germany integrated militarily into the European power blocs. Despite the tension between the superpowers, their leaders attempted to moderate their differences by holding discussions to air grievances.

In the early 1960s, the superpowers had a frightening confrontation when the Soviet Union placed missiles in Cuba. The world stood at the brink of nuclear war, but the Soviet Union removed its missiles from Cuba, and the threat passed.

SUGGESTED SOURCES

Beschloss, Michael R., *Mayday: Eisenhower, Khrushchev, and the U-2 Affair* (1986). A fascinating, dramatic, and well-researched work on the U-2 crisis and its background.*

Garthoff, Raymond L., *Reflections on the Cuban Missile Crisis* (1987).*

Gelb, Norman, *The Berlin Wall* (1986).*

LaFeber, Walter, *America, Russia and the Cold War, 1945–1980* (1980). A readable account that concentrates more on U.S. motives than on those of the Soviet government.*

Leuchtenberg, William E., *A Troubled Feast*, updated ed. (1983). A concise and lively survey of U.S. history since 1945.*

Mastny, Vojtech, *Russia's Road to the Cold War* (1979). An excellent analysis of Soviet diplomatic aims from 1941 to 1945.*

Medvedev, Roy A., *Khrushchev* (1982). The best biography, by a Soviet dissident.*

Smith, Bradley F., *Reaching Judgment at Nuremberg* (1979). A penetrating study of the corrupting effects of Nazism.* (Also a film, *Judgment at Nuremburg*.)

Smoke, Richard, *National Security and the Nuclear Dilemma*, 2nd ed. (1987). A trenchant overview of the post-World War II arms race, from a U.S. perspective.

Ulam, Adam B., *The Rivals: America and Russia since World War II* (1971). A stimulating treatment by an expert on the Soviet Union.*

Weisberger, Bernard A., *Cold War, Cold Peace: The United States and Russia since 1945* (1985). A superb narrative focusing primarily on the period up through the Cuban missile crisis; especially good on the U.S. actions and reactions.*

*Paperback available.

23

The United States and Latin America after World War II

After World War II, the United States enjoyed twenty years of economic growth accompanied by social reforms. During the 1960s, however, the pace of change, the war in Vietnam, and other problems provoked social divisions and convulsions. In Latin America, pressures against the elite establishment continued to build, not only from traditional reform groups but also from Marxist revolutionaries. As Marxist influence grew in Latin America, the United States, operating from Cold War presumptions, returned to its earlier policy of intervention.

THE UNITED STATES: FROM PROSPERITY TO SOCIAL CONVULSION

Economic Boom and the Attack on Poverty

In the two decades after World War II, Americans wished to lay down the burden of wartime responsibilities and take advantage of rising economic prosperity. During most of this period, wages rose faster than prices, and goods and services were cheap. The Cold War kept defense and related industries humming, and unemployment was relatively low. American families enjoyed increased purchasing power and spent their money on appliances, television sets, automobiles, and other consumer goods. Fewer people worked on farms and in factories; more Americans now held white-collar jobs in business and government. An increasing number of families moved out of the central cities to the new suburbs, where they could own a home with a yard and a garage and live near others of similar backgrounds. Auto-oriented suburban shopping malls sprang up, weakening central business districts in cities. By the early 1960s, as prosperity continued to increase, many families were purchasing second cars, vacation cottages, campers, and sporting equipment.

For almost twenty years after 1945, Americans supported the New Deal heritage but were not interested in major extensions of the welfare state. In Congress, a coalition of conservative Democrats and Republicans controlled the political process, no matter which party had a legislative majority or held the presidency. The Cold War abroad cast its shadow on domestic society. President Truman joined Congressional conservatives in the Red Scare, a controversial campaign against internal subversives. Truman also had the support of both parties when he created the national security state, which included the first large peacetime army, the Department of Defense, the National Security Council, and the Central Intelligence Agency. When Truman tried to go beyond the New Deal by introducing federal aid to education and national health insurance, however, conservatives in Congress rejected his proposals. On the other hand, Congress maintained the welfare state by increasing Social Security benefits and the minimum wage and approving more public housing for the poor. Truman's successor, President Eisenhower, was a popular, genial war hero who generally left Americans alone to pursue their private goals. In the 1950s, bipartisan support enacted public works programs such as the interstate highway system and the St. Lawrence Seaway through the Great Lakes.

By the mid-1960s economic prosperity, increased government revenue, and a resurgence of political liberalism prompted President Lyndon Johnson to launch the "Great Society." Johnson's program markedly expanded the welfare state, in which the federal government took the lead in providing opportunities for all Americans to have a better life. Congress made education a high priority, pouring money into every level. The administration supported mass transit systems and also created programs to fight decay in the central cities. Congress also enacted Medicare, a health insurance program for the aged.

A key element of the Great Society was the "War on Poverty." The federal government provided many of the poor with opportunities for legal aid, job training and youth employment, food stamps and school lunches, medical care, and special educational programs. In the first decade after the launching of the Great Society, the proportion of Americans living below the poverty level was cut by one-third.

Social Progress and Social Discord

While the United States was enjoying economic prosperity, it was also experiencing increased social tensions. Throughout U.S. history, white males of northern European extraction had controlled the economic, social, and political life of the country. Women and minority groups, particularly blacks, faced discrimination, both legally and in practice. In the post–World War II period, this pattern began to crumble as blacks, supported by a few white allies, began to press for equal treatment. Influenced by growing black voting power in large cities, the Truman administration desegregated the armed forces and sponsored unsuccessful civil rights legislation. Meanwhile, federal courts outlawed restrictive covenants in housing and ordered the desegregation of graduate education

Finding a Way to Attack Racism

[At Moorehouse College] I read [Henry David] Thoreau's *Essay on Civil Disobedience* for the first time. Fascinated by the idea of refusing to cooperate with an evil system, I was so deeply moved that I reread the work several times. This was my first intellectual contact with the spirit of nonviolent resistence.

Not until I entered Crozier Theological Seminary in 1948 . . . did I begin a serious intellectual quest for a method to eliminate social evil. . . . I came early to Walter Rauschenbusch's *Christianity and Social Crisis,* which left an indelible imprint on my thinking by giving me a theological basis for the social concern which had already grown up in me as a result of my early experiences. . . .

My study of Gandhi convinced me that true pacifism is not nonresistance to evil, but nonviolent resistance to evil. . . . It is rather a courageous confrontation of evil by the power of love. . . . *

Here the young Reverend Martin Luther King, Jr., shortly after his successful leadership of the Montgomery, Alabama, bus boycott, describes the ideas that influenced his technique of nonviolent group action to remove barriers to black civil rights. The ideas of Reinhold Niebuhr and Hegel, and Marx's concern for the welfare of the masses, also influenced King. At first King was impressed with the power of Nietzsche's attack on Christian pacifism, but came to believe that Gandhi's approach of nonviolent resistance overcame Nietzsche's position. King's outlook and tactics represent a blending of thought from all over the world; he applied these ideas while leading the civil rights movement in the United States in the 1950s and 1960s.

in southern state universities. In 1954, the Supreme Court, in *Brown v. Board of Education of Topeka,* declared racial segregation in the public schools unconstitutional. Southern whites responded with "massive resistance" to racially mixed schools.

In the decade following the *Brown* decision, blacks mounted an increasingly effective civil rights movement. Led by Baptist minister Martin Luther King, Jr., blacks used nonviolent direct action and civil disobedience techniques similar to Gandhi's tactics in India. In the early 1960s, blacks staged sit-ins, freedom rides, and marches, particularly in the South. Their protests sought to end segregation in transportation, local businesses, and public buildings, and to win the right to vote in the South. Whites resisted by means ranging from legal maneuvers to beatings, firebombings, and killings. By the mid-1960s the national political establishment had conceded that the time for civil equality had come. After first trying to evade the matter, President Kennedy endorsed the movement. Texas-born President Johnson, quoting the civil rights workers' song ''We Shall Overcome,'' pressed Congress into enacting important legislation, particularly the 1964 Civil Rights Act, that banned legal inequality on the basis of race. These civil rights laws, supported by Supreme Court decisions, changed the South by eliminating segregated public accommodations and enabling blacks to vote and hold political offices. In the North, however, the federal government was less vigorous at enforcing laws banning school segregation and bias in housing and employment.

Along with the black civil rights movement came an expansion of individual civil liberties. The Supreme Court, led by Chief Justice Earl Warren, restricted certain police and prosecution practices and extended the concept of due process of law so that the poor and uneducated would have access to fair trials. The Warren Court reduced the scope of censorship of printed and visual materials and widened the rights of free speech. In addition, the Court altered many traditional practices connecting church and state; for example, all state-sponsored devotional Bible reading and prayers in public schools were declared unconstitutional. The Supreme Court also promulgated the ''one man, one vote'' doctrine in apportioning legislatures, increasing the political power of cities and suburbs, which had previously been shortchanged by rural interests.

Meanwhile, the success of the black civil rights movement inspired others, such as American Indians, Hispanics, and women, to challenge discrimi-

Civil right leaders: Martin Luther King, Jr., Robert Kennedy, Roy Wilkins of the NACCP, and then Vice-President Lyndon B. Johnson meet in 1963. All are now dead, two by assassination. (UPI/Bettmann Newsphotos)

nation. Indians tried to recover lost western land rights. Hispanics organized political groups and Cesár Chavez's United Farm Workers. Feminists won federal bans against employment and credit bias and founded the National Organization for Women (NOW) to seek full legal equality. The radical wing of the women's movement questioned traditional standards of appearance, sexual roles, and family structures.

By the early 1970s the reform impulse extended beyond civil rights. Many Americans became concerned about the deterioration of the environment and resulting threats to health. They celebrated "Earth Day," cut back on some sprays and plastics, and launched local recycling efforts. In response, Congress established the Environmental Protection Agency to monitor a network of new legislation designed to regulate strip mining, industrial and automobile contaminants in the air, and polluted water. Other legislation mandated automobile safety equipment and attempted to protect individuals from harmful additives in food and beverages. Governments at all levels also moved to preserve portions of the environment from industrial and residential development and exploitation.

Dissenting young people spearheaded several, often socially divisive, movements during the 1960s. Prosperous and numerous due to high birth rates, American young people increasingly questioned the life styles and values of their parents. The "hippies" waged a cultural rebellion, trying to fashion a new society by the way they thought and lived. Often children of affluence themselves, members of the counterculture turned their backs on the materialism, competition, and emotional repression of mainstream society. Hippies glorified nature and leisure. They encouraged sharing and tried to shed inhibitions and express inner feelings. Their long hair, rock music, casual sex, and drug use shocked and angered elders, but the counterculture would soon leave its mark on adult society.

Although hippies often dropped out and ignored public issues, other young people became political activists. The "New Left," led by the Students for a Democratic Society (SDS), organized the poor, joined civil rights causes, and led campus protests. Rising opposition to the Vietnam War expanded the ranks of the New Left. Masses of young Americans marched in the streets, chanting, "Hey, hey, LBJ, how many kids have you killed today?" As draft calls passed 30,000 a month, students mobilized against the war, first holding teach-ins and sit-ins, then turning to draft resistance and evasion. As the SDS became more radical in ideas and tactics, it turned from peaceful to violent action against the war and nourished dreams of revolution. By the late 1960s government repression and internal factionalism had torn the SDS apart. Declining draft calls in the early 1970s lessened the urgency of antiwar protest. Meanwhile, the political establishment recognized the importance of the new generation by lowering the voting age in federal elections to eighteen. Many states lowered the age for marriage, contracts, and other adult privileges to eighteen as well.

Movements seeking social change also produced frustration, division, and counterattacks. Environmental causes had broad support, but businesses and some unions complained about added costs and lost job opportunities. Many men, threatened by feminist demands for legal and economic equality and new male-female relationships, both ridiculed and attacked the women's movement. The Great Society and the Warren Court also drew heavy criticism. Many Americans believed that civil liberties reforms favored criminals and stimulated crime. They complained that social welfare programs gave their tax money to undeserving people who refused to work. Furthermore, the challenge to traditional values by the counterculture and New Left horrified many. Both young people and adults from blue-collar families resented the cultural and political radicalism of youthful dissenters.

Meanwhile, the civil rights movement sparked explosive reactions among Americans of both races. Despite progress toward legal and political equality, poor blacks saw little improvement in their jobs, housing, and public services. Their frustration boiled over in a series of riots, primarily in northern and western cities. As the civil rights movement met white resistance, a few blacks mocked King's talk of love and peace. They turned to movements such as the separatist Nation of Islam (Black Muslims) and the radical Black Panthers. Each rejected the reformist style and goals of the civil rights movement, and each used confrontational language that frightened the white majority. Racial tension accelerated in April 1968 when a white assassin shot King. Blacks rioted and looted in scores of cities.

At the same time, the civil rights movement was shifting its focus from legal to economic issues and from the South to the North. These developments created a "white backlash." While many supported the idea of equality in general, they did not want to integrate their neighborhoods and workplaces, and they opposed busing to achieve racial balance in their schools. By the end of the 1960s, opposition to the pace of social change had swelled so much that it overcame Johnson's Great Society vision. Appealing to the resentments of what he called the "silent majority," Republican Richard Nixon captured the presidency, defeating liberal candidates in 1968 and 1972.

SOCIAL CHANGE IN LATIN AMERICA

While revolution and war had swept much of the world during the first half of the twentieth century, Latin America, except for Mexico, had been relatively quiet. Most of the region had been officially independent for over a hundred years and had therefore escaped the trauma of the independence struggle mounting in Africa and Asia. There had been only one major war between Latin American nations in the twentieth century, and Latin America was only marginally involved in the world wars. During the postwar period, however, the region was increasingly caught up in social turmoil and became enmeshed in the global Cold War. Most Latin American nations still retained the feudal two-culture society, and the gap between the few rich and the many poor remained wide. Meanwhile, the trend toward urbanization, underway earlier in the century, intensified after World War II. As

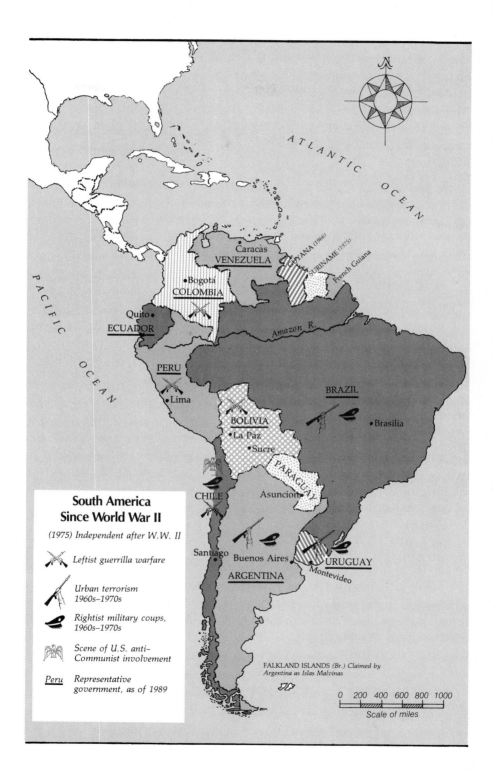

South America Since World War II

(1975) Independent after W.W. II

Leftist guerrilla warfare

Urban terrorism
1960s–1970s

Rightist military coups,
1960s–1970s

Scene of U.S. anti-
Communist involvement

Peru Representative
government, as of 1989

FALKLAND ISLANDS (Br.) Claimed by
Argentina as Islas Malvinas

0 200 400 600 800 1000

Scale of miles

VENEZUELA
Caracas
GUYANA (1966)
SURINAME (1975)
French Guiana
COLOMBIA
Bogota
Quito
ECUADOR
Amazon R.
PERU
Lima
BRAZIL
BOLIVIA
La Paz
Sucre
Brasilia
PARAGUAY
Asuncion
CHILE
Santiago
Buenos Aires
ARGENTINA
URUGUAY
Montevideo

ATLANTIC OCEAN
PACIFIC OCEAN

the rural population kept growing in an area already suffering from a labor surplus, it appeared to many families that their only chance to survive would be to find work in the city. Consequently, swollen by a massive influx of *campesinos,* the cities of Latin America grew enormously after World War II. In 1930, only one city contained a million people; by 1988 twenty-eight cities had attained that size. Mexico City, with over eighteen million people in 1988, was the second largest city in the world. Some of the arrivals from the countryside found employment in the new industries, but most found only part-time or marginal work and some found no jobs at all. As had happened earlier under the same circumstances in Europe and the United States, Latin American city administrators could not handle the massive influx of outsiders and were unable or unwilling to supply adequate housing, sanitation, transportation, water, schools, or police protection. *Villas miserias* (misery towns) that contained hovels constructed of scraps of tarpaper, wood, tin, and concrete sprang up around the cities, creating a stark contrast to the new luxury apartments and skyscrapers.

After World War II, Latin America remained an economically underdeveloped region, its standard of living trailing far behind that of the United States. Agriculture remained inefficient and the region continued to import more food. Even in those nations that expanded their economies, a rapidly expanding population often outstripped economic growth rates. Most were dependent on the fluctuating international market prices of such staples and raw materials as coffee, cocoa, bananas, sugar, cotton, wheat, meat, hides, wool, timber, copper, tin, and petroleum. After World War II, the Latin American share of the world market actually decreased.

After the Depression of the 1930s, staple prices dropped to a disastrous low, and leaders in larger Latin American nations sought to diversify the economies of their nations through industrialization. "Modernization" and "development" became key terms in Latin America, as many nations rushed to develop factory systems. Latin American governments often accompanied their industrial expansion with the expropriation of foreign holdings. In the process, many nations ran into difficulties. Instead of developing basic industries such as iron and steel, textiles, and machinery, they concentrated on producing a spectrum of consumer goods ranging from automobiles to toothpaste. As a result, Latin American nations not only continued to import basic industrial products but also had to pay for the materials, machinery, technicians, and patents necessary to produce consumer products. They also found that such goods could not compete on the world market with those of the more efficient, established industrial powers, and discovered further that their own populations were too poor to buy such products.

Argentina: Social Change from the Right

After World War II, several nations, following the lead of Mexico and Chile, instituted social reforms that narrowed the gap between the rich and the poor. One nation that moved in this direction, if somewhat unintentionally, was Argentina. Argentina was one of the larger and more industrialized nations of Latin America. In the early 1940s, a conservative military clique controlled the government. One of the ruling group of officers was Juan Perón, a charismatic political adventurer who recognized, as had Vargas in Brazil, that the mass of urban workers, if organized, could become a powerful political force. As minister of labor under the military government, Perón wooed the workers with pay raises and bonuses and organized them into unions loyal to him. When Perón was placed under house arrest, massive demonstrations by the workers freed him, and in the election of 1946, with the backing of the *descamisados* (the shirtless ones), Perón swept into the presidency. Argentinians of every background rallied behind him as he nationalized foreign industrial and transportation holdings. He embarked on a massive program of social services, wage increases, pensions, and low-cost vacations for the urban workers, who in turn rallied to him with intense gratitude and support.

In a broad sense Perón became a dictator, with personal characteristics reminiscent of Mussolini. He was genial instead of cruel, *muy macho* (a he-man) in image. A dynamic speaker at mass rallies, he harangued the crowds, who chanted back "Perón cumple!" ("Perón delivers the goods!") Perón did not hesitate to manipulate the media and the educational system and to rig his reelection. He often used mobs and arrests to intimidate political rivals. Perón was substantially aided by his former mistress and new wife, Eva Duarte Perón, an attractive and ambitious woman who had risen from poverty to become a radio star. She saw to it that women were enfranchised, and headed a foundation that provided food, services, and jobs for the poor. "Evita" was widely beloved by the common people (but hated by most of the rich), and when she died in 1952 there was a campaign to canonize her. Juan and Eva together represented Latin American "personalist" rule at its ultimate.

Despite his personal dynamism and the intimidation of his opponents, Perón finally made too many mistakes and was driven from power. Perón ignored the *campesinos* and had little support in the countryside. His social programs and nationalization efforts were costly and created massive national debts and inflation. Late in his rule, he picked a useless quarrel with the Catholic Church. In 1955, the military, with the backing of the upper class, drove Perón into exile in Spain, but it did not tamper with much of his social legislation. Perón remained popular with many Argentinians, and returned to power in 1973 at the age of seventy-seven, remarking: "It is not that we are so good, but those who followed us were so bad that they made us seem better than we were." Now conservative, he served only a year before his death. Although his genuine commitment to reform was debatable, Perón's social programs remained deeply embedded in Argentina's national life.

Guatemala: Social Change from the Left

Until the late 1940s, reforms in Latin America had been for the most part either inspired by the Mexican Revolution or liberalism, or engineered by rightist opportunists. In the 1940s, however, beginning with a secondary role in Guatemala, Marxism also began to play an increasing role in social change. A tiny foreign and domestic oligarchy controlled this small Central American nation, owning the land and the export crops, which were bananas, sugar, and coffee. The largest foreign enterprise in Guatemala was the United Fruit Company, owned by U.S. investors. The bulk of the population were Indian descendants of the Mayas—poor, illiterate serfs destined to die young.

In the 1940s, a movement toward social reform began in Guatemala. Reformers drew up a new constitution that prohibited great estates, permitted compensated expropriation, and created a new labor code to protect the rights of urban and rural workers. A small but well-organized labor movement, increasingly dominated by the Communist party, became active in politics. In 1952, Jacobo Arbenz became president and proceeded to accelerate the reorganization of Guatemalan society. He nationalized some foreign holdings and instituted a program for social security and improvements in education. He expropriated unused lands on private estates, sometimes encouraging Indians to occupy land not yet confiscated. After allowing a small compensation, Arbenz expropriated over 400,000 acres of unused United Fruit Company land, and he allowed no appeals to the courts. By 1954 Guatemala was a nation working its way toward social and economic justice.

THE COLD WAR COMES TO LATIN AMERICA

Although the Cold War began in Europe in the late 1940s, by the early 1950s it was spreading to other areas of the world, including Latin America. As noted previously, long before the United States had adopted its policy of containing communism in Europe and Asia, it had repeatedly intervened in the affairs of Caribbean nations to protect its economic and strategic interests there. By 1934, with no threats of European intervention in Latin America, with its power established in the Caribbean, and faced with mounting hostility in the region, the United States inaugurated a new policy of nonintervention. After World War II, however, a second period of interventionist outlook set in. U.S. leaders, worried about the spread of Marxism, scrutinized the Caribbean area for any signs of Communist penetration. From their point of view, Communists coming to power in the region constituted a threat to the United States and would have to be dislodged.

Guatemala: The Overthrow of Arbenz

The Guatemalan moves that curtailed the power of U.S. businesses first brought the Cold War to Latin America. Substantial property was at stake, and Communists were involved in the changes taking place. The United Fruit Company and conservative Guatemalans clamored for help and played up Communist strength in Guatemala. As a consequence, the Eisenhower administration de-

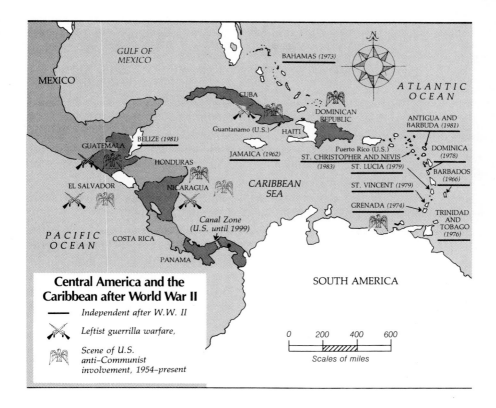

Central America and the Caribbean after World War II

——— Independent after W.W. II

✗ Leftist guerrilla warfare,

🦅 Scene of U.S. anti–Communist involvement, 1954–present

cided to overthrow Arbenz. The United States trained and armed a small group of Guatemalan rebels in neighboring Honduras and Nicaragua. The rebels invaded in 1954; CIA-piloted planes assisted by bombing Guatemala City and other locations, and the Guatemalan army joined the invaders. Arbenz was driven from power and military/elite rule was reimposed. The new rulers canceled land reform and dispossessed the peasants, while Communists were jailed and murdered. Some leftists took to the hills and began a small guerrilla movement. Violence plagued Guatemala intermittently over the next decades.

Cuba: Marxist Social Change during a Cold War Struggle

In Cuba, despite Cold War harassment, Marxist revolutionaries brought about a thoroughgoing social transformation. In the 1950s, under Batista, Cuba had been one of the more prosperous nations in Latin America. Cubans, especially in the cities, enjoyed—by Latin American standards—a high per capita income, high literacy and low death rates, and better-than-average life expectancy. Still, the per capita income of Cubans was one-sixth that of people in the United States. In the rural areas, where a few Cuban families and foreign businesses owned most of the land, many *campesinos* lived in poverty. U.S. investors

The Making of a Revolutionary Leader

I had been a political illiterate when I entered the university [of Havana]. As the son of a landowner, . . . I had brought nothing more than a rebellious temperament and the uprightness . . . they had inculcated into me in the Jesuit school. . . . [M]y first questionings of an economic and social kind arose when I was a student at the university, studying political economy and capitalist economics. . . . How could there exist overproduction of some goods, causing unemployment and hunger? . . . [Some concepts of Marx, Engels, and Lenin] seemed to me truly unquestionable: for example, the idea that society is divided into classes with antagonistic and irreconcilable interests. . . . [Such] intellectual interests inclined me more and more towards political struggle. . . .

[B]efore the tenth of March [Batista's overthrow of the Cuban republic in 1952 and imposition of a dictatorship] I had been thinking of legal means, of using the Parliament as a point of departure from which I might establish a revolutionary platform and motivate the masses. . . .

When the coup d'etat . . . took place, everything changed radically. . . . [W]hen none of [the established political] leaders showed they had either the ability or the realization of the seriousness of purpose or the way to overthrow Batista, . . . I finally worked out a strategy of my own.*

In the passage above Fidel Castro, interviewed in 1965, reflects on his path to leadership of the revolutionary movement in Cuba. When Batista seized power in Cuba, twenty-five-year-old Fidel Castro, just two years out of law school, was one of many young radicals who were active in politics. After the takeover, Castro presented a brief to the Court of Appeals in which he demanded one hundred years imprisonment for Batista for destroying the republic. After his brief was dismissed, he turned to insurrection. When the radicals led by Castro finally triumphed in 1959, they proceeded to bring about a social revolution along Marxist lines, but they created a political dictatorship instead of restoring the republic.

*From *Castro's Cuba, Cuba's Fidel* by Lee Lockwood. Copyright © 1986 by the MIT Press. Used with permission.

owned 40 percent of the sugar crop and controlled sugar refining, mining, communications, and tourism.

In 1959, Castro came to power and began to transform Cuban society. The international confrontation that resulted has already been discussed, and while it was developing Castro continued his social revolution. Landholding was restricted to a maximum of 165 acres, and all holdings in excess of that were expropriated, a move that brought three-quarters of all the land in Cuba under government control. Most of the land was not redistributed to the peasants but held in large national cooperatives owned in theory by all Cubans and on which all rural Cubans found work. Former landowners, U.S. and Cuban, were offered limited compensation in the form of bonds. The Castro regime stressed the dignity of farm labor and discouraged migration to the cities.

Castro at first tried to diversify the economy, but his programs failed. By the 1970s, the Cuban government had again begun to stress the importance of sugar production, but Castro failed to raise per capita sugar production above that of the 1950s. The United States and most OAS members refused to trade with Cuba, hindering Cuban economic growth. Loss of the U.S. sugar market forced Castro to sell sugar to the Communist bloc and anywhere else he could find buyers. Sugar prices fluctuated markedly, falling to a low level in the late 1970s but recovering somewhat in the 1980s.

In the meantime, Castro's government gave Cuba the most complete array of social services in Latin America. Cubans were provided with free medical care, and malnutrition was eliminated. Life expectancy rose to seventy years, the highest in Latin America, and close to that in the United States. The regime provided Cubans with free education and employed young Cubans to teach their illiterate elders to read and write. In 1980, the literacy rate stood at 94 percent, one of the highest in Latin America. The government constructed public housing projects, schools, and nurseries, and inaugurated a complete pension plan. The new social programs were too expensive for a poor nation to afford, however, and the Soviet Union had to sustain them through massive infusions of aid.

Politically, Castro turned Cuba into a Communist totalitarian state. The government was altered several times over the years, with Castro's grip on

Latin revolutionaries Castro (center left) and Che Guevara (center right) review a parade. (UPI/Bettmann Newsphotos)

power becoming ever tighter. Although Castro's regime encouraged Cubans to participate in politics and instituted voting for a national assembly, the real power rested with the small, reorganized Communist party controlled by Castro and a small group of military leaders. The government molded the media and the education system into propaganda props for the state and encouraged Cubans to spy on one another. Castro banned opposition groups and expressions of criticism, and thousands languished in jails as political prisoners, although there were few executions after the initial purge. Approximately 700,000 Cubans, mostly from the middle and upper classes, representing about 8 percent of the population, fled the nation after 1959, disillusioned with life under Castro. Nevertheless, most Cubans apparently believed that Castro was interested in their welfare, and, despite shortages and other economic problems brought on by the boycott and the mistakes of the government, gave at least lukewarm support to the regime.

Besides appreciating the social benefits of Castro's regime, most Cubans, Marxist and non-Marxist alike, supported Castro in his roaring attacks on the Colossus of the North. He declared, for example, that "If there ever was in the history of humanity an enemy who was truly universal, an enemy whose acts and moves trouble the entire world, threaten the entire world, attack the entire world in any way or another, that real and really universal enemy is Yankee imperialism." Such denunciations engendered enthusiastic approval and made Castro popular throughout Latin America.

Castroism outside Cuba

While Castro was building a Marxist state in Cuba, his promise to export revolution caused enormous concern throughout Latin America. As the United States headed toward confrontation with the Soviet Union over Cuba in 1960–62, it demanded support for its policy of isolating Cuba. This put most Latin American nations in a painful dilemma. Traditionally, most Latin American nations were hostile to instances of U.S. pressure, but the conservative regimes in power in most of those nations were terrified of Castro-induced social revolution. Finally, most members of the Organization of American States reluctantly agreed to invoke economic sanctions against Cuba and to cut off diplomatic relations. Mexico, proud of its revolutionary tradition and of its independence from the United States, refused to go along, and Venezuela agreed only to limited measures.

During the 1960s, Castro followed through on his announced intention to spread Marxist revolution to the rest of Latin America. Cuban guerrilla warfare experts went to Central America, Colombia, Bolivia, Venezuela, and Peru to encourage peasants to rise against their governments. Ernesto "Che" Guevara, a heroic symbol of Marxist revolution to radicals around the world, went to Bolivia in 1966 to revive the armed bands that had controlled Bolivia in the 1950s. The United States countered with military aid and advisors to the Bolivian government.

In the Dominican Republic, next door to Cuba, the United States went further. Fearing that Castro supporters were involved in political unrest there, President Johnson sent in U.S. troops in 1965, the first direct U.S. armed intervention in thirty years and a violation of the charter of the OAS. As it turned out, there was little Communist activity in the Dominican Republic, and a great hue and cry in opposition to U.S. intervention broke out both in the United States and throughout Latin America. The Johnson administration saved face by persuading the OAS to set up an international peace-keeping force headed by a Brazilian general; a year later, all foreign troops left the Dominican Republic.

In addition to military assistance and armed intervention, the United States also attempted to combat the turn toward communism in Latin America through the selective granting of economic aid. The Eisenhower and Kennedy administrations realized that impoverished Latin Americans might find communism attractive. They concluded that economic aid would be effective in forestalling communism only if it was used as a prod to Latin American governments to institute effective economic, social, and political reforms. The Eisenhower administration established the Inter-American Development Bank, which linked economic assistance to reforms. The Kennedy administration created the much-heralded Alliance for Progress, a ten-year plan with an initial funding of $1 billion. To receive this money, Latin American nations were to demonstrate progress in creating democratic institutions, improving health and education, and redistributing income. The Alliance demanded too much from most Latin American regimes, however. Members of the upper and middle classes were generally not willing to make the sacrifices required, fearing that if significant reforms were undertaken to satisfy the United States, the lower classes would take over. Instead, Latin American governments, stressing the threat of Communist subversion, diverted the money to military build-ups to combat real or potential guerrillas. By the early 1970s the Alliance was dead.

Castro's hopes for the triumph of Marxism through guerrilla warfare fizzled during the 1960s. American military aid and the lack of interest among the peasants led to the collapse of Castroite guerrilla movements in the countryside. Guevara was betrayed and shot in Bolivia in 1967. Castroites turned to terrorism in the cities, primarily in Brazil, Uruguay, and Argentina, committing kidnappings, robberies, bombings, and assassinations. Eventually, military forces also crushed these urban guerrillas. By the early 1970s it appeared that Cuban-inspired revolutionary forces had ceased to be a significant factor in Latin America.

No longer fearing Cuba, some Latin American nations began to drop their anti-Cuban stances and resumed diplomatic and trade relations with Cuba. The U.S. government also lessened its hostile stance. It lifted passport restrictions and allowed limited U.S. tourism to Cuba. Americans and Cubans ranging from baseball teams to birdwatchers became the beneficiaries of the improved international climate. For a period in the mid-1970s, complete normalization of relations appeared to be at hand.

SUMMARY

After World War II, the United States enjoyed economic prosperity, and many went on a "buying spree" for a wide range of consumer goods. In the 1950s, the nation was not interested in extensive political change, but by the mid-1960s the Johnson administration had embarked on its Great Society program, which greatly diminished poverty and expanded the welfare state. During this period, blacks struggled for their civil rights, and by the mid-1960s had made substantial gains in eliminating segregated facilities and barriers to voting. At the same time, Supreme Court rulings curtailed government controls over the civil liberties of individuals.

Social problems arose in the United States as opposition to the Indochina war grew steadily and as some more militant blacks rioted in the cities for improved economic and social conditions. Other minorities and some women began to apply pressure for an end to discriminatory practices. Environmental concerns mounted. Some young people protested against social injustices by peaceful means, but others resorted to violence and still others became hippie dropouts.

In many respects, Latin America after World War II was unchanged from earlier generations. Agriculture remained the dominant aspect of the economy, but many nations tried to diversify by supporting industrialization projects. Population increases swallowed up most economic gains, and Latin American cities grew so rapidly that they were beset by a number of social problems. The United States continued to dominate the region economically and resumed its interventions when Cold War interests dictated.

The region also experienced substantial changes. Its nations became more nationalistic, anxious to remove foreign economic controls and to steer an independent course in international relations. Some nations, even conservative ones, created extensive government controls over key elements in the economy. Perhaps the greatest change in Latin America was the movement in several nations toward ending the traditional two-culture society of the elite few and the impoverished masses. While the upper classes in many nations tried to repress the movements for social and economic change, some nations made efforts to provide social services, employment, and land. Change came sometimes from the Right, as in Argentina; sometimes from the Left, as in Guatemala. In Cuba, Castro created a new Marxist society, but his attempts to bring Marxist regimes to power elsewhere in Latin America were defeated. Acting from Cold War motives, the United States intervened in various ways throughout the Caribbean.

SUGGESTED SOURCES

Bremner, Robert H., and Gary W. Reichard, eds., *Reshaping America: Society and Institutions, 1945–1960* (1982). Historians' essays on social history topics, such as rural and urban life, women and families, business and labor, crime and education.

Chafe, William H., *The Unfinished Journey: America since World War II* (1986). An outstanding one-volume history, notable for its lively style and its strong interpretive dimension.

Evita (1979). A Broadway musical that gives a relatively realistic picture of the life and times of the Argentine cult figure Eva Perón.

García Márquez, Gabriel, *One Hundred Years of Solitude* (1971). A novel giving an impressionistic view of life in Latin America.*

Goodsell, James Nelson, ed., *Fidel Castro's Personal Revolution in Cuba, 1959–1973* (1975). A helpful introduction to the political, economic, cultural, and international aspects of Fidelismo.*

Hamby, Alonzo L., *Liberalism and Its Challengers: F.D.R. to Reagan* (1985). Essays on leading political figures, covering most postwar presidents but also including Martin Luther King, Jr., and Robert F. Kennedy.

Matusow, Allen J., *The Unraveling of America: A History of Liberalism in the 1960s* (1984). The rise and collapse of liberalism, traced through economic and reform policies of Kennedy and Johnson as well as the youth and black movements.

O'Neill, William, *Coming Apart* (1971). A spirited account of the United States in the turbulent 1960s.*

*Paperback available.

24

Asia in the Aftermath
of World War II

Besides its legacy of destruction and death, World War II also inspired many Asians to demand social reforms and freedom from all outside controls. During its early phase, the triumphant Japanese army and navy had evicted every European colonial power from every colony in Asia east of India and had tried to rally popular support with the cry, "Asia for the Asians." Although the Japanese turned out to be harsher and more arrogant rulers than the Europeans, Asians were nevertheless in no mood for compliant acceptance of the return of European colonialism once the Japanese had been defeated.

World War II had also drastically altered the power equation in Asia. Japan, which had dominated East Asia for half a century, lay prostrate in 1945, its military and economy in ruins and its home islands under foreign military occupation for the first time in its history. China, Japan's first victim, emerged a victor in the war, its international status enhanced. It had gained equality among nations in 1943, after a century of unequal treaties, and now stood as one of the Big Five victorious powers, a founding member of the United Nations and a permanent member of the Security Council. The United States hoped in 1945 that a friendly, strong, and united China under a KMT government would become the anchor of postwar Asia. However, the war had mortally weakened the Nationalist government, at the same time giving a new lease of life and unprecedented opportunities to the CCP. The Soviet Union, which had entered the war against Japan at its very end, reaped many benefits as a victor. With its Chinese Communist allies victorious in China in 1949, the Communist movement seemed poised to make new gains, and indigenous Communist parties in several Asian nations took heart. These developments and the threat of further spread of communism in Asia became a major worry to the United States, which sought countermeasures. Asia thus became a key theater in the Cold War.

340

THE TRIUMPH OF COMMUNISM IN CHINA

During the Sino-Japanese War of 1937–1945, the CCP took advantage of the widespread patriotic movement in Japanese-occupied areas and used its expertise in guerrilla warfare to organize and control the resistance forces in the nominally Japanese-occupied countryside. As Mao Tse-tung said about guerrilla war, "The people are the water, the soldiers are the fish"; that is, a successful war of resistance needed popular support. Whereas the CCP had 40,000 party members and 30,000 troops in several small bases in 1937, at the end of the war it claimed 1.2 million party members, eighty million people under its control, a military force of almost a million regulars, and two million militiamen. These spectacular gains proved Chiang Kai-shek right when he said during the darkest days of the anti-Japanese war that whereas the Japanese were a disease of the skin, the Communists were a disease of the heart threatening his government.

By comparison, the KMT government was beset by troubles. War destroyed its modern base in the coastal areas. Driven inland, it was forced to rely on local conservative gentry for support, and, as a result, the government also became more conservative. Wartime conditions and the overwhelming needs of the military reinforced existing tendencies toward authoritarianism and militarism, costing the KMT support among the people. Still, China hung on until circumstances outside it brought about the defeat of Japan.

Eight years of war against Japan had devastated China. Twenty million Chinese soldiers and civilians had perished, and fifty million people had moved to the interior. The government in 1945 was faced with a shattered economy, galloping inflation, and millions of refugees awaiting resettlement.

Communist Victory in the Civil War

The removal of the Japanese once again brought the competition for power between the KMT and the CCP to the forefront, and civil war erupted over control of formerly Japanese-occupied areas. The United States, which had become deeply involved in China during the war, was committed to playing a role in the evolution of postwar Chinese politics. Initially, the United States aided the KMT by airlifting its troops from south and west China to the major population centers in the north so that the KMT could take control before the CCP moved in from the northern countryside. When the U.S. government later recognized how strong the Communists were, it attempted to mediate a solution to the KMT-CCP conflict. Conditioned by its own political tradition, however, it visualized the two parties in China as similar to the two political parties of the United States, and asked the two sides to give up their independent armies and come together in a coalition government. General George Marshall, with all his prestige as the architect of Allied victory in Europe, was sent to China in December 1945 to attempt a reconciliation between the two Chinese groups.

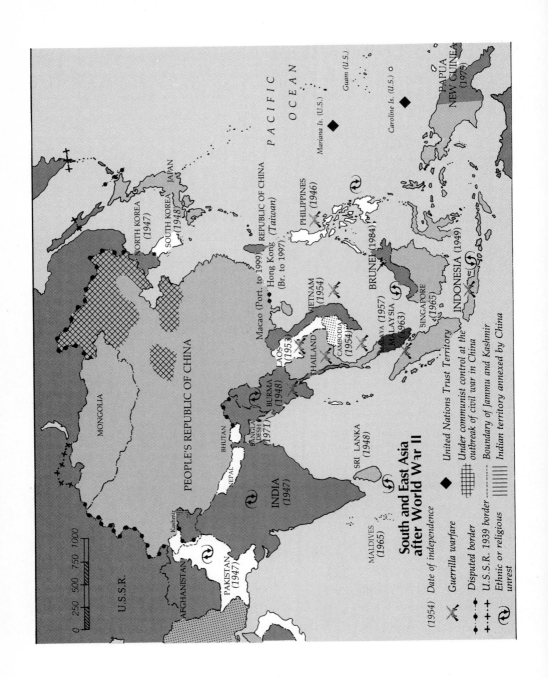

**South and East Asia
after World War II**

(1954) Date of independence

◆ United Nations Trust Territory

⊞ Under communist control at the
  outbreak of civil war in China

✕ Guerrilla warfare

••• Disputed border

+·+·+ U.S.S.R. 1939 border

⦚⦚⦚ Boundary of Jammu and Kashmir

▥▥▥ Indian territory annexed by China

↻ Ethnic or religious
  unrest

PEOPLE'S REPUBLIC OF CHINA

MONGOLIA

U.S.S.R.

AFGHANISTAN

PAKISTAN
(1947)

Kashmir

NEPAL

BHUTAN

INDIA
(1947)

BANGLA-
DESH
(1971)

BURMA
(1948)

SRI LANKA
(1948)

MALDIVES
(1965)

LAOS
(1953)

THAILAND

VIETNAM
(1954)

CAMBODIA
(1954)

MALAYA (1957)
MALAYSIA
(1963)

SINGAPORE
(1965)

BRUNEI (1984)

INDONESIA (1949)

Macao (Port. to 1999)

Hong Kong
(Br. to 1997)

REPUBLIC OF CHINA (Taiwan)

PHILIPPINES
(1946)

NORTH KOREA
(1947)

SOUTH KOREA
(1948)

JAPAN

PACIFIC

OCEAN

Guam (U.S.)

Mariana Is. (U.S.)

Caroline Is. (U.S.)

PAPUA
NEW GUINEA
(1975)

0 250 500 750 1000

342

However, neither party trusted the other, and neither would give up its hope of eventual total control. Thus Marshall's mission ended in failure.

In 1949, the CCP won the civil war, and the KMT government and part of its military forces fled to the island of Taiwan. Many factors—military, economic, political, and morale—contributed to this outcome. Militarily, the KMT army, with about three million men in 1946, opposed approximately one million CCP soldiers and two million militiamen, but in taking over all areas formerly under Japanese occupation, it had become overextended. Its strategic doctrine was to hold cities and other strongly fortified positions. Conversely, the CCP army resorted to guerrilla tactics, destroyed railroads, controlled the countryside, and avoided battle unless on terms favorable to itself. It put into practice Mao's dictum: "The enemy advances, we retreat; the enemy camps, we harass; the enemy tires, we attack; the enemy retreats, we pursue." The results were brilliant. The isolated KMT units, which also often suffered from corruption and poor command, either surrendered or were cut to pieces.

The military debacle was partly caused by the collapse of the KMT government. Eight years of anti-Japanese war had taken a heavy toll. The loss or destruction of its economic base had forced the KMT government to wage its war against Japan by printing more and more paper money; at the end of the war, the volume of notes issued was 465 times that at the war's outbreak. After 1946, the need to finance a civil war led to continued deficit spending and runaway inflation that especially impoverished the urban population, and caused chaos, corruption, and loss of confidence in the government. When its currency collapsed in late 1948, so did the remaining civilian support for the Nationalist cause.

On the other hand, the Communist cause exemplified strict military discipline, high morale, and coherent leadership. Although the CCP had carried out only moderate land reforms in areas it controlled during the war, it reverted to violent land reform tactics in its areas at the war's end and promised similar drastic programs for all of China. The poor and dispossessed backed the Communists because of this promise, and many students and intellectuals gradually came to support them also.

The international situation, including, ironically, U.S. aid, also helped the CCP. To prevent Mao from taking over China, the United States sent over $2 billion in aid to prop up the KMT government. While U.S. arms equipped the KMT army, U.S.-style reorganization of the army only furthered confusion and rivalry between units under different commands. The withdrawal of U.S. support in 1948 contributed to the further demoralization of the KMT government and speeded its collapse.

Finally, the Soviet Union also contributed to the CCP triumph. Stalin, after extracting concessions favorable to the U.S.S.R., committed himself in wartime agreements to recognize the KMT government as the only legal one in China and not to aid the CCP. He did not have a high regard for the CCP, as exemplified by his wartime characterization of the Chinese Communists as "margarine" (not the genuine article) or "radish" (red outside, white inside) Com-

Mao Zedong reviews parade at Square of Heavenly Peace in Peking, celebrating the fourteenth anniversary of Communist victory in 1963. (NCNA/Camera Press)

munists. Nevertheless, Stalin helped the CCP by timing Soviet withdrawal from Manchuria to ensure that the CCP captured all surrendered Japanese arms, by providing sanctuary to CCP units in North Korea and the U.S.S.R., and by rallying international support to the CCP cause.

On October 1, 1949, standing atop the Gate of Heavenly Peace in Peking, Mao Zedong[1] proclaimed the establishment of the People's Republic of China (hereafter, China). It was immediately recognized by the Soviet Union and other Communist nations, and early in 1950, India and several other nations in Asia and Europe followed suit. Among the major Western powers, only Great Britain, concerned for its huge investments and the safety of its Hong Kong colony, extended recognition.

China Fails to Modernize

Although minor political parties acceptable to the CCP were allowed to exist, the government of the People's Republic was a totalitarian one that carried out policies set by the Communist party. Nationwide mass organizations controlled by the Communist party, such as the All China Federation of Trade Unions, paralleled the structure of the party and the government. These organizations reached individuals in their professional or social roles and carried out party directives.

Mao Zedong sought to reshape the thinking and behavior of everyone so that he could create a new society of "collective man." To do this, he initiated

---

1. Hereafter in the text, spelling of Chinese names will follow the *pinying* system, adopted in 1949, for China, and the Wade-Giles system for Taiwan, in accordance with each government's convention.

campaigns to abolish old loyalties and patterns of thought and to instill new values and obedience to the state. New marriage and divorce laws were enacted to eliminate the old patriarchal family and give women equality. The government required its citizens to attend frequent meetings to learn Marxist ideology and the party lines, and to criticize themselves and each other. To keep China on the "correct course" and to emphasize the importance of being "Red" rather than "expert," people were forced to attend frequent meetings where they studied Mao's thoughts and memorized his sayings, which they repeated on all occasions, for example, "All reactionaries are paper tigers." Children sang songs to praise Mao rather than nursery rhymes, and at nursery schools, the first words they learned to write were Mao's name. The government also used force to ensure obedience. It declared whole classes of people enemies of the revolution, and between 1951 and 1953 exterminated or jailed millions of "landlords" and redistributed their land. The social and economic influence of the gentry-landlord class was totally ended.

In economic development, the party stressed Soviet-style planning and rapid modernization, and received massive technological assistance from the Soviet Union. The First Five-Year Plan (1953–57) stressed building up heavy industry and collectivizing agriculture, but despite rapid progress in the first five years, vast problems remained. This led Mao, who stressed humans as the "decisive force in history," to ignore objective economic realities and to embark in 1958 on a crash program called the Great Leap Forward. It involved the mass mobilization of labor, establishment of communes, and the building of backyard furnaces to smelt iron.

Instead of instant development, the Great Leap Forward brought nothing but disaster. Most early statistics of initial gains made under the Leap were either wildly exaggerated or faked. Figures show that about 600,000 backyard furnaces were built, but the iron they produced was of such low quality that it was almost useless. By 1959 the economy had been crippled by the follies of the Leap, the people were exhausted and demoralized. Bad weather exacerbated the man-made disaster and starvation stalked the land. Economists estimate that the Leap caused a loss of $66 billion to the economy; the government admits that about eighteen million people, perhaps more, died as a result. When the Central Committee of the CCP met in 1959, even Mao had to admit the magnitude of the disaster facing China. Many of his senior associates were disillusioned with the way he had run the government and eased him out of direct control of the party and the government, although he retained the title of Chairman of the Communist party. They preferred a pragmatic approach to China's problems, and they had their way between 1959 and 1966, as they undid the damage that his policies had inflicted and began rebuilding again.

Alliance with the Soviet Union

China's foreign policy was based upon several factors. Still a weak nation and barely on its feet, China at first derived strength from its close ties with the Soviet Union. It needed both economic aid and protection from the Soviet Union to forestall possible Western intervention, as had happened in Russia after the Bolshevik Revolution. To secure this, Mao went to Moscow in 1950, his first trip abroad. He paid obsequious tribute to Stalin, in such statements as the following:

> Everyone knows that Comrade Stalin had an ardent love for the Chinese people and believed the might of the Chinese revolution to be immeasurable. To the problems of the Chinese revolution he contributed his sublime wisdom. And it was following the theories of Lenin and Stalin and with the support of the Soviet Union . . . that the Chinese Communist Party . . . won its historic victory.

As a result of the trip, a Sino-Soviet Treaty of Friendship and Alliance was signed in 1950, in which Stalin granted Mao a military alliance, provided credit, and promised tens of thousands of Soviet military and civilian experts to help China modernize its armed forces and industries. In the next decade, the Soviet Union, at a time when it had barely recovered from the devastations of World War II, transferred massive amounts of technology to China. It also returned to China the equipment it had looted from Manchuria at the end of World War II.

Understandably, in the light of China's century-long history of humiliation by Western and Japanese imperialism, the new government sought recognition as a great power. Mao proclaimed that in international affairs, China would "lean to one side," that is, the Marxist side, in the Cold War. The Soviet Union surrendered its remaining privileges in China and accorded it the position of associate leader in the international Communist movement. In 1957, it promised to assist China in its nuclear development. For its part, China orchestrated its foreign policy to aid the international Communist movement, and, in so doing, also abetted its drive for leadership in Asia and position in the world. For example, in sending a million "volunteers" to aid North Korea in the Korean War and in assisting North Vietnam's struggles, China not only furthered the Communist cause in Asia, but also reasserted its traditional role as the protector of small states on its borders. In 1956, China mediated in the disputes between the Soviet Union and its East European satellites, thus helping to maintain Soviet dominance in the socialist bloc, while asserting its position as associate leader in the international Communist movement.

At the same time, China sought to become the leader of all Asia and also of the Afro-Asian bloc of newly independent nations. Thus it championed the themes of coexistence and anti-Western imperialism. China won recognition as the leader of the Afro-Asian nations at the Bandung Conference held in 1955. Its successes became an inspiration to many underdeveloped nations.

The balance sheet of the first decade of the People's Republic showed considerable successes, not only in the domestic field (up to the Great Leap Forward), but also in world affairs. China had not only thrown off the shackles of imperialist domination, but was even reasserting its traditional role as the dominant power in its part of the world. In instituting the communes during the

Great Leap Forward, it was attempting to put itself on a higher ideological plane than the Soviet Union, and even gloated that it was ahead of the U.S.S.R. in its progress toward the socialist utopia.

DECOLONIZATION IN ASIA

World War II not only ended Japan's dream of empire in Asia; the victorious nations found that they, too, had to divest themselves of their empires. Weakened by two world wars, the European colonial powers in particular found that they could not hold back the rising tide of Asian nationalism, whether peacefully or violently expressed. Between 1946 and 1957, the people of every major colony in South and Southeast Asia became citizens of new nations. The United States led the way in 1946, granting full independence to the Philippines. Great Britain, however, demonstrated the full magnitude of the collapse of colonialism when, in 1947, it departed from the most valuable possession of any colonial empire, the Indian subcontinent, leaving in its wake the new nations of India and Pakistan. One year later, it granted independence to Burma and Sri Lanka (Ceylon). In 1949, the Netherlands reluctantly left Indonesia rather than risk losing U.S. economic aid trying to prolong a war of independence it could not win. In 1954, the French were driven from Indochina after losing a war of independence. In 1957, the British granted independence to Malaya, their last major colony in Asia, and combined it with several smaller neighboring British colonies to form the federation of Malaysia. This section will concentrate on events in India, Pakistan, and Indochina.

India's Continuing Struggle for Freedom

Since 1909, Great Britain had reluctantly but steadily granted ever-increasing measures of self-rule to India and Burma; this process led the way for the other nonwhite British possessions in Asia and Africa. Had World War II not occurred, India could possibly have attained final independence before 1947. However, preoccupation with global war, and the worsening relations between Hindus and Muslims during the war, compelled Great Britain to postpone the steps toward complete independence until the war had been won.

Great Britain declared war against Nazi Germany in 1939 and against Japan in 1941 on its own behalf and on behalf of India and its other possessions and dominions. While most Congress leaders supported British war aims against the Axis, they nevertheless objected to India's automatic entry into the war without prior consultation with Indian leaders. In protest, Congress-controlled provincial governments resigned. The British government, maintaining that World War II was a life-and-death struggle, countered by taking control of the provinces and dissolving the India Act of 1935. Congress then began a new *Satyagraha* campaign throughout the land, for which the British arrested 1,400 Congress leaders, including Gandhi and Nehru.

Muslim fear and dislike of the Congress cause prompted Muslim League President Mohammed Ali Jinnah, called "Great Leader" by his followers, to declare the closing of Congress ministries in the eight provinces a "Day of Deliverance and Thanksgiving." The Muslim League and League-controlled provinces cooperated with the British administration throughout the war. Muslim confidence and separate consciousness increased during the war period. Jinnah exemplified Muslim opinion when he said in a speech in 1940 at the annual meeting of the Muslim League:

> Hindus and Muslims belong to two different religious philosophies, social customs, literature. . . . To yoke together two such nations under a single state, one as a numerical minority and the other as a majority, must lead to growing discontent and final destruction of any fabric that may be so built up for the government of such a state. . . . The only course open to us all is to allow the major nations separate homelands for dividing India into "autonomous national states."

Following that speech, the League passed the "Pakistan Resolution," which called for a separate Muslim state. Pakistan, or "the Land of the Pure," was to consist of those areas of the Indian subcontinent where Muslims formed the majority of the population.

Most Indians actively aided Great Britain in fighting the Axis. Much more than during World War I, Indian troops fought in the Middle East, in Africa, and in Southeast Asia and defended India against a threatened Japanese invasion, acquitting themselves well. Some who passively resisted the war effort did so not so much out of pro-Axis feelings as out of frustration over India's political status. A few Indians actively supported the Japanese, but they failed to gain a popular following.

A number of British missions came to India during the war years to offer concessions that would mollify the Congress. They suggested formulas for the transfer of more power to Indians during the war and also promised full independence immediately afterwards. However, all British offers failed, either because of Congress intransigence on timing or because of the stumbling block of Muslim-Hindu communal hostility. Congress now called on Britain immediately to "Quit India"; the Muslim League responded by insisting that independence must result in the creation of two successor states, India and Pakistan. This was the deadlocked situation at the war's end.

Independence Comes to India and Pakistan

In July 1945, general elections brought the Labour party to power in Great Britain under Prime Minister Clement Attlee. Never sympathetic to imperialism, the new government declared its intention to grant independence to India immediately and appointed Lord Louis Mountbatten, a war hero and able diplomat, to accomplish that task. Even then, the final stages of British withdrawal were delayed by Hindu-Muslim antagonism. Communal riots in many parts of

India took on the character of full-scale battles, and civil war threatened. Finally Gandhi agreed that it was preferable to let Muslims have Pakistan than to engulf the whole land in civil war, and secured Congress's consent that areas with a Muslim majority in the northwest and northeast should be allowed to become Pakistan. Mountbatten appointed a Briton to head an impartial commission to draw up the boundaries, a most difficult task that pleased neither side. Indian princes, who had made separate treaties in the nineteenth century that put them under the protection of the British crown, were told that they could join either India or Pakistan, but could not become independent.

Compared to political transitions elsewhere in Asia, Indian nationalism triumphed with little bloodshed against the foreign ruler. At the stroke of midnight on August 14, 1947, India became a sovereign nation within the British Commonwealth. At the invitation of the Indian parliament and in gratitude for his efforts, Mountbatten stayed on as governor-general (representative of the British sovereign) of India until June 1948. At the same time, peoples of the predominantly Muslim northwest and northeast declared their independence as the new nation of Pakistan.

Fearful of their fate in East and West Pakistan, Hindu minorities sought safety by crossing over into India, and, equally frightened, many Muslims fled into Pakistan. More than fifteen million people took part in this massive human migration, with nine million resettling in India and six million in Pakistan. Approximately 600,000 people died. Some were killed in riots and street battles in their towns and villages by members of the opposing religion; others died in attacks by hostile mobs as they tried to make it to their new nation; still others died of starvation or diseases while making their grueling flights. The disturbances immediately threatened to engulf the two new nations in war.

Gradually, the panic and frenzy diminished. Fifty million Muslims remained in India, and Prime Minister Nehru labored to ensure that they received protection. Similarly, Jinnah (who became governor-general of Pakistan, which also opted to remain in the British Commonwealth) worked to protect the remaining Hindu minority of ten million in Pakistan. The wounds of partition never healed, however.

More heartsick than anyone over the carnage, Gandhi, the champion of nonviolence, undertook personal missions of peace to the disturbed cities and villages in India. He also began a fast for an end to communal hatred, which had a sobering effect on the violent mobs. On January 30, at a prayer meeting, he was assassinated by a Hindu extremist who believed that he had been too generous to the Muslims.

Prime Minister Nehru found the task of governing India an extremely difficult one, as indeed did the leaders of all newly independent nations. He said:

> Sometimes as I reached a gathering, a great roar of welcome would greet me
> . . . Victory to India! I would ask them unexpectedly what they meant by
> that cry, who was this Mother India whose victory they wanted? My

question would amuse them and surprise them, and then, not knowing exactly what to answer, they would look at each other and at me.

One problem was how to feed the inexorably growing population. Over 80 percent of Indians were rural, and most were desperately poor. With a high population density, primitive agricultural methods, and almost total dependence on monsoon rains, the land could not produce enough food for the population. Tragically, every improvement made in food production, sanitary facilities, and public health further boosted the population growth. In 1947, life expectancy for an Indian who survived infancy was thirty-two years; by 1969, it had reached fifty-two. Increased longevity put such a strain on Indian food resources that Nehru was led to remark, "India must run very fast just to stand still."

There was also the language problem. The 1950 constitution recognized sixteen official languages, including English, and many more were spoken. A government plan to make Hindi the national language angered the majority of Indians, who did not speak Hindi, and riots broke out. In retreat, the parliament passed a law (embarrassing to nationalist leaders) to retain English as the national language until the indefinite time when the non-Hindi-speaking peoples would accept Hindi; the matter remained unresolved.

Politically, Nehru and his Congress party favored democracy and opposed the existence of the almost 600 princely states ruled more or less autocratically by maharajas, many of them colorful and eccentric. After independence, all princely states were integrated, some by force, into seventeen states within the Indian federation, each with its own legislature. On the national level, the government was modeled after the British parliamentary system, with certain features of the U.S. congressional system added. The prime minister was India's political leader and presided over the Council of Ministers, or cabinet, which was chosen by the majority party in the parliament. India proudly counted itself as the most populous democracy in the world, and the living proof that democracy could thrive despite illiteracy and poverty. Because of high illiteracy, the Indian ballot was marked by symbols such as the cow and plow to designate political parties.

Economically, the Congress governments encouraged industrial development as a solution to India's backwardness, and abandoned the Gandhian ideal of traditional village handicrafts. To maximize development, Nehru and his successors opted for a "mixed economy," in which the government owned or controlled the basic industries but encouraged foreign investments and private enterprise. To develop industry, modernize agriculture, and stimulate trade, Nehru launched his first Five-Year Plan (1951–56). Such plans were continued by successive governments. About 10 percent of the capital needed for these five-year plans came from foreign aid programs funded by the United States, the Soviet Union, other nations, and international agencies. Because of India's poverty and its importance to both sides in the Cold War, it became the largest single recipient of foreign aid in the post-World War II era. Between 1947 and 1980, India received over $9 billion in U.S. aid. It now ranks as the tenth industrial power of the world.

The Indian government's main goal in its economic development program was to raise the pitifully low standard of living of the average Indian. The an nual per capita income in 1951 was $53, and Indians had to spend up to 90 percent of their income on food, in contrast to U.S. citizens, who spent 16 percent. The goal of improving the standard of living and literacy rate was constantly frustrated by the alarmingly fast growth in the population, which was in turn caused, in part, by illiteracy and poverty that perpetuated traditional values, including a desire for large families.

India chose a foreign policy of nonalignment with either power bloc in the Cold War. Its unwillingness to become a member of a bloc headed by the United States and Great Britain was a reaction to its colonial experience and an expression of its residual resentment against Great Britain, and, by implication, its ally the United States. Nehru also hoped that India could become the leader of a bloc of neutral nations and could thereby mediate in disputes between the major powers. Nehru announced India's commitment to peace, which, however, did not prevent him from going to war against Pakistan or sending troops to evict the Portuguese from Goa, their colony on the Indian coast.

Pakistan was and remained India's primary concern. In addition to the bitterness created by partition, India and Pakistan had problems over the distribution of water from the Indus River for irrigation. Kashmir, however, was the major bone of contention between the two nations. Both India and Pakistan claimed ownership of this area, which was a princely state, 80 percent of whose people were Muslim. In 1947, India and Pakistan fought over Kashmir, and continued to fight until a U.N.-imposed cease-fire went into force in 1948, in effect partitioning Kashmir. A U.N. observer force remained there. Jinnah and his successors demanded a plebiscite, which Nehru and his successors rejected, since they feared that the Muslim majority would vote to join Kashmir with Pakistan. India and Pakistan fought again in 1965 over Kashmir, but agreed to a cease-fire mediated by the Soviet Union, with no boundary changes.

Although Nehru encouraged good relations with Communist nations, he had no tolerance for native Communists and once remarked that India had more Communists in prison than any other nation. Nor was he successful in maintaining friendly relations with China. During the 1950s, Indians often professed in a slogan that "Indians and Chinese are brothers," but border disputes ended those good feelings when war broke out between the two nations in 1962. The Chinese soundly defeated the Indian army and occupied sections of disputed territory in the Himalayas. However, the Chinese did not press their advantage, withdrew from certain advanced positions, and called for negotiations. The border disputes were not settled and Sino-Indian relations remained strained.

Pakistan after Independence

Most of the problems that plagued India also affected Pakistan, a wretchedly poor nation with primitive agricultural methods, little industry, many refugees, and one of the fastest-growing populations in the world. Furthermore, Pakistan had an impossible geography. West Pakistan was located along the Indus valley and East Pakistan was situated on the Ganges delta; the two were separated by almost 1,000 miles. From the beginning, the bizarre geopolitical structure of the state—two separate halves that had little in common except Islam—was the most serious threat to the survival of Pakistan. The capital city was in West Pakistan, and West Pakistanis, who formed less than half of the total population, made up 70 percent of the civil service and 80 percent of the officer corps. Most of the foreign aid and export earnings went to develop industries and services in West Pakistan. Finally, West Pakistanis tended to regard the physically and linguistically different East Pakistanis as inferiors.

A year after independence, Jinnah, the father of Pakistan, died of cancer. In 1951, his successor, Liaquat Ali Khan, was assassinated. The deaths of these two leaders left Pakistan with a heritage of political instability. The military took control in 1958, dissolved the parliament, and instituted a system of modified and indirect elections that was termed "Basic Democracy." Except for brief intervals of civilian rule, Pakistan remained under army control.

Pakistan's foreign policy was dictated by fear of its bigger neighbor, India, and its inordinately large military was maintained at a huge cost to ensure safety against India. Since India maintained a neutralist foreign policy with a pro-Soviet leaning, Pakistan allied itself with the U.S.-led CENTO alliance.

France is Forced from Indochina

Unlike Great Britain and the United States, France had done little to satisfy nationalistic aspirations in Indochina prior to World War II. Vichy France surrendered Indochina to Japanese occupation peacefully, but during World War II, Nationalist China aided a broad spectrum of Indochinese nationalists who resisted Japan, among whom the Communists were the most effective. On Japan's surrender, the Communist Vietnamese leader Ho Chi Minh established his headquarters in Hanoi and declared the independence of all Indochina. France refused to accept Ho's claim, offered only limited reforms, and reoccupied Indochina. The nationalists totally rejected France's proposals, and war between the Indochinese and France broke out in late 1945.

The struggle for independence centered in Vietnam. A pattern of French control in South Vietnam and Ho's control of the north soon emerged. Ho used his considerable influence as Vietnam's foremost nationalist leader to assimilate and dominate the other Vietnamese nationalist movements. With his subordinate, General Vo Nguyen Giap, Ho perfected guerrilla warfare tactics to fight a war of attrition. They avoided open battles and concentrated on terrorist activities and sabotage. The French could not distinguish the peaceful citizen from the guerrilla fighter, who often worked at an ordinary job by day and took up arms at night. By 1954, French forces in Vietnam, including 200,000 Vietnamese soldiers plus Foreign Legionnaires, numbered 420,000. They confronted a Vietminh army almost as large. For every Frenchman killed, perhaps ten Vietnamese on the opposing side died.

The climax of the war for independence came at the siege of Dien Bien Phu in 1954, in which 15,000 of France's best troops were hopelessly trapped in a fortress city by General Giap's forces, now heavily strengthened by arms from the Soviet Union and China. France appealed to the United States, which was already shouldering 80 percent of the cost of the war, to intervene with land and air forces. President Eisenhower, who had just extricated the United States from a deadlocked Korean War, refused to become involved. Without direct U.S. aid, Dien Bien Phu fell. By this time, the war-weary French public was ready to quit Vietnam and pressured its government to comply. France had already agreed to the independence of Laos and Cambodia and now departed from Vietnam.

THE PROBLEMS OF NEW NATIONHOOD

During the first decade of independence, the new nations of Asia faced similar problems of varying degrees of severity, but a major problem to all was that their economies had been dislocated and devastated by World War II. The Philippines had suffered most from the fighting. Only Warsaw was more war-damaged than Manila. Burma and Vietnam had also suffered from military campaigns. All the new nations needed outside economic assistance, but the source and amount of that aid were dictated by the foreign policies of the newly independent nations, particularly as they related to the Cold War. For example, the United States gave the Philippines large quantities of aid, both from a sense of responsibility for the islands' colonial past and because the new republic was willing to accept U.S. military bases on its land and to be allied with the United States. Similarly, the British remained in Malaya until 1960 to clean up the remnant Communist guerrilla forces, even though Malaya had become independent in 1957. Great Britain and several Commonwealth nations also gave Malaya economic aid. Burma, however, opted out of the Commonwealth at independence and took a strictly neutralist stand in international affairs; it rejected all economic aid from all parties. North Vietnam, on the other hand, received significant military and economic aid from the Soviet Union, and from the People's Republic of China after 1949, in its struggle against France.

The task of running a government was difficult in all cases, especially since many of the leaders had no previous experience. Every nation had ethnic or religious minorities; in many cases these minorities were disaffected from the government, and some revolted to overthrow the government or to establish their own nations. Thus the Muslims of Mindanao revolted and waged civil war against the government of the Philippines, as did the non-Burmese hill tribesmen in northern Burma against the Burmese government.

In other cases, the nationalistic leaders of the new nations persecuted ethnic minorities in their lands, as happened to the Indian minority in Burma and the Chinese minority in Indonesia. Only in Malaya was there relative harmony between the three racial groups—Malays, Chinese, and Indians. Political inexperience, poverty, and traditional attitudes also resulted in rampant corruption, which occurred regardless of the system of government, and was particularly notorious in the democratic Philippines as well as authoritarian Indonesia. While Malaya and the Philippines continued with the democratic experiment, Burma's elected government was soon replaced by the military, and in Indonesia Sukarno became dictator under the guise of president for life and a "Guided Democracy."

Each Southeast Asian nation was also faced with severe social problems, which were closely linked with economic ones. In all nations a wide gulf divided the rich from the poor, but the coming of independence unleashed energies that demanded social reforms, such as greater equality for women, and economic improvements that the new governments could not or did not wish to implement. Meanwhile, improvements in medicine and public health resulted in an inexorable population increase that wiped out any economic gains.

In North Vietnam, the problem of economic disparity was tackled by forced land reform accompanied by the killing and jailing of former landlords. In non-Communist Asian nations, social and economic inequities made the Communist call for revolt attractive to some. In the Philippines, where no reform took place, land hunger by the poor peasants led to a Communist-led uprising known as the Huk Rebellion. Although largely put down by 1954, the insurgency never died out because the conditions that caused the rebellion were never adequately remedied.

A spellbinding speaker, President Sukarno of Indonesia addresses a giant rally. (AP/Wide World Photos)

THE COLD WAR IN ASIA

After World War II, Asia became one of the theaters of the Cold War. When the Communists emerged victorious in the Chinese civil war in 1949, President Truman initially did not consider the People's Republic a threat to U.S. interests in Asia; he appeared resigned to its conquest of Taiwan and considered recognizing it as the government of China. The outbreak of the Korean War in 1950 and Chinese participation in the war quickly altered U.S. perceptions of the goal of the Communist bloc in Asia. Later, as Communist insurgency movements cropped up in the Philippines, Malaya, and Burma, and threatened their newly independent and unstable governments, the United States became increasingly concerned over the spread of communism across the continent, as it was over similar Communist expansion in Europe. These fears strengthened U.S. resolve to contain the spread of communism on both continents.

The Korean War and its Aftermath

Allied leaders had agreed at wartime summit conferences to restore an independent Korea, but had worked out no details of its implementation. When the Soviet Union declared war on Japan, Soviet troops immediately invaded Korea. As the Soviet Union and the United States had agreed, their representatives took the Japanese surrender north and south of the 38th parallel respectively. As it turned out, they created two nations.

In the north, the Soviet Union proceeded to establish a state headed by a young Korean Communist named Kim Il-Sung, and an army guided by Soviet advisors. The government quickly implemented Communist policies, and in the process drove one million of its citizens to seek refuge in the south. In the south, the United States hoped to help establish a democratic government with popular representative institutions, but had no definite blueprints to realize its goals. It allowed exiled patriots to return home, among whom was seventy-year-old Syngman Rhee, veteran opponent of Japanese imperialism. Rhee proceeded to organize an authoritarian anti-Communist government in South Korea.

In 1947, the United States placed the Korean problem before the United Nations, which appointed a commission to supervise elections. Rhee's party won the elections in 1948 and declared the establishment of the Republic of Korea, thus terminating the U.S. military government. Elections were also held in North Korea, but without the presence of the U.N. election commission, after which the government proclaimed itself the Korean Democratic People's Republic. Soviet troops withdrew from North Korea but left in place a well-trained and well-equipped North Korean military force.

Both Korean governments were dedicated to unification, each on its own terms. On June 25, 1950, North Korea launched a surprise attack on the South. In the months before the attack, the United States government had sent confusing signals as to whether South Korea was inside the U.S. "defense perimeter." Once the attack occurred, President Truman, mindful of the lesson of the 1930s in China

The Korean War

❶ *Furthest North Korean advance, Sept. 1950*
❷ *U.N. landing at Inchon, Sept. 15, 1950*
❸ *Furthest U.N. advance, Nov.–Dec. 1950*
❹ *Furthest Chinese and North Korean advance, Jan. 1951*
❺ *Armistice line, July 27, 1953*

CHINA
U.S.S.R.
Yalu R.
NORTH KOREA
P'yongyang
SEA   OF
Panmunjom
38th parallel
Inchon
Seoul
JAPAN
SOUTH KOREA
YELLOW
SEA
Pusan
JAPAN

0   50   100   150   200
Scale of miles

and Europe—that unchecked aggression invited more of the same—decided to commit U.S. troops for the defense of South Korea against the North's aggression. In deciding to defend South Korea, Truman also was mindful of the security of Japan, Okinawa, and the Philippines. He also secured the support of the United Nations Security Council, which condemned North Korea for aggression against another sovereign state and called on member states to contribute military units collectively to repel the aggressors. The Soviet Union, which had been boycotting the Security Council for six months to protest the presence of Nationalist China on the council, was not there to cast its veto.

South Korea contributed about one-half of the ground forces of the United Nations command, in a war formally termed a "police action." The United States contributed the navy, air force, and two-fifths of the army; the remainder came from Great Britain, a number of Commonwealth nations, Turkey, and others—in all, fifteen nations. President Truman termed Korea "the Greece of the Far East," where the U.S. must contain Communist expansion.

United Nations Commander-in-Chief General Douglas MacArthur turned the tide of the Korean War in a brilliant tactical maneuver by landing at Inchon

Inspiration from the West

It must be remembered that the great ambition which led me to the mission school was to learn English, and English only. This ambition I quickly achieved, but I soon discovered I was learning something of far greater importance than the English language. I was imbibing ideas of political equality and liberty. Those who know anything about the political oppression to which the masses of the Korean people were subject can imagine what a revolution took place in the heart of a young Korean Yangban [upper class] when he learned for the first time that people in Christian lands were protected against the tyranny of rulers. I said to myself, "It would be a great blessing to my downtrodden fellow men if only we could adopt such a political principle. . . . "

Let us gather all our powers and make our nation like the nations of wealthy, powerful and civilized people. Keep independence in your own hearts. The most important part is to cast out hopelessness. We must become diligent workers. Our own individual dedication is the seed from which will grow the harvest of a sound nation.*

Syngman Rhee was born into an aristocratic Korean family. He became a student activist when studying in a missionary school, and founded the Independence Club, which opposed the government's submissive policy toward Japan and advocated modernization; for this he was imprisoned from 1897 to 1904. This passage comes from a book written by Rhee during the years he spent in prison. He became a lifelong crusader against Japanese rule over Korea and became president of independent South Korea after World War II. As president, he emphasized nationalism rather than democracy and ruled as a strongman. His government was overthrown as a result of student riots in 1960.

*From *Syngman Rhee: The Man Behind the Myth* by Robert T. Oliver. (Quoted from Syngman Rhee, *The Spirit of Independence*.) Copyright © 1954 by Dodd, Mead, and Company.

in the rear of the North Korean forces. He then proceeded to drive the North Koreans out of South Korea and through North Korea toward the Chinese border. As the war changed from one of repelling aggression to one of conquering North Korea, Cold War tensions rose high. China became anxious as U.N. troops approached its border, partly since the remnants of the North Korean air force were still attacking U.N. troops from Chinese air bases. In October 1950, Chinese troops, allegedly "volunteers," began crossing into Korea and by December were driving U.N. forces back into South Korea. The front sta-

President Syngman Rhee of South Korea thanks General Douglas MacArthur, commander-in-chief of U.N. forces, after the liberation of Seoul, capital of South Korea, from North Korean invaders in October 1950. (UPI/Bettmann Newsphotos)

bilized in 1951 close to the 38th parallel, the original boundary between the two Koreas.

During the retreat from North Korea, and as the war settled into a stalemate, MacArthur and his military and civilian supporters pressed to use Nationalist Chinese troops and U.S. air and naval power to attack and defeat the Chinese. President Truman and his civilian and military advisors, pressured by nervous European allies, decided that such proposals were unacceptable because they risked bogging down the United States in a major war against China that might widen into a conflict with the Soviet Union. When MacArthur began publicly to challenge Truman's decision, the president relieved him of his command for insubordination.

The stalemated war dragged on until an armistice was signed in 1953. The United States suffered 142,000 casualties, the fourth largest number in its history; South Korean casualties were estimated at 300,000, North Korean at 520,000, and Chinese at 900,000. Many Americans were indignant over the dismissal of MacArthur and were frustrated that the United States had not clearly won the Korean War. These two issues were added to the already acrimonious political debate in the United States over responsibility for the "loss of China." Together, they contributed to the election of Republican presidential candidate Eisenhower in 1952.

To clarify its intentions and instill confidence among anti-Communist Asian nations, the United States concluded a mutual defense treaty in 1954 with South Korea, on which basis U.S. troops continued to be stationed in that nation. In addition, the United States committed large sums for the military build-up of the South Korean armed forces and the economic rebuilding of the terribly devastated land. To President Rhee's government fell the responsibility of postwar reconstruction. Autocratically inclined, he put nationalism ahead of democracy in a state threatened by invasion and Communist subversion, and used strong-arm tactics to bring dissidents into line. Rhee was toppled in 1960 by student demonstrations, but as the faction-ridden political parties were unable to produce unified leadership, the army seized power in 1961. The generals inaugurated a five-year plan for stimulating capitalist economic development. Successive economic plans, fueled in part by U.S. economic aid and investments, and after 1965 by Japanese investments, put South Korea on the road to prosperity. Although civilian rule was ostensibly restored in 1963, the elections returned a general to the presidency and the military continued to play a leading role in politics.

North Korea was one of the purest examples of a monocracy (government by one man)—Kim Il-Sung, who concentrated in himself supreme power over the Korean Workers' Party (Communist), the armed forces, and the government. It received large quantities of Soviet and Chinese aid and, until 1958, the continued protection of Chinese troops. North Korea had a smaller population than the South, but greater natural resources and more industries, which the Japanese had built. Its economic build-up was accomplished under tight discipline imposed by Kim's government. By the late 1960s, however, South Korea had outdistanced the North.

Each Korea maintained its ultimate goal of reunification, by force if necessary. An uneasy truce continued, punctuated by incidents of sabotage, infiltration, and armed provocation by North Korea, along one of the most tightly guarded and tense borders in the world. Since the peninsula remained divided and provocations from North Korea continued, the U.N. Command in South Korea remained, and the United States continued to maintain over 40,000 military personnel south of the Demilitarized Zone (DMZ). The governments of both Koreas remained committed to the eventual reunification of the peninsula, and Kim, who still ruled North Korea in 1989, harassed South Korea time and again through assassinations and other terrorist acts. Much as it longed for reunification, South Korea appeared unlikely to start a war against the North. Nor did the United States wish a confrontation, showing restraint when North Korea captured a U.S. surveillance vessel, the *Pueblo,* in 1968, and killed two U.S. officers in the DMZ in 1976. Thus, while tensions remained high on the Korean peninsula, they were unlikely to lead to renewed war.

U.S. Anti-Communist Policies in Asia during the 1950s

By the early 1950s the United States was faced with the fact that communism was spreading fast in Asia. Mao Zedong had come to power in China in 1949, and in 1950 Communist North Korea had nearly wiped out South Korea, followed by a bloody stalemate between U.N. and Communist Chinese troops. Communist-led guerrilla insurgents were active in several newly independent nations of Southeast Asia, and Ho Chi Minh's guerrillas were getting the upper hand in Indochina. U.S. leaders believed that Stalin had a master scheme to make the world Communist, which he was now putting into effect in Asia with the aid of China. Asia had long been an area of U.S. imperialist and commercial interest, and many Americans were up in arms over "losing" China and "not winning" in Korea.

Under these circumstances, the United States, determined that no more of Asia should be "given away," extended to Asia the containment doctrine that it had first applied to Europe in the late 1940s. As one major aspect of containment, the U.S. government began to supply military and economic aid to friendly anti-Communist governments in Asia. In doing so, it failed to perceive an important difference between Western Europe and Asia. Most Asian nations were newly independent and beset by social upheavals, mainly from peasant demands for land ownership and other reforms. Since communism promised fundamental social and economic reforms, many Asians were attracted to local Communist movements. Failing to understand this phenomenon, the United States gave support to reliably anti-Communist governments in Asia, many of which lacked popular support because they opposed or were insensitive to needs for economic and social reforms. In effect, the United States, as it had in Latin America, put itself in the position of supporting governments that opposed reform, a position that would bring trouble in the decades to come.

Another goal of containment was to try to neutralize China. The Korean War had made the United States especially hostile toward China. It refused to recognize the government headed by Mao as the legitimate government of China and used its veto to block its admission to the United Nations. It also opposed a Chinese conquest of Taiwan (seat of the Nationalist government since 1949) and interposed the Seventh Fleet in the Taiwan Strait.

To forestall Communist expansion and to prevent non-Communist nations from falling under communism like a row of dominos, the United States built up a network of alliances with anti-Communist governments in the region. Bilateral mutual defense treaties were concluded with Japan, the Philippines, South Korea, and the Republic of China on Taiwan (hereafter, Taiwan). These treaties with individual nations were reinforced by the Southeast Asia Treaty Organization (SEATO), established in 1954, which included Great Britain, France, Australia, New Zealand, Thailand, and the Philippines in a collective defense of the region. Another treaty (ANZUS) put Australia and New Zealand under U.S. military protection and gave U.S. armed forces access to military bases in the Southern Hemisphere. When SEATO and other Asian bases were linked with U.S. bases in Pakistan (under CENTO) and with NATO, U.S.-led alliances had ringed the Communist bloc. The U.S. attempt to halt the spread of communism in Indochina will be taken up in Chapter 29.

Both the Chinese Communist and Nationalist governments were agreed that there should be only one China. The Communist government, anxious to complete its victory, sought to destroy the Nationalists on Taiwan. In 1955 and 1958, China bombarded the tiny Nationalist-held off-shore islands of Quemoy and Matsu, seemingly as prelude to an assault on their 100,000 defenders. Since by their Mutual Defense Treaty the United States was obliged to supply the Nationalist garrisons, direct conflict between the United States and China became a distinct possibility. The United States stood firm in its commitment to support the Nationalists and threatened to use nuclear weapons should the Communists attempt to invade Taiwan, but it also ordered its supply boats to respect Chinese territorial waters by staying outside the three-mile limit. After the attempt to wrest the islands had obviously failed, China ordered its artillery to fire only on alternate days, thus allowing U.S. supply ships to reach the islands. Hostilities wound down finally to firing propaganda leaflets from both sides. The United States also pressured Chiang Kai-shek to renounce any intentions of attacking the mainland. Thus the tensions over the Taiwan Strait gradually subsided.

SUMMARY

After suffering eight years of Japanese invasion, China was immediately engulfed in civil war after the victory against Japan. The Chinese Communists, despite preventive efforts by the United States, defeated the corrupt and inefficient Nationalist government in China. After 1949, Mao Zedong and other Communist leaders transformed the world's most populous nation into a totalitarian Communist state, the People's Republic of China, and placed it firmly in the socialist camp as an ally of the Soviet Union. It aided North Korea with over a million soldiers in the Korean War and gave material and training aid to the Vietnamese Communists, but its economic backwardness and the domestic turmoil that Mao brought on with the Great Leap Forward prevented it from playing a larger role in the Cold War in Asia.

Between 1945 and 1960, most of the former colonies in Asia gained independence. Great Britain and the United States led the way, as they had done before World War II, and made peaceful and orderly transfers of power. They retained, for the most part, the good will of their former colonies. Most former British colonies remained in the Commonwealth, while the Philippines became an ally of the United States. France and the Netherlands were less farsighted and withdrew from Asia only when they had no options.

In many cases, independence brought to the forefront ancient regional disputes and internal problems that had lain submerged during colonial rule. Thus Hindus and Muslims in India resurrected ancient rivalries that predated

British control and remained smoldering for decades. Several other newly independent nations almost immediately became embroiled in civil wars or insurrections by ethnic or religious minorities. Economic and social problems
plagued most of the new nations and often defied both foreign aid and local
efforts to find solutions, even when there was a will to do so. Ancient and modern local rivalries and nationalistic ambitions became entwined with Cold War
politics, embroiling the new nations in alliances or leading them to policies of
nonalignment.

As the leader of the non-Communist world, the United States became
deeply involved in combating the spread of communism in Asia. American
forces were dispatched to Korea to prevent the Communist conquest of South
Korea. On the other side, China entered the war to prevent the U.S. conquest
of North Korea. The armistice that ended the fighting reflected a stalemate that
continued into the 1980s. The United States also protected the Nationalist refugee government on Taiwan from invasion by China, sent aid to Southeast Asian
nations to combat Communist guerrillas, and created a number of formal military alliances, collectively and individually, with nations of the area. When
victorious Communist-dominated forces threatened to overrun all Vietnam and
wrest it from war-weary France, the United States and other great powers intervened to partition the former colony and restrict the Communists to the northern half. Thus, on two major and several minor occasions, the Cold War in
Asia erupted into hot wars and left a legacy of three divided lands.

SUGGESTED SOURCES

Bloodworth, Dennis, *An Eye for the Dragon: Southeast Asia Observed, 1945–1970* (1970).
A long-time resident in Southeast Asia, the author gives insights into the peoples,
forces, and events that have shaped the area in a turbulent era.*

Collins, Larry, and Dominique Lapierre, *Freedom at Midnight* (1980). A gripping account of the last stages of India's struggle for independence.*

Elegant, Robert, *Dynasty* (1978). A novel of a Hong Kong Anglo-Chinese family, whose
exciting lives are intertwined with important events in China from the Boxer Rebellion to the Cultural Revolution.*

Fifield, Russell H., *Americans in Southeast Asia: The Roots of Commitment* (1973). A
survey of twentieth-century U.S. involvement in the region.

Fitzgerald, Charles, *Revolution in China* (1966). The author focuses on the indigenous
forces underlying the Chinese Communist revolution.

Jeffrey, Robin, ed., *Asia—The Winning of Independence* (1981). A concise summary of
how each nation won its independence.

Lewis, John Wilson, ed., *Peasant Rebellion and Communist Revolution in Asia* (1974).
Explains the relationship between traditional peasant rebellions and twentieth-
century Communist-led revolutions.

Liang, Heng, and Judy Shapiro, *Son of the Revolution* (1983). A poignant autobiography about growing up in Mao's China.*

"Lord Mountbatten: The Last Viceroy" (1984). TV series that dramatizes the people
and events preceding the independence of India and Pakistan.

Masters, John, *Bhowani Junction* (1954). A novel set amid the excitement of the independence and partition of the Indian subcontinent.* (Also a film and video.)

Mehta, Ved, *A Family Affair: India under Three Prime Ministers* (1982). A critical study of the politics and personalities of Indian leadership.

Pu Yi, ed. Paul Kramer, *The Last Manchu* (1987). An autobiography of the tragic life of the last emperor of China.* (Also a film, "The Last Emperor" [1987].)

Russ, Martin, *The Last Parallel* (1959). A marine's first-hand account of fighting in Korea.*

Ward, Barbara, *Women in the New Asia: The Changing Social Roles of Men and Women in South and Southeast Asia* (1977). An insightful description of social relations and changing roles of women.

*Paperback available.

25

African Struggles for Independence

After World War II, Africa began to move from a continent of colonies to a continent of independent states. As in Asia, most European colonial nations, their strength eroded by two world wars, no longer had the power or even the will to hold on to their empires in the face of mounting nationalist pressure. Rapid industrialization, urbanization, and increased contact with Western technology and culture caused radical alterations in the traditional patterns of African society; this accelerated the various movements toward independence. As the peoples of Africa loudly demanded control over their own political and economic destinies, it became evident that the small number of Europeans living in northern and eastern Africa could not hold back the forces favoring national self-determination. By 1963 virtually all of the northern two-thirds of Africa consisted of independent states. In southern Africa, however, white minorities still clung to power (see Chapter 31).

The struggle for independence took different forms throughout Africa. In some cases, as in Tunisia, Morocco, or Uganda, the imperial powers granted independence under prearranged conditions. In Libya, for example, the United Nations played a key role in establishing an independent political entity. In these instances, Africans secured independence with a minimum of bloodshed. On the other hand, in areas where there were well-entrenched European white settlers or where the imperial powers were determined to maintain control, the struggles for independence were protracted and often violent. In Algeria and Kenya, and later throughout much of southern Africa, African nationalists were often forced to resort to guerrilla warfare and armed attacks against the imperial powers. These guerrilla wars, or "wars of liberation," as they were often known in the Third World, followed the same pattern as that in Vietnam.

Just as the imperial powers had differed in their approaches to their African empires, so too did they adopt contrasting policies toward the newly independent nations. Some, in particular France, attempted with notable success to maintain close cultural and economic ties. Indeed, former French colonies remained economically and linguistically tied to France decades after independence had been secured. Former British possessions tended to adopt more independent approaches to economic and cultural development. Others, most notably Belgium in the Congo, abdicated responsibility for their former holdings. A selective look around the African continent will reveal in more detail how most of the colonies finally secured independence and how the various European imperial powers approached their former colonies.

NORTH AFRICA: INDEPENDENCE THROUGH BOTH NEGOTIATION AND WAR

In North Africa, nationalist sentiments had gained enormous popular support by the end of World War II. In the face of this groundswell for national liberation, France, after limited struggles, granted independence to Tunisia under Habib Bourgiba and Morocco under King Mohammad V in 1956. Both Bourgiba and Hassan II, Mohammad's son, continued to rule into the 1980s. Similarly, Libya secured its independence under King Idris through the auspices of the United Nations. The traditional monarchy of King Idris was overthrown by a military coup led by Muammar Qaddafi in 1969. By the end of the 1960s, huge petroleum revenues transformed Libya from one of Africa's poorest nations into one of the richest.

In contrast, in order to obtain their independence, the Algerians, led by the National Liberation Front (FLN), fought a bloody war (1954–62) against the French, who were unwilling to give up what the government had for a century considered to be an integral part of France. The French *colons* were particularly vociferous and determined to keep Algeria as an integral part of France; they even went so far as to establish their own secret army to fight the Algerians and those French who supported independence. The FLN used attacks on urban centers populated by the *colons* and other guerrilla warfare tactics similar to those employed in Vietnam; these included hit-and-run tactics and what has been called the "bombs in a basket" approach, whereby women and children would carry out attacks on the *colons* and the French military. The French retaliated by bombing villages, removing families from the countryside, and, in some instances, torturing Algerian suspects. General de Gaulle, who came to power in 1958, concluded that France could not win the struggle and should negotiate a settlement. After protracted negotiations, continued violence within Algeria, and assassination attempts on de Gaulle, Algeria finally achieved independence in 1962. Upon independence most of the *colons* left Algeria and settled in France or Spain. The Algerian war cost a million Algerian deaths and thousands of French casualties. In many ways, it divided French society much as the Vietnam War later split U.S. society.

Following independence, Algeria was in the vanguard of revolutionary Arab states, but later it established more friendly relations with the United States. Algeria had substantial revenues from its petroleum resources but nevertheless had enormous economic problems. Unemployment was high among

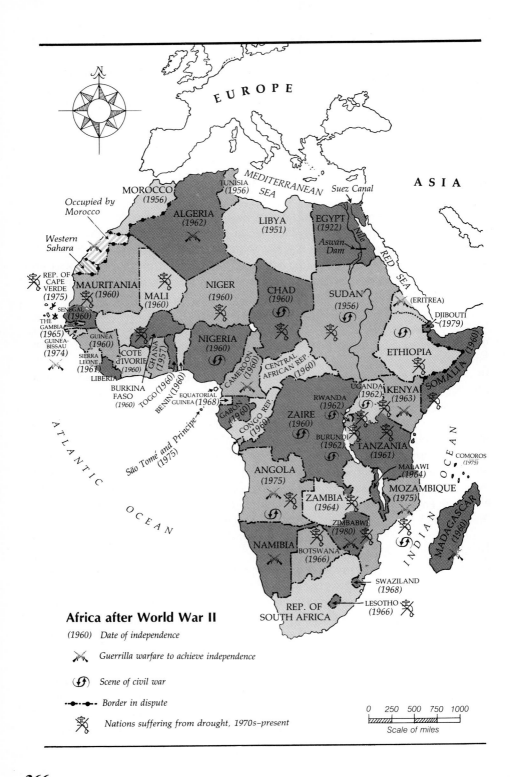

Africa after World War II

(1960) Date of independence

Guerrilla warfare to achieve independence

Scene of civil war

Border in dispute

Nations suffering from drought, 1970s–present

EUROPE

ASIA

MEDITERRANEAN SEA

Suez Canal

MOROCCO
(1956)

Occupied by
Morocco

Western
Sahara

TUNISIA
(1956)

ALGERIA
(1962)

LIBYA
(1951)

EGYPT
(1922)

Aswan
Dam

Nile

RED SEA

REP. OF
CAPE
VERDE
(1975)

MAURITANIA
(1960)

MALI
(1960)

NIGER
(1960)

CHAD
(1960)

SUDAN
(1956)

(ERITREA)

DJIBOUTI
~(1979)

SENEGAL
(1960)

THE
GAMBIA
(1965)

GUINEA-
BISSAU
(1974)

GUINEA
(1960)

SIERRA
LEONE
(1961)

LIBERIA

COTE
d'IVOIRE
(1960)

GHANA
(1957)

BURKINA
FASO
(1960)

TOGO *(1960)*

BENIN *(1960)*

NIGERIA
(1960)

EQUATORIAL
GUINEA *(1968)*

São Tomé and Príncipe
(1975)

CAMEROON
(1960)

CENTRAL
AFRICAN REP.
(1960)

GABON
(1960)

CONGO REP.
(1960)

ZAIRE
(1960)

RWANDA
(1962)

BURUNDI
(1962)

UGANDA
(1962)

KENYA
(1963)

SOMALIA
(1960)

ETHIOPIA

TANZANIA
(1961)

COMOROS
(1975)

ANGOLA
(1975)

ZAMBIA
(1964)

MALAWI
(1964)

MOZAMBIQUE
(1975)

ZIMBABWE
(1980)

NAMIBIA

BOTSWANA
(1966)

SWAZILAND
(1968)

LESOTHO
(1966)

REP. OF
SOUTH AFRICA

MADAGASCAR
(1960)

ATLANTIC
OCEAN

INDIAN
OCEAN

N

0 250 500 750 1000

Scale of miles

its youth, which, as in many of the newly independent nations, formed a large sector of the total population. All of France's former North African imperial holdings retained close economic ties with the former imperial power, with the majority of their imports and exports coming from and going to France. Following independence, Algeria became a leader of the Third World, and it often played a key role in mediating between Third World nations and Western superpowers.

DECOLONIZATION IN WEST AFRICA

As indicated previously, western Africa, particularly the Gold Coast (Ghana), had been in the forefront of African national movements. In 1949, Kwame Nkrumah formed his Convention People's party, with its demand for "self-government now." Strikes and boycotts, accompanied by some violence, were directed against the British administration. As a result, Nkrumah was imprisoned, but internal unrest persisted.

Finally, in 1957, the British agreed to grant Ghana independence under the leadership of Nkrumah; in the view of many African nationalists, Ghana's independence was the first step toward independence for all of black Africa. By 1960 Nkrumah had declared himself president for life. Along with seeking further economic and educational development within Ghana, Nkrumah also portrayed himself as the leader of the Pan-African movement. As a result, he incurred the enmity of rival African leaders and, more important, alienated other Ghanaians who were more concerned over economic development. Consequently, Nkrumah was overthrown by a military junta in 1966. Attempts to return Ghana to stable civilian government met with varying degrees of success, and as in so many newly independent nations in the twentieth century, the army remained an important force. As a result of poor management and political instability, Ghana was plagued with economic problems, smuggling, and profiteering.

In Nigeria, one of the largest and most populous African nations, the British attempted to solve the problem of ethnic and cultural heterogeneity by forming a federated system that, in theory at least, was to give full local rights to the three main ethnic groupings within the nation. However, riots in 1953 demonstrated the major differences between the predominantly Muslim north and the predominantly Christian Ibos in the southeast. Attempting to reconcile these differences, the British declared Nigeria an independent nation in 1960. The carefully prepared constitution called for a federated nation, but the basic ethnic hostilities remained.

In 1967, the Ibos attempted to secede and to establish their own nation, which they called Biafra. The civil war that followed was characterized by bloody violence and extreme hardship; thousands died of starvation. The war dragged on until 1970, when war-weary and often starving Biafrans surrendered and the military regime of Colonel Yakubu Gowon reunited the nation.

After independence, Ghanaians proudly wore
clothes imprinted with pictures of their
nationalist leader, Nkrumah. (Keystone Press)

In contrast to the British approach, the French tried to retain a close union
with their West African empire. As early as 1944, General de Gaulle had promised a French union, which was to be a more highly centralized version of the
British Commonwealth, but which theoretically would respect indigenous societies. However, de Gaulle's attempt to keep some degree of French control
over its empire failed to fulfill the national aspirations of the West Africans
living under French control.

Thus, in spite of considerable financial benefits from the French government,
nationalists continued to press for independence. After World War II, Felix
Houphouet-Boigny played the leading role in forming a political alliance to fight
for the independence of the Ivory Coast. Joined by nationalists from other French
colonies in West Africa, the move triggered a series of violent confrontations. When
de Gaulle returned to power in 1958, he proposed holding an election whereby
West African nations could choose to participate as autonomous units within a
French union or could choose complete independence. In the 1958 elections, only
Guinea, led by Ahmed Sekou Touré, voted for complete political and economic
separation from France. Sekou Touré ruled Guinea until his death in 1984; subsequently, military officers led a takeover of the government and moved to restore civil liberties and build up the nation's faltering economy.

By 1960, France had granted the rest of its West African colonies full independence. Some, such as Senegal under the noted poet Leopold Senghor, proved remarkably stable. In the Ivory Coast, one of the most prosperous West African nations, a lively artistic heritage, particularly in the fields of ceramics, weaving, and metalsmithing, was continued and expanded. Other nations, such as Togo, Cameroon, and Benin, were plagued by continual military coups and countercoups. Indeed, military dictatorships became the predominant political force in most of West Africa; as Yukubu Gowan, the military president of Nigeria, emphasized, "The trouble with military rule is that every colonel or general is soon full of ambition. The navy takes over today and the army tomorrow." Throughout Africa, military regimes were often able to put down regional disputes and tribal conflicts, but the costs were high. Many smaller ethnic groups were largely decimated by military leaders representing larger or more powerful forces.

Importantly, most former French colonies maintained fairly close economic and cultural ties with France. In contrast, the former British colonies often went their own ways and established economic ties with other outside nations. Through organizations such as the Ghana-Guinea Union, some West African nations also attempted to bridge the linguistic and cultural divisions which had been created by British and French colonial policies.

CHAOS IN ZAIRE

All of the general patterns of African struggles for independence were apparent in the Belgian Congo (later Zaire). There was some violence and bloodshed; the superpowers became involved, and the United Nations attempted to mediate the conflict. While both the British and the French had tried to prepare and to educate at least an elite to take over the governments of new independent states, the story was quite different in the Congo, because Belgian paternalism had kept the Congo under rigid controls. Much as they tried, however, the Belgians could not isolate the Congo from the nationalist fervor of its neighbors. A number of local nationalist movements developed, including one based in Katanga led by Moise Tshombe and another led by Patrice Lumumba.

In the face of growing nationalist sentiments, the Belgian government abruptly announced Congolese independence in 1960. The new state was immediately threatened by conflicting local rivalries. Tshombe announced the secession of the mineral-rich Katanga province. Lumumba called for the intervention of the United Nations. The Congo became the arena for some private companies and the superpowers to meddle in African affairs. Hired mercenaries further complicated the situation.

Finally, U.N. police actions in 1963 reunited Katanga with the rest of the Congo, but the fighting continued even after the U.N. troops left in 1964. After Lumumba's assassination in 1961, the Congolese government was troubled with military threats and political instability. Following a relatively bloodless coup,

General Joseph Mobutu became head of the government in 1965 and proceeded with the tasks of unifying the badly divided nation, changing its name to Zaire. The government of Zaire used part of the capital earned from the nation's tremendous mineral wealth to build roads, lines of communication, and educational facilities. However, the government also allocated a large portion of Zaire's economic wealth to maintain a large army and to quell rebellions by groups opposed to the military or by those who had been systematically excluded from power.

PEACE AND WAR IN BRITISH EAST AFRICA

As in West Africa, the British moved toward granting *uhuru* (freedom) in East Africa after World War II. Unlike West Africa, however, East African nations came to independence through war as well by peace. Tanganyika, economically the least developed of British possessions in East Africa, secured its independence in 1961 after a decade of gradual steps toward autonomy. Unified with neighboring Zanzibar in 1964, it became the Republic of Tanzania. Tanzania emerged as a one-party nation led by Julius Nyerere's United Tanganyika Party (TANU). Nyerere, one of Africa's leading champions of state socialism, promptly initiated a series of grass-roots development projects aimed at increasing agricultural output and providing better social services. China provided much technical and financial assistance for development, but most of the rural population remained poor.

In Kenya, the move toward independence was complicated by the presence of the white minority, most of them farmers in the Kenyan highlands. These white settlers, like the *colons* in Algeria, wished to keep their dominant position. In contrast, the British government had embarked on a gradual program of increased self-determination based on a multiracial cooperation that would also include the Indians, Kenya's other racial minority. These concessions failed to alleviate African grievances, particularly among the Kikuyu, one of the largest of Kenya's ethnic groups. As white salaries and standards of living continued to rise, the economic position of blacks deteriorated. The Kenya African Union under Jomo Kenyatta persistently demanded that these inequities be eradicated and that blacks be given a larger proportion of the important government positions. When these demands were ignored, the independence movement became more radical.

In 1952, there were widespread demonstrations as the Kikuyu organized into a national resistance group popularly known in the West as the Mau Mau, centered mainly in the countryside. Guerrilla warfare ensued, but the actual number of assassinations and violent acts perpetrated by the Mau Mau was widely exaggerated in the Western media. In a futile effort to destroy the Mau Mau, the British imprisoned Kenyatta, but the resistance continued. Finally, the British and white settlers admitted defeat and Kenyan independence was proclaimed in 1963.

Kenyatta quickly emerged as the leader of a single-party state. Through a series of political maneuverings, and with the advantages of relative economic prosperity and his own charismatic appeal, Kenyatta managed to unify the various Kenyan groups into a fairly cohesive nation. While many of the white settlers left Kenya, some remained as new Kenyan citizens. Under Kenyatta's leadership, the Kenyan government remained relatively stable and survived Kenyatta's death in 1978. Although the majority of political power certainly rested in the executive branch, Kenya was unusual in that it managed to retain civilian government and a cohesive national identity even after the demise of its first generation of nationalist leadership.

THE BLACK STRUGGLE FOR FREEDOM IN SOUTHERN AFRICA

Pressure on Southern Rhodesia and the Portuguese Colonies

In southern Africa, the Portuguese led by the dictator Salazar and the white-dominated regimes elsewhere in the area were far more determined to maintain their supremacy than were the colonial powers in the rest of Africa. In Rhodesia, for example, the white settlers announced their determination to retain their dominant political and economic position. On the other hand, the British government sought to avoid South African problems by agreeing to grant independence to Southern Rhodesia along the lines of equal representation. As British Prime Minister Harold Macmillan noted on a visit to South Africa, "The wind of change is blowing through [Africa], and whether we like it or not this growth of national consciousness is a political fact . . . and our national policies must take account of it." Such an approach meant that the small white population would no longer enjoy the position of privilege it had had under the old regime. The white minority bitterly opposed the British plan and, in open defiance, unilaterally declared its independence as the state of Rhodesia in 1965. With the exception of the white-controlled Republic of South Africa, no nations recognized the new Rhodesian government under Ian Smith, and the United Nations declared an economic boycott of Rhodesia. However, Rhodesian tobacco and minerals continued to be channeled to Western markets, and the economic boycott seemed to have little effect.

As the pressure mounted, African states surrounding Rhodesia became involved. South Africa assisted the Smith regime, while black African nations supported the growing forces of revolutionary black Rhodesians. Armed insurrections became commonplace throughout the Rhodesian countryside. Both Great Britain and later the United States tried to mediate the dispute and to reach a settlement based on equal black participation in the government, with no success.

At the same time that Rhodesia was falling under siege, blacks in the Portuguese colonies of Mozambique and Angola increased their pressure for independence. Portuguese dictators Antonio Salazar and Marcello Caetano refused to grant independence or greater autonomy to the last vestiges of Portugal's four-hundred-year-old colonial empire. Indeed, in 1955, the Salazar regime attempted to extend its centralized control by referring to the colonies as "overseas provinces," an approach that was similar to the French concept of Algeria as an integral part of France. Just as the concept of Algeria as French had failed, so, too, did the Portuguese attempts to incorporate its African colonies. Condemnations of Portuguese policies in Africa by the United Nations were ignored. As a result of nationalist sentiments and Portuguese repression, rebellion broke out in Angola and Mozambique in 1961. A decade of war followed.

Racial Repression in the Republic of South Africa

Much of the struggle for independence in the southern third of Africa focused on the Republic of South Africa. One of the richest and strategically important African nations, its society was still dominated by the conservative Dutch Afrikaners. During World War II, many Afrikaners, who had long chafed under British domination and attempts to liberalize the society, openly favored the Nazi regime. The Dutch Reformed Church reinforced the Afrikaners' philosophy of racial supremacy.

After the war, the Afrikaners in the Republic of South Africa enacted the policy of apartheid, a government-endorsed and -enforced system of strict racial segregation. Apartheid legalized the dominance of 4.5 million whites over 800,000 Asians (mostly Indian shopkeepers), 2.8 million "colored" (people of mixed racial origin), and 22 million blacks, restricting their civil rights and allowing no political power. In addition, it called for the complete segregation of the races in housing, education, religion, and government. It separated black Africans from Asians, both of these from the colored, and all three of them from the white population. In many cases, it forced families who lived in areas designated as white, colored, or black to move if they were of the wrong color. Huge, largely black bedroom townships developed around the outskirts of largely white cities. Blacks were permitted into these cities to work in industry or white homes during the daytime, but they had to leave the cities during the evening hours. Blacks had to carry identification cards at all times; to be caught without a card or after curfew in areas designated as white meant possible imprisonment or the loss of a pass to work in cities, which meant unemployment and further impoverishment. The Afrikaner government justified these repressive measures on the ground that they helped to suppress Communist activities.

In the decades after World War II, black society and white society moved further and further apart. Landless blacks began to seek jobs in the growing industrial centers, which were profiting from South Africa's great natural wealth in diamonds, uranium, and gold. Here, too, skilled white workers held the highest-paying positions; blacks were given the lowest-paid jobs as manual laborers. Gradually, all whites, even in unskilled jobs, were paid a higher wage simply because of skin color.

The apartheid policy and the repressive tactics that accompanied it pro-

---

Resisting Apartheid

A short while later [1953] my first ban was served on me in terms of the Riotous Assemblies Act and the Criminal Law Amendment Act. In comparison with my later bans it was a mild affair. I was debarred from entry into all the larger centres of the Union. I was not allowed to attend public gatherings anywhere.

   This last provision at once raised the question of attendance at public worship. My church took up the matter with the Department of Justice and told me that while they did not *think* that the police would interfere with my religious activities, I should apply for permission to be present at public worship.

   In the winter of 1954, when the new battery of ruthless laws was freshly in place on the Statute Book, my ban expired. It was not immediately reimposed. I suppose I was being given a chance to go straight. I immediately misbehaved.*

Luthuli, the grandson of a Zulu chief, describes an episode in his struggle against apartheid in South Africa. He was President of the African National Congress and a leader in the Pan-African movement. He was awarded the Nobel Peace Prize in 1961.

*From *Let My People Go* by Albert Luthuli. Copyright © 1962 by William Collins Sons & Company, Ltd.

---

voked nonwhite leaders to resist. Initially, they stressed nonviolence after the pattern set by Gandhi, who had spent part of his early life in South Africa. Numerous black leaders, including the Nobel Peace Prize winner Albert Luthuli, were imprisoned. Others, like white novelist Alan Paton, who was outspoken in his opposition to the regime, were censored and placed under virtual house arrest. The African National Congress (ANC), under Luthuli's leadership, sought a unified and racially integrated society in South Africa and led the struggle for nonviolent tactics and passive resistance against apartheid.

   Black nationalists also initiated a series of strikes and demonstrations. These culminated in the 1960 Sharpeville incident, where police opened fire on the unarmed crowd, killing dozens and wounding many. Condemning the ANC as revolutionary, the white South African government declared the organization illegal in 1961. Nelson Mandela, one of the leaders of the ANC, evaded arrest but was ultimately caught and tried under the Suppression of Communism Act. Mandela, who was not a member of any Marxist party, and seven other nationalist leaders were sentenced to life imprisonment; although Mandela has remained a prisoner for over twenty-five years, he has continued to be the symbol and leader of black nationalism in southern Africa. When Great Britain and other members of the Com-

Blacks are massacred at Sharpeville in South Africa in 1960. (Keystone Press)

monwealth criticized apartheid and the repression of black nationalist leaders, South Africa retaliated by leaving the Commonwealth in 1961.

To alleviate growing internal and international criticism, the South African government in 1966 announced the creation of Bantustans, or black states, within South African territory. The Bantustans of Bophuthatswana and Transkei were, in fact, large black reservations. Permits were required for blacks to leave the Bantustans and to go to any area designated as white. White South Africans argued that the Bantustans were created as a logical extension of the apartheid principle of separate development. However, the Bantustans were on only 13 percent of the total land area, generally exceedingly poor, territorially fragmented, and dependent for communication and transport lines on white South Africa. Their foreign affairs were also controlled by the South African government. In 1966, Prime Minister Henrik Verwoerd, a leading proponent of apartheid, was assassinated by a mentally disturbed Greek immigrant, but his successors continued the policies. As hopes for concessions faded, black nationalists began to turn to violence (see Chapter 31).

NEW MOVEMENTS TOWARD PAN-AFRICAN UNITY

Many African leaders, from Nkrumah to Nasser, saw Pan-Africanism, a concept born between the wars, both as a means to improve standards of living and as a way of giving Africans more political and economic clout in the international arena. African union was encouraged through various Pan-African conferences during the decades of the 1950s and 1960s. The Bandung Conference in 1955 gave enormous impetus to the movement for Afro-Asian cooperation. Similarly, the First World Congress of Black Writers and Artists, held in Paris in 1956, was an important cultural event in bringing together English- and French-speaking Africans. The next logical step occurred in May 1963, when representatives of the newly independent African states met in Addis Ababa and created the Organization of African Unity (OAU). Much of northern Africa also considered itself part of the Arab world, and leaders such as Nasser in Egypt argued that the predominantly Muslim and Arab nations of Africa belonged to both the circles of Arabism and of Africanism.

However, in spite of their broad emotional appeal, both African and Arab unity appeared to be a distant dream. African union was verbally championed by most African leaders, but concrete attempts for unity generally failed, for a variety of political and economic reasons. Personal rivalries for dominant positions among conflicting African leaders drove wedges between African nations. Most of the educational institutions and economic relations of African states were plugged into Western nations; there was very little, if any, economic interdependence that would facilitate the movement toward political union. Thus, economic rivalries heightened political differences. The Western powers aggravated the differences among African states by economic and political interference, and later occasionally by direct or surrogate military interference, as in Zaire.

SUMMARY

With the notable exceptions of Algeria and Kenya, independence came relatively peacefully in northern and central Africa in the 1950s and 1960s. By the 1960s all western and eastern African nations had become independent. Many of these new, struggling nations experienced political upheavals, and military dictatorships often became the norm. In Zaire, there were particularly bloody conflicts which were exacerbated by superpower involvement.

In southern Africa, levels of violence rose as colonial and white settler regimes in the Portuguese colonies and Rhodesia clung to power year after year in the face of growing African discontent. The institution of apartheid widened the gulf between the races in South Africa. The white minority in South Africa remained determined to keep the black majority from participating in the political system. In reaction to Afrikaner refusals to allow equality, blacks turned first to nonviolent methods to force changes, but as the white minority clung to power, black activists turned to violence.

Independent African nations were troubled with economic crises and persistent political instability, which often led to military interference. Attempts at union, either political or economic, were impeded by cultural differences, outside interference, and political weaknesses.

SUGGESTED SOURCES

Achebe, Chinua, *No Longer at Ease* (1963). A historical novel, a sequel to *Things Fall Apart,* where the hero returns to Nigeria after living in Britain.*

Calvocoressi, Peter, *Independent Africa and the World* (1984). A survey of Africa and superpower involvement since the 1950s.*

Horne, Alistair, *A Savage War of Peace: Algeria 1954–1962* (1979). A moving description of the Algerian revolution.*

Omer-Cooper, J. D., *A History of Southern Africa* (1987). Analytical study of origins of contemporary South African societies.*

Paton, Alan, *Too Late the Phalarope* (1953). On the psychological dimension of apartheid, by a noted novelist.*

Winnie and Nelson Mandela (1986). Powerful biographical film about the two most famous black South African nationalists.

*Paperback available.

26

Continued Crisis
in the Middle East

Middle Eastern nations achieved independence after World War II, but the region's vital oil fields and its strategic importance in terms of the Cold War meant that the superpowers constantly sought to secure allies and influence in the area. While the petroleum-rich nations were able to finance vast and far-reaching development programs, the poor nations without oil revenues continued to suffer the problems of underdevelopment. In addition, inter-regional rivalries and the ongoing Arab-Israeli conflict contributed to tensions and intermittent warfare.

INDEPENDENCE AFTER WORLD WAR II

As war clouds gathered in Europe, Great Britain took steps to quell the growing nationalist storms in the Middle East. Great Britain wanted to ensure loyalty, or at least quiet, in the Arab world because of the area's vital strategic location. Consequently, the British tried to placate Arab nationalists, many of whom were prone to favor the Axis powers. Arab support for the Axis powers did not generally stem from ideological agreements with them, but was based on the old expression "an enemy of my enemy is my friend." Encouraged by Nazi propaganda and hating the British presence in the area, Arab nationalists were encouraged to believe that if the Germans won the war they would grant the Arabs complete independence.

In the Palestine mandate, the British tried to pacify Palestinian Arab opposition by limiting Jewish immigration and by promising independence to Palestine in the future. Due to the anti-Semitic basis of the Nazi regime, Great Britain knew that world Jewry would support the Allied war efforts. Thus assured of Jewish support, Great Britain felt safe in making friendly gestures toward the Arabs. This policy angered the Zionists, who believed all Jews in the diaspora (Jews scattered throughout the world) had the right to settle in Palestine.

In other parts of the Arab world, Great Britain attempted to secure its interests through censorship, military control, repression of Arab nationalists, and pro-Allied propaganda campaigns. After the fall of France and the creation of the pro-Nazi Vichy regime, Allied forces gradually occupied French-held Syria and Lebanon. In spite of French protests, the U.S. and British governments encouraged nationalist sentiments, particularly in Syria and Lebanon. By 1945 when the war ended, most Middle East nations had achieved national autonomy; however, the Western powers were still anxious to maintain their military and petroleum interests in the region.

To protect their vital interests in the Middle East, the British encouraged the creation of the Arab League, which was designed to foster interstate cooperation; however, the League was continually disrupted by feuds among the various independent Arab nations. After the war, interdynastic disputes among the Hashimites in Jordan and Iraq, the Saudi monarchy in Saudi Arabia, and Faruk in Egypt were major stumbling blocks to Arab unification. After 1952, the Arab world was divided by rivalries between the conservative, generally pro-monarchy forces (Saudi Arabia and Jordan) and the so-called revolutionary forces in Egypt under Nasser, in Syria, and in Iraq.

THE ARAB–ISRAELI CONFLICT

After World War II, the Arab-Israeli conflict became the major political and military problem in the Middle East. After 1945, both the Zionists and the Palestinian Arabs pushed for the creation of their own individual nations; the problem was that each of these nationalist groups sought to express its independence within the same geographic territory. The Palestinians, who in 1945 were about two-thirds of the local population and owned about 80 percent of the land, believed the territory was theirs. On the other hand, the Zionists believed that through historical and religious involvement, the territory was theirs. In addition, Jewish national claims had enormous emotional support in the West and among Jewish survivors of the Holocaust, as a result of the tremendous suffering of the Jewish communities within Nazi-controlled Europe. The Holocaust, with its untold horrors, caused many Westerners to conclude that the Zionists were correct in advocating a Jewish national state that would protect the religious and political rights of the Jewish people. In opposition, the Palestinians and the Arabs generally viewed anti-Semitism and the Holocaust as Western problems for which they were not responsible and for which they should not be forced to pay.

In this situation, the British, who had played Palestinian and Zionist nationalisms against each other, were caught on the horns of a dilemma. If the British continued to support the creation of a Jewish state and the further immigration of the survivors of the Holocaust to Palestine, Great Britain would lose support in the Arab world, with its petroleum resources and strategic locations. On the other hand, by attempting to limit Jewish immigration into Palestine, the British were placed in the untenable moral position of opposing and

Jewish immigrants who fled Nazi persecution in Europe enter Palestine in 1939 despite British laws. (AP/Wide World Photos)

often imprisoning Jewish immigrants coming directly from the concentration camps in Europe. The British administration in Palestine also faced increased armed opposition by both the Zionists and the Palestinian Arabs. Furthermore, the British had severe domestic economic problems, and were forced to cope with mounting nationalist demands throughout the empire. The British solved their dilemma by washing their hands of it. In 1947, the same year as Indian independence, Great Britain turned the problem over to the United Nations, which promptly formed a committee to investigate the problem. The U.N. committee (UNSCOP) recommended in its majority report that Palestine be divided into a Jewish state and an Arab state. Partition had been suggested on previous occasions, but was not overwhelmingly popular. The Palestinians immediately opposed the proposed plan, which allocated approximately 50 percent of the territory, including the more fertile coastal areas, to the Jewish state. The Zionists reluctantly accepted the idea of partition but were dissatisfied because the plan did not allot to them all the area of ancient Israel.

Despite the mounting violence in Palestine, in November 1947 the United Nations voted for the partition plan that was to be implemented when the British withdrew in May 1948. In the interim, violence spread throughout Palestine as both sides began to prepare for battle. On May 14, 1948, as the British hastily withdrew, David Ben-Gurion, who was fairly confident of U.S. support, announced the creation of the state of Israel.

The surrounding Arab states and the Palestinian Arabs refused to recognize the new state, and the first Arab-Israeli war promptly began. The Arab forces, saddled with corrupt leadership, divided chains of command, faulty weapons, and no clear-cut military strategy, were no match for the well-organized, trained, and spirited Israelis. The Israelis won the 1948 war, expanding Israeli territory by approximately one-third more than granted under the original U.N. partition plan. The West Bank, which had been apportioned to the Arab state under the U.N. plan, was incorporated into Jordan. Jerusalem was divided under Israeli and Jordanian control. The Gaza strip was administered by Egypt.

One way or another, all Palestinian Arabs found themselves under the control of others. Before and during the war, thousands of Palestinians, particularly the peasants, fled their farms and homes. The Arabs maintained that the refugees, who clustered in southern Lebanon, the West Bank, and the Gaza strip, had been forced to leave because of Zionist terrorism and violence. The Israelis argued that they were not responsible for the refugees, who, according to Israel, had left as a result of Arab pressures or of their own free will. There are cases supporting both allegations, but there is no doubt that the 1948 war left almost a million Palestinians homeless. Receiving meager support from the U.N., these refugees by the 1980s numbered almost two million, but they remained determined to return to their homeland. The guerrillas of the Palestinian liberation organizations that were active from 1967 onward came predominantly from the refugee camps.

With enormous domestic economic and political problems of their own, the Arab governments did little to solve the refugee problem and, indeed, often used the Palestinians for their own political aims. As the former Algerian leader Ahmed Ben Bella once remarked, "The Arabs in power bargain on the backs of the Palestinians." On the other hand, the Israelis generally refused responsibility and were reluctant to accept the return of the refugees, who they maintained would become a subversive presence within Israel. In addition, the Israelis stressed that the return of the Palestinians would alter the basic ethnic and religious structure of Israel and would, thereby, change its Zionist basis. Thus, although Israel won the 1948 war, no peace treaties were concluded, and the borders of Israel and the surrounding Arab nations remained tense.

THE 1956 WAR AND AFTER

Events in Egypt soon led to a second Arab-Israeli war. Following the 1952 overthrow of the corrupt Faruk monarchy by a group of nationalist military officers, Gamal Abdel Nasser announced far-reaching programs for industrial and agricultural development. The Aswan (high) Dam, described as "more magnificent and seventeen times greater than the Pyramids," was the cornerstone of Nasser's program for economic development. The dam was to increase reclaimed agricultural land by one-third and was to provide low-cost electrical power for villages and for industrialization. Ironically, by the time the dam was

Attacking Imperialism

We, the whole generation, began to move towards violence. I confess
. . . that political assassinations blazed in my inflamed mind.

I remember one night in particular. . . . We had prepared
everything. . . . We selected one to put out of the way. . . . The plot
was to shoot him as he returned home at night.

The appointed night came and I went out myself with the squad
of execution. Everything went as we imagined. The person came and
bullets were fired. . . .

I got home, threw myself on the bed, my mind in a fever, my
heart and conscience incessantly boiling. . . . Suddenly I found myself
exclaiming, "I wish he would not die." I rushed anxiously to the morning papers. I was happy to find that the individual whose assassination
I plotted was destined to live.*

---

*Gamal Abdel Nasser describes how he and many other idealistic and na-
tionalistic young people fought against the corrupt monarchy of King
Faruk and British imperial control over Egypt in the years prior to World
War II. Nasser became politically active in his late teens, and as a military officer led the 1952 revolution that ousted Faruk. Between 1952 and
his death in 1970, Nasser was the dominant political power in Egypt and
a powerful charismatic force throughout the Arab world.*

*From *Philosophy of Revolution* by Gamal Abdel Nasser. Copyright © 1959 by Smith,
Keynes, and Marshall, Buffalo, N.Y.

completed, Egypt's population had increased by one-third, thereby undercutting the per capita improvements originally anticipated.

At the time of its inception, the Aswan Dam was the largest project of its
type in the world and required enormous expenditures of monies and technical
skills. Without petroleum revenues, Nasser hoped to secure assistance from
the West and the World Bank. Initially, the United States and other nations
were highly supportive of the project, but as Nasser moved to improve Egyptian
relations with the Soviet Union, China, and neutral Third World nations, Western support waned. In particular, U.S. Secretary of State John Foster Dulles
was opposed to neutralism, which he believed was thinly disguised communism. After Nasser failed to receive military arms from the United States, he
concluded an arms deal with Czechoslovakia. In light of these developments,
Dulles abruptly announced the withdrawal of U.S. assistance for the Aswan
Dam.

In Cairo, the refusal was correctly interpreted as an insult to Egypt and
as a direct slap in the face to Nasser. In retaliation, on July 26, 1956, to the

Egyptian President Nasser chats with Chinese Premier
Zhou Enlai in Cairo in 1965. (UPI/Bettmann Newsphotos)

astonishment of many Western officials, Nasser nationalized the Suez Canal,
which had previously been administered by the Suez Canal Company, whose
stockholders were predominantly European. Furious, the British and French
decided to take back the canal and to topple Nasser. The French government
was also anxious to overthrow Nasser in order to stop his support for the
Algerians, who were fighting for independence. For political and military reasons, the Israelis were also willing to join in military actions with the French
and British. The Israelis were being harassed by commando raids along their
borders and feared Nasser's success in mobilizing Arab supporters throughout
the region. An agreement was reached whereby Israel would launch an attack
across the Sinai peninsula but would stop short of the Suez Canal. The British
and French were then to intervene between the Israeli and Egyptian forces and
occupy the canal. The scenario anticipated the immediate downfall of Nasser,
followed by a more malleable or pro-Western Egyptian government.

In late October 1956, the Israelis successfully launched their attack and
occupied the Sinai peninsula. After some delay, the British and French bombed
Egyptian airfields and parachuted troops along the Suez Canal. The tripartite
collusion, which the British, French, and the Israelis publicly denied for many
years, was a military success, but a political fiasco. Contrary to Western expectations, Nasser did not fall. In fact, the war strengthened his argument that

The Arab-Israeli Conflict

- ◼ Israel according to U.N. partition plan, 1947
- ▨ Territory annexed by Israel, 1948
- Territory occupied by Israel, 1967
- ▨ Territory restored to Egypt, post-1973 war
- Territory restored to Egypt in stages, 1979–1982
- ▨ Annexed by Israel, 1982
- Occupied by Israel, 1982–1985
- Occupied by Syria, 1976
- X Areas of Palestinian refugee camps

MEDITERRANEAN SEA

LEBANON

Beirut ● X

SYRIA

X

Damascus

Golan Heights

West Bank

X

Tel-Aviv ●

● Amman

Jerusalem (Annexed, 1948, 1967)

Gaza Strip

X

ISRAEL

JORDAN

Suez Canal

E G Y P T

SINAI PENINSULA

● Cairo

Nile

GULF OF SUEZ

Gulf of Aqaba

Elat

SAUDI ARABIA

Sharm al-Sheikh

RED SEA

0   25   50   75   100

Scale of miles

the Western powers and Israel had imperial designs in the Middle East. The United States had opposed the use of military force and was placed in the awkward position of having to confront its closest allies, Great Britain and France; meanwhile, the Soviets played up the confrontation in order to divert attention from their invasion of Hungary. This divergence led to strained relations among the NATO allies. Eventually, the British, French, and Israeli forces withdrew from Egyptian territory, but Israel secured free access through the Straits of Tiran to its southern port of Eilat. This acquisition, which the Egyptians and the Arab world never recognized, was to be the immediate cause of the 1967 Arab-Israeli war.

Following the 1956 war, a wave of anti-Western and pro-Nasser sentiments swept the Middle East. Pro-Western Arab governments, particularly the conservative monarchies, were severely threatened by pro-Nasser forces. After some delay, the Soviets agreed to lend financial and technical assistance to build the Aswan Dam. In 1958, revolutionary activity in the region reached its peak. The conservative Hashimite monarchy in Iraq was overthrown by a military junta, which was ousted in its turn in 1963 by a military group from the Ba'ath party, which espoused Arab unity and socialism. In the following two decades, Ba'athists continued to rule in Iraq, while a more conservative Ba'athist group ruled in Syria under Hafiz al-Asad. The precarious throne of King Husayn, the Hashimite monarch of Jordan, was saved only by British parachutists.

In 1958, U.S. marines intervened in a civil war in Lebanon, acting under the proviso of the Eisenhower Doctrine that the United States would intervene in support of governments fighting communism. Actually, the Lebanese civil war was largely a conflict between conservatives and the leftist pro-Nasser forces; the war was temporarily settled by the creation of a moderate coalition government of Christian and Muslim Lebanese. However, the coalition perpetuated the problem of religious communalism in Lebanon.

THE 1967 "SIX DAY" WAR AND AFTER

Because there had been no peace settlement following the 1956 war, both sides had continued to prepare for the next violent confrontation. In May 1967, Nasser, in an attempt to regain his preeminent position as leader of the Arab world, asked that the U.N. forces stationed on Egyptian territory, particularly those along the vital Straits of Tiran at Sharm al-Sheik, be withdrawn. Acting according to U.N. mandates that troops could be placed in sovereign territory only with the consent of the concerned nation, U Thant, the U.N. Secretary General, reluctantly agreed to withdraw the troops. After the 1956 war, Israel had announced that it would consider any attempt to close the Straits of Tiran as cause for war. Quickly, both Israel and Egypt began to prepare for yet another confrontation. Syria and Egypt already had a mutual defense pact; although King Husayn of Jordan had been feuding with Nasser, he soon joined Egypt. Both the United States and the Soviet Union attempted to defuse the growing tensions, but while negotiations and talks were still in progress, Israel launched a preemptive strike against the air fields of the major Arab nations, destroying Arab air strength within six hours.

The 1967 June war lasted six days, but was really won by Israel within those first six hours. The Israelis, with complete air supremacy, soon defeated the Arab forces and occupied the Gaza strip, the entire Sinai peninsula, the West Bank (including the rest of Jerusalem), and the Golan Heights, from which Syria had been bombarding Israeli settlements.

The 1967 war was a dramatic victory for the Israelis and a complete humiliation for the Arab world. In the face of the massive defeat, Nasser resigned, but the stunned Egyptian masses demanded his return. The Israelis were initially optimistic that their military victory would force peace negotiations. At first, they were willing to discuss the return of most of the occupied territories with the exception of Jerusalem, which they proclaimed as the unified capital of the nation. However, the United Nations and the international community refused to recognize this gain, which was against the U.N. charter provision expressly forbidding territorial gains made through armed conflict. Israel refused to withdraw from the occupied territories until there were direct peace negotiations and full recognition of its existence by the Arab nations. The Arab nations refused to enter into direct negotiations or to accept Israel's right to any of the territory secured in the war. They also continued to demand the recognition of Palestinian rights to a homeland of their own. The 1967 war also increased the refugee problem, since over 200,000 refugees crossed from the West Bank to the East Bank in Jordan. Only a small fraction of this number returned to the occupied territories once the war had ended. Thus the stalemate was complete—no war, no peace. Various attempts were made to mediate the dispute, particularly by the United States, but all failed.

In the interim, the Palestinians concluded that no outside powers, including the Arab governments, would secure an independent Palestinian state. Consequently, a number of Palestinian guerrilla groups emerged from the disasters of the 1967 war and formed loose alliances under the umbrella of the Palestine Liberation Organization (PLO). The largest and most well-known of these groups was al-Fatah, led by Yasir Arafat. The PLO began a series of raids and attacks into Israeli territory; when these tactics failed to secure the objective of a Palestinian state, some Palestinians expanded the struggle to targets outside the Middle East and to all powers or individuals who supported Israel. These tactics including skyjackings, assassinations, and bombings. Israel retaliated with raids and attacks into surrounding Arab nations and ultimately with assassinations of Palestinian leaders. Thus the cycle of mounting terrorism spread around the globe.

The PLO was particularly strong in Jordan, where about half the population was Palestinian. As it became clear to King Husayn that he was close to losing control of his government to the PLO, he launched an armed attack against Palestinian units in Jordan in September 1970. There followed a bloody war that the Jordanian forces won, inflicting heavy casualties on the Palestinians. Nasser, in one of his last accomplishments before his death in September

1970, effected a settlement between the warring factions. Following the Jordanian civil war, the PLO moved its main base of operations to Lebanon.

EGYPT AND ISRAEL: WAR, THEN PEACE

Anwar Sadat, a fellow army officer with Nasser, succeeded as Egyptian president following Nasser's death. Most observers predicted that Sadat would not survive long, but their analyses were proven wrong as Sadat revealed far more political acumen than had been anticipated. With strong fortifications along the Suez Canal, the Israelis were confident that the Egyptians could never cross. In October 1973, after several years of preparation, each of which he had termed his "year of decision" and which some Egyptians had dubbed his "years of indecision," Sadat launched a successful attack across the canal. Several weeks of tank and air battles in the Sinai followed and culminated in the Israelis' making a counter-crossing onto the western bank of the canal; Israeli and Syrian troops also clashed along the Golan Heights. Big-power intervention, led by the United States, brought about a cease-fire. Militarily, both sides claimed a victory.

Following the war, Sadat was hailed as the Arab leader who had taken the resolution of the Arab-Israeli conflict off the "back burner" and placed it at the forefront of international attention. With this limited victory, Sadat moved to enter open negotiations. The 1973 war also brought the United States into the conflict as a mediator. The United States was anxious to secure a settlement of the conflict, to maintain a balance with the Soviet Union in the region. It also wanted to ensure the continued free flow of petroleum that Arab petroleum producers, led by Saudi Arabia, had threatened to restrict for all nations that supported Israel. The United States feared a total "Arab boycott" of petroleum, but while supplies diminished, the cutoff never materialized.

Several years of negotiations followed, characterized by U.S. Secretary of State Henry Kissinger's shuttle diplomacy from Tel Aviv to Cairo to Damascus, and back again. The outgrowth of these protracted negotiations was the reopening of the Suez Canal and the partial withdrawal of Israeli troops from the Sinai and the Golan Heights. Although further direct negotiations were to have been held in Geneva, the issue of Palestinian participation prevented a settlement. The Arabs demanded that the Palestinians, represented by the PLO, be participants in negotiations that were to deal with their vital national interests, and the Israelis refused to include them.

As events dragged on with no resolution in sight, Sadat, who was anxious for a settlement in order to concentrate needed finances on domestic development within Egypt, decided to take matters into his own hands. In November 1977, he made a dramatic personal visit to Israel. During his speech to the Knesset, the Israeli parliament, he urged direct peace settlements. Sadat's visit, the first public visit by an Arab leader to Israel, altered the psychological atmosphere of distrust and led to direct negotiations between Egyptian and Israeli leaders. These talks intensified during the Camp David meetings in the United

States in the fall of 1978, when President Jimmy Carter directly mediated between Sadat and Israeli Prime Minister Menachem Begin.

The talks culminated with the signing of a peace treaty between Egypt and Israel in the spring of 1979. However, the rest of the Arab world, particularly the Palestinians, opposed the agreement, which implemented the gradual return of the Sinai peninsula to Egypt but which did not address the issue of Palestinian self-determination or the continued Israeli occupation of the West Bank and the Gaza strip. Likewise, there was no agreement on the status of Jerusalem, a city with sacred meaning for Jews, Christians, and Muslims. Israel refused to negotiate with the PLO, which Israelis considered a terrorist organization. On the other side, Arab nations refused to recognize Israel until Palestinian demands for a homeland were fulfilled. The assassination of Sadat in October 1981 by militant Muslims, and President Hosni Mubarak's subsequent attempts to develop good relations with the Arab nations and the Soviet Union, turned the settlement between Egypt and Israel into what has been called a "cold peace."

MODERNISM VERSUS FUNDAMENTALISM: THE IRANIAN REVOLUTION

On the domestic front, the newly created state of Israel concentrated on building new economic, political, and military structures while moving to assimilate large numbers of Jewish immigrants. By the 1970s Israel's multi-party system

In March 1989, President Sadat of Egypt, President Carter of the United States, and Prime Minister Begin of Israel signed a peace treaty ending the war between Egypt and Israel, but the treaty failed to settle the conflict between the Israelis and the Palestinians. (UPI/Bettmann Newsphotos)

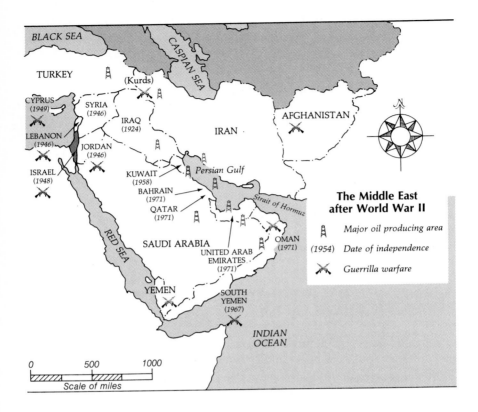

The Middle East after World War II

Major oil producing area

(1954) Date of independence

Guerrilla warfare

had led to increased political divisions and infighting. Golda Meir, a leading Labor politician and prime minister, joked that if four Israelis met in a room they would create five political parties. The elections in the 1980s failed to give either the conservative Likud party or the Labor party a clear-cut majority, and they were therefore forced to create a kind of dual government in which both shared power. By 1988 it was clear that the Israeli population was fairly evenly divided between those who wished to keep the Occupied Territories and those who wished to reach a settlement with the Palestinians and return at least portions of the territory. Economically, the kibbutzim, collective agricultural settlements created by the early Zionist immigrants, became less important as the nation's economy was increasingly geared toward manufacturing in the form of small factories, particularly those producing armaments and small-cut diamonds.

Within the Arab world, Middle Eastern nations after World War II generally sought to create secular nationalist states similar to those found in the West. They often copied plans for agricultural and industrial development from the West and placed great stress on advanced technologies. The continued conflict between Israel and the Arab states, however, forced the nations in the Middle East to expend increasing amounts of their GNP on large armies and defense expenditures.

In spite of political problems and continued warfare, the Arab governments attempted, with various degrees of success, to improve the standard of living of their people. They improved education—for girls as well as boys—

and provided other social welfare projects. By the 1960s and 1970s, when pe- troleum revenues became substantial, economic development surged dramat- ically, particularly in the petroleum-rich nations of Saudi Arabia, Libya, and the sheikdoms of the Arab/Persian Gulf. These areas, which previously had been among the poorest in the Middle East, were able with so-called "petro- dollars" to embark on ambitious programs to build new hospitals, homes, schools, airports, and roads. Often, as in Kuwait, the governments provided free education through the university level, low-cost or free housing, free med- ical care, including dental and eye services, and even low-interest loans for starting new businesses. However, the nations without petroleum, such as Egypt, which had the largest Arab population, remained desperately poor and constantly had to struggle to provide even minimum services for their peoples.

By the 1970s continued economic, political, and social problems had caused many people in the region to question and ultimately to reject the Western-based secular nationalist programs that their governments had insti- tuted. As the governments, often military dictatorships, failed to satisfy the demands of the people, to solve the Arab-Israeli conflict, and to avoid entan- glements with or dependency on the superpowers, many in the Middle East— as elsewhere in the world—began to turn toward religion. Increasingly, mili- tant Muslims argued that the Western-based models, whether from the United States or the Soviet Union, were foreign, artificial imports that did not reflect the realities of Middle Eastern societies. They advocated the institution of Islamic governments ruled not by secular, essentially Western, legal codes, but by the *Sharia,* the Islamic law. The move away from secularism was not lim- ited only to Muslims; the Maronite Christians in Lebanon and some Israelis, particularly many new immigrants from the United States, pushed for increased religious participation in government and in society in general. Thus the ongo- ing trend of tension between the secular and the spiritual was brought into clear focus. This conflict would break out into open warfare in Lebanon and would form the basis of sweeping revolutionary changes in Iran.

The modernizing state of Iran had become one of the cornerstones of U.S. foreign policy after World War II. The pro-United States ruler Mohammad Reza Shah built up a huge military complex using U.S. foreign aid and petroleum revenues that rose sharply during the 1970s. He also implemented the "White Revolution," which was to develop Iran agriculturally and industrially while improving living standards for all Iranians. Economic development seemed rapid, but it was accompanied by growing inflation, corruption in the highest levels of government, an actual decline in some agricultural sectors, and in- creased political repression. Disaffected Iranians from the political Left and from the strongly entrenched Shia clergy joined forces to overthrow the shah in 1979. The shah and his family went into exile, and an Islamic republic was instituted with the Imam (referred to in the West as the Ayatollah) Ruhollah Khomeini acting as the final voice of authority.

The revolutionary government vowed to eradicate the abuses of the old regime, to champion traditional Islamic values, and to improve living condi- tions. The Iranians denounced the United States as "the Great Satan" for its support of the old regime, and demanded that the shah be returned to stand trial for his alleged crimes. After the United States refused, the U.S. embassy in Iran was occupied in November 1979 and the staff taken hostage. For over a year there ensued threats, negotiations, denunciations, financial retaliations in which Iranian assets in the United States were frozen, and one major abortive rescue mission. Finally, in January 1981, a complex agreement was reached and the hostages were released.

The furor over the hostages, particularly in the United States, often obscured the severe domestic problems faced by the new regime. Within Iran, there were open clashes as a number of different parties, particularly from the Left and the Right, sought to gain power. The religious Right emerged victorious, with the *mullahs* (clergy) becoming the dominant political force in Iran. They championed the creation of Islamic governments, not only in Iran, but throughout the vast Islamic world. The religious forces also pushed for the implementation of strict, traditional values in all aspects of society, including traditional dress and codes of behavior for women.

THE IRAN–IRAQ WAR

The Islamic fervor of Iran threatened not only the secular Arab governments but also the Saudi monarchy, which, although it based its legitimacy upon Islam, maintained close relations with the West, particularly the United States. Other Islamic political groups in Egypt, Tunisia, Lebanon, and elsewhere in the Muslim world were encouraged by the successes of the Iranian revolution and occasionally (as in Lebanon) even received direct support from Iran.

After Iran called for Islamic revolution in neighboring Iraq, the Ba'athist government there moved to defuse the Islamic revolution and to settle old grievances by attacking Iran in September 1980. The war dragged on as Iran refused to compromise with the Iraqi regime, or what Iranians called the "Great Satan's Puppet Ba'ath party." By 1988, the eighth year of the war, there had been over a million casualties and the two nations had spent more than $450 billion—more than the United States had expended in all the years of fighting in Vietnam. Attempting to win the war, Iran used waves of men, some as young as fourteen, to clear mine fields, while Iraq used poison gas; the capital cities of both nations were periodically attacked by missiles.

Because of Iran's and Iraq's petroleum reserves, military potential, and strategic location, the Gulf war was of vital interest to both superpowers. Attacks on petroleum tankers in the Persian Gulf by both Iran and Iraq broadened the war and caused international involvement, including the direct military presence of the United States. The region remained one of the most explosive in the world.

By the summer of 1988 the Iranian regime, which was finding it increasingly difficult to secure young volunteers to fight the war and which was suffering under continued Iraqi attacks, had moved to negotiate through the offices of the United

Nations. An uneasy armistice was arranged aimed toward securing a final peace settlement; although there have been periodic flare-ups along the borders, neither Iraq nor Iran had the political or economic will to resume the conflict. Khomeini's death in 1989 left a major political vacuum in Iran, and initially at least, a group of somewhat more pragmatic clergymen came to power.

RECENT SUPERPOWER RIVALRY IN THE MIDDLE EAST

To complicate matters further, the Middle East, with its vast petroleum reserves and strategic location, was of major importance to both the United States and the Soviet Union. Since World War II, both nations periodically became directly and indirectly involved in various regional disputes. For example, in December 1979, the Soviet Union moved into Afghanistan. The collapse of the pro-American Iranian regime and the unstable nature of the revolutionary Iranian government caused both the Soviet Union and the United States to reassess their positions in the region. Since World War II, Afghanistan had remained one of the poorest and least developed nations in the area, one in which numerous political factions constantly attempted to gain power. Following a cycle of coups and countercoups, Babrak Karmal, backed by the Soviet Union, emerged as the leader of Afghanistan.

To protect the dependent Karmal regime, the Soviet Union moved over 80,000 troops into Afghanistan. The presence of foreign troops and political hostility to the Karmal regime led to an armed resistance movement which was dominated by militant Muslims who largely emulated the Iranian revolution and who received military assistance from the United States. As fighting in Afghanistan escalated, over a million refugees fled into Pakistan, which already had severe population problems. Soviet involvement in Afghanistan largely isolated the Soviet Union from much of the Islamic world. The traditional governments in the Middle East, particularly Saudi Arabia and the petroleum-rich sheikdoms of the Persian Gulf, fearing both the spread of the Iranian revolution with its particular brand of radicalism and the Soviet influence in the region, condemned the Soviet actions in Afghanistan. Because the mountainous terrain was ideal for guerrilla warfare, Soviet forces, even with superior military equipment, found it impossible to eradicate the Afghan opposition. Between 1988 and 1989, the Soviets withdrew from Afghanistan, leaving the pro-Soviet Afghan government and the *Mujahideen* (Islamic fighters) to struggle for control over the nation.

Meanwhile, the United States moved to establish closer relations with other Middle Eastern nations. During the Cold War, Turkey had become one of the cornerstones of U.S. military strategy against the Soviet Union. However, the status of the strategic island of Cyprus off the Turkish coast was a major area of disagreement among Turkey, Greece, and the United States. The population of Cyprus was mixed, with a majority of people who were of Greek heritage and a minority of Turkish ancestry. Some Cypriots wanted an independent nation, and others wanted to merge with Greece. Following an attempted Greek coup d'etat and a Turkish armed invasion in 1974, a so-called Green Line manned by U.N. forces divided Cyprus into Greek and Turkish sectors. The U.S. government tended to favor Turkish claims because of the close military alliance, but public opinion in the United States was overwhelmingly pro-Greek. Consequently, Turkey gradually moved further away from the U.S. orbit, and Cyprus remained an area of heightened tension in the eastern Mediterranean.

During the 1970s and 1980s, the United States relied on Egypt, Saudi Arabia, Israel, and U.S. military strength in the Red Sea and the Persian Gulf to counter the Soviet presence. Following Sadat's assassination in 1981, U.S. reliance on Israel and Saudi Arabia increased. The main thrust of U.S. military power in the region was through the Rapid Deployment Force, whereby armed units could be moved into the area. However, although the Saudis pressured for increased armaments (including sophisticated reconnaissance planes such as the AWACs), most nations in the Middle East were reluctant to accept the permanent stationing of U.S. forces on their territories. Nonetheless, the United States created a substantial informal military presence in Egypt and Saudi Arabia. The United States also concentrated on extending its military links with nations around the Persian Gulf. For the first time in its history, the United States established a permanent naval force in the Indian Ocean, with a new naval base at Diego Garcia; the United States also developed facilities in Somalia. Although the Soviets built up bases in South Yemen, Ethiopia, and the Indian Ocean, on balance, the United States, Great Britain, and France maintained military superiority in the region.

CHAOS IN LEBANON

Meanwhile, Lebanon became a battleground for both domestic and regional disputes. After 1970, Palestinian border raids from Lebanon into Israel increased, and the Israelis retaliated with ground and air strikes, including the bombing of Lebanese villages. The continued domestic tensions and border violence resulted in a protracted and bloody civil war that, in effect, divided Lebanon into several distinct sections. The Lebanese civil war, which continued intermittently after 1975, was partially caused by communal differences between Muslims and Christians. It was also brought about by political splits between the Left and Right; by the presence of the Palestinians in the nation; by outside interference by Israel, Syria, and other surrounding Arab nations; and by interventions by Western powers. Indeed, Lebanon became a surrogate battleground for wider conflicts. The war resulted in the Syrian occupation of parts of Lebanon, while the United Nations stationed troops along the border with Israel. Using southern Lebanon as a base, Palestinians launched attacks on Israel, which responded in turn by raiding southern Lebanon in an attempt to eradicate Palestinian power. Hundreds of Lebanese and Palestinians died. None of these measures stopped the fighting or solved the problems.

In the early 1980s, armed confrontations continued in southern Lebanon, where Palestinian and leftist Lebanese forces clashed with the Israelis and the Israeli-supported enclave in southern Lebanon. Clashes among the various forces also continued in Beirut. Mediation efforts by the United States, Saudi Arabia, and other nations from 1975 to 1981 failed to remedy the cycle of violence that turned Beirut, once one of the loveliest cities in the Middle East, into the scene of bombings, random assassinations, and extensive destruction.

In June 1982, Israel launched a full-scale invasion of Lebanon with the primary intention of destroying the PLO military presence there. In the ensuing war, Israel bombarded Lebanese cities by land, sea, and air. Thousands of people were killed, injured, and made homeless. After bloody combat with the Palestinians and their Lebanese allies, the Israelis and their Lebanese Christian allies besieged West Beirut. Following weeks of protracted Israeli bombings of the city, the PLO fighters and leaders were evacuated under the auspices of international peace-keeping forces. Bashir Gemayel, son of one of the leading rightist Lebanese Christians and leader of the largest private militia, was elected president of the war-torn nation. His assassination in September led Christian militiamen to massacre hundreds of Palestinians in Sabra and Shatila, the large Palestinian refugee camps in West Beirut under Israeli control.

After 1982, as Israeli and Syrian forces remained in occupation of the southern and eastern sections of the small nation, Lebanese religious and political militias continued to fight among themselves. International peace-keeping forces, including U.S. marines, attempted to control the situation. However, as the United States was gradually drawn into the conflict, U.S. installations and personnel became targets. In the spring of 1983, the U.S. embassy in Beirut was bombed by pro-Iranian forces, and in October over 200 marines were killed by truck-bombs.

As the "peace-keeping" forces had clearly failed, they ultimately withdrew. The brutal Lebanese civil strife continued, with all Westerners increasingly becoming targets for kidnappings, particularly by the Iranian-backed Hizbollah (Party of God) groups. Although the Israelis finally withdrew from much of southern Lebanon, they continued to occupy a ten-mile so-called "security zone" in Lebanon; likewise, the Syrians continued to maintain a large military force in Lebanon. Owing to threats and violence, the parliament was unable to meet to elect a new president in 1988, and Lebanon moved increasing toward a de facto partition, with separate Muslim and Christian governments. It appeared that until solutions for the issue of Palestinian national self-determination and a settlement of the wider Arab-Israeli conflict were devised, there was little likelihood of a resolution to the warfare in Lebanon, which constantly threatened to expand into a full-scale Middle East war. Lebanon also demonstrated the continued problems inherent in its confessional system, in which a citizen's religious affiliation forms the basis of national identity and participation in political, social, and economic institutions.

ISRAELIS AND PALESTINIANS

The 1982 war was a severe blow to the Palestinian liberation movement, but it also caused serious political divisions within Israel. The ultimate status of the West Bank and the Gaza strip, which had remained under Israeli occupation since the 1967 war, became the focal point of the controversy. Israelis were widely divided on the issue. The Likud, the conservative party of the Right, generally aimed to keep all of the Occupied Territories; the Labor party generally advocated a "land for peace" solution, in which some of the territories would be traded for a settlement of the ongoing conflict with the Palestinians. However, the Palestinians demanded that the PLO be their sole representative, and the Israeli government firmly refused to deal with the PLO. Meanwhile, the number of Israeli settlements in the Occupied Territories continued to increase, and the 1.4 million Palestinians in the Occupied Territories became increasingly disenchanted with Israeli military control. After intermittent confrontations, the conflict broke out in a full-scale uprising (*Intifadah*) in December 1987. Palestinians, particularly the young people, demonstrated, went out on strike, boycotted Israeli goods and services, and threw stones. The Israeli army retaliated with an "Iron Fist" policy, in an attempt to repress the uprising. By 1989, over 500 Palestinians and several dozen Israelis had been killed, and the conflict showed no signs of abating. The uprising caused political debates within Israel and among Jewish-Americans over possible solutions. In a sweeping move, the PLO in 1988 declared the independence of Palestine (the West Bank and Gaza), recognized the existence of Israel, and called for a negotiated settlement of the conflict. Dozens of nations recognized the new Palestinian state and lauded the move toward peace, and the United States finally agreed to protracted negotiations with the PLO. However, Israel intensified its repression over the Palestinians in the Occupied Territories, a move that guaranteed the continuation of the *Intifadah*. Consequently, it appeared certain that the conflict would continue until the two major parties—the Israelis and Palestinians—were able to reach a compromise or some negotiated settlement.

SUMMARY

Regional differences, territorial disputes, and domestic problems made the Middle East one of the most volatile regions in the world. Like most of the Third World, the Middle East was an area of rapid change and uncertainty. The political fights between leftists and conservative forces within Middle Eastern nations and among the various governments of the region led to upheavals. The Arab-Israeli conflict and the failure to achieve a solution to Palestinian demands for self-determination also contributed to violence in the region. Lebanon became the surrogate battleground for many of these disputes. The emergence of various militant religious groups radically altered the nature of many Middle

Eastern governments and societies; in addition, both the superpowers had problems dealing with the new independent and dynamic nations.

Regional problems were further complicated by the geopolitical interests of the United States and the Soviet Union. Because of their strategic locations and their regional position as the world's largest producers of petroleum, Middle Eastern nations were of vital concern not only to the superpowers but also to all industrialized nations.

SUGGESTED SOURCES

Aroian, Lois A., and Richard P. Mitchell, *The Modern Middle East and North Africa* (1984). A concise and up-to-date survey.

Awwad, Tawfiq Yusuf, *Death in Beirut* (1978). A novel tracing the political and religious divisions of Lebanese society before the civil war.*

Fernea, Elizabeth Warnock, ed., *Women and the Family in the Middle East: New Voices of Change* (1985). Collection of firsthand accounts including poems and short stories by Middle Eastern women.*

Halliday, Fred, *Iran: Dictatorship and Development* (1979). An in-depth analysis of Iran before the 1979 revolution.*

Hiro, Dilip, *Islamic Fundamentalism* (1988). Incisive account of role of Islam in culture and politics.*

Khouri, Fred, *The Arab-Israeli Dilemma,* 3rd ed. (1985). A factual narrative of complex conflict.*

Mosley, Leonard, *Power Play: Petroleum in the Middle East* (1973). Focuses on personalities involved in the development of the petroleum industry in the Middle East.*

Neff, Donald, *Warriors at Suez* (1981) and *Warriors for Jerusalem* (1984). Highly entertaining yet informative descriptions of personalities behind the 1956 and 1967 wars.

Sadat, Anwar, *In Search of Identity, An Autobiography* (1979). The Egyptian leader describes his political life and beliefs.*

*Paperback available.

27

Détente and the New Europe

Following the Berlin crisis of 1961 and the Cuban missile crisis of 1962, the superpowers pulled back from confrontation, and there was a movement toward détente (a lessening of tensions) in the Cold War. Beginning in the 1960s, Western European nations, especially France, became less dependent on the United States. Eastern European nations, thanks in part to the Sino-Soviet split, were able to achieve a little more autonomy than the Soviet Union had previously allowed. During the 1970s, U.S. diplomatic initiatives toward Communist China further contributed to transforming the bipolar U.S.-Soviet global rivalry into a more multipolar global balance of power. Events in Czechoslovakia in 1968 and Poland in 1981, however, indicated that the Soviet Union was still determined to keep Eastern European countries firmly within its orbit. In the late 1970s and early 1980s, tensions between the superpowers again intensified before once more starting to improve beginning in 1985.

THE DAWN OF DÉTENTE

The Cuban missile crisis had been frightening, and in its aftermath many world leaders became interested in lessening tensions and thus reducing the chances of nuclear war. In 1963, the major atomic powers, joined by over one hundred nations, signed the Nuclear Test Ban Treaty, which prohibited testing in outer space, in the atmosphere, and underwater. France and the People's Republic of China refused to sign; the French wished to do more testing to catch up with the advanced nuclear powers, and the Chinese needed tests to complete the development of their first atomic bomb. In 1964, the People's Republic exploded a bomb and became a new and potentially powerful member of the atomic club.

The Chinese bomb spurred international action to deal with the growing threat of nuclear proliferation. The established atomic powers took the position that the world would be safer if no more nations created their own atomic bombs. The United States, the Soviet Union, and Great Britain prepared a draft treaty for the United Nations in which the signatories agreed not to develop atomic weapons. Eventually, ninety-eight nations signed the Nuclear Non-Pro-

396

liferation Treaty. Again, France and China refused to sign; India, Pakistan, Israel, and other nations undertaking nuclear weapons research also refused.

Meanwhile, the United States and the Soviet Union proceeded with a number of bilateral agreements. Taking a lesson from the Cuban missile crisis, they agreed to install a "hot line," a direct personal telephone connection between the U.S. president and the Soviet premier that might defuse a developing crisis. A new trading era began between the two nations when the United States agreed in 1963 to sell large quantities of wheat to the Soviet Union at a time of shortage. Soon the United States was regularly selling a wide variety of products to the Soviet Union. Tourism was encouraged, and ordinary U.S. citizens found themselves looking at Lenin's Tomb in Moscow or visiting the Hermitage Museum in Leningrad, while Soviet officials viewed New York from the Empire State Building or visited the Lincoln Memorial. There were also cultural exchanges, as the Bolshoi Ballet and Louis Armstrong crossed the Atlantic to perform.

THE COMMON MARKET AND DE GAULLE

In 1967, the European Economic Community (EEC or Common Market), founded in 1957, joined with the European Coal and Steel Community and the European Atomic Energy Community to form the European Communities (EC), later simplified to the European Community. In 1968, the EEC, which continued to exist within the EC, attained its goal of ending tariffs between member nations (France, West Germany, Italy, Belgium, the Netherlands, and Luxemburg). Some trade barriers, however, remained, as a result of factors such as differing product standards and government contracts. In 1973, Great Britain, Ireland, and Denmark became members of the EC; Greece (1981), Spain (1986), and Portugal (1986) joined later. As the organization grew, its organs, including a Council of Ministers and a European Parliament, also increased in significance.

Members of the EC and other European nations continued their postwar economic recovery, and during the 1960s became serious economic rivals to the United States. West Germany, especially, impressed the world by its strong postwar economic performance. The U.S. government became concerned that EC tariffs on U.S. goods entering EC nations would be undersold by comparable goods from nations trading within the EC. Thus the United States bargained strenuously to reduce tariffs to make its goods more competitive, but U.S. families nevertheless purchased an increasing number of European automobiles, television sets, and other products. Coupled with U.S. military expenditures in Europe, this helped to bring about a U.S. balance-of-payments deficit in Europe's favor that increased throughout the 1960s. The devaluation of U.S. currency in 1971 and 1973 against European currencies clearly indicated that the U.S. dollar no longer dominated Europe as it once had.

If the European Community was one symbol of growing European independence, General Charles de Gaulle personified another: the desire to end European political dependence on the United States. He came to power in 1958, after the French Fourth Republic had produced twenty-seven governments in thirteen years. In the midst of a governmental crisis revolving around Algeria, de Gaulle was invited by the French Assembly to rule while a new constitution was drawn up. The new constitution provided for much stronger executive powers than in the past. It created a president elected for a seven-year term, who appointed the prime minister; the president was given other powers that clearly made him the dominant figure in the government. De Gaulle was elected to the post in 1958 and remained the president of France until he resigned in 1969.

De Gaulle was an aloof and haughty figure—he once said: "When I want to know what France thinks, I ask myself." Roosevelt had stated that de Gaulle imagined himself another Joan of Arc. A nationalist in every inch of his imposing frame, he was continually concerned with the greatness and prestige of France. One of his first priorities was resolving the costly Algerian war, and by 1962 he had finally persuaded the French to acquiesce in Algerian independence. Another major step toward his goal of bolstering French prestige was to extricate France from the embrace of the United States. De Gaulle began to remove French troops from the U.S.-dominated North Atlantic Treaty Organi-

General Charles de Gaulle in French Africa shortly before being elected president of France in 1958. (UPI/Bettmann Newsphotos)

zation (NATO) as early as 1959, and by 1967 he not only had withdrawn all French forces from NATO, but also had requested all NATO forces to leave French soil. Since the United States would not allow the French to control U.S. nuclear weapons, de Gaulle no longer allowed such weapons in France. From the beginning of his presidency, de Gaulle encouraged France to develop its own atomic capability, and in 1960 France tested its first atomic bomb.

De Gaulle envisioned France as the head of a Third Force that would stand between the United States and the Soviet Union. He hoped that most Western European nations would follow his lead; in part, that meant a leading role for France in the Common Market. During the 1960s, he blocked British entry into the organization because he feared the rivalry of Great Britain and its close ties with the United States. He also tried to improve relations with the Soviet Union and the Eastern European nations, recognized the People's Republic of China, and traveled to such areas as Latin America and Canada in an effort to exercise global statesmanship. Although France did not gain the leading role he envisioned, de Gaulle did make a major contribution to the growing sense of independence in Europe.

In May 1968, students at several campuses of the University of Paris openly revolted against authorities, the police, and the French government. The student revolt in Paris was matched by student demonstrations in the United States, Great Britain, Italy, West Germany, and other nations during the late 1960s. Causes for Western student unrest varied: the boredom bred by an affluent, technological civilization; the impact of New Left ideologies influenced by Mao Zedong and Castro; the opposition to the Vietnam War; local student grievances; and a whole host of others. In Paris, the students were soon joined by leftist political leaders and by a large number of workers who went on strike. De Gaulle's regime was at first threatened with chaos, but wage concessions to workers, promises of university reforms, and support from French citizens opposed to the unrest helped him restore order. Nevertheless, the events were a blow to his prestige; and when the nation refused to approve an administrative reorganization referendum in 1969, de Gaulle resigned.

THE SOVIET UNION: BREZHNEV TO CHERNENKO

In October 1964, Nikita Khrushchev's colleagues ousted him from power. He was not imprisoned or executed, but he was forced into retirement and kept under close supervision until he died in 1971. The other Soviet leaders forced Khrushchev to retire for a number of reasons: a poor harvest in 1963, along with a sluggish economy; foreign policy failures, including the Cuban missile crisis and a growing split with China; an increasingly abrasive, authoritarian, and incautious political style; and a backlash against his attack on Stalin and Stalinists. Leonid Brezhnev replaced Khrushchev in the key position of first secretary of the Communist party, while Alexei Kosygin took over as premier.

After 1964, Brezhnev was the dominant figure in Soviet politics. Like Khrushchev, he was not a dictator but the most prominent of a small group of political leaders in a one-party state. Like most of them, Brezhnev had a technical background and a long history of party work.

During the Brezhnev era, the Soviet Union in some areas continued to follow the path marked out by Khrushchev. The government gradually improved the living standard of the average Soviet citizen throughout most of the late 1960s and 1970s, but military spending remained the top priority. The government continued to develop the nation's rich resources in petroleum, gas, and minerals at a slow but steady pace. On the other hand, agriculture remained the most troubled area of the Soviet economy. Crop failures in 1972 and 1975 forced the Soviet government to make large grain purchases from the United States. From 1979 through 1982, the U.S.S.R. experienced four poor harvests in succession, and Soviet economic growth slowed considerably. Despite some experiments in economic liberalization, the party and government kept tight control over the national economy.

A major difference between the two eras was that Brezhnev put an end to Khrushchev's "de-Stalinization" campaign. Khrushchev's overall record on literature and intellectual life was considerably more liberal than Stalin's had been, and once writers experienced this thaw, the party discovered it was difficult to contain them. Nevertheless, in 1966, Brezhnev and his colleagues apparently decided matters had gone far enough: Andrei Siniavsky and Yuli Daniel were tried for "anti-Soviet propaganda," although their only crime had been to send literature to the West for publication. They were sentenced to seven and five years respectively in Soviet labor camps.

During the 1970s, the dissident movement continued despite government efforts to repress it. It was fueled by opposition to the Siniavsky-Daniel and other trials and by realistic fears of increased official sympathy for the Stalinist past. Underground literature and the number of manuscripts sent abroad increased. The underground *Chronicle of Current Events,* published regularly from 1968 to 1972 and sporadically thereafter, reflected the opposition of scattered intellectuals, religious groups, and ethnic minorities. While the party continued to sentence dissidents to prison, labor camps, and mental institutions, it also allowed or forced some of the more prominent ones to leave the U.S.S.R., as Alexander Solzhenitsyn did in 1974. By the early 1980s there were few active, free dissidents of stature left.

Meanwhile, the vitality of the aging Soviet leadership was also declining. Brezhnev himself suffered a stroke in 1976 and, in the words of the Russian historian Roy Medvedev, "he gradually found it more and more difficult to carry out the most simple protocol functions and could no longer understand what was going on around him." He finally died in 1982. Between late 1982 and early 1985, the party had two more leaders whose health was poor and who soon died in office: Yuri Andropov and Konstantin Chernenko. After Chernenko's death, the Communist leadership finally turned to a younger man and made Mikhail Gorbachev, age fifty-four, head of the party.

EASTERN EUROPE IN THE 1960s

If de Gaulle and some other Europeans resented early postwar U.S. domination of Western Europe, Eastern Europeans were even more hostile to Soviet hegemony over them, and sought ways to reduce it. The Sino-Soviet split of the early 1960s encouraged this desire; but only small Albania, which sided with China, was able to leave the Soviet orbit. While Rumania remained a Soviet ally—and politically oppressive—its government insisted on a measure of independence in economic and foreign policies. In 1963, when COMECON attempted to hamper Rumanian industrial advancement, Rumania refused to cooperate. In its foreign relations, Rumania was on better terms with China and Israel than was the Soviet Union; on occasion it also voted differently at the United Nations.

Some Eastern European nations also pursued policies that were more liberal than those in the U.S.S.R. In Hungary, the János Kádár regime improved economic conditions by relaxing centralized economic planning and allowing more local initiative. The government also permitted more personal freedom; in 1964, for example, more than 100,000 Hungarians were allowed to visit Western nations. In Poland, most of the farmland, unlike that in the Soviet Union, remained in private hands. Poland and Rumania, as well as Hungary, also allowed more religious freedom.

There were, however, limits to how much autonomy the Soviet Union would allow among its satellites, and in 1968 Czechoslovakia passed those limits. During the mid-1960s, discontent spread in Czechoslovakia under the Stalinist Antonin Novotný. In December 1967-January 1968, he was replaced by Alexander Dubček as first secretary of the Czechoslovak Communist party. Soon afterward, encouraged by public opinion, Dubček and his colleagues began to carry out a policy of liberalization. They greatly reduced censorship, recognized civil liberties, rehabilitated victims of past party injustices, and allowed autonomous political groupings to emerge. Relations with Western nations grew warmer, and Dubček displayed a desire to place Soviet-Czechoslovakian ties on a more equal footing.

Soviet leaders became increasingly alarmed about the liberalization policies and feared that they might spread like a virus to other Eastern European nations. Dissent in the Soviet Union, already a problem for the regime, might also be encouraged if the Czechoslovakians were allowed such freedoms. In addition, Czechoslovakia's strategic position between the U.S.S.R. and West Germany undoubtedly magnified Soviet fears. The Soviet Union began to pressure the Czechoslovakian leaders to rescind their reforms, but they refused to give way. On August 21, 1968, Soviet, East German, Polish, Hungarian, and Bulgarian troops invaded Czechoslovakia. Believing it would be suicidal to offer armed resistance, the nation's leaders and people simply offered a sullen and passive noncooperation. Dubček was soon forced out of office, and Gustav Husák became head of the party. The "Prague Spring" of 1968 and the accompanying hopes for a more humane socialism were dead.

Prague, Czechoslovakia, 1968: Soviet tanks and troops suppress the liberal Communist regime of Alexander Dubček. (Keystone Press Agency)

Following the invasion, Husák gradually restored Czechoslovakia to the status of a "police state" on which the Soviet Union could rely, and Soviet leaders elaborated their justification for interference—Western observers would label it the "Brezhnev Doctrine." It stated that "every Communist party is responsible not only to its own people but also to all the socialist countries," and that "the sovereignty of individual socialist countries cannot be counterposed to the interests of world socialism."

THE FLOWERING OF INTERNATIONAL DÉTENTE

Despite the strained feelings stimulated by the Vietnam War and the 1968 invasion of Czechoslovakia, the "spirit of détente" was well under way when Richard Nixon became president of the United States in 1969. Nixon had been a hard-line anti-Communist "Cold Warrior" in the 1940s and 1950s, but he had now shifted his position and intended to make his mark in history by easing Cold War tensions. In particular, he expected to improve relationships with both the Soviet Union and China. These two nations had become antagonists, and Nixon hoped to utilize their fears of one another, and the fear of each that the other would warm up to the United States, to improve U.S. relations with both. To carry out his initiatives, Nixon relied on the diplomatic skills of the dynamic Henry Kissinger, who sought to replace the Cold War with a more complex multipolar balance of power.

The core of the tension between the United States and the Soviet Union lay in the nuclear arms race, and both nations were ready to consider means to slow it down. The Soviet Union had, at great cost to its economy, achieved a rough parity with the United States in tonnage of deliverable atomic destruction, but was increasingly distracted by its split with China. The United States was staggering under the economic burden of the Vietnam War, and its society was distracted by social unrest. In addition, both nations were faced with the costs of implementing two major new weapons systems now deemed necessary to keep abreast or ahead in the arms race. One was the antiballistic missile (ABM), a defensive missile designed to destroy incoming missiles. The special attraction and also danger of this weapon was that the first nation that believed itself fully protected by its ABMs would be tempted to launch a successful attack on its less well-defended adversary. To increase the sophistication of the offense against the ABM, military technicians had created another weapons system, the multiple independently targeted reentry vehicle (MIRV). The MIRV consisted of several warheads, each programmed to hit a different target, all mounted on a single rocket.

In 1969, Nixon and Brezhnev agreed to arms limitation talks. By 1972 the basic agreement had been hammered out, and Nixon traveled to Moscow to sign the Strategic Arms Limitation Treaty (SALT). The treaty suspended the building of ICBMs, capped the number of missile-firing submarines that could be employed, and limited the deployment of ABMs. Even with these limitations, both nations remained capable of "overkill"; that is, destroying their opponent many times over. The spirit of accord was enhanced in 1973 when Brezhnev visited Washington; some commentators claimed that the Cold War was over. Meanwhile, a number of bilateral and multilateral agreements were hammered out, including a pact not to deploy nuclear weapons on the ocean floor and one not to manufacture bacteriological weapons. At Vladivostok in Soviet Siberia in 1974, President Gerald Ford and party leader Brezhnev signed a preliminary agreement designed to extend strategic arms limitations into the 1980s. The same year, the two nations also agreed not to conduct underground nuclear tests of more than 150 kilotons.

The series of agreements between the United States and the Soviet Union were important for world peace, but it was the sudden rapprochement between the United States and China in 1971–72 that startled and excited the world. Since 1950, there had been a "bamboo curtain" between the United States and China; they had no diplomatic, economic, or cultural relations, and the two governments constantly attacked each other in public statements. The Chinese had conducted a relentless propaganda campaign against "the paper tiger of American imperialism," while the U.S. government encouraged anti-"Red China" attitudes among Americans. Both nations, however, had reasons to change their policies. China feared the Soviet Union and also feared that improved U.S.-Soviet relations would isolate China and reduce its influence. China was also worried that if the United States reduced its involvement in Asia, the vacuum would be filled by Japan and the Soviet Union. All these factors crystallized at a time when China was emerging from the turmoil of the Cultural Revolution (see Chapter 29). At the same time, the United States was extracting itself from a disastrous war in Indochina, attempting to negotiate a settlement on some basic issues with the Soviet Union, and rethinking some of its belief that an expansionist China must be "contained."

Late in 1969, secret negotiations began toward the "normalization" of Sino-U.S. relations. In 1971, the United States refrained from employing its veto while the United Nations expelled Taiwan and seated the People's Republic in the General Assembly and in China's permanent seat in the Security Council. In 1972, amid mixed feelings both at home and around the world, Nixon traveled to Beijing, where he had a polite but restrained welcome. Nixon met briefly with Mao and participated in discussions with other Chinese leaders. At the Great Hall of the People, Nixon and his hosts banqueted, toasted one another with potent mao tai cocktails, and before departing exchanged gifts— Nixon received two giant pandas, Hsing-Hsing and Ling-Ling. The Americans and Chinese did not come to any major agreements, being satisfied at that time to air their differences. The final communiqué ambiguously noted that "the United States acknowledges that all Chinese on either side of the Taiwan Straits maintain there is but one China and that Taiwan is part of China." Shortly thereafter, the two nations agreed to begin cultural and economic contacts to open China to U.S. tourists and to open "liaison offices" (embassies in all but name) in each other's capitals. The momentum established by the Sino-U.S. rapprochement quickly extended to China's relations with Japan, and later that same year Japan recognized the Communist government of China and established normal diplomatic relations.

After 1972, the main obstacle to complete normalization between the United States and China continued to be China's insistence that the United States withdraw its recognition of Taiwan and abrogate its mutual defense pact with that island's government. The United States feared that China would attack Taiwan if the United States withdrew its pledge of military support. In 1978, the administration of President Carter, apparently receiving tacit assurances that China would not attack Taiwan, agreed to China's two principal conditions. On January 1, 1979, the two nations opened their embassies in Beijing and Washington. Normalization was now complete, although the United States and China remained wary of each other. The United States continued to retain economic and cultural ties with Taiwan. In 1984, President Reagan visited China. As a result, the United States increased its technical aid and agreed to sell China certain weapons.

The spirit of détente in the 1970s also extended to settling lingering disputes in Europe, most of them centering on Germany and some of them going back to World War II. Much of the credit for this, and a Nobel Peace Prize, went to Willy Brandt, head of the Social Democratic party and since 1969 the chancellor of West Germany. Brandt urged the creation of an Ostpolitik, "a hand offered to the East." In 1972, the two German nations formally recognized each other. The United States recognized East Germany and the Soviet Union pledged not to block access to Berlin. That year, both Germanies were admitted to the United Nations. At Helsinki in 1975, the process of détente expanded to Europe as a whole. In addition to affirming respect for human rights, thirty-three European nations plus the United States and Canada agreed in effect that the existing boundaries in Europe, including the German-Polish border, were "inviolable." The results of World War II had been ratified at last.

During the 1970s, despite the easing of political tensions and despite a series of agreements on nuclear testing and proliferation and on strategic arms limitations, the arms race expanded. Nuclear powers continued to test underground frequently, and China still tested above ground. Even though the 1972 SALT treaty limited the number of nuclear weapons, the Soviet Union and the United States continued to improve their nuclear weapons in speed, range, accuracy, and, above all, power. By 1978 the two nations were in a state of approximate nuclear parity. They possessed over 40,000 strategic nuclear warheads with a total destructive force equal to 1.5 million bombs of the magnitude that fell on Hiroshima. Experts pronounced the arms race at the stage of Mutually Assured Destruction—MAD.

In addition to the potential for nuclear devastation from the "limited" bombs and missiles, military scientists had developed or were developing weapons not limited by treaty. Such weapons included the low-flying "cruise" missiles that could escape radar detection; the neutron bomb, which killed people with little damage to property; laser beams, the "ray gun" of science fiction now made reality; and space satellites and platforms that could fire missiles and lasers.

WESTERN EUROPE: 1970–1988

Western Europe entered the 1970s after several decades of economic growth. Only Great Britain continued to have serious economic problems; a sluggish economic growth rate, balance-of-payments deficits, labor unrest, and inflation all troubled the Labour party government that had taken over from the Conservatives in 1964 and continued in power until 1970. Nevertheless, even in Great Britain, the standard of living of most individuals continued to improve.

In 1974 and 1975, however, increased food and petroleum prices and an economic recession temporarily shook Western European nations used to prosperity. West Germany's inflation rate had been under 2 percent in 1969, but by 1974 had risen to 7 percent. Great Britain's was a little under 6 percent in 1969, but by 1975 it was close to 25 percent. Italy's inflation and unemployment rates in 1974 were among Europe's highest. It was perhaps no accident that the men chosen to head the French and West German governments in 1974, Valery Giscard d'Estaing and Helmut Schmidt, had both been finance or economics ministers in previous governments. In Great Britain, after four years out of power, Labour party chief Harold Wilson, an economist by training, was also voted back into office in 1974.

Paradox: During the 1970s, the superpowers pursued a policy of détente while at the same time continuing their post-World War II arms race. Above, Soviet President Brezhnev plants one of his trademark kisses on the cheek of U.S. President Carter at the 1979 SALT II conference in Vienna; below, Soviet missiles on parade through Moscow. (AP/Wide World Photos)

By the late 1970s Western European nations gradually had begun to re-cover from the economic shock of the earlier part of the decade. By 1978 the inflation rate in Great Britain had fallen to about 9 percent and in West Germany to 2 percent. Although the British continued to be plagued by longstanding eco-nomic problems, they increased production of North Sea petroleum, reducing dependence on foreign sources. By 1981 several Western European nations were listed among the wealthiest in the world. Switzerland, Sweden, Denmark, West Germany, Norway, and Belgium all had a higher per capita GNP than the United States; the Netherlands and France were not far behind. During the early 1980s, however, the global recession brought to Western Europe its highest unemployment since World War II. Economic growth increased from 1984 through 1988, with 1988 registering the most growth in over a decade. But unemployment remained high, hovering around 11 percent in the Common Market nations during the same five-year period.

Despite Europe's economic ups and downs, European politics remained fairly stable, with moderately conservative and moderately socialist parties being the most dominant. Even Italy's frequent changes of government—averaging slightly over one a year in the postwar decades—became so common that they seemed almost routine. In Portugal and Spain, where right-wing governments had long ruled, the people restored democracy in 1975–77 and maintained it with less difficulty than many predicted.

By 1988 Western European Communist political parties were on the decline. Some Europeans thought communism less relevant in a Europe of high technology and consumerism and a smaller percentage of blue-collar workers. A more moderate socialism, however, continued to appeal to many voters, especially in Scandinavia and in southern Europe (Greece, Spain, and Portugal), where socialist governments predominated. These governments, however, increasingly tended to be pragmatic and sympathetic to business growth. The most important European socialist was French president Francois Mitterrand, elected in 1981 and reelected to another seven-year term in 1988.

Two of Europe's other dominant political figures during the 1980s were the Christian Democrat (moderately conservative) Helmut Kohl, who replaced the Social Democrat (moderately socialist) Helmut Schmidt as West Germany's chancellor in 1982, and Margaret Thatcher, who became prime minister of Great Britain in 1979 and who by 1988 had been in power longer than any British prime minister of the century. Sometimes compared to President Reagan because of her conservatism, she pursued a policy (privatization) aimed at reducing Britain's welfare state and turning more and more of its functions over to free enterprise. Her supporters claimed that she revived the British economy, and her opponents charged that she benefited the rich at the expense of the poor.

Regardless of differing political views, however, conservatives like Thatcher and socialists like Mitterrand all worked in the 1980s to augment European prosperity. Toward that aim, the nations of the European Economic Community agreed in 1987 to go beyond eliminating tariffs between them and to try by 1992 to eliminate a variety of other financial, commercial, and customs barriers that hampered the free flow of goods within the community. If successful, the plan would open up a market of over 300 million consumers for unfettered trade.

Although most Western Europeans seemed content with their governments, all was not calm in the political waters. Radical leftist terrorists plagued

Germany and Italy, in particular, by sporadically staging bombings, kidnappings, and assassinations. In 1981, Pope John Paul II was wounded by a Turkish terrorist with apparent connections to the Bulgarian secret police. Basque separatists in Spain also committed acts of violence in their campaigns for independence, as did members of the radical Irish Republican Army (IRA), which struggled to separate Northern Ireland from the United Kingdom and join it to the Irish Republic. In 1981, several IRA prisoners gained wide attention as they starved themselves to death as a protest to British policy in Northern Ireland.

In the 1980s, ethnic and racial differences also increased in some European nations where they had previously been less of a problem. By 1988 almost a million blacks and Asians were living in London, and incidents of racial conflict were becoming more common. The numbers of Africans and Asians living in France also increased. In the 1988 presidential contest in France, right-wing candidate Jean-Marie Le Pen stirred racist fears by blaming many of his nation's problems, such as crime and unemployment, on these minorities.

EASTERN EUROPE: 1970–1985

In the 1970s and early 1980s, Eastern European nations continued efforts to be something more than mere puppets of the U.S.S.R. Some, such as Hungary, experimented with economic reorganization, and in general, Eastern European governments made greater attempts to appease their citizens through improving living standards than did the Soviet Union. While adequate housing remained scarce, personal incomes rose, and television sets, washing machines, and refrigerators became much more common. By the beginning of the 1980s, one family out of four in Hungary and two out of five in East Germany owned an automobile. Travel to other nations, primarily within the Eastern bloc, continued to increase significantly. The process of urbanization and industrialization also proceeded at a rapid pace. By 1980 only Albania and Yugoslavia were more rural than urban. East Germany and Czechoslovakia had a higher percentage of urban population than did the Soviet Union. Improved living standards, however, were in large part dependent on stable prices, large loans from the West, and favorable trade relations with the U.S.S.R., which, for example, furnished energy and raw materials below world prices. The increased prosperity of the 1970s—growth was especially strong in the first half of the decade—was thus based on an unstable foundation.

The fragile economic and political status of Eastern Europe became especially evident in the early 1980s during the development of an extended crisis in Poland. In 1980, the Polish government attempted to increase meat prices, and disturbances broke out. Earlier, in 1970 and 1976, price increases had also led to demonstrations. This time, however, unrest was so intense that the government was forced to recognize Solidarity, a powerful new independent labor union. The government agreed to salary increases and made concessions regarding political prisoners, censorship, additional religious access to the mass media, and a number of other worker demands. Communist party leader Gierek was replaced by Stanislaw Kania, and for the next year liberalization proceeded at a rapid pace, as Solidarity, under the leadership of Lech Walesa, prodded the government. The Catholic Church, headed by the Polish Pope John Paul II, was sympathetic to the union and supported the push for liberalization.

As the Poles gained more freedom, Soviet leaders became increasingly alarmed and resorted to a variety of measures to express their displeasure. In an effort to appease Soviet leaders and to bolster the declining prestige of the party, the Central Committee of the Polish Communist party in October 1981 replaced Kania as first secretary and put in his place General Wojciech Jaruzelski. In December 1981, Jaruzelski, without warning, declared a state of national emergency, established martial law, and set up a Military Council of National Salvation to run the nation. Armored units appeared in the streets of Warsaw and other cities. Solidarity leaders were arrested and union activities suspended. A few months later, the Polish government increased food prices.

Alarmed by Poland's precarious economic position and upset by the crackdown on Solidarity, Western governments became either hostile to or cautious about further credit. Already worried about rising worldwide indebtedness, Western governments became increasingly concerned about the large debts of Eastern European nations. By early 1982 the six Soviet satellites owed over $50 billion to Western governments and banks. At about the same time, the Soviet Union, beset by its own economic problems and debts to the West, began to reduce its energy deliveries to Eastern Europe and to charge prices more in line with world prices. As a result of these factors, as well as a global recession, the rate of increase in living standards leveled off sharply in the early 1980s; in some cases, living standards even declined. While the Soviet Union encouraged its satellites to meet the situation by becoming less dependent on the West, some Eastern bloc leaders appeared to believe that the best solution was more economic reform and better relations with the West. By late 1982 the Polish government had freed most of those who had been arrested in December 1981 and had lifted many of the restrictions imposed at that time. Partly as a consequence of these actions, Western governments and banks agreed to the rescheduling of Polish debts.

THE FADING OF DÉTENTE

By the late 1970s earlier optimism that the Cold War was over had begun to fade. President Carter's emphasis on human rights—he once called it "the soul of our foreign policy"—and his sympathy for Soviet dissidents irritated the Soviet leadership. The continued Soviet military build-up of the 1970s alarmed some U.S. political leaders, and the movement toward international accords lost momentum rapidly, as Cold War discord flared in the Middle East, Africa, and Latin America. The movement of Soviet troops into Afghanistan in late 1979 especially soured relations. In the United States, hostility and suspicion toward the Soviet Union claimed a major casualty when the 1979 SALT II agreement was not ratified. In the summer of 1980, as a response to the Soviet presence in Afghanistan, the United States boycotted the Olympic games in Moscow and placed an embargo on U.S. grain shipments to the Soviet Union.

During the presidency of Ronald Reagan in the early 1980s, a number of events contributed further to the decline of détente—a term Reagan disliked because he believed the Soviets had benefited from it more than had the United States. Soviet fears were nourished by Reagan's determination to increase U.S. military spending and by Reagan's harsh words, such as his calling the Soviet Union an "evil empire." In part provoked by the threat to Western Europe caused by the recent deployment of Soviet SS-20 and other missiles in the western Soviet Union, the U.S. government proceeded with the previously scheduled deployment of Pershing II and cruise missiles in Western Europe. In reaction to the new missile deployments, the Soviets broke off arms talks in Geneva in late 1983. At the same time, Soviet leader Andropov had angry words for President Reagan's newest weapons plan: the Strategic Defense Initiative (SDI), or, as often referred to less respectfully, "Star Wars." Andropov charged that by advocating a space-based defense system which would destroy Soviet missiles before they could reach U.S. territory, Reagan hoped to prevent the Soviets from launching any type of retaliatory strike if the United States decided to attack the U.S.S.R. first.

The United States, on the other hand, was angered by the major role that the Soviet Union had played in turning back the Solidarity movement in Poland. It responded with limited sanctions not only against Poland but also against the Soviet Union, which the United States charged bore a "heavy and direct responsibility for the repression in Poland." In 1983, the Soviet air force shot down over Soviet territory a Korean civilian jetliner, which the Soviet military apparently believed was a spy plane. Although later U.S. intelligence information seemed to contradict him, President Reagan declared that "there is no way a pilot could mistake this for anything other than a civilian airliner." He condemned the act and cited it as evidence of the barbaric nature of the Soviet system. In 1984, the Soviet Union and many other Communist nations friendly to the Soviet Union refused to take part in the summer Olympics in Los Angeles.

Along with sports, other areas of interaction and cooperation fostered by détente suffered as relations deteriorated. U.S.-Soviet trade and Jewish emigration from the Soviet Union, both of which had increased during the 1970s, declined in the early 1980s. Only in 1985, with the coming to power of Mikhail Gorbachev, would U.S.-Soviet relations reverse their downward spiral (see Chapter 32).

SUMMARY

From the Nuclear Test Ban Treaty of 1963 through most of the 1970s, superpower relations were generally characterized by a spirit of détente. Both the

United States and the Soviet Union attempted to find points of agreement and succeeded in expanding trade and cultural contacts and agreeing on a strategic arms limitation treaty. In the 1970s, the United States and China ended a long period of hostility and established diplomatic, cultural, and economic relations with each other. Most of the international community, which displayed an increasing tendency toward multipolarity, joined in signing a number of treaties designed to limit the testing and proliferation of nuclear weapons. Meanwhile, however, the uninterrupted postwar arms race produced ever more destructive weapons. From time to time, international events, such as the war in Indochina and the Soviet invasion of Czechoslovakia in 1968, stalled progress toward improved relations. The appearance of Soviet troops in Afghanistan in December 1979 and events of the early 1980s signaled that the spirit of détente had faded and that the arms race was accelerating.

From the 1960s into the 1980s, some of the European allies of the two superpowers made attempts to lessen their dependence on the United States or on the U.S.S.R. The Common Market, Western European economic prosperity, and de Gaulle all encouraged this trend in the West, while the "Prague Spring" of 1968, certain Rumanian and Hungarian policies, and the activities of Poland's Solidarity union reflected the desire for more independence in Eastern Europe.

While Europe remained, in general, economically and politically stable, there were some serious problems. The economic recessions of 1974–75 and 1981–82 shook Western European nations. Unstable governments, youth unrest, and outbursts of terrorism also plagued some of these nations for various periods during the 1960s and the following decades. The early 1980s also displayed a number of Eastern European economic shortcomings, including heavy indebtedness to Western governments and banks.

SUGGESTED SOURCES

Ash, Timothy G., *The Polish Revolution: Solidarity* (1985). An excellent discussion of the events in Poland in the early 1980s.*

Craig, Gordon A., *The Germans* (1982). An examination of the German people in the early 1980s from a historical perspective.*

Dornberg, John, *Eastern Europe* (1980). A look at Eastern Europe in the 1970s.

Edmonds, Robin, *Soviet Foreign Policy: The Brezhnev Years* (1983). An insightful, brief account.*

Hyland, William, *Mortal Rivals: Superpower Relations from Nixon to Reagan* (1987). A good overview by a leading U.S. expert on foreign affairs.*

Jenkins, Peter, *Mrs. Thatcher's Revolution: The Ending of the Socialist Era* (1988). A distinguished British journalist offers his insights into a decade of "Thatcherism."*

Konwicki, Tadeusz, *A Minor Apocalypse* (1979). A novel by one of Poland's leading writers which captures well the anguished condition of the country.*

Laqueur, Walter, *Europe since Hitler*, rev. ed. (1982). A description of economic, social, political, and cultural developments in Europe from 1945 to the beginning of the 1980s.*

Lewis, Flora, *Europe: Tapestry of Nations* (1988). A U.S. journalist looks at the similarities and differences between European nations, both east and west.*

Shipler, David K., *Russia: Broken Idols, Solemn Dreams* (1984). An observant account of Soviet life by a *New York Times* correspondent.*

Smoke, Richard, *National Security and the Nuclear Dilemma,* 2nd ed. (1987). A concise and informed history of the U.S. role in the arms race and in détente.*

*Paperback available.

28

The United States and Latin America in Recent Years

In the years following the late 1960s, several broad patterns emerged in the United States and Latin America. In the United States, a conservative era set in, as Americans cut back on the welfare state and lost interest in reforms and change. In Latin America, there were contradictory trends. Conservative military regimes were in the ascendancy in the 1970s, but largely gave way to civilian governments in the 1980s. Meanwhile, both revolutionary and democratic Marxism gained ground, opposed at every step by the United States.

THE CONSERVATIVE ERA IN THE UNITED STATES

The Troubled 1970s

During the 1970s, as the United States gave up on the war in Indochina, the economy began to run into increasing difficulties. Already drained by the expense of the war, the economy suffered from low worker productivity, nagging unemployment, and, most destructive of all, a steadily increasing rate of inflation. One source of inflation was a rising national debt resulting from spending large sums on both the Vietnam War and on expanded social programs at home. Another cause of inflation was a sharp rise in the cost of imported petroleum, accompanied by a relative decline in the amount of petroleum available. This, in turn, stemmed from price-fixing by the petroleum-producing nations and from the refining and distribution practices of the major petroleum companies. The era of cheap fuel for Americans ended as they faced long gasoline lines and skyrocketing heating bills. The automobile industry, long a mainstay of the domestic economy, sagged as consumers switched from large U.S. cars to small, energy-efficient imports from Japan. Because of inflation, many families found their real incomes dropping and their prospects for the future narrowing. They were not able to attain the higher standard of living they had hoped to achieve, and in many cases they found themselves compelled to give up luxuries they had come to expect.

Government struggled unsuccessfully with the economic problems of the 1970s. President Nixon put aside his conservative instincts when he adopted a planned budget deficit to stimulate the economy and a wage-price freeze to control inflation. Gerald Ford, Nixon's successor, tightened spending and credit; the resulting recession may have cost him the 1976 election. The victor, Democrat Jimmy Carter, did no better. An Iranian oil embargo worsened the existing energy crisis. High inflation, high interest rates, and persistent unemployment contributed to a "misery index" that the Republicans used as one of their political weapons to take back the White House in 1980. The existence at the same time of inflation, slow growth, and a high jobless rate was unprecedented and baffled politicians and economists alike. Their failure to master the economy increased public mistrust of those in high places.

Already alienated from government by the war and economic stagnation, the public grew more cynical still as a result of the political and constitutional firestorm of the Watergate affair. Evidence indicated that President Nixon and his chief administrative aides had engaged in a criminal conspiracy to obstruct justice by attempting to cover up a Republican party break-in of Democratic party headquarters. When the House of Representatives Judiciary Committee voted bills of impeachment, and it appeared that both Democrats and Republicans would vote to convict him, Nixon resigned the presidency on August 9,

Watergate: Senators Howard Baker and Sam Ervin examine a witness during Congressional hearings pertaining to the break-in of the national headquarters of the Democratic party. This investigation led to the resignation of President Nixon and the jailing of several Republican administration leaders. (George Tames/The New York Times)

1974. His successor, Gerald Ford, pardoned him, and Nixon went into seclusion. The Watergate affair, Nixon's misuse of intelligence and internal security agencies, and the controversy surrounding the conduct of the war in Indochina convinced many that an "imperial presidency" had evolved that had gotten out of control. Congress created legislation, supported by Ford and Carter, that gave it more effective oversight of the conduct of foreign and military policy and brought the intelligence agencies under more supervision.

Meanwhile, economic uncertainties helped bring about a changed social mood. The Americans of the "me-decade" 1970s, preoccupied with their own employment and security concerns, were little interested in social change and gave scant attention to national or international issues. Meanwhile, trend setters among affluent Americans stressed personal development, physical fitness, and a "laid back" life of self-indulgence that in some ways echoed the counterculture of the 1960s. College students, once in the vanguard of political activity, now concentrated on compiling good grades to give them an edge in getting jobs in a tightening economy.

Meanwhile, conservative forces were gaining strength. Economic conservatives called for lower taxes on, and less regulation of, business. Increasing numbers of Americans objected to high property and income taxes, called for an end to "throwing money" at social problems, and advocated cuts in welfare programs. Interest in social reform faded as more Americans became skeptical that government regulations could solve social ills. The proposed Equal Rights Amendment guaranteeing equal legal treatment for women, at one time seemingly destined for ratification by the states, twice failed. Social conservatives called for an end to abortions, the return of prayers to the schools, the censorship of pornographic and literary materials, limitations on the social and occupational roles of women, and more jails and tougher punishments for criminals.

Public policy reflected the conservative forces that gained strength in the 1970s. Nixon's revenue-sharing program illustrated the new drive to reduce the role of the federal government. In this instance, the U.S. government turned over a small portion of its revenues to the states to be spent under loose federal guidelines as each state determined. The movement away from big government found support from both parties. During the Democratic Carter administration, Congress reduced regulation of airlines and truckers, allowing carriers to compete in the marketplace. Beginning in 1969, a series of appointments to the Supreme Court made that body less likely to continue the innovative role it had had under Earl Warren. While the Court broke new ground when it upheld the constitutionality of abortions under certain conditions, it slowly reduced procedural protections for persons accused of committing a crime.

The Reagan Era

In 1980, conservative forces won their greatest triumph, putting Republican Ronald Reagan in the White House and gaining effective control of Congress. Once a New Deal Democrat, Reagan was a former movie star and California governor who united traditional economic conservatives with cultural conservatives of the "New Right." Unlike Carter and Ford, Reagan left a firm imprint on public policy. Declaring that government was the problem, not the solution, Reaganites did some pruning on the extensive welfare state that had grown since the New Deal. While programs with a strong middle-class following like Social Security escaped the budget ax, Congress slashed Great Society supports for the poor, such as food stamps, school lunches, and Medicaid. In addition, Congress enacted the biggest tax cut in the nation's history, with the wealthy reaping the greatest benefits. Moreover, Reagan ordered a major increase in military spending but at the same time curbed environmental and occupational safety programs.

Economic results were mixed. Inflation, a vexing problem for a decade, plunged sharply. Interest rates also fell. These gains, however, came at considerable cost. The percentage of the population living in poverty moved upward. The worst economic tailspin since the 1930s pushed jobless rates above 10 percent in 1982. Although the economy recovered and the unemployment rate declined significantly, many never reclaimed their high-paying jobs in basic industry. Increasingly, the U.S. moved toward becoming a service economy, with many persons in non-union, low-paying jobs with few or no fringe benefits. The "rustbelt" states of the Midwest and Northeast staggered as corporations "outsourced," shifting the manufacture of autos, clothing, electronics, and other products to low-wage labor markets outside the United States. Corporations also invested their capital in a series of "takeovers" of smaller firms, encouraged by the government's green light for business mergers. Meanwhile, the combination of tax cuts and accelerated military funding caused the national debt to climb to unprecedented levels. By the late 1980s Americans were buying so many products from the Asian Rim and Western Europe that a huge trade deficit joined the budget deficit. The government's debt burden grew, and the value of the dollar on world money markets sank. Foreign investors bought ever larger shares of U.S. economic assets. Once the world's economic giant, the United States watched as Japan and other East Asian nations seized the economic initiative.

Social trends of the 1980s continued to follow the conservative paths of the 1970s. The earlier "me decade" had its counterpart in the "Yuppies," or young urban professionals. Whereas earlier popular songs had celebrated social changes "blowin' in the wind," a widely admired singer of the 1980s proudly claimed that she was "a material girl." Concerned with their private lives rather than public issues, Yuppies spent freely on possessions and leisure pastimes. For many, a comfortable standard of living depended on both husband and wife holding full-time, long-term, well-paid employment. To further their financial security and individual satisfaction, more couples than ever before delayed children or chose to remain childless. These trends reflected greater educational and occupational opportunities for women, the heritage of the previous two decades.

Still another mark of the conservative mood of the 1980s was the continued growth and assertiveness of the nation's fundamentalist Christians. Although by the late 1980s they had not enacted their program of school prayer, "creation science" in the classroom, and an end to abortions, they entered politics in increasing numbers and set the political agenda. Evangelists, using television and mass mailing, built large followings and raised substantial sums of money. In the late 1980s, however, sexual and financial scandals tarnished the "televangelists'" image in the eyes of some.

Substance abuse and public health were major national concerns of the decade. Here conservatives often, but not always, took the initiative. Public opinion surveys ranked drug abuse as one of society's chief problems. The counterculture's marijuana remained popular, but use of highly addictive cocaine spread rapidly, ensnaring victims of all races and social classes. First Lady Nancy Reagan urged the public to "just say no," while the authorities tried both suppression and treatment, with little success. Substance abuse counseling and treatment programs ballooned, and government pushed through ever harsher enforcement legislation. Attitudes toward liquor underwent change as well. Social drinking declined in some circles, and state and local sanctions against drunk driving intensified, partly in response to lobbying by groups like Mothers Against Drunk Drivers. Tobacco smokers found themselves increasingly on the defensive. Federally required health warnings had already appeared in advertising and packaging; now employers and state and local governments banned or restricted smoking in workplaces, public buildings, and public carriers.

Two aspects of the 1980s clearly illustrated the conservative mood of the decade. Although some reports showed lessening crime rates due to the declining youth population, crime remained a major public concern. States built more prisons and carried out the death penalty more frequently. A vigorous gun lobby used fears of crime to block federal handgun restrictions, even in the wake of an attempt on President Reagan's life. Meanwhile, the mid-1980s saw the appearance of a deadly disease, AIDS. Striking down mainly homosexuals and intravenous drug users, the AIDS epidemic provoked a tangle of highly emotional concerns, among them sex, drugs, medical research, and the right of privacy.

As the decade neared its end, the 1988 election sustained the conservatives as Reagan's Vice-President, George Bush, won the presidency. Bush's campaign stressed patriotic symbols (the Pledge of Allegiance to the flag, as well as the flag itself) and appealed to the public's fear of violent crime. On the other hand, the more liberal Democrats increased their seats in Congress and in state governments. Americans continued to be political pragmatists, putting their conservative political, social, and economic instincts in the hands of Republican presidents and their support for a slimmed-down welfare state in the hands of a Democratic Congress.

STAGNATION IN MEXICO

While social change swept through much of Latin America after World War II, Mexico—the model for many Latin American reformers—had stagnated, its revolutionary fervor dissipated. The modest social and land reform programs in augurated before World War II had been eroded by a huge increase in population, and wage increases had been eaten up by inflation. The nation, particularly its swollen cities, teemed with unemployed and marginally employed citizens. In the early 1970s, abundant petroleum reserves encouraged Mexico to borrow money to build steel mills, power plants, and other capital improvements. Many U.S. corporations took advantage of low wage levels in Mexico to set up manufacturing and assembly installations, thus adding to the nation's income. The profits from these projects mostly benefited the rich, however, and the large gap between the rich and the poor remained unchanged. The drop in petroleum prices in the late 1970s prevented Mexico from earning enough money to reduce the principal on its debt, which stood at $100 billion by mid- 1989. The government was forced to institute austerity programs, to devalue the currency, and to dedicate the bulk of its petroleum earnings to paying the interest on the debt, with little immediate hope of reducing the principal.

Relations between Mexico and the United States remained uneasy. Millions of illegal Mexican immigrants and hundreds of thousands of seasonal workers crossed into the United States. A huge drug traffic from Mexico to the United States flourished. Proud of being an emerging world economic power, Mexicans remembered historic wrongs by the United States and resented being the butt of patronizing stereotypes about bandits and siestas. On the other hand, Mexico was interested in selling its staples to the United States and in encouraging trade and tourism, and the United States was interested in buying Mexican petroleum and natural gas. Frequent meetings between the leaders of the two nations helped to avoid serious ruptures in political and economic relations.

During the 1980s, the economic and social problems of the Mexican people began to change their political behavior. Since the 1920s, the government had been in the firm grip of the Party of Revolutionary Institutions, many of whose leaders were accused of enriching themselves while in office. Opposition parties and a free press were tolerated as long as they posed no real threat to the control of the PRI, but any signs of violent opposition, such as student unrest or illegal strikes, were quickly smashed by the government. By the 1980s, however, many Mexicans had become tired of the graft and inefficiency of the PRI. In the July 1988 presidential elections, the PRI faced formidable opposition for the first time. Strongly opposed by parties from the Left and Right, the PRI presidential candidate Carlos Salinas lost the cities, but, with support from the rural peasants who had benefited from land reform, squeaked through with a bare majority amid cries of fraud. The once overwhelming PRI majority in the national legislature was sharply reduced. Whether Mexico was about to have a true multi-party political system in which the PRI would surrender power if defeated at the polls remained to be seen.

MILITARY AND CIVILIAN GOVERNMENT: A PENDULUM

By the 1960s the established order in many Latin American nations, including some practicing democracies, had become alarmed by high inflation, sporadic violence associated with social reform programs, and Castroite subversion. They also feared that reforms might embolden the lower orders to rise up and destroy their privileges. As a consequence, they often turned to the military for security. In the process, representative government disappeared in many nations. By the late 1980s, however, the military of most Latin American nations, faced with economic problems they could not solve, had either turned over the government to elected civilian leaders or taken steps in that direction. By 1989, it appeared that civilian governments, while more supportive of constitutional rights, were about as ineffective as their military predecessors in combatting the economic woes of their nations.

The Pendulum in Brazil and Argentina

In 1964, the Brazilian military ousted a leftist president and terminated the civilian government. These officers did not make the promise often made by the instigators of twentieth-century military *golpes* (blows, or coups) that they would return Brazil to democracy after immediate problems had been solved. Rather, they were prepared to rule the nation indefinitely, proclaiming themselves the embodiment of the whole Brazilian people and promising a program of revolutionary changes to benefit all citizens. The military abolished political parties and tinkered constantly with the organization of the government until they were satisfied they had created an arrangement that would give them tight control over the nation. They muzzled political opposition and repressed scattered vi-

Wealth and poverty in Latin America: shantytown suburbs and downtown office buildings in Caracas, Venezuela. (Peter Menzel/Stock, Boston)

olence from the Castroites. Private right-wing death squads killed individuals believed to be subversive. The Brazilian officers intensified industrial development, presuming the benefits of this would trickle down to the impoverished masses. They did not make social reforms or redistribute the land. Their economic program was apparently successful; production increased sharply, as did per capita income. Other nations hastened to copy "the Brazilian miracle."

By the late 1970s, however, the "miracle" in Brazil had faded. The industrialization program emphasized producing consumer goods, but the cost of providing raw materials, machinery, technicians, and other supporting factors led to inflation. The increase in per capita income masked the fact that profits from industrial expansion were going to the rich and that the gap was widening between the rich and the poor. The illiterate rural and urban workers continued to live in abject poverty, with one of the lowest life expectancy rates in Latin America. They could not buy the consumer products manufactured by the new industries.

Despite these failures, the military continued in power with the support of the upper classes until the 1980s, when many Brazilians, including many in the military, had become disillusioned with the regime's floundering economy and a massive debt ($124 billion in mid-1989). Faced with increased unrest from the middle class and workers, and under mounting foreign creditor pressure, in 1985 the ruling officers began to turn the government over to elected civilians in stages. Unable in its turn to cope with the huge debt, the Brazilian government in 1987 unilaterally suspended interest payments to foreign commercial banks; by 1989 there were rumblings of popular discontent as the government appeared to be losing ground to Brazil's many economic problems.

In Argentina, the second Perónist government, headed by Perón's second wife, Isabel Perón, who had taken over after the death of her husband, was overthrown in 1976. The armed forces and right-wing death squads suppressed sporadic violence by leftist guerrillas and proceeded to imprison, torture, and execute those believed to be opposed to the new military regime.

After several years in control, the Argentine junta, like the military in Brazil, found itself unable to grapple with an array of economic and social problems. Hoping to regain popular support, the government embarked on a military adventure that in fact backfired and destroyed the regime. Since 1820, Argentina had claimed the Islas Malvinas in the South Atlantic, but Great Britain had taken these islands in 1833 and had held them ever since as the Falkland Islands dependency. In 1982, Argentine forces seized the islands in a surprise attack. British forces recaptured the islands, in the process smashing the Argentine navy and air force and capturing thousands of soldiers. The discredited junta arranged for free elections in 1983; Raul Alfonsin, whose centrist party defeated the Peronistas, won in an upset. The Alfonsin government put on trial some of the officers who had been responsible for the reign of terror, but his government had to move cautiously because the army was restive, and military revolts occasionally occurred. Alfonsin's other major task was to cope with Argentina's many economic woes, including inflation and a large national debt.

In 1987, Alfonsin was able to refinance the debt, then standing at $53 billion, but economic problems continued. By 1989 the debt stood at $60 billion and food riots and hyperinflation threatened democratic institutions in Argentina.

The Death of Democracy in Chile

In Chile, multi-party democratic politics, which had been the rule since 1938, existed in uneasy conjunction with widespread poverty, a traditional social elite, and economic domination by a few families and foreign investors. Although the Mexican Revolution had already produced a rather strong social welfare program by Latin American standards, Castro's domestic program in Cuba inspired Chile's reformers, particularly its Marxist political parties, to press further. In 1970, despite CIA efforts to prevent it, Marxist Salvador Allende, supported by a coalition of leftist parties, was elected president in a divided field with 36 percent of the popular vote. Allende's government proceeded to nationalize foreign holdings without compensation, justifying the act with the claim that the companies owed back taxes to the government. He also greatly accelerated the land reform program, but not fast enough for Chilean radicals, who encouraged *campesinos* to seize land not yet expropriated. Allende expanded the social welfare program and sold food to the poor at low prices. Wages rose and unemployment dropped. In the 1973 legislative elections, Allende's party, although still without a majority in Congress, gained ground. By 1972–73 it appeared that Chile was becoming the world's first democratically elected Marxist state.

During 1973, Allende's program ran into trouble. Agricultural production dropped and more food had to be imported. A decline in copper production, coupled with a drop in the price of copper on the world market, limited national income and drove the government further into debt. Landless peasants continued unauthorized and sometimes violent land seizures. At the same time, the Nixon administration, believing that Chile was controlled by pro-Cuban and pro-Soviet enemies of the United States, embarked on a program to "destabilize" Allende's government. The CIA spent over $13 million to foster opposition inside Chile, and the United States cut off aid to Chile and discouraged private investment there. Meanwhile, the Chilean middle class, fearing social revolution, fought back against Allende, mounting an increasing number of strikes and demonstrations as truckers refused to haul freight and shopkeepers closed their stores. In September 1973, the military moved in and Allende was killed in the takeover.

Like the military in Brazil and Argentina, the Chilean military government, led by General Augusto Pinochet, that ruled in the 1970s and 1980s rested for the most part on the firm support of the upper and middle classes. The new military rulers eliminated the legislature and political parties, censored the press, and became one of the most repressive regimes in Latin America, imprisoning, torturing, and killing thousands of Chileans. Pinochet halted land redistribution, canceled wage increases, and returned some nationalized business to private ownership. During the early 1980s, pressure mounted on the military junta. As the declining price of copper brought on an economic depression, various groups began to demonstrate and strike. Pinochet's government stood fast. By the late 1980s, an increase in consumer goods production and copper output and a flourishing foreign trade brought prosperity to the upper classes, but the standard of living for the lower classes fell.

Meanwhile, the junta began to work on building up a long-term basis for conservative rule. In 1980, it created a new constitution, approved by plebiscite, that provided for a strong president with a single eight-year term and put severe limitations on freedom of expression, political activity, and the right to strike. Marxist groups and other organizations "contrary to public morality, order, or national security" were banned. Pinochet was to be president until 1990; meanwhile, presidential and congressional elections were to be held in 1989 and civilian government restored in 1990.

Despite economic prosperity for the upper classes under the military junta, Chileans nevertheless apparently wished to return to civilian government, and in 1988 they delivered a severe blow to the regime. The military government called for a plebiscite to determine if Pinochet would be the first president under the fully enacted constitution, and in a fair election 55 percent of the voters voted against him. It remained to be seen if the junta would now allow constitutionally mandated elections in 1989 so that civilian government could be restored in 1990.

THE COLD WAR RETURNS TO CENTRAL AMERICA AND THE CARIBBEAN

In the early 1970s, it had looked as though revolutionary Marxism in Latin America had faded away outside Cuba. During the middle and late 1970s, however, guerrilla warfare led by leftist forces began to break out in Central America. The unrest generally stemmed from wretched living conditions in a region that was generally the poorest in Latin America. The insurgents were dedicated to ending the privileges of the few and were generally hostile to the United States. The guerrilla movements increasingly came under the influence and leadership of Marxists, although it was not always clear to what extent these groups considered themselves allies of the Soviet Union.

In the 1970s and 1980s, opinion in the United States was divided over how to respond to the unrest in Central America and the Caribbean. On one hand, politicians in both parties were more likely than in earlier decades to realize that poverty was likely to cause revolution and war in poor nations. Also, there was more understanding among U.S. politicians of the hostility engendered in Latin America by perceptions of "Yankee imperialism" held by many there. These attitudes led the United States to once again step up economic aid to relieve poverty and to pressure conservative governments into instituting reforms. On the other hand, as has already been discussed, U.S.

leaders continued to be extremely sensitive about the presence of Marxism in the Caribbean and Central America and remained ready to take whatever actions they deemed necessary to keep Marxists out. For example, in 1983 the United States invaded the tiny island of Grenada, toppling a pro-Castro Marxist regime there.

By the late 1980s, however, the Cold War in the Caribbean area appeared to be on the wane. The Soviet Union, concerned with economic and political change at home (see Chapter 32), began to scale down its military aid for revolutionary movements in Central America and economic aid for Cuba. Castro's regime, facing an economy straining to support Cuba's effective but expensive social programs, gave only modest support itself to the Central American guerrillas. Politics in the United States moved toward supporting economic and diplomatic measures appropriate to the region and away from military solutions.

Panama: Phasing Out Imperialism

The situation in Panama was primarily one of resentment of U.S. imperialism. After World War II, nationalist Panamanians had increased their pressures on the United States to cede the Canal Zone to Panama and to surrender control of the canal itself to Panama. During the 1970s, the Panamanian dictator Omar Torrijos stressed that the Panama Canal complex was a flagrant example of outdated Yankee imperialism. He also asserted that frustrated nationalism might become radical and endanger the canal itself. The canal was partly obsolete, since it could not handle the new petroleum supertankers, and was difficult to defend against sabotage and guerrilla attacks. With one eye on the situation in Nicaragua (see below), the Democratic administration of President Jimmy Carter concluded an agreement with Panama in 1978 that provided that the United States would complete a phased withdrawal from the Canal Zone by the year 2000, after which Panama would operate the canal as a neutral waterway. The United States reserved the right to intervene militarily to keep the canal open. With great reluctance about losing a prized symbol of U.S. power, the United States Senate ratified the treaty in 1979.

Although many Panamanians realized that they had economically benefited from the presence of the United States, they remained very sensitive to the history of U.S. controls over Panama. In 1988 and early 1989, when the United States tried to oust strongman Manuel Noriega because of his dictatorship and his alleged role in the international drug traffic, he stood fast, claiming that Panama was faced with yet another instance of Yankee imperialism.

Nicaragua: The Triumph and Tribulations of Revolutionaries

The revolutionary struggle building in Central America in the 1970s achieved success in Nicaragua. A poor and thinly populated nation, Nicaragua was under the control of Anastasio Somoza, the latest in a family line of dictators. Somoza's rebel adversaries called themselves "Sandinistas" in honor of Augusto

César Sandino, a Nicaraguan rebel who died opposing the U.S. occupation of Nicaragua in the 1920s and 1930s. The Sandinistas were composed of a spectrum of Somoza opponents ranging from moderates to Marxist revolutionaries; Cuba supplied them with some arms. Many were given sanctuary in Costa Rica, a neighboring democracy that had previously suffered harassment from Somoza. In 1979, the Sandinistas drove Somoza out and installed a leftist government, which instituted land reform and built schools and hospitals. The Carter administration, sensitive to charges of past U.S. overreaction in Cuba, the Dominican Republic, and Chile, concluded that the Sandinistas were not Communist allies of the Soviet Union and extended recognition and aid to the new government.

In the years that followed their triumph, however, the ruling Sandinista junta, led by Daniel Ortega, moved steadily toward the left, bringing in teachers, doctors, and military training personnel from Cuba. The Sandinistas became increasingly anti-United States in tone, while harassing political opponents, censoring the press, and heavily regulating private business. Beginning in 1981, the Republican administration of Ronald Reagan took the position that guerrilla warfare in Central America, while in part a product of repressive economic and social conditions, was also the result of a plan by the Soviet Union to spread communism throughout the region by funneling arms and advisors from the U.S.S.R. through Cuba and then through Nicaragua to the guerrillas in El Salvador (see below). The Reagan administration considered Nicaragua a Marxist ally of Cuba and the Soviet Union, and despite resistance by some in Congress, employed the "destabilization" approach used against Guatemala, Cuba, and Chile. The United States applied economic pressures, such as refusing to buy Nicaraguan sugar, cutting off foreign aid, and opposing loans to Nicaragua by international financial agencies. Anti-Sandinista Nicaraguans, called "Contras," many of them supporters of the deposed dictator Somoza, were trained and supplied by the United States in neighboring Honduras and sent into Nicaragua to drive out the Sandinista government. The United States encouraged another set of anti-Sandinistas to attack Nicaragua from neighboring Costa Rica. U.S. land and air forces went on maneuver in Honduras, while U.S. warships and observation planes watched traffic in and out of Nicaragua. The CIA and other covert organizations harassed Nicaragua with sabotage, air raids, and mining of harbors. The Sandinista junta responded by obtaining economic and military aid from the Soviet Union.

By 1988 the Contras had made little headway against the Sandinistas, and Congressional political and economic support for them wavered. Meanwhile, U.S. economic and military pressure, plus ineffective economic programs of the Sandinista government, brought increasing hardship to the Nicaraguan people. In 1988, hyperinflation reached an astounding 20,000 percent, and by 1989 the junta was forced to announce a 44 percent cutback in the public sector of the national budget. Thousands of public employees were fired, and money outlays for land reform, housing, public health, education, and food subsidies were cut. As domestic support for the regime eroded and the United States remained a powerful adversarial presence, and faced with increased signs of ebbing Soviet support, the Sandinistas vacillated. At different times, they allowed opposition and an open press and suppressed them; called for open elections and either rigged or postponed them; uttered scathing attacks on the United States and made conciliatory statements; negotiated with mediating Latin American nations and ignored them.

Guerrilla Warfare in El Salvador and Guatemala

In the early 1980s, it appeared as though revolutionary forces might repeat their Nicaraguan triumph in other Central American locations. Communist guerrillas became a formidable force in El Salvador, where tens of thousands of civilians died. Some were killed by guerrillas, but most died in army sweeps through the villages and at the hands of right-wing death squads that eliminated those suspected of supporting the guerrillas or of working for land reform. Those killed or missing included leftist politicians, labor organizers, and those working for the Peace Corps and for the Agency for International Development. In El Salvador, the Roman Catholic Church, which supported moderate reforms, was particularly hard hit. Victims included U.S. nuns, Salvadorian priests, and the archbishop of San Salvador, murdered in the cathedral chapel.

The United States, perceiving another instance of Communist subversion, acted. Operating under the principle of the Truman Doctrine, it provided military supplies and advisors to El Salvador during the 1980s to assist the Salvadorian army in defeating the guerrillas. At the same time, the United States attempted to eliminate domestic conditions fostering guerrilla warfare in El Salvador by stepping up economic aid, denouncing the death squads, and supporting moderate politicians such as José Napoleon Duarte, who was elected president in 1984. Most of the U.S. public, however, still mindful of the Vietnam experience, appeared reluctant to have the United States intervene directly. Meanwhile, the guerrillas received military aid from Nicaragua and apparently from Cuba.

As the war dragged on into the late 1980s, the government emphasized bombing villages presumed to be in sympathy with the rebels; the guerrillas attacked military installations, blew up utilities, and assassinated village officials. By 1988 the war in El Salvador was in a rough stalemate; over 60,000 civilian and military personnel had been killed in the struggle, and the standard of living in the tiny, densely populated nation was the lowest of the century. In a less publicized Marxist insurgency in Guatemala, over 100,000 persons had been killed and 60,000 were missing since 1972, most at the hands of the government and of right-wing death squads.

Throughout the 1980s, Latin American nations, particularly those located around the Caribbean basin, brought forth a series of peace plans in hopes of bringing the warfare in Central America to an end. At one point, the most hopeful sign for eventual peace in the area was the proposal put forth in 1987 by Oscar Arias, the president of Costa Rica, who received the Nobel Peace Prize.

Signed by the presidents of Guatemala, El Salvador, Honduras, Nicaragua, and Costa Rica, the plan called for negotiations between their governments and unarmed internal opposition groups, cease-fires with guerrillas, cessations of states of emergency and the restoration of civil rights, and an end to outside aid to insurgent forces. The period after the signing was not auspicious, however. The Sandinistas and the Contras started talks but broke them off; the United States agreed in principle, but ignored the plan in fact; and nothing changed in Guatemala and El Salvador. In 1989, the five Central American presidents signed an accord in which the Contras' bases in Honduras would be dismantled in return for guarantees of free elections in Nicaragua. Whether this agreement would bring peace to Nicaragua remained to be seen.

SUMMARY

During the 1970s and 1980s, the United States moved away from the expansion of the welfare state and from the social turmoil that characterized the preceding decade. Americans of the 1970s were harassed by fuel shortages, inflation, political scandal, and the distasteful aftermath of the Indochina war. Liberal causes, such as equal rights for women, fared poorly as political and social conservatism grew stronger.

During the "Reagan era" of the 1980s, conservatives curbed inflation, cut taxes, built up the military, and trimmed back the welfare state, but the United States also faced a huge budget deficit and a large imbalance in foreign trade. Social conservatives were unable to make much headway in their particular causes. U.S. society as a whole, as in the 1970s, appeared to put its emphasis on material success rather than on social reform.

In the 1970s and 1980s, the success of movements toward social justice and political democracy fluctuated dramatically in Latin America. By the 1970s, military governments supported by groups fearful of social change dominated Latin America. Meanwhile, in Central America, frustrated proponents of change turned to guerrilla warfare to achieve social and economic change for the masses. By the 1980s failure to solve social and economic problems had put several South American military regimes into retreat. By 1988, nearly all Latin American nations had civilian governments; even Chile, long under an oppressive junta, appeared to be on the road back to democracy. There were also signs that Mexico's traditional one-party state might be on the road to a competitive party system.

After World War II, the Cold War shaped much of the history of the Caribbean and Central America. The United States, fearing the growth of Soviet influence in the region, agreed to return the Panama Canal to Panama to lessen anti-imperialist hostility in the region. On the whole, however, the U.S. responded to the presence of Marxism by increasing its intervention. The United States intervened with varying degrees of success in Chile in the 1970s and in Grenada and throughout Central America in the early 1980s. Leftist revolutionaries triumphed in Nicaragua and held on in the face of formidable pressures from the United States; U.S.-backed governments in El Salvador and Guatemala remained locked in a bloody, inconclusive struggle with Marxist guerrillas.

SUGGESTED SOURCES

Anderson, Thomas P., *Politics in Central America* (1982). An examination of the social and economic context for recent political developments in El Salvador, Guatemala, Honduras, and Nicaragua.*

Argueta, Manilo, *One Day of Life* (1983), tr. Bill Brow. A novel set in El Salvador that captures well the peasants' daily struggle for existence and their dealings with church and state.*

Barrett, Lawrence I., *Gambling with History: Reagan in the White House,* rev. ed. (1984). A full account of Reagan's first term, treating both domestic and foreign policy.*

Bremner, Robert, et al., eds., *U.S. Choices: Social Dilemmas and Public Policy since the 1960s* (1986). Historians' essays on major social issues spanning the 1960s and 1970s, including poverty, women's issues, civil rights, the environment, and the economy.

Carroll, Peter N., *It Seemed Like Nothing Happened: The Tragedy and Promise of America in the 1970s* (1982). A comprehensive and lively overview of the era, covering both politics and social trends, but giving greater attention to the latter area.

Lewis, Oscar, *Five Families* (1976). A study of Mexican families from the poorest to the richest.*

Lukas, J. Anthony, *Common Ground: A Turbulent Decade in the Lives of Three U.S. Families* (1985). A controversial and widely read exploration of race, class, and the urban crisis, centering on the school desegregation conflict in Boston in the 1970s.

Wesson, Robert, ed., *New Military Politics in Latin America* (1982). A collection of essays dealing with the long-lasting military dictatorships in Argentina, Brazil, Chile, and Uruguay.

*Paperback available.

29

Asia in Recent Decades

Several major themes dominated events in Asia from the 1960s to the late 1980s. China plunged into revolutionary turmoil and chaos as factions of the Communist leadership struggled for power. In the new nations, the period was one of internal conflicts, unfulfilled promises, and uneven development. Major power rivalries continued in Asia, as in other parts of the world. In formerly French Indochina, the Cold War once again became a hot war that directly embroiled the United States for over a decade.

THE SINO-SOVIET SPLIT AND THE CULTURAL REVOLUTION

From 1959 to 1966, after the debacle of the Great Leap Forward had relegated Mao Zedong to the mainly honorary position of Chairman of the Communist party, the so-called pragmatists ruled China. They repaired the economic damages caused by the Great Leap by dismantling the communes and restoring incentives to peasants and workers. China for a few years enjoyed relative quiet.

Meanwhile the Sino-Soviet relationship, which Mao once described as "lasting, unbreakable, and invincible" was steadily deteriorating. There were several reasons for this. One was ideological: Mao Zedong claimed that his ideas contributed to the ideological development of Marxism-Leninism and were especially applicable to revolutionary movements in the non-Western world. The Soviet Union firmly rejected such Maoist claims. Mao, moreover, claimed to be the senior worldwide Communist leader after Stalin's death in 1953, another claim that the Soviet Union absolutely denied. In addition, there were historic differences between the Chinese and Soviet Communist parties, territorial disputes between the two nations that went back to the nineteenth century, and Khrushchev's de-Stalinization campaign, which he had launched without prior consultation of Mao. Mao was especially upset with the dismantling of Stalin's personality cult because he was busily building up his own.

The two Communist giants were clearly on a collision course. In 1960, the Soviet Union abruptly ended all technical aid to China and recalled its technicians together with their blueprints. The split widened in 1962, when Khrush-chev bowed to U.S. pressure and withdrew nuclear missiles from Cuba with-out consulting the Chinese, who called him a coward for doing so. When China and India clashed over boundary disputes in 1962, the Soviet Union sided with India. Relations had eroded to such a low point by 1964 that when China det-onated a nuclear device, the Soviet Union considered launching a preemptive strike to destroy its nuclear industry. Although this did not happen, border skir-mishes erupted in 1969 over disputes. Chinese fear of the Soviet Union, espe-cially the possibility that the Russians might apply the Brezhnev Doctrine to China (i.e., as the senior Communist state, the U.S.S.R. had the right to use military force to enforce the correct practice of communism in other Commu-nist states), led Mao to rejoin the international community.

Meanwhile, Mao was plotting to end his enforced retirement, oust his ri-vals, and reverse their pragmatic practices. Since the regular party structure and bureaucracy were controlled by the pragmatists, Mao, his wife Jiang Qing (a former actress who until now had played only a minor public role), and some allies went to the campuses of universities and secondary schools, where they enrolled millions of young people into the Red Guards and used them to roust the party cadres and bureaucrats from power. Mao called his campaign to seize power and implement his radical vision for China the Great Proletarian Cul-tural Revolution. He dreamt of a China in which material incentives played no part and in which ideological purity counted for more than expertise. An old man, he had little time left in which to attempt to realize his dream. Between 1966 and 1968, China was thrown into a frenzy of turmoil as Red Guards shut down the schools, government offices ceased to function, and factories stopped producing. Mao especially hated intellectuals, whom he derided as "swollen in head, weak in legs, sharp in tongue but empty in belly." His supporters hu-miliated, tortured, and jailed millions of party officials, bureaucrats, teachers, and managers, including chief of state Liu Shaoqi and party secretary-general Deng Xiaoping. Many of his victims were killed, and others committed suicide in despair. Mao returned to power, elevated in a personality cult that even Stalin might have envied. By 1969 China was in utter chaos, as rival Red Guard units began to battle each other in power struggles. Mao then called in the army to put down the Red Guards, after which many young people were sent to the countryside to work on farms. Although normalcy began to return slowly after 1970, the era of the Cultural Revolution did not really end until Mao's death in 1976 and the purging of his wife and other radicals soon after.

The decade of turmoil wreaked widespread devastation on China and turned the clock back in that nation while other nations in East Asia were forg-ing ahead in rapid development. At Mao's death, the nation was on the verge of bankruptcy, with industry and agriculture in chaos, the schools barely func-tioning, and the party and bureaucracy a shambles. As Communist leaders at-tempted to rebuild China, they call the decade of the Cultural Revolution the Ten Disastrous Years, the worst in Chinese history. The damage affected three generations: an older one sent to prison and menial labor and denied opportunities for research and teaching, the Red Guard generation who were denied education and training, and a younger generation denied schools and facilities and teachers as they reached school age.

In retrospect, almost all in and out of China agreed that while Mao was a great revolutionary, he was a disastrous ruler once his revolution had succeeded. As one of his colleagues reportedly said several years after his death:

> Had Chairman Mao died in 1956, there would have been no doubt that he was a great leader of the Chinese people. . . . Had he died in 1966, his meritorious achievements would have been somewhat tarnished.
> However, his achievements were still very good. Since he actually died in 1976, there was nothing we can do about it.

THE NEW NATIONS STRUGGLE TO SURVIVE

After 1960, Asia entered the post-colonial era. Aside from Hong Kong and Macao, which Britain and Portugal had agreed to return to China before the end of the century, all former colonies had gained independence. However, after several decades of nationhood, the new states presented a mixed scorecard as they struggled to cope with problems that faced them, often with inadequately trained and inexperienced leadership.

The Search for Political Stability

Faced with massive economic and social problems, it was not surprising that the new Asian nations found it difficult to attain and maintain political stability. Great Britain and the United States had given their possessions some training in the democratic process, and upon independence these new nations possessed democratically elected governments and relatively well-developed political infrastructures. India enjoyed elected governments except between the years 1975 and 1977, when Prime Minister Indira Gandhi (daughter of Nehru and no relation of Mahatma Gandhi) suspended the constitution and ruled under emergency laws. When she allowed free elections in 1977, the Indian electorate demonstrated its commitment to democratic principles by throwing her and her Congress party out of office. The Janata party that replaced her was ineffective and unstable, however, and Indira Gandhi was swept back to power in the 1980 election. When Mrs. Gandhi was assassinated in 1984 by her Sikh bodyguards, leaders of the Congress party quickly elevated her son Rajiv to the prime ministership. Rajiv Gandhi was at first popular because he was young, not corrupt, and a supporter of modernization, and above all because of the circumstances of his succession; but he was handicapped by political inexperience. Since independence, except for almost three years of Janata rule, the Congress party had governed India, and the Nehru-Gandhi family had held the prime ministership for all but two years during the Congress era. Although India was a democracy, some critics charged that the dominance of the Nehru-Gandhi family in post-independence politics showed that the electorate was really very traditional and even feudal in its attitude toward leadership.

Pakistan had some early episodes of parliamentary governments, but after 1964 was under either direct or veiled military control. In 1977, General Mohammad Zia ul-Haq seized power in Pakistan from elected prime minister Zufilkar Ali Bhutto. After ruling for twelve years, Zia was killed in an airplane crash in 1988. In elections held in late 1988, the People's party, headed by Benazir Bhutto (daughter of the former prime minister), won a handy victory. As a result she was named prime minister, the first woman head of government in a Muslim country.

In the 1970 elections, more populous East Pakistan won a majority, whereupon the generals, who were West Pakistani in origin, decided to postpone convening the National Assembly. This was the last straw for the East Pakistanis, who resented their second-class citizenship. Led by Sheikh Mujibur Rahman, leader of the winning political party, called the Awami League, East Pakistan declared its independence and renamed itself Bangladesh in 1971. A bloody civil war ensued, in which over a million people lost their lives as the army sent from West Pakistan sought to crush the rebellion. Ten million fled to seek refuge in neighboring India. India seized the opportunity to humble its enemy Pakistan and to restore peace and return refugees. It forced Pakistan to give up its attempt to reconquer the east. The military ruled Bangladesh for most of its post-independence years.

The Philippines' constitution established a U.S.-style democratic system that worked turbulently under a two-party system through the 1960s. Ferdinand Marcos was elected president in 1965, and reelected in 1969. In 1972, masking his quest to perpetuate his personal and family rule by asserting that he needed more powers to put down a Communist revolt, Marcos suspended the constitution and declared martial law, which continued until 1981. During the 1980s, an ailing Marcos shared power with the military and his wife Imelda. Meanwhile, long-active Communist and Muslim (mostly on Mindanao island) insurgencies continued. Under U.S. and mounting domestic pressure, Marcos held presidential elections in 1986. He was opposed by Corazon Aquino, widow of an opponent who had been assassinated. Massive fraud allowed Marcos to declare himself the winner, but by now the United States had switched its support to Mrs. Aquino. A military coup led by reform-minded officers finally toppled Marcos; Mrs. Aquino was inaugurated president, and democracy was restored to the Philippines. Although personally upright, Mrs. Aquino was politically inexperienced and her government was plagued by instability.

In Indonesia, Sukarno ruled in an authoritarian and eccentric fashion as president for life under the guise of a ''Guided Democracy'' until 1965. In the face of deteriorating health, he held onto power by playing off the army against the Communist party of Indonesia (PKI) and its front organizations, which he seemed to favor increasingly. In a sequence of events that remained unclear afterwards, the PKI staged a coup against the army in 1965 and killed a number of senior officers. It failed to capture several key leaders, one of whom,

Suharto, seized leadership and crushed the rebellion, killing between 150,000 and 500,000 people in the process. Sukarno was stripped of power and died in 1970. Suharto remained in power in an essentially authoritarian regime, although several general elections were held. Suharto's government emphasized political consensus, a tradition highly regarded in Indonesia.

The Struggle for Economic Development

In the decades after 1960, the new nations of Asia continued to give first priority to developing their economies to improve the standard of living of their people. Their fast-increasing populations, however, often posed a problem. India, for example, had a population of about 350 million at independence. Improved public health and medical care caused the population to skyrocket to about 800 million in 1988; Pakistan registered a similar rate of increase, from 32.5 million in West Pakistan in 1947 to nearly 100 million in 1988. In 1988, Bangladesh had about 110 million people, Indonesia 177 million, the Philippines 57 million. In all cases, the population had much more than doubled since independence. To feed, clothe, and educate such rapidly increasing populations was difficult for naturally well-endowed nations such as Indonesia, but virtually impossible for resource-poor lands such as Bangladesh, even with massive foreign aid. Prime Minister Indira Gandhi coined the slogan "Stop at two (children)" and attempted to force some Indians to undergo sterilization in an attempt to slow the growth rate during the time that she suspended the constitution. Her tactics so enraged tradition-minded Indians that this policy contributed in part to her electoral defeat in 1977, and successive Indian governments had to softpedal the issue from then on. The exceptions to the population problem were Japan and more recently Singapore and Taiwan (see Chapter 30), which achieved moderate population growth rates comparable to advanced Western nations.

On balance, India achieved much after 1960, due to large infusions of foreign aid from both Eastern and Western blocs (over $9 billion from the United States between 1947 and 1980) and a combination of state planning and private enterprise. Economic advances were especially rapid after the advent of Rajiv Gandhi, who favored private enterprise and high technology. For example, India's middle class (defined as people with disposable income after payment for the necessities of life) became larger than the total population of the United States.

In another remarkable achievement, India, which since the earliest times had suffered from sporadic famines such as that in 1900, began to produce enough food to feed its huge population. This was due to the "green revolution" begun in the 1960s, which introduced high-yielding hybrid seeds, the clearing of virgin lands, and large, new irrigation projects, which made possible double-and triple-cropping. However, the progress also brought pollution and erosion. There was also a widening gap between the rich and poor, as many small farmers who could not afford the necessary capital to invest in farm machinery, chemical fertilizers, and pesticides were squeezed out.

Several factors, however, held India back from an even faster rate of development. India committed a large part of its resources to the military, to watch hostile Pakistan and to sustain its pretensions to being the regional power of South Asia. India's fast population growth had many troublesome ramifications. For example, in 1950 the government had established a goal that by 1960 all children up to age fourteen would be in school. A high birth rate, however, had prevented its realization. In fact, illiteracy barely decreased, and only about 25 percent of the people could read and write. Thus India remained a poor Third World nation. The average annual per capita income of Indians was $53 in 1951, $150 in 1977, and $240 in 1988.

Bangladesh was one of the ten poorest nations on earth, with a per capita income of $150 in 1988. With an estimated population of 110 million people in 1988, it was the eighth most populous nation in the world, and with land area approximately the size of Wisconsin, it was also one of the most densely populated. Its low-lying land was vulnerable to disastrous floods, and it lacked natural resources for industrial development. It received massive foreign aid, but lacked the infrastructure to distribute that aid properly.

The Philippines was another nation that remained on the verge of economic ruin, partly due to mismanagement and corruption during the Marcos decades (1965–1986). Marcos rewarded members of his family and supporters, and created a system dubbed "crony capitalism," in which wealth wound up in the hands of a small group of families and individuals. While peasants were pushed off the land, large estates thrived on producing for export. Lacking pe-

Indian Prime Minister Indira Gandhi meets leader of Bangladesh, a nation that owed its independence to India. (Keystone Press)

troleum deposits, the Philippines imported petroleum at increasingly high prices and, despite extensive U.S. aid, chalked up a huge foreign debt of $26 billion. After 1986, the Aquino government checked the downward spiral but had not initiated land reform, reduced corruption, or generated enough confidence to attract investments and thus begin economic recovery.

Persistent Racial, Ethnic, and Religious Conflicts

Communal problems in India preceded independent nationhood and continued afterwards. Hostilities between Hindus and Muslims had delayed its independence and resulted in the partition of the subcontinent into India and Pakistan. In post-independence India, Hindu-Muslim communal antagonisms persisted and occasionally erupted into rioting. Other minority groups, such as the Gurkas, who lived near Nepal, and the tribal people in Assam, agitated or revolted for special treatment or autonomy. The most serious troubles for India, however, came from the Sikhs, a religious minority of about sixteen million people who lived in the northern state of Punjab. The Sikhs were a successful people who had done well in the government and military, and their province was one of the richest in the land. However, when the Indian government refused special recognition for their religion and greater autonomy for Punjab, extremists resorted to armed terrorism and began to store arms in the Golden Temple in Amritsar, Sikhism's holiest shrine. In 1984, Prime Minister Indira Gandhi ordered the Indian army to oust Sikh terrorists from the Golden Temple, in the course of which hundreds were killed and the temple damaged. After disgruntled Sikh officers in her bodyguard assassinated her, Rajiv Gandhi negotiated an accord with moderate Sikh leaders that included greater autonomy for the Punjab and other concessions. The extremists, however, who would have been satisfied only with an independent Sikh state, were not mollified, and sporadic acts of terrorism continued.

Despite India's own troubles with minority separatism, it intervened in the ethnic conflict in neighboring Sri Lanka. The Buddhist Sinhalese majority politically controlled that island, and the Hindu Tamil minority there resorted to terrorism to gain autonomy or to secede. India at first allowed the Tamil rebels to use southern India for training and refuge and supplied them with arms. It did so to assert its claim as the regional power of South Asia and because the large population of Tamils in southern India sympathized with the plight of their kindred in Sri Lanka. In 1987, the Indian government forced a mediated settlement and landed its troops to enforce its terms, but it became mired in Sri Lanka battling the Tamils, who were dissatisfied with the terms of the settlement.

Throughout Southeast Asia, the status of Chinese minorities presented a special problem. There were Chinese populations in every nation, numerically small but economically very influential. The success of the Chinese excited envy, and often retaliation and victimization. For example, it was customary for Filipino politicians to shake down local Chinese-Filipinos; and during the army countercoup in Indonesia in 1965, many of the victims were local Chinese who were killed because of their wealth. The recent rise of militant Islam among the Malays in Malaysia added to the disquiet of the Chinese and other minority groups, and threatened the political stability that characterized Malaysia's post-independence years.

Walking the Cold War Tightrope

The foreign policy of every new Asian nation was affected by the continuing Cold War, and each nation's relation to the Cold War was in turn affected by its particular ideology, colonial experience, and relationships with its neighbors. Some nations chose alignment with one of the superpowers, while others chose neutrality or non-alignment.

India professed neutrality in superpower politics, but in practice tilted toward the Soviet Union. When India's initially friendly relations with China deteriorated to war in 1962, the Soviet Union rewarded India with weapons and diplomatic support. India and Pakistan continued to be each other's worst enemy, intermittently threatening each other with war. On the other hand, Pakistan chose a pro-Western stance, and after 1962 also became pro-Chinese. When India detonated a nuclear device in 1974, its intended eventual target was undoubtedly Pakistan.

The Indian threat motivated Pakistan to hastily develop its own nuclear capability, which it reputedly achieved in 1986. Although the United States opposed nuclear proliferation, it continued to assist Pakistan because that nation was playing the leading role in supporting anti-Soviet guerrilla fighters in Afghanistan. Pakistan gave refuge to over three and one-half million Afghans who had fled their homeland, allowed its territory to be used as a staging ground for the Afghan guerrillas to strike back into Afghanistan, and became a conduit for U.S. military and economic aid to the insurgents. Anxious to continue receiving U.S. aid after Soviet withdrawal from Afghanistan, Prime Minister Benazir Bhutto announced in 1989 that Pakistan would not build nuclear weapons. India, on the other hand, refused to criticize the Soviet Union for its activities in Afghanistan.

The remaining non-Communist states of southeastern Asia, with the exception of neutralist Burma, tended to tilt toward the West in the Cold War. However, after the United States withdrew from the Indochina war, some of them, for example, Thailand, became fearful of antagonizing their powerful Communist neighbors and so began to distance themselves from the United States. An uneasy relationship also developed between the U.S. and the Philippines. The two largest U.S. overseas bases, Clark Air Force Base and Subic Bay Naval Station, were located in the Philippines. The United States paid the Philippine government handsome rent for use of the facilities, and the bases generated much-needed income for the Filipino economy. Nevertheless, many Filipinos resented the massive U.S. presence in their nation as a symbol of the nation's residual colonial status. In 1988, an agreement was signed between the two countries which extended the lease until 1990 in exchange for an increased rent and aid package from the United States.

India, together with Egypt and Yugoslavia, sponsored the Nonaligned Movement, organized in 1961. Its Asian members included Bangladesh, Indonesia, Malaysia, and Singapore. In 1967, Indonesia, Malaysia, the Philippines, Singapore, and Thailand founded the Association of Southeast Asian Nations (ASEAN) to promote economic and political cooperation between these non-Communist nations (Brunei was admitted after independence). Through frequent consultations, ASEAN nations achieved mutual tariff reductions, sponsored joint economic projects, and in other ways worked to further the interests of all member nations. Burma, however, was conspicuous in refusing to join multinational endeavors.

THE CONTINUING COLD WAR IN ASIA

The Great Powers Partition Vietnam

The economic, political, and international relations of all nations of Asia were profoundly affected by the intrusion of Cold War superpower interests into Indochina after France's withdrawal in 1954. The mixture of communism and nationalism in Indochina also ensured that the major powers would become embroiled in the decolonization process. Where communism was not an issue, the United States supported independence for Asian peoples. Thus it had pressured the Netherlands to relinquish control over Indonesia. However, it opposed the Communist-led independence movement in Indochina, first by supporting the French. When that failed, it endorsed an international conference, convened at Geneva, Switzerland, in 1954, where representatives of the United States, Great Britain, and France met with those of the Soviet Union and China and with Vietnamese leaders. At the conference, the great powers agreed temporarily to partition Vietnam at the 17th parallel, the north to remain under Ho Chi Minh's control, and the south to be under a non-Communist government that France had installed. They also agreed that elections, to be held within two years of the agreement in both parts of Vietnam, should determine the future of the land, and asked the United Nations to supervise the elections. Laos and Cambodia became independent and neutral nations. The United States and South Vietnam did not sign the Geneva Agreement because Ho Chi Minh was allowed to control the north, but the agreement nevertheless went into effect and France withdrew from Indochina.

The two halves of Vietnam quickly polarized into a Communist and an anti-Communist nation. North of the 17th parallel, Ho Chi Minh established the Democratic Republic of Vietnam, with its capital at Hanoi. With economic and military aid from the Soviet Union and China, Ho proceeded to build a strong and effective regime in the north based on the Chinese model. His brutal land reform and other policies led to the flight of a million northern-born Vietnamese, mostly Catholics, to the south and triggered a peasant revolt which had to be suppressed with troops.

In the south, the Republic of Vietnam established its capital at Saigon.

After 1955, President Ngo Dinh Diem, a Catholic in a predominantly Buddhist land, ruled there autocratically. About 90,000 supporters of Ho fled north, which made Diem's task of consolidating the south easier. With the support of the French-trained army, Diem suppressed various armed religious sects and promulgated a constitution in 1956 which gave him extensive powers. Diem was a nationalist, but his regime became increasingly unpopular because his government was corrupt and authoritarian and because he favored the Catholic minority. The United States supplied economic aid to South Vietnam and, fearing a Communist victory, encouraged the South Vietnamese government not to hold the elections, with which it readily agreed.

The Second Indochina War

In 1958, South Vietnamese Communists, who called themselves the Viet Cong for short, launched a revolt against the government of South Vietnam. In 1959, Ho began infiltrating Communist southerners who had gone north in 1954 back to their homeland, and within a year these Communist cadres had fused together the disparate anti-Diem elements into the National Liberation Front of South Vietnam (NLF). Meanwhile Laotian and Cambodian Communist guerrillas had also launched revolts against their governments, turning the hostilities into a general Indochina war.

The superpowers soon turned these civil wars, especially the one in South Vietnam, into a Cold War conflict. The Soviet Union and China hailed their side's goal as a "war of national liberation," but initially gave little more than moral support. The United States under President Eisenhower invoked the Truman Doctrine and began to send military aid and advisors to build up the South Vietnamese army, called ARVN for short. President Kennedy continued and expanded aid to South Vietnam and gave aid also to anti-Communist forces in neighboring Laos in what he called a "flexible response" policy.

As the United States became more involved in South Vietnam, the Soviet Union, China, and other Communist bloc nations countered by supplying North Vietnam with weapons, economic aid, and technical advisors. China also sent labor batallions to replace North Vietnamese who had been drafted into the army. These supplies, and, after 1964, North Vietnamese troops, were funneled through Laos and Cambodia into South Vietnam along the Ho Chi Minh Trail. In South Vietnam, the Viet Cong fought a war of ambush and assassinations while they controlled peasants in the countryside by intimidation and won their support by land reforms.

Meanwhile, Diem's anti-Buddhist policies led the Buddhist clergy to widespread protests; several monks shocked the world by publicly setting themselves afire. Late in 1963, the United States gave tacit approval to a plot by disaffected ARVN generals to overthrow the Diem government. In the resulting coup, Diem and his hated brother, the security chief, were both killed. Political instability followed, as a succession of generals tried and failed to organize governments that enjoyed widespread public support.

PEOPLE'S   REPUBLIC   OF   CHINA

BURMA

Dien Bien Phu

Hanoi

Haiphong

Gulf of
Tonkin

NORTH

Luang
Prabang

VIETNAM

Vientiane

L
A
O
S

South

China

17° Parallel

Sea

THAILAND

Mekong R.

Hue

Da Nang

SOUTH

Bangkok

C A M B O D I A

VIETNAM

VIETNAM

Cam
Rahn
Bay

Phnom Penh

**The Second
Indochina War
1957–1975**

Saigon

Ho Chi Minh Trail

Soviet supplies

Chinese railroad supply line

Area substantially under Communist
control throughout the war

U.S. bases

U.S. troops and supplies

Tonkin Gulf incident

Area of Communist guerrilla operations

0   50   100   150   200

Scale of miles

438

A Buddhist monk burns himself to death in Saigon in 1963 in protest against the Diem regime. (UPI/Bettmann Newsphotos)

Lyndon Johnson, who succeeded Kennedy as president in 1963, sharply escalated U.S. involvement in Indochina. Johnson used an engagement between U.S. naval vessels and torpedo boats of North Vietnam to maneuver the Congress into passing the August 7, 1964, Tonkin Gulf Resolution, which authorized the president to "take all necessary measures to repel any armed attack against the forces of the United States in order to prevent further aggression." After Johnson won election to a full term in 1964, he gradually increased U.S. troop levels until they reached half a million in 1968. He also authorized air strikes against military targets in North Vietnam and along the Ho Chi Minh Trail.

It was extremely difficult for U.S. forces, despite better arms, equipment, and supplies, to fight disciplined guerrillas in an oppressively hot climate among peasants of an alien culture. The United States was further hampered by having to work in tandem with a poorly led conscript South Vietnamese army, and with an inexperienced and graft-ridden South Vietnamese government.

By 1968 the United States and North Vietnam were shouldering the main burden of the fighting in South Vietnam. Although the U.S. and its allies (Australia, Thailand, South Korea, and several other nations also sent troops) were engaged in conflict with a Communist state supported by the senior members of the Communist bloc, the major powers tacitly agreed that the conflict should not be enlarged into a nuclear war.

The Tet (lunar new year) offensive of 1968 was the turning point in the war. Taking advantage of a traditional holiday when their adversaries were off guard, the Communists launched heavy simultaneous assaults on all important towns in South Vietnam and inflicted heavy casualties, although they were eventually driven back with severe losses. The Tet offensive dashed hopes of a quick end to the war, and many weary Americans and their leaders began to look for a way out. In 1968, the United States and North Vietnam began discussions to end the war.

Unpopular because of his role in leading the U.S. into a wider war, Johnson did not seek reelection. Republican candidate Richard Nixon announced that he had a plan to end the war "with honor." President Nixon ended U.S. involvement in the war by improving relations with the Soviet Union and China, heavily bombing North Vietnam to persuade it to negotiate seriously, increasing aid to strengthen the ARVN, and slowly withdrawing U.S. troops from South Vietnam.

On January 27, 1973, the United States and North Vietnam signed an agreement that called for a cease-fire, the complete withdrawal of U.S. troops in sixty days, and U.S. aid to both North and South Vietnam. Chief negotiators Henry Kissinger and Le Duc Tho received the Nobel Peace Prize in 1973, but fighting continued in South Vietnam until 1975, when the North Vietnamese and Viet Cong crushed the South Vietnamese government. The thirty-year struggle for a united, independent Vietnam was over, on Communist terms. In 1976, representatives from North and South Vietnam voted to create the unified Socialist Republic of Vietnam; Saigon was renamed Ho Chi Minh City (Ho had died in 1969). Communist governments also took over in Laos and Cambodia.

Communist Quarrels after the War

Contrary to fears engendered by the domino theory, Communism spread no further in Asia after 1975. Instead, the Communist nations of Asia began to fight each other, demonstrating that nationalism and imperialism were often stronger impulses than common political and economic ideology. Historical Vietnamese imperialism, which had been halted by French colonialism and U.S. intervention, now triumphed across Indochina. Vietnam invaded Cambodia in 1977 to expel one set of local Communist leaders (the murderous regime of Pol Pot) and installed their puppets, but Cambodian guerrilla resistance tied down a large Vietnamese occupation force. Vietnam also established control over Laos. The Vietnamese military, fifth largest in the world, battle-tried and well armed with Soviet and Chinese weapons and captured U.S. armor, became widely feared by the militarily weak non-Communist nations of Southeast Asia. Many Southeast Asian nations, once afraid of the giant presence of the United States, now rued the day of U.S. withdrawal.

On the other hand, Vietnam's ambitions received a check from its erstwhile ally and mentor, China. Sino-Vietnamese enmity was a historic fact of long standing, especially felt by Vietnamese, who feared the long shadow cast by much larger and historically dominant China. As a result, Vietnam cultivated close ties with the Soviet Union to counter China. For its part, China feared that Vietnam, and by inference the Soviet Union, would extend its influence in Southeast Asia. Alleging Vietnamese mistreatment of ethnic Chinese in Vietnam and accusing Vietnam of imperialism in its control of Cambodia, China launched a punitive campaign against Vietnam in 1978, but the inexperienced Chinese units did not perform well against the battle-hardened Vietnamese. In any case, after a limited invasion, China declared that it had punished Vietnam and withdrew, threatening to return should Vietnamese behavior require it in future.

The Chinese incursion put Vietnam squarely in the Soviet camp. Numerous Soviet technicians were sent to Vietnam, and large sums of Soviet aid poured in to keep afloat the inefficient and war-damaged Vietnamese economy. In return, the Soviet navy obtained Camranh Bay, with its excellent natural harbor and U.S.-built installations, as a base from which it could challenge the U.S. navy at Subic Bay and exert power in Asian and western Pacific waters.

In the late 1980s, no Asian nation, with the possible exception of the Philippines, appeared likely, short of outside conquest, to turn communist. Almost all of them were more prosperous and had made larger economic gains than the nations under communism. The Philippines was an exception, because its population was miserably impoverished, its economy was in ruins and near bankruptcy, the government was unstable, and the Communist insurgency had not been controlled.

SUMMARY

Until after Mao Zedong's death in 1976, China was mired in ideological disputes and power politics within the Communist leadership that brought the nation to near-bankruptcy. The newly independent nations found themselves beset by common problems, namely population explosion, poverty, economic backwardness, and ethnic and communal conflicts. While India (except for a short interlude) had enjoyed stable, democratic governments, Pakistan and Bangladesh had fluctuated between elected governments and military rule, while the other nations had experienced almost everything in between. Economic progress had also been uneven. While some, such as Indonesia, had made good use of their resources, the Philippines had mismanaged itself into near-bankruptcy, while economists despaired as to whether Bangladesh could ever progress beyond its desperate poverty. In international affairs, Asian nations had been drawn into either the Eastern or Western blocs, or maintained a precarious and sometimes a tilting neutrality.

Two of the most dangerous East-West confrontations of the postwar period had been in Asia. Although the actual fighting of the Korean War ended in

1953, the Korean peninsula remained divided and a potential danger point. In formerly French Indochina, a second war was fought that pitched the United States against a Communist state that had the backing of the Soviet Union and China. The United States failed to stem the advancing tide of communism in Indochina, which after 1975 was ruled by Communist governments and dominated by Vietnam. However, the domino theory did not prove applicable beyond Indochina, and in fact the change in Indonesia from a pro-Communist to a pro-Western neutral nation had redressed the balance and contributed to the stability of Southeast Asia.

SUGGESTED SOURCES

Bhutto, Benazir, *Daughter of Destiny, An Autobiography* (1989). A moving book by a courageous woman.

Butterfield, Fox, *Alive in the Bitter Sea* (1983). A moving account of life in China.*

Caputo, Philip, *A Rumor of War* (1977). A thoughtful account of the war in Indochina by a marine who fought there.*

Cheng, Nien, *Life and Death in Shanghai* (1987). A victim's account of the horrors of the Cultural Revolution in China.*

Clubb, O. Edmund, *20th Century China*, 3rd ed. (1978). An authoritative history.*

FitzGerald, Francis, *Fire in the Lake* (1972). Perhaps the best overview of the culture and politics of Vietnam and of the nature of the war there.*

Grey, Anthony, *Saigon* (1982). An epic novel that intertwines French, American, and Vietnamese lives from 1925 to 1973.

Herring, George C., *America's Longest War: The U.S. and Vietnam, 1950–1975* (1979). A concise, well-written narrative.*

Hsu, Immanuel C.Y., *The Rise of Modern China*, 3rd ed. (1983). A good, comprehensive history of China from the nineteenth century.

Karnow, Stanley, *Vietnam: A History* (1983). A balanced account of the war. (Also made into a thirteen-part television series.)

Romilo, Beth Day, *Inside the Palace: The Rise and Fall of Ferdinand and Imelda Marcos* (1987). An insider's look of the Marcos regime by the American journalist wife of a prominent Filipino.

*Paperback available.

30

The "Asian Rim": A New Economic Powerhouse

Beginning in the 1960s, a new center of capitalist power, often referred to as the Asian Rim, arose to challenge the two traditional economic powerhouses, the United States and Western Europe. The Asian Rim nations—Japan, South Korea, Taiwan, Hong Kong, and Singapore—all shared a heritage of Chinese culture, particularly a Confucian moral and social system that honored strong family ties, revered education, and promoted a work ethic. Japan led the pack in economic progress, but by the 1980s the other four had made amazing advances that earned them the nickname of "little Japans," a term that they viewed with a mixture of pride and resentment.

ECONOMIC RISING SUN: POSTWAR JAPAN

The story of postwar Japan was that of the phoenix rising from its ashes, alive but significantly changed. Wartime agreements between Allied powers stipulated that Japan be stripped of its conquests since 1895, which the emperor's unconditional surrender implicitly accepted. Crushed in war, Japan in September 1945 was open to change to a degree that was unique in history. On the basis of its recent past, it had the potential to follow either a democratic or a totalitarian path, but U.S. occupation directed its political and social restructuring along democratic lines.

The United States Rebuilds Japan

The catalyst that sent Japan along the road to recovery and prosperity was the seven-year U.S. occupation of the islands. What happened to Japan after the war differed significantly from what happened to Germany. Japan was occupied by the United States rather than by forces from many nations. Although General Douglas MacArthur was Supreme Commander for the Allied Powers (SCAP), in reality he took orders only from the government of the United States.

Unlike Germany, Japan was not directly governed by the occupation forces; rather, it retained its emperor and government, which was closely supervised by the SCAP.

After their decisive defeat, most Japanese had no wish to return to their imperial past. With their former sense of national mission shattered, they proved amenable to change and cooperative with the occupiers, whom they found surprisingly benevolent. With the Cold War spreading rapidly from Europe to Asia, the United States had an added impetus to rebuild Japan economically and to restructure its government along parliamentary and democratic lines. The United States assumed that a prosperous and democratically governed Japanese people would not find communism attractive and would be less likely to disturb world peace again.

The immediate task for the U.S. occupation authorities was to help feed a large population that included six million returned soldiers and colonial personnel. U.S. food prevented starvation until the Japanese could rebuild their shattered economy. The next task was to create a new political structure, based on a new constitution. The emperor was retained as a stabilizing force, but was stripped of his formerly divine status, which he renounced on January 1, 1946, in the Declaration of Humanity. In addition to a small number of leaders who were tried and punished for war crimes, about 200,000 former military officers, officials, and industrialists were forbidden to hold office or continue in business. The removal of the old guard allowed a young generation of Japanese to rise to power.

General MacArthur closely supervised the writing of the new constitution, which was promulgated in 1947, accompanied by a Bill of Rights. These documents contained elements from the Declaration of Independence, the U.S. Constitution, the Gettysburg Address, and the British parliamentary system. The constitution proclaimed the Japanese people sovereign, enfranchised women, and provided a bicameral legislature (the Diet), with members of both chambers elected by universal suffrage. The executive was made directly responsible to the Diet, and the judiciary was independent of the executive. The constitution renounced war and the right of belligerency forever and declared that "land, sea, and air forces, as well as other war potential, will never be maintained." This provision made the Japanese constitution unique among constitutions. Later the United States encouraged Japan to create a small Self-Defense Force.

SCAP also instituted economic and social changes, designed to break the authoritarian and paternalistic pattern in Japanese society and to promote democratic and egalitarian ideals. In a sweeping land reform program, SCAP sanctioned a drastic rent reduction, set a limit on land ownership, and sold excess land at a low price to existing tenants. Over a million families benefited from the reforms, which were as sweeping as those in Communist China, but accomplished without violence.

Equally fundamental was the breakup of the *zaibatsu*. Ten family-owned holding companies and dozens of industrial and trading companies were dissolved and their stocks were sold to the public. The Diet passed laws modeled on U.S. antitrust legislation, established a Fair Trade Commission to police business practices, and abolished laws restricting the labor movement and trade unions.

SCAP made fundamental changes in education. Under its supervision, the Diet extended compulsory education from six to nine years, although most students went on to twelve. The Diet also changed the content of education, emphasizing democratic principles. Girls were given more opportunities, and all young people were given more chances for higher education.

In the long run, the reforms brought about changes in attitudes which shaped Japan for decades. On April 11, 1951, the Japanese were greatly shocked when President Truman dismissed General MacArthur in a dispute over the conduct of the Korean War. This event served as a great object lesson in democracy—that a message from a civilian leader could bring down a great military proconsul who had seemed all-powerful, an event that would had been undreamed of in prewar Japan.

Independence Restored

In the early 1950s, Japan moved quickly toward independence. It had always been presumed that the United States would occupy Japan for a limited time; further, the Communist victory in China, followed by the Korean War, emphasized Japan's importance as an anti-Communist bastion. The United States decided to end the occupation quickly so that Japan could take its place among

Japanese schools are strict and maintain high academic standards. Students in this class are attentive and well prepared. (Michal Heron/Woodfin Camp & Associates)

democratic nations of the world. As a major step, Japan and forty-eight victor nations in World War II signed a peace treaty in San Francisco in 1951. The Communist bloc nations refused to sign, and neither of the Chinese governments was included because each claimed to represent all of China. A separate treaty was soon signed between Nationalist China and Japan.

In 1952, the occupation of Japan came to an end. The United States and Japan signed a treaty of mutual cooperation and security that allowed the United States to retain bases in Japan and forbade Japan to grant military bases to any other power without U.S. consent. Japan became in effect a U.S. military protectorate, which made some Japanese unhappy, although most were glad to enjoy the security provided by the U.S. nuclear umbrella. With U.S. protection, the Japanese did not need to change their constitution to allow them to spend large sums of money to ensure national security.

The Japanese economy recovered rapidly during the 1960s. U.S. aid in the amount of $2 billion between 1947 and 1952, and military procurement orders during the Korean War, had helped send Japan on the road to economic recovery. Per capita income rose from $146 in 1951 to $395 in 1960; during the same decade, the GNP increased at an average annual rate of close to 9 percent. The dynamic of Japan's economic success was based on a combination of new imported equipment, the work ethic of a highly literate labor force, a high rate of savings, agricultural improvements, a low birth rate, and government encouragement.

Just as Adenauer guided West Germany toward recovery and rehabilitation in the postwar years, Yoshida Shigeru did the same for Japan during the decade between 1945 and 1955, called the "Yoshida Years." Yoshida served as a diplomat before World War II but opposed the imperialistic policies of the military, for which he suffered brief imprisonment. A staunch anti-Communist and a conservative, he worked well with SCAP to build a new Japan, concentrating on economic recovery and efficient government. When SCAP restored free elections, the two major conservative political parties of the prewar era emerged under new names as the Liberal party and Democratic party. Yoshida headed the Liberal party as prime minister. When various left-wing parties merged to form the Socialist party in 1955, the two conservative parties did the same thing, forming the Liberal Democratic party, which held power in Japan throughout the postwar period, relegating the Socialists to the status of a permanent opposition. The persistent domination of the Liberal Democratic party has led some to call the recent Japanese political system the one-and-half party system.

The most important guiding principle of Japan's post-occupation foreign policy was to maintain close ties with the United States, in intergovernmental as well as educational and cultural affairs. When the two nations revised their treaty in 1960, the Japanese obtained more favorable terms than they had under the 1952 treaty; for example, the Japanese government now had to be consulted before the United States brought nuclear weapons into Japan.

A second guiding principle was to support an open and expanding world trading order. Toward that end, Japan agreed to pay reparations to several newly independent nations in Southeast Asia for World War II damages. Japan then established diplomatic relations with these nations, and supplied them with loans, credit, and other forms of economic aid. Following the lead of the United States, Japan maintained diplomatic relations with Nationalist China on Taiwan, which became an important trading partner.

Japan Becomes a World Economic Power

After 1960, Japan scored one economic success after another, enjoyed political stability, and began to develop a new sense of national confidence. It enjoyed a steady growth based on the newest plants and equipment, a cooperative attitude between workers and management, government encouragement of business, and a determined work ethic. A German industrialist who visited Japan in the late 1960s remarked that the Japanese worked the way Germans used to work. Japan's economic growth was also facilitated by the light burden of military spending, stipulated by its U.S.-dictated constitution. Whereas the United States spent nearly 10 percent, the Soviet Union close to 20 percent, and Western European nations around 5 percent of their GNP on their respective military establishments, Japan's defense spending was consistently less than 1 percent of its GNP.

The success of Japan's rapid recovery produced sweeping changes that affected every aspect of life. Significantly, it was the first Asian nation to bring population growth under control. Peace and better medical care brought about a baby boom in the immediate postwar years; between 1945 and 1950, the population increased 15.6 percent, from seventy-two to eighty-three million. In 1948, prodded by SCAP, the government legalized abortion for economic and medical reasons in the Eugenics Protection Law. Then the increase tapered off, due to the Act and changing social mores. It stood at an estimated 121 million in 1987, a demographic revolution achieved in one generation. Still, Japan remained one of the most densely populated lands on earth.

The new Japan was basically urban. In 1972, one out of nine Japanese lived in greater Tokyo, and one out of four lived in the Tokyo-Osaka industrial belt. In this urban society, a social revolution steadily took place. Better-educated women claimed and obtained greater equality in fact as well as in law; smaller, nuclear families became the norm; and material goods increasingly became a goal, especially among the young.

By the mid-1960s, the humiliation of defeat was replaced by a growing national self-confidence, but this new nationalism was diffuse, like that of other modern states, and not accompanied by a reemergence of militarism or emperor ideology. Japan had its social problems, mainly caused by rapid change, but Japanese society in the 1980s lacked many of the ills that afflicted Western societies. There was no drug problem, the crime rate was low, guns were tightly controlled, and politics were stable as the Liberal Democratic party returned to power after each election.

The postwar decades were not uniformly ones of success. Japan suffered several severe shocks in the early 1970s. Two occurred in 1971 and came from the United States, which the Japanese dubbed the "Nixon shocks." To counter an adverse balance of trade, mainly against West Germany and Japan, the U.S. Congress passed a trade bill that placed a 10 percent surcharge on all imports and floated the dollar. Later that year, President Nixon announced that he was planning to visit China to mend Sino-American relations, which had been marked by hostility since the Korean War. Both the United States and China were motivated by a mutual fear of the Soviet Union. In 1973 came the "petroleum shock," as OPEC nations raised petroleum prices by 450 percent and some refused to sell petroleum to Japan because of its friendly relations with Israel. Since Japan imported all its petroleum, 80 percent of which came from the Middle East, the shock was considerable. Although the problem of supply was solved quickly, Japan suffered from double-digit inflation in 1973 and 1974. Moreover, OPEC action raised the possibility that other producer nations might form similar cartels, a frightening prospect for resource-poor Japan, which imported 100 percent of its iron ore, bauxite, wool, rubber, and phosphates, and high percentages of other industrial raw materials. Japan's response in the following years was a "raw materials diplomacy." A nation that thrived and depended on free trade, Japan had also continued to support global free trade. It negotiated long-term agreements with raw material-producing nations, from petroleum for technology with China to joint ventures with Australia, Canada, and the United States.

The crises of the 1970s also led to a larger debate in Japan over its long-term policies and goals. The Japanese decided to favor a slower growth rate than they had pursued in the preceding decades, and to shift from smokestack industries such as steel and chemicals to "clean" industries such as computers, opticals, and high technology. After debating how to distribute the fruits of future growth, the Japanese agreed increasingly to divert profits and revenues to higher wages, better living conditions, and actions to protect the environment.

Japan thus weathered the economic crises of the 1970s, and during the 1980s continued to sustain an impressive growth rate anchored in a stable democratic system. With the second largest GNP (it surpassed the Soviet Union in 1987), Japan had become an industrial giant, a global trading nation, and a major aid giver. The Liberal Democratic party continued to win every election, so that although the premiership rotated among LDP leaders, Japan enjoyed political stability and a continuity of policy. It had an open, diverse, and modern society, with characteristics more akin to those found in Europe and North America than to other nations in Asia.

Japan's economic strength, however, provoked a series of international problems. It chalked up enormous trade surpluses against most nations, especially its largest trading partner, the United States. Both governments worked to redress the imbalance by such measures as a sharp upward revaluation of the yen and the removal of many import restrictions; Japan significantly lowered tariffs (except on agricultural goods, so that it could remain self-sufficient in production of basic food such as rice). Japan also became a major foreign aid giver to poor nations and an international investor. Despite these measures, Japan continued to enjoy a huge trade surplus, mostly against the United States. In 1987, the Diet overcame a great psychological block and voted to increase defense spending over the previous limit of 1 percent of the GNP. The Japanese became worried about rising protectionist sentiments in much of the world, and in particular, in 1988, about a U.S. protectionist trade bill. To maintain its competitive edge, Japan encouraged research that placed it well in the forefront of advanced technology, where its main competitor was the United States. It was in a race with the United States to develop a "seventh-generation" artificial intelligence machine, a ceramic engine, and ever more sophisticated computers. With an average per capita income of over $23,000 in 1987 (compared with $18,000 in the United States), Japan was a high-cost labor nation that had to resort to robots at home and in overseas manufacturing plants to keep its products cost-competitive.

Japan was not entirely successful in pursuing a foreign policy of having "no enemies." The victims of its past aggression, especially in Asia, still harbored residual resentment. For example, the Chinese and Koreans were deeply offended by Japan's efforts to introduce school history textbooks that soft-pedaled its past brutal imperialist policies, and by some chauvinist remarks by the minister of education. They protested so vehemently that the minister was fired and some of the objectionable passages in the books were changed. Lingering hostility between the Soviet Union and Japan prevented an agreement that would have let Japanese capital and technology develop the mineral resources of Siberia on terms acceptable to Japan. Dependence on imported raw materials, rising labor costs, an aging population, and sizeable government budget deficits were additional problems that troubled an otherwise successful industrial giant.

THE RISE OF THE FOUR DRAGONS
OR "LITTLE JAPANS"

From the 1960s on, Taiwan, South Korea, Singapore, and Hong Kong followed Japan's path in economic advancement and become trading nations. They were variously dubbed "the Little Japans," "the Four Dragons," or "the Four Tigers." Taiwan was the most successful among the four, and within a generation had been transformed from an agricultural society to an industrial power. After arriving on the island in 1949, the Nationalist government made peaceful land reforms and introduced technological innovations that increased farm production. It also built up the physical and social infrastructure and developed light industries. Resource-poor, it had to rely on trade. The nation developed labor-intensive and export-oriented light industries in the 1960s, followed by heavy industries in the 1970s and high-technology industries in the 1980s.

The modernization program required capital, qualified personnel, and scientific management. U.S. economic aid provided much-needed capital until the

early 1960s, when it was phased out. Political stability and favorable investment conditions attracted foreign capital. Taiwan created an excellent educational system; there were nine years of free and compulsory education, although
most students went on to finish twelve grades, and over 25 percent of post-
secondary young people were in colleges and universities, thus producing the
qualified manpower for development. Many of the brightest youths went on to
graduate schools on the island and abroad, providing the necessary personnel
for research and management. Taiwan enjoyed under 2 percent unemployment,
low inflation, and fast growth. Its economy grew to be forty times as large in
1987 as it had been in 1969, and its foreign trade grew from twenty-first in the
world in 1978 to twelfth in 1988, at about $110 billion. In 1988, it was second in
the world, after Japan, in foreign currency reserve holdings. It was almost unique
in its simultaneous achievement of rapid economic growth and equitable distribution of wealth (the ratio of the highest and lowest 20 percent of wage-earners
in 1978 was 4.18:1, a smaller gap than in the United States). Per capita income
reached $7,000 in 1989 (from less than $60 in 1950). By all criteria, Taiwan was
almost a fully developed nation.

Despite its impressive development, Taiwan had its share of problems.
Environmental degradation, pollution, and various social problems accompanied rapid development and awaited solution. However, timely liberalization
and political reforms began in 1987, preempting serious protests and preclud-
ing disturbances such as those that had recently clouded the otherwise equally
impressive economic progress of South Korea. Although democratization was
proceeding apace, the government retained many authoritarian powers. The
most difficult problem facing Taiwan, however, was its political future in the
face of China's demand for reunification. Prosperous and increasingly democratic, the twenty million people of Taiwan opposed reunification with China
on the latter's terms.

Like Taiwan, South Korea progressed from a poor agricultural nation,
ravaged by war and flooded by refugees, to an economic power. Similarly, it
received economic aid from the United States until the economy had reached
a take-off point; economic grown had been phenomenal despite huge national
defense burdens. Again like Taiwan, South Korea implemented successful land
reform and followed that by developing the agricultural sector and light industries.
After 1962, it built up heavy industry and export-oriented industries. Despite a
lack of petroleum and mineral resources, South Korea's economy grew by leaps
and bounds, and in the 1980s some of its products, for example, Hyundai automobiles, competed with those of Japan in foreign markets. As time went on,
the prospect of reunification of the more populous South (forty-three million
people) with the North (twenty million) became less and less attractive. In the
late 1980s, South Korea and Taiwan ran neck-in-neck in their GNP, their export share, and the upward revaluation of their currencies. Both had opened
their markets to imports, and both were keenly apprehensive about the potentially damaging effects of the 1988 U.S. trade bill. Unlike Taiwan, however,
South Korea had a foreign debt of about $45 billion.

Hyundai shipyards and others make South Korea the world's second largest shipbuilding nation. (Reuters/Bettmann Newsphotos)

Many South Koreans believed that they had paid a heavy price in recent years for their progress. Benefits had not filtered down equitably to all citizens, and they had been ruled by heavy-handed generals. Student-led demonstrations resulted in the resignation of General Chun Doo Hwan as president, but divided opposition parties ensured the election of Chun's colleague in the Democratic Justice party as president in 1988. Continued student demonstrations and some worker strikes hurt South Korea's economy, one reason that Taiwan had overtaken it in international trade. On the other hand, South Koreans were proud of their successful hosting of the 1988 summer Olympic Games in the face of North Korea's threats to disrupt them.

The third dragon, Singapore, was another showcase of success. Singapore had separated from Malaysia in 1965, and became an independent nation within the Commonwealth. At 239 square miles, the island nation was smaller than New York City, but its population of 2.7 million, most of whom were ethnically Chinese, had made it a banking, commercial, and industrial center of Asia. It had extensive ship repair facilities, had recently developed both heavy (such as petroleum refining) and light industries, and stressed free trade.

Although it had a democratically elected legislature, Prime Minister Lee Kuan Yew was its only leader after independence, and as time passed he developed authoritarian tendencies. Lee promoted Confucianism as the national ideology, to the discomfiture of the 23 percent of Singaporeans who were not ethnically Chinese. Singaporeans enjoyed the highest standard of living in Asia next to the Japanese (an average per capita income of $6,500 in 1986), and many social and welfare programs. Demographically and socially, it resembled advanced Western nations more than many of its Asian neighbors.

Most of Hong Kong's five million people were refugees from China. British rule and free trade policy had allowed its people to build up a bustling and thriving capitalist economy. The bright lights and free life style of Hong Kong were the envy of millions of Chinese across the colony's border and the target of tens of thousands of refugees from China and Vietnam every year. In 1984, Great Britain signed an agreement with China whereby Hong Kong would be returned to China in 1997, upon the expiration of the lease of part of the territory now administered by Great Britain. China agreed to allow Hong Kong a separate administration and to respect its economic and social systems for fifty years. After 1984, however, Chinese representatives exerted an increasing influence on the way Hong Kong was ruled. For example, in accordance with Chinese wishes, the British government postponed implementing laws that would have increased Hong Kong's representative institutions, and passed a law to curtail future press freedom. A lack of confidence in the future caused Hong Kong's better-educated and more affluent citizens to seek new homes in Canada, the United States, and Australia.

SUMMARY

United States occupation of Japan after World War II ensured Japan's development as a democratic, pluralistic society. It enjoyed political stability under the uninterrupted leadership of the Liberal Democratic party. Initial U.S. aid and the hard-working habits of the Japanese, aided by a supportive Japanese government, created an economic miracle despite the nation's lack of energy and other raw materials. Independent Japan benefited from U.S. military protection and remained a firm member of the Western community of nations. In recent years, Japan played a constructive role as trading partner, loan supplier, and aid provider to other nations in Asia.

A common heritage of Chinese-based culture, with a Confucian ideology, strong family patterns, and respect for learning, characterized Japan and the Four Dragons of the Asian Pacific Rim, explaining in part their success in recent decades. Of the Four Dragons, Taiwan and South Korea made enormous economic progress to become emerging industrial nations. Both received U.S. economic aid, which allowed them to take the initial steps toward industrialization and military protection against their Communist neighbors. Singapore and Hong Kong, although minuscule in size, developed strong industrial and commercial bases and enjoyed remarkable prosperity.

SUGGESTED SOURCES

Clough, Ralph N., *Island China* (1978). A good overview of Taiwan from 1949 through the 1970s.

Gibney, Frank, *Five Gentlemen of Japan: The Portrait of a Nation's Character* (1973). An examination of the impact of the occupation on Japanese life through sketches of the emperor, a farmer, an admiral, a newspaperman, and a steelworker.*

Gold. Thomas, *State and Society in the Taiwan Miracle* (1985). Study of the factors that made Taiwan's rapid progress possible.

Harries, Meirion and Susie, *Sheathing the Sword: The Demilitarization of Post-War Japan* (1987). Thought-provoking book on U.S.-Japanese relations since World War II.

"Hirohito: The Chrysanthemum Throne," video (1980). Leaders of the 20th Century Series (Coronet). On the Japanese economic miracle.

Lau, Lawrence J., ed., *Models of Development: A Comparative Study of Economic Growth in South Korea and Taiwan* (1986). Good analytical comparisons of two success stories.

Lincoln, Edward J., *Japan Facing Economic Maturity* (1988). Summary of Japanese economic development since the 1970s, with prediction of possible future developments.*

Shataro, Ishinomori, *Japan, Inc. An Introduction to Japanese Economics* (*The Comic Book*) (1988), tr. Betsey Scheiner. The Japanese take their comics seriously. This book is about Japanese pop culture and how the Japanese view their astonishing success.*

*Paperback available.

31

African Problems and Promise

In the 1970s and 1980s, Africa, like the rest of the developing world, endured a multitude of problems, but also showed signs of promise for economic, social, and political improvement. East Africa was one area of major disturbance, but the chief spot that attracted international concern was southern Africa, dominated in the early 1970s by European imperial powers and white minority governments. As superpowers and their surrogates began to play a significant role, the Cold War, already a major factor over much of the world, affected eastern and southern Africa. Meanwhile, the independent nations of Africa faced common problems of political factionalism and of conflict between the industrial and rural sectors. Many of these problems were typical of those faced by Third World nations around the globe, but others were unique to Africa.

TURMOIL IN NORTH AND EAST AFRICA

North African Rivalries and Negotiations

North African nations have struggled with a variety of regional rivalries while playing a substantial role in Arab, African, and international politics. Libya under Muammar Qaddafi used petroleum revenues not only to launch spectacular development and agricultural programs but also to champion Islamic revolutions throughout the Middle East and much of Africa. Qaddafi's particular brand of Islamic-based social revolution, which was explained in his Green Books (similar to Mao's more famous Red Book), was often opposed by both the United States and the Soviet Union. Both nations correctly viewed Qaddafi as a threat to their own aims in the region. In contrast, Algeria steered a neutral path between the two superpowers and became a successful mediator between the West and the Third World. Because of its reputation as "an honest broker," Algeria was able to mediate the release of the U.S. hostages from Iran in 1980–81.

However, rivalries among North African nations for the dominant role in the region contributed to the allocation of needed resources toward increasing military expenditures. For example, as early as the 1960s Algeria and Morocco clashed over control of parts of the Sahara, which is rich in natural resources. This dispute over control of the western Sahara turned into a protracted war through the 1970s and the 1980s between the Polisario, armed revolutionaries seeking an independent Sahara Arab Democratic Republic, and Morocco. Determined to exercise sovereignty over the area, Morocco constructed a 1,000-mile wall of earth, which enclosed the most valuable part of the western Sahara and severely impeded guerrilla activity. In 1988, all the involved parties reluctantly agreed to disengage and hold a referendum for the Saharwis (inhabitants of the Sahara) to decide their political future. Depending on its military presence and increased economic expenditures, Morocco was confident that most Saharwis would vote for affiliation with Morocco. Such conflicts limited the effectiveness of North African leaders like Qaddafi in their attempts to formulate and dominate Arab and African policies. They also undermined programs for economic development in North Africa.

Uganda's Nightmare

Uganda, one of Great Britain's most prosperous colonies, went down a calamitous road of death and devastation after it received its independence in 1962. Lacking a broad base of support, the government fell to a military coup led by Milton Obote; in turn, while outside Uganda attending a Commonwealth conference, Obote was ousted by Idi Amin in 1971. Obote finally took up residence in neighboring Tanzania.

Idi Amin was an officer from a tiny Muslim tribe in a predominantly non-Muslim nation. His rule was characterized by a bizarre combination of flamboyance, cruelty, and personal eccentricity. He delighted in sending long, rambling telegrams to Queen Elizabeth and Richard Nixon and offered public advice on how they should govern. At the same time, he himself was instituting a reign of terror, massacring his political and tribal opponents by the thousands. In 1972, Amin gave the Asian population, which was mostly engaged in business, ninety days to leave Uganda. Using his Islamic allegiance, he established close ties with many Arab nations and was vociferous in his antipathy to Israel, South Africa, and Western imperialism.

The mounting violence in Uganda made its neighbors increasingly hostile. After Amin's ill-considered attempt to invade Tanzania in 1978, Tanzanian president Nyerere moved Tanzanian forces into Uganda in January 1979. Libya, under Qaddafi, openly supported Amin. In the ensuing chaos, Amin escaped, eventually taking up residence in Saudi Arabia. The new compromise Ugandan government was plagued with internal divisions, violence, economic ruin, refugees, and uncertainty. Only large amounts of foreign aid, mostly from Arab nations, saved the nation from total economic collapse. Rebuilding and developing this formerly prosperous area remained an enormous task.

War and Revolution in the Horn of Africa

Owing to its strategic geographic location, the Horn of Africa (a collective name for the eastern sector of the continent projecting into the Indian Ocean) became one of the major areas of the U.S.-Soviet competition. Ethiopia, a centuries-old Coptic Christian kingdom, regained its independence in 1941 when British forces defeated the Italians and returned Emperor Haile Selassie to Addis Ababa. In 1952, Eritrea, with its predominantly Muslim population, was federated within Ethiopia in spite of Eritrean preference for independence and closer association with Arab states. Eritreans and other ethnic groups within Ethiopia, particularly the Somali minority in eastern Ethiopia, viewed themselves as victims of both Ethiopian and European imperial ambitions, and continued armed opposition to all Ethiopian regimes.

Haile Selassie was extremely pro-Western in his foreign policies, and Ethiopia soon became a major pivot in U.S. policies for Africa. The United States built a radar-tracking station and a major military base in Ethiopia and provided large sums of foreign aid. In addition, Israelis were brought in to train army officers and to provide technical skills. Israeli involvement in Ethiopia typified a pattern whereby each superpower encouraged its allies to further the superpower's interests in a region.

In spite of substantial foreign aid, Ethiopia remained a desperately impoverished nation. The peasants, who composed over 90 percent of the population, were among the poorest in the world. The Coptic church and the emperor's family kept tight control over a largely feudal system. With minimal natural resources and a terrain of high plateaus separated by deep valleys that made travel difficult, Ethiopia faced major obstacles to economic development. The emperor's regime was further weakened by its disregard of the widespread starvation brought on by several years of drought and famine.

In 1974, as a consequence of these problems, a group of army officers led by Mengistu Haile Mariam rebelled, ousted the emperor, and created a military government. The new Ethiopian government adopted a pro-Soviet stance and remained a major center for Soviet influence and naval presence in Africa.

Neighboring Somalia, formerly an Italian colony, became independent in 1960. In 1969, the conservative Somali government was replaced by a military-led socialist regime that was originally friendly to the Soviet Union. Somalia claimed the Somali-populated Ogaden region in Ethiopia and in 1977 began aiding guerrillas in that area. Thousands fled from the war zone to gather in huge refugee camps. War, drought, and famine made living conditions in Somalia among the worst on earth. Political rivalries, corruption, and red tape prevented the massive foreign aid programs and food shipments from stopping the human suffering and starvation.

As Ethiopia moved closer to the Soviet Union, Somalia moved closer to the United States. Both superpowers were anxious to control the vital shipping routes of the Red Sea and the Suez Canal. Furthermore, the Horn was a strategic area from which both the United States and the Soviet Union serviced naval units watching the petroleum-rich Arabian peninsula. With its enormous economic problems and regional rivalries, the Horn of Africa continued to be a focal point of tension in Africa.

FREEDOM STRUGGLES IN SOUTHERN AFRICA

Independence in Mozambique, Angola, and Zimbabwe

As the Portuguese in Angola and Mozambique and the white minorities in Rhodesia and South Africa fought to keep control of those areas in the 1970s and 1980s, the black majority populations intensified their struggle for independence, increasingly resorting to guerrilla warfare.

Both sides sought and received outside support. From the first, independent black African nations assisted the liberation movements of southern Africa; later, the Soviet Union and Cuba also gave support. Nations along the borders of South Africa, such as Mozambique, became known as "front-line states." These nations provided training bases, often run by Marxist and Chinese advisors, for guerrillas operating in the target areas. On the other side, the white South African regime assisted the white regime in Rhodesia; at the same time, Great Britain and the United States, both of which had substantial economic investments in mining and raw materials in South Africa, continued to maintain substantial economic ties there. South Africa and Western nations also argued that the sale of arms was necessary because of South Africa's strategic location on the southern Cape and because of its steadfast opposition to the Soviet Union.

The Portuguese colonies of Angola and Mozambique were the chief scenes of nationalist guerrilla warfare in the early 1970s. The Angolan Liberation Movement (MPLA) and the Mozambique Front (FRELIMO) both escalated guerrilla attacks against the Portuguese army and the *prazeros* in a classic example of wars of national liberation. Both MPLA and FRELIMO received aid from the Soviet bloc and sympathetic African nations. Although Portugal received some military assistance from European NATO nations, the colonial wars severely drained its already weak economy. Finally, by 1975 new leaders in Portugal had moved toward a settlement of the conflicts. In a relatively peaceful transition, Mozambique declared its independence in June 1975. The new Mozambique regime, dominated by Marxist leaders from FRELIMO, launched programs for improving health care facilities and other social welfare plans and, in 1978, announced a massive campaign to increase literacy. In addition, the regime was openly friendly to other African liberation movements, particularly in Rhodesia.

As in Mozambique, nationalist guerrillas forced the Portuguese to leave Angola, but in this case a second Angolan war broke out before a stable government could be created. In 1975, competing nationalist groups, each supported by different ethnic and linguistic groups and by different opposing superpowers, vied for power. South Africa, which opposed the Soviet-backed MPLA, occupied parts of southern Angola; the United States and private mercenaries assisted moderate nationalist groups. Finally, Cuban troops moved in to bolster the MPLA, which took control of the government and declared independence in February 1976.

By 1978 the situation had temporarily stabilized, and the Marxist Angolan government attempted to turn its attention to rebuilding the nation's economic base, which had been largely destroyed by over a decade of warfare. On the other hand, continual internal rivalries impeded development. The revenues from Angola's petroleum resources helped in the reconstruction, but in part because of its petroleum, Angola remained a nation of interest to the superpowers and to its neighbors.

After Mozambique and Angola, the liberation movement focused on Rhodesia. South Africa supported the Ian Smith regime, but the rest of Africa and the international community refused to recognize the white minority government. In the face of increasing violence on the domestic front and mounting international opposition, Smith finally granted token black representation in 1978, but it was a far cry from true participation. The move failed to satisfy the demands of black nationalists, who tended to become more radical as their legitimate aspirations for self-determination were continually rejected by the small white minority. Escalating tensions induced many white Rhodesian farmers to leave; however, those that remained continued to cling to power.

Fearing the growing Cuban and Soviet presence in the region, Great Britain and the United States launched another series of negotiations in 1979. These protracted discussions, complicated by domestic rivalries, led to relatively free elections in the spring of 1979 and independence in 1980.

The new nation, named Zimbabwe (for an ancient African culture in that area) and led by Robert Mugabe, moved to deal with the continuing problems of superpower involvement, rivals for power, and internal development. Although the infant nation faced massive problems of internal economic development and political divisions, coupled with continued hostility from South Africa, Zimbabwe became a relative success story. Negotiations ultimately succeeded in avoiding the worst excesses of total civil war, the parliamentary system remained intact, and the white minority continued to participate in the political system. Ian Smith even became a member of Parliament.

Apartheid versus Equality in South Africa

Despite objections around the world, successive Afrikaner leaders continued the segregation policies of apartheid. Black African nationalist leaders were imprisoned or forced underground or escaped into exile. After the African National Congress (ANC) was outlawed in 1960, the leaders, including Nelson Mandela and Oliver Tambo, reluctantly concluded that only force of arms would end apartheid. After trials for sabotage in 1964, Mandela was sentenced to life imprisonment; Tambo escaped into exile. Many of the armed ANC members operated out of the front-line states of Zambia, Tanzania, and Angola. Sabotage bombings and attacks increased within South Africa, and in 1973 there were massive strikes. The most serious racial violence occurred in Soweto in 1976, when schoolchildren demonstrated against the use of Afrikaans as the major language of instruction; violence soon spread throughout South Africa and indicated that many blacks had become radicalized. The South African government responded with a new series of repressive tactics, typified by the death under mysterious circumstances of Steven Biko, a leading nationalist spokesman, while in prison.

International organizations widely condemned South Africa for its racial policies, and in 1984 a major critic of apartheid, Bishop Desmond Tutu, was awarded the Nobel Peace Prize. Both Tutu and the Reverend Allan Boesak called for economic boycotts of white businesses and divestiture by Western interests as a means of undercutting the apartheid regime and forcing changes. However, outsiders continued to purchase South African goods, to operate industries, and to sell armaments to the regime.

The South African system of apartheid and its continued domination of Namibia were annually condemned by the United Nations. In addition, many church leaders, including the pope, and other activist organizations around the world voiced their opposition to apartheid. In attempts to lessen its growing isolation in international forums, South Africa modified racial barriers to allow multiracial memberships on sports teams. By means of such compromises, South Africans, who were keen sports enthusiasts, hoped to be readmitted to international competitions. Strict censorship regulations had prohibited many publications and mass media productions from depicting blacks in roles of equality, but in 1976 the government was pressured into allowing television broadcasts. Job restrictions among the races and other racially based laws were modified, but limitations on citizenship were augmented.

A new constitution, implemented by Prime Minister P. W. Botha in 1984, permitted Asians and colored minorities technically to become junior partners in the political system, but further entrenched the complete exclusion of the black majority. During the 1987 elections, a political button, "If voting could change the system, it would be illegal," encapsulated the problem. Blacks and sympathetic whites engaged in large-scale demonstrations against apartheid, both in South Africa and in other nations, but the South African regime showed few signs of changing its racial policies and in 1985 took Emergency Powers to crush black opposition. It forced more and more blacks into the Bantustans, now renamed "homelands" to appease world opinion. Identity cards were gradually replaced with "travel documents" (passports). South Africa was on its way to becoming the first African nation with no black African citizens.

The black liberation movement was impeded by the poverty of its people, by old ethnic divisions which the white South African government continually sought to intensify, and by the overwhelming military power of the government. In addition, although the movement had the sympathy of the rest of Africa, most African nations were too weak and poor to offer much direct as-

In Althone, South African police use rhinoceros hide whips to beat anti-government demonstrators in 1985. (Detroit Free Press photo by David C. Turnley)

sistance. The longer the apartheid system continued without indication of change or compromise, the greater became the likelihood of massive civil war. Many black and some white South Africans, who had long hoped and worked toward a peaceful solution of full national rights for all, became increasingly pessimistic. The escalation of the conflict into neighboring nations (see below) and the scarcely veiled involvement of both the United States and the Soviet Union on opposing sides contributed to the danger of full-scale warfare.

South Africa against Black Africa

The government of the Republic of South Africa believed that the black independence movements outside its borders were perhaps a greater threat to apartheid in the foreseeable future than was black opposition inside the nation. This outlook translated into taking the military offensive by denying independence to Southwest Africa (now generally called Namibia) and retaining it as a buffer against black African and Marxist governments from the north. The offensive also entailed punishing the new front-line states of Mozambique and Angola, which were supporting the ANC, training guerrillas, and in general becoming focal points for extensive black opposition to the white South African regime.

Namibia was the last African colony, in the sense of being a region of Africa ruled by an outside white government. South Africa had held Namibia as a League of Nations mandate, and in spite of U.N. opposition had annexed the territory in 1949. In retaliation, the United Nations censured South Africa for its racist policies. In 1966, the South African Peoples Organization of Namibia (SWAPO) launched an armed struggle against South African domination. Although South Africa responded quickly with armed force, the struggle continued. As the Namibian forces escalated their attacks, the South African regime moved swiftly to arrest and imprison SWAPO leaders, but by 1972 armed confrontations were commonplace. The United Nations declared 1975 the deadline for South African withdrawal; however, the deadline came and went with no appreciable changes in policy.

Meanwhile, SWAPO continued its attacks and consistently boycotted all South African attempts at elections to further the establishment of Bantustans in Namibia. SWAPO had the open support of its African neighbors and the Communist bloc, but political divisions among various nationalist groups in Namibia also became apparent as the situation polarized leftist and more conservative forces.

The South African government consistently used economic, political, and military means to eradicate the support that neighboring black nations were giving to Namibian independence and to the blacks in South Africa. From 1982 on, Angola was subject to continuing retaliatory raids by South African armed forces, which, along with a civil war fought with U.S.-supported guerrillas, impeded and ultimately largely destroyed Angola's economic and social progress. South Africa also conducted raids into Mozambique and gave support to a rebel insurgency group so cruel that the whole world, including the United States, condemned it. South Africa also used its economic power, particularly its control over much of the railroad system of southern Africa, to intimidate Zimbabwe and Botswana. In a very real way, Mozambique, Angola, and even Zimbabwe and Botswana were victims of the continuation of apartheid in South Africa. Negotiations to ease both Angolan support for SWAPO and South African attacks and to secure independence for Namibia continued, and by 1988 a U.N.-sponsored settlement seemed to be leading to South African disengagement and independence for Namibia. However, few were optimistic that, barring the dismantling of the South African apartheid regime, a long-term resolution could be achieved. Hence, the region remained one in which an East-West confrontation could easily degenerate into an armed conflict involving the superpowers.

PROBLEMS AMONG NEW AFRICAN NATIONS

Several major problems confronted African nations after their independence. First, all African leaders had to deal with widespread poverty and often starvation. Economic problems contributed to preexisting religious, ethnic, and regional divisions that made it difficult and often impossible to forge national unity. Frequently, the national boundaries drawn by the European colonial powers did not reflect the cultural, ethnic, or linguistic patterns of the peoples living within them. Consequently, the newly independent African nations often had to deal with a multitude of different and sometimes hostile ethnic groups within one nation. Border disputes among neighboring nations also deflected energies and much-needed economic resources away from internal development and toward expenditures for armaments and the military.

These problems and the failures of the civilian governments to solve them frequently led to open interference by the military. Military coups and countercoups became the rule rather than the exception. The preeminence of the military in government also meant that large portions of national revenues were expended on the military sector. Military leaders often lacked the expertise to formulate and implement much-needed development projects. This was particularly true in the agricultural sector, in which the overwhelming majority of Africans worked. Hence, the tasks of nation-building and economic development often proved more difficult than the struggles for independence had been.

AGRICULTURE: CRISIS AND POTENTIAL

After independence, African nations had faced a number of political, social, and economic troubles. In the 1970s and 1980s, inadequate food supply, a problem that had previously been primarily localized, became a major specter across much of Africa. In a continent where most of the people were still small independent farmers, low agricultural productivity, droughts, and famines plagued many areas.

Africa has particular environmental problems. The highest rainfalls are around the equator, but the majority of the continent is either semi-arid or desert. Rains tend to be unpredictable and often fall in such torrents that soil erosion becomes a major problem. The tsetse fly, which carries the deadly trypanosomiasis parasitic infection, infests the humid or sub-humid regions where agriculture and cattle farming are climatically possible, and has proved to be a major impediment to development.

In the 1970s and 1980s, social and economic circumstances contributed to the problem of food supply. One African child in every seven died before his or her fifth birthday. Uncertainty about children surviving, as well as local traditions, made most parents want large families, thus contributing to high population growth in many nations. As a consequence of these environmental conditions, many African nations were not able to increase agricultural output fast enough to keep pace with the growing population. Ironically, advanced Western technological "solutions," such as gigantic dams, often exacerbated the problems and contributed to increased soil depletion and declining production.

The problem of ever-larger populations, droughts, and the resultant famines was particularly acute along the Sahel, a hot, dry stretch of land running from West Africa south of the Sahara (which itself was rapidly advancing) into Ethiopia and Somalia in the east. From 1977 to 1984, this region had one of the worst refugee problems in the world, as people moved from their homes to

Lusaka, the capital of Zambia, typifies the modern and rapidly expanding African city where a wide variety of manufactured goods are available for the few who can afford them. (Ray Ellis/Photo Researchers)

escape the devastation caused by prolonged droughts (in some areas 90 percent of the livestock perished) and continuing regional conflicts.

By 1984 the drought had spread to large sections of eastern and southern Africa and had become the main contributor to a major famine during the late 1980s. In Chad, the Sudan, Ethiopia, and Mozambique (nations also plagued by civil war), over 600,000 persons had died of starvation, and the lives of nineteen million starving people were threatened throughout the Sahel and East Africa. An estimated 150 million others were rapidly running out of food; even with increased rains by mid-decade, famines continued because there was no seed to plant; massive numbers of people had left their traditional farm holdings; livestock had long since been killed or had died; and deforestation was widespread. There were numerous charges that the affluent nations were too slow to recognize the problem and that the relief agencies and the governments of the afflicted nations were inefficient in distributing the food.

On the positive side, individual projects, such as Burkina Faso's public health blitz that inoculated three-quarters of its children against measles, meningitis, and yellow fever, and Ethiopia's well-digging project in Bale province, were remarkably successful. Other grass-roots and self-help projects that required minimal outside monies or support systems often worked out well.

Despite their plethora of troubles, many Africans saw a promise of improvement in the future. Agroforestry (tree farms), more efficient use of animal and human resources, land reclamation through water-harvesting in microbasins, planting of fast-growing trees, and water conservation all promised to reverse the agricultural crisis. The best procedure to bring about long-term success for these projects appeared to be a combination of market and government projects, mainly for urban areas, and locally run projects in rural areas with the use of appropriate technology. Some decades before, India had faced a future of continued agricultural shortages, yet had become self-sufficient in food. There was a similar potential for Africa.

SUMMARY

North African nations were plagued by border disputes and internal problems of development. However, Libya, with vast oil revenues, launched massive and largely successful development projects. Algeria, which also had petroleum, devoted considerable resources to domestic development; but with a much larger and generally young population to feed and provide services for, economic growth was not as rapid or extensive.

Military dictators became the rule in much of sub-Sahara Africa. Some, such as Idi Amin in Uganda, were particularly repressive and were eventually overthrown in countercoups. African nations, particularly in the Horn of Africa and the southern sector, had also been the scenes of outside intervention from neighboring nations and from outside powers. In the process, a number of African nations had become the battlegrounds for superpower rivalry that often exacerbated already volatile situations. In southern Africa, levels of violence had continued to rise as the South African government clung to the apartheid system, which excluded the majority black population from all political and many economic fields. There was been little evidence that the problem could be resolved peacefully.

Mounting economic troubles also exacerbated religious, ethnic, and regional divisions that made it difficult and often impossible to forge national unity. Regional disputes also directed much-needed resources toward armed conflicts and away from economic development programs. There were some success stories in the agricultural field, but drought, under-production, and famines continued to ravage much of Africa. Thus, by the end of the 1980s, Africa remained a powder keg that might easily explode into higher levels of violence. The leaders of the superpowers recognized the danger, but the vast natural resources, agricultural potential, and labor force in Africa made the continent important to the industrialized world.

SUGGESTED SOURCES

Chazan, Naomi, R. Mortimer, J. Ravenhill, and D. Rothchild, *Politics and Society in Contemporary Africa* (1988). An insightful narrative on the complexities of African politics.*

Finnegan, William, *Crossing the Line: A Year in the Land of Apartheid* (1986). A Western perspective on life under apartheid.*

Harrison, Paul, *The Greening of Africa: Breaking through in the Battle for Land and Food* (1987). Rare optimistic look at success stories in African development projects.*

Lamb, David, *The Africans* (1983). A timely and fascinating survey.*

Legum, Colin, *The Battlefronts of Southern Africa* (1988). A history of current crisis in southern Africa and the forecast for greater violence.*

Nkosi, Lewis, *Home and Exile* (1983). A black South African examines his society and the outside world.*

Wallbank, T. W., *Contemporary Africa: Continent in Transition* (1980). Analysis and readings on Africa.*

A World Apart (1988). A film about the personal story of a white girl growing up in an apartheid society which her family opposes.

*Paperback available.

32

The Changing Marxist World

Beginning in the late 1970s, Communist leaders, first in China and then, after 1985, in the Soviet Union, made a dramatic attempt to cut loose from some old dogmas and sail into uncharted waters toward what they hoped would be more promising shores. The move to modify traditional Communist practices was motivated by a number of factors, including technological, economic, and cultural considerations. The economic shift was the most dramatic in China, but political changes moved at a more rapid pace in the Soviet Union. Taken all together, these radical changes represented the greatest shift in the Marxist world since the Chinese Communists came to power in 1949.

EARLIER ALTERNATIVES TO STALINISM AND MAOISM

Prior to 1985, when Mikhail Gorbachev became general secretary of the Communist party of the Soviet Union, most people in the West equated Communism with the totalitarian systems developed to their fullest under Stalin and Mao Zedong. In these systems, a powerful leader directed a Communist party that attempted to dictate all phases of economic, social, and cultural life. The party instituted five-year economic plans that determined the amount and price of all legally produced goods and services. The term "consumer demand" had little meaning, and the needs of the military and heavy industry received first priority. The party also rigidly controlled all media and allowed no deviations from party doctrine.

Even before Gorbachev, and before the reforms initiated in China in the late 1970s by Deng Xiaoping, however, other Communist models existed or had been proposed. During the Soviet New Economic Policy period (1921–28), there had been considerably more economic and cultural freedom than there was after Stalin fully consolidated his power toward the end of the decade. Under Khrushchev in the late 1950s and early 1960s, Stalinism was denounced and some of its worst features attacked.

At times, the Stalinist model had also been rejected outside the Soviet Union. After his break with the Soviet Union in 1948, Yugoslavia's Tito—and his successors after his death in 1980—gradually instituted a more decentralized, participatory, and market-oriented Communist system than the Soviet Union had practiced from the late 1920s to the mid-1980s. When the Soviets crushed the reform movements in Hungary in 1956 and Czechoslovakia in 1968, little attention was paid in the West to the fact that both of these challenges to traditional Communism were supported by reformist Communist leaders, Nagy in Hungary and Dubček in Czechoslovakia. In 1968, the same year as the crushing of Czechoslovakian reform, the Hungarian "New Economic Mechanism" was introduced—the first of a number of major steps that eventually made the Hungarian economy more market-oriented. Although it still remained overwhelmingly a planned-command economy, it became less so than that of either the Soviet Union or its Eastern European Communist neighbors.

DENG XIAOPING AND REFORMS IN CHINA

Frail and senile, Mao Zedong died in September 1976. His death was followed shortly by the downfall of his widow Jiang Qing and her radical supporters, all of whom had risen to power during the Cultural Revolution. It was also followed by the rehabilitation of Deng Xiaoping, who had twice been disgraced for following the "capitalist road," that is, for advocating pragmatic economic policies. In 1981, the government tried and condemned Jiang and other members of the "Gang of Four" for prosecuting three-quarters of a million people and executing 34,375, and for other crimes. Although Mao was not on trial, their conviction also convicted him by implication. Later in 1981, a special meeting of the Central Committee of the Chinese Communist party passed a resolution that said: "The 'Great Cultural Revolution' from May 1966 to October 1976 caused the most devastating setback and heavy losses to the party, the state, and the people in the history of the People's Republic, and this 'Great Cultural Revolution' was initiated and led by Comrade Mao Zedong." With this assessment of Mao's final years, the Maoist era finally came to an end.

Domestic Reforms and Reactions

After 1978, Deng Xiaoping was China's paramount leader, and although he elevated his younger supporters to the forefront in the late 1980s, he remained the most powerful man in China. With China near bankruptcy and comparing unfavorably with the economic miracle that was Taiwan, there was enormous pressure for reform. Moreover, the Chinese leaders knew about the positive results that Hungary and Yugoslavia had achieved in their experiments in economic reform since the 1960s. These results compared favorably with China's Soviet-style centrally planned economy, with its inefficiencies that included institutionalized corruption, irrational prices, lack of contact between supplier and consumer, and emphasis on quantity rather than quality. Shortages were pervasive, morale was low, and there was growing alienation from the regime.

Something had to be done urgently, and the pragmatic Deng was willing to try whatever might work. "It doesn't matter," he had noted earlier, "if a cat is black or white so long as it catches mice."

The attempt to revive a moribund socialist economic system—called *gaige* in Chinese and *perestroika* in Russian—began in 1978 with tentative rural reform in Sichuan province, a rich agricultural region whose l00 million people were close to starvation because of mismanagement. The peasants of Sichuan (close to 80 percent of the Chinese population were peasants) were offered private plots of land to farm, and after delivering to the state a contracted amount of grain they could dispose of the rest of their produce as they saw fit. The results were so good that by 1984 all of China's 54,000 communes had been abolished. Agricultural output soared and peasant income nearly tripled. To encourage the peasants to make long-term improvements, the government gave them land-use contracts of up to fifty years. Surplus farm laborers were absorbed into small rural cooperative industries that sprang up. Although prosperity was uneven, substantial new farmhouses mushroomed throughout China, testifying to the overall success of the program.

Deng's strategy of starting economic reform with the farmers was a sound one, for he thereby enlisted 800 million supporters and had results and converts before he set about tackling the more complex problem of restructuring other sectors of the economy. In particular, *gaige* in the industrial sector was more complex than privatizing agriculture. In 1980, according to official estimates, 60 percent of Chinese industrial plants and technology were completely obsolete. Although Deng encouraged some private enterprise and foreign investment (by early 1984, for example, 128 U.S. firms had offices in Beijing), many industries remained state-run, the government still allocated key resources, and the state de-

Deng Xiaoping's reforms have allowed Chinese peasants to sell their produce in free markets like this one, near Canton. (Jiu-hwa Upshur)

termined who received foreign capital and technologies. One of the most pressing problems was the difficulty of adjusting prices to reflect production costs and demand. In a society accustomed to government price-setting and subsidies for basic commodities, a market-oriented pricing system could easily lead to inflation and social discontent.

There were many opponents to reform: senior party leaders who genuinely believed in a Soviet-style centrally planned economy, generals faced with a reduced share of the pie for the military, middle-ranking party bureaucrats who feared that reforms would take away their "perks," and ordinary workers accustomed to the "iron rice-bowl," lifetime tenure in jobs that were low-paying but that expected little of them and gave them subsidized housing and food. Some workers were also hostile to the thought of the unemployment and inflation that accompanied a freer market-oriented system.

Slowly, Deng convinced many senior colleagues who opposed him to retire and placed his supporters in key positions. He persuaded military leaders to demobilize 20 percent of their forces (a million troops) and cut their share of the GNP from 11.7 percent in 1978 to 6.7 percent by 1985, with the argument that a revitalized industrial sector would make possible more sophisticated military technology later. Some factory managers were won over by the promise of more decision-making power and less state interference, and this meant at times that the state allowed factories to select their own managers and to hire and fire based on performance.

Deng continued his new program throughout the 1980s. China sent ever-larger contingents of scholars and graduate students to universities in the United States, Canada, Japan, and Western Europe. From a trickle in the late 1970s, the number had increased to 40,000 in the United States alone in 1989. China needed the knowledge and skills its students acquired in the West if it were to sustain progress and succeed in modernizing. But the opening of China to outside influences inevitably brought about yearning for political reform and democratization, especially among students and intellectuals. Restructuring brought about other results too. It brought on high inflation, inequitable distribution, rampant corruption, increased worker unrest, and some unwanted outside influences. Conservatives feared these outside forces would corrupt many Chinese, especially the youth, and launched several campaigns to curtail what they called "spiritual pollution." They also denounced the uneven development brought about by market forces as un-Marxist. Since they proposed no overall viable alternative, however, they were forced to fight a rearguard action.

Two more problems confronted the reformers: the pace of reform and its direction and scope. Some within Deng's camp, such as general secretary of the Communist party Hu Yaobang, wanted reforms to proceed at a faster pace. Inevitably, the reforms heightened expectations and exposed shortcomings. At first, in 1978 and 1979, the people of Beijing enjoyed the privilege of airing their grievances and criticizing their leaders on a "Democracy Wall" in the city where they could post their views. In 1980, the government abruptly ended the practice and silenced critics. Several dissidents were tried and given harsh sentences in labor camps. After the Communist party halfway denounced Mao in 1981, no further denunciations were allowed. In 1986, students became frustrated with reality versus promise and took to the streets in demonstrations. They were sternly put down; some educators and journalists who had spoken out for greater freedom were disciplined. Hu Yaobang was dismissed for being too outspoken about the need for faster economic change and for a freer political climate. (Hu had been ridiculed for some of his proposals, for instance when he said that the Chinese should abandon using chopsticks and eat with knives and forks instead.)

Following the dismissal of Hu in early 1987, the battle over the pace and scope of reforms continued. At the Thirteenth Communist Party Congress, in the fall of 1987, Zhao Ziyang (a Deng protegé) was appointed Communist party general secretary and proclaimed that since China was only in the "primary stage of Socialism," whatever worked would be considered ideologically permissible. This was a 180-degree reversal of earlier Maoist claims and prescriptions for China. The appointment of Zhao, however, was balanced off with that of Li Peng as premier: Li was a Soviet-educated engineer and a more moderate reformer who was comfortable with a planned economy under party control. In September 1988, faced with soaring inflation, Deng Xiaoping himself admitted that the rate of economic development had been "too fast." Top party leaders pledged to slow it down, to check the spiraling inflation (at over 30 percent during 1988), and to restore some of the previously dismantled centralized controls.

One of the darker sides of Communist rule from its inception had been its anti-intellectualism. Although Chinese intellectuals gained some freedoms in the Deng era, they feared that what little freedom they enjoyed might be reversed. Scientists, teachers, and professionals had time and time again been humiliated, sent to the countryside to do manual labor, imprisoned, and killed. Their place was often taken by revolutionary party zealots with little education. That Deng, like Mao, mistrusted intellectuals was clearly proven by events in the spring of 1989. The seventieth anniversary of the May 4th movement and the death of reform-minded Hu Yaobang were catalysts that propelled university students in Beijing to demonstrate and petition the government to check corruption and grant reforms such as freedom of speech. Refusal by Deng even to discuss student demands led to huge peaceful student demonstrations that were supported by workers and citizens in the capital city, followed by similar demonstrations throughout China. Deng viewed these as threats to his personal power and called out the army to crush the demonstrators. Zhao Ziyang and other moderate leaders were ousted from power for being too sympathetic to student demands and replaced by hardliners. Deng and his allies then imposed martial law, arrested many demonstrators, tightened censorship, and suppressed the democracy movement.

Nevertheless, a decade after Deng's advent to power, most Chinese were better fed, clothed, and housed than they had been under Mao Zedong. Despite the inflationary surge of 1988 and their continuing relative poverty—the per capita income on Taiwan, for example, was in 1988 fifteenfold that of China—the Chinese were able to buy more goods such as televisions, cameras, motorcycles, refrigerators, and cosmetics. Per capita consumption of consumer products, including some made abroad, more than doubled between 1981 and 1987. Nevertheless, the tragic massacre at Tiananmen Square in Beijing in June 1989 and the government's subsequent harsh treatment of leading demonstrators were bound to have negative domestic and international repercussions that could hinder further economic progress.

A Pragmatic Foreign Policy

Just as China's domestic policies became more practical under Deng, so did its foreign policy. Already under Mao Zedong, fear of the Soviet Union and its military build-up along China's border had nudged China closer to the West. In 1972, Richard Nixon became the first U.S. president to visit China, and all subsequent presidents followed his example. In 1979, the United States established diplomatic relations with China and severed formal ties with Taiwan. Under Deng Xiaoping, China steadily increased its Western trade, its participation in international organizations, and it virtually abandoned providing even moral support for revolutionary movements in the Third World.

On the whole, Chinese foreign policy in the 1980s was characterized by pragmatism and flexibility. It significantly toned down its denunciations of both the United States and the Soviet Union. It generally supported U.S. policy in Asia, especially toward Afghanistan and Indochina, but it agreed with the U.S.S.R. in condemning the U.S. Strategic Defense Initiative (SDI).

Foremost among China's goals was reunification with Taiwan. In 1986, the Central Committee of the CCP declared four principles it intended to adhere to. They included adherence to Marxism-Leninism and a monopoly of power by the CCP. Taiwan, meanwhile, was moving toward political liberalization and democratization. Such political divergence and the economic gap between the two Chinas made peaceful reunification difficult to foresee.

Even before Deng cracked down on the 1989 demonstrations for democracy, the Chinese leadership had taken steps to lessen the possibility of outside influences contaminating its citizens. It required them to obtain special passes before they could enter the four special economic zones their government had set up to attract foreign investments and technology. After the student disturbances of 1986–87 the government increased ideological indoctrination in the schools and tightened the screening of students for study abroad. But as the government found out in 1989 from students in touch with the world beyond China, it was becoming more and more difficult in the Information Age to combat unwanted outside influences.

GORBACHEV AND PERESTROIKA

Although the changes in China were noted in the U.S.S.R., Soviet leaders also recognized that the two Communist giants were very different. Three major differences were: (1) a centrally planned economy with no legal private enterprise had existed for much longer in the Soviet Union than it had in China under Mao Zedong; (2) non-Russian nationalities, some quite resentful of the Russians, made up almost 50 percent of the total population of the U.S.S.R., whereas in China the non-Han Chinese minority made up only about 5 percent of the total population; and (3) the Soviets, unlike the Chinese, had an "empire"—the Eastern European Warsaw Pact nations. The first difference meant that economic change in the face of more ingrained economic habits would probably be more difficult in the Soviet Union than in China. The second and third differences indicated that Soviet leaders would have to consider more than did the Chinese the potential consequences of their reforms on minorities and on other nations.

Domestic Reforms and Reactions

Despite the potential difficulties, Gorbachev began pushing for a whole series of changes in Soviet society soon after being selected as the general secretary of the Communist party in March 1985. Although he was influenced by the previous Chinese example and Hungary's experiment with a less centralized economy and society, Soviet domestic considerations, including important economic and social pressures, offered more of a stimulus. The Gorbachev domestic program was soon characterized by three words: *glasnost* (openness), *perestroika* (restructuring), and *demokratizatsiia* (democratization).

Glasnost encompassed the ideas of more freedom of expression and less censorship and government secrecy, and by 1988 there was considerably more of such freedom in the Soviet Union than in China. As a result of *glasnost,* some dissidents were freed, permission to emigrate and travel abroad increased significantly, and many Soviet intellectuals supported Gorbachev's policies. Films, plays, and books that had long been forbidden suddenly appeared, including Boris Pasternak's long-suppressed novel *Doctor Zhivago.* New historical interpretations, especially ones critical of the Stalin and Brezhnev eras, came forth, but by the end of the 1987–88 school year they had not yet had time to be incorporated into textbooks. Therefore, since (according to the Soviet newspaper *Izvestia*) the old history books were full of "lies," the government canceled all final history exams for primary and secondary school students. The government even tolerated some demonstrations and strikes. Gorbachev also pushed for a more tolerant attitude toward religious believers and for broadening the legal rights of Soviet citizens. In December 1988, the government suspended the jamming of foreign radio broadcasts, including the Russian-language programs of U.S.-financed Radio Liberty.

Perestroika, although a term eventually used to symbolize all of Gorbachev's reforms, originally referred primarily to economic restructuring, and the reorganization of the Soviet economy remained a top priority. During the decade prior to 1985, the growth of the Soviet economy had slowed considerably compared to earlier periods. For example, it grew at less than half the rate that it had maintained during the 1960s; some economic supporters of Gorbachev even declared that there had been no real growth in national income during the early 1980s. Moreover, the economy continued to be plagued with various structural defects, including poor worker productivity, shortages of housing and consumer goods, and persistent agricultural shortcomings. Despite having more farmers than all of the industrialized West and Japan put together, the Soviets were forced year after year to spend precious hard currency in order to import Western grain. Not only did Soviet peasants produce much less than Western farmers—roughly one-seventh per capita—but as much as a third of the vegetable crop spoiled each year before it could reach consumers. High defense expenditures presented another major problem. Although roughly equal to that of the United States, Soviet military spending represented a much greater burden, since the per capita GNP of the U.S.S.R. was less than half of that of its superpower rival.

Another important factor motivating change was the challenge of the Information Age. At a time when computers and telecommunications were becoming increasingly important in business and economic affairs, the Soviet Union was falling further behind in their civilian uses—and not only behind the United States, but also behind many other nations in Europe and Asia. (This was part of the reason why it now took five or six Soviet workers to produce what one Japanese worker could.) As late as 1988, personal computers in the Soviet Union numbered in the tens of thousands, while numbering about 20 million in the United States. The director of Moscow's Institute for Space Research even admitted that to find adequate computers for his institute, he had to buy U.S.-made ones on Moscow's "black market."

Earlier Soviet leaders, especially Khrushchev, had experimented with piecemeal economic reforms, but Gorbachev and his backers soon came to realize that more radical measures were needed. Therefore, the Soviet government permitted individuals and cooperatives to offer some lawful alternatives to state enterprises, especially in the long-neglected area of services, such as restaurants and repairs. It also established joint ventures with foreign businesses—including Pizza Hut, McDonald's, and Baskin-Robbins—which signed agreements to provide for a variety of needs, from fast foods to dental fillings and hotel construction.

More long-range economic plans called for reducing centralized control of the economy and allowing more local initiatives to factories, farms and peasants, and limited private enterprise; increasing worker productivity and quality control; and restructuring prices and salaries to more adequately reflect real market values. Gorbachev and his supporters also increasingly called for *perestroika* to be applied to various other areas of Soviet life, such as the government, society, and culture.

Gorbachev's third watchword, *demokratizatsiia,* meant providing for increased participation of Soviet citizens in the political process. This issue received special attention in mid-1988 at the Nineteenth Communist Party Conference, where Gorbachev told delegates that the party's history of monopolizing power and exercising centralized control had "straight-jacketed

Under Gorbachev, joint ventures with foreign businesses such as Pepsi-Cola (Pizza Hut's parent company) have increased. (Walter Moss)

society.'' He therefore proposed reducing the role of the Communist party in the everyday political and economic life of the nation, and the conference approved a series of party and government changes designed to accomplish this.

These changes mandated secret-ballot, multiple-candidate (although not multiple-party) elections to Soviet bodies at all levels and limited elected government officials to a maximum of ten years in any position—the party had earlier agreed to similar changes for itself. The measures also increased the powers of a streamlined Supreme Soviet and its president, both to be selected by secret ballot by a newly proposed Congress of People's Deputies.

In the spring of 1989, after mainly contested elections, the new congress of 2,250 deputies met in a spirited two-week televised session that presented to Soviet citizens the most open political debates they had ever witnessed. Before adjourning, the congress elected a new 542-member Supreme Soviet and Gorbachev as its president.

Pronouncements and resolutions before, during, and after the 1988 party conference made clear the interconnection of Gorbachev's three political slogans. If a meaningful restructuring of the economy was to be accomplished, especially in the Information Age, Soviet citizens would have to become willing participants in the transformation. In his opening speech to the conference, Gorbachev indicated how democratization was related to *perestroika*. He told the delegates that ''we must have the courage to admit that if the political system remains immobile and unchanged, we will not cope with the tasks of *perestroika*.'' In his closing speech to the conference, Gorbachev said that ''no problems can be truly resolved without the people's intellectual and moral potential.'' Thus, *glasnost* would facilitate tapping this potential and the airing of opposing views, which Gorbachev hoped would lead to the selection of the best solution to any problem, whether economic, social, or political. One of the conference's resolutions noted still another connection between the three watchwords when it stated: ''A consistent broadening of *glasnost* was an indispensable condition for unfolding the process of democratizing every aspect of public life.''

By mid-1989 it was clear that Gorbachev desired to transform the Soviet Union more than any other Soviet leader had done since 1928. His criticism of Stalin and his Communist party conference proposal (which was accepted by other party leaders) to build a monument to Stalin's victims indicated that he wished to create a system very different from the totalitarian and terroristic one under Stalin. Although he did not envision for the Soviet Union a Western-style multi-party government with a free-enterprise economy, nevertheless the type of socialist society he pointed toward, if actually realized, promised to be far more humane than any of its Soviet predecessors.

The difficulties in front of him, however, showed no signs of abating. Despite a number of party personnel changes designed to strengthen his position, he still faced ingrained habits and fear of change, especially among the long-privileged elite, which stalled, delayed, and, at times, compromised reforms.

On the other hand, some of his supporters among the intelligentsia thought that he was trying to carry out ''democratic reforms through undemocratic plans.'' The words were those of Andrei Sakharov, whom Gorbachev had earlier freed after almost seven years of exile. Like most observers, Sakharov thought that the new government changes would strengthen Gorbachev's power. Despite what Sakharov considered Gorbachev's ''good intentions,'' he believed it would be a ''dangerous development'' to concentrate too much power in any one man.

In addition, despite statistics indicating modest economic growth from 1985 to 1988 and plans for significant future increases in government spending for food processing, consumer goods, and housing, many Soviet citizens grew increasingly impatient with promises, and with increasing rationing and shortages. Declining alcohol and petroleum revenues—as the world's largest oil producer, the U.S.S.R. suffered from falling prices—contributed to budget deficits and increased the country's economic problems. Gorbachev's ''vodka reform,'' which had helped lead to the deficits, was unpopular with many and had increased alcohol prices while making it more difficult to obtain, an effort to stem Soviet alcoholism and its effects on worker productivity. Although in late 1988 the government eased back a bit on its earlier anti-alcohol measures, there was by then increased grumbling about the high prices that some of the new cooperatives and private entrepreneurs were charging for other goods and services.

Gorbachev's policies also awakened the long-repressed aspirations of some of the Soviet nationalities. Conflict between Armenians and Azerbaijanis in the Caucasus occurred sporadically in 1988, leading to some deaths, massive demonstrations, strikes, and the flight of some 180,000 people from their homes before a devastating earthquake hit the region and, at least temporarily, diverted nationalistic rivalries. In the three Soviet Baltic republics of Estonia, Latvia, and Lithuania, nationalism took another form. "Popular front" organizations, created in all three republics in 1988, increasingly pushed for more national autonomy. Spurred on by the Estonian Popular Front, the Estonian Supreme Soviet (in the past a rubber-stamping organization) declared the Estonian republic sovereign in all areas except foreign affairs and defense, and affirmed its own right to approve or reject any all-union laws passed in Moscow. Gorbachev himself recognized that all these open displays of nationalist feelings were both stimulated by *glasnost* and *perestroika* and, if not kept within bounds, a grave threat to their continuance.

A "New-Thinking" Foreign Policy

While Gorbachev and other Soviet leaders used the term *perestroika* to symbolize his domestic reforms, they often chose the words "new thinking" to characterize his foreign policy. It was indeed new in many ways. Gorbachev admitted that the Soviet Union bore some responsibility for the past arms race, and the 1988 party conference declared that "foreign policy activity should contribute ever more to releasing the nation's resources for peaceful construction, for *perestroika*." At about the same time, Deputy Foreign Minister Vladimir Petrovsky stated that his nation had "a different way of seeing the world since 1985." He elaborated by saying that his government had been wrong not to give its full support to the United Nations because the world needed a stable structure for international affairs. In the sphere of regional conflicts, Petrovsky declared that "you can't export revolution or counterrevolution." He also expressed his government's desire to help find regional solutions to conflicts in such places as Angola, Cambodia, and the Middle East.

The Gorbachev foreign policy reflected the new orientation in deeds, as well as in words. Although not forsaking a Marxist viewpoint that criticized Western neocolonialism and Western attempts "to undermine the developments of the socialist states," Gorbachev nevertheless by the end of 1988 had met with U.S. President Reagan on five occasions in a little over three years. This unprecedented burst of personal meetings helped produce agreements which reversed the deteriorating relations of the early 1980s. Most important of these was an Intermediate Nuclear Forces (INF) treaty, ratified in 1988, which mandated the destruction of all (some 2,800) Soviet and U.S. land-based nuclear missiles in the 300–3,400 mile range. Other agreements provided for increased exchanges of students, cultural programs, scientific research, and nuclear testing information. And despite Gorbachev's strong objections to President Reagan's SDI—"What we need is Star Peace and not Star Wars," he quipped on one occasion—Soviet negotiators continued discussing with U.S. representatives a strategic arms reduction treaty (START) which would cut long-range nuclear weapons on each side by 50 percent.

Gorbachev and Regan at their first summit (Geneva, November 1985). (Reuters/ Bettmann Newsphotos)

On a visit to New York and the United Nations in December 1988, Gorbachev also announced that within two years the Soviet Union would unilaterally reduce its military by 500,000 troops, withdraw 50,000 Soviet troops from Eastern European bloc countries, and reduce overall Soviet European forces—in Soviet Europe and in the other bloc countries—by 10,000 tanks, 8,500 artillery systems, and 800 combat aircraft.

Improving U.S.-Soviet relations also facilitated the solving of regional conflicts such as Afghanistan, from which the U.S.S.R. removed the last of its troops in early 1989 (see Chapter 26).

The Afghanistan accord also helped the Soviet Union improve its relations with China—its Afghan intervention had been a major source of Sino-Soviet friction. Some Soviet troop reductions along the Chinese border, along with promises of more future cutbacks and Soviet encouragement of Vietnamese troop withdrawals from Cambodia, also helped ease tensions. In June 1989, Gorbachev visited China, and as a result, relations between the two Communist giants were normalized after almost thirty years of strain.

Gorbachev's efforts to improve Soviet-Chinese relations were symptomatic of his efforts to better Soviet relations in both Asia and Europe. He sought increased trade on both continents and talked of obtaining help from Asian capitalist nations for Siberian development. Japan, along with Western European nations, became his chief source of foreign loans, which increased considerably in 1988 in order to step up investment in modernizing Soviet food processing and the consumer goods industry.

To the extent that Japan and Western Europe provided credits, advanced technology, and know-how which could help Gorbachev restructure his economy, the Soviet Union thereby reduced its need for U.S. assistance, which was less forthcoming.

Gorbachev especially stressed Soviet links with Europe, advocating "the end of the schism of Europe" and referring to it as our "common home." In the fall of 1988 alone, he met with the heads of government of Italy, West Germany, and France, and received promises of major new loans. Gorbachev also applied some "new thinking" to Eastern Europe. Before further considering his policies there, a review of the region's internal changes is necessary.

REFORM AND THE SMALLER COMMUNIST STATES

Although some of the other Communist nations displayed little enthusiasm for reform—for example, Albania and North Korea—nevertheless the changes in China and the Soviet Union made an impact on many others. Some of the Communist nations of Eastern Europe, in particular, became interested in exploring new economic and political options.

Eastern Europe

By early 1985 Eastern Europe, like the Soviet Union, faced serious economic difficulties. Although living standards varied considerably from East Germany to Rumania, in Eastern Europe as a whole consumers were noticeably worse off than in Western Europe in regard to the availability of both goods and services. Economic growth rates from 1980 to 1984 were only approximately one-fourth of what they had been in the early 1970s, and on a per capita basis only about one-sixth. Although national economies in many other areas of the world had also suffered due to the global recession of the early 1980s, future prospects in Eastern Europe were much gloomier than, for example, in Western Europe. There was a growing technological gap between the two parts of Europe, especially in regard to computers and telecommunications. This gap was broadened in the late 1970s and early 1980s, as Western Europe invested much more heavily in a whole range of modernized and energy-efficient machinery. Foreign debt also promised continuing hardships, especially for Poland, as in another way did the region's polluting industries.

Lack of popular support for many of the area's governments exacerbated these economic problems. This was seen most clearly in Poland, where the standard of living declined noticeably from what it had been in the late 1970s and the Communist government seemed unable to reverse the stagnation. The government refused to deal with the outlawed Solidarity union, and most Polish workers refused to cooperate with a government in which they had little faith. The lack of popular backing made many of the region's nations reluctant to risk introducing measures of economic austerity, even though some of the funds used to buttress living standards were badly needed to pay off debts and for investing in industrial research and modernization.

Soviet insistence that they would not allow change in Communist Eastern Europe to undermine Soviet security had always been a major limitation on reform movements, as Hungary, Czechoslovakia, and Poland had learned in 1956, 1968, and 1981. The appearance of Gorbachev on the Soviet scene opened up a whole new range of possibilities, however, because he did not grudgingly tolerate reform, but actively encouraged it. His thinking seemed more akin to Alexander Dubček's than to that of Brezhnev, who had intervened to overturn the Czechoslovakian leader in 1968.

Gorbachev did not, of course, ignore Soviet security interests, but there were numerous indications that he defined them differently from the way his predecessors had. Economic stagnation in the Soviet bloc and a costly arms race appeared to him more threatening to Soviet security than Eastern European political reforms. He encouraged economic restructuring throughout the bloc, signed the INF agreement, which removed a whole class of Soviet missiles from Europe, promised unilateral reductions of Soviet European forces, and pushed for more European cooperative efforts and reductions in both nuclear and conventional forces throughout Europe.

Such a Soviet foreign policy orientation was popular with most Eastern European political leaders, who, for various reasons, desired better relations with the West. Increased East-West trade was especially important to them. The attitude of political leaders to Gorbachev's economic reforms, however, was more varied. Among leaders in Poland and in Hungary, there was enthusiasm; in 1988, Hungary announced plans to expand free enterprise considerably, beginning in 1989. East German, Czechoslovakian, and Rumanian authorities were less enthusiastic. With the most prosperous economy in the Soviet bloc, the East Germans, who possessed an economy more centralized than Hungary's, displayed little desire to move in the direction Gorbachev was advocating for the Soviet Union. Czechoslovakian leader Husak also seemed reluctant to embrace meaningful economic changes, and even though he was replaced in late 1987 by Milos Jakes, by mid-1989 Czechoslovakia had still not jumped on the *glasnost-perestroika* bandwagon. In Rumania, independent-minded party chief Nicolae Ceauşescu was more concerned with personal power and continuing to reduce his foreign debt than with restructuring the most miserable economy in the Soviet bloc. For his part, Gorbachev emphasized a willingness to tolerate different economic approaches among the nations of Eastern Europe, especially if, as in the case of the East Germans, they had achieved some success.

In all Eastern European Communist parties, as in the Soviet Union itself, there were varying degrees of both enthusiasm and distaste for Gorbachev's political reforms. Again, there was less enthusiasm among East German and Rumanian leaders and more support among party bosses in Poland and Hungary, who already allowed more freedom in their nations than existed in the U.S.S.R. In Poland, General Jaruzelski praised Gorbachev's policies and declared that the Soviet Union and Poland were now moving in the same direction and that "Poland had not experienced such a happy convergence for the whole of the past millennium." A series of strikes in the summer of 1988 and continuing economic misery—high inflation, with real wages down 20 percent from their 1980 level—nudged Polish leaders further along the road to reform. The Polish Communist government agreed to once again legalize Solidarity, to revamp Poland's parliament, and to allow Solidarity to run candidates for all 100 seats of a new upper house and for 35 percent of those of the lower house. In elections in June 1989, Solidarity candidates won all but one of the seats they were allowed to contest. Several months later, with the agreement of President Jaruzalski, former solidarity newspaper editor Tadeusz Mazowiecki formed a new government. In Hungary, party chief Karoly Grosz, who in 1988 had replaced Janos Kadar, boasted to reporters that Gorbachev told him that "it was probably the Hungarian endeavors and the Hungarian perceptions that were the closest now to those of the Soviet Union." In 1989, Hungarian Communist leaders finally bowed to pressure and recognized former Premier Nagy, overthrown by the Soviets in 1956, as a martyr and hero, not a traitor. They also began holding round-table talks with opposing political forces and committed the government to multi-party elections no later than in 1990.

The remarkable progress toward democratization in Poland and Hungary during 1989, coupled with an increasing interest in these nations by Western political and financial leaders and some uncertainty as to the limits of Soviet flexibility, indicated that the future of these two countries could be especially interesting and significant.

Among East European intellectuals and the population in general, some expressed hope that Gorbachev's influence would contribute to more freedoms and better living conditions, but others were skeptical. In mid-1987 in East Berlin, German youths reflected such hope when they shouted "Gorbachev, Gorbachev" along with "Down with the [Berlin] Wall."

Although Yugoslavia was not part of the Soviet bloc, it was still an Eastern European Communist nation which experienced some of the same problems and challenges as some of the bloc nations. Most troubling by late 1988 were the highest inflation rate in Europe—over 200 percent in 1988—and ethnic conflicts that threatened to rend apart a state which was a patchwork of nationalities.

Authoritarianism in North Korea and Vietnam

In the smaller Asian Communist nations, reform had made less headway than in China, the Soviet Union, or Eastern Europe. This was seen most clearly in North Korea, one of the most regimented and least open societies on earth. The aging Kim Il Sung remained in total power, one of the last to survive from the early post-World War II years, grooming his son Kim Jong Il to succeed him. Kim's· personality cult was complete and his presence was ubiquitous in North Korea. He had given himself many titles, two of which were "Ultimate Savior of All Mankind" and "Infinitely Resourceful Commander-in-Chief." With an estimated population of twenty million, North Korea maintained a larger army than South Korea, which had twice the population. Few visitors were allowed in, and North Koreans were not allowed to have contact with anyone outside the nation, including relatives in South Korea. The Kim government had resorted to numerous measures against South Korea, including assassinations and blowing up airplanes. It was therefore not surprising that tentative talks in the 1980s between the governments of the two Koreas had achieved nothing. North Korea demanded to co-host the 1988 summer Olympic Games in Seoul with South Korea, and, upon its rejection, boycotted the games. Neither of its big brothers, the Soviet Union and China, had any clear influence over this government.

In Vietnam, on the other hand, a number of forces, particularly economic considerations and Soviet influence, encouraged some halting attempts at reform. Although the war had ended over a decade earlier, by the mid-1980s Vietnam's economy was still a shambles, due to the rigid, anti-incentive policies of the northerner-dominated and aging leadership, which performed better in war than in peace. It maintained the fifth-largest army in the world, at 1.2 million strong, of whom an estimated 150,000 were in Cambodia to prop up a pro-Vietnamese regime, and an unknown number in Laos fighting Lao insurgents. It also still exercised a harsh agricultural collectivization policy, had abolished the private sector, and persecuted people associated with previous regimes and the ethnic Chinese; hundreds of thousands of its citizens fled. The plight of the "boat people" from Vietnam, who risked death in leaky boats and at the hands of cruel pirates to flee their native land, captured international attention. Vietnam's unwillingness to satisfy U.S. demands regarding its servicemen still missing in action from the war hampered the establishing of diplomatic relations with the United States, and the trade and aid that might have come in its wake.

Meanwhile, the Soviet Union enjoyed the use of the Camranh Bay naval base and air bases in Vietnam that bolstered its presence in Southeast Asia and the Indian Ocean, and it began to display its unhappiness with Vietnam's misuse of Soviet aid and mismanagement of its economy. The Soviet Union exerted pressure on Vietnam to negotiate a Cambodian settlement that would be acceptable to the United States and China and that would lead to a withdrawal of Vietnamese troops from that nation. It also pressured Vietnam to introduce reforms into its economy.

Thus, in 1987 Vietnam elevated men with some economic expertise to high positions. New Communist party leader Nguyen Van Linh announced plans for economic decentralization and reforms and loosened up censorship controls—the party's role regarding the arts, he said, had been "undemocratic, despotic, and overbearing." He also began talks on the future of Cambodia (Kampuchea), which eventually led to a Vietnamese troop withdrawal by the fall of 1989. However, in the spring of 1988, the government sentenced to jail five writers, including one of the nation's most prominent ones. That action, and a concurrent inflation surge, were indications of a rocky road ahead for the economically troubled nation.

SUMMARY

Beginning with China in 1978, important reforms began in the Communist world. Although some nations such as Albania, Rumania, and North Korea, were scarcely touched by the breath of reform, the major Communist powers, China and the Soviet Union, witnessed momentous developments. These changes were caused by a variety of forces, including technological, economic, and cultural factors. By the mid-1989 changes had already been underway for a decade in China, and in the Soviet Union they had developed faster under Gorbachev's leadership than anyone had dared predict when he came to power in 1985. Moves toward democratization in Poland and Hungary, in response to continuing economic and social pressures, were exciting. Nevertheless, Communist reforming governments sailed in dangerous waters. They wished to leave behind economic stagnation and political, social, and cultural malaise and sail forward toward prosperity, more popular support, and improved relations with the West. But those who attempted to ease up on central planning and to allow market forces some room to operate soon discovered the task to be more perilous and complex than they had imagined. The waves of high inflation experienced by China, Poland, and Yugoslavia in 1988 were just one indication of this difficulty. In addition, the winds of political dissent, while at times propelling them forward, also threatened to pick up and endanger their cautious crossings, as was demonstrated by the Chinese student demonstrations and the government's brutal reaction to them in the spring of 1989. By this time in Poland and Hungary there were glimmers of hope for an evolution toward democracy, but events in China in 1989 were a reminder that some Communist leaders, even economic reformers like Deng Xiaoping, were willing to react with utmost force at any perceived challenge to their power. As the 1980s came to a close, many different paths still seemed open for Communist governments and their peoples to traverse.

SUGGESTED SOURCES

Brown, Harrison, ed., *China among the Nations of the Pacific* (1982). Articles by experts on China's internal and external problems and prospects.

Cracraft, James, ed., *The Soviet Union Today: An Interpretive Guide,* 2nd ed. (1988). An up-to-date collection of thirty essays covering all aspects of contemporary Soviet life.*

Dawisha, Karen, *Eastern Europe, Gorbachev and Reform: The Great Challenge* (1988). An excellent introduction to the many problems facing the region's political leaders.*

The Editors of Time, *Mikhail S. Gorbachev: An Intimate Biography* (1988). A readable introduction for general readers and students.*

Goldman, Marshall I., *Gorbachev's Challenge: Economic Reform in the Age of High Technology* (1987). A good overview not only of the Soviet economic scene, but also of the Chinese, Hungarian, and East German economic experiences and their relevance for the Soviet Union.*

Goldman, Minton F., *The Soviet Union and Eastern Europe,* 2nd ed. (1988). A useful overview, plus thirty-seven articles from the world press; part of the annual Global Studies series.*

Gorbachev, M. G., *Perestroika: New Thinking for Our Nation and the World* (1987). An elaboration of some of the major ideas of the Soviet leader.

Harding, Harry, *China's Second: Revolution: Reform after Mao* (1987). A good summary and analysis of changes in China and a prediction of future directions.*

Hsu, Immanuel C. Y., *China without Mao: The Search for a New Order* (1982). A short summary of changes in the first five years after Mao's death.*

Lewin, Moshe, *The Gorbachev Phenomenon* (1988). An excellent short analysis of the social forces affecting Gorbachev's reforms.

Liang, Heng and Judith Shapiro, *After the Nightmare* (1986). The authors of *Son of Revolution* revisit China to report recent changes.*

Theroux, Paul, *Riding the Iron Rooster: By Train through China* (1988). An entertaining account by a keen observer.*

*Paperback available.

33

The Twentieth Century:
The Past and the Present

As the world approaches the last decade of the twentieth century, the five interrelated issues important in 1900 are still major motivating factors around the globe. At the end of 1988, two cosmonauts returned after 365 days in orbit. This odyssey in space was a far cry from the thirty-minute flights of the Wright brothers' experiments. The communications revolution has swept the world, and car phones are as popular in Riyadh, Saudi Arabia, as in Detroit, Michigan. Although technological and scientific achievements have bettered the quality of life for millions of people, they still have not conquered a host of old and new problems. At the very time that diphtheria, the scourge of the early twentieth century, has been virtually eradicated, a new virulent plague, AIDS, has spread around the world.

Contemporary societies face the paradox that at the very time in history when technological potentials offer the possibility of incredible advances, there is an equal threat to the continued existence of both the quality and quantity of life on earth. At the same time that scientists like Professor Stephen Hawking at Cambridge might be close to explaining the history of the universe, major man-induced ecological crises such as the greenhouse effect from the lessening of the ozone layer seem to defy easy solutions. One U.S. senator summed up the feelings of many when he noted in 1988, "We only have one planet. If we screw it up we have no place to go."

Increased technological sophistication has also contributed to the development of more deadly weapons that now have the capability of destroying life on earth. In particular, the use of nuclear weapons poses the threat of long-term biological, genetic damage. As President Carter said in 1981, more people could be killed in the first few hours of a nuclear war than have been killed in all previous wars in history. Indeed, the destructive potential of modern weapons often seems to exceed human abilities to control or to limit their use and proliferation. Nation after nation, from France to China to India, has developed nuclear capabilities. It has been estimated that by 1990, some thirty nations will have the capability to produce atomic weapons. The proliferation of

Improved health care here in northern India and elsewhere raised living standards but also contributed to the population explosion. (WHO photo by P. K. J. Menon)

atomic weapons increases the possibility of nuclear confrontation not only between the superpowers but also between smaller rival nations. As the possession of nuclear weapons has spread, the power of the United States and the Soviet Union to prevent nuclear confrontations has diminished.

Ironically, technologically advanced nations have also become more vulnerable to certain forms of armed attack. One or two strategically placed bombs at electric power stations or water supply installations could paralyze sprawling urban centers and could spread panic among people accustomed to the luxuries of running water and electricity. Traditional rural life can often be sustained in spite of continuous attack by conventional weapons, as the United States discovered in Indochina, France in Algeria, and the Soviet Union in Afghanistan.

In addition, humans have often developed skills and knowledge in the scientific and technological fields at a far faster rate than in social and political fields. As a result, political and social institutions have frequently failed to deal effectively with the impact of twentieth-century technology. Often, technological changes have occurred so rapidly that societies have not been able to absorb or to understand their impact.

Because of rapid economic and technical growth in the developed world, the gap continues to widen between rich societies with access to and control of modern technology and poor societies with outdated agricultural and industrial systems. Thus, while modern science and technology may well possess the ability to control and to solve the most pressing problems, many societies may lack the resources, will, and determination to finance or to implement the solutions. How to cope with and, perhaps, how to conquer these paradoxes remain the greatest challenges of science and technology.

In the late 1980s, Nintendo—a Japanese-manufactured video game series—became the latest craze among young people in the Western world. As Nintendo and a myriad of other high-tech Japanese goods have swamped the Western markets, the Japanese economy has enjoyed unprecedented prosperity and arguably has become the new power center of the capitalist world, which in 1900 was overwhelmingly Western-dominated.

As the twentieth century draws to a close, struggles for economic power remain one of the most divisive factors in world affairs. Capitalist systems based on private enterprise vie for ascendancy, as the economies of Western Europe, the United States, and the Asian Rim nations dominated by Japan compete with one another for larger shares of the global markets in the same manner that imperial colonial systems did in 1900. The competition between the so-called "free-enterprise" economies and the Marxist world that evolved during the century also continues to affect international economic developments.

Meanwhile, a gap between rich and poor nations has persisted throughout the century, although some nations have been able to cross the gap. The basic problem of the unequal distribution of wealth remains unsolved: Many nations are caught in a cycle of poverty while a few industrialized nations continue to prosper. A 1987 United Nations report indicated that the world continues to face interlocking economic and environmental problems that only international cooperation can begin to solve. The problems of hunger, poverty, population growth, military expenditures, and unequal distribution of wealth are all related. Hence, just as the famine in India at the beginning of the century had interrelated causes, so, too, do the famines threatening so many African nations at the end of the century. How and whether national governments and multinational organizations will move to resolve these problems remains uncertain.

Many nations suffer under a mounting burden of foreign debt, owed largely to Western nations or banks. In 1988, French President Mitterrand proposed a plan to relieve the crushing debt owed by the poorest African nations. Under the Mitterrand plan, France moved to cancel one-third of the debts owed to it by African nations with less than $500 per capita annual income. Latin American nations such as Brazil, Mexico, and Argentina have amassed such huge debts that they have little hope of repayment. During his 1988 address to the United Nations, Soviet leader Mikhail Gorbachev urged the international economic community to settle the debt crisis in multilateral forums and to search for means to reduce debts owed to commercial banks.

In 1987 and 1988, young black students in South Africa and young Palestinian students in Israeli-occupied Gaza and the West Bank led massive strikes to demand political self-determination. Protesting against the continued repres-

Palestinian refugees remained homeless in camps from 1948 to the present
(Courtesy of Tor Eigeland/Aramco World)

sion by the white-dominated South African government, on one hand, and on the
other hand against Israeli occupation, black Africans in southern Africa and
Palestinians in the Occupied Territories hurled stones and chanted slogans calling
for freedom. Just as Emma Goldman and her allies in the early twentieth century
had a vision about what sort of societies they wished to create, so, too, did South
African blacks and Palestinians have dreams for self-determination and full participation in the political and economic spheres of their nations. As the parties to
these conflicts—the white Afrikaners, the South African blacks, the Israelis, and
the Palestinians—all sought outside allies to support their particular goals, these
struggles also assumed international importance. As nations around the world have
become increasingly interdependent, regional domestic social and political struggles have often become international problems.

The struggle between liberal and conservative forces also continues to
characterize political life in Western nations. In the 1970s and 1980s, elections
in Great Britain, the United States, Canada, and, to a lesser extent, Germany

marked victories for the Right. The Thatcher and Reagan administrations moved to reverse the tendencies toward "big government" in their nations and initially adopted hardline Cold War policies. On the other hand, elections of socialist governments or socialist-moderate coalitions in Portugal, Spain, France, Greece, and Cyprus were successes for the Left. These governments often enlarged the range of state controls and increased levels of public services. In Latin America, freely held elections in Argentina, Brazil, Chile, and other Latin American nations reinforced the move against military dictatorship and toward the creation of workable, albeit fragile, democracies. During the 1980s, in the Marxist world, Deng in China and Gorbachev in the Soviet Union inaugurated major domestic changes that promised to liberalize their nations economically and socially. However, events in China during 1989 indicated a return to more repressive domestic policies. Liberalization in the Soviet Union caused an upsurge in local nationalist sentiments which threatened Russian hegemony within the federated Soviet system.

Another twentieth-century development, the use of guerrilla wars to bring about sweeping changes in a nation, continues to play an important role in modern society and politics. Such wars are often stimulated by cheap, mass-produced radios and other forms of modern communications technology that bring messages of change and hope to downtrodden populations. Originally primarily a method to win independence from colonial masters, guerrilla warfare has increasingly occurred in poor agricultural nations where leftist revolutionaries struggle with national armed forces controlled by the traditional elite. Still a major presence in Latin America and also a factor in Southeast Asia, the guerrilla fighter, along with the transistor radio, would appear for the foreseeable future to play a part in the process of bringing social change.

In the past three decades, some nationalist forces and individuals have adopted what has been termed "the politics of desperation." Such groups as the Irish Republican Army, the Basques in Spain, blacks in southern Africa, Sikhs in India, and the Palestine Liberation Organization (PLO) have been unable to achieve their nationalist goals through existing international organizations or by conventional economic and political means. As a consequence, they have adopted the policy of striking, with whatever forces are available, at any enemy target, civilian or military. This mode of attempting to achieve goals by intimidation, or terrorism, has become commonplace in the last quarter of the twentieth century and poses major domestic and international problems for superpowers and many rich industrialized nations.

Meanwhile, in the newly independent nations, leaders are engaged in the lengthy and difficult task of creating political, social, and economic institutions that reflect the characteristics of their own societies. They are also working, with varying degrees of success, to forge national unity from diverse peoples and cultures. Nationalism continues to be a source of domestic and international tension.

In 1987 and 1988, President Reagan and Premier Gorbachev met to discuss mutual problems of the superpowers. Their face-to-face meetings underscored the growing cooperation between the two Cold War rivals and reinforced the movement toward agreements regarding the spiraling arms race and economic crises. The INF treaty, whereby the two superpowers agreed to dismantle some land-based, intermediate-range nuclear missiles, marked a concrete first step toward control of the arms race. Although major differences and distrust remain, the meetings between the leaders of the two major superpowers seem to mark the beginning of a possible new era of cooperation. Rather than intervening militarily to resolve problems, as in the case of the Boxer Rebellion, the superpowers seem to be headed toward increased cooperation and negotiation.

The United States and the Soviet Union remain the dominant global powers, and their rivalry continues to encompass economic, cultural, and military spheres. Although both continue to maintain complex alliance systems and seek to include neutral Third World nations in those alliances, the superpowers have reluctantly realized that maintaining the balance of power has become increasingly difficult and expensive. Whether the newest move toward détente will indeed signify the end of the Cold War and the beginning of continued steps toward disarmament and toward economic, political, and cultural collaboration remains uncertain.

Although the United States and the Soviet Union are still dominant, the emergence of new nations, the mounting power of the multinational corporations and the petroleum-producing nations, the economic clout of Japan, and the growing strength of China have all diminished U.S. and Soviet political control over global affairs. The unity of Western Europe with the United States and of Eastern Europe with the Soviet Union is undermined by conflicting political and economic forces within each bloc. Eastern European leaders sometimes pursue policies that to some degree conflict with Soviet policies. Likewise, France and Japan frequently adopt economic policies that clash with those of the United States.

Importantly, the leaders of more and more nations have come to realize that many of the major problems facing their societies necessitate international cooperation. No one nation can solve the environmental crises caused by industrialization and overpopulation. No one nation can institute effective legislation to regulate multinational corporations, and no one nation can resolve the complex problems of inflation, indebtedness, and scarcity. In the twentieth century, nations must work together on global problems that threaten the quality of life everywhere. Ironically, many of these problems—inflation, abuses of the multinational corporations, pollution, the arms race—are so huge and so complex that individuals despair of understanding or solving them and find solace in alliances with local nationalistic loyalties. Thus, at the very time that fruitful international relationships are more vital than ever before, there is also an opposing tendency in much of the world toward commitment to nationalisms based on smaller ethnic and regional identities.

In 1988, the grand old man of Egyptian literature, Naguib Mahfouz, received the Nobel Prize in Literature. Unaware that he had even been nominated, Mahfouz stressed that he was only one of many meritorious Arab writers. Like Nietzsche nearly a century before, Mahfouz had often been criticized for his harsh depictions of modern life and his secular approaches to sex and family life. After leaders from al-Azhar, the famous Islamic university, complained, the serialization of his trilogy on Cairo was banned by the Egyptian government, which feared reprisals from Muslim fundamentalists were the series to be published. Similarly, Christian fundamentalists in the West demonstrated against the showing of the film *The Last Temptation of Christ.*

Increased religious fervor has not been limited to Islamic societies; during the later decades of the twentieth century, Christian, Hindu, and Jewish communities have all experienced a resurgence of religious fervor and sometimes of religious fanaticism. To some extent, the increase of militant and fundamentalist religion has been precipitated by the failures of secular societies to solve human problems. Disillusionment and fear over the uncertainties created by the modern technological age have also caused many to turn toward spiritual goals.

In the twentieth century, scientific and political changes have occurred at a dizzying pace. As a result, all societies have experienced some form of "culture shock." These changes, first apparent in the industrialized nations, have spread throughout the world. Initially, Western societies eagerly embraced the changes that seemed to offer the opportunity for unlimited progress. Western artists explored revolutionary dramatic, literary, and artistic styles, and many people have experimented with totally new life styles.

The effects of technology and Western life styles have been particularly traumatic in traditional societies. Although most societies have embraced the use of manufactured goods which offer immediate improvements in daily lives—refrigerators, radios, trucks—modernization has often meant Westernization, which has entailed the loss of long-held values and beliefs. Many traditional societies have refused to give up their own institutions and beliefs for new Western ways that seem to them not only foreign but also highly undesirable.

Thus, in many traditional societies, and ultimately in the West as well, attempts have been made to balance the uncertainties of modern existence by returning to traditional values. By the closing decades of the twentieth century, two contradictory cultural trends are apparent. On one hand, there is a movement toward continued change and experimentation; on the other, there is a growing trend toward the return to conservative, traditional ways. The resurgence of militant Islam throughout the Middle East—most notably in the Iranian revolution—is just one evidence of this trend. Many organized religious movements have recently experienced an increase in adherents throughout the world, and many groups have begun openly to question the value of the cultural and societal changes that occurred in previous decades.

In social, cultural, and economic fields, many traditional methods are also being revitalized. For many nations, the highly sophisticated technology of the industrial world is inappropriate to their social and economic needs. Early in the century, Mohandas Gandhi advocated the use of labor-intensive pragmatic approaches in rural areas. Faced with hard economic and ecological choices, many Third World and even industrialized nations are recognizing the validity of Gandhi's approach.

Many nations are increasingly using traditional methods, adaptations of Western approaches, and so-called appropriate technology in their agricultural and industrial development plans. Traditional irrigation schemes are being revitalized, and labor, a surplus commodity in much of the Third World, is being used instead of machinery. Architects such as the Egyptian Hasan Fathi have advocated the revival of age-old earthen or mud architecture to provide inexpensive yet artistically pleasing housing for the poor around much of the world. The use of mud architecture has also been adopted by some wealthy persons in parts of the southwest United States and Europe. Similarly, many artists around the globe are infusing their work with old cultural designs, music, and themes to produce new artistic expressions.

All societies, Western and traditional, have been irrevocably altered by the political, military, and scientific changes of the twentieth century. Societies that wish to maintain their traditional values must still deal with the problems of incorporating technical advances and changes within older, established institutions. Many societies continue to debate the role of women and the family in social, cultural, and political fields. What direction world societies will take remains one of the most perplexing and difficult problems of the century. As the twentieth century draws to a close, the observation of historian Eric Hobsbawm serves as a guidepost for the future: "The only certain thing about the future is that it will surprise even those who have seen furthest into it."

Appendix A

World Geography

INTRODUCTION

The history of every nation has been and is, to a great extent, determined by its geography. Physical geography considers the patterns of landforms, climate, soils, and other natural factors that form the setting for human activities and often impose limitations on them. Cultural geography studies population, urbanization, and the significance of languages, religions, and settlement, among other phenomena, in creating the human mosaic. Finally, economic geography concerns itself with the ways in which people pursue their livelihoods. Patterns of agricultural and industrial development, resource utilization, differential wealth and poverty, trade and transportation, and environmental impacts are analyzed with a view to understanding the complex human struggle for economic advancement, or perhaps only survival. In the following section, the world's major geographical regions are briefly summarized, with particular attention to their economic development, population growth, and changes in resource utilization.

THE WORLD POPULATION

There were approximately 1.6 billion people on earth in the year 1900, and about two-thirds lived in Asia, which, including European Russia, embraced about one-third of the earth's land surface. Europe contained the next largest population, with nearly 400 million people. By comparison, the other land areas were more sparsely populated, with 81 million in the United States and Canada, 63 million in Central and South America, 118 million in Africa, and only 6 million in Australia and Oceania. Antarctica was (and remains) an unpopulated land. Every continent contained large areas unsuitable to human habitation because of extreme heat or cold, too much or too little rain, infertile soils, or high altitudes. As a result, approximately 90 percent of the people lived (and still live) on less than 10 percent of the land. Thanks to medical and technological advances, the present world population is 4.5 billion, and, at the current rate of increase, will reach 7 billion by the year 2000.

ASIA

This is the largest continent, by far the larger part of the Eurasian land mass.

Japan

Japan lies on the eastern extremity of Asia. It is an island nation the size of California, which in 1900 had approximately forty million people. Only 16 percent of the land was arable, and agriculture was labor-intensive. Rice was the main crop, with other cereals, tea, and mulberry for silkworms as the secondary crops. As a result of government intervention and encouragement, Japan developed a core of basic and light industries. These industries were fueled by a very limited coal supply and later by abundant hydroelectricity from harnessed mountain streams. Japan lacked industrial resources and had to depend on importing raw materials and exporting manufactured products for survival. In 1900, it was the only Asian nation to have industrialized successfully, and its people enjoyed the highest standard of living in Asia. Today Japan is an industrial giant that enjoys the second highest gross national product (GNP) among all nations and continues to maintain the highest standard of living in Asia; in addition, the Japanese enjoy the longest life span. Tokyo, capital of Japan, vies with Shanghai in China for the title of the most populous city in Asia, with about twelve million people.

China

China lies to the west of Japan. It is a giant nation in size, and in 1900 was the most populous, with over 400 million people. However, most of China was unsuitable for habitation. Great mountains rim its northwest. Mount Everest, highest peak of the towering Himalayan Mountains, bestrides its southwestern border. Its northern frontier is rimmed by the Gobi and Karakorum deserts, an area inhabited by Mongol and other nomadic tribes. However, following the construction of railroads, peasants from farther south steadily encroached on the old pastures of the Mongols and other nomads.

Only 10 percent of China was arable; most of this area lay along the Yellow River and Yangtze valleys and near the coast. Over 80 percent of the population lived on this farmland and, as elsewhere in Asia, were mostly subsistence farmers. In the cool, dry north, farmers grew wheat and other cereals. In the warmer and wetter south, rice was the main crop, and double- and triple-cropping eked out more food from tiny farms. The diet of most peasants was protein-poor, the result of poverty and lack of grazing land. The main source of meat was the pig, a scavenging animal. Extreme changes in weather brought floods and famine, the endemic scourge of all Chinese peasants. The peasant sometimes owned his own land, but often rented. Because of the custom of equal division of land among all male heirs, there were few large estates in China. The nation had significant deposits of coal and iron ore, but in 1900 China had few modern industries and railroads, and those were mostly owned and developed by foreign nations.

Today, the People's Republic of China remains an economically underdeveloped nation. However, extensive petroleum deposits have been discovered. Now, as then, about 80 percent of the population remains rural (total population has risen to about one billion). Agriculture has been collectivized but follows the ancient pattern of backbreaking hand labor. Despite water conservancy works, floods and droughts still periodically wreak havoc over the land. Industrialization lags because of lack of capital. China's aim is to become a modern nation by the year 2000.

India

India constitutes another great geographical entity in Asia. It is a self-contained subcontinent, rimmed in the north by the Himalayas and the Hindu Kush ranges, south of which stretch the great Ganges-Brahmaputra and Indus valleys. Low-lying mountains and plateus, flanked by coastal plains, cover central and southern India. Monsoon winds demarcate the seasons and provide rainfall critical to agriculture. In 1900, about 30 percent of the land was arable, and it was sown with rice, wheat, other cereals, cotton, tea, and sugar cane.

The Indian peasant was poor, illiterate, and debt-ridden, whether a tenant or landholder. In most cases, poverty and religious prohibitions made peasants vegetarians. They might own an ox as a draft animal, but many of the cattle seen in the Indian countryside and cities were "holy cows" and made little economic contribution. India had few modern industries except for some textile mills in Bombay and Calcutta. A system of British-built trunk roads and railroads linked the various regions of the land.

Today, the subcontinent includes the nations of India, Pakistan, and Bangladesh. Despite ambitious five-year plans, foreign aid, and local efforts, each nation remains poor and underdeveloped. All suffer from rapidly increasing populations that have defied sporadic efforts at control. Thus, increased production from irrigation projects and the green revolution (high-yield, disease-resistant strains of grain and other crops) have not increased the standard of living. To date, no large petroleum deposits have been found. As a result, all three nations are heavily dependent on petroleum imports and have suffered acutely from OPEC price increases.

Southeast Asia

Southeast Asia contains two regions: the Indochinese peninsula, which consists of Vietnam, Laos, Cambodia, Malaysia, Thailand, and Burma; and the two island groups of Indonesia and the Philippines. Accessibility to the sea makes water rather than land the means of transportation within the area, and made the area open to outside influence in times ancient and modern. There is also great similarity in the topography and climate of most parts of Southeast

Asia. The climate is either equatorial or tropical monsoon, with abundant rainfall. As a result, living patterns tend to be similar. Most people in 1900 were farmers. Rice was generally the main crop, and was tended by human hands, not machines. After the late nineteenth century, with Western capital and management, large areas were opened to plantation farming, most notably rubber in Malaya and Vietnam, tea and coffee in Java (an island of Indonesia), and sugar cane in Java and the Philippines. Many of the plantations depended on Chinese or Indian labor, as did newly opened mines, such as the tin mines in Malaya.

Today, Southeast Asia suffers from rapid population increases, which have resulted in intense pressure on the land. Virgin forests are being chopped down at a rapid rate to provide more crop land, without regard to ecological results. Although the green revolution has helped to increase yields, it has also squeezed out the small farmer who cannot afford the improvements. The dispossessed have flocked to cities and created huge slums of unemployed. Industrialization has come too slowly to absorb the large reservoir of workers. Malaysia, with a small population and abundant resources, is relatively well off. Indonesia, with major petroleum deposits, is also reasonably prosperous.

The Middle East

The Middle East, or Southwest Asia, forms a unit because of similarities in geography of the area and the religion of the majority of the people. Except for coastal plains, river valleys, and oases, the area tends to be arid, with much desert. Mountainous terrain dominates large parts of Persia (Iran) and Turkey and all of Afghanistan.

While the majority of the people in 1900 were farmers and village dwellers, a minority were, and remain, nomadic. In Persia and Afghanistan, the tribes followed their herds up and down the mountain slopes in a vertical migration pattern. They and their sedentary village cousins wove colorful rugs, each tribe or village with its distinctive pattern. In the dry plains and desert lands were nomads called Bedouins, who herded sheep, horses, and especially camels. Each group followed strictly defined migration routes, whose violation resulted in tribal wars. Nomads traded their animals to villagers for products of the land.

Today, as a result of the discovery of large petroleum deposits, the Middle East has become more significant economically and strategically. Petroleum has made Iraq, Saudi Arabia, Iran, Kuwait, and other Persian Gulf states very prosperous: Their per capita income in some cases exceeds that of advanced Western nations. Lack of petroleum keeps the remaining nations poor. Large sums of petroleum revenue have been spent by Iran and Saudi Arabia for modernization.

AFRICA

Africa is physically dominated by plateaus and low tablelands. Such large river systems as the Nile, Congo, Niger, and Zambezi drain parts of the continent, but only parts of each of these rivers are navigable. Rainfall is sparse in the north and south, and very abundant in the equatorial zones. The continent has played a subordinate role in the modern commercial world and, with few exceptions, remains underdeveloped.

North Africa

North Africa is arid, except for a relatively narrow strip along the coast and the Nile valley, where there is adequate moisture through rainfall or irrigation for agriculture. In 1900, North Africa, where both native Arabs and Europeans lived, was the most urbanized part of the continent. There were many good harbors, for example, Alexandria, Tripoli, and Algiers. The economy was a mixture of the old and new, represented by native subsistence farms and European-organized plantations for such commodities as cotton and grapes. A few nomads roamed the marginal dry lands. Today, the European-controlled plantations are gone, although the land continues to be used for food products. Modern industries are still of minor importance, due to a lack of most of the resources necessary for developing manufacturing complexes. The Aswan High Dam has brought more acreage into cultivation along the Nile. Egypt has a huge population and little petroleum, while Libya and Algeria have huge petroleum and natural gas reserves and small populations.

West Africa

West Africa's interior is linked by rivers, but the long coastline lacks good ports. With abundant rainfall, much of the area is suitable for tropical crops, and a reliable local labor supply made possible the development of cacao, palm oil, rubber, coconut, and cotton plantations in the late nineteenth and early twentieth centuries under European domination. Europeans also developed tin, gold, bauxite, and other mines in the interior. Despite commercialization, many local peoples, especially in the interior, remained primitive subsistence farmers. Sleeping sickness and river blindness carried by the tsetse fly and mosquito made herding and farming difficult. No Europeans settled in the area.

Today, continued demand for tropical products by the outside world has maintained the present-day economy of the area. Mining has become important in Zaire, and the petroleum discovered in Nigeria has made it a rich nation. However, the general dependence of West Africa on exports makes it a victim of world economic viscisitudes.

East Africa

East Africa, from Ethiopia in the north to Tanganyika (Tanzania) in the south, has no uniform topography, but forms a distinctive unit because it possesses the most favorable conditions in tropical Africa for human habitation and successful agriculture. Much is highland, between 3,000 and 6,000 feet, with a temperate climate. Coastal East Africa had long been known to Arabs, Indians, Chinese, and Europeans, and was important through most of the nineteenth century for the export of gold, ivory, spices, and slaves.

In the late nineteenth century, British and German colonists found the area inhabited by indigenous black subsistence farmers who were dominated by Bantu herders and farmers. European settlers introduced commercial agriculture and produced sugar, coffee, tea, and tobacco. Indian laborers developed roads and railroads, after which many stayed to become retailers and professional people. While some blacks became plantation workers, most remained herders and farmers.

Today, Kenya and Tanzania are relatively prosperous because of continued development brought by local efforts and foreign aid. Wars and civil disturbances have all but ruined the economies of Ethiopia and Uganda.

Southern Africa

Southern Africa was modified by Europeans more than any other part of the continent. It attracted European settlers because of its equable climate and land suitable for European-style farming and grazing. It was also populated sparsely by peoples of simple culture who were easy to subdue.

By 1900 Europeans had spread from South Africa to the Rhodesias (Zambia and Zimbabwe). The discovery of gold and diamonds made the area even richer and more glamorous.

Today, South Africa, together with the Soviet Union, mines most of the world's gold and diamonds. Together with Southwest Africa (Namibia), it is also rich in silver, uranium, copper, and a host of other minerals. South Africa also has huge coal reserves. Thus, South Africa is the wealthiest and most advanced African nation, with extensive modern mining and manufacturing centers and large cities.

EUROPE

Europe is situated on the western tip of the Eurasian land mass. Its coastal location and the belt of prevailing westerly winds give much of Europe a temperate climate and sufficient rain. However, Eastern Europe suffers from the extremes of heat and cold typical of continental climates, while the Mediterranean basin has a dry summer climate. There are no deserts. Even the highest mountain ranges, such as the Alps, the Pyrenees, and the Carpathians, are minor barriers compared with the Himalayas in Asia and the Rockies and Andes in North and South America. The Danube and Rhine rivers, flowing into the Black Sea and Atlantic Ocean respectively, dominate central and western portions of the continent. In 1900, Europe, along with the United States, had undisputed leadership in the economic world, including an almost monopolistic position in manufacturing: It supplied most of the world with machine-made goods and commanded most of its trade. Western Europe was the most advanced part of the continent.

Great Britain

In 1900 Great Britain was the leading economic power. The Industrial Revolution began in England in the eighteenth century; it was made possible by water power in Lancashire and Yorkshire and coal mines in the Midlands and south Wales. Dominance of the seas permitted Great Britain to colonize and trade around the world and to bring food and raw materials from many lands. Great Britain became a great investor nation and London became the financial center of the world.

Today, Great Britain has lost its preeminent position. The growing industrial might of the United States, Germany, Japan, and others has deprived Great Britain of old markets. It has lost its empire and investments, its industrial plants are outmoded, and its labor and management practices are antiquated. One bright spot is that with its North Sea petroleum wells flowing, Great Britain is again energy self-sufficient.

France

France is the largest nation in Europe outside of the Soviet Union, about four-fifths the size of Texas. With frontage on both the Atlantic Ocean and the Mediterranean Sea, it has long been a transition zone between nations of the Mediterranean and northern Europe.

Since the early nineteenth century, France had had a fairly stable population and so had avoided the problems of overpopulation. This stability had been a disadvantage in its effort to maintain its position in Europe vis-à-vis the faster-expanding populations of Great Britain and Germany.

French agriculture enjoyed a strong tradition. France was one of the first nations to adopt modern farming practices in the nineteenth century, and these had proved so successful that the French peasant was reluctant to leave the farm for factories, or to adopt twentieth-century practices. Unlike Great Britain, France was self-sufficient in its basic food needs.

In 1900 France lacked major iron ore deposits (the Lorraine ore fields were then under German control) and abundant coal. To compensate for these deficiencies, French industry had been characterized by high-quality products. For example, although it produced all types of textiles, it was especially noted for fashion fabrics. The same situation prevailed in most other types of manufacturing. Handicrafts continued strong.

Today, France has recovered from the damage of two world wars. With the loss of its empire, it is now even more dependent on imports of fuel and industrial raw materials. France exports textiles, automobiles, chemical and electrical equipment, weapons, and wines; the last is not high on the list when measured by value but is one of the oldest and steadiest earners for foreign exchange.

Germany

Germany is east of France in the center of Europe. It occupies an exceedingly favorable position for international trade, with good land, river, and sea routes radiating in all directions. Its climate is reasonably suitable for agriculture. Above all, it is abundantly supplied with coal and minerals such as iron ore, copper, lead, and zinc. By 1900 it was vying with Great Britain for economic leadership in Europe.

Germany had many industrial centers, of which the most important was and is the greater Ruhr industrial district, a focal point of world industry. The Ruhr area contained the largest deposits of high-grade coal in Europe, as well as other minerals. It was situated on the Rhine River complex of water and land routes. As a result, the Ruhr attracted huge primary iron and steel plants, as well as heavy metal fabricating mills that produced locomotives, automobiles, machinery, chemicals, cement, paper, synthetics, textiles, and electrical equipment.

Today, Germany is partitioned into two parts, which have been almost completely divorced economically from each other. Partition has produced dislocations in the German economy. East Germany's economy has been largely integrated with that of the Soviet Union and its satellites. The more populous West Germany is a member of the European Economic Community and has integrated its economy with that of Western Europe. Despite the handicap of partition, West Germany has emerged as an industrial giant, and ranks fourth in global GNP. East Germany also ranks as one of the ten leading industrial nations.

Italy

In 1900 Italy was not as strong economically as Great Britain, France, and Germany, but was the leader among Mediterranean states. Italy lacks natural resources, is mountainous, and has little productive farm land. Its agricultural-industrial core was and is the north Italian plain and the bordering Alpine and Apennine foothills. Here, textile, metal, and chemical industries relied on hydroelectric power, or "white coal." The rest of Italy was rural and poor. Southern Italy was closer geographically and economically to other Mediterranean lands than to northern Italy. Generally speaking, the level of poverty increased as one moved south.

Today, Italy continues to have problems in supporting a large population on poor agricultural land. In manufacturing, Italians find it difficult to compete with nations more plentifully endowed with resources. Emigration, which acted as the safety valve for an increasing population, has for the most part ended. Thus, Italy must resort to more efficient farming and manufacturing to improve its living standard.

The Iberian Peninsula and Greece

Iberia includes Spain and Portugal, and is a peninsula cut off from Europe by the difficult Pyrenees Mountains and more accessible to Africa across the Strait of Gibraltar. Much of the land in each nation is too rugged and dry for farming and is more suitable for grazing. Most of the agriculture of this area and North Africa in 1900 was based on the cultivation of grapes and citrus fruits. Roads and railways were expensive to build and maintain. Nor was there abundant coal or iron ore. Thus, industrial development was slow.

Today, Spain, Portugal, and Greece are more prosperous than before because of closer integration with the economies of the rest of Western Europe. Tourism is booming, due to the mild, sunny climate and abundant historical ruins.

Eastern Europe

Broad lowlands and rivers characterize the northern section of Eastern Europe, whereas much of the landscape in the Balkans to the south is cut up by rugged mountains. Poland, Hungary, Bulgaria, and Rumania were traditionally grain-growing areas, but only small pockets of land were cultivable in Yugoslavia and Albania.

Agriculture was the main mode of livelihood in 1900. Industries were developed only in Silesia (then Germany, now Poland) and Bohemia (then the Austro-Hungarian Empire, now Czechoslovakia). Before World War II, all nations in the area exported food to Western Europe in exchange for industrial products.

Today, the Soviet Union dominates the entire area, and all governments, except that of Austria, are Marxist. The result has been state planning of the economy to coordinate with the developments in the Soviet Union (except for Yugoslavia). Until the 1960s, the economies of Poland and Czechoslovakia in general emphasized industry, while the other nations concentrated on food crops and industrial raw materials.

Northern Europe

Northern Europe consists of Scandinavia (Norway, Sweden, Denmark) and Finland. Except for Denmark, which is situated on a low peninsula suitable for farming and grazing, the area is mountainous and heavily glaciated. The nature of the terrain and the northerly latitude render most of the land unsuitable for agriculture and normal grazing. There are extensive forests, and as a result of coastal indentations, much of the land is close to the sea. Therefore, forest industries and fishing have played, and still play, important roles in the economy.

Today, Scandinavia is highly industrialized. Since coal is lacking, most industries are fueled by hydroelectricity (except for Norway, which has recently developed abundant petroleum deposits beneath the North Sea). The area is notable for its effective use of natural resources such as iron ore and uranium; such use has produced a high level of prosperity. It ranks high in the world in per capita production and in economic and cultural standards. Illiteracy is virtually unknown, and health and sanitary conditions are unsurpassed anywhere.

Russia (later the Soviet Union)

This nation comprises large portions of both Europe and Asia. It is about as large as all of North America. Most of Russia is situated north of 50 degrees latitude, with the result that most of the land ranges from cool temperate to arctic in climate, although small areas near the Black Sea are subtropical. Some major rivers flow northward into the Arctic Ocean, while others, such as the Volga and Dnieper, flow into the Caspian and Black Seas.

Russia in 1900 was primarily an agricultural nation. It was an exporter of grain and forest products. In Asiatic Russia, the population was very sparse. There, Great Russians and other people of European descent lived in farming, mining, or penal communities, amid nomadic or semi-nomadic natives of Turkic and Mongolian racial background. In Central Asia, people were Muslim in religion.

The Industrial Revolution did not come to Russia until the late nineteenth century. In 1900, it was far behind Great Britain, Germany, and France in key aspects of industrial development. Moreover, Russian industries were limited to small areas close to the western extremity of the empire. They were in the St. Petersburg (Leningrad)-Baltic coastal region, where communications with the rest of the world were best; in the Moscow region, because it was a focal point of water routes; and in the Ukraine-Crimea area to the south, where there were coal and iron ore deposits.

Today, European Russians have been moved to populate the rest of the Soviet Union, and in some areas they now outnumber the indigenous population. This has been offset, however, by larger population increases among some of the hundred-plus nationalities that populate the Soviet Union, especially those of Muslim background in Central Asia. Today, the various non-Russian nationalities make up almost 50 percent of the Soviet population, and have higher birthrates than do European Soviet citizens. Nevertheless, European parts of the Soviet Union remain more developed and enjoy a higher standard of living.

With its GNP third in the world after those of the United States and Japan, the Soviet Union is now an economic giant. A succession of Five-Year Plans has substantially built up Soviet industry. New industrial centers dot the Soviet Union from the Baltic to the Pacific, and even above the Arctic Circle. The most important of these are in the Caucasus and Volga districts in Europe, in the Urals, in the Kuzbass mineralized area of Siberia, in Central Asia, and in the Baikal and Far Eastern districts in Asia. Soviet agriculture has been collectivized but remains inefficient and poorly mechanized. As a result of difficult climate, bad soil conditions, and collectivization, yields per acre for most crops in the Soviet Union are much lower than in the United States; the Soviet Union is not self-sufficient in grain. The standard of living of the Soviet citizen is much lower than that of Europeans and North Americans.

NORTH AMERICA

The Western Hemisphere has three distinctive divisions: North America, Middle America, and South America. North America was the first area in the New

World to experience the Industrial Revolution. As a result, it possesses the most advanced economies.

Canada

In 1900, most of Canada's eleven million people were congregated in the southeastern corner. The southern prairie lands were mostly given to grain farming, and in the north were cold forests and frozen wastes. Canada today has some twenty-two million people. Discovery of petroleum and minerals has made it wealthy, but lack of population and capital and a formidable climate make development difficult.

The United States

The United States is well endowed in assets. About two-thirds of the land is lowland, and much of this possesses some of the best soils for agriculture as well as favorable climates. In 1900, U.S. farming was the most efficient in the world. Out of a population of seventy-four million, about thirteen and one-half million were farmers, who grew enough to export large quantities. The economic heartland region of the United States was situated in the northeast quadrant from the east bank of the Missouri to the Atlantic, and north of the Ohio and Potomac rivers. This area was noted for agriculture, mining, manufacture, and commerce. The coastal stretch between Boston and Baltimore contained a number of large urban centers. New York City was a major world center of finance and culture.

The southeastern part of the United States was primarily agricultural, with some industries. Land west of the Missouri River up to the Rocky Mountains was sparsely populated and devoted to agriculture and ranching. Further west lay the Rocky Mountain region of rugged terrain and forests. The economy there centered on gold, silver, tin, copper, and other minerals. Along the Pacific coast, an agricultural economy was developing.

Today, the United States is the industrial giant of the world. Agricultural products are still major items of export, as are machinery, manufactured goods, and technology. However, in recent years, some of its manufacturers have faced stiff competition from more efficient German, Japanese, and Asian Rim industries. Dependence on foreign sources for about half its petroleum needs has restricted industrial growth. Within the United States, there has been a shift of industries and population from the old centers in the northeastern "frost belt" to the "sun belt" in the South and Southwest.

MIDDLE AMERICA

Middle America consists of Mexico, Central America, and the Caribbean islands. The former two regions are situated within a major belt of high mountains, with narrow coastal plains and some interior basins, and are populated by Indian- and Spanish-descended peoples.

Mexico

In 1900 half of the people in Mexico were concentrated in the areas around Mexico City, where high plateaus and valleys supported agriculture. Northern Mexico was too arid for large populations, and the southern part was debilitatingly hot and humid. Corn was the staple grain, cultivated by subsistence farmers or laborers on large estates. Sugar was a major crop. There was some mining and a little manufacturing. Today, Mexico has more factories and mines. Recent discovery of large petroleum and natural gas fields have promoted prosperity, but population increases have been too rapid for absorption of new manpower into the labor force.

Central America

Central America is broken up into numerous small nations. Rugged terrain and areas of dense rain forest prevented good land communications in 1900. Unstable governments frightened away investors. Except for enclaves of modern plantation agriculture, most people were, and remain, subsistence farmers, not much touched by modern influences. The Panama Canal, situated at the base of Central America, provides a route of communication between the Atlantic and Pacific Oceans.

The Caribbean Islands

The Caribbean Islands were colonized by many European powers and were mainly populated by descendants of African slaves. In 1900 the economies were export-oriented and were dominated by sugar and other tropical crops. Today, the newly independent republics rely heavily on tourism for income.

SOUTH AMERICA

Northern South America

Northern South America is dominated by Brazil. The rain forests of the Amazon River basin spread through much of the interior of Brazil and northern South America, much of which was underdeveloped in 1900. Population was concentrated along the coastal regions and engaged in sugar and coffee production and ranching. Brazil encouraged immigration from both Europe and Asia. Today, Brazil's economy is booming, with rapid development of industry and mining. Efforts are being made to open up the Amazon valley, which will, however, also have severe ecological repercussions.

Other nations in northern South America are Colombia and Venezuela, plus the Guiana colonies. In 1900 most inhabitants were farmers and herders, whose use of the land was dictated by the mountains. Coffee was grown, and gold and emeralds were mined. Today, coal and petroleum have provided the basis for the development of some manufacturing. Venezuela in particular is petroleum rich; its export revenues have provided boom economic conditions. Guyana, French Guiana, and Surinam remain poor today.

Western or Andean South America

Consisting of Chile, Bolivia, Peru, and Ecuador, this narrow strip of land extends from the equator to 50 degrees south latitude. The rugged Andes isolated this area from the rest of South America in 1900, as few roads penetrated the mountains to connect with the rest of the continent.

Ecuador in the north was predominantly a land of Indians who persisted in a meager traditional life of farming and herding. The urban and commercial sector was dominated by *mestizos* (Indian-Spanish mixed bloods) and people of Spanish descent. Peru fell to Spanish conquistadors in the sixteenth century because of its gold and silver.

Today, foreign-owned companies have expanded the area of exploitation (little gold and silver remain) to copper, lead, zinc, and some petroleum and coal. Although *guano* (fertilizer made from bird-droppings) was once the main export of coastal Peru, this is today superseded by cotton and sugar and by an important fishing industry. Peru's difficult terrain and tradition-minded Indians have slowed modern development.

Bolivia is a land-locked, high-altitude Andean nation. Very few Spaniards settled in this area, with the result that over half the people remain full-blooded Indians. Other than subsistence agriculture, which involved most the the population in 1900, it is tin mining that formed and continues to form the basis of Bolivia's commercial life.

Chile's favorable climate attracted many Spanish and other European settlers. In 1900, it was one of the most advanced nations in South America. Today, it has modern urban centers and diversified manufacturing. It has commercial rather than subsistence farming in the temperate coastal valleys.

Argentina, Uruguay, and Paraguay

These are located in southern South America. The former two nations enjoy a favorable location for trade on the Atlantic coast, temperate climate, and good soils. These two nations attracted European immigrants, who came bringing new skills and technology. Except for the Chaco waste region in the north and parts of Patagonia in the extreme south, most of the land is suitable for farming and grazing. The main products in 1900 were commercially raised maize, wheat, cattle, and sheep, which were exported to Europe. Today, Argentina is an important commercial, manufacturing, and agricultural nation. In contrast, land-locked Paraguay remains underdeveloped and poor.

AUSTRALASIA

Australasia is the smallest, most recently developed, and most sparsely populated geographical area. The dominating feature of this region, the continent of Australia, was too arid for intensive settlement in the interior in 1900, and the population was concentrated along the south and east coasts. Most Australians were of British descent. Agriculture prevailed mostly along the east and south coasts and some inland plains with adequate rainfall. Ranching of both sheep and cattle took place in the more arid parts of the interior, while the vast core of the continent remained relatively empty. Until recently, Australia exported products of the land in exchange for industrial products. Today, manufacturing has become important in such coastal cities as Sydney and Melbourne, and discovery of important mineral deposits such as diamonds, coal, natural gas, petroleum, and aluminum has led to the development of the Outback as well as increasing Australia's importance as a resource producer. New Zealand was even more recent in British settlement than Australia and remains rural and pastoral. The total present population of Australasia, including the peoples on the scattered islands of Oceania, is under twenty million.

Appendix B

Wealthy Nations, Poor Nations, 1986

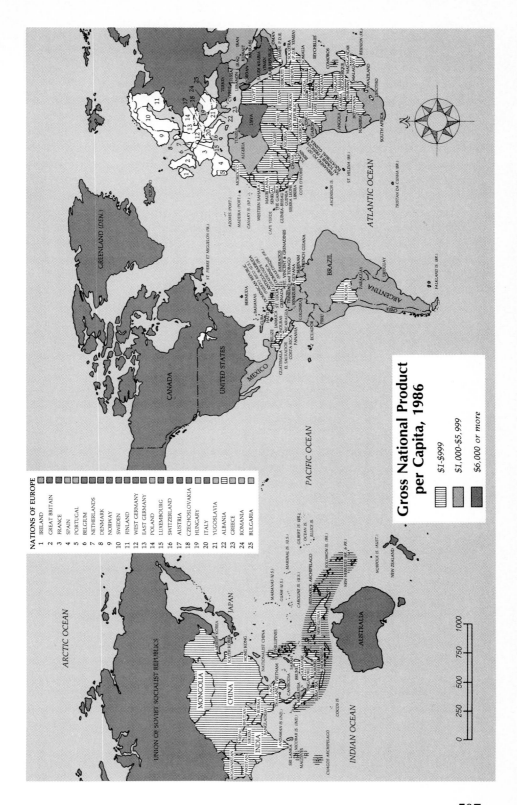

Gross National Product per Capita, 1986

$1–$999

$1,000–$5,999

$6,000 or more

NATIONS OF EUROPE

1. IRELAND
2. GREAT BRITAIN
3. FRANCE
4. SPAIN
5. PORTUGAL
6. BELGIUM
7. NETHERLANDS
8. DENMARK
9. NORWAY
10. SWEDEN
11. FINLAND
12. WEST GERMANY
13. EAST GERMANY
14. POLAND
15. LUXEMBOURG
16. SWITZERLAND
17. AUSTRIA
18. CZECHOSLOVAKIA
19. HUNGARY
20. ITALY
21. YUGOSLAVIA
22. ALBANIA
23. GREECE
24. ROMANIA
25. BULGARIA

Per Capita Military Expenditures and Gross National Product by Region, 1975, 1980, 1985 (in constant 1984 dollars)

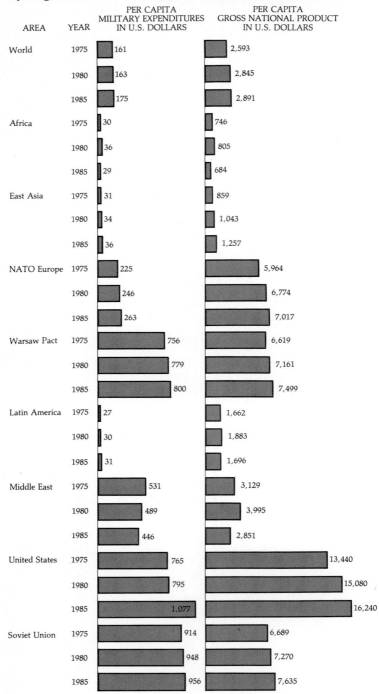

AREA	YEAR	PER CAPITA MILITARY EXPENDITURES IN U.S. DOLLARS	PER CAPITA GROSS NATIONAL PRODUCT IN U.S. DOLLARS
World	1975	161	2,593
	1980	163	2,845
	1985	175	2,891
Africa	1975	30	746
	1980	36	805
	1985	29	684
East Asia	1975	31	859
	1980	34	1,043
	1985	36	1,257
NATO Europe	1975	225	5,964
	1980	246	6,774
	1985	263	7,017
Warsaw Pact	1975	756	6,619
	1980	779	7,161
	1985	800	7,499
Latin America	1975	27	1,662
	1980	30	1,883
	1985	31	1,696
Middle East	1975	531	3,129
	1980	489	3,995
	1985	446	2,851
United States	1975	765	13,440
	1980	795	15,080
	1985	1,077	16,240
Soviet Union	1975	914	6,689
	1980	948	7,270
	1985	956	7,635

Figures are taken from U.S. Arms Control and Disarmament Agency.

Index

The World in 1989

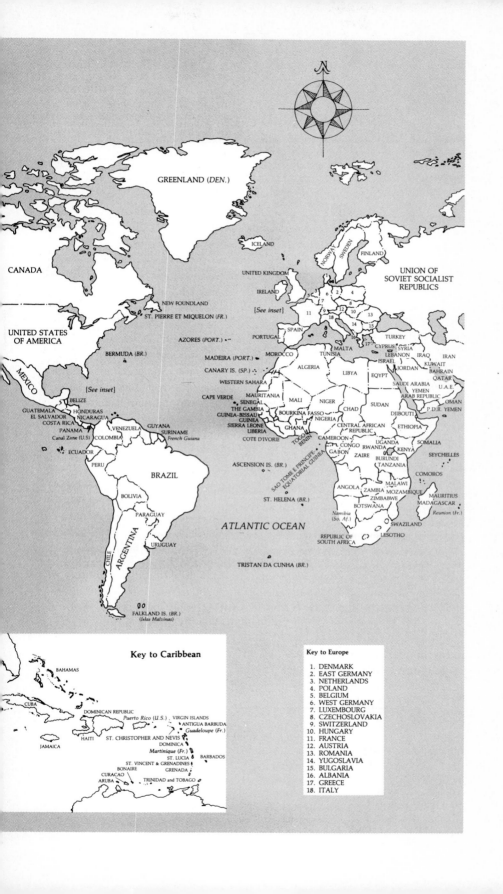

GREENLAND (*DEN.*)

ICELAND

NORWAY SWEDEN FINLAND

CANADA

UNITED KINGDOM

IRELAND

UNION OF
SOVIET SOCIALIST
REPUBLICS

NEW FOUNDLAND

ST. PIERRE ET MIQUELON (*FR.*)

[*See inset*]

UNITED STATES
OF AMERICA

BERMUDA (*BR.*)

AZORES (*PORT.*)

PORTUGAL

SPAIN

6   2   4
7
9   12
11   10   13
18   14   15
16
17   CYPRUS SYRIA IRAQ IRAN
LEBANON   KUWAIT
ISRAEL JORDAN   BAHRAIN
QATAR
U.A.E.

TURKEY

MALTA

MADEIRA (*PORT.*)

CANARY IS. (*SP.*)

WESTERN SAHARA

CAPE VERDE

MOROCCO

ALGERIA

TUNISIA

LIBYA

EGYPT

SAUDI ARABIA
YEMEN
ARAB REPUBLIC

OMAN
P.D.R. YEMEN

MEXICO

[*See inset*]

BELIZE
GUATEMALA   HONDURAS
EL SALVADOR   NICARAGUA
COSTA RICA
PANAMA
Canal Zone (U.S)   COLOMBIA
VENEZUELA   GUYANA
SURINAME
French Guiana

ECUADOR

PERU

BRAZIL

BOLIVIA

PARAGUAY

MAURITANIA
SENEGAL
THE GAMBIA
GUINEA-BISSAU
GUINEA
SIERRA LEONE
LIBERIA
COTE D'IVOIRE

MALI

BOURKINA FASSO

NIGER

CHAD

SUDAN

DJIBOUTI

GHANA
TOGO
BENIN

NIGERIA

CENTRAL AFRICAN
REPUBLIC

ETHIOPIA

CAMEROON
CONGO
GABON   RWANDA
ZAIRE   BURUNDI
TANZANIA

UGANDA
KENYA

SOMALIA

SEYCHELLES

ASCENSION IS. (*BR.*)

SAO TOME E PRINCIPE
EQUATORIAL GUINEA

ANGOLA
ZAMBIA
ZIMBABWE

MALAWI
MOZAMBIQUE

COMOROS

MAURITIUS
MADAGASCAR

Reunion (*Fr.*)

ST. HELENA (*BR.*)

Namibia
(So. Af.)

BOTSWANA

SWAZILAND

ATLANTIC OCEAN

ARGENTINA

CHILE

URUGUAY

REPUBLIC OF
SOUTH AFRICA

LESOTHO

TRISTAN DA CUNHA (*BR.*)

FALKLAND IS. (*BR.*)
(*Islas Malvinas*)

Key to Caribbean

BAHAMAS

CUBA

DOMINICAN REPUBLIC

Puerto Rico (*U.S.*)   VIRGIN ISLANDS
ANTIGUA BARBUDA
Guadeloupe (*Fr.*)

JAMAICA

HAITI   ST. CHRISTOPHER AND NEVIS
DOMINICA
Martinique (*Fr.*)
ST. LUCIA   BARBADOS
ST. VINCENT & GRENADINES
BONAIRE   GRENADA
CURACAO
ARUBA   TRINIDAD and TOBAGO

Key to Europe

1. DENMARK
2. EAST GERMANY
3. NETHERLANDS
4. POLAND
5. BELGIUM
6. WEST GERMANY
7. LUXEMBOURG
8. CZECHOSLOVAKIA
9. SWITZERLAND
10. HUNGARY
11. FRANCE
12. AUSTRIA
13. ROMANIA
14. YUGOSLAVIA
15. BULGARIA
16. ALBANIA
17. GREECE
18. ITALY

About the Authors

RICHARD GOFF received his A.B. degree from Duke University, M.A. from Cornell University, and Ph.D. from Duke University. He specializes in teaching the early national period of United States' history and has taught twentieth century world history since 1975. He is the author of *Confederate Supply* and encyclopedia articles on southern history and culture. He is currently editing a world history text scheduled for publication in 1991.

WALTER MOSS received his B.S. degree from Xavier University (Ohio) and his Ph.D. from Georgetown University. He has taught at Eastern Michigan University since 1970, specializing in Russian history. He has written numerous book reviews and several articles and is currently completing a work on the era of Alexander II of Russia.

JANICE TERRY is a graduate of the School of Oriental and African Studies, University of London. She is the author of *The Wafd, 1919–1952: Cornerstone of Egyptian Political Power* and *Mistaken Identity: Arab Stereotypes in Popular Writing*. She has also published many articles on the Middle East in anthologies and periodicals. Dr. Terry has lived and traveled extensively throughout the Middle East and Africa. She is a co-author of a world history text scheduled for publication in 1991.

JIU-HWA UPSHUR received her B.A. from the University of Sydney (Australia) and her M.A. and Ph.D. from the University of Michigan. She is the author of articles and book reviews on Chinese history and two catalogs on Chinese art and has completed a monograph on Koumintang China. She is a co-author of a world history text scheduled for publication in 1991.